STUDIES ON CHINA

A series of conference volumes sponsored
by the American Council of Learned Societies.

18. *Voices of the Song Lyric in China,* edited by Pauline Yu,
University of California Press, 1994.

19. *Education and Society in Late Imperial China, 1600–1900,*
edited by Benjamin A. Elman and Alexander Woodside,
University of California Press, 1994.

20. *Chinese Historical Micro-Demography,* edited by Stevan Harrell,
University of California Press, 1994.

21. *The Waning of the Communist State: Economic Origins of Political Decline in China
and Hungary,* edited by Andrew G. Walder, University of California Press, 1995.

22. *The Consumer Revolution in Urban China,* edited by Deborah S. Davis,
University of California Press, 2000.

23. *Becoming Chinese: Passages to Modernity and Beyond,* edited by Wen-hsin Yeh,
University of California Press, 2000.

24. *Ways with Words: Writing about Reading Texts from Early China,*
edited by Peter Bol, Stephen Owen, Willard Peterson, and Pauline Yu,
University of California Press, 2000.

Becoming Chinese

*This volume, and the conference from which it resulted,
was supported by the Joint Committee on Chinese Studies
of the American Council of Learned Societies
and the Social Sciences Research Council,
in collaboration with the Academia Sinica Committee
on Cooperation in Humanities and Social Sciences.*

Becoming Chinese

Passages to Modernity and Beyond

EDITED BY

Wen-hsin Yeh

UNIVERSITY OF CALIFORNIA PRESS

Berkeley   Los Angeles   London

University of California Press
Berkeley and Los Angeles, California

University of California Press, Ltd.
London, England

© 2000 by
the Regents of the University of California

Library of Congress Cataloging-in-Publication Data
Becoming Chinese : passages to modernity and beyond / Wen-hsin Yeh, editor.
    p.   cm. — (Studies on China ; 23)
Includes bibliographical references and index.
    ISBN 0-520-21923-6 (alk. paper). — ISBN 0-520-22218-0 (pbk. : alk paper)
    1. China—Civilization—20th century.   2. Cities and towns—China—
History—20th century.   3. National characteristics, Chinese.
I. Yeh, Wen-hsin.   II. Series.
DS775.2.B43   2000
951.05—dc21   99-11019
                                                  CIP

Manufactured in the United States of America

08   07   06   05   04   03   02   01   00   99
10   9   8   7   6   5   4   3   2   1
The paper used in this publication meets the minimum requirements
of ANSI/NISO Z39.48-1992 (R 1997) (*Permanence of Paper*). ♾

Chapter 7 is a revised version of materials published
as "Sources of Individual and Modern Chinese Identity,"
Chinese Social Sciences Quarterly 9 (November 1994): pp. 51–84.
The revised version is reprinted here by permission.

CONTENTS

PART TWO · THE NATION AND THE SELF

ILLUSTRATIONS

FIGURES

MAP

ACKNOWLEDGMENTS

This volume is the product of a series of activities jointly sponsored by the American Council of Learned Societies/Social Science Research Council (ACLS/ SSRC) and the Academia Sinica Committee on Cooperation in Humanities and Social Sciences, and organized by the Center for Chinese Studies at the University of California at Berkeley. The objective is to capture the results of new scholarship on Chinese experience in the first half of the twentieth century, which has been carried out in the fields of history, literature, political science, anthropology, and sociology, among other disciplines. We gratefully acknowledge the support of the ACLS/SSRC Joint Committee on Chinese Studies, which made it possible for a planning workshop to be held in Monterey, California, in October 1993. Discussions at the workshop led to the organization of a conference that took place in June 1995 in Oakland, California, with the funding support of the Academia Sinica's Republic of China Committee for Scientific and Scholarly Cooperation with the United States, for which we are grateful.

The conference was organized around four modules: the cities and the countryside, the rise of the nation, modernity and the practices of everyday life, and war and violence. David Strand, Sherman Cochran, Leo Lee, and Paul Pickowicz prepared review papers for the discussion of these modules. The essays collected in this volume reflect the results of intense discussions over a period of three days. The authors wish to acknowledge the critical and constructive comments made by Professors Ch'en Yung-fa, Chang Yu-fa, Yen-p'ing Hao, Cho-yun Hsu, Philip Kuhn, Jonathan Spence, Vivienne Shue, Wei-ming Tu, and Ying-shih Yu.

Drs. Herbert Ma and Cho-yun Hsu of the Academia Sinica and Stanley Katz and Jason Parker of the ACLS offered invaluable guidance and support for the project, for which we are grateful.

Joan Kask and Elinor Levine of the Institute of East Asian Studies of the University of California at Berkeley coordinated the workshop and the conference respectively. Ms. Levine took on, in addition, the critical task of coordinating the publication of this volume. Wen-hsin Yeh contributed by serving as the convenor of both the workshop and the conference.

Sheila Levine of the University of California Press has been unfailingly astute with her editorial comments and encouraging with her support. We are grateful for her guidance in steering the project through the final process of publication.

Introduction:
Interpreting Chinese Modernity,
1900–1950

Wen-hsin Yeh

One of the most active fields of academic research in recent years concerns the history of modern China, especially China's experience with modernity during the first half of the twentieth century. From a modest start in the 1970s, with a relatively small number of researchers working on a limited range of topics, the field has grown exponentially over the past two decades to encompass more than a dozen active research centers, scores of doctoral students, several academic journals, numerous research workshops and conferences, a large number of collaborative projects with scholars based in China, and an international network of researchers who bring to the field a diversity of perspectives.[1]

Several factors contribute to the extraordinary concentration of scholarly interest and energy focused on this period. With Deng Xiaoping's policies of modernization and the reopening of China to the West after 1979, scholars have gained, for the first time since the 1940s, significant access to archival materials and library collections on the Chinese mainland. These collections range from central government archives (the Number Two State Historical Archives in Nanjing), provincial and municipal papers (the Shanghai Municipal Archives and the Sichuan Provincial Archives, for example), and local county holdings (the Baxian Archives in Sichuan and the Wujiang Archives in Jiangsu) to materials held at research institutions, labor unions, factories, financial institutions, film studios, writers' associations, schools, colleges, universities, libraries, Communist Party branches, military headquarters, museums, and local history bureaus. In addition, published collections of newspapers, periodicals, memoirs, biographies, letters, diaries, and photographs are available, along with films, documentaries, and the results of oral history projects. A growing number of Western researchers travel to China to visit libraries and archives, to carry out interviews, and to conduct fieldwork. Chinese custodians of source materials, meanwhile, have enhanced the availability of sources not only by reproducing them using copying machines and printing presses but also by storing them on microfilm and posting them on the Internet. The wealth of information, the richness of research experience, and the dynamics of interaction with Chinese intellectuals have combined to permit the exploration of a much broader range of modern historical topics from fresher perspectives than ever before.

A second source of intellectual energy comes from recent developments in social science theories and cultural studies, especially in the disciplines of anthropology, sociology, and literature. Until fairly recently, Chinese historical research in the United States tended to be dominated by a Weberian sociological conception as interpreted by Talcott Parsons and his followers. Scholars influenced by this conception of social change paid special attention to the study of late imperial Chinese politics and institutions, and their work was by and large characterized by a functional and structural approach to historical problems. These research projects, inspired largely by Max Weber's seminal text *The Religion of China,* have gone a long way toward explaining long-term institutional features of Chinese society. They have also contributed enormously to a practical understanding of how the late imperial Chinese political system "worked." The functional approach, as it deals with social categories rather than individuals, tends to marginalize the import of human agency and overlook factors of contingency. Not only were models of rationality constructed at the expense of a more supple and sophisticated appreciation of culture, but much of the analysis was predicated upon a linear conception of universal historical progress.

These characteristics have come under sharp review in recent years, as China scholars gained exposure to a broad range of new writings in the social sciences and humanities. The sources of inspiration ranged from Foucault, Bourdieu, Barthes, de Certeau, Ricoeur, and Habermas to Anderson, Gellner, Said, Chatterjee, and Jameson, among others. The rise of new sensitivities led to the problematization of new issues as well as the reconceptualization of old ones. It also led to a critical reflection on some of the unexamined assumptions embedded in the intellectual frameworks of an earlier time.

The availability of source materials and the development of social science theories did not in themselves, of course, lead to the articulation of a new research agenda. For years, scholarly interest regarding the first half of twentieth-century China had been guided by a desire to explain the rise of the Chinese Communist movement and the founding of the People's Republic in 1949. The explanations provided tend to be informed by both an unquestioning acceptance of a centralized, hierarchically arranged, and unified political system—*Da yitong* (grand unification)—as the normative imperative of the Chinese world order and a placement of the Chinese nation-state as the implied subject in a linear scheme of historical evolution. This leads, on the one hand, to a narrative convention that treats the first half of the century as a transient period between the fall of the Qing and the creation of the People's Republic and, on the other, to an interpretive understanding of modern Chinese history via the lens of "stages of revolution" that culminated in the resurrection of a centralized political authority in Beijing nearly four decades after the fall of the imperial government.[2]

The revolutionary paradigm of modern Chinese history was certainly not without earlier detractors.[3] In the late 1980s, especially in the aftermath of the Tiananmen Square Incident in June 1989, the paradigm became a focus of critical review and radical reconceptualization. Few scholars these days would continue to embrace the Chinese Communist revolution as the key to a structural solution to all of China's problems in modern times. In response to the profound changes taking place in the Chinese world, many have turned their attention to a new set of research problems that range from urban society, civic politics, migrant laborers, and income disparity to business practices, legal culture, technology transfer, and global capitalism, all set against the backdrop of a reevaluation of China's encounter with the modern West. Furthermore, as research contacts have increased between scholarly communities in and outside China, Western and Chinese scholars become fellow participants in debates over a broad range of historical issues that promise to radically revise our earlier understanding of fundamental questions such as the nature of Chinese revolution, the promises of Chinese modernity, and the dynamics of Sino-Western interaction.

Two general trends deserve special attention in this regard. Instead of a focus exclusively on a territorially bounded "China" that manifested itself through the institutionalized means of a centralized state, there now emerges in scholarly conception a view of a culturally defined Chinese universe with negotiated boundaries, in which the attributes of "Chineseness" are not culturally predetermined and immutable, but are the products of an ongoing historical process of nation building dating back to the recent past. And, instead of an unqualified acceptance of a linear conception of progress through historical time, there has now developed in scholarly approaches a heightened sensitivity to the differential attributes of a variety of spatial domains and to a multiplicity of historical subjects in the discourse of Chinese modernity. Instead of grand narratives and comprehensive explanations, scholars break down conventional divisions, such as those separating the Nationalist from the Communist era, and examine structural tension, spatial fragmentation, temporal duality, and unintended consequences, along with unsuspected links of continuity. While attention to China's quest for wealth and power—the birth of the Chinese nation and the rise of the modern state—remains high on the scholarly agenda, there has developed, at the same time, a critical approach to structures of authority and the patterns of material culture in individual lives on an everyday basis.

Each essay in this volume represents an effort to treat Chinese experience in the first half of the twentieth century in a new way.[4] Moreover, the volume highlights the city and the nation as the twin loci for the construction of a Chinese modernity. There is a growing literature on the urban culture and commerce in Shanghai in recent years, which has laid the foundation of scholarly understanding of the Chinese modern.[5] The essays in this volume, in contrast, go beyond a focused examination of Shanghai to engage the issue of urban network and civic culture in Republican China. They recount the politics of the Westernized educated professionals, along with the transnational orientation of an emerging bourgeois class, and draw attention to the transformative capacity of the modernizing state as well as the expanding new business enterprise.

What, then, becomes of the self and the individual in the context of Chinese modernity? Beyond the cosmopolitan flair and the professional finish, what does it mean to be Chinese under the discipline of the new state and emerging economy, with their open border and industrializing technology? How did the individual fare in a century of violence and mobilization, war and revolution? Did the rise of the city and the nation, in the final analysis, set the condition for an epistemic shift in established systems of knowledge and power, in discourse as well as in institutions? How did patriotism and consumerism, for example, conjoin to rearrange social relationships and undermine patriarchal authority?

The essays collected here each stem from larger projects with their own integrity. But when read as a collection, they reveal points of convergence that lie at a deeper level; these points become clear as we approach the essays as both a dialogue among themselves and a set of revisions against conventional wisdom. The volume, revolving around discussions of the city and the nation, raises questions about the condition of the modern Chinese self in a rapidly changing society. The goal of this introductory essay is not, then, merely to present a synopsis of individual essays, but also to offer an interpretive reading of all the pieces together. The objective is to help highlight the connections among these diverse projects, as well as to stimulate reflection upon both the sum and the parts as we sketch the contour of Chinese modernity.

THE CITY AND THE MODERN

In his interpretive reading of the Shanghai publishing culture in the opening chapter of this volume, Leo Lee tackles the problematic of Chinese modernity. He examines the production and consumption of print culture in Shanghai from the late Qing through the 1930s, and identifies a mode of urban modernity at the popular level that linked the project of intellectual enlightenment to the rise of a new style of urban life.

It was in Shanghai, Lee argues, that Chinese modernity was born. This modernity was the product of a print culture launched in the first decades of the century by a handful of Westernized publishing houses. The new publishers sought to call into being a new Chinese nation at the same time as they defined a new reading public. Propelled by the wheels of commerce, this print-mediated modernity was subsequently transformed into a popular culture of images and styles that, according to Lee, "do not necessarily enter into the depth of thought but nevertheless conjure up a collective imaginary" in the visual culture and surface glamour of urban life. Shanghai modernity thus connected an elitist project of enlightenment with a populist commodification and consumption of images of a Westernized cosmopolitan style of life. The publishing industry and the printing technology that facilitated the education of a new citizenship thus simultaneously served the goals of a new urban consumerism.

Shanghai modernity, by Lee's descriptive analysis, was operative on at least two different levels. It encompassed, as the publishing enterprises of the Commercial Press suggest, a conscious effort by an emerging class of professional writers, editors, publishers, and translators—cultural mediators and interpreters in a broad sense—to map out a new system of intellectual categorization and construct a new genealogy of knowledge. This project of enlightenment was the product of complex dynamics of cultural encounters between China and the modern West. It was instrumental, within the Chinese context, both in the opening up of the spatial horizon that let in the outside world and in the celebration of a Western-engineered material culture of machines, gramophones, moving pictures, neon lights, steamboats, trains, automated vehicles, and telegraphs—the energy, dynamism, light, and power of *sheng, guang, dian, hua* that concretely altered everyday experiences with time and space.

A second dimension of Shanghai modernity concerns, in Lee's analysis, the collective surfaces and the semiotics of daily life—the daily practices that became a desired way of life for a growing number of urbanites in the 1930s. Modernity, in this sense, was epitomized by the commercially produced images of modern women that adorned, for example, the cover pages of pictorial magazines such as *Liangyou*. The open circulation and public display of these images, often based on photographs of real individuals, featured realism as well as glamour. These women, shown to combine classic charm with a Westernized touch and depicted in a variety of styles of clothing, further introduced into daily life a dress-consciousness that was indexed, Lee observes, to a functional division of domestic versus public spaces. The commodification of the female images not only was part of a larger commodification of daily practices that extended to a consciousness of interior decoration and furniture but was the most tangible expression of modernity as consumerism.

Modernity at this collective, popular level, as Lee shows, did not necessarily have much to do with ideas, knowledge, reflection, or understanding. As the product of the commercial packaging of a whole way of life (whether concerning the rise of the nuclear family, the discovery of childhood, the attention to personal hygiene, the near obsession with individual well-being, or the renegotiation of gender boundaries between men and women), these mechanically reproducible images were not only the medium of advertising but also themselves products of a commercialized print culture for visual entertainment.

Commerce and commercialization do not in themselves, one might argue, produce conditions of modernity; otherwise we might be obliged to discover modernity in the urban culture of, say, Kaifeng and Hangzhou during the Song dynasty. Nor is modernity simply a function of enlightenment, whether in the form of a re-categorization of knowledge, the refashioning of women, the redistribution of cultural authority, the reconstitution of social space, or the rearrangement of everyday life. Significant as these changes were, radical reorganizations of knowledge were not without precedents, such as during the coming of Buddhism in the fifth century. But, in Lee's presentation, early-twentieth-century Chinese modernity did break new ground, precisely insofar as it blurred the distinctions between the elitist and the popular, the reflective and the unself-conscious. "Enlightenment" in this sense was, to be sure, commodified and promoted for a profit. Commercial imperatives, meanwhile, became the engine propelling the rise of a new culture. Shanghai modernity thus went well beyond the pet projects and cultural defiance of a handful of intellectuals to become a materially based way of life with its own logic and economy.

In his discussion of Shanghai modernity, Lee emphatically rejects the conventional bifurcation that opposes "tradition" and "modernity." Instead, he sees "tradition within modernity" and points to the poster calendars of the 1930s as tangible artifacts of this modernity. Two sets of time markers—Chinese and Western, lunar and solar, traditional and modern—invariably came together on Shanghai poster calendars of this period. The coexistence of the dual marking systems suggests how a modern scheme of temporal organization has been inscribed on the traditional and vice versa. Even as the Shanghai urbanites timed their comings and goings to the ticking of the mechanical clock, they also punctuated their seasonal temporal rhythm with the observation of religious festivals and communal holidays. Time was simultaneously "emptied," with the value of each unit of time seen as being equal to the others in a commodified scheme of exchange, and "charged," with no two moments endowed with the same significance derived from custom and faith. Chinese modernity, in Lee's conclusion, was far from a simple break with the Chinese past.

To sum up, several points stand out in Lee's characterization of Chinese modernity. First of all, it was embedded in an urban-based print culture responsive to the logic of the marketplace. Furthermore, it was by no means exclusive of a continued involvement with the Chinese past, either in content or in form. It was tangible in its celebration of a new form of material culture—the utility rather than the rationality of science and technology. It was about a new scheme of demarcation of space, private as well as public, and a new coding system of time, socially as well as culturally. Finally, it was the product of a commodified culture of consumption that had profoundly changed the semiotics of everyday practices at the popular level.

The full revisionist implication of Lee's approach is thrown into sharp relief once it is set against the established historiography on the May Fourth Movement, even though Lee himself does not engage in this comparison. The May Fourth Movement, in this established view, has often been presented as a moment of cultural iconoclasm and intellectual enlightenment.[6] It has often served, in historical writings produced in English as well as in Chinese, as the point of initiation in a narrative convention that links this unprecedented "cultural revolution" to the revolutionary politics of the succeeding half century. For decades, textbooks have taught that the May Fourth Movement, with its unqualified acceptance of Western values of science and democracy and its commitment to political activism, ushered in Chinese modernity.

By naming Shanghai instead of Beijing as the birthplace of a new culture and by focusing on styles and images instead of ideas and ideologies, Lee has outlined an alternative to the conventional view of Chinese modernity. Implicit in his approach is the argument that modernity was about business rather than politics, the quest for a good life rather than a just society, the transformative capacity of private enterprises rather than collective action. Modernity came into being not by the committed break with the past effected by a handful of the awakened mobilizing themselves for revolutionary politics, but as the sum total of the daily practices by ordinary people going about their business as publishers and readers, advertisers and consumers, innovators and entrepreneurs, and so forth. Modernity was about the material transformation of everyday life for the hundreds of thousands, rather than the organizational mobilization of an elitist few for a well-articulated cause.

Lee's implicit critique of an interpretive tradition that privileged the political over the economic, the ideological over the imagined, as the agents of Chinese modernity is further developed in chapter 2 by Sherman Cochran, who offers a close examination of the marketing and advertising practices of the new drug business of Huang Chujiu (1872–1931), the founder of Shanghai's Great China-France Drug Store and a leader of the city's New Medicine Trade Association.

Huang was a resourceful entrepreneur and a self-made man who built one of Shanghai's largest new medicine businesses from scratch. His two leading products, Ailuo Brain Tonic and Human Elixir, were both indigenous formulas that pretended to be imports. The drugs offered unproven medicinal benefits. Huang promoted them nonetheless as inspired, cutting-edge Western cures for age-old Chinese ailments and built a major enterprise out of their sale on the basis of marketing prowess. He put together a distribution system featuring scores of franchised outlets in central and south China, and promoted sales with vigorous advertising campaigns, both in print and on the radio. His advertising team churned out tens of thousands of calendar posters featuring close-ups of modernized city women who nonetheless maintained traditional poses of modesty and compliance. These poster images of "beauties" (*meiren*) followed the set formulas masterminded by a handful of artisan painters (e.g., Zheng Mantuo and Hang Zhiying) and were routinely executed with minor variations by a hired team of studio painters. The machine-reproduced copies of these drawings were then liberally distributed throughout middle Yangzi townships and cities. With the relentless push of their merchandising operations, Cochran shows, private entrepreneurs such as Huang Chujiu contributed significantly to the transformation of the visual culture at a popular level that reached well beyond Shanghai's urban boundaries.

Cochran's essay raises important questions about the outer reach of Shanghai's commercialized culture of modernity. What, for instance, was its capacity either to transform or form the foundation of a whole way of life beyond the city? What about the urban-rural dichotomy and the socioeconomic gap between the coastal cities and the inland villages, so well developed in left-wing Chinese social criticisms of the 1930s that they were accepted as incontestable points in subsequent Chinese historiography? Cochran's essay strongly implies that these issues deserve a careful reexamination.

While Cochran analyzes the transformative dynamics of Shanghai and challenges the rigidity of the rural-urban dichotomy, in chapter 3 David Strand reconsiders the major attributes of modern Chinese cities and explores the making of an urban China. What, Strand asks, was the meaning of the "urban" in places beyond Shanghai? Was there an urban network in Republican China that facilitated the flow among cities? Strand draws attention to Lanzhou, the northwestern center of camel-caravan trade and the spot marking the geographical center of China. By the 1930s, Lanzhou was linked to Shanghai by cross-continental railroads that cut across several regions and connected other major stops, including Nanjing, Guangzhou, Beijing, and Wuhan. The railroad lines, along with telegraph wires, printed media, and paper currency, helped to engender a heightened sense of connection among cities and between urban China and the rest of the country. With these means of communication in place, separate cities supplied a common perspective derived from interactive and circulating publics, movements, markets, and models of reform.

But even as Lanzhou's prosperity showed its ties to distant markets and its dependency on the regional as well as the national economy, there was, Strand argues, no national urban network that patterned itself after a hierarchy. What the material connections and mobility among the cities had promoted was, first of all, a mental picture rather than a physical reality of city life as one of continuous and simultaneous activity. The "conscious," "systematic" use of urban China referred, therefore, less to a realized vision and more to a cultural or polemical artifact of processes that were no doubt diffuse and uneven. There was, on the one hand, metropolitan Shanghai, busily keeping pace with other urban centers around the world. There were, on the other hand, cities that revealed a "counterfeit localism" as they projected the appearance of keeping up with the coastal urban complex. Too many factors, ranging from a reality of unevenness imposed by political upheaval, staggered treaty-port openings, and the vagaries of global economic change to the progressive modernization of transport, intervened to permit the configuration of a hierarchically patterned urban system within the national boundary.

Strand, then, departs from the Skinnerian model of an urban hierarchy of late imperial Chinese cities. He problematizes the conventional bifurcation of the local versus the global and the rural versus the urban, and redefines the cities as nodal points of an ongoing relationship of exchange—of reciprocal patterns of interaction involving merchandise, population, images, and ideas.

Modernity in Strand's conception is not, however, only about a cosmopolitan way of life or a technology-powered form of material culture that distanced the country from the city. It is also about the organizational power of the state and the technology of control. The private entrepreneurs and the urban consumers described by Lee and Cochran shared time and space with a municipal administration of bureaucrats and technocrats, engineers and planners, who take center stage in Strand's discussion. Strand's essay thus not only raises new questions about the role of the modernizing city in modern Chinese politics—the classic issue that had concerned Weber in a different context—but also draws attention to questions of power, technology, and the darker side of modernity.

In his earlier work Strand has shown that the late imperial Chinese city "supplied a tradition of self-management of urban society and a sense of balance between state and society that encouraged cost-effective approaches to urban problems." After the turn of the century, amid the gathering social crises, modernity "provided an impulse to mobilize and deploy resources beyond the limits imposed or assumed by the old urban order and in ways that were both creative and destructive."[7] All three sectors of municipal politics—the city administration, the trade and professional associations, and the urban labor force—were profoundly affected by this new condition. The workers discovered a new form of power through populist movements, while the urban professionals gained new means to facilitate the formation of social networks. Among the municipal administrators, meanwhile, there emerged in the 1920s and 1930s a statist ideology that looked toward bureaucratic initiatives and technological means to regulate public life and to reform urban society. This new ideology was accompanied by the creation of new institutions that enabled such changes to take place from above.

The central theme of Republican civic politics, in Strand's view, was thus not the democratization of municipal polity but the rise of municipal administrative absolutism. The rise of the modern city could not have failed to assert an overall liberalizing effect on Chinese political system. However, the liberalization went only so far, as municipal administrators resisted central government authority and strove to operate with a higher degree of municipal autonomy. The rise of the city thus led to a decentralization of political power. But while urban political participation and state building both picked up momentum in the first half of the century, Strand believes the development of electoral institutions and representative assemblies lagged behind after the early republic. In fact, the peak of institutional commitment to elections and assemblies in Shanghai may have come in 1909 under Qing reformers. The Republican trend in municipal governance, in contrast to that of the late Qing, was toward a less accountable, more authoritarian administration. If there were any particular trajectories in modern Chinese political life to be spoken of, they surely did not follow a pattern of linear progression, nor did they ever take the form of democratic liberalization of civic politics.

Strand's essay defines the nature of Republican polity from the perspective of municipal governance. In chapter 4, which continues the discussion of technology and organization in modern politics, William Kirby approaches this question by examining the very nature of the Nationalist party-state. The landscapes outlined and the sources consulted differ significantly between these two essays, which nonetheless converge on the common theme of the rise of a statist ideology driven by technology.

In a direct challenge to one of the most basic assumptions in the revolutionary paradigm, Kirby argues that in the longer perspective of a larger history, the twentieth century is better understood as a century of global industrialization rather than permanent revolution, of international technology rather than international communism, of the "Tekhintern" rather than the Comintern. In the case of China, the early Republican years witnessed the birth of a transformative Chinese state that would be the leading agent of industrialization.[8] In policies as well as in political vision, technology and industrialization were at the heart of the nation-building strategy of the Nationalist government during the critical decade of relative peace, 1928–1937. The young Chinese Republic, following an ambitious blueprint of "national reconstruction" laid down by its revolutionary leader Sun Yat-sen, sought to erect a state-of-the-art modern national capital, electrify the country, dam the Three Gorges, tie the country together in networks of railroads, motor roads, and even air routes, and build overnight China's heavy industries. It emphasized the nurturing of a pool of technocratic talent. Driven by a self-imposed expectation to guide and manage the nation's industrial transformation "scientifically," it also organized its governmental agencies, allocated its economic resources, set its educational agendas, and forged its collaborative relationships with advanced industrial nations accordingly, all on the basis of the nation-building tasks thus defined.

Despite the right-wing social effects of many of its policies, the Nationalist government, according to Kirby, was thus the first modernizing Chinese state to plot out the integrated economic and industrial development of a reunified China, and was the institutional and even ideological forerunner of its socialist successor, which later featured the world's largest Soviet-style economic bureaucracy. The Nationalists, to be sure, observed a form of "mixed economy" in public and private ownership of industrial projects. They also used the state industrial planning agencies more for bureaucratic regulating, technological advising, resource allocation, and deal-making than for downright state ownership.[9] Nonetheless, they shared with their Communist foes and successors comparable practices in large areas of economic and industrial policy, ranging from planning, standardizing, engineering, zoning, funding, and allocating to technology transfer and control over joint enterprises. Both regimes placed a high priority on China's industrial-military self-sufficiency and displayed a firm determination to achieve this goal as soon as possible.

The prime movers of this Republican vision of industrial modernity were neither ideologues nor activists but engineers and bureaucrats of elite background and advanced Western technological training. These men's political standing and work conditions, Kirby shows, were far more dramatically affected by the century's warfare—especially the wartime economy of control—than the turmoil of the socialist revolution. The Chinese Engineering Association, which had insisted on a certain professional autonomy and self-regulation in the earlier years of the Republic, became progressively nationalistic and reliant upon the state as the century wore on. The National Resources Commission, one of the largest state employers of engineering experts, emerged from the Sino-Japanese War serving the immediate interest of the state leadership, although it became, at the same time, a highly professional, bureaucratized, and politically insulated entity. The commission managed to steer clear of ideological bickering over its social agenda, but it was seldom ever really above the fray in bureaucratic infighting. Its technocratic claim and unchallengeable expertise nonetheless assured the strength and endurance of this elite bureaucratic agency over two decades—straddling the birth of "New China" in 1949 that has so often been seen as such a decisive divide between autocratic reaction and revolutionary breakthrough.

Several key points inform Kirby's overall argument, which lays the foundation of a new interpretive framework. First, it locates the sources of China's long-term transformative capacity in visions of industrial modernity rather than in strategies of socialist revolution. It sees continuous state formation and nation building, rather than continuous revolution, as the more significant trends in twentieth-century Chinese political history. It draws attention to policies and institutions rather than politics and movements, and highlights the role of total warfare rather than total revolution as the agency of enduring social change. Above all, it challenges a simpleminded opposition between the Nationalists and the Communists, thereby sketching the outlines of an alternative historical narrative that breaks the constraints of the revolutionary chronology.

Kirby and Strand both draw attention to a modernizing elite that did little to liberalize China's political system. By the intellectual tenets of the 1930s, science and politics were not expected to mix. Indeed, it was almost imperative for the Western-educated technical bureaucrats of the National Resources Commission to detach themselves from political concerns in order to safeguard the "purity" of the agency's technical expertise and scientific rationality.

But the politics of these newly emergent urban entrepreneurs and professionals was clearly a factor of critical importance in Republican politics. Richard Madsen in chapter 5 and Helen Siu in chapter 6 each take up this same question from a different set of perspectives.

Madsen's essay, which devotes considerable attention to French Jesuit missionary activities in north China, considers the educational formation of a key sector of Tianjin's industrial and commercial elite—those individuals of affluent family background who acquired their technical training in engineering and business in the Catholic Gong Shang College (L'Institut des Hautes Etudes Industrielles et Commerciales de Tientsin).

The French Catholic founders of Gong Shang College, according to Madsen, had two goals in mind for the school: to train French-speaking Chinese managers and engineers for French businesses in China and to serve as "the best agent of French propaganda in China." However, they were soon forced by changing circumstances to retreat from these objectives—so much so as to redefine, time and again, what it meant for the school to be either "Catholic" or "French." A growing number of non-Catholics within the student body ensured the development of a secular, Chinese campus culture in extracurricular activities that was markedly patriotic. The school meanwhile retained a hierarchical, clerically controlled quality that, as it demanded deference and docility, reflected the organizational characteristics of the Catholic Church and discouraged student activism. Students who came to Gong Shang College in the 1930s, Madsen observes, appeared to be mostly those willing to submit to such hierarchical Jesuit attitudes. This produced an apolitical school atmosphere in a decade of warm-blooded student nationalism elsewhere in north China, where students of Qinghua, Beida, and Nankai mobilized to demand immediate armed resistance against the Japanese by the Nationalist government.[10]

It came as no surprise, then, that the Jesuits of Gong Shang College were quick to collaborate with the Japanese once the War of Resistance broke out. Most of the students went along with it, and Gong Shang alumni came to occupy key positions in Tianjin's financial, industrial, and commercial enterprises in the 1940s. The implications are clear: professional training under the auspices of the French Jesuits had prepared middle-class Chinese youth well for positions in the ranks of the city's businesses and industries. Their exposure to a Western curriculum, however, did little to either prepare them for active engagement in public affairs or challenge old-fashioned regard for hierarchy and community. Indeed, Jesuit respect for church hierarchy buttressed rather than vitiated established Confucian habits vis-à-vis paternalistic authority, communal bonds, and social subordination.

The merchants of the Pearl River delta were no more engaged in Republican politics than Tianjin professional elites, says Siu, although for a different reason. Siu examines historical records concerning merchant groups in the delta in the Ming and Qing and concludes that leading merchants in those years "were able to create vigorous dialogues with the state by engaging in a language of orthodoxy. The dialogues took place in the local arenas of lineage, temple, guild, and academy." Siu takes issue with the stereotypical characterization of the merchants as apolitical, and she presents them as critical linchpins in communications between the country and the city, between the center, the region, and the locale. As adherents of orthodox cultural practices and as participants in rituals as well as festivals in late imperial China, the merchants mediated between the urban-centered political culture of the imperial bureaucracy and the village-based popular practices of the locale. They were cosmopolitan in cultural outlook and political visions within the Chinese context.

Things changed, however, after 1900. On the margins of the delta and from the fringes of the rural society there emerged a class of local bosses who did not mind realizing their goals through the use of brute force and sheer violence. This took place against the backdrop of the rise of regional militarism. In the early years of the century, the rule of Confucian bureaucrats gave way to that of modernized militarists, and the warlords took charge of the provincial capitals. The contention among rival militarists signaled the disintegration of the old Chinese empire and undercut the merchant elite's ability to maintain its ties to the rural community. The urban-based merchants, who had been busily forming business ties that criss-crossed the South China Sea, were able, meanwhile, to reach out to a cultural horizon that was cosmopolitan in a new and different way.

Mercantile cultural cosmopolitanism of maritime China, in Siu's analysis, rose in tandem with the decline of the sovereign power of the old continental empire. The Republican merchants in the Pearl River delta, unlike their Ming and Qing predecessors, were no longer facilitators of communications up and down the imperial hierarchy via orthodox cultural practices. They became, instead, vectors of new cultural norms as well as agents of differential rates of social change. They were drawn to the Nationalist government and local society, Siu observes, in vastly different but equally intense ways. The challenge that they faced in the twentieth century was thus in part a challenge to construct a new language of the nation-state that accommodated merchant interests, and to create alternative territorial bonds that attached local regions to the Republican state. Neither set of tasks, however, was satisfactorily accomplished. Republican merchants thus found themselves un-grounded in the Chinese political universe despite their cultural cosmopolitanism.

The essays discussed above focus our attention on the activities of a broad spectrum of the urban educated across the country. These included the publishers and advertisers (Lee), the private entrepreneurs and consumers (Cochran), the municipal planners and administrators (Strand), the engineers and bureaucrats (Kirby), the managerial and industrial experts (Madsen), and the mercantile elites (Siu). These individuals built railroads and industries, developed commercial networks, transformed styles and mentality, planned cities, and dreamt up a modernized Chinese nation.

Their daily activities, whether at work or at home, transformed the physical landscape, the material foundation, the institutional framework, and the technological arrangement of modern Chinese lives. Yet with the exception perhaps of the municipal administrators mentioned in Strand's essay, few of these elites appeared to have developed strong commitments; nor did they appear to have taken it upon themselves to articulate a new set of social or cultural values.

This is certainly not to suggest that urban-educated Chinese in the Republican years were simply apolitical or morally unconcerned. It does, however, raise questions about culture and politics in the context of Chinese modernity. Specifically, Madsen's essay notes that the acquisition of modern technical knowledge bore little relevance in challenging the authoritarian and hierarchical nature of Chinese social relationships. Similarly, Strand's essay suggests that blueprints of industrial modernity facilitated rather than discouraged the rise of a municipal form of administrative absolutism. Kirby's essay hardly encourages the hope that highly placed American-trained technocrats in the Nationalist government would necessarily have a liberalizing impact upon Republican political life. Nor do the essays by Lee, Siu, and Cochran suggest connections between commercial practices and the regeneration of values, especially liberal democratic values, despite all the freedom and sophistication that accompanied the flow of capital and goods. What, then, was the political significance of the emergence of an urban professional class of technocrats and managers against the backdrop of a culture of consumerism? In what way did the rise of the cities interact with the constitution of the modern Chinese nation-state?

THE NATION AND THE SELF

Many have noted the authoritarian and hierarchical character of Chinese social relationships. Such characteristics have often been traced to the Confucian political order of late imperial days. The political scientist Lucian Pye, for instance, holds the view that in the Chinese mentality there was special sensitivity to the importance of authority, which was evidenced in familial as well as political relationships.[11] The literary critic Fredric Jameson observes that in Chinese texts, just as in other Third World texts, "the story of the private individual destiny is always an allegory of the embattled situation of the public third-world culture and society." But unlike Pye, Jameson does not see this as the product of Chinese cultural traits. He attributes it instead to the oppositional relationships between the First and Third Worlds.[12] The fusion of individual experience with that of the nation-state and an absence of a distinct sense of the self nonetheless remain key characteristics of modern Chinese intellectual identity.

In his essay reexamining the political and philosophical ideas of Zhang Taiyan, Wang Hui takes on the question of the place of the individual in modern Chinese political thinking. Wang focuses on the crucial period between 1906 and 1908, when many of Zhang's most influential ideas—such as his call for a Han ethnic revolution against the Manchus and his unique brand of ethnically based modern Chinese nationalism—were taking shape. Wang goes about his task through a close analysis of the discursive mode in Zhang's writings and argues that Zhang's affirmation of the individual was the product of a process of negative reasoning. It stemmed from his rejection of the ontological reality of collective entities such as the "nation," the "state," and the "people," all seen as constructs in abstraction. Furthermore, the autonomy of the individual was seen as actualizing itself not in terms of inalienable rights but in terms of an ability to stand apart and say no—to resist collective demands on individual allegiance as misplaced, denounce universal principles as partial, reject the imperatives of social norms as coercive, and place the individual above and beyond the collectivity.

Implicit in Zhang's rejection of the collectivity, Wang Hui suggests, was thus a much broader rejection of the ontological assumptions and epistemological positions that naturalized the rise of nation-states as a universal historical process for all people. In his effort to affirm the absolute existence of the individual, Zhang had thus rejected, according to Wang, the scientism of material determinism and universal law, on the one hand, and the ethic of evolutionary progress and linear historical time, on the other. Zhang's affirmation of the individuated subject—which was not the "self" in a corporal, material sense but a participant in a collective stream of subjectivity—was accomplished ultimately with the help of Buddhist metaphysics that denied the ontological reality of the self. In the final analysis, Zhang's concept of the individual was intended as both a substitute and an opposition to rival subjects such as the "public" and the "community" in a Chinese discourse of modernity. In its rejection of an evolutionary scheme of time, it was opposed to power as well as modernity. By rescuing the individuated subject from the materially determined collectivity, Zhang had sought, according to Wang, to reestablish a foundation of moral choices and action.

Wang's objective in this essay, however, was not to rewrite intellectual history so that Zhang could be presented as a champion of indigenous Chinese notions about the absolute autonomy of the individual. On the contrary, Wang goes on to show that Zhang's individuated self was freed from the materially determined collectivity only to be subsumed in a broader stream of subjectivity. Zhang's ultimate concern did not, according to Wang, rest either with issues of metaphysics or individuality, but with the revolutionary politics of the late Qing. To the extent that his treatises on Buddhism were meant to supplement his political pronouncements, his espousal of the concept of the individual was delimited, conversely, by the discursive practices that defined the burning political issues of his day.

Zhang's concept of the absolute autonomy of the individual, Wang Hui argues, thus did not necessarily exhaust the full logical potential of the notion. Instead of a three-way consideration of relationships among self, society, and the nation-state, Zhang followed a binary logic that opposed the individual exclusively against the nation-state. This particular positioning of the self, Wang believes, was a direct result of Zhang's intellectual rivalry with his political opponents, chiefly Yan Fu and Liang Qichao. The latter, as they sought the wealth and power of the Chinese nation, had accepted the political legitimacy of the Qing state. They pressed for reform rather than revolution, and were willing to strengthen the political center at the expense of the locale, despite the fact that the ruling house was ethnically Manchu. The debates between Zhang and Liang were thus not only debates over fundamental philosophical principles but also manifestations of tangible political struggles between the Constitutionalists (Liang) and the Revolutionaries (Zhang). It was a contest between two different strategies of mobilization: a top-down model that would enhance the state's capacity to extract resources and tighten up control, and a bottom-up model that would call into being, in the process of revolutionary change, the power of the people consisting of a multitude of individuals.

May Fourth individualism, which had played such a crucial role in the iconoclastic attack against China's cultural past, was, according to Wang Hui, different from Zhang's individualism, and the product of a different genealogy. Zhang's concept of the individual, as it was defined in opposition to the veneration of the modern nation-state, could not enter the mainstream of May Fourth intellectual current, for the latter was, in the final analysis, patriotic and nationalistic. Nonetheless, Zhang's ideas did serve as the foundation of a new moral criticism in the new literature—especially in the works of Zhang's leading disciple, Lu Xun. Although Zhang's may seem to be the case of a lone voice and a solitary enterprise far removed from the main scenes of political action, its significance should not be understated.

But even more important, Zhang's intellectual biography speaks directly to a number of critical issues. It demonstrates, first of all, that modern Chinese acceptance of the authority of the collectivity, far from being a matter of tradition, was a relatively recent development spurred by the quest for national wealth and power. Second, it shows that this acceptance was the product of specific historical circumstances rather than essentialized cultural attributes. The binary opposition between the collectivity and the individual, between the nation-state and the individuated subject, Wang shows, followed no logical necessity, let alone cultural imperatives. It was the product not only of the political goals and intellectual tasks that Zhang had set for himself—a matter of strategic choice rather than logical necessity—but also of the linguistic constraints and discursive mode of the moment, which were themselves shaped in time.[13]

The implications of Wang Hui's critical and revisionist interpretive position within the current Chinese intellectual context can hardly be exaggerated. In rereading Zhang, Wang has identified, in the intellectual life of the 1900s, an alternative conception of the individual in the formation of modern Chinese identity. This discovery helps to throw into sharp relief the intellectual genealogy of the much celebrated May Fourth conception of the individual, exposing the latter's materialistically deterministic foundation and its politically coercive nature at the same time. The ontological issues raised in the essay thus help to denaturalize the primacy of the nation-state as the one and only uncontested and conceivable subject of modern Chinese history.[14] In that sense, the essay delivers a forceful critique of a misplaced ardor for the wealth and power of the nation-state, a willingness to sacrifice the individual for the sake of the collectivity, and a tendency to compromise the moral for the expediency of the political.

Wang Hui does not deny the authoritarian and hierarchical nature of modern Chinese social relationships. Nor does he deny that Zhang Taiyan's conception of the individual was instrumental in nature. A recognition of these characteristics serves, in fact, as a point of departure in his search for an alternative genealogy of Chinese modernity. The conclusion that he offers points to viable strategies for escaping that past.

It is worthwhile to note that the critical spirit, which informs Wang's essay, is in itself a product of China's intellectual climate in the 1980s. In the post–Cultural Revolution decade, a whole new generation of Chinese scholars and intellectuals has come forward, willing to reexamine China's revolutionary history in this century from a critical perspective.

Much of this critical reflection has resulted in an intense search for the place of the individual and the meaning of human existence in Chinese society. Wang Hui's work, along with that of many others, including the philosopher Li Zehou, the literary critic Liu Zaifu, and the Marxist thinker Wang Ruoshui, is a fine example along these lines. How the individual has fared in China's twentieth century is, of course, a function not merely of metaphysical thinking, but also of discursive practices and cultural politics. The fate of the individual in this century of war and revolution has been inextricably bound to, above all, the rise of nationalism and socialism as hegemonic discourses, to the disciplining of a modern citizenship by the power of the party-state, and to the growth of a political culture of violence that these practices have spawned.

This culture, as chapter 8 by David Wang and chapter 9 by Frederic Wakeman illustrate, has been expressed in manifold ways, ranging from a festive celebration of bloodshed in class struggles against the landlords to the citizen patriots' cult of "blood, sweat, and tears" during the War of Resistance against the Japanese. Wang and Wakeman explore this culture from different perspectives—by rereading some of the most celebrated fictional works conventionally honored in standard literary history textbooks published in post-1949 China, and by an archival reconstruction of the lives of Shanghai's proresistance assassins who set upon Chinese collaborators. These essays take us beyond the charmed circles of municipal reformers, urban professionals, ingenious entrepreneurs, and sophisticated urbanites into the minds of comrade revolutionaries and citizen patriots. They permit us a glimpse into the darker side of Chinese modernity, where the political parties and the state, with the help of print media and new technology, worked toward disciplining the masses.

David Wang's essay, which examines scenes of crime and punishment in Chinese literary works from the late Qing to the late 1940s, addresses the issue of critical intellectual stances vis-à-vis the state and outlines a literary trajectory that progressed from a representation of violence to the transformation of literature into sites of violence. Wang begins with an analysis of Liu E's turn-of-the-century novel *Lao Can's Travels*, and notes the appearance of a modern consciousness of violence and injustice in its pages. Violence and injustice sprang from where they were least suspected, in the ostensibly impartial courtroom presided over by the incorruptible judge Gang Yi. This disparity opens up a literary space that enabled the author to set up a contest between poetic justice and legal justice, displacing the latter with the former and thereby renegotiating the terms of justice and violence in real lives as well as in literary representation.

A major thrust in the writing of modern Chinese literature, Wang notes, has been this compulsion to address social justice—a "high-strung, contentious call for justice" that turned the printed pages into veritable courtrooms of public appeal. This impulse to expose wrongs and this self-assigned mission to indict injustice in China's modern literature had much to do with its moment of birth in the midst of the May Fourth Movement, Wang suggests, as well as with May Fourth proponents' unrelenting assault on all traditional norms and relationships as systems of coercion.

In the 1930s, as sparks of cultural iconoclasm gave way to a full-blown ideology of socialist revolution, left-wing literary attacks on the past grew increasingly violent in imagery and imagination. Social justice became progressively fused with literary violence. Chinese literature under the auspices of leftist aesthetics, which began as a literary crusade against social injustice, evolved into a form that embraced violence.

After the outbreak of the War of Resistance, many left-wing writers joined the Chinese Communist Party in its wartime base areas in the various border regions of north and northwestern China. In the Communist capital of Yan'an, under the governance of the party, many lent their voices to the service of the Chinese Communist Party. The pen was mobilized not only to serve the politics of opposition in a war of resistance but also to launch attacks in party-led class warfare. With the transformation of the writers from critics into champions, poetic justice was subsumed by revolutionary justice.

Through a rereading of Ding Ling's *The Sun Shines over the Sanggan River,* David Wang makes his case about the total identification of the authorial voice with the grand narrative of a Communist-led socialist revolution. In the pages of Ding Ling's much celebrated contribution to the genre of revolutionary literature, class enemies were subjected to "the arbitrary will of the newly empowered," and "punishments are performed with an aim to arouse bloody festivity." Ding Ling's novel on land reform fuses the theater, the courtroom, and the site of punishment. The animal instincts exhibited by the newly empowered in this piece of fiction are shown "as a *logical* outcome rather than a momentary human reversion to the bestial." The ink, in other words, was spilled not to lament, but to demand bloodshed as a historical necessity. Modern Chinese literature in this sense has espoused the socialist revolution as a final and total solution of all the crimes and injustices that deserved punishment. It fused poetic justice with class struggle and celebrated violence as justice. As the writers blended their voices with that of the party, their writings lost the critical dimension of self-reflection.

The new revolutionary literature of the left wing, David Wang argues, ultimately facilitated the disciplining of a new citizenship by reducing the role of "the *man* of the new era" to "the role of the *woman* of the prerevolutionary era." The "hero" becomes, at best, an emasculated male—someone who earns his place in the master narrative through continuous acts of self-sacrifice, self-denial, and selfless penitence for the higher goals of the collectivity: in other words, he displays virtues conventionally gendered female rather than male. Such a hero is honored for his willingness to permit the loss of his individuality and humanity to the inexorable forces of the law of history. With protagonists such as these taking center stage, literary crusades against social injustice came to an end, and violence in modern Chinese literature was finally stabilized, Wang concludes, "in the form of self-imposed crimes and self-inflicted punishments."

The crime and punishment in Wang's essay, which tested the mettle of the revolutionary hero, were the exploitative deeds of one's class and ensuing fire and death in the purgatory of class warfare. The crime and punishment in Wakeman's essay, which explores the phenomenon of *hanjian* in the context of the War of Resistance, were fused with collaboration and resistance, and the hero, who loved his country instead of the people, fought the collaborators instead of the landlords. However, the war hero was no more a master of his own deeds in the patriotic campaigns of resistance than was the revolutionary hero in the struggles for justice, as Wakeman so aptly shows with his analysis of the discursive context of *hanjian*.

A *hanjian* in the twentieth century, Wakeman tells us, is an ethnic Chinese who had gone over to the enemy and betrayed his own people. The term combined ethnic transgression with political betrayal: it connected "ethnocultural treachery and the crossing of boundaries by collusion with foreigners," which was "linked in turn with bestiality, sexual violation, and demonic behavior." In other words, popular attacks on *hanjian* were grounded in two sets of understanding. The term suggested, first, the primacy of a communal identity that was ethnocultural, instead of socioeconomic, ethical-religious, or political. Second, as it fused deeds of treachery and transgression, it blurred the distinctions between issues of citizenship and identity.

Identity, in the discursive practices centered upon the campaigns against *hanjian*, was, as Wakeman demonstrates, not only a matter of communal belonging on the basis of ethnicity but also the very foundation of one's claim to humanity. Those who had transgressed the bounds had gone beyond the pale of the civilized world and were no longer human, and thus were the rightful targets of elimination. Conversely, those who remained within the ethnic bounds not only were the cherished members of a blood brotherhood, but they could claim superior human understanding.

Chinese citizenship in this discourse of *hanjian* was, by Wakeman's analysis, thus a product of one's ethnic identity. Ethnic allegiance not only determined one's civic obligations but also functioned as a substitute for the latter. Meanwhile, to the extent that those within the ethnic bounds could claim superior human understanding, the duties of citizenship necessarily entailed a moral imperative to launch attacks on the traitors, since by committing treason the latter had forfeited their claims to humanity. "*Hanjian*," Wakeman writes, "did not deserve to be killed only because they were 'treacherous merchants' smuggling black market rice and driving up the price for decent Chinese; or because they opened up opium supply bureaus to 'poison' (*duhua*) their compatriots; or because they heedlessly 'extorted' (*sougua*) higher and higher taxes from the farmers the Japanese permitted them to govern; or because they sold out Chinese economic interests to their masters in Tokyo. They deserved to be killed just because they were *hanjian*, and that was all there was to it."

Those who performed deeds of patriotism, as they followed a logic of ethnic identity couched in terms of moral obligation, thus could hardly claim moral agency and individual autonomy. But the heroes of resistance, Wakeman argues, were products of larger forces in yet another sense.

The term *hanjian,* Wakeman shows, did not originate with the twentieth century. Its first usage can be traced back to the Song dynasty, when it described Han Chinese officials who spied for the Jurchen Jin dynasty. In the twentieth century, as a matter of discursive practice the meaning of the term did not stabilize until after the retreat of the Nationalist government from Wuhan in December 1938—in an atmosphere of loss and defeat—when many Chinese appeared to have wavered on their resolution to fight the Japanese. The Nationalists and the Communists, allies in the United Front, consciously resolved to polarize the distinction between the "traitors" and the "heroes" in an effort to mobilize popular support for armed resistance. Under the orchestration of the state and the two major political parties, resistance fighters were portrayed in the press as good heroes, while pacifists, would-be collaborators, and collaborators alike were branded as villains. This stark opposition between the heroes and the villains grew out of a willful determination to overlook the complexity and ambivalence of collaboration. The good and the evil, once separated, were then accorded sharply dichotomized treatments. "Those who continued to be traitors to the people (*minzu pantu*), who continued to act publicly as puppets or to behave clandestinely as *hanjian,* not only risked the wrath of Heaven, but they also faced public elimination by their fellow citizens." A whole generation of young men were taught, meanwhile, not only to love their country, but also to set upon the traitors.

In a richly textured account based on the files of the Shanghai Municipal Police, Wakeman offers a close look at patriotic deeds on the streets of Shanghai as wild-eyed young men were recruited as assassins for the military intelligence service of the Nationalist government in Chongqing. There was a certain glamour to the deeds of violence and the lore of heroic assassins in popular culture on Shanghai streets, Wakeman shows. The committed killers included a destitute printer completely dependent upon relatives, a teenager unable to find a job since graduating from primary school, a waiter with a friend in the guerrillas, a laid-off clothing salesman, and a number of country folks in the city who shared an attic with bosom friends. These men gunned down, hacked open, chopped up, clubbed to death doctors, writers, journalists, financiers, industrialists, politicians—eliminating anyone suspected of dealings with the enemy. Most of these assassins also died young themselves, captured, tortured, and killed either by the Japanese military police or agents in the service of Chinese collaborators.

Even as these young men were spilling blood to defend the community's ethnic integrity, the top leaders of the war in Chongqing, Nanjing, northern Jiangsu, and Tokyo were subtly adjusting themselves to the changing dynamics in the battlefields. The leaders struck deals and formed tactical alliances that redrew political boundaries. The firm lines drawn between the hero and the traitor, the good and the evil, Wakeman concludes, were fully subject to redefinition by expediency.[15]

Wang Hui's essay, as we have seen, is a search for the standing of the individual vis-à-vis the collectivity in modern Chinese life. The essays by David Wang and Wakeman underscore, in contrast, the largely collective and authoritarian characteristics in Chinese social relationships, which are seen as the products of modern discursive practices as much as inherited practices from the old. Wang and Wakeman recognize that, for the multitude who lived through this century's wars and revolutions, the constitution of the self was both a function of the possible ranges of their own actions and a matter of ontological assumptions. They sketch a social space in which not only did the "hero" depend on his opposition to the "villain" for self-definition, but heroism entailed, on the one hand, a willingness to submit to emasculation by party discipline, and, on the other, resulted in betrayal by pragmatism and political contingencies.

Not everyone, of course, strove to be a hero. Few, however, could elude the disciplining power of the hegemonic discourse. Socialist revolution and nationalist resistance, according to the analysis by Wang and Wakeman, each produced its version of a tragic hero. But modern hegemonic discourse shaped public as well as private lives, and reconfigured domestic as well as civic spaces. Both socialism and nationalism demanded undivided allegiance of all Chinese. The emergence of such discursive practices not only forcefully rearranged the distribution of symbolic resources but also—much as did the power of commodification analyzed by Leo Lee—altered the semiotics of everyday life. The modern nation-state, working through a variety of means at its disposal, not only posed a powerful challenge to all established forms of corporatist power and authority; it structured a whole system of representation and set the terms of individual self-representation. It was within this context that the traditional patriarchal system of authority, as Prasenjit Duara in chapter 10 and Paul Pickowicz in chapter 11 suggest, was significantly reconfigured in modern times. The new nationalist discourse had a large part to play not only in the lives of men but also of women.

Duara's essay, which explores the representation of women in modern Chinese nationalist discourse, examines at the same time the subversion of such discourse by the women themselves. Two very different nationalistic representations of women have emerged in China, according to Duara. On the one hand, there was the May Fourth representation of the radically anti-Confucian, antifamilial, nationalist woman, and on the other, the varieties of more conservative constructions of woman as the representative of the soul of tradition. Politically, the former was associated with the Communists, while the latter was more commonly aligned with the Nationalist and social reformers. The iconoclastic woman, liberated as she appeared to be, turned out to be a political liability: communism itself was delegitimized by its association with such representations in the 1920s and 1930s, because radical women and their behavior threatened to corrupt the inner purity of Chinese culture. By contrast, conservative women, tradition-bound as they seemed to be, were brought into the modern world and established at the center of a "new nationalist patriarchy."

Why did the political fallout from these two female representations sort itself out as it did? The answer, Duara suggests, lies in the larger question of the construction of national identity, especially the authentication of an interior space that was stable and inviolable, in the context of modernity. Modernity, as we know it, is predicated on a sense of time that is linear and progressive, ceaselessly chang- ing and perpetually forward-moving. For the self to recognize itself in this stream of time, it is logically imperative that there be a space of authenticity—an un- changing essence from the past that serves the necessary function as the subject of a linear history. This interior space consists of "a repeatedly reconstituted repre- sentation whose historicity is concealed by its pace of change, which is not syn- chronous with change in other spheres." "All nations and societies that see them- selves as subjects progressing or evolving through linear time need to constitute an 'unchanging core' in order to recognize themselves in their ever-changing circum- stances," according to Duara. In the case of Republican China, the aporia of hav- ing to be "of the past and also not of it" happened to overlap the spatial question about being both Eastern and Western. The result was "an imbrication between Easternness, national or cultural essence, and the space of authenticity, each func- tionally different, but each authorizing the other." Since the Chinese space of au- thenticity had to be a space off-limits to Westernizing influence, it was necessarily constituted as the feminine, domestic, spiritual, and traditional. In the new dis- course of nationalist patriarchy that subsequently emerged, women were thus "to participate as modern citizens in the public sphere of the nation, but they were also expected to personify the essence of the nation or civilization."

Just how exactly were Chinese women supposed to personify the essence of the national tradition? This, Duara shows, was of course a matter of many pragmatic possibilities and diverse political ramifications. Leading Republican figures, from Sun Yat-sen and Wang Jingwei to Lu Xun, each had their thoughts on the subject. The critical consideration in this context, Duara notes, was how nationalist patri- archy came into being by appropriating the categories of traditional patriarchy to serve the nation. Thus a woman might be able to affirm her traditional attri- butes—steadfastness and compassion (qualities that Chinese men presumably did not have), hence public-mindedness and patriotism—in the new discursive con- text of the nation-building project.

How the categories of traditional patriarchy were appropriated to serve the purposes of the new nationalist patriarchy was examined further at close range in the context of the emergence of the Morality Society, a middle-class elite associa- tion, as it operated in Manzhouguo under Japanese sponsorship in the 1930s. An elite association closely supervised by the Japanese authorities, the Morality Soci- ety boasted a membership including top officials, merchants, and landowners at all levels of Manzhouguo society from the major cities to the subcounty townships. It was, Duara acknowledges, a *jiaohua* (moral education) agency with a strong propagandizing urge, spreading messages of peace, morality, and spiritual salva- tion of the world by Confucian East Asia. It countered the West, characterized as material, with an East that was moral rather than spiritual in the sectarian tradi- tion, in part as a result of its close relation with the state. It sought no radical break with the cults of chaste widows and virtuous wives. Its middle-class patriarchal sponsors made common cause with the Manzhouguo state by representing the family as strong, the husbands as righteous, and the wives as obedient. Women as a constituted subject were represented as repositories of the essence of tradition—of the virtues of filiality, devotion, self-sacrifice, and even obedience to patriarchs.

Duara agrees that this pedagogy was far from meaningless. Buttressed by the educational institutions and the propaganda machinery at the command of the state and the middle-class patriarchy, nationalist patriarchy placed constraints on the permissible for women and gave them the terms in which to think of their own subjectivity. Not all was lost, however. Through a close reading of over three hundred pages of personal narratives and testimonials—of the female leaders and teachers of the Morality Society who taught in its charitable schools and went around the country in the mid-1930s giving lectures on morality—Duara shows that a gap existed between women as the constituted subject and the enunciating subject. The very fact that these women participated in the Morality Society, Duara argues, was itself an ideal way to "control their activities outside the home." Furthermore, the positive evaluation of the realm of the social or public in modern ideologies created opportunities for women to define as their proper space of action an expanded community of moral service. Women as enunciating subjects were thereby able to construct a sphere of autonomous activity outside the prescribed traditional feminine domain, even as they were represented in these terms once again in the new nationalist patriarchy. The women lecturers of Manzhouguo's Morality Society were thus people who maneuvered the language in the same moment as they were constituted by it, successfully defying the latter even as the bonds remained.

The construction of women in modern Chinese nationalist discourse, by Duara's analysis, thus cuts both ways. While the logic of national identity and nationalistic patriarchy demanded that women be represented as the repository of female virtues according to the categories generated in the traditional system of patriarchal authority, the very valorization of the nation in a patriarchal discourse opened up a new space for female action and autonomy. This inner connection between nationalism and patriarchy, which, in Duara's presentation, was simultaneously a product of the opposition between the First and the Third Worlds and of the imperatives of nation building, resulted in new dynamics that defied simple dichotomized divisions phrased either as "tradition versus modernity" or as "progressive versus conservative."

The historical connection between modern nationalism and traditional patriarchy was, of course, operative in a variety of contexts. While Duara sees it in the representation of women by the morality associations of the Manzhouguo middle-class elite, Pickowicz finds it in the popular Shanghai films made in the late 1940s on China's wartime experience. Duara, as has been noted, sees in this connection certain irreducible psychological imperatives plus an epistemological necessity—he argues, in other words, that the connections are *necessary* so that the national subject recognizes himself or herself in an evolutionary scheme of time, authenticating a space of interiority that is off-limits to the West. Pickowicz, by contrast, does not make a case about either the functional or the contextual necessity of this connection. He sees, instead, a *pragmatic* isomorphism between the nation and the family—in how family narratives functioned as national allegories in the popular films of the 1940s. The films, to be sure, were meaningful fabrications that corresponded to certain lived experiences while contributing to their representation. Between the contextual necessity and the cultural pragmatics of such linkages, Duara and Pickowicz map out the deeper psychological terrain of Chinese modernity.

Disillusionment and despair were facts of postwar life in China, Pickowicz shows. The majority of Chinese endured utter devastation, which occurred over large parts of China during the War of Resistance. They emerged from the battlefields feeling dislocated and defeated, despite China's final victory over Japan.

A series of postwar films appeared in the late 1940s that confronted the problem of such malaise in the Shanghai area. Following a formulaic representation that recounted China's war experience in the form of epic narratives about how Chinese families endured, these films were immediate box office successes that sold out to full house capacity for months on end. The films, which captured a pervasive urban mood in the late 1940s, helped to articulate a sense of injustice and dislocation in postwar China that turned victory into an experience of defeat. Although the Nationalist government was not blamed, many negative characters in the films were Chongqing-bound wartime profiteers. Thus the films most likely contributed to the mounting criticism of the Nationalist regime and its eventual collapse. For this reason they have conventionally been labeled as politically "progressive" in film histories produced after 1949.

Pickowicz's close analysis of the classics in this genre—notably *Far Away Love, Eight Thousand Miles of Cloud and Moon,* and *A Spring River Flows East*—shows, however, that there was nothing revolutionary in them when it comes to the representation of the family. The family values and cultural politics expressed in them were in fact decidedly conservative. The patriotism and unselfish public-spiritedness of all the positive characters were natural extensions of their old-fashioned, neo-Confucian cultural orientation. All negative characters, however, were simply the ones who had betrayed these time-honored family values. The villains had transgressed cultural boundaries, become corrupted by Western styles and alien ways, and given themselves to greed, decadence, callousness, and selfishness that virtually prepared them for collaboration with the enemy—much as the *hanjian* traitors described in Wakeman's essay. There was, Pickowicz notes, an unmistakable antimercantile and antibourgeois thrust that informed all these films. All the positive characters, by contrast, had endured and persevered through thick and thin, their sense of self and of Chineseness remaining intact whether in life or at the moment of death, thanks to the traditional norms that authenticated their sense of worth and being. Thus, instead of spearheading cultural iconoclasm, these postwar "progressive" films had in fact aligned themselves with a nationalist discourse that used traditional symbols and norms to constitute its national subject as well as safeguard its purity.

We should note, however, that the postwar films about families in war were not simply allegories about the nation; they were allegories about a nation in distress. The family relationships that the films depicted were not simple expressions of traditional patriarchal norms either, but showed the patriarchal order in disarray. War films capture the crisis by showing a redistribution of attributes between men and women. In the examples offered by Pickowicz, decency, strength, loyalty, and dedication were often exhibited by women but not men. Moral degeneration, emotional weakness, failure to resist colonialism, and evidence of wavering and withdrawal were the sins of men but not women. The war, Pickowicz notes, appeared to have brought out the best in Chinese women and the worst in Chinese men.

The strain placed on patriarchal order in moments of national distress might have brought forth admirable heroines, discredited male characters, and disrupted the familial institutions. But it did not necessarily delegitimize patriarchal authority, nor did it endow women with greater autonomy. Those who survived the war by drawing strength from traditional feminine virtues such as patience, endurance, self-sacrifice, and caring for others, Pickowicz shows, were not rewarded with triumph at the end of the war. These women emerged from trial and tribulation heroic in moral stature, only to be betrayed and rejected by their impure spouses. Heroines who denounced the immorality of their kin and broke the bonds of their bourgeois families fared no better, if a higher degree of autonomy was among the objectives. The logic of their own moral superiority dictated that they join a new patriotic collective and submit themselves to its patriarchal authority. Their virtue thus won them an expanded space for selfless service and total dedication. As much as they appeared to have stepped out of the confines of the home to join the public, the communal, and the collective, women as the constituted subject in a positive role continued to be represented by those very qualities traditionally gendered as feminine.

Whether Chinese women had fared better or worse with the emergence of a nationalistic patriarchal system of authority is, of course, an issue for further research and debate. Pickowicz and Duara, through examinations of different sets of materials under separate circumstances, have mapped out comparable sets of problems. Both essays offer the suggestion that, with the rise of a new nationalist discourse, women's space for action had expanded beyond the domestic confines traditionally prescribed. The valorization of the nation and public opened up new spheres for women's activities. The disruption of the family and the rise of the collectives, however, also placed them under the patriarchal authority of the state in an unprecedented way. Unlike the middle-class Manzhouguo women lecturers in Morality Society, women in collectives depicted in the films were no longer housewives endeavoring to extend the bounds of their prescribed space. They were, through their devotion to the fatherland, desexualized women comrades and warriors who had earned for themselves a place in public, as well as in the master narrative.

The discursive practices that Pickowicz has exposed shed light on the representation of the female subject as pedagogically constituted. They raise questions about how the three-way realignment of power relationships among the nation, the patriarch, and the woman played themselves out in China's century of war and revolution. Whether the realignment resulted in a regendering of the feminine and a recoding of social spaces in the context of Chinese modernity is a question, as Leo Lee's essay suggests, that awaits further exploration. What Duara and Pickowicz have eloquently shown, along with Wang Hui, David Wang, and Wakeman, is the steady and unrelenting rise—whether by logical necessity or by sheer happenstance, with benevolent intent or authoritarian command—of the power of the nation-state and its ever-expanding capacity to intervene in the production of modern Chinese identity.

The expanding state, as we learn from Kirby and Strand, was able, on its way up, to muster the service of a whole generation of modern professional elites while claiming their allegiance. These individuals built the institutional foundation of the modern Chinese polity. Yet despite the overseas exposure and maritime contacts in their social and educational background, they were far less effective in articulating an alternative set of principles that posed a challenge to entrenched cultural and political norms.

In Shanghai and other coastal cities, meanwhile, forces unleashed by the trade of goods and ideas worked steadily to redefine social relationships and the material foundation of everyday life. The cosmopolitan flair and the entrepreneurial drive, so central to a vision of Shanghai modernity in the 1930s, brought to life a new era of public culture and civic activism in the years leading up to the War of Resistance. Yet barely a decade later, the energy and sophistication of this prewar urban efflorescence seemed, from the perspective of a war-torn China, remote and removed indeed. Nonetheless, as the chapters in this volume will show, the high hopes for enlightenment as well as the deep despair over war, the street-corner poetry as well as the state-sponsored violence, were irreducible parts of modern Chinese historical experience. As we follow the passages of middle-class elites sojourning across a fragmented landscape from the coast to the interior and back, we can explore both the meaning of becoming Chinese and the legacies of that quest.

NOTES

1. As this is a volume that seeks to problematize Chinese modernity and does not purport to be a comprehensive treatment of modern Chinese history in the first half of the twentieth century, it is organized with a certain selectivity and does not attempt to engage all issues of historical importance. Specifically, recent scholarship has made significant contributions to a better understanding of the early history of the socialist revolutionary move-

ment; political economy and mobilization in the hinterland; urban working-class collective action; issues of gender, class, and ethnicity; and questions of legal reform and institutional change. These issues are not highlighted in this volume.

2. For a succinct, classic, paradigmatic statement of the thesis of "stages of revolution" in modern Chinese history, see Mary C. Wright, "Introduction: The Rising Tide of Change," in *China in Revolution: The First Phase, 1900–1913*, ed. Mary C. Wright (New Haven: Yale University Press, 1968).

3. There were lively debates over the nature of the Chinese revolutions of 1911 and 1927, as well as that of 1949, along with competing interpretations of their relative success and failure at each stage. For an overview of relevant research results, see John K. Fairbank and Albert Feuerwerker, eds., *The Cambridge History of China*, vol. 13, *Republican China, 1912–1949*, pt. 2 (Cambridge: Cambridge University Press, 1986), especially chapters 3, 11, and 12.

4. Modernity is seen in this volume as multifarious and complex. It operates simultaneously on several levels. The topics include projects of intellectual enlightenment, urban cosmopolitanism and consumerism, global enterprises and transnational capitalism, bureaucratic rationalization and industrial technology, the transformation of material culture, municipal planning, urbanization, professionalization, the rise of the nation-state, the disciplining of a new citizenry, and the emergence of a nationalist discourse.

5. For a discussion of the prominent themes and wealth of information in this area of research, see Wen-hsin Yeh, "Shanghai Modernity: Commerce and Culture in a Republican City," *China Quarterly*, no. 150 (June 1997): 375–94.

6. There is a large body of scholarship on the May Fourth Movement. Standard texts on the subject include Chow Tse-tsung's groundbreaking work, *The May Fourth Movement: Intellectual Revolution in Modern China* (Cambridge: Harvard University Press, 1960), and more recently, Vera Schwarcz, *The Chinese Enlightenment: Intellectuals and the Legacy of the May Fourth Movement of 1919* (Berkeley and Los Angeles: University of California Press, 1986).

7. David Strand, *Rickshaw Beijing: City People and Politics in the 1920s* (Berkeley and Los Angeles: University of California Press, 1989), 2. See also Strand, "Conclusion: Historical Perspectives," in *Urban Spaces in Contemporary China: The Potential for Autonomy and Community in Post-Mao China*, ed. Deborah S. Davis, Richard Kraus, Barry Naughton, and Elizabeth J. Perry (Washington, D.C.: Woodrow Wilson International Center for Scholars; and New York: Cambridge University Press, 1995), 394–426.

8. On the state as a transformative force in modern Chinese political structure, see the seminal work by Philip Kuhn, "Local Self-Government under the Republic: Problems of Control, Autonomy, and Mobilization," in *Conflict and Control in Late Imperial China*, ed. Frederic Wakeman Jr. and Carolyn Grant (Berkeley and Los Angeles: University of California Press, 1975), 257–98. See also Prasenjit Duara, *Culture, Power, and the State: Rural North China, 1900–1942* (Stanford: Stanford University Press, 1988).

9. William C. Kirby, *Germany and Republican China* (Stanford: Stanford University Press, 1984). For related discussion, see Thomas B. Gold, *State and Society in the Taiwan Miracle* (New York: M. E. Sharpe, 1986).

10. See John Israel, *Student Nationalism in China, 1927–1937* (Stanford: Hoover Institution, 1966); and John Israel and Donald W. Klein, *Rebels and Bureaucrats: China's December 9ers* (Berkeley and Los Angeles: University of California Press, 1976).

11. Lucian W. Pye, *The Spirit of Chinese Politics* (Cambridge: MIT Press, 1968), xviii.

12. Fredric Jameson, "Third World Literature in the Era of Multinational Capitalism," *Social Text* 15 (1986): 69.

13. Note that Wang Hui's treatment of authoritarianism in Chinese culture is different from Madsen's, which postulates respect for authority as a traditional Chinese cultural trait.

14. See also Prasenjit Duara, *Rescuing History from the Nation* (Chicago: University of Chicago Press, 1995); Peter Zarrow, *Anarchism and Chinese Political Culture* (New York: Columbia University Press, 1990); and Arif Dirlik, *Anarchism in the Chinese Revolution* (Berkeley and Los Angeles: University of California Press, 1991).

15. Frederic Wakeman Jr., *The Shanghai Badlands: Wartime Terrorism and Urban Crime, 1937–1941* (New York: Cambridge University Press, 1996).

PART ONE

The City and the Modern

ONE

The Cultural Construction
of Modernity in Urban Shanghai:
Some Preliminary Explorations

Leo Ou-fan Lee

The issue of Western modernity has been thoroughly treated—and critiqued—in recent scholarship; however, that of Chinese modernity remains to be examined. This essay represents an initial attempt to look at Chinese modernity from the perspective of cultural history by situating it in the emergent urban culture of Shanghai in the 1930s.

Modernity in China, as I have argued elsewhere, was closely associated with a new linear consciousness of time and history, which was itself derived from the Chinese reception of a social Darwinist concept of evolution made popular by the translations of Yan Fu and Liang Qichao at the turn of the century. In this new temporal scheme, present (*jin*) and past (*gu*) became polarized as contrasting values, and a new emphasis was placed on the present moment "as the pivotal point marking a rupture with the past and forming a progressive continuum toward a glorious future."[1] This new mode of time consciousness was, of course, a "derivative" discourse stemming from the Western post-Enlightenment tradition of modernity—an intellectual package now being severely criticized by postmodern theorists for the positivistic and inherently monological tendencies embedded in its faith in human reason and progress. One could further argue that the very same post-Enlightenment legacy has infused the expansionist projects of the colonial empires, particularly those of England, and that one of its political by-products is the modern nation-state. However, once transplanted into China, the legacy served to add a new dimension to Chinese semantics: in fact, the very word *new* (*xin*) became the crucial component of a cluster of new word compounds denoting a qualitative change in all spheres of life: from the late Qing reform movement (*Weixin yundong*), with its institutional designations such as new policies (*xinzheng*), to new schools (*xinxue*) to Liang Qichao's celebrated notion of new people (*xinmin*) and the May Fourth slogans such as new culture (*xin wenhua*) and new literature (*xin wenxue*). Two terms that gained wide popularity in the 1920s were *shidai* (time or epoch) and *xin shidai* (new epoch), based on the Japanese word *jidai*. This sense of living in a new epoch, as advocated by May Fourth leaders such as Chen Duxiu, was what defined the ethos of modernity. By the 1900s, another Japanese term was adopted: *wenming* (*bunmei*), or civilization, which came to be used with words like *dongfang* (east) and *xifang* (west) to form the common May Fourth vocabulary of "Eastern" and "Western" civilizations as dichotomous and contrasting categories.[2] The underlying assumption was that Western civilization was marked by dynamic progress made possible by the manifestation of what Benjamin Schwartz has called a "Faustian-Promethean" strain that resulted in the achievement of wealth and power by the Western countries.[3]

Schwartz's pioneering study of Yan Fu has not covered the rapid spread of these new categories of value and thought in the Chinese popular press. In newspapers like *Shenbao* (Shanghai news) and magazines like *Dongfang zazhi* (Eastern miscellany) published by the Commercial Press, such new vocabulary terms became a regular feature of most articles. Thus by the 1920s, it came to be generally acknowledged that "modernity" was equated with the new Western civilization in all its spiritual and material manifestations. Whereas conservative or moderate commentators in *Dongfang zazhi* and other journals voiced concern with the possible bankruptcy of Western civilization as a result of World War I, all radical intellectuals continued to be firm believers in modernity as formulated above.

The center of cultural production of such ideas of modernity was indisputably Shanghai, in which the large majority of newspapers and publishing houses were located—in fact, congregated in one small area around Foochow Road. It is also worth noting that the earliest use of the Western calendar was found in *Shenbao*—a newspaper originally owned by a Westerner—which began to place both Chinese and Western calendar dates side by side on its front page in 1872. But it was not until Liang Qichao proclaimed his own use of the Western calendar (in his 1899 diary of his trip to America, which he published) that a paradigmatic change in time-consciousness was effected. Typical of his elitist aspirations, Liang simply announced that, as he declared his own transformation from provincial person to "man of the world," his use of the Western calendar was in keeping with the general trend toward unifying the measurements of time.[4] By coincidence, Liang announced his adoption on December 19, 1899, as he departed from Tokyo for Hawaii, on the very eve of a new century! By the 1920s, if not earlier, the commercial calendar poster had become a popular advertisement item for Shanghai's tobacco companies and a fixture in urban daily life. (See section 3.)

It was against such a "timely" background that a Chinese nationhood came to be "imagined." Benedict Anderson's widely cited book has led us to believe that a nation was first an "imagined community" before it became a political reality. This new community was itself based on a conception of simultaneity "marked by temporal coincidence and measured by clock and calendar."[5] The technical means for representing this "imagined community," according to Anderson, were the two forms of print culture—newspapers and the novel—that first flowered in the eighteenth and nineteenth centuries in Europe.[6] However, Anderson does not go into much detail in fleshing out the complicated process in which these two forms were used to imagine the nation (aside from citing two Philippine novels). Another theorist, Jurgen Habermas, has likewise pointed to the close connection between periodicals and salons that contributed to the rise of the "public sphere" in England and France.[7] But neither Anderson nor Habermas has seen fit to connect the two phenomena: nationhood and the public sphere. In my view, this was precisely what constituted the intellectual problematic for China at the turn of the century, when the intellectuals and writers sought to imagine a new community (*chun*) of the nation (*minzu* or *guojia* but not yet *minzuguojia*) as they tried to define a new reading public.[8] They attempted to draw the broad contours of a new vision of China and disseminate such a vision to their audience, the newly emergent public of largely newspaper and journal readers and students in the new schools and colleges. But such a vision remained a "vision"—an imagined, often visually based evocation of a "new world" of China—not a cogent intellectual discourse or political system. In other words, this visionary imagination preceded the efforts of nation building and institutionalization. In China, modernity, for all its amorphousness, became the guiding ethos of such a vision, as yet without the Weberian concerns of rationalization and disenchantment that the practical workings of instrumental rationality inevitably entail.

Thus I argue that the nation as an imagined community in China was made possible not only by elite intellectuals like Liang Qichao, who proclaimed new concepts and values, but, more important, by the popular press. It is interesting to note that the rise of commercial publishing—particularly the large companies such as the Commercial Press (*Shangwu yinshu guan,* or literally the shop that printed books for commercial purposes) and China Bookstore (*Zhonghua shuju*)—also predated the establishment of the Republican nation-state in 1912. (In this regard we might give Homi Bhabha's term about nationalism another twist in meaning: "dissemi-Nation" indicated, thus more literally and less ironically, that the knowledge about the new nation must first be *disseminated.*)[9] As this chapter will show in detail, these commercial ventures in publishing were all in the name of introducing the textual sources of modernity, of which the general journals such as *Dongfang zazhi* and *Xiaoshuo yuebao* (Short story monthly) served as showcases. In a way, they are comparable to the eighteenth-century French "business of Enlightenment" as described by Robert Darnton, in which the ideas of the philosophes were popularized and vigorously disseminated by a network of printers and booksellers.[10] However, in the name of promoting new culture and education, books in China were sold quite cheaply as something of a study aid for students in new-style schools and for other readers who were deprived of schooling. In short, from its beginning Chinese modernity was envisioned and produced as a cultural enterprise of enlightenment—*qimeng*, a term taken from the traditional educational practice in which a child received his first lesson from a teacher or tutor. That the term took on the new meaning of being "enlightened" with new knowledge in the national project of modernity should come as no surprise.

In this essay, for obvious reasons I cannot survey the whole "enlightenment industry"; I will instead focus on the textbook production of the Commercial Press, as seen in the advertisements of the press's leading journal, *Dongfang zazhi*, in order to throw some new light on this little-studied terrain of China's modern print culture.[11] Before I do so, perhaps a few words about the journal are in order.

1.

The Business of Enlightenment: Journals and Textbooks

Dongfang zazhi may be considered a middlebrow publication under the aegis of the Commercial Press for the urban readership. Begun in 1904 as a monthly, it was changed into a fortnightly, and it continued publication until 1948. Sales for each issue could be as high as fifteen thousand copies.[12] Its table of contents shows its eclectic quality, combining journalistic reports, political commentary, and cultural criticism with translations and learned articles. The journal's "miscellaneous" contents may have lacked a distinct character, but herein lies its purpose and appeal. The lead article in the July 1919 issue of the journal spells out clearly the functions of this general magazine. Whereas on a lofty level the magazine is supposed to live up to three purposes—scholarly pursuit (*yanjiu xueli*), enlightenment (*qifa sixiang*), and correction of customs and mores (*jiaozheng xisu*)—its real function, on a mundane level, is like that of a grocery store (*zahuo dian*): the goods are diverse and trivial, seldom precious and valuable, but they are nevertheless daily necessities. The article also sets three more goals for the magazine of the future: to stay abreast of world trends, to be adaptable to present conditions, and above all to be suitable for practical life.[13] As an indication of its "world trends" orientation, the journal devoted considerable attention to the European war—with photos, a chronology of events, articles, and translations. The writings of Du Yaquan, its editor, and other authors reveal an obvious disillusionment with the West in general, which led them to caution against excessive Westernization. At the same time, however, the journal contained extensive coverage and discussion of postwar European political, intellectual, and cultural trends and focused rather excessively on discussions of nationalism and socialism (the latter especially after 1919). Conscious of the continued impact of knowledge from the West, the journal's editors and leading authors groped toward a moderate position by seeking compromises between Western modernity and Chinese tradition, which they considered to be still relevant.

During the period 1915–20, the journal had voluminous coverage of subjects related to science and technology. A large number of articles described new weaponry used in the European war, in particular the submarine and the dirigible (thus feeding the fascination with underwater and air gadgetry in late Qing fiction). But the journal also carried rather learned articles on evolutionary theory, Freud's theory of dreams as a form of science, and various technological inventions that were already shaping and transforming human life: not only telegraphs, trolleys, telephones, and automobiles but also typewriters, gramophones, and movies. The sum total of the articles—some were translations from British, American, and Japanese popular journals and textbooks—conveys a continuing obsession with what in the late Qing discourse was referred to as the four major categories of modern technology: sound (*sheng*), light (*guang*), chemistry (*hua*), and electricity (*dian*)—a discourse later fleshed out in Mao Dun's novel *Midnight*. At the same time, however, some of the journal's articles sounded worried: if the triumph of modern civilization was inevitable, they seemed to argue, the Chinese should nevertheless be wary. In one article, titled "Machines and Life" (paraphrased from an article by Arthur Ponsonby in the British journal *Contemporary Review*), the author duly warned about the danger of the fast progress of all the new mechanical inventions, which, he stated, should not be equated with the progress of civilization.[14] Thus behind the journal's surface attitude of compromise and moderation lurks a sense of ambiguity and ambivalence, if not anxiety, toward the civilization of Western modernity, caused, ironically, by the journal's success in introducing it.

Although *Dongfang zazhi* was the flagship of the periodicals published by the Commercial Press, it still vied for attention with at least eight others by the same company. An advertisement lists the nine in the following order: *Dongfang zazhi*, *Jiaoyu zazhi* (Education magazine), *Xuesheng zazhi* (Student magazine), *Shaonian zazhi* (Young magazine), *Funü zazhi* (Women's magazine), *Yingwen zazhi* (English magazine), *Yingyu zhoukan* (English language weekly), *Xiaoshuo yuebao* (Short story monthly), and *Nongxue zazhi* (Agricultural study magazine). *Short Story Monthly*, in particular, has been widely described in post–May Fourth accounts as having been a bastion of the old-fashioned Butterfly school of popular fiction until Mao Dun assumed editorship in 1920 and turned it overnight into a journal of New Literature. Still, the imposition of a May Fourth interpretation has certainly not done full justice to this and other journals of the Commercial Press. Even a reading of the advertisement can reveal a common purpose: simply put, it is to provide readers with a certain practical knowledge for their everyday lives. Publication of the nine magazines also represented a new way of categorizing this practical knowledge; whereas *Dongfang zazhi* had the most comprehensive coverage—from politics, literature, science, business, and news to encyclopedic learning (*baike zhi xue*), according to the attached explanation in the advertisement—each of the other journals clearly catered to a specific readership: teachers, college and high school students in the new school system, youths, women, students enrolled in agricultural schools, and, most interestingly, self-taught readers. As the Commercial Press's only literary journal, the *Short Story Monthly* was intended originally for such self-taught learners. Another full-page advertisement for the journal mentioned not only its increasing sales (six thousand copies per issue), its inclusion of color pages, and the translations of Lin Shu—China's most productive translator, who had rendered more than a hundred Western novels into classical Chinese—but also the fact that its choice contents were meant to provide "entertainment for the family, and [that] the new knowledge is particularly good for daily use, hence [the journal is] a must-read for household residents [*ju jiazhe*]"—a term that in all likelihood referred to urban housewives.[15] No wonder the enormously popular genre "butterfly fiction" became a useful item! Still, the fact that it was entertaining does not detract from its seriousness of purpose: the words *xinzhi* or *xin zhishi* (new knowledge) and *chang shi* (common knowledge) became ubiquitous in these advertisements. Even the two English journals were geared toward a practical purpose, as they provided how-to lessons in composition, grammar, translation, and letter writing, as well as "literature" for easy reading. They were also connected with the dictionary projects, such as *Webster's*, as well as correspondence schools sponsored by the Commercial Press and by an American company in Pennsylvania.[16] In one ad, the Berlitz method was highlighted.

In accordance with the stated purpose of the Commercial Press magazines, the women's publication, *Women's Magazine*, was designed as an aid to women's education (*nüxue*). The history of women's education in this transitional period deserves a long monograph and is too important to be summarized here. However, it is noteworthy that a distinctly modern quality is underscored by the ads and articles in the magazine. In an ad for the "big improvement" of *Women's Magazine*, published in 1916, the name of the new editor is prominently mentioned: a certain Mrs. Zhu Hu Binxia from Wuxi, a modern woman who had been educated in a women's school in Tokyo and who then went to America for an additional seven years of education, gaining a B.A. from Wellesley and research experience at Cornell.[17] An American degree (printed in block characters) thus added prestige to the journal, which May Fourth leaders like Hu Shi also played to their maximum advantage. The magazine's ads marked a transition of cultural capital: whereas the prime movers of the late Qing reform movement were scholars and officials who knew no foreign language and had to rely on translations, mostly from Japanese, the new generation of elite intellectuals were largely Western educated—some in fact had contributed articles to *Dongfang zazhi* from abroad—and the countries and educational institutions where they studied were also prominently attached to their names (an editorial practice continued to the present day in some journals in Hong Kong and Taiwan).

Dongfang zazhi carried a number of articles about Western universities, particularly those in the United States; it also featured or reprinted from other newspapers and journals accounts of Chinese universities, including the curriculum of Beijing University. But the main goal and market of the educational enterprise of the Commercial Press, insofar as we can gather from its advertisements, was primary and secondary education. From the magazine's founding in 1904 until its closing some forty years later, almost every issue of *Dongfang zazhi* is filled with advertised lists of textbooks of various sorts, revealing a feverish publishing activity closely geared to the educational policies and laws of the government. Thus we can safely say that the Commercial Press played a seminal role in the modernization of the educational system: it was a gigantic task that fulfilled a national need after the abolition of the civil service examination system in 1905.

The Commercial Press was not the first to publish textbooks; two smaller companies—called Wenming (Civilization) and Guangzhi (Expanding wisdom)—had published a set of textbooks by four Wuxi schoolteachers sometime before 1903.[18] Their textbooks were called *mengxue duben,* or texts for "primary studies"; the term refers to the traditional notion of *tongmeng,* or children whose "beclouded" minds need to be cleared by the instruction of moral texts (according to the Confucian injunction), which in turn leads to the notion of *qimeng,* that is, *qifa mengmei,* or open up the children's state of ignorance, hence "enlightenment." By 1903, the Commercial Press, together with its chief rival, the China Bookstore, began to dominate the textbook market when it started its own textbook enterprise in a big way by setting up a new printing plant, hiring three Japanese advisors, and appointing an editorial board headed by Jiang Weiqiao, of which Wang Yaquan was also a member in charge of science textbooks.[19]

The founding of the Republic was enthusiastically advertised by the Commercial Press: it capitalized on the big event of the Wuchang Uprising in 1911 with a detailed account in *Dongfang zazhi* and the publication of thirteen volumes of photos and other illustrations, as well as more than three hundred postcards! Not surprisingly, the press also began to issue in 1912 a new set of textbooks, a series appropriately titled Textbooks of the Republic (*Gongheguo jiaokeshu*). The advertisement in *Dongfang zazhi* was headed by the following solemn announcement: "With the founding of the Republic, the political polity has been changed to that of a republic. The educational policy is consequently changed. . . . In view of the present changing circumstances, [this press] respectfully observes Decree No. 7 of the Ministry of Education, and has revised the various textbooks of the primary school level. All knowledge necessary to a national citizen of the Republic, as well as the origins of this Revolution, has been given in detail in them, so as to cultivate the complete Republican citizen."[20]

The subject of the national citizen—the Chinese word is *guomin*—thus formally entered the new textbooks. A special *Primer for a National Citizen of the Republic* (Gonghe guomin duben) was issued, clearly a revision of the original *Primer for the National Citizen of the Constitutional Era* (Lixian guomin duben, referring to the late Qing constitutional period of 1910–11). It also became a topic in the brand-new primary-school textbooks on *xiushen,* or cultivation—a term preserved from premodern primers on Confucian teaching. The new textbooks for the primary levels included not only the major subjects of Chinese (*guowen*), arithmetic (*bisuan*), history (*lishi*), geography (*dili*), and English but also quite a number of other subjects, including use of the abacus, singing, physical exercise, brush drawing, sewing, science, agriculture, commerce, and handicraft. Under the history category we find Chinese history, East Asian history, and Western history; and under geography,

Chinese geography, foreign geography, and human geography. In addition, there were textbooks on botany, biology, mining, physiology, physics, chemistry, arithmetic, geometry, trigonometry, algebra, general physical exercise, military exercise, and several others.[21] This is a most impressive list apparently intended to comprise an equally impressive curriculum.

I do not intend to discuss the pedagogic contents of the textbooks and curriculum. Rather, I would like to reveal how a publishing company, through concerted effort, succeeded in its self-assigned task of enlightening the public and, in so doing, aided in the nation-building effort of the Republican government. The compilation of textbooks for the education of its new *guomin* was definitely a priority in the government agenda, since the Ministry of Education publicized, as early as 1912, a set of provisional guidelines for general education. The old term for schools, *xuetang*, was changed to *xuexiao*. In the schools, coeducation was allowed for the primary level; reading the classics was abolished, as were some of the Qing dynasty legal codes.[22] In particular, the agency established two bureaux for compiling and censoring textbooks. To be sure, the practice had already started in the Qing period, but the new guidelines made some specific points about how textbooks' approach and contents should be handled, together with procedures for examination and approval by the agency.[23] The Commercial Press turned this new government policy to its own advantage by quoting in its textbook ads the seal of approval of the Ministry of Education (*jiaoyu bu shending*) together with the ministry's comments on particular texts. Most of the quoted comments are of a practical nature: for instance, "the choice of materials is excellent, the divisions clear; [the textbook] can be used for the physical sciences in higher primary schools." But occasionally a vaguely ideological phrase or sentence enters: "The wording is clear and succinct, and contains rather lively interest; *extremely well equipped with the knowledge and morality necessary for the national citizen*" (in reference to *Jianming guowen jiaokeshu* [The concise textbook for Chinese literature]; emphasis mine). All these endeavors pointed to the overriding objective of training the nation's people to be good citizens.

How should the people of a new nation be trained properly? The decrees issued by the Ministry of Education reflected many changes in approach. Whereas the 1912 decrees seemed to focus on practical education (primary-school curriculum must include handicraft, physical exercise, use of the abacus, etc.), the 1914 decrees—reflecting the power of the then president, the conservative warlord Yuan Shikai—restored the classics and honored the words of Confucius, with the special injunction that the curriculum in education must "emphasize the special national character of the people of this nation."[24] In 1919, two years after the Literary Revolution, the ministry formally decreed the use of the modern vernacular and new punctuation in all textbooks for the beginning two grades of primary schools.[25]

Given the turmoil of the period, we cannot be sure whether these changes in policy were strictly followed by the publishing companies. The Commercial Press, being the largest, might have developed its own views on education, which, while not contradicting government policy, might have extended the prescribed curriculum. The advertisements give the impression that the textbooks were meant not only for a school curriculum but for extracurricular activities as well; some books clearly aimed at the urban cultural arena outside the schools. For such "outside" needs, the press seemed to pay special attention to children and young adolescents, with a very large selection of titles of fables, translated stories, picture books, cartoons, color postcards, maps, simple how-to primers on arithmetic, games, and toys. It obviously reflected a commercial move to seize a new segment of the urban market—children, together with their mothers. At the same time, the company's extracurricular publications had gone far beyond the confines of the school system to the world of urban adults who could not attend school and had to work for a living. In my view, it is in this public arena of urban society that the Commercial Press's task of enlightening the public performed a crucial role as it served to promote a vision of modernity beyond the ideological confines of government policy.

The Business of Enlightenment: Repositories

How does one provide basic knowledge in a way that makes it accessible to everyone in society? In addition to school textbooks, the Commercial Press launched two well-known repositories (*wenku*): *Dongfang wenku* (Eastern repository [1923–34]) and *Wanyou wenku* (Comprehensive repository [1929–34]). The *Dongfang wenku*, in which some of the major articles printed in *Dongfang zazhi* were collected (together with other treatises and translations that did not appear), totaled more than 120 pamphlet-sized volumes—a device clearly intended for the task of inculcating new knowledge. The roster of its authors is distinguished and includes both academic and nonacademic intellectuals representing a wide spectrum of backgrounds and positions. The subjects and titles (mostly translations) are even more impressive, as they cover an immensely wide range. I can give only a rough classification of the subjects covered, as follows: literature (19 titles), philosophy (17), sciences (13), society (9), economy (7), politics (6), foreign countries (6), diplomacy (6), history (5), geography (5), art (5), women (5), culture (4), psychology (3), law (3), scholarship (3), education (3), military affairs (2), migration (2), and journalism, language, archeology, religion, and medicine (1 each).[26] This rundown serves to give us merely a general impression, and it does not reveal the specific contents of the volumes. It seems to disclose a fairly heavy concentration on the humanities (literature and philosophy), which is followed by natural and social sciences. A considerable number of titles are concerned with diplomacy and foreign countries (12). Among the titles in literature, six are collections of stories from foreign countries: Anglo-American, French, Russian, European, Japanese, and Indian (the works of Tagore). But a more intriguing feature is the diversity of some of the other titles. To give one small example, a book written by Du Yaquan titled *Chushi zhexue* (A philosophy to cope with the world) turns out to be based on a Japanese translation of a work by Schopenhauer. It is collected in a box (volumes 32–50) that also includes works on journalism, East-West cultural criticism, Chinese society and culture, ethics, psychology, contemporary philosophy (mainly on Dewey), Bergson and Eucken, Kropotkin, Gandhism, the philosophy of war, two volumes of Bertrand Russell's essays, and a volume on the fundamentals of science.

Still, *Dongfang wenku* is dwarfed by comparison with its sister repository, *Wanyou wenku*, whose conception was even more ambitious, for it was designed to fill up nothing less than a modern library. This is clearly what its chief editor Wang Yunwu had in mind when he embarked upon the two gigantic series comprising *Wanyou wenku*, each containing more than a thousand volumes. By purchasing the two series, a newly established library acquired a basic collection in the most economical and systematic fashion—economical as a result of modern printing, and systematic because of the new index system based on Mr. Wang's own four-corner system.[27] This may have been the most ambitious effort in the categorization and dissemination of knowledge for the general public during the Republican period.

From his own preface about the origin of the repository project, we see that Wang's basic design derives from the traditional *congshu* (collectanea) formula, and that he had seen fit to add a considerable number of new collections to the series Basic Collectanea of National Learning (*Guoxue jiben congshu*). We find such collections as *Baike xiaocongshu* (Mini collection of encyclopedic knowledge) and *Xinshidai shidi congshu* (History and geography of the new era), as well as separate *congshu* for agriculture, industry, commerce, normal school education, arithmetic, medicine, and athletics, all of which were meant to be "disciplinary tools."[28] By the time Wang edited the second series, he had further enlarged the collections of both Western translations and "national learning," and, instead of the disciplinary texts, had included two new collections: a collection on natural sciences (*Kexue xiaocongsu*) and a collection on "modern problems" (*Xiandai wenti congshu*); the most complex task, he admitted, was the compilation of the latter, because "there were few precedents in the publications in the nation and abroad."[29]

A glance through the catalogue of the two series is sufficient for some revelations. The editorial board for the first series lists Wang Yunwu as chief editor and a dozen other editors. At the end of the preface Wang also acknowledges the help of such "friends"—all intellectuals of great renown—as Cai Yuanpei, Hu Shi, Li Shizeng, Wu Zhihui, Yang Xingfo, and others. The editorial guidelines list the following four basic purposes: (1) the repository is intended to "inculcate in the general reading public the knowledge that is necessary for human life"; (2) "the standard of collection is based on necessity"; (3) "the whole collection is clearly systematic and complete in all categories; the categories have the effect of mutual enlightenment and do not have the blemish of duplication"; and (4) "what is deemed most necessary for all categories [of knowledge] is provided for the library or individual collector at the lowest price; students of the middle school or below, or teachers of primary schools, can establish a rudimentary library when they purchase a complete set of this repository."[30] To facilitate such purchases, a cleverly designed mail-order scheme, with installments for payment, was attached to a pamphlet that announced the series. It is evident that this massive project surpasses the textbook project in its ambition to spread the "knowledge of human life" to a reading public created by the publishing market.

In its own way the project is certainly comparable to that of the French Encyclopedists and their disseminators.[31] The crucial difference, however, lies in the systems and contents of categorization. Let us leave aside the 400 titles of "Chinese learning" in the two series (100 in the first series and 300 in the second) and look into the 250 titles of translations of "world classics" (100 in the first series, 150 in the second), as well as the 200 titles of "natural science" and 50 titles of "modern problems"—a total of 500 titles of what might be called "Western learning." Even at a glance, the catalogues are most impressive. The following is a selective listing of the categories and the significant Western authors and titles contained therein.

There are fifteen categories of translations in the first series.

1. Philosophy: Descartes's *Discourse on Method*, Spinoza's *Ethics*, Hume, Kant's *Critique of Pure Reason*, Schopenhauer, William James, Kropotkin, Nietzsche's *Thus Spoke Zarathustra*, Eucken, Bergson, Dewey, and Westaway's *Scientific Method*

2. Psychology: W. James's *Psychology: Brief Course*, Freud's *Psycho-analysis*, J. B. Watson's *Psychology from the Standpoint of Behaviorism*, K. Koffka's *The Growth of the Mind*

3. Sociology: H. Spencer, Kropotkin, Durkheim

4. Political science: Plato's *The Republic*, Aristotle's *Politics*, Hobbes's *Leviathan*, Bentham's *Introduction to the Principles of Morals and Legislation*, J. S. Mill's *On Liberty*, W. Bagehot's *Physics and Politics*, E. Jenks's *History of Politics*, Harold Laski's *Grammar of Politics*

5. Economics: Adam Smith's *The Wealth of Nations*, List, Proudhon, Marx's *Value, Price, and Profit*, Ingram, Hobson's *Modern Capitalism*, Webbs's *History of Trade Unionism*, D. S. Kimball's *Principles of Industrial Organization*, A. L. Bowley's *Elements of Statistics*

6. Law: Gropius, Montesquieu, Maine, Dicey, Lombroso, Duguit

7. Education: Rousseau's *Emile*, Herbart, Spencer, Dewey's *Democracy and Education*

8. Natural sciences: Newton, Lamarck, Faraday, Darwin, Huxley, Pasteur, Russell, Einstein

9. Anglo-American literature: Shakespeare's *Hamlet*, Milton's *Paradise Lost*, Defoe's *Robinson Crusoe*, Swift's *Gulliver's Travels*, Benjamin Franklin's *Autobiography*, Goldsmith's *The Vicar of Wakefield*, Walter Scott's *Ivanhoe*, Dickens's *David Copperfield*, Washington Irving's *Tales of Alhambra* (most of the preceding Anglo-American literature was translated by Lin Shu), G. B. Shaw

10. French literature: Rousseau's *Confessions,* Molière's *The Miser,* Hugo's *Les Miserables,* Dumas père's *The Three Musketeers,* Dumas fils' *La Dame aux Camelias* (translated by Lin Shu), Maupassant's *The Heritage*

11. German literature: Goethe's *Egmont,* Schiller's *Wallenstein,* Hauptmann's *Der rote Hahn*

12. Russian literature: Gogol's *The Reviser* or *Inspector General,* Turgenev's *Fathers and Sons,* A. Ostrovsky's *Poverty No Vice,* Tolstoy's *Childhood, Boyhood, and Youth*

13. Literature of other countries: Homer's *Odyssey,* Cicero's *Orations, The Arabian Nights,* Dante's *Divine Comedy,* Cervantes's *Don Quixote,* Ibsen's plays, Bjørnson's *In God's Way,* Maeterlinck's *The Blue Bird,* Tagore's *The Crescent Moon,* a collection of Japanese stories translated by Zhou Zuoren

14. History: Robinson's *New History,* Wells's *Outline of History*

15. Geography: Huntington and Cushing's *Principles of Human Geography,* Bowmen's *The New World*

In the second series, the translations of Western titles are divided into the following categories (italics indicate new or added categories): *culture and cultural history,* philosophy (Bacon, Leibnitz, Comte, Nietzsche), psychology, *logic* (Aristotle's *Logic*), ethics, sociology (Durkheim, Morgan, Malthus), *statistics,* political science (Rousseau's *Social Contract,* Moore's *Utopia*), *world diplomacy,* economics and *finance,* law, *military affairs,* education, *industry, family and marriage,* general science, mathematics, biological sciences, physics, applied sciences (more specialized than in the first series), geography and *travel, biographies* (of Napoleon, Bismarck, von Hindenburg, Tolstoy, and Edison, and including the autobiographies of J. M. Mill and Andrew Carnegie), *historiography,* history of Europe and America, history of Asia, general literature, and national literatures, with the latter including collections of works from countries including Japan, India, the United States, England, Germany, France, Italy, Spain, Russia, Poland, Denmark, Hungary, Norway, Sweden, and Romania, and the works of individual authors, such as Carlyle, Thackeray, Charlotte Bronte, J. M. Barrie, Drinkwater, Hardy, Galsworthy, Hawthorne, O. Henry, Frank Wedenkind, J. Freytag, Theodor Storm, Zola, Romain Rolland, Balzac, Octave Mirabeau, Paul Geraldy, Anatole France, Andreyev, Dostoevsky, Gorky, Dante, Euripides, Sophocles, Aeschylus, Knut Hamsum, Sienkiewicz, Ibanez, and K. Palamas.

To the above we may add the 200 titles of the natural sciences collection in the second series, which comprise the following ten categories: general discourses on science; astronomy; physics; chemistry; biology; zoology and anthropology; botany; geology, mining, and geography; biographies of famous scientists; and other. Almost all of the titles are translations (with Zhou Jianren, Lu Xun's younger brother, and Zhang Ziping, otherwise known as a popular novelist, taking a conspicuous share). These titles alone would earn the collection a particularly prominent position in the repository. Then, we must also add the 70 titles in the natural sciences section and the 30 titles in the applied sciences section of the "mini encyclopedia" collection of the first series. Thus, in the two series, titles related to the sciences alone (excluding subjects such as industry, statistics, psychology, etc.) come to 336—roughly the same as the "Chinese learning" collection. If we then add to this the other titles in the translation collections, the balance definitely tilts in favor of "scientific learning." Perhaps a majority of the science titles bear on aspects of practicality in modern life. (By comparison, titles on the "pure" sciences were apparently included in the textbooks.) This is not surprising, given the practical nature and goals of the repository.

What ultimately seems most relevant are the 50 titles in the second series in the category "modern problems." What can be categorized as modern problems (which is itself problematic)? In the second series catalogue we find the category divided into two parts: China (24 problems) and the world (26 problems). A mere listing of the titles already tells a story of nationalism as conceived and categorized in a popular imagination. Given the background of the Commercial Press, one cannot expect such a story to have a radical revolutionary projection. Rather, the problems in the section on China clearly focus on the recently established nation-state: namely, constitution, local self-government, village reconstruction, land, water conservancy (*shuili*), transportation, finance, taxation, international trade, cotton, silk, tea, compulsory education, adult education, women, labor, consular jurisdiction, recovery of the Northeast, development of the Northwest, Mongolia, Tibet, Sino-Japanese relations, Sino-Soviet relations, and overseas Chinese. The problems represent a preoccupation with issues of social and economic development; territorial and diplomatic issues also seem to demand attention. The latter is clearly reflected in the second section, whose titles address problems of the "world," with Japan, Soviet Russia, America, India, and the Philippines (its independence) occupying the center of attention. But an overwhelming amount of attention is focused on international issues, above all the reform of the League of Nations, international jurisdiction, and national self-determination, but also military weapons, food, fuel, unemployment, migration, monetary regulations, eugenics, sale of narcotic drugs, and rationalization (*helihua*). Together they give a political context that realistically reflects the situation of the world between the two world wars, in which the new Republic of China emerged as a new nation concerned with its territorial sovereignty and domestic development.

However, if we compare the titles in the category above with the revolutionary programs of the Chinese Communist Party, whose activities during the same period (1929–34) marked a transition from the urban to the rural phases, it is clear that some of the basic revolutionary premises are missing from the "fifty modern problems" covered in the series: problems of the urban proletariat, workers' strikes, theories of socialism, revolutionary literature, and above all peasantry and its revolutionary potential. The discrepancy reveals not only a difference between political orientations (Wang Yunwu's editorial board consisted of moderates and conservatives) but also a gap between the urban and rural imaginations. In other words, the entire repository enterprise was both urban based and addressed to an urban public. It deserves our attention because it provides the basic intellectual stuff of which an urban idea of Chinese modernity is made. At the very least, the above listings should be sufficient to give us a taxonomy of what constituted new knowledge in the early Republican era.

I hope that my narrative centered on the Commercial Press has also conveyed a sense of how its commercial enterprise evolved—from an educational enterprise based on textbook production to a cultural enterprise based on its journals and repositories. Together they forged a modern trajectory in terms of both time and space: the press's introduction of new knowledge was definitely animated by a desire to bring China abreast of what was going on around it, at the same time that it sought to support the effort of nation-building by providing intellectual resources for both the state and its "people." However, its definitions of the *guomin* remained vague, reflecting a nationalist echo of Liang Qichao's earlier slogan—and unfinished intellectual project—to have a "people made new" (*xinmin*) by renovating their collective mind and spirit. Whereas elitist intellectuals from Liang to Chen Duxiu and Lu Xun, perhaps following a Confucian precedent, continued to emphasize the issue of how to cultivate the intellectual and spiritual "essence" of a people, the less elitist intellectuals were perhaps less driven by such a moral impulse; they may have been more interested in the task of *popularization*—to make knowledge more general and accessible to the "new people" (who were "created" after all by their textbooks and newspapers), thus infusing urban society with the "temper" of a new era.

2.

My strategy in my search for urban modernity is based on the assumption that, contrary to the elitist approach of conventional intellectual history, which tends to discuss only the essential ideas of individual thinkers, the task of a cultural historian is to explore what may be called the "cultural imaginary." Since a cultural imaginary may be defined as itself a contour of collective sensibilities and significations resulting from cultural production, we must also wrestle with both ends of this interpretive strategy—namely, both the social and institutional context of this cultural production and the forms in which such an imaginary is constructed and communicated. In other words, we must not neglect the "surfaces"—images and styles that do not necessarily enter into the depth of thought but nevertheless conjure up a collective imaginary. In my view, modernity is both idea and imaginary, both essence and surface. I shall leave the idea part to other scholars—or to another book—and direct my energies to the surface, by boldly attempting to "read" a large number of pictures and advertisements in the journals and newspapers. For such purposes, I will base my analysis on data provided in another journal, a pictorial magazine called *Liangyou huabao* (The young companion [1926–45]), which was the longest-running large-sized pictorial journal in modern China. Before I get into the pictorials themselves, I must give a brief background of this cultural enterprise that, though smaller in scale than the Commercial Press, played an equally important role in the history of modern Chinese publishing—and in the shaping of a Chinese modernity.

The "Good Companion"

Liangyou tushu yinshua gongsi (literally, the Good friend books and printing company), established in Shanghai in 1925, clearly followed in the footsteps of the Commercial Press. Its founder, Wu Liande, an enterprising businessman who had once worked for the Commercial Press, was able to enlist such literary luminaries as Zhao Jiabi, Zheng Boqi, Ma Guoliang, and Zhou Shoujuan as editors. With its flagship journal, *Liangyou huabao*, the company quickly carved out a market for pictorial journals and other popular magazines. Following the example of the Commercial Press, it also sponsored the publication of collectanea and repositories, of which the most famous were *Liangyou wenxue congshu* (Liangyou's collectanea of literature), *Liangyou wenku* (Liangyou repository), and *Zhongguo xinwenxue daxi* (Compendium of new Chinese literature)—the last item has remained a useful compendium for all students of modern Chinese literature.[32] In an advertisement announcing the expansion of the company, it boasted about "the creation of a new era in the field of printing," since it was the first publishing company to specialize in photography. It also sponsored publication of half a dozen journals: in addition to *Liangyou huabao*, we find a cinema monthly—among the first of its kind—*Silver Star* (*Yinxing*); a journal entitled *Modern Woman* (*Jindai funü*); a weekly on the arts (*Yishu jie*), edited by the four "decadent" aesthetes Zhu Yingpeng, Zhang Ruogu, Fu Yanchang, and Xu Weinan; and a quarterly devoted to the world of athletics (*Tiyu shijie*). These magazine titles suggest the company's chief commercial direction: arts and entertainment. That such magazines satisfied an urban demand seems self-evident, but it is also likely that the demand was created by the magazines themselves.

At first glance, *Liangyou huabao* immediately impresses the reader with its large size—it is larger than *Dongfang zazhi*. For a pictorial, it contains a fairly heavy dose of written material, but its attraction obviously lies in its visual features. On the cover of each issue is a photograph or portrait of a moderately modern woman, with her name printed underneath. This may have been a continuation of a convention established by late Qing courtesan newspapers, in which a number of "famous flowers" (mostly courtesans who were acquaintances of the editors) appeared on the covers. But instead of courtesans *Liangyou huabao* covers featured "new-style" women of considerable renown. For instance, Lu Xiaoman, the coveted paramour and later wife of the famous poet Xu Zhimo, appears on the September 1927 issue. A photograph of the famous actress Anna May Wong (Huang Liushuang) appears on the cover of the June 1927 issue—a personal gift from her to the editor Wu Liande (her inscriptions are in English). This public display brings a sense of both realism and glamour. However, beginning in 1927, the journal also featured portraits of "fantasy" women. For example, the woman on the June 1928 issue sports not only rather chic high-heeled shoes but also, as was apparently the fashion of the period, a big fur scarf, which is prominently displayed on her shoulders, and earrings. Yet both her dress and her facial features remain "traditional," and they blend harmoniously with the background of what seems like a traditional Chinese painting. On closer inspection, however, we realize that she is not so demurely traditional after all: one of her arms is half exposed and leans against the back of what seems to be a modern (rocking) chair, and with the other hand on her crossed legs she strikes a slightly flirtatious pose. Her dress patterns are more flowery and elaborate than would be expected for an average woman—and she definitely looks rather rich (or pretends to be) with her fur scarf and earrings. As in each issue, the title of the magazine appears in both Chinese and English: whereas the Chinese characters loom large, they are not as artfully designed as the English title—*The Young Companion*. When we read the entire cover, both word and image, a subtitle or even subtext easily suggests itself: the young, rich, and alluring woman is (made to appear as) a "young companion" to the reader: thus this fantasy woman is designed to lure the reader into the magazine's written contents, which provided genuine "intellectual companionship."

I am not prepared to argue that the women on the front covers served no other purpose than as commodified "objects" intended to arouse male desire. Rather, I think the magazine's intended readership may have consisted of more women and school-age youths than adult men. Self-identified as a good companion (*liangyou*) to the reading public, the journal could not flaunt prurient interests but had to maintain a *good* reputation in order to maintain its large circulation. This good reputation was established, however, not through any intellectual clout or scholarly depth, but through good-natured gestures of *friendliness*. The editor's words in the front pages of the beginning issues certainly give us such an impression—that the journal serves as a good and constant companion in the daily lives of its readers. In the third issue (April 15, 1926), the editor, assuming the guise of a spirit (*Liangyou zhi shen*), greets the readers on the front page:

> Good morning, dear good friends:
>
> As you open the first page this morning and meet me, I am really a little abashed, and I don't know what to say. So I'll just say good morning and wish you good health. I was an ignorant youth, but thanks to your loving care I have been on friendly terms with you for about two months. I am even more grateful to you for not forsaking me due to my ignorance, and from now on I vow to be a good person, a reliable person, and your trusting and loyal friend.

In another issue the "Words from the Editor" column brings the "friend" even closer to the quotidian lifestyle of the intended reader: "When you are tired from work, pick up a copy of *Liangyou* and read through it; you can be assured that your energy will revive and you'll work better. When you're in a movie theater before the music begins and the curtain is drawn up, pick up a copy of *Liangyou* and read it; it's better than looking around. When at home you have nothing else to do, reading *Liangyou* is better than playing mah-jongg. When lying in bed, and your eyes are not tired, it's better to read *Liangyou* than to stare and indulge in silly thoughts."[33]

To attribute the above merely to the ingenuity of the editor would be too easy, since behind such words lurk both a conscious intention and a cultural context. Just as the editors of *Dongfang zazhi* and *Wanyou wenku* capitalized on the obvious need for new knowledge, the editors of *Liangyou huabao* sensed and exploited the public need for a new urban lifestyle on the quotidian level. Naturally this need was better served by a pictorial magazine. A useful comparison can be made between the journal and its late Qing predecessor, *Dianshizhai huabao* (Pictorial from the stone-tablet studio), which revealed the popularity of such a medium. In the late Qing intellectual context, the *Dianshizhai* pictorial, which consists entirely of drawings in the traditional style (with no photography), is more "fantastic" in content but nevertheless aimed to inform and enlighten the reader with new knowledge by illustrating the wonders of the world. By the time *Liangyou huabao* was published, that intellectual task was being accomplished by the Commercial Press. At least in Shanghai, modernity, as evidenced by the transliterated term *modeng*, could be seen as an emergent urban style of life. Thus *Liangyou huabao* ushered in a second phase of pictorial journalism, one that reflected this urban taste for the modern life—which, beginning in the early 1930s, became further glamourized by the numerous movie magazines. It is in this context that I wish to pay more attention to its coverage of women and youth, for I believe that from this coverage unfolds another story of Chinese modernity.

Not only do women grace the front covers of *Liangyou huabao*, they also occupy a central position in the magazine's contents, of which the first and last few pages are entirely devoted to photographs; other photos and illustrations, including comic sketches (*manhua*), are interlaced with written articles. We can only imagine how an issue of the magazine was read by readers of the time, but the reading process would inevitably involve an experience of both visual and written "pleasures." The reader, if reading in sequence, would first look at the front cover and then the photos on the first few pages of the magazine before reading the articles. Or a reader might look at all the pictures and then choose a few articles to read. In either case, a chain of visual links is formed, with or without the written contents. It is highly unlikely that a reader of a pictorial magazine would read only the written and ignore all the visual materials. Thus I would like to attempt a rudimentary visual reading by focusing on pictures of women.

The woman on the cover may not have much to do with the contents of the issue; still, her look and dress serve to establish an initial surface impression that may be linked to other pictures inside the magazine. In some cases, some of the photos inside are variations (more photos or paintings) of the same cover woman as she models seasonal fashion. For instance, Ms. Yang Aili wears a spring or summer dress on the cover of the May 15, 1926, issue, but inside she wears a winter garment complete with a big fur. As the reader scans the other photos (credited by a line in English: "supplied by A. L. Varges, International Newsreel Corp. of New York"), she or he is introduced to the different dress styles. In this issue, there is a whole page of six photos of women modeling different clothes, some of whom may have already become familiar due to their appearances on the magazine's covers. The reader is then drawn into a seasonal fashion fantasy in which different facets of the fantasy woman's social life (ordinary dress in the house, cape worn to a ballroom, etc.) are featured and further variations typecast her into one of several stock social categories. This last trait is clearly an ideological inscription taken from traditional Chinese culture: for instance, terms like *miaoling nülang* (young girl at a tender age), *guinü* (young maiden), *dajia guixiu* (cultivated maiden from a well-to-do family), and *yanzhuang shaofu* (gorgeously dressed young lady or housewife) often accompany the fashion photos.

I argue, however, that fashion-consciousness plays only a small part in these photos and drawings about women's fashion. (There were no fashion models then, as there was no such profession yet.) Rather, they reflect a consciousness of *dress* itself, which provides an index to a new range of sensibilities in the lives of urban women of the middle and upper classes. For I believe that the photos delineate a set of domestic and public spaces in which these categories of the "well-dressed woman" live and move: from the bedroom to the ballroom, and from the living room to the movie houses and department stores. Thus it is not surprising that by 1930 dress-consciousness had widened to include a consciousness of interior decoration and furniture. In issue No. 50 (1930) we find well-dressed women sitting in different rooms of "a typical modern home": two photos of the parlor with modern furniture; two photos of the bedroom with emphasis on the colors and tones of the wallpaper; and the children's bedroom with a bed, chair, and large drawing of an animal on the wall.

On the basis of these photos, it would seem that woman's place is *still* at home, albeit in a modern space, together with her children. In fact, this domestic link—women and their children—is repeated in almost all the advertisements. At first glance, this domestic picture seems to contradict the earlier May Fourth discourse, which centered on the image of an emancipated Nora—an independent woman who, like Ibsen's character, leaves her traditional family to lead an independent life. Still, I argue that this does not necessarily indicate a conservative retreat from the radicalism of the previous decade. The narrative that can be derived from reading through the *Liangyou huabao* is one that revolves around women's new roles in a modern conjugal family into which are woven other aspects of an evolving style of urban bourgeois life. Whereas, as these advertisements suggest, women's new roles are still in the home, it is a home made anew by all the modern conveniences and interior design. The domestic space of the household is now fully "publicized" in the open, and as such has become a public issue. As indicated in the numerous photos and articles in the journal, this public discourse of new domesticity pays great attention to physical health and family hygiene. Some medicine ads are especially revealing in this regard.[34]

Advertising Modernity

In a revealing study of the medical ads in the newspaper *Shenbao*, Huang Kewu has concluded that social life in Shanghai was besmeared by the problems of contagious and sexual diseases, and of opium-smoking and its prohibition; the ads also showed some significant changes in women's lives, of which freedom from foot binding was a major phenomenon. My own preliminary findings, drawn from the ads in *Dongfang zazhi* and *Liangyou huabao,* indicate that there were other issues as well. For instance, the advertisements for Dr. Williams' Pink Pills for Pale People invariably contain illustrations of people to show the positive functions of the drug. In the other samples, I have found the recurrent motif of a modern conjugal family of husband and wife, sometimes with one or two children or an occasional grandfather or grandmother. Together these ads, it seems to me, tell an imagined story of a modern couple for whom marital happiness based on good health becomes a central element. If read together with Huang's findings, the ads project an urban lifestyle in which the errant husband is more likely to contract sexual diseases outside but the wife remains healthily at home. (Of course, he will stay healthy so long as he stays at home with his wife.) In contrast to the implied "evil" space outside, home is portrayed as a safe and clean place in which, in one ad, a woman is seen brushing her teeth with Colgate's Ribbon Dental Cream (when she is not using Colgate's Fab, which "Safely Washes Fine Fabrics"), and in another, holding her baby on top of a can of Momilk by American Brewer and Company, beside a long passage describing the dangers of wet nurses who, in a predictable transference, are the transmitters of sexual and other contagious diseases.[35]

Even in the ubiquitous cigarette ads, we find a picture of domestic comfort as an elaborately dressed wife (in the same style as the cover portrait cited earlier) offers a tin of Golden Dragon Cigarettes to her traditionally clothed husband sitting on a modern sofa. The four lines of Chinese words placed into a square form an awkward and blatantly exploitative message: "Beauty is lovely; cigarettes are also lovely. The cigarette that is a national product, it is even more lovely." Perhaps the most revealing is a set of three ads for Quaker Oats, which gives us three variations of the same story: in the first one, a wife wearing an apron is holding a bowl of Quaker Oats to give to her seated husband, who is reading a newspaper (with the heading "Ideal Breakfast"); in the second, a mother is holding her beloved baby and feeding him a spoonful of Quaker Oats; in the third, there is no direct representation of the cereal but the picture of two youngsters, a boy and a girl, carrying their satchels and running to school. The health message reads: "Give the energy, nourish the soul: youngsters in school consume a lot of energy, and the development of their bodies and hearts consumes even more. For nourishment, this is proper food." From the three ads we can easily piece together a Quaker Oats story: the healthy life of a couple leads to a healthy family, which in turn strengthens the children's bodies and souls. This American product, therefore, contributes its share to the education of a healthy people. This crude bildungsroman is given a shot of nationalism in the two lines of another Momilk ad: "Strengthening the nation must begin with strengthening the people; strengthening the people must begin with strengthening the children."[36]

The emphasis on children is further evidenced by the many photos of naked babies in *Liangyou huabao*'s issues. The magazine proceeded in late 1926 to sponsor, together with the Momilk company, a competition for the healthiest babies, with an award totaling four hundred yuan for the top thirty. Hundreds of photos of eager entrants appeared in subsequent issues. The whole enterprise is but a "healthy" echo of an American beauty contest, which the journal also featured in its twentieth issue. The Chinese headings for the beauty contest used three terms: *meiren* (beautiful person), *meinü* (beautiful woman), and *renti mei* (beauty of the human body). The last also became the recurrent theme of a series of photographs displaying the female body with an increasing degree of nudity. The issues of 1926 featured Western sculptures and paintings of nudes and photos of Japanese women in bathing suits. These were accompanied by drawings by contemporary Chinese artists (for instance, issue No. 15 [1927] featured the works of Wan Laiming). In issue No. 30 (1928), a number of nude poses appeared together with an ad for a book of Wan Laiming's paintings. This was the first time that photos of a Chinese nude model appeared: four photos showing the contours of a woman's back. In issue No. 40 (1929) a "photographic study" by Chang Chien Wen shows a full-page nude facing a mirror—with the explanatory remarks lauding the naturalness of her body: "a healthy body is the first principle of beauty." In issue No. 50 (1930), another photo of a frontal nude also takes up a whole page, with the English title "Under the shade of a willow tree (a photo by P. C. Chen)"; the Chinese title again lauded "a healthy and beautiful body."

It would take a long treatise to put the public display, artistic or otherwise, of the female body in a modern Chinese cultural context. (It would be relatively easy to see it as an invasion of Western culture and aesthetics that inscribes a long history of the Western human body on the Chinese mind.) As Mark Elvin has shown in a long article, the discourse on the body in traditional Chinese culture is full of complexities. The Chinese word for body, *shen*, is translated by Elvin as "body-person" as it is often connected with extraphysical attributes of person, self, life, or lifetime.[37] Both Confucianism and Taoism were, of course, much obsessed with the physical side of the human body. But according to Elvin the reason for this was above all to preserve longevity: "Late-traditional Chinese were hypochondriacs, obsessed with diets, medicine, and health generally"[38]—all presumably for such a purpose. One should add that these hypochondriacs were mostly men. Elvin notes that "the body-person is also the heart-mind's most important single resource. It is (obviously) the carrier of physical beauty, both female and male. It is the repository of 'face,' both in the all-or-nothing sense of social credit-worthiness and in the incremental-decremental sense of prestige. Even its wealth seems to stick to it like a physical characteristic, and affects how it is perceived by others. The expected dowries and inheritances of the sons and daughters of the rich are discussed in the same breath as their appearance and their behavior. Female bodies have a precise market value. It goes without saying that this is so for the young ladies—far from the most unfortunate in this society—who are purchased as investments when young by the madames who run the houses of pleasure, and sell them off later as secondary wives to rich businessmen in whom a besotted lust has been artfully introduced."[39]

The relevance of this observation for our purposes is that this last instance may well have been preserved in the cultural memory of readers of *Liangyou huabao*. As I argued earlier, the journal's effort to maintain a healthy respectability and friendliness may have stemmed from an awareness of the popularity of countless journals, as well as the gossip sheets put out by the "mosquito press," devoted to the pleasure quarters. Catherine Yeh has demonstrated that in the late Qing period, such journals about courtesans also held beauty competitions; each "famous flower" had her own literati following.[40] The vogue faded from the publishing scene after (so Yeh surmised) such journals were replaced by movie magazines. Courtesan literature, in fact, did not fade from modern Chinese literature: only its "public image" was displaced by photographs and paintings of modern, and more respectable, women. Thus to display the female body either as a work of art (Western) or as an embodiment of physical health marked the beginnings of a new discourse that was made problematic precisely because it was derived from the previous courtesan journals, in which female bodies indeed carried a market value. Insofar as it portrayed young ladies, a new pictorial like *Liangyou huabao* had to reinvest the female body with an entirely new meaning and ethical value. The new women portrayed or photographed are *not* poor, or at least not from poor families. And when they are placed in a interior setting of a modern family, they are made to embody a totally different style of life. Their bodies, therefore, are placed in new "persons": to follow Elvin, their new house would be where they could *an-shen* (settle down in life), just as their *chu-shen* (upbringing) and *shen-fen* (personal status) are purposefully given a "dressing up" of bourgeois wealth and respectability. Thus fashion—the styles of dressing up—became a modern element in a culture that did not have such a tradition except in a fleeting form (according to Elvin, "chiefly hairdo and makeup, it seems").[41]

To move from the portrait of a fashionable woman to that of a nude female generated further anxiety for readers living in that still transitional age, because the drawings of naked female bodies in traditional Chinese culture were found largely in pornographic books. The invention of photography and its adoption by the modern newspaper and magazine added a mimetic dimension: the nude figure looks like a real person. This new "shock of recognition" could incur all kinds of "misinterpretations" by the average readers of the time—most of all those derived from male gaze and lust, hence leading to objectification and commodification of the female body—a familiar view in current feminist and postcolonial theories. But what if some (even large numbers) of the readers were women? And what if pages of nudes were placed in the journal together with pictures of Chinese and world leaders, sporting events, and Hollywood movie stars? The issue here is not confined to the female body alone: I argue that the display of the female body became part of a new public discourse related to the modernity of everyday life, a subject that has received considerable theoretical attention in the field of cultural studies because, among other reasons, it addresses directly the problematic of the (Western) culture of modernity and postmodernity.[42] As mentioned before, in the Chinese context of the early twentieth century, the theme of everyday life was a construction of print media and was structured and governed by a semiotics of *material* culture. The contours of such a material world can be detected, again, in the advertisements in the magazines. In the above discussion I have mentioned Quaker Oats, Momilk, Colgate's Ribbon Dental Cream, and Fab detergent. These products already fulfill, functionally, the family's needs for the morning ritual: the family can clean their teeth with the dental cream and breakfast on oatmeal and milk; yesterday's laundry can be cleaned with detergent. From the ads we can easily reconstruct a list of daily necessities and luxuries for the modern urban household: electric cooking pots (*zhufan dianlu*) as sold by the Oriental Trading Company, Limited; automatic firepots or gas burners (*zilai huolu*) from the Shanghai Gas Company, Limited (the ad notes that "recently Chinese people have largely replaced coal burners with gas burners, and that [a gas burner] is especially suitable for Chinese houses in winter for purposes of hygiene for the whole family"); cameras; camera studios; Agfa and Kodak film (featured in a journal that took great pride in photography); Eveready batteries; gramophones and records (Pathe and RCA)—though not yet the telephone—and fountain pens. A full-page ad in issue No. 7 (1926) for the Hong Kong branch of the Wing On Department Store presents a neat mosaic of these items: Conklin fountain pen (and a Western-clothed man using it), various kinds of cotton cloth, Swan brand silk stockings and cotton socks, Pilsner Art Export Beer, and a copy of *Liangyou huabao*. The necessities for daily comfort for an urban household, both inside and outside, seem complete.

By the early 1930s, an entire imaginary of urban modernity was constructed in the pages of *Liangyou huabao*. There appeared more and more photos showcasing the various attractions of the city itself. Issue No. 87 in 1934 includes a two-page photographic extravaganza billed in English as "Outline of Shanghai"; its Chinese title is even more revealing: "So This Is Shanghai: Sound, Light, and Electricity." Other photos show Shanghai's famed department stores, hotels, ballrooms, cinemas (together with movie stars), and women. An issue in 1934 presents a photographic mosaic with headings in both English and Chinese—"Intoxicated [*sic*] Shanghai" and "Duhui de ciji" (Excitements of the metropolis)—with photos of a jazz band, a new twenty-two-story skyscraper, scenes of horse and dog racing, a movie poster of King Kong, and two parallel scenes showing a row of women baring their legs in athletics and cabaret dancing.[43] At the center is a young Chinese woman wearing a fashionable *qipao*—a gown of "Manchu cut" widely popular at the time—with high slits, who is seated in an alluring pose. Lest the photos be considered too seductive, the journal, in an apparent act of self-criticism, printed in a subsequent issue another series of pictures, titled "On the Sidewalks of Shanghai," showing other aspects of the city: used books and magazine stands, professional scribes whose business was to read and write letters for the illiterates at a modest price, four men gawking at pictures of women on a street wall, a newsstand, a bucket of cheap fountain pens, two men and a boy reading old pictorial storybooks, and beggars with their open letter to the public unfolded on the ground.[44] These photographs combine to reveal an intriguing self-reflexivity: the city to which the journal owed its very existence was first glamorized and then critiqued, as if to show that the imaginary modernity contained in its photographs was but a fantasy pieced together by a clever arrangement in print; at the same time, however, the mimetic intent of the photographs seemed to imply that this fantasy was based on reality. No matter how hard the journal's editors sought to present the other side of Shanghai, it was this modern fantasy that began to take hold of the popular imagination of its readers. What makes the story of *Liangyou huabao* worth telling, lies precisely in its conscious effort in advertising modernity, thereby helping to construct it in Shanghai's urban culture. As such, it marked not only a significant chapter in the history of modern Chinese journalism but a historical step in representing the progress of Chinese modernity itself.

Calendar Posters

It remains for me to discuss one last specimen in this series of commercial advertisements for modernity—perhaps the most significant one, as it provides the crucial temporal scheme of everyday operation—the commercial calendar.

The commercial calendar began as an advertising gimmick introduced by Western capitalism—principally the British and American tobacco, medicine, cosmetic, textile, and oil companies. As early as the second decade of the twentieth century, the American Tobacco Company (*Yingmei yancao gongsi*) had introduced offset lithographic printing, formed its own advertising department, and set up an art school for the sole purpose of training commercial artists. But its domination was soon challenged by native Chinese entrepreneurs, in particular Huang Chujiu, the owner of the Great Eastern Dispensary and the Great World Amusement Building, who spotted the artistic talent of a Hangzhou painter, Zheng Mantuo, and promoted him.[45] Thus calendar posters painted by Zheng and his disciples became most sought-after items, thereby establishing a new tradition of commercial art that combined traditional Chinese painting techniques with modern design (sometimes framed with art deco patterns) and utility. In the 1920s and early 1930s, the calendar poster reached a peak of popularity.

The basic composition of the commercial calendars is the same for each: an oblong rectangular frame, like that of a traditional Chinese painting, with the portrait of a woman occupying about two-thirds of the frame, and at the bottom a calendar; on top of either the large frame or the calendar is printed the name of the company advertising its commodity: usually cigarettes or medicine. In some ways this makes for a perfect summation of some of the central elements I have discussed in this chapter: the calendar poster features not only the veneer of modernity as seen through advertisements but also the paraphernalia associated with the women in the pictures. In fact, the cover women in *Liangyou huabao* and the women in the calendars bear some striking similarities in terms of fashion, posture, and facial expression, and the background landscapes are similar. The calendar portraits also exhibit a painting technique that, while clearly linked to traditional brush styles and popular roots (such as the *nianhua*, or New Year pictures, in rural households), nevertheless added some innovative touches. This new vogue was popularized by Zheng Mantuo and his friends and disciples. A special technique of Zheng's was to begin drawing the woman's face with charcoal powder and then touch up with colored hues, thus creating a tender, subdued look. This kind of "portrait of a lady in modern dress" (*shizuang shinu tu*) became a representative fixture of the calendar, and the discerning viewer or collector supposedly could even see "her eyes following people."[46]

Allow me to read one such woman depicted on a calendar that I own (see figure 1.1).[47] This is one of the more traditional varieties of the calendar, and it advertises Hatamen brand cigarettes. It is painted with a special 1930 technique of light-colored brushwork (*caibi dancai hua*) first used by the artist Zheng Mantuo in the late Qing period.[48] In this particular case, the body of the woman is not lengthened, as sometimes is necessitated by the oblong shape of the frame. She sits sideways by a patch of water where a pair of swans swim together; in the upper and lower right corners are branches and grass painted in the traditional style. The ambiance seems to transport us away from the modern reality. In my view, it also evokes the fictional world of the Butterfly school (also known as the Mandarin Duck and Butterfly school); the pair of swans in particular is a visual reference, metonymically, to mandarin ducks. This common traditional style may serve to tone down the blatantly foreign (English) origin of the cigarettes. However, in order to spotlight the commodity, the cigarette pack in the grass next to her is red.

As we gaze at the picture of the woman, we find that although her clothes are traditional—she wears a simple and tastefully light-colored *qipao*—there are some very modern touches that distinguish her from the myriad traditional women who graced magazine covers. For one thing, the big flower she wears near her collar is a striking pink, which contrasts with the pale green color of her gown (with slim pink stripes to match), thereby both bringing out and toning down the familiar aesthetic association of prime colors (red and green). The pointed position of the flower of course also serves to point to the woman, thus giving rise to the familiar poetic metaphor for woman: *yizhi hua*—a solitary flower of (faded) splendor that

Figure 1.1. Calendar poster, 1930.

conveys a vague feeling of passion soured by pity and sadness. What kind of flower is she wearing? A rose, a peony, or even a pear flower (as in the evocative poetic line: "A pear flower, bringing spring and rain" [*Yizhi lihua chun dai yu*]). I may be intentionally overreading the flower associations because I find her face reminiscent of the famous movie actress Ruan Lingyu, who rose to great fame around 1930—definitely a great icon and a legendary woman of passion, who later committed suicide for love. In fact, movie actresses often served as models for these commercial calendars (another famous example is the actress Li Lihua, who posed for a poster advertising *yindanshilin bu*, a blue-colored textile fabric commonly used for women's clothes).[49] As on movie screens, the women on the calendars are displayed objects who nevertheless make a subjective visual impact on individual viewers. What distinguishes a good calendar from a mediocre one lies precisely in this particular combination of the striking and the stereotypical, the real and the fantastic. The woman on a calendar, I suspect, becomes the key factor for the buyer's choice (if the calendar is not given out by the company as a New Year gift, according to custom then and now), and the tobacco company's "legendary" reputation may have something to do with its posted, hence fetishized, woman. Thus the woman figure, like the cigarette, became a commodity.[50]

But the real function of this calendar, hence the real content of this "text," is the calendar itself, which is reduced to the lower half but framed with a striking art deco design. What makes it immediately relevant to my purposes is the fact that the calendar in this case uses two sets of modern year-marks: 1930 of the Western calendar on the left and the nineteenth year of the Republic of China on the right. The rest of this yearly calendar is divided by the months, which are further divided into weeks. At this point the traditional lunar dates also enter into the charts. I have no idea when this calendrical arrangement became the standard, but the cultural significance cannot be overemphasized. Not only does the standard calendar bring two clear time-markers together (Chinese and Western, both notably modern), but the two also combine to inscribe a modern organizational scheme of time on the traditional. The division of months, days, and weeks is manifestly Western and modern, and by this time governed the everyday lives of Chinese urbanites; a few seasonal dates from the lunar calendar are placed on the month column on top—perhaps as a reminder of the important rituals people still needed to perform or, as is still practiced now, as a form of "fortune-telling" to alert the modern city-dwellers to equate their modern date-keeping with a tabulation of divine fortune: which day may be auspicious for which ritual? All of these have become common features in the Chinese calendars used today. But the invention of the calendar poster must be duly accredited. For I believe that time—and the system of calendrical dating—is the foundation on which modernity is constructed. This is also the underlying thesis in Anderson's book, that nationalism could be imagined only as a result of a fundamental change in the conception of time: the imagined community of the nation springs from an idea of "homogeneous, empty time, in which simultaneity is, as it were, transverse, cross-time, marked not by prefiguring and fulfillment, but by temporal coincidence, and measured by clock and calendar."[51] To bring Anderson's abstraction to the level of urban Shanghai, we could almost say that the daily life of the kind of "imagined modernity" I have described was also measured by the clock (there was a big one on top of the Shanghai Customs House) and the calendar.

3.

In this essay I have surveyed two highly successful journals, *Dongfang zazhi* and *Liangyou huabao*, and their related commercial enterprises in order to explore the ways in which an imaginary of modernity was constructed in Shanghai's urban culture. The two also bore institutional linkages: Wu Liande, the founder of *Liangyou huabao*, once worked for the Commercial Press, and the Liangyou company clearly followed some of the publishing projects of the Commercial Press with its own resounding success. The most impressive and enduring of the Liangyou projects was surely the ten-volume *Zhongguo xinwenxue daxi* (Compendium of new Chinese literature) edited by Zhao Jiabi, which after its publication in the early 1930s soon attained canon status.[52] Other ambitious projects, such as *Liangyou wenku* (Liangyou repository) and *Yijiao congshu* (Ten-cent series), were cheap editions composed of works by renowned authors of modern Chinese literature and thought. But certainly the major legacy of modern Chinese print culture was its pictorial pages, which literally and figuratively contributed to the making of a modern Chinese imaginary.

Throughout the essay I have used the term *imaginary* in the sense of a cluster of linked images that collectively represent an imagined ideal (of Chinese modernity). An imaginary is different from a theory because it also concerns the way ordinary people imagine their surroundings; intellectual theory is the creation of a small intellectual elite, whereas social or cultural imaginary can be shared by large groups of people through the circulation of print and visual media. It aims at a common understanding that makes possible common practices and a sense of legitimacy.[53] Throughout this essay I have also emphasized the process of cultural construction rather than consumption, for reasons that should by now be clear. For I believe that this imaginary of modernity was still in the making during the early Republican period. I have further suggested that, following Anderson, such a modern imaginary was also related to the formation of the modern Chinese nation first as an imagined community. That this imagined community was being legitimized with the organization of a social imaginary can be evidenced in Liangyou's weighty pictorial album *Zhonghua jingxiang* (originally translated as *China as She Is: A Comprehensive Album*) published in 1934.[54] What lies behind this photographed collection of national scenery (*jingxiang*) seems to be a clear impulse to define the boundaries of the new nation. Further research is necessary to establish the exact relationship between this cultural and commercial enterprise and the policies of the modern Chinese state, particularly in education. It would not be surprising to find that the kind of imaginary that was being constructed conformed largely to the prescriptions of the state.[55]

Likewise, we need to explore further the connection and interplay between editors and readers, producers and consumers. What was the composition of the urban readership? How diverse was it? Would different kinds of readers respond to different content in different journals? So far my evidence is merely textual: I have tried to gauge the range and size of the readerships from the printed articles and advertisements in the journals themselves, though there is danger that the journals are guilty of self-serving exaggeration. However, my purpose in this essay is not to describe empirical research but to explore the possibilities of a new approach, that of cultural history. Some of my interpretations can be taken as hypotheses subject to further proof. However, not all interpretations are based on empirical evidence, and no amount of research can ever establish the final picture. I hope that I have at least blazed a small trail by shifting our scholarly attention from the elitist domain of lofty ideas and grand narratives to a more popular realm of urban print culture.

NOTES

1. Leo Ou-fan Lee, "In Search of Modernity: Reflections on a New Mode of Consciousness in Modern Chinese Literature and Thought," in *Ideas across Cultures: Essays in Honor of Benjamin Schwartz*, ed. Paul A. Cohen and Merle Goldman (Cambridge: Harvard East Asian Monographs, 1990), 110–11.

2. The term *wenming* is included in appendix D, "Return Graphic Loans: Kanji Terms Derived from Classical Chinese," in Lydia Liu's *Translingual Practice: Literature, National Culture, and Translated Modernity—China, 1900–1937* (Stanford: Stanford University Press, 1996), 308.

3. Benjamin Schwartz, *In Search of Wealth and Power* (Cambridge: Harvard University Press, 1964), 238–39.

4. Rengong [Liang Qichao], "Hanman lu," *Qingyi bao* 35 (1899): 2275–78.

5. Benedict Anderson, *Imagined Communities: Reflections on the Origin and Spread of Nationalism* (New York: Verso, 1983).

6. Ibid., 31–36.

7. Jurgen Habermas, *The Structural Transformation of the Public Sphere* (Cambridge: MIT Press, 1989), 40–41, 50–51.

8. But this is not the same as Habermas's "public sphere," as China did not share the same preconditions as Europe in the eighteenth century. Thus I differ from those who believe there was a Chinese public sphere or civil society. Still, the concept of a reading "public" does open up notions of the "public space" as well as urban space, which may constitute a "semipublic sphere" within the framework of urban society. But even so, some of the standard manifestations Habermas sees in eighteenth-century French salons or English pubs and journals did not take place in China.

9. Homi K. Bhabha, "Dissemination: Time, Narrative, and the Margins of the Modern Nation," in *Nation and Narration*, ed. Homi K. Bhabha (London: Routledge, 1990).

10. Robert Darnton, *The Business of Enlightenment: A Publishing History of the Encyclopedie* [*sic*] (Cambridge: Harvard University Press, 1968).

11. There has already been scholarly treatment of both *Dongfang zazhi* and the Commercial Press in Western languages. Thus, I do not intend to go into their backgrounds. For a comprehensive study of the latter, see Jean-Pierre Drege, *La Commercial Press de Shanghai, 1897–1949* (Paris: Institute des hautes etudes chinoises, College de France, 1978). See also the valuable collection of reminiscences *Shangwu yinshugan jiushinian* (Ninety years of the Commercial Press) (Beijing: Shangwu yinshuguan, 1987).

12. Ma Xuexin, Cao Junwei, et al., eds., *Shanghai wenhua yuanliu cidian* (A dictionary of cultural sources in Shanghai) (Shanghai: Shanghai shehui kexueyuan chubanshe, 1992), 199.

13. Jing Cang, "Jinhou zazhi jie zhi zhiwu" (The duty of the magazine world from now on), *Dongfang zazhi* (hereafter *DZ*) 16, no. 7 (July 1919): 3–5.

14. Lu Lu, "Jiqi yu rensheng" (Machines and life), *DZ* 16, no. 10 (October 1916): 47–54.

15. *DZ* 8, no. 1 (March 1911): 38.

16. Apparently English-Chinese dictionaries were in great demand, and the Commercial Press had to make every effort in order to beat other publishers to the market. Most dictionaries were patchworks stitched together from English and Japanese dictionaries. In the case of publishing *Webster's Dictionary*, the Commercial Press had to pay a sizable sum as a result of the lawsuit brought by the original company. See Xie Juzeng, *Shili yangchang de ciyang* (Silhouettes on the Bund) (Guangzhou: Huacheng chubanshe), 50.

17. Actually, Mrs. Zhu was editor in name only; the real editor was a man, Zhu Yunzhang, a member of the press's staff, who nominally consulted her and wrote some articles under her name. See Xie Juzeng, *Shili yangchang de ciyang*, 38.

18. See "Jiaokeshu zhi fakan gaikuang" (The general situation of the publication of textbooks), in *Zhongguo jindai chuban shiliao chubian*, ed. Zhang Jinglu (Shanghai: Zhonghua shuju, 1957), 220.

19. Ibid., 228. The Japanese connection proved to be a mixed blessing; the press eventually severed it. This may have been the reason, though an undocumented one, why the Japanese bombarded and destroyed the press's printing plant and other buildings during the air raid on January 28, 1932.

20. This announcement and the advertisements for the photo and postcards can be found in *DZ* 8, no. 11 (November 1911).

21. *Zhongguo jindai chuban shiliao chubian*, 243–44.

22. *Zhongguo jiaoyu daxi* (The grand compendium of Chinese education) 2 (1994): 2221–22.

23. *Zhongguo jindai chuban shiliao chubian*, 242–43.

24. Ibid., 246.

25. Ibid., 221.

26. I am indebted to my student Mr. Chen Jianhua for these statistics and for other research assistance.

27. Wang Yunwu, "Wangyou wenku di yierji yinxing yuanqi" (The background for the publication of the first and second series of the *Wanyou wenku*), in *Zhongguo xiandai chuban shiliao yibian* (Shanghai: Zhonghua shuju, 1954), 290–91. Drege discusses Wang Yunwu's reorganization efforts (Drege, *Commercial Press*, 89–94), and in the appendix section of *Commercial Press* are listings of the periodicals distributed by the press, as well as *congshu* and dictionaries (185–98), but not textbooks.

28. Ibid., 290–91.

29. Ibid., 293–94.

30. "Wanyou wenku bianyi fanli" (The guidelines for the compilation of *Wanyou wenku*), *Wanyou wenku diyiji yiqianzhong mulu* (Catalogue of one thousand titles of Wanyou wenku, 1st ser.) (Shanghai: Shangwu yinshuguan, 1929), 2.

31. The relevance was noted by Li Shizeng, a renowned intellectual of the time, who is reported to have remarked that he admired two historical figures: Ji Xiaolan, the Qing dynasty compiler of the *Siku quanshu,* and Diderot, the French philosophe of the *Encyclopedie.* See Qian Huafo and Zheng Yimei, *Sanshinian lai zhi Shanghai* (Shanghai of the past thirty years) (1946; reprint, Shanghai: Shanghai shudian, 1984), 46–47.

32. Ma Xuexin et al., *Shanghai wenhua yuanliu cidian* (Shanghai: Shanghai shehui kexueyuan chubanshe, 1992), 379. For an analysis of the making of the *Compendium of New Chinese Literature,* see Lydia Liu, *Translingual Practice,* 214–38.

33. *Liangyou huabao,* 6 (July 15, 1926): 18.

34. Huang Kewu, "Cong Shenbao yiyao guanggao kan minchu Shanghai de yiliao wenhua yu shehui shenghuo" (Shanghai's medical culture and social life as seen in Shenbao's medicine advertisements), *Zhongyang yanjiu yuan Jindai shi yanjiu suo jikan* (Quarterly journal of the Modern History Institute, Academia Sinica), no. 17 (December 1988): 141–94.

35. *Liangyou huabao* 6 (July 15, 1926): 18.

36. *Liangyou huabao* 11 (December 15, 1926).

37. Mark Elvin, "Tales of Shen and Xin: Body-Person and Heart-Mind in China during the Last 150 Years," *Zone 4: Fragments for a History of the Human Body,* pt. 2 (New York: Zone, 1989), 275.

38. Ibid., 277.

39. Ibid., 295.

40. This is from a talk given at the Workshop on Chinese Cultural Studies, Fairbank Center, Harvard University, Cambridge, March 9, 1995.

41. Ibid., 268.

42. See, for instance, Henri Lefebvre, *Everyday Life in the Modern World,* trans. Sacha Rabinovitch (New Brunswick and London: Transaction Publishers, 1990). But Lefebvre's interpretive scheme is too contemporary and Western to be relevant to the Chinese materials treated in this essay.

43. *Liangyou huabao* 85 (1934): 14–15.

44. *Liangyou huabao* 103 (1935): 34–35. For sampling these photos I am grateful to my student Ezra Block, whose senior thesis at Harvard (June 1996), "Modeling Modernity: The *Liangyou huabao* in the 1930s," is also on the journal.

45. Zhang Yanfeng, *Lao yuefenpai guanggao hua* (Advertisement paintings in old calendars), vol. 1 (Taipei: Hansheng zazhi, 1994), 65.

46. Cai Zhenghua and Fan Zhenjia, "Yuefen pai" (Calendars), in *Bainian Shanghai tan* (The Shanghai treaty-port during the last one hundred years), ed. Ye Shuping and Zheng Zu'an (Shanghai: Shanghai huabao chubanshe, 1990), 120–22.

47. This is a gift from William Tay, who purchased it in Hong Kong. A photo reproduction of it is included in Zhang Yanfeng, *Lao yuefenpai guanggao hua,* 1:18. Apparently a widespread nostalgia for such old artifacts is now sweeping Hong Kong, Taiwan, and Mainland China.

48. Zhang Yanfeng, *Lao yuefenpai guanggao hua,* 1:10.

49. Ibid., 42.

50. Francesca Dal Lago, at New York University, has written a master's thesis on the subject. Contrary to my sedate and "conservative" reading, her argument states that the

central figure on the poster is the "New Woman," who looks morally loose; hence the figure is associated with concubines or high-class prostitutes. See her paper "Modern Looking and Looking Modern: 'Modern Woman' as Commodity in 1930s Shanghai Calendar Posters" (paper delivered at the symposium "Visual Cultures and Modernities in China and Japan," Institute of Fine Arts, New York University, October 26, 1996).

51. Anderson, *Imagined Communities*, 30.

52. For a perceptive discussion, see Lydia Liu, *Translingual Practice*, chapter 4.

53. These remarks are indebted to Charles Taylor, who spoke of the "social imaginary" at several conferences that I also attended.

54. As advertised in *Liangyou huabao* 87 (April 1934) in the second printing; the first printing of three thousand copies quickly sold out.

55. It would be intriguing to see whether Chiang Kai-shek's conservative "New Life Movement" had a visible impact on the pictorial contents of *Liangyou huabao*. I have glanced through the issues from 1930 to 1937, but I did not find any definite changes, except that there were no more pictures of nudes after 1934, and the more alluring portraits of the urban pleasures of Shanghai were toned down.

TWO

Marketing Medicine and Advertising Dreams in China, 1900–1950

Sherman Cochran

Today ... calendar posters are popular with ordinary people in Chinese society. The women in calendar posters are sick. Not only are calendar painters unskilled but the subjects of their paintings are disgusting and depraved. China has lots of women who are strong and healthy, but calendar painters only draw sickly ladies so weak that they could be knocked down by a gust of wind. This kind of sickness does not come from society. It comes from the painters.

LU XUN (1930)

Here Lu Xun, the most brilliant writer in China during the first half of the twentieth century, took a position that challenges anyone interested in advertising in Chinese history.[1] According to his analysis, advertising was traceable to one of two sources—commercial artists or society—and in his opinion the images of Chinese women then appearing in calendar posters were attributable to commercial artists rather than society. Was Lu Xun right? Was advertising wholly an expression of commercial artists' "sick" fantasies and not at all a reflection of society at large? If so, then why did calendar posters and other advertisements become, in Lu Xun's words, "popular with ordinary people in Chinese society"?

Lu Xun was undoubtedly right not to adopt the common and untrustworthy assumption that advertising directly reflects social reality or simply expresses popular attitudes. While it is tempting to imagine that advertising is a mirror that reflects a true image of society and popular thought, specialists on advertising in Western history have convincingly shown that at most it has been, in the words of the American historian Roland Marchand, "not a true mirror but a Zerrspiegel, a distorting mirror[;] ... a fun-house mirror [that] not only distorted, it also selected."[2] If Lu Xun was right not to attribute advertising simply to society, he was wrong to attribute it solely to commercial artists. As will be noted later in this essay, certain Chinese commercial artists did play crucial roles as creators of advertising images (especially images of women), but they were not the only or even the principal historical figures responsible for making and popularizing advertisements in China during the first half of the twentieth century. More pivotal in the process of making and popularizing advertising were Chinese entrepreneurs who took the lead not only in producing advertising on the drawing boards (as shown in the first three parts of this essay) but also in distributing it across space and sustaining it over time (as shown in the last two parts). To illustrate how entrepreneurs made and popularized advertising, this essay draws upon the history of "new medicine" (*xinyao*), Chinese-made Western-style patent medicines that were probably the most intensively and extensively advertised goods in China during the first half of the twentieth century. In particular, the focus here is on Huang Chujiu (1872–1931), a manufacturer and distributor of "new medicine," who was known in early-twentieth-century China as the King of Advertising (*guanggao da wang*).[3]

THE DREAM OF WESTERN SOLUTIONS
TO CHINESE PROBLEMS

Huang Chujiu based his first major advertising campaign on the premise that, at the beginning of the twentieth century, Chinese yearned for Western solutions to their medical problems. He tested the popularity of this belief by introducing China's first Chinese-made drug that appeared to be Western. He distributed the drug in bottles under a Chinese name, *Ailuo bunaozhi* (Ailuo Brain Tonic), which sounded like a Chinese transliteration of a Western name, and he had China's biggest publishing house, the Commercial Press, print instructions on the label in English. On the label and the outer paper wrapper he added, also in English, that the product was invented by Dr. T. C. Yale. Thus, on the outside, this medicine gave every indication of being Western.[4]

Chinese Origins of a "Western" Alternative.   Huang presented Ailuo Brain Tonic as Western even though he had no Western partner or Western financial backing, had never been in the West, and had never studied Western pharmacology or received any Western education. Born in 1872 in Taoyuan village, Yuyao county, Zhejiang province, 120 kilometers south of Shanghai, he had grown up as the son of a Chinese herbal doctor and had learned about Chinese medicine as an apprentice in his father's clinic. In his home village, until the age of fifteen he had attended a private school (*sishu*) of the kind that rejected Western educational reforms in favor of traditional Chinese learning.[5] Only once, after the death of his father in 1887 had prompted him and his mother to move to Shanghai, had he been exposed to a Western-oriented institution, when he had enrolled briefly at the Qingxin Academy (*Qingxin shuyuan*). But in Shanghai he had soon discovered opportunities to make money selling medicine as a street peddler, so he had begun skipping classes and then dropped out of school and ended his formal education altogether. Thereafter he had gradually built up a business selling Chinese medicines, first as a hawker in teahouses and wineshops around the Temple of the City God (*chenghuang miao*) and then as the proprietor of a small traditional drugstore, which he and his mother had opened in Shanghai's old walled city.[6]

In 1890, when Huang moved his business into Shanghai's French Concession, he took his first step toward identifying it with Western medicine by converting his shop from an old-style drugstore into a new-style one. He dropped its original, traditional-sounding name, Hall of Long Life (*Yishou tang*), which ended in *tang* (hall), as the names of many old-style Chinese drugstores did, and he adopted an explicitly foreign-sounding name that was appropriate for Shanghai's French Concession, the Great China-France Drug Store (*Zhongfa da yaofang*), which ended in a new Chinese term, *yaofang* (drugstore). He also gave his new drugstore a name in English, the Great Eastern Dispensary, which he included along with its Chinese name on his shop sign and in the letterhead of his stationery. Later, he moved his drugstore one last time in Shanghai, from the French Concession into the International Settlement.[7]

While Huang's drugstore and the label on his Ailuo Brain Tonic might have appeared to be Western, there was in fact nothing Western about the contents of this medicine. He bought the recipe for it from a Chinese pharmacist, Wu Kunrong, who had intended that it be used as a sedative. Huang employed forty Chinese workers to produce and bottle it, and he distributed it through his and other Chinese-owned new-style drugstores. He promoted it in advertising campaigns exclusively through Chinese-language media—newspapers, handbills, and posters— and in this advertising he concentrated on promoting his "Western" medicine by locating it in a Chinese medical context.[8]

Huang's advertising urged Chinese to try his "Western" brain tonic to make up for the deficiencies of Chinese medicine. He traced these deficiencies to the traditional Chinese medical theory of the five yin orbs and six yang orbs (*wu zang liu fu*) and found fault with it for focusing too sharply on relations or functions in the body and not enough on relations or functions in the brain (*naozhi*). From Western medical theory he had learned, he said, that the brain was a sixth yin orb, and, on the basis of this discovery, he claimed to have formulated a new synthesis—the theory of the *six* yin orbs and six yang orbs (*liu zang liu fu*).[9]

In his advertising, Huang invoked Western medical theory as the key to his insights and as the basis for his product, Ailuo Brain Tonic, but he delivered this message in terminology and logic that remained firmly embedded in Chinese medical theory. Whereas Huang claimed to be adopting a Western medical perspective, he described the body entirely in terms of orbs (*zang*), not organs, even though, as the medical historian Manfred Porkert has pointed out, "statements bearing on a certain orb can under no circumstances be made to agree completely with statements bearing on the corresponding organ in Western thought. . . . [It is fallacious to assume] that congruence may be achieved between the description of a Chinese orb and the characteristics that Western medicine postulates for its substratum."[10] Huang made no comment on the differences between Chinese and Western modes of thinking about orbs and organs or, for that matter, about health and disease in general. Instead, keeping his advertisements strictly in Chinese terms, he boasted that he had discovered the "Western" theory of the sixth yin orb, and that it revealed the Chinese need for "brain health" (*jiannao*)—precisely the need that his product would satisfy.[11]

Overcoming Objections to Claims of Westernness.   Huang's product had barely hit the market before he faced two challenges to the claims in his advertising. In 1907, less than a year after Huang introduced Ailuo Brain Tonic, he was approached by "a little American bum" (*Meiguo xiao wulai*—to quote the characterization given in the Huang family's version of the story) who demanded royalties because he claimed to be the son of T. C. Yale, the inventor identified on the label of Ailuo Brain Tonic. Recognizing this as a minor threat, Huang disposed of it by paying off this Mr. Yale quietly in exchange for his signature on a legal document granting to Huang's Great China-France Drug Store all rights to Ailuo Brain Tonic.[12]

Later in 1907 another complaint was lodged by a Portuguese physician named Yale. This doctor, an established medical practitioner in Shanghai's International Settlement, sued Huang for using his name to promote a drug without his permission and filed charges in the Mixed Court of the International Settlement. This time, unable to settle quietly out of court, Huang confronted his Western accuser and used the occasion to generate publicity for himself and his business.

Pleading innocent, Huang claimed that he had used the name T. C. Yale on the label because it was the Western equivalent of his own name. He explained that his name, Huang, means yellow, and since Yellow was not a common Western surname, he chose a common Western surname that sounds like Yellow: Yale. As for the initials T. C., these were the first letters of his two given names, Chu and Jiu, as romanized to represent the sounds of these two characters when pronounced in his native dialect.[13]

Huang's performance in the courtroom was mesmerizing. The judge found in his favor and dismissed the charges, and newspaper reporters described his victory in sensational stories. As a result, Huang's reputation as a slippery character (*huatou*) spread widely.[14] Even among Shanghainese (who have often been stereotyped by Chinese from elsewhere as "wily"), he became known jokingly as "one of the two and a half slipperiest characters in town."[15]

Following the trial, Huang quickly earned high profits on Ailuo Brain Tonic. He priced it at 2 yuan per bottle and sold 500 bottles per day. Since each bottle (containing 168 cc of medicine) cost only .40 yuan to make, his rate of profit was 400 percent. As the profits rolled in, Huang used them to buy a fancy automobile, renovate a three-story building made of reinforced concrete, and begin distributing his goods in China outside Shanghai. By 1911, he had reinvested enough profits in the Great China-France Drug Store to make it the second-largest new-style Chinese drugstore in Shanghai, with capital of 68,000 yuan, annual sales revenue of 250,000 yuan, and annual profits of 50,000 yuan. At that time, in 1911, he made his business officially Western. By paying several hundred yuan to the Portuguese consul in Shanghai, he bought the citizenship of a deceased Portuguese resident of Shanghai, and he registered the Great China-France Drug Store as a Portuguese enterprise. Thereafter the letterhead on its stationery proclaimed in Chinese as well as English that it was a Portuguese business.[16]

By successfully introducing Ailuo Brain Tonic and defending it in court, Huang set precedents that opened the way for the sale in China of Chinese-made "new medicine" that appeared to have foreign origins. Impressed by his high profit rates, several Chinese drugstores began making their own new-style medicines, which became known as "goods under local trademarks" (*benpai chanpin*). By the mid-1930s the Great China-France Drug Store manufactured more than 500 such drugs under its local trademark, and it was by no means unique. Several other Chinese-owned new-style drugstores each made a comparable number of drugs under their local trademarks, and one, the Five Continents Drug Store (*Wuzhou da yaofang*), made as many as 780.[17]

Popularizing Western Solutions to Chinese Medical Problems. Why did Huang Chujiu's advertising for Ailuo Brian Tonic become popular? The above account shows that Huang personally played the leading role in devising specific advertising campaigns for merchandising his goods, but how did he make his advertising effective? Was it (in Lu Xun's terms) because Huang's advertising ideas and images came from society or from the advertiser?

In this particular case, such questions are difficult to answer because scholars are still debating the history of Chinese popular attitudes toward medicine—a field worthy of future research. On the basis of work done thus far, it seems that Huang's emphasis on a Western solution as a viable alternative to Chinese medicine was an idea espoused at the time only by a segment of China's intellectual elite and was not representative of popular thought in Chinese society as a whole. Intellectual and political historians have shown that advocates of modern Western medicine (*xiyi*) and defenders of traditional Chinese medicine (*Zhongyi*) battled fiercely and mobilized substantial organizations against each other during the first half of the twentieth century,[18] but their studies of these factional rivalries concentrate exclusively on the educated elite—intellectuals, political leaders, physicians—and leave open the question of whether other Chinese thought of medicine in these dualistic Sino-Western terms.

On the basis of studies of Chinese medical practice, it seems likely that during the first half of the twentieth century Huang advertised in a society where most Chinese thought of their medical options not dualistically in Sino-Western terms but eclectically in a framework of "medical pluralism." As Nathan Sivin has observed, "the abiding problem of medical pluralism" is central to any understanding of Chinese medical practice before and throughout the first half of the twentieth century. According to his summary, "Chinese chose freely throughout history—as freely as their social and financial circumstances permitted—among priests, spirit mediums, magicians, itinerant herbalists and acupuncturists, classical physicians, and other healers." Writing in 1987, Sivin noted that this wide variety of choices was then still available in some Chinese communities on the periphery of the mainland, although in the People's Republic "most of them have been eradicated as superstitious, and the pluralism of the past has given way to the dualism of traditional and modern medicine."[19]

Sivin's thesis that pluralism in Chinese medicine did not give way to a Sino-Western dualism before the founding of the People's Republic has not yet been tested by historical research on healing services in China during the first half of the twentieth century, but it is convincing because it has strong support from his own historical research on pre-twentieth-century China and from several anthropologists' studies of Chinese medical practices in Taiwan and Hong Kong during the 1960s and 1970s.[20]

Huang thus popularized his medicine as Western in a society where Western medicine had not become widely popular. Faced with this marketing challenge, he devised a strategy for promoting Western medicine that differed from the one adopted by members of China's intellectual elite. As shown here, he advertised in familiar Chinese medical terms (body orbs) rather than unfamiliar Western scientific ones (body organs), and he thereby made his product seem intelligible and unthreatening to Chinese consumers even while it retained its appeal as an (apparent) import from the exotic Occident. In Lu Xun's terms, one might say that Huang's advertising came from both himself (through his adaptation of Chinese intellectuals' advocacy of Western medicine) and society (through his accommodation to popular unfamiliarity with Western medicine).

THE DREAM OF THE TRIUMPH
OF ECONOMIC NATIONALISM

In 1911, emboldened by his success with "Western" Ailuo Brain Tonic, Huang Chujiu began to make an imitation of a Japanese-made medicine called Humane Elixir (a two-character name pronounced *Jintan* in Japanese and *Rendan* in Mandarin). Eventually, during an anti-Japanese boycott in China four years later, Huang began to compete with the Japanese manufacturer of this medicine by introducing nationalistic "buy Chinese" advertising, but initially he viewed it as a model for his own business.

Huang's Japanese Model: Humane Elixir.   From Huang's point of view, Japanese-made Humane Elixir was the obvious choice as a model for his own product because it was by far the most popular foreign-made medicine in China. According to the American consul general in Shanghai at the time, Humane Elixir's sales in China were nearly equal to those of all other foreign-owned pharmaceutical companies combined.[21] Its popularity was not traceable to its therapeutic efficacy, at least not according to an analysis done at the time by the American Medical Association, which concluded that Humane Elixir "possessed no material potency" because it lacked "potent alkaloids" and consisted mostly of sugars that were "highly aromatized, suggesting 'breath perfumes' like 'sen sen.' "[22]

But if the medical efficacy of Humane Elixir's product was open to doubt, the commercial potency of the company's marketing system in China was undeniable.

Humane Elixir's Japanese founder, Morishita Hiroshi, had an eye on China even before opening the company at Osaka in 1893. Throughout his life he had been interested in "Chinese medicine" (*kanpo* in Japanese), and while serving with the Japanese army in Taiwan he had conceived the idea of making Humane Elixir.[23] After consulting a Japanese sinologist and a Japanese journalist specializing in China, he chose for the product a name deeply rooted in Chinese tradition—humaneness was the very first of the five Confucian virtues (followed by righteousness, propriety, wisdom, and faithfulness), and elixir was the term long used to describe Daoist potions and other traditional Chinese tonics[24]—and soon set up a distributing system for it in China.

By 1908, Humane Elixir maintained sales offices in three Chinese cities (Shanghai in the lower Yangzi, Hankou in the middle Yangzi, Tianjin in north China) and made each of these offices responsible for distribution in a sales territory encompassing five or six of China's provinces. At the Shanghai office, it established Toa and Company, capitalized at 500,000 yen, to serve as its headquarters in China. Through Toa it lured Chinese-owned drugstores away from rival Western pharmaceutical firms and convinced them to sell Humane Elixir exclusively by granting them seven to ten months' credit (compared to only three months' credit from Western companies) and by protecting them from fluctuations in market prices. Whenever the market rose above the agreed-upon price, it allowed them to keep surplus profits, and whenever the market fell below the agreed-upon price, it allowed them to pass their losses along to it.[25] By using this strategy, Humane Elixir distributed its goods throughout China before Huang Chujiu entered the market at Shanghai. As the American consul at Shanghai remarked about Humane Elixir at the time, "This company has spared no pains, either in canvassing or publicity campaigns, to exploit thoroughly and systematically the whole of China, so that even in remoter interior sections it is difficult to escape the familiar poster extolling the virtues of 'Jintan' [Humane Elixir]."[26]

As suggested by these references to Humane Elixir's "publicity campaigns" and its "familiar poster," the Japanese company armed its large-scale distributing system with a full arsenal of advertising weapons. By 1910 it was already the number-one advertiser in Japan,[27] and it set its sights on the same goal in China. While sending its message through a wide range of media—newspapers, magazines, billboards, posters, handbills, calendars, and parades—Humane Elixir focused attention sharply on a single image: its trademark. This trademark was well designed to reach illiterate as well as literate Chinese consumers, according to an American advertising analyst who was sent by the United States Department of Commerce to spend eighteen months in 1919 and 1920 surveying advertising in China, Japan, and the Philippines. "The best 'chop' is nearly always pictorial, supplemented in most cases with a few easily read Chinese characters," he observed in his report on advertising in China, and he cited Humane Elixir as his prime example: "One of the very best chops is that used by the Japanese 'Jintan' [Humane Elixir] ... which is advertised and used all over China. The chop consists of nothing but the head and shoulders of a man wearing a distinctive kind of hat, together with two simple Chinese characters that even the most illiterate coolie can read and remember."[28] This description of the two characters in Humane Elixir's name as "simple" is no exaggeration. Each is written in only four strokes.

In the second decade of the twentieth century, Humane Elixir made its trademark familiar to illiterate as well as literate Chinese by featuring it in outdoor advertisements over and over again, especially on billboards and in parades of sandwich-board carriers.[29] In fact, it eventually made the Humane Elixir man's face on its trademark so familiar that he had an effect on men's fashions in China. Adopting his heavy black mustache as their model, many Chinese men grew similar mustaches and were seen wearing this kind of mustache in China's cities (including Beijing, as noted by novelist Lin Yutang) and in China's countryside (as portrayed in Wu Zuxiang's short story "Fan Village").[30] Even today, long after the image of the Humane Elixir man has ceased to occupy a prominent place in China's landscape, the term "Humane Elixir mustache" (*rendan huzi*) continues to be used to describe mustaches worn by Chinese men in China.

Imitating the Japanese Model.   Favorably impressed by this Japanese company's success, Huang Chujiu tried to make a new medicine indistinguishable from Humane Elixir. He named his new medicine Human Elixir, which was pronounced exactly the same as Humane Elixir (*Rendan* in Chinese and *Jintan* in Japanese); even the tones used to say the two names were identical. To make Human Elixir, Huang founded the first Chinese-owned foreign-style mechanical pharmaceutical manufacturer, the Dragon and Tiger Company (*Longhu gongsi*) and assigned it the task of duplicating Humane Elixir. According to the Dragon and Tiger Company's analysis, Humane Elixir turned out to contain peppermint, borneol, cloves, and catechu, which were all readily available in China. So Huang used these ingredients in his effort to make Human Elixir resemble Humane Elixir as closely as possible.[31]

In advertising, as in manufacturing, Huang initially made his product appear to be similar to its Japanese counterpart. In July 1911, his first advertisement for Human Elixir in *Shen bao*, one of China's two biggest newspapers, established his theme by emphasizing his product's universal applicability. It should be "in every person's pocket and in every family's medicine chest," this advertisement proclaimed.[32] In it and subsequent advertisements during the next four years, Huang made no effort to differentiate his product from Japanese-made Humane Elixir, no mention of his product's Chinese origins, and no appeal to his Chinese customers' patriotism. In fact (following the example of Huang's Ailuo Brain Tonic), his advertising included un-Chinese, Western images such as an orchestra that featured brass horns and a bass drum (known in Chinese as foreign instruments, *yanghao* and *yanggu*).[33]

Using this strategy of imitation, Huang made a poor start with Human Elixir. Initially he was unable to raise sales above a hundred cases per year.[34] Nonetheless, he stayed with the same strategy until 1915, when Japan imposed on the Chinese government the Twenty-one Demands—a wide-ranging set of economic rights and privileges for Japanese in China—which provoked Chinese protests, including a boycott against Japanese-made goods.

Selling "National Goods."   On March 23, 1915, less than two months after the Twenty-one Demands were made public, Chinese leaders of Shanghai's twenty major guilds formed the Society for the Use of National Goods (*Quan yong guohuo hui*) and started a boycott against Japanese-made goods that was largely devoted to the promotion of Chinese-made substitutes. Though officially banned by the Chinese government in Beijing, this organization quickly extended its reach, opening offices at seventy locations in China by May 1915.[35] As the boycott spread, Huang Chujiu tried to capitalize on it by advertising Human Elixir as one of the "national goods."

Between May and August of 1915 Huang filled his newspaper advertisements with nationalistic slogans in support of Human Elixir. These advertisements exhorted Chinese consumers to "Stop the Economic Drain [Abroad]" (*louzhi*), "Restore Economic Rights [to Chinese]" (*wanhui liquan*), and "Buy 100 Percent National Goods" (*wanquan guohuo*).[36] Conceding that Huang's Human Elixir had once tasted less good than his foreign rival's product did, his advertising insisted that it had been worth buying even then because it had always been an effective medicine and had always been a 100 percent national product. Besides, as of 1915, Human Elixir tasted "not a bit inferior to foreign goods [*waihuo*]," his advertising claimed, because he had improved it by combining raw materials from China with "the most up-to-date manufacturing techniques from the West."[37] To enhance their visual appeal, Huang's newspaper advertisements contained nationalistic drawings along with nationalistic slogans. One advertisement from 1915, for example, employed the emotionally charged imagery of the flag and flagpole: the Chinese character for country (*guo*) formed the flagpole's base; the character for China (*zhong*) was the pole; and a flag emblazoned "Human Elixir" flew from the top of the pole.[38]

While adopting the rhetoric of modern nationalistic competition, Huang did not abandon the imagery of traditional Chinese harmony. Instead he blended the two together. In 1915 he revised Human Elixir's trademark so that it contained representations of both nationalistic competitiveness and traditional harmony. To signify nationalism, he highlighted in circles Chinese characters meaning Chinese national goods (*Zhonghua guohuo*); and to invoke tradition, he pictured a dragon and a tiger, which, according to traditional Daoist symbolism, produced a divine elixir by bringing together yang (the dragon) and yin (the tiger) in a harmonization of opposites.[39] This trademark gave the impression that Human Elixir was an official product as well as a nationalistic and traditional one by declaring that it had received special recognition from three governmental agencies: approval from the Ministry of Health, tax-exempt status from the Ministry of Finance, and official registration from the Trademark Bureau.[40] To reinforce this impression, Huang bought for himself honorific official titles, including one as "presidential advisor" (*da zongtongfu ziyi*) to Yuan Shikai, who presided over China's republican government in 1915.[41]

Even while Huang used nationalistic and traditional imagery to differentiate his product from his Japanese rival's, he adopted more of his Japanese rival's financial and promotional techniques to strengthen his company's distributing system. In 1915 he converted his business into a limited liability company and recruited several Chinese investors to help him raise its capital to 100,000 yuan. With this backing, he began offering exactly the same credit to Chinese distributors as his Japanese rival had offered them, allowing them to hold goods up to ten months before they were required to make any payment. To supply these distributors with advertising, he followed step-by-step in his Japanese rival's tracks, sending out advertising teams to put up posters wherever Humane Elixir's advertising appeared in Shanghai and dispatching another four or five teams to do the same in other cities, towns, and villages outside Shanghai. These teams hired local children to parade around in tall hats and white gowns while marching to the beat of drums and handing out leaflets.[42]

And yet, despite all of this fanfare, Huang did not earn high profits. At the end of the boycott against Japan's Twenty-one Demands in August 1915, he was so disappointed in the sales of Human Elixir that he sold it to two Chinese publishers, Lufei Bohong and Shen Zhifang, the president and vice-president of the Zhonghua Book Company. A year later, after these new owners fared even less well and lost all of the 60,000 yuan they had invested in order to improve Human Elixir, Huang bought it back from them for 20,000 yuan, half as much as they had paid him for it.[43]

Thereafter, Huang continued to sell Human Elixir, with results ranging from poor to mediocre. In average years, he sold 200–300 cases of it. He regularly underpriced Human Elixir by 20 percent and at times by as much as 80 percent and, as a result, frequently suffered losses on Human Elixir and covered them by dipping into profits from Ailuo Brain Tonic. He recorded his highest sales, 1,000–1,260 cases per year, in conjunction with two anti-Japanese boycotts, one during the May Fourth Movement of 1919 and the other during the National Salvation Movement of 1931. But even selling at these levels Human Elixir was no match for its Japanese rival. During the boycott of 1919, it yielded profits of 20,000 yuan—less than half of the average annual profits on Huang's Ailuo Brain Tonic at that time—and during the boycott of 1931 its sales amounted to no more than one-thirtieth of its Japanese rival's sales in China (1,260 cases compared to 37,800 cases).[44]

Popularizing Economic Nationalism.   Why was Huang's advertising for Human Elixir not as effective as advertising for his other products? As with Ailuo Brain

Tonic, he took command of the product's promotional campaign, but he had far less impressive results. Was his advertising's relative failure attributable to society or himself? These questions, like the ones raised earlier about popularizing Western medicine, are difficult to answer because of the limited amount of research available on the subject. Judging by available studies, it seems likely that Huang was less successful at popularizing Human Elixir at least in part because his advertising for it did not accommodate popular attitudes as inventively and as fully as his advertising for Ailuo Brain Tonic did.

As with Ailuo Brain Tonic, Huang devised an advertising campaign using ideas and images that had been introduced by members of China's intellectual elite. Since the turn of the century, Liang Qichao and other Chinese thinkers had advocated nationalist causes, and during the first third of the century Chinese intellectuals and students led an extraordinary number of Chinese antiforeign boycotts—each sparked by a political or diplomatic incident—that were directed primarily against Japan (in 1908, 1909, 1915, 1919–21, 1923, 1925–26, 1927, 1928–29, and 1931–32) and secondarily against Britain (in 1909, 1925–26, and 1927). Undoubtedly Huang adopted and continued to use "national goods" slogans because some of these boycotts were effective. As C. F. Remer has shown, when one of these boycotts spread widely and lasted more than a year in China, it reduced the sale of foreign-made goods by as much as 25–40 percent in the lower Yangzi region and south China and by 10 percent in north China.[45] Citing this evidence, economic historian Chi-ming Hou has gone so far as to conclude that economic nationalism gave Chinese-owned businesses a major advantage over foreign-owned rivals in their battles for China's market.[46] But perhaps this conclusion overestimates the extent to which consumers' preferences were based on a sharply defined Sino-foreign dualism in Chinese popular thought.

The rivalry between Huang's Human Elixir and his Japanese rival's Humane Elixir provides additional evidence to show that Chinese consumers practiced "medical pluralism" rather than choosing between Chinese medicine or Western medicine as distinct alternatives. In the case of Ailuo Brain Tonic, as noted in the first part of this essay, Huang took advantage of the lack of a sharp distinction between modern Western medicine and traditional Chinese medicine by advertising his supposedly Western product in familiar, un-Western, Chinese terms. In the case of Human Elixir, he tried once again to mix seemingly contradictory ideas and images: new, unfamiliar notions of Western-style competitiveness (in the nationalistic rhetoric of boycotts) and old, familiar representations of Chinese-style harmony (in the traditional images of the dragon and the tiger). Since a similar strategy had worked with Ailuo Brain Tonic, it might well have worked with Human Elixir too, but this time Huang had met his match. In competing with Japanese-owned Humane Elixir, not only did Huang have to contend with a company whose production and distribution were superior to his own, but he also had to compete with a foreign rival that advertised successfully on Chinese terms (as none of Ailuo Brain Tonic's Western rivals did). So the outcome of Huang's ri-

valry with Humane Elixir in advertising seems attributable not simply to his alignment of an economic nationalist (Human Elixir) against an economic imperialist
(Humane Elixir), but also to his failure to combine modern Western-style imagery
with traditional Chinese-style imagery as effectively as his Japanese competitor
did. Although Huang undeniably lost out in this competition, perhaps he should
not be judged too harshly. After all, none of the manufacturers of Humane Elixir's
competitors during the early twentieth century (or since) has invented such a concise and memorable Sino-Western syncretism as the one found in Humane Elixir's
own trademark: a man modeled after Bismarck whose uniform, hat, and epaulets
represent Western-style power, and two simply written Chinese characters whose
meanings express the core values of Confucianism and Daoism.[47]

THE DREAM OF WOMEN'S BODIES

While Huang Chujiu had at best sporadic and limited advertising success with
nationalism, he popularized advertising more consistently by using pictures of
women to promote Ailuo Brain Tonic, Human Elixir, and several other products.[48] To produce these portraits, he recruited two Chinese commercial artists,
Zheng Mantuo (1888–1961) and Hang Zhiying (1900–1947), who eventually became widely known in early-twentieth-century China for their calendar posters of
women, especially nudes.

Unveiling Nudes. In 1914 Huang took his first and perhaps biggest step toward
successfully commodifying women when he discovered Zheng, then an unknown
twenty-six-year-old portrait painter. At the time, Zheng was painting portraits of
classical Chinese beauties (*shinu hua*), and after migrating to Shanghai from
Hangzhou only a few months earlier, he was hoping to sell his paintings by putting
them on display at Zhang Garden in the heart of Shanghai's commercial district
on Nanjing Road.[49]

When Huang saw Zheng's paintings, he immediately recognized the potential
for advertising. He was particularly impressed by Zheng's rendering of classical
Chinese beauties through the use of a new technique, light-colored brushwork
known as rub-and-paint (*cabi dancai*).[50] Apparently Zheng had invented this technique on the basis of his experience working at the Erwoxuan Photography Studio in Hangzhou in 1913, and he used it to make his female subjects lifelike (*xuxurusheng*) and comely—"seemingly available at a viewer's beck and call," as art critic
Zhang Yanfeng has recently observed.[51] Zheng thus differed from the most prominent Chinese artists then painting advertisements in China. His training was in
painting portraits, whereas theirs was in painting New Year's pictures (*nian hua*)
and drawing magazine illustrations, and his experience with photography made
him more attentive to gradations of light and shade than they were.[52]

Upon seeing Zheng's paintings, Huang hired him on the spot and put him to
work transforming the image of Chinese women in advertisements. Almost im-

mediately Zheng's advertising images became widely recognized because of their new technique and their new subject: women's bodies, including nudes. Prior to the twentieth century, Chinese artists had tended not to paint nudes or even show the shapes of women's figures. "Except in erotica," the art historian Marsha Weidner has noted, "figures in traditional Chinese paintings are invariably clothed and usually heavily draped.... Until the early twentieth century, when Chinese artists working in Western modes began to draw from nude models, the question of participation in life-drawing classes simply did not arise."[53] In comparative terms, according to another art historian, John Hay, before the twentieth century "no Chinese painter ever produced a 'nude' in the sense of that cluster of culturally defined anatomical shapes and surfaces so prominent in Western art."[54] Not until 1914 did a few Chinese artists paint nude models in private, and not until the mid-1920s did they begin to display paintings of nudes in public exhibitions.[55] Nor did photographers publish pictures of Chinese nudes at the time. As Perry Link noticed in surveying literature published in popular Chinese magazines, "Beauties in magazine photographs of the 1910s are always heavily clothed from the neck down."[56]

And yet, as early as 1914, while other Chinese artists and photographers continued to obscure women's bodies in heavy clothing, Zheng Mantuo began painting seminudes for Huang Chujiu's business, and Huang wasted no time publishing them in calendar posters advertising his medicine. For Zheng's very first calendar poster, he chose a familiar subject, Yang Guifei (719–56), royal consort to the Xuanzong emperor during the Tang dynasty, who had long been regarded as one of the four leading Chinese classical beauties, and he placed her in a hot springs as other Chinese painters had done before him. But unlike previous portraitists—even ones emphasizing Yang Guifei's seductiveness and the Xuanzong emperor's salaciousness—Zheng revealed the contours of Yang Guifei's body by showing her wearing a transparent silk bathrobe. Under the title *Yang Guifei Emerging from Her Bath* (*Guifei chuyu*), this painting appeared on the calendar poster that Huang's business distributed to its wholesalers, retailers, and customers for the year 1915.[57]

For painting Yang Guifei's head, Zheng had numerous models available to him. He was able to consult paintings of Chinese classical beauties, which continued as in the past to be a popular subject with Chinese artists. In addition he could look at the heads of Chinese classical beauties in advertisements that had been published and distributed by foreign- and Chinese-owned businesses in the first years of the twentieth century before Zheng joined Huang's staff.[58] Without seeing a copy of *Yang Guifei Emerging from Her Bath*, it is not possible to say precisely what model Zheng chose for Yang Guifei's head, but in light of his other early calendar posters of women, it seems likely that he endowed her with the stereotypical facial features of a classical Chinese beauty: almond-shaped eyes (*xing yan*), eyebrows like moth antennae (*e mei*), cherry lips (*ying chun*), an egg-shaped face (*e dan lian*), and hair piled high with a bun on top.[59]

For Yang Guifei's semiclothed body, Zheng could consult no comparable models of Chinese women in paintings and advertisements. So he modeled her body after the bodies of nude Western women as they appeared in magazines imported from the West. Before moving to Shanghai, Zheng had studied English at Hangzhou's Yuying Academy (*Yuying xueyuan*), and in Shanghai he used his reading knowledge to track down English-language magazines containing photographs of nudes. By copying a Western woman's nude body, adding Yang Guifei's head, and adjusting for scale, he produced the first painting showing a woman's body to be published as an advertisement in China.[60]

With the publication of this and subsequent calendar posters, Zheng Mantuo's work was soon in great demand. Huang Chujiu tried to retain Zheng, and, by the standards of the time, Huang spent heavily on advertising, paying an annual salary of 2,400 yuan each to his leading commercial artist, his best writer of advertising copy, and his advertising manager.[61] Despite Huang's tempting offers, Zheng soon left the Great China-France Drug Store, opened his own studio, and began to accept commissions. His minimum price for a basic design was 500 yuan. He offered his clients the opportunity to suggest additions and revisions, and he charged 100 yuan for each change that they required. Even billing at these high rates, Zheng was overwhelmed with orders, receiving so many that he had the luxury of holding over late requests for calendar posters from one year until the next.[62]

Keeping Up with Fashions.   After Zheng left Huang's business, Huang began to pay commissions to a younger man, Hang Zhiying, who eventually surpassed Zheng as China's most influential painter of women in advertisements. During the second decade of the twentieth century, as a teenager working in the advertising department at the Commercial Press in Shanghai, Hang had learned Zheng's techniques by literally stealing from him—sneaking into Zheng's office at the Commercial Press and making off with original copies of his drawings.[63] Then in 1925 Hang left this job, founded his own business, and began to introduce innovations. His new techniques were adapted mainly from the work of Walt Disney (whose cartoons were shown in Shanghai's movie theaters beginning in the late 1920s). Like Disney, Hang named his business after himself (calling it Zhiying Studio), trained students there (serving as master for scores of apprentices before his death in 1947), and organized teams of artists to work collectively on each painting. In his business's hierarchy, he held the top position and signed his name (allowing no other) on all of the paintings that were done; below him were two immediate subordinates, Li Mubai (1913–91) and Jin Xuechen (1904–); below them were seven or eight other paid artists; and at the bottom of the organizational structure were unpaid apprentices. According to available evidence, all of these artists were men. Indeed, all identifiable Chinese calendar painters working for Hang or anyone else were men.[64]

Hang differed from Zheng in his portrayals of Chinese women's heads and bodies. On their faces, he put broad smiles—smiles so broad that he bared their teeth. His modern women smiled with pleasure as they attended social occasions and engaged in Western-style sports—bicycling, tennis, golf, archery—and even his classical beauties broke into grins (rather than keeping their mouths closed behind demure "cherry lips").[65] Interested in women's heads quite apart from their bodies, Hang was the first Chinese to design calendar posters that showed contemporary women only from the neck or shoulders up. Prior to that time Chinese artists had avoided painting close-ups of heads, apparently because of a popular belief linking pictures of heads with beheadings and bad deaths. Breaking this taboo, Hang deliberately confined himself to heads in numerous paintings, which became known as "portraits of great beauties' heads" (*da tou meinu hua*).[66]

In his portraits of women's bodies, Hang also introduced innovations. Initially he followed Zheng Mantuo's example in showing classical Chinese beauties sometimes draped in traditional costumes that left their figures seemingly formless and sometimes clad in transparent bathrobes that made them seminude.[67] But later he showed women in two types of modern fashions, one Western and one Chinese. When dressing them in Western clothes, he exposed their unbound feet and breasts by showing them in tight-fitting shorts, bathing suits, unbuttoned blouses, untied halters, and evening gowns with plunging necklines.[68] When dressing them in modern Chinese style, he clothed them in the *qipao*, a Chinese adaptation of a Manchu costume that had a high collar, slits up the sides, and buttons running from the neck across the chest, under the right arm, and down the right side. Whereas earlier painters, including Zheng Mantuo, had shown Manchu and Chinese women in *qipao* that were waist-length jackets with long sleeves and were worn with loose-fitting long skirts or pants, Hang pictured Chinese women in *qipao* that were sleeveless floor-length dresses which clung tightly from the waist up and fell open at the slit, exposing the women's legs from the thigh down.[69] Whether dressing women in Western or Chinese costumes, he and his all-male staff of artists apparently painted them for men, placing them almost invariably in frontal positions and compliant poses and showing them gazing out from calendar posters as though eyeing male spectators.

Hang became renowned for his portraits of nudes and seminudes, and he received orders for calendar posters from lots of entrepreneurs besides Huang Chujiu. These orders came from Chinese-owned businesses—generally based in Shanghai, south China, and Southeast Asia, not in the northeast, north or northwest—and from foreign-owned businesses. Even the British-American Tobacco Company, proud possessor of the biggest advertising department of any business in China, eventually commissioned Hang to supply fully half of all its advertising paintings in China. Each year during the late 1920s and 1930s, Hang's Zhiying Studio produced more than eighty advertising paintings and earned over 240,000 yuan.[70]

Popularizing Women's Bodies.   Why were Huang's calendar posters of women's bodies his most popular advertisements of all? As emphasized by Lu Xun in the quotation cited at the beginning of this essay, Chinese commercial artists played important roles as painters of the images of women in advertisements; but as shown here, it was the entrepreneur Huang Chujiu who discovered Zheng Mantuo, the first and eventually most influential Chinese commercial artist of his time, and it was Huang who hired Zheng and put him to work constructing the first advertising images of Chinese women. As in campaigns for Ailuo Brain Tonic and Human Elixir, Huang thus played the leading role in the creation of advertising images. Once again his actions raise the question of whether his ideas came from himself or society at large, and once again this question is difficult to answer for lack of detailed studies of Chinese popular taste during the first half of the twentieth century.

If the bold analysis by the historian Mark Elvin is any indication, then Huang had available to him no conceptions of the human body as an aesthetic object except those discovered by members of the Chinese elite through contact with the West in the early twentieth century. Prior to the late nineteenth century, Elvin has argued, Chinese elites traditionally viewed the "body-person" (*shen*) as nothing more than "a peg-doll, a carrier of attributes," and, accordingly, they dressed in loose-fitting clothes and had "almost nothing corresponding to 'fashion.'"[71] This "overall Chinese syndrome" in pre-twentieth-century attitudes toward the human body is traceable, according to Elvin, to a "fundamental historical difference between Chinese thought and Western thought. Chinese traditionally assumed that there was a deep gulf between the morally proper and the morally improper.... There was no accepted dialogue, either philosophical or artistic, between the correct-upright (*zhehng* [*zheng*]) and the depraved-oblique (*xier* [*xie*]), or between the public-impartial (*gong*) and the private-personally based (*si*)." Thus, "virtue" remained uncompromising, unrealistic, and sterile, and "vice" remained human and vital but irredeemable, instead of enriching each other by their interaction, as seems to have happened in the classical, medieval, and early-modern West.[72]

Only after this Western "dialogue" reached China in the early twentieth century, Elvin has asserted, did Chinese begin to view the unclothed human body as an aesthetic object, and only then did Chinese artists begin to depict clothed women in postures that made viewers conscious of bodies beneath the clothing.[73]

While concentrating mainly on the Chinese elite's conceptions of the body, Elvin has also concluded that the elite's exposure to Western images of the body did not decisively change popular Chinese attitudes. The Western "dialogue" between the "correct" and the "depraved" appealed only to the elite in China's largest cities and "was felt by most Chinese to be a deadly allurement... and also a source of general social anomie, precisely because it weakened the barriers between the 'correct' and the 'depraved' aspects of life. They lacked the cultural resources needed for the easy handling of this powerful, if peculiar, Western aberration."[74]

When applied to the case described here, Elvin's thesis is helpful only insofar as it highlights Western influence on the Chinese commercial artists who painted

Huang's calendar posters. Elvin's heavy emphasis on the newness and Western-ness of Chinese conceptions of the body in the early twentieth century is borne out in this case to the extent that Zheng Mantuo copied his first nude women's bodies from photographs in Western magazines and Hang Zhiying chose Walt Disney's studio as a model for his business organization. But Elvin seems to have overestimated Western influence and underestimated Chinese "cultural resources," at least as manifested in the history of advertising. In fact, Huang succeeded where previous advertisers had failed precisely because his artists portrayed women as Chinese and evoked images of beauties from China's past as well as its present. During the first decade of the twentieth century, Western businesses had exported to China Western-made advertising showing Western women, and had been disappointed to find Chinese consumers unreceptive or even hostile to these images.[75] Not until Huang's artists began to feature Chinese women in advertising during the middle part of the succeeding decade did he (and subsequently his imitators, including Western businesses) become satisfied with the results. Huang's successful strategy of prominently showing classical Chinese beauties as well as contemporary Chinese women in advertising suggests that in the early twentieth century Chinese artists and their audiences retained a greater non-Western legacy of "cultural resources" and possessed a greater capacity for imagining and portraying Chinese women's bodies than Elvin has supposed.

This conclusion and the conclusions to the first two parts of this essay all have characterized Huang Chujiu as a pivotal figure taking ideas and images from the Chinese elite and popularizing them in Chinese society. Up to this point, his success at popularization has been inferred from the sales of his products and the satisfaction that he expressed with his advertising. But in efforts at popularization, how far did he and other sellers of "new medicine" reach? Was their advertising popular only with the elite in restricted localities or more widely throughout China and Chinese society? Clues to the answers lie in the extent to which medical advertisements were distributed in China.

MASS ADVERTISING

During the first half of the twentieth century, businesses published and distributed advertising for "new medicine" in China on a grand scale. They made pictorial advertisements accessible to all social classes, including illiterate as well as literate observers, and they circulated these advertisements in all of China's nine macro-regions (lower, middle, and upper Yangzi, northeast, north, northwest, southeast, south, and southwest).[76] The biggest of the Chinese-owned drugstores conducted nothing less than mass advertising by operating marketing systems on three tiers: at Shanghai headquarters, in regional branches, and through local franchises.

Shanghai Headquarters.   In the early twentieth century, Shanghai pulled ahead of its rivals as the city of choice for the headquarters of Chinese-owned businesses selling "new medicine." As early as 1907–8, Shanghai became China's print capital and leading exporter of newspapers and advertising, and between 1911 and 1936, Shanghai surpassed Guangzhou as the most popular base for businesses selling and advertising "new medicine." As late as 1911, Shanghai ranked about the same as or slightly behind Guangzhou as a center for this trade, with each city housing 28 Chinese-owned new-style drugstores and with Shanghai handling 10 percent of China's imported drugs compared to Guangzhou's 12.2 percent. But by 1936 Shanghai far surpassed Guangzhou as the trading center for Chinese sellers and importers of new-style medicine, serving as home for 166 Chinese-owned new-style drugstores compared to Guangzhou's 84 and receiving 77 percent of China's imported drugs compared to Guangzhou's 5.9 percent (and Tianjin's 9.2 percent).[77]

Among Chinese entrepreneurs, Huang Chujiu was one of the first to establish formal headquarters at Shanghai, and for this purpose he designed buildings that themselves served as advertisements. In the 1920s, he deliberately selected sites for his buildings on corners at busy intersections in Shanghai so that they would attract attention. He housed his headquarters in his two most prominent office buildings, one at the corner of Beijing Road and Zhifu Road and the other at the corner of Fuzhou Road and Shandong Road. In 1928, when he decided to build them, he formulated "Basic Guidelines for the Design of the New Stores," which he gave the architects and builders to follow. In these guidelines, he emphasized the importance of big plate glass windows to showcase eye-catching displays, and he allowed no steps at the entrances because he wanted the buildings accessible to all, particularly the frail and elderly in search of medicine. Once completed, the buildings were ringed on the ground floor with windows whose design and construction (not counting displays) cost more than 30,000 taels. Each building stood five stories tall and was topped with a roof of gleaming ceramic tiles, one yellow and the other green. Even Huang's medicine factory attracted attention because he gilded its sign with twenty ounces (*liang*) of real gold.[78]

Of all Huang's buildings, the one with the greatest advertising value was the Great World (*Da shijie*), a five-story amusement hall that he opened in 1917 in Shanghai's French Concession at the corner of Tibet Road and Avenue Edouard VII (today's Yan'an Road). At the Great World, Huang installed distorting mirrors, staged Chinese regional operas, and supplied other forms of popular entertainment that attracted huge crowds—an average of twenty thousand paying customers per day—and as the pleasure seekers moved from one floor to the next in this rambling building, he exposed them to walls covered with advertisements for his medicines. Outside the building he also used the Great World to spread his advertising. On its facade he affixed billboards, and from its tower he launched advertising stunts, flying a huge kite, for example, that dropped advertising leaflets onto surrounding neighborhoods. Day after day he tied so much advertising to the Great World that people at the time began jokingly calling the place "Huang Chujiu's 'Commercial World'" (*Shangpin shijie*).[79]

Besides designing buildings, Huang Chujiu and his staff also designed advertising at his Shanghai headquarters. He established a specialized advertising section (*guanggao ke*) and heavily funded it, allocating to it between 60 and 75 percent of the budget for his most popular medicines (leaving only 25–40 percent for the cost of manufacturing and distributing these goods). Part of this advertising budget covered salaries for painters and writers who, as noted earlier, were well paid by the standards of the time. Another part of the advertising budget financed the founding and operation of a radio station, Mainland Radio (*Dalu diantai*), a wholly owned subsidiary of Huang's business, which broadcast commercials for his medicines as sponsors for serialized adaptations of Chinese classics such as *The Story of the West Wing* (*Xixiangji*) and other programs every day. A third part of the advertising budget covered the cost of making visual commercials—slide shows and short films preceding feature-length movies at theaters. And a fourth part of the budget was spent on newspaper advertisements, including some of an unprecedented kind. In the 1920s, for example, Huang Chujiu was the first in Shanghai to take out full-page newspaper advertisements—a practice subsequently adopted by several other new-style drugstores. In 1923, when he launched a new medicine called "Machine for Long Life" (*bailingji*), he ran full-page advertisements for it in newspapers once or twice every month; at the same time he separately published his own magazine, *Long Life Pictorial* (*Bailing huabao*), which was devoted largely to advertisements for this product.[80]

In Shanghai, besides broadcasting commercials over the radio and running advertisements in newspapers, Huang and other sellers of new medicines distributed published advertisements through a merchandising hierarchy of wholesalers and retailers. At the highest level were the sixteen biggest Chinese-owned drugstore chains, each capitalized at more than 100,000 yuan. They made their own advertising and distributed it through their own chains of drugstores. By 1936, some had six wholly owned branch stores apiece in Shanghai, and altogether the sixteen biggest drugstore chains accounted for 68.3 percent of sales of "new medicine" in Shanghai at the time. At the next level were medium-sized drugstores capitalized at an average of 15,000 yuan, with sales of 30,000 yuan per year. From these medium-sized drugstores, Huang's firm and other big drug companies rented window space for their advertising. Still lower in the hierarchy were small drugstores capitalized at an average of 2,000 yuan, with sales of 15,000–30,000 yuan per year, and below them were restaurants, tobacconists, and other commercial vendors, including itinerant peddlers. Big drugstores supplied advertising to these retailers either directly or indirectly through wholesalers.[81]

In the absence of detailed data, it is difficult to assess the effectiveness of this advertising in Shanghai, but the available evidence suggests that by 1936 it helped new-style drugstores (which all carried heavily advertised "new medicine") to outsell old-style drugstores (which all carried unadvertised traditional Chinese medicine).[82] As shown in table 2.1, even though in 1936 new-style drugstores in Shang-

TABLE 2.1   A Comparison of Chinese-Owned New-Style
and Old-Style Drugstores in Shanghai, 1936

	No. of Stores	Capital (in Yuan)	No. of Employees	Sales Volume (in Yuan)
New-style	166	7,550,000	2,012	41,510,000
Old-style	498	13,530,000	5,400	41,880,000

SOURCE: Shanghai shehui kexue yuan jingji yanjiu suo, comp., *Shanghai jindai xiyao hangye shi* (Shanghai: Shanghai shehui kexue yuan chubanshe, 1988), 120, 123.

hai were far less numerous, less well capitalized, and less well staffed than old-style drugstores were, they generated about the same amount of total sales revenue.

Shanghai-based new-style drugstores advertised more intensively in Shanghai than in other cities (and most intensively of all in Shanghai's foreign concessions, where their headquarters were concentrated), but they did not confine their advertising to this one city.

Regional Branches.   Outside Shanghai, as within it, the biggest new-style drugstores established wholly owned branch drugstores, and they modeled these branches after the ones in Shanghai. As in Shanghai, they tended to locate each branch conspicuously on a corner at an intersection in the heart of a highly commercial area. Over each entrance they placed a large wooden signboard proclaiming that this drugstore was a branch of the Shanghai-based parent company. They designed branches as new-style drugstores, which, by contrast with old-style Chinese drugstores in each city, were multistoried buildings featuring clock towers, plate glass windows, and brightly lit interiors for displaying medicines to passersby and coaxing them inside.[83]

From their Shanghai headquarters, the biggest drugstores paid directly for newspaper advertising in their regional branches' localities. By the 1930s advertisers could take advantage of newspapers originating in every province of China. In 1935 China had 313 "big dailies" (consisting of one big sheet or more in each issue) plus 600 small and irregularly published newspapers. Altogether, according to an estimate at the time by Lin Yutang, 30 million Chinese read newspapers every day.[84]

The biggest Chinese drugstores distributed their own advertisements—which had been published in Shanghai—to their regional branches. As early as 1916 Huang Chujiu sent advertising teams outside Shanghai to put up posters and organize parades for distributing handbills in other cities. By 1936, several new-style drugstores based in Shanghai owned regional branches in metropolises at the cores of six of China's macroregions (lower, middle, and upper Yangzi, north, south, and southeast), leaving them without branches in the remaining three (northeast, northwest, and southwest).[85] Their branches, in turn, distributed advertising and goods to the parent companies' local franchises.

Local Franchises. Without investing in additional branches, big new-style drugstores extended their sales networks by recruiting independently owned drugstores to serve as local franchises (*lingpai lianhao*). They arranged for local Chinese shopkeepers to affiliate with them by seeking out interested parties, negotiating deals, and signing contracts.

From the standpoint of the parent companies, their affiliations with franchises provided an inexpensive means of advertising their products in untapped markets. They added new franchises only in cities and towns where they had not previously opened a regional branch or designated a franchise, and they assumed no legal responsibility for a local franchise's losses. They tried to persuade each franchise to sign exclusive dealing agreements in which the franchise holder promised to sell only the medicines of the parent company, not of any rival, but they frequently accepted franchises where the local owners rejected this provision.[86]

For a local drugstore, the principal advantage of becoming a franchise took the form of advertising. The direct financial benefits for the local franchise were minimal—small discounts, early notification of sales, year-end commissions depending on the franchise's sales volume—and provided no guarantees of compensation in case of losses. But the amount of advertising supplied by the parent company was plentiful. The local franchise named its shop after the parent company, declaring on its shop sign that it was a branch (*fenzhi*), and became, in the words of a recruiting brochure used by one of the big drugstores based in Shanghai, part of "a well-organized advertising network penetrating every corner of the country."[87]

This claim that a company "penetrated every corner of the country" might sound like an advertising agent's cliché, but in fact between 1912 and 1936 the biggest new-style drugstores did reach all nine of China's macroregions by means of franchises. As shown in table 2.2, the three biggest drugstore chains distributed goods and advertising nationwide to 162 local franchises in 105 of China's cities and towns, and they marketed outside China through 15 local franchises in Taiwan, Hong Kong, Singapore, Indonesia, Malaya, and Thailand.

Advertising for Chinese-owned new-style drugstores also was distributed outside cities and towns. Its success at reaching down the urban hierarchy into rural China is evident in the fact that Chinese peasants were still using pre-1949 calendar posters to decorate their homes in the early 1990s. In 1992, when the art critic Zhang Yanfeng began searching in China for forms of pre-1949 commercial art, she and her research assistants found little in the cities, where, they were told, such bourgeois remnants had survived until the 1960s but had been destroyed during the Cultural Revolution. So they extended their search outside the cities into the countryside in four regions—the lower Yangzi, north China, northeast China, and south China—where they eventually discovered 586 pre-1949 calendar posters hanging on walls in the homes of peasants.[88]

TABLE 2.2   Regional Branches and Local Franchises
of Three Shanghai-Based Drug Companies (China and the West,
China-France, and Five Continents), 1912–1936

Region of China or Country or Colony outside China	No. of Cities and Towns with Regional Branches	No. of Towns with Regional Branches	No. of Cities and Towns with Local Franchises	No. of Local Franchises
Lower Yangzi	6	23	41	65
Middle Yangzi	5	7	17	28
Upper Yangzi	1	2	2	3
Northeast China	0	0	4	6
North China	4	5	23	30
Northwest China	0	0	6	8
Southeast China	1	1	5	11
South China	1	1	5	8
Southwest China	0	0	5	3
Taiwan	0	0	5	4
Hong Kong	0	0	1	4
Singapore	0	0	1	1
Indonesia	0	0	—	3
Malaya	0	0	1	1
Thailand	0	0	—	2

SOURCE: Shanghai shehui kexue yuan jingji yanjiu suo, comp., *Shanghai jindai xiyao hangye shi* (Shanghai: Shanghai shehui kexue yuan chubanshe, 1988), 95–96, 98–99, 391–92.

Reaching a Mass Audience.   Did this advertising reach a mass audience in China? In their article on the beginnings of mass culture in China, Leo Ou-fan Lee and Andrew Nathan have defined mass culture as "culture that is nationwide, universal to all classes, and consciously engineered and controlled from above," and using this definition they have concluded that in China "it was not until after 1949 that a truly mass audience was created."[89] If taken literally, this definition sets unrealistic standards for assessing mass culture in Chinese history. In a country so large and diverse, it is doubtful whether any cultural medium even up to the present has become nationwide and universal to all classes, and it is questionable whether in any country culture is ever engineered and controlled entirely from above. Nonetheless, this definition has the advantage of specifying three useful criteria—the reach across space, reach across classes, and control over production.

By each of these three criteria, advertising for "new medicine" functioned as a formidable medium of mass culture in China before 1949. As shown above, in accordance with the first criterion, it reached nationwide to the extent that it circulated in all of China's macroregions (not to mention Southeast Asia). In keeping with the second criterion, it became "universal to all classes" to the extent that it used pictorial representations and itinerant drummers to reach the literate and the illiterate, the peasants and the urban dwellers. And in conformity with the third criterion, it was "consciously engineered and controlled from above" to the extent that entre- preneurs like Huang Chujiu supervised its design, production, and distribution.

This conclusion is valid for the years 1912–36, as documented in table 2.2, but did advertising for "new medicine" continue to function as a medium of mass cul- ture over a longer period of time? In an era of political turmoil and military con- flicts, its durability was put to the test.

MARKETING IN PEACE AND WAR

While Huang and other sellers of medicine extended their advertising across all re- gions and down urban hierarchies in China and Southeast Asia, they also sustained the distribution of their advertising to these far-flung locations over time. They did so despite attempts by governments to introduce official restrictions on medical ad- vertising in the 1930s and 1940s. After being spared any such restrictions prior to 1930, they responded by effectively postponing, deflecting, or evading new policies proposed by each successive government: Chiang Kai-shek's Nationalist govern- ment, 1927–37; the Japanese occupying forces and the collaborationist government of Wang Jingwei, 1937–45; and the Nationalists again, 1945–49.

Delaying the Implementation of Nationalist Regulations, 1927–37.   When the Nation- alist government came to power, it established a Ministry of Health that was re- ceptive to long-standing demands for official regulation of "new medicine" in China. Since the passage of the Pure Food and Drug Act in the United States in 1906, Chinese and Western members of the Chinese Medical Association had been campaigning for this kind of regulation.[90] Of all the leaders of the campaign, the one best positioned to influence official policies was Wu Liande, a Western-trained Chinese physician who first gained fame for leading a campaign against a plague of epidemic proportions in Harbin, 1910–11, and who subsequently held official appointments as a medical administrator in each of China's successive central governments (Qing, Beiyang, and Nationalist) during the first third of the twentieth century.[91] In 1929, Wu summed up the main arguments and expressed the tenor of this campaign when he urged the leaders of the Nationalist government to levy a tax on new-style medicines. These medicines, he said, were "needless and even harmful luxuries" and were sold in "enormous" quantities in China. If they remained untaxed and unregulated, then Chinese would continue to be, according to Wu, even more vulnerable to new-style drug companies' newspaper advertising and other marketing techniques than people were in other countries: "The gullibility of the general public is proverbial in every country, but in China this takes on an extreme form, for both the educated and uneducated readily swallow all the lies and exaggerations which appear in print."[92]

In February 1930 the Nationalist government's acting minister of health, Liu Ruiheng, responded to Wu and other advocates of regulation by issuing the "Proposed Regulations Governing Patent and Proprietary Medicines." All of these medicines, according to the draft regulations, had to be properly tested, registered, labeled, and packaged, and all medical advertising had to be free of "false and pretentious claims, or the use of a third person as guarantee, or any misleading statement." Violators were subject to fines and other punishments.[93]

Written by four Chinese scientists, including one Western-trained pharmacologist, the draft regulations delighted the physicians who had been critical of new-style Chinese medicines and drugstores. Upon hearing news of the proposal, Bernard Read, a distinguished research scientist at Peking Union Medical College, spoke for many doctors when he published his endorsement of the draft regulations in the *National Medical Journal of China* (Shanghai) and the *China Medical Journal* (Beijing) and expressed his relief that new-style medicines, a "group of drugs flooding the China market," would finally be put under the "most rigid control . . . to protect the medical profession and the public against fraud, undesirable secrecy and proprietary advertising."[94] But this declaration of victory for the medical profession over new-style drugs and drugstores proved to be premature.

Even before the proposed regulations were announced, Huang Chujiu and other sellers of "new medicine" had already organized resistance to them. In January and February 1927, as Chiang Kai-shek's troops were preparing to take Shanghai, Huang Chujiu convened in his home two meetings of twenty of his fellow Chinese owners of new-style drugstores. At the first meeting he proposed the formation of a trade association, and at the second he announced the founding of the Shanghai New Medicine Trade Association (*Shanghai xinyaoye gonghui*) and the election of himself as its first president. Once before, in 1909, on the eve of the founding of the Chinese republic, Huang and a few other Chinese drugstore owners had established the Foreign Medicine Guild (*Yangyao gongsuo*) in anticipation of the need for a lobbying organization to deal with a new government that, as it turned out, was established with the founding of the Chinese republic in 1912. Now, on the eve of the Nationalists' founding of another new government, Huang formed a trade association in anticipation of the same need.[95]

Huang also took advantage of his informal contacts with people who had direct access to Chiang Kai-shek. He had a close relationship, for example, with Huang Jinrong, the very first person from Shanghai to call on Chiang after the Nationalist leader's arrival in the city in 1927.[96] Huang Chujiu and Huang Jinrong were from the same native place, Yuyao, and Huang Chujiu had cultivated a friendship with Huang Jinrong since 1917, when Huang Chujiu had constructed his first large building in Shanghai's French Concession—an area where Huang Jinrong wielded immense power because he held a position as a detective in the French police force and used elaborate networks of Chinese "disciples" (*xuesheng*) to control an underworld organization known as the Green Gang.[97] Through Huang Jinrong, Huang Chujiu also formed alliances with two younger Green Gang leaders, Du Yuesheng and Zhang Xiaolin. According to an investigation in 1931 by Tan Shaoliang, superintendent in the police force of Shanghai's International Settlement, Huang Chujiu was "friendly" with Huang Jinrong, Du Yue-sheng, and Zhang Xiaolin, although he was not involved in the opium trade and gambling rackets as they were.[98]

Besides befriending these powerful underworld figures, Huang Chujiu formed alliances with the second person to call on Chiang after the Nationalist leader's arrival in Shanghai in 1927: Yu Ziaqing, president of the Shanghai Commercial Federation (*Shanghai shangye lianhehui*).[99] Since 1915, Yu had been a major shareholder in Huang's Great China-France Drug Store, and during the same period Huang had served with Yu in the Shanghai General Chamber of Commerce and other merchant organizations.[100]

As head of the Shanghai New Medicine Trade Association, as a friend of Shanghai's leading underworld figures, and as a business associate of Shanghai's leading merchants, Huang Chujiu proved to be an effective lobbyist. In 1930, as soon as the Nationalist government's Ministry of Health announced its proposed regulations governing patent medicines, he formally protested in the name of the Shanghai New Medicine Trade Association, and in all likelihood he informally used his personal contacts to mobilize support for this protest. In response, the government agreed to delay implementation of the regulations. According to the draft regulations, the new laws were to be promulgated in July 1931 and were scheduled to go into effect after a grace period of six months, in January 1932.[101] But in actual practice the regulations were not enforced in 1932, or later. In 1933, according to D. Barat, an officer in the association of licensed pharmacists in Shanghai, "all these regulations exist only on paper." He cited a survey by the Health Authorities of the Foreign Settlement, which found that 90 percent of Shanghai's pharmacies were "run by unqualified people, and the importance and sale of pharmaceutical products is in the hands of laymen." As a result, Barat complained, not only Shanghai but the country as a whole had acquired a dubious distinction: "China is regarded by smaller as well as bigger manufacturing enterprises as the only country in the world that can be flooded with all kinds of worthless medicines."[102]

Meanwhile, advertising for these "worthless medicines" also went unregulated. In 1936 Lin Yutang wrote in his history of the press that "China is the ideal land for quack doctors, which is really a new evil arising only in modern times from the growth of periodicals." He was particularly disturbed by the large number of advertisements run by these "quack doctors" in the most widely circulated newspapers. Based on an analysis of one of China's two biggest newspapers, *Shen bao*, he concluded that it "is carrying on different days [in May 1936] not one, but four... 'medical supplements' and 'health supplements,' run by different groups of doctors with different medicines to sell."[103]

In January 1937 the Nationalist government promulgated a new Patent Medicine Law that closely resembled the one passed in 1930.[104] Even if, as the government vowed, it intended to enforce this law with greater resolve, it had little opportunity to do so before the Japanese military invasion of China in the summer of 1937.

TABLE 2.3   New-Style Chinese-Owned Drugstores in Four Cities, 1882–1949

Years	Shanghai	Guangzhou	Beijing	Hankou
1882–1912	28	28	—	20+
1912–1937	166	84	—	107
1937–1945	652	153	130+	—
1945–1949	636	300	200	—

SOURCES: Shanghai shehui kexue yuan jingji yanjiu suo, comp., *Shanghai jindai xiyao hangye shi* (Shanghai: Shanghai shehui kexue yuan chubanshe, 1988), 79, 350–57; Chen Xinqian and Zhang Tianlu, *Zhongguo jindai yaoxue shi* (Beijing: Renmin weisheng chubanshe, 1992), 31, 33–34, 39–41, 43.

withdrew from China in 1945 and Chu Minyi was executed for treason at Nanjing in 1946, Xu Xiaochu was not only exonerated but celebrated for his wartime activities. He was officially declared to have been an undercover agent for Chiang Kai-shek's Nationalist government, and he became an influential figure in postwar business and politics under Nationalist rule. He recruited onto the board of directors of the Great China-France Drug Store other politically influential figures, notably Chen Guofu, chair of the Nationalist Central Finance Committee, and Zhao Dihua, director of the Bank of Communications, and he formed a close relationship with the military leader Bai Chongxi. Like himself, Bai was a Muslim, and on Bai's recommendation Xu attended the government's National Congress as a Muslim representative.[112]

Politically well connected, Xu's Great China-France Drug Store distributed medicine and advertising extensively in postwar China. It was finally free of its long-standing rival, Japanese-owned Humane Elixir, which retreated to Japan with the defeated Japanese military forces in 1945; and the Chinese company's management filled the vacuum by casting a wide net for its own Human Elixir. In 1946 it signed "special sales contracts" (*teyue jingxiao hetong*) specifying sales territories, setting commissions, granting credit, and taking responsibility for advertising with thirty sales agents in fifteen Chinese provinces and three Southeast Asian countries, and in 1947 its staff formulated an advertising plan for blanketing all regions of China with billboards and posters at every level of the urban hierarchy, down to the levels of county (*xian*) and rural market town (*zhen*). By 1949 it reached all nine of China's macroregions and all bordering regions except Tibet, and it sold 75 percent of its product, Human Elixir, outside Shanghai.[113]

Meanwhile, it advertised intensively as well as extensively. In the late 1940s its opportunities for intensive advertising increased because new-style drugstores proliferated, as shown in table 2.3. Thus in the late 1940s the Great China-France Drug Store and other sellers of "new medicine" had an unprecedented opportunity to advertise in more than a thousand new-style drugstores in China's three biggest cities alone, not to mention the rising number opened in other cities and towns.[114]

Although civil war between the Nationalists and Communists began in 1946 and raged throughout the late 1940s, not until late 1948, when the Communists' victory seemed assured, did Xu Xiaochu and other owners of big new-style drug companies begin to withdraw from China. Between October and December 1948, Xu transferred approximately US$35,000 worth of the Great China-France Drug Store's assets to Taiwan, and on February 26, 1949, he fled there. At about the same time, several other owners of big new-style drug companies left China for Taiwan or Hong Kong.[115]

On January 1, 1951, less than two years after the Communists had won the civil war and founded the People's Republic, the new government took over the marketing of Human Elixir in China. The government recruited the Great China-France Drug Store's manufacturing division, Zhonghua Medicine Mill (*Zhonghua zhiyao chang*), to be the first pharmaceutical company to sign an official purchasing agreement (*baoxiao hetong*), which guaranteed that the government would supply all of Human Elixir's raw materials and would buy and distribute all of its finished goods. Lacking these guarantees, Human Elixir's rivals could not compete with it, so they soon either signed similar purchasing agreements with the government or became more fully nationalized as jointly managed companies (*gongsi heying*). On January 1, 1956, the Great China-France Drug Store's Zhonghua Medicine Mill finally became a jointly managed company—it was the last major pharmaceutical plant in China to do so—but by then it had lost all control over the marketing of its goods. The signing of its purchasing agreement with the government five years earlier had effectively brought to an end the marketing of medicine in China by itself and other large-scale presocialist commercial enterprises.[116]

POACHING AND POPULARIZING

This chapter has shown that Huang Chujiu and other sellers of "new medicine" produced images of the West, economic nationalism, and women and widely distributed these and other images through advertising in China over a sustained period of time during the first half of the twentieth century. It has argued that Huang as an entrepreneur played a pivotal role in advertising by taking ideas and images from the Chinese elite and disseminating his version of these ideas and images in promotional campaigns. By way of conclusion, it is worth considering some of the historiographical and theoretical implications of this argument.

According to intellectual historians of early-twentieth-century China, the Chinese responsible for introducing Western ideas into modern Chinese discourse bore little resemblance to Huang Chujiu. Compared to him, these Chinese were highly educated and cosmopolitan intellectuals, as characterized in biographies, collective portraits, and, most recently, cultural studies.[117] In Tani Barlow's words, the Chinese-educated elite "monopolized the appropriation of Western ideas, forms, signs, and discourses [in early-twentieth-century China]."[118]

If the Chinese intellectual elite "monopolized" the appropriation of ideas from the West, the case of Huang Chujiu demonstrates that the process of appropriation did not stop there. It is true that Huang, lacking the education and cosmopolitanism shared by members of the intellectual elite, did not appropriate ideas, forms, signs, and discourses directly from the West. But as emphasized in this essay, it is also true that he did appropriate "Western" ideas, forms, signs, and discourses from the Chinese intellectual elite, and he made use of them for his own purposes. As shown in the first three parts of this essay, Huang co-opted some of the Chinese intellectual elite's most cherished causes—advocacy of Western medicine, economic nationalism, and women's liberation—and commodified them to promote his products. In the process, he substantially altered the contents of the Chinese intellectual elite's formulations, freely substituting familiar Chinese terms (like *body orbs* in Chinese medicine) for unfamiliar foreign ones (like *body organs* in Western medicine), loosely mixing old notions (such as traditional harmonization of opposites) with seemingly contradictory new ones (such as competitive economic nationalism), and unabashedly depoliticizing images (such as pictures of liberated women, whom he portrayed as fashionable beauties rather than as serious campaigners for women's rights).

In a word, Huang poached on the Chinese intellectual elite's modern discourse. This term *poach* has been coined by the theorist Michel de Certeau to describe a process in which consumers actively "use" (rather than passively accept) representations, rituals, and laws in any society. By poaching, according to Certeau, consumers defend themselves against whatever culture has been imposed upon them, and their poaching has the effects of subverting and transforming the imposed culture.[119] In general, this notion of poaching seems apt as a characterization of what Huang made of the Chinese intellectual elite's ideas and images.

And yet, Certeau's concept of poaching encompasses only part of the process by which Huang's and other entrepreneurs' advertising had subversive and transformative effects on Chinese culture during the first half of the twentieth century. These advertisers did more than defensively poach ideas and images from an intellectual elite. They also aggressively popularized their advertising by producing it in massive quantities, distributing it through large-scale marketing networks, and publicizing it in wartime as well as peacetime. Only with both concepts, poaching and popularizing, is it possible to make a reasonable reply to Lu Xun as he was quoted at the beginning of this essay. Advertisers' success in both poaching and popularizing helps to explain why, as Lu Xun acknowledged, advertising became "popular with ordinary people in Chinese society," and it also helps to explain why advertisers seemed to Lu Xun, as a member of China's intellectual elite, to be "sick."

NOTES

It is customary for contributors to conference volumes to express thanks for conference participants' comments on earlier drafts of essays, but I owe a much deeper debt to my colleagues at this conference than is customary. In this case, the participants not only made comments but tape-recorded them so that I could hear them despite the fact that I was unable to attend the conference. For this special consideration, I am deeply grateful. I also wish to thank Zheng Liren for his invaluable help with research on this essay.

1. Lu Xun, "Lu Xun zai Zhonghua yishu daxue yanjiang jilu" (Transcript of Lu Xun's lecture at the China College of Art), recorded by Liu Ruli, February 21, 1930, in *Xuexi Lu Xun de meishu sixiang* (Studying Lu Xun's thoughts on art) (Beijing: Renmin meishu chubanshe, 1979), 2–3.

2. Roland Marchand, *Advertising the American Dream: Making Way for Modernity, 1920–1940* (Berkeley and Los Angeles: University of California Press, 1985), xvii.

3. Shanghai shehui kexue yuan jingji yanjiu suo (Shanghai Academy of Social Sciences, Institute of Economics), *Shanghai jindai xiyao hangye shi* (A history of the modern medicine trade in Shanghai) (Shanghai: Shanghai shehui kexue yuan chubanshe, 1988), 236. Hereafter cited as *Xiyao*.

4. Gong Jimin, "Huang Chujiu zhuan" (A biography of Huang Chujiu), pt. 3, *Zhuanji wenxue* (Biographical literature) 60, no. 3 (March 1992): 75–77; Kong Lingren et al., eds., *Zhongguo jindai qiye de kaituozhe* (Pioneers in modern Chinese enterprises), vol. 2 (Jinan: Shandong renmin chubanshe, 1991), 427–28.

5. On private schools, cf. Evelyn Sakakida Rawski, *Education and Popular Literacy in Ch'ing China* (Ann Arbor: University of Michigan Press, 1979), 162–67.

6. Gong, "Huang," pt. 2, 60, no. 2 (February 1992): 53–56, 72–74; Guan Zhichang, "Huang Chujiu," *Zhuanji wenxue* (Biographical literature) 47, no. 3 (September 1985): 138; *Xiyao*, 231–32; Shanghai shehui kexue yuan jingji yanjiu suo (Shanghai Academy of Social Sciences, Institute of Economics), ed., *Longteng huyao bashi nian: Shanghai Zhonghua zhiyaochang chang shi* (Eighty years of the dragon soaring and the tiger leaping: A factory history of the Zhonghua medicine factory of Shanghai) (Shanghai: Shanghai renmin chubanshe, 1991), 2. Hereafter cited as *Longteng*.

7. *Longteng*, 2.

8. Guan, "Huang," 138; Kong, *Zhongguo*, 2:427–28; Gong, "Huang," pt. 3, 60, no. 3 (March): 74–75.

9. Gong, "Huang," pt. 3, 60, no. 3 (March): 72–73.

10. Manfred Porkert, *The Theoretical Foundation of Chinese Medicine: Systems of Correspondence* (Cambridge: MIT Press, 1982), 107 and 161.

11. Gong, "Huang," pt. 3, 60, no. 3 (March): 75.

12. Ibid.; Guan, "Huang," 139; Kong, *Zhongguo*, 2:428.

13. Gong, "Huang," pt. 3, 60, no. 3 (March): 75; Guan, "Huang," 138–39.

14. Guan, "Huang," 139.

15. The other "one and a half" were Shi Dezhi, a man of mixed Sino-Western descent who sold fake antiques, and Wu Jiangang, a fortune-teller. Ping Jinya, "Mantan Huang Chujiu jiqi 'shiye'" (Random remarks on Huang Chujiu and his "industry"), in *Wenshi ziliao xuanji* (Collection of cultural and historical materials) (Beijing: Renmin chubanshe, 1963), 146–47.

16. *Xiyao*, 36–37, 41, 233–35; Gong, "Huang," pt. 3, 60, no. 3 (March): 73–75; Shanghai Municipal Police Files, "File on the Affairs of the Late Huang Cho Chiu," D-1949 (1931).

17. *Xiyao*, 93; Gong, "Huang," pt. 4, 60, no. 4 (April 1992): 94.

18. Ralph C. Croizier, *Traditional Medicine in Modern China: Science, Nationalism, and the Tensions of Cultural Change* (Cambridge: Harvard University Press, 1968); Zhao Hongjun, *Jindai Zhong Xi yi lunzheng shi* (A history of disputes between Chinese and Western medicine in modern China) (Hefei: Anhui renmin chubanshe, 1989).

19. Nathan Sivin, *Traditional Medicine in Contemporary China* (Ann Arbor: Center for Chinese Studies, University of Michigan, 1987), 195.

20. Arthur Kleinman, *Patients and Healers in the Context of Culture* (Berkeley and Los Angeles: University of California Press, 1980); Emily Ahern, "Chinese-Style and Western-

Style Doctors in Northern Taiwan," in *Culture and Healing in Asian Societies*, ed. Arthur Kleinman (Cambridge: Schenkman, 1978); Marjory Topley, "Chinese Traditional Etiology and Methods of Cure in Hong Kong," in *Asian Medical Systems*, ed. Charles Leslie (Berkeley and Los Angeles: University of California Press, 1976); Jack M. Potter, "Cantonese Shamanism," in *Religion and Ritual in Chinese Society*, ed. Arthur P. Wolf (Stanford: Stanford University Press, 1974).

21. Thomas Sammons, *Proprietary Medicine and Ointment Trade in China*, Department of Commerce, Bureau of Foreign and Domestic Commerce, Special Consular Report no. 76 (Washington, D.C.: Government Printing Office, 1917).

22. "Jintan," *China Medical Journal* 30, no. 2 (March 1916): 150.

23. *Tsuien kinencho* (A commemorative album in honor of the ancestors) (Osaka: Morishita Jintan kabushiki kaisha, 1959); Ito Yoichiro, "Morishita Hiroshi o o shinobu" (Remembering the venerable Morishita Hiroshi), *Keizai jin* 7, no. 1 (1953): 387.

24. *Jintan kara JINTAN e: Morishita Jintan hyakushunen kinenshi* (From Jintan [in characters] to JINTAN [in capitalized roman letters]: Commemorating Morishita Jintan's 100th anniversary) (Osaka: Morishita Jintan kabushiki kaisha, 1995), 34.

25. *Tsuien; Longteng*, 1–2, 5; *Xiyao*, 56–57.

26. Sammons, *Proprietary Medicine*, 4.

27. Johannes Hirschmeier and Tsunehiko Yui, *The Development of Japanese Business, 1600–1973* (Cambridge: Harvard University Press, 1975), 181.

28. J. W. Sanger, *Advertising Methods in Japan, China, and the Philippines*, U.S. Department of Commerce, Bureau of Foreign and Domestic Commerce, Special Agents' Series no. 209 (Washington, D.C.: Government Printing Office, 1921), 67.

29. *Tsuien.*

30. Lin Yutang, *Moment in Peking: A Novel of Contemporary Chinese Life* (New York: John Day Company, 1939), 576; Wu Tsu-hsiang (Wu Zuxiang), "Fan Village," in *Modern Chinese Stories and Novellas, 1919–1949*, ed. Joseph S. M. Lau, C. T. Hsia, and Leo Ou-fan Lee (New York: Columbia University Press, 1981), 404.

31. *Xiyao*, 121, 234; Guan, "Huang," 139; Gong, "Huang," pt. 4, 60, no. 4 (April): 93.

32. *Shen bao*, 7 and 25 July 1911.

33. *Shen bao*, 26 July 1911.

34. *Longteng*, 3.

35. C. F. Remer, *A Study of Chinese Boycotts with Special Reference to Their Economic Effectiveness* (Baltimore: Johns Hopkins Press, 1933), 47; Kikuchi Takaharu, *Chugoku minzoku undo no kihon kozo: Taigai boikotto no kenkyu* (The structure of Chinese nationalism: A study of antiforeign boycotts) (Tokyo: Daian, 1966), 164–65; Joseph T. Chen, *The May Fourth Movement in Shanghai* (Leiden: Brill, 1971), 93.

36. *Shen bao*, 18 and 23 May and 30 August 1915.

37. *Shen bao*, 30 August 1915.

38. *Guohuo diaochalu* (A record of research on national goods), vol. 3 (Shanghai: n.p., 1915).

39. For a graphic visual representation of this image, see the thirteenth-century painting *Dragon and Tiger Embracing* (Long hu tuzhu), formerly attributed to Chen Rong, at the Museum of Fine Arts, Boston.

40. Zhang Yanfeng, *Lao yuefenpai: Guanggao hua* (Old calendar posters: Advertising paintings), *Han sheng zazhi* (Echo Magazine) (Taipei) 2, no. 61 (1994): 47; *Shen bao*, 30 August 1915.

41. Guan, "Huang," 139; Gong, "Huang," pt. 4, 60, no. 4 (April): 94; *Xiyao*, 234.

42. Gong, "Huang," pt. 4, 60, no. 4 (April): 93–94; *Xiyao,* 235; *Longteng,* 4 and 6–7.

43. Guan, "Huang," 139; *Xiyao,* 234–35; *Longteng,* 6.

44. *Longteng,* 7–8, 11; *Xiyao,* 131, 235, 315; Gong, "Huang," pt. 4, 60, no. 4 (April): 93.

45. Remer, *Study,* 245.

46. Chi-ming Hou, *Foreign Investment and Economic Development in China, 1840–1937* (Cambridge: Harvard University Press, 1965), 151–55.

47. *Jintan,* 34.

48. Zhang, *Lao yuefenpai,* 1:29.

49. Ibid., 88.

50. The art historian Ellen Laing has given the following lucid explanation of the "rub-and-paint" technique: "In this method, a layer of carbon powder was applied on the space where the image would go. The carbon in what were to be areas of shadow was gently rubbed into the paper, creating a sort of faint sketch; water pigments were then applied. The result was a realistic rendering of volume and mass. Colors became softer." See Ellen Johnston Laing, "Commodification of Art through Exhibition and Advertisement" (paper prepared for the annual meeting of the Association for Asian Studies, Chicago, March 13–16, 1997).

51. Zhang, *Lao yuefenpai,* 1:88.

52. Bu Ji, "Jiefangqian de 'yuefenpai' nianhua shiliao" (Historical materials on preliberation New Year's calendar posters), *Meishu yanjiu* (Research on art) 2 (1959): 51–52; May-ching Margaret Kao, "China's Response to the West in Art: 1898–1937" (Ph.D. diss., Stanford University, 1972). By thus distinguishing himself, Zheng became the most prominent of the second wave of commercial artists in China. On Zhou Muqiao, the most prominent Chinese commercial artist in the first wave, see Sherman Cochran, "Transnational Origins of Advertising in Early Twentieth Century China," in *Inventing Nanjing Road: Commercial Culture in Shanghai, 1900–1945,* ed. Sherman Cochran (Ithaca: Cornell East Asia Series, in press).

53. Marsha Weidner, "Women in the History of Chinese Painting," in *Views from Jade Terrace: Chinese Women Artists, 1300–1912,* ed. Marsha Weidner et al. (New York: Indianapolis Museum of Art and Rizzoli, 1988), 23.

54. John Hay, "The Body Invisible in Chinese Art?" in *Body, Subject, and Power in China,* ed. Angela Zito and Tani E. Barlow (Chicago: University of Chicago Press, 1994), 43.

55. Kao, "China's Response," 77 and 110–11.

56. E. Perry Link Jr., *Mandarin Ducks and Butterflies: Popular Fiction in Early Twentieth-Century Chinese Cities* (Berkeley and Los Angeles: University of California Press, 1981), 66.

57. Bu Ji, "Jiefangqian," 51; Ellen Johnston Laing, "Chinese Palace-Style Poetry and the Depiction of *A Palace Beauty,*" *Art Bulletin* 72, no. 2 (June 1990): 291; Zhang Muhan, "Cong meiren hua kan nuxing mei" (The ideal of feminine beauty as reflected in paintings of classical beauties), in *Lidai meiren huaxuan* (Selected paintings of beauties through the ages) (Taipei: Yishu tushu gongsi, 1984), 24.

58. Cochran, "Transnational Origins."

59. On this stereotype, see Zhang, "Cong meiren," 26. For examples of Zheng's earlier calendar posters of women, see *Lao yuefenpai,* 2:10.

60. Bu Ji, "Jiefangqian," 51.

61. Huang's advertising manager was Zhou Minggang, and his best writer was Xu Zhuodai, a popular humorist known for his "comic stories" (*huaji xiaoshuo*). On Xu, see Link, *Mandarin Ducks,* 158.

62. *Xiyao*, 113–14; Gong, "Huang," pt. 4, 60, no. 4 (April): 96; Bu Ji, "Jiefangqian," 52–53.

63. Ding Hao, "Ji lao Shanghai guanggao huajiaqun" (On advertising artists in old Shanghai), in *Lao Shanghai guanggao* (Advertising in old Shanghai), ed. Yi Bin (Shanghai: Shanghai huabao chubanshe, 1995), 13–17.

64. Zhang, *Lao yuefenpai*, 1:29, 33, 89, 90; Bu Ji, "Jiefangqian," 53; Wu Hao, Zhuo Botang, Huang Ying, and Lu Wanwen, *Duhui modeng: Yuefenpai 1910s–1930s* (Calendar posters of the modern Chinese woman) (Hong Kong: Sanlian shudian youxian gongsi chubanshe, 1994), 5 and 161–64.

65. Zhang, *Lao yuefenpai*, 1:28, 33, 60, 84; 2:18, 121.

66. Ibid., 1:77–78; Bu Ji, "Jiefangqian," 55.

67. Zhang, *Lao yuefenpai*, 1:33; 2:22–24.

68. Ibid., 1:29, 60; 2:14, 86, 121.

69. Ibid., 2:10, 11, 88, 95, 96, 106, 117–21; Cochran, "Transnational Origins."

70. Zhang, *Lao yuefenpai*, 1:65,70–71, 77–78, 85–86, 90; Bu Ji, "Jiefangqian," 53, 55.

71. Mark Elvin, "Tales of *Shen* and *Xin:* Body-Person and Heart-Mind in China during the Last 150 Years," *Zone* 4, pt. 2 (1989): 267–68 and 275.

72. Ibid., 268.

73. Ibid., 292 and 312.

74. Ibid., 268.

75. Cochran, "Transnational Origins."

76. On the delineation of these "macroregions," see G. William Skinner, "Regional Urbanization in Nineteenth-Century China," in *The City in Late Imperial China*, ed. G. William Skinner (Stanford: Stanford University Press, 1977), 211–49.

77. Leo Ou-fan Lee and Andrew J. Nathan, "The Beginnings of Mass Culture: Journalism and Fiction in the Late Ch'ing and Beyond," in *Popular Culture in Late Imperial China*, ed. David Johnson, Andrew J. Nathan, and Evelyn S. Rawski (Berkeley and Los Angeles: University of California Press, 1985), 368–70; Chen Xinqian and Zhang Tianlu, *Zhongguo jindai yaoxue shi* (A history of modern medicine in China) (Beijing: Renmin weisheng chubanshe, 1992), 31, 39; *Xiyao*, 66–67, 79.

78. Shanghai shehui kexue yuan jingji yanjiu suo (Shanghai Academy of Social Sciences, Institute of Economics), ed., *Zhongxi yaochang bainian shi* (A history of one hundred years at the China and the West Medicine Factory) (Shanghai: Shanghai shehui kexue yuan chubanshe, 1990), 12–13, hereafter cited as *Zhongxi*; *Xiyao*, 114; Gong, "Huang," pt. 4, 60, no. 4 (April 1992): 97.

79. *Xiyao*, 237; Guan, "Huang," 139; Gong, "Huang," pt. 4, 60, no. 4 (April 1992): 96 and pt. 5, 60, no. 5 (May 1992): 105, 107.

80. *Xiyao*, 109, 114–15, 235–36; *Zhongxi*, 23.

81. *Xiyao*, 80, 95, 108, 114, 240; Chen and Zhang, *Zhongguo*, 37.

82. On the contrast between the advertising policies of "old-style" and "new-style" drugstores, see Huang Kewu, "Cong *Shen bao* yiyao guanggao kan minchu Shanghai de yiliao wenhua yu shehui shenghuo, 1912–1926" (Medical advertisements in *Shen bao* as reflections of medicine, culture, and social life in early republican Shanghai, 1912–1926), *Zhongyang yanjiu yuan jindai shi yanjiu suo jikan* (Journal of Academia Sinica, Institute of Modern History) (1988): 150–53.

83. *Wuzhou da yaofang sanshi zhoujinian kan* (A commemorative volume on the thirtieth anniversary of the Five Continents Drugstore) (Shanghai: n.p., 1936).

84. Lin Yutang, *A History of the Press and Public Opinion in China* (Chicago: University of Chicago Press, 1936), 143–49.

85. *Longteng*, 6; Gong, "Huang," pt. 4, 60, no. 4 (April): 93; *Xiyao*, 98; and also see table 2.2.

86. *Xiyao*, 94–98.

87. Ibid., 96–98.

88. Zhang, *Lao yuefenpai*, 1:3, 104.

89. Lee and Nathan, "Beginnings," 360 and 375.

90. Physicians launched their first major campaign to restrict medical advertising in China in 1909. See *China Medical Journal* 23, no. 2 (March 1909): 107–10; 23, no. 3 (May 1909): 215–18; 23, no. 4 (July 1909): 256–57; 23, no. 5 (September 1909): 267–73, 365–68; 23, no. 6 (November 1909): 405–6, 421.

91. Howard L. Boorman and Richard C. Howard, eds., *Biographical Dictionary of Republican China*, vol. 3 (New York: Columbia University Press, 1970), 440–42.

92. Wu Lien-teh, "Financing Public Health in China," *National Medical Journal of China* 15, no. 1 (February 1929): 51.

93. "Proposed Regulations Governing Patent and Proprietary Medicines," *China Critic* 3, no. 21 (22 May 1930): 500; and 3, no. 22 (29 May 1930): 522.

94. Bernard F. Read, "The Chinese Pharmacopoeia," *National Medical Journal of China* 16 (1930): 282; and Read, "Chinese Pharmacopoeia I. 1930," *China Medical Journal* 44, no. 6 (June 1930): 520–21.

95. *Xiyao*, 298–99.

96. On Huang Jinrong's visit with Chiang, see Joseph Fewsmith, *Party, State, and Local Elites in Republican China: Merchant Organizations and Politics in Shanghai, 1890–1930* (Honolulu: University of Hawaii Press, 1985), 117.

97. Zhang Jungu, *Du Yuesheng zhuan* (A biography of Du Yuesheng), vol. 1 (Taipei: Zhuanji wenxue chubanshe, 1968), 80–109.

98. Shanghai Municipal Police Files, "File on the Affairs of the Late Huang Cho Chiu."

99. On Yu's visit with Chiang, see Fewsmith, *Party*, 117.

100. *Xiyao*, 235; Shanghai Municipal Police Files, "File on the Affairs of the Late Huang Cho Chiu."

101. *Xiyao*, 309.

102. Quoted in "The Pharmaceutical Situation in China," *Chinese Medical Journal* 47, no. 4 (April 1933): 405.

103. Lin, *History*, 143: Lin Yutang, *Shen bao de yiyao fukan* (*Shen bao*'s medical supplements), *Yuzhou feng* 18 (June 1, 1936): 270–71.

104. "Patent Medicine Law," *Chinese Medical Journal* 51, no. 1 (January 1937): 99–101.

105. Chen and Zhang, *Zhongguo*, 32–33; *Xiyao*, 170–73.

106. *Xiyao*, 149, 241–44, 279–80.

107. Boorman and Howard, *Biographical Dictionary*, 1:467–68; *Xiyao*, 170–171, 239; *Longteng*, 11–12.

108. *Xiyao*, 242–43.

109. *Xiyao*, 154, 160, 170–71, 240–44; Chen and Zhang, *Zhongguo*, 32–33.

110. *Xiyao*, 171–72, 242–43, 268–69, 280; *Zhongxi*, 34; Wang Ke-wen, "Collaborators and Capitalists: The Politics of 'Material Control' in Wartime Shanghai," *Chinese Studies in History* 26, no. 1 (fall 1992): 46–47.

111. *Xiyao,* 171–72, 300–302; Wang, "Collaborators," 49–50.

112. *Xiyao,* 244.

113. *Longteng,* 12–20.

114. On smaller cities and towns, see Chen and Zhang, *Zhongguo,* 44.

115. *Xiyao,* 245, 256–57, 289.

116. *Longteng,* 33–39.

117. For biographies, see Maurice J. Meisner, *Li Ta-chao and the Origins of Chinese Marxism* (Cambridge: Harvard University Press, 1967); Jerome Grieder, *Hu Shih and the Chinese Renaissance: Liberalism in the Chinese Revolution, 1917–1937* (Cambridge: Harvard University Press, 1970); Guy Alitto, *The Last Confucian: Liang Shu-ming and the Chinese Dilemma of Modernity* (Berkeley and Los Angeles: University of California Press, 1979). For collective portraits, see Jonathan D. Spence, *The Gate of Heavenly Peace: The Chinese and Their Revolution, 1895–1980* (New York: Viking, 1981); Vera Schwarcz, *The Chinese Enlightenment: Intellectuals and the Legacy of the May Fourth Movement of 1919* (Berkeley and Los Angeles: University of California Press, 1986); Arif Dirlik, *The Origins of Chinese Communism* (New York: Oxford University Press, 1989). For cultural studies, see Tani E. Barlow, "Theorizing Woman: *Funü, Guojia, Jiating,*" in *Body, Subject, and Power in China,* ed. Angela Zita and Tani E. Barlow (Chicago: University of Chicago Press, 1994).

118. Barlow, "Theorizing Woman," 262.

119. Michel de Certeau, *The Practice of Everyday Life,* trans. Steven F. Randall (Berkeley and Los Angeles: University of California Press, 1984), xi–xii and chap. 12.

THREE

"A High Place Is No Better Than a Low Place": The City in the Making of Modern China

David Strand

AN URBAN FRAME OF REFERENCE: LANZHOU, SHANGHAI, AND OTHER URBAN CENTERS

Lanzhou, the capital city of Gansu Province, stands at the geographical center of China. Located in a region notorious in the late imperial period for treacherous travel conditions, the city was, and is, a long way from centers of Chinese political, economic, and cultural life.[1] How far away depended, of course, on mode of transport. In the Republican era, Xi'an to Lanzhou by car took four to seven days (or three hours by once-a-week air flight).[2] A journey by camel from the nearest railhead at Baotou lasted forty days.[3] In an essay published in Mao Dun's 1936 compilation of vignettes, "One Day in China," Qian Julin, newly arrived in Lanzhou, made the city seem like the end of the world. A temple fair on Wuquan Mountain overlooking Lanzhou reminded him of the Festival of the Bathing of the Buddha in Jingan Temple in Shanghai. But he also lamented that in "lifeless and lonely Lanzhou," Mount Wuquan is the only "attraction" in an otherwise "dreary" place.[4] Sketching a hectic scene of pilgrims, beggars, prostitutes, peddlers, policemen, country girls dressed in "old and very out of fashion" clothes, "a few modern girls from the south," and a lone Christian evangelist, Qian also reported seeing a sign on the temple library that read, "'A High Place Is No Better Than a Low Place.' I say," he concluded enigmatically, "Lanzhou is no better than Shanghai."[5]

High in what sense? No better in what way? Shanghai towered over Lanzhou and nearly every other Chinese city in terms of marketing functions, political and cultural centrality, wealth, and population. But Shanghai apparently was no better for all that and Lanzhou no worse for being dreary. Reasons for this bleak comparison may lie in the author's personal desolation as an exile who both missed and deplored Shanghai, a city as famous for decadence and disorder as for progress and modernity.[6]

98

Cities in the first half of the twentieth century were high in that they held the commanding heights of most technological, cultural, and political change and low in their apparent inability to translate this advantage into a stable, urban-based economic, political, and social system capable of governing China. Cities like Beijing and Shanghai failed to produce or command a powerful nation-state. However, through media like newspapers, professions like writer, banker, and businessman, and disciplines like urban planning and social criticism, urban China did help produce a growing consciousness of being modern and Chinese. Among the parallel tracks and countercurrents left by failed republics, lost wars, and cultural humiliation was a heightened sense of connection among cities and between urban China and the rest of the country. High or low, Qian Julin saw Lanzhou through memories of Shanghai and Shanghai from his new vantage point in Lanzhou. He wrote his essay on Lanzhou within the framework of a common urban reality connected by camel, boat, horse or mule cart, car, train, and plane that also extended into the countryside and out into the world.

Distances were shrinking, however fitfully and unevenly, increasing the likelihood of finding the commodities and institutions of coastal Shanghai at the end of a long journey to a city of the interior like Lanzhou. Things one might buy in these out-of-the-way places, like cigarettes or patent medicine, were available as part of a national market. They were advertised, as Sherman Cochran shows in chapter 2 of this volume, with the help of recognizably Chinese and non-Chinese images. Alien and hybrid forms abounded. Western buildings with Chinese roofs, and political parties with citizens ordered in what political writers of the day described as "pagoda-style" hierarchies, achieved a generic presence in big cities and small towns. Meanwhile, temple festivals were still celebrated in modern, cosmopolitan Shanghai.

Urban zones and bands of influence widened beyond treaty-port enclaves. The building of motor roads, such as the highway from Shanghai to Nanjing, laid out new urbanized corridors along older commercial routes.[7] In good weather, one could drive from Xi'an to Lanzhou in four days, because by 1935, a new road, complete with service and aid stations equipped with telephones, had been completed between the two cities.[8] Railway construction, though disrupted by war and political instability, tied cities together in ways that supplemented and superseded the water routes of the late imperial period. Connections and mobility promoted a mental picture of city life as one of continuous and simultaneous activity. Standing in the train station outside Qian Gate in Beijing, one could visualize disembarking outside Yudai Gate in Hankou.[9] With a further act of imagination one might anticipate completion of the 1901 plan to link Beijing to Guangzhou by direct rail.[10] By midcentury, rail lines would reach Lanzhou as well.

Six years after Qian Julin sent his ironic message from the interior, Cai Mengjian, the mayor of Nationalist-held Lanzhou, gave an optimistic speech celebrating the city's progress while still acknowledging the burden imposed by Lanzhou's remote location.[11] By 1942, the war against Japan had given Lanzhou's old roles as Silk Road way station and imperial outpost new strategic import as the city became a link in supply lines running to and from the Soviet Union.[12] The Japanese invasion had also driven businesses and refugees west, stimulating economies and swelling populations in "rear-area cities" (*houfang chengshi*). From 1937 to 1940, the population of the city almost tripled to more than 150,000.[13] But in reporting on a recent trip taken to Chongqing to attend a political meeting, Mayor Cai lamented that, of the two hundred officials present at the Chongqing convocation, only eighteen had ever visited Lanzhou. The remainder pictured Lanzhou as "a desolate or uncivilized place," an image the mayor had tried to correct.[14]

Listening to the reports of other municipal officials also kindled the mayor's own sense of what kind of place Lanzhou ought to be: "In comparing Lanzhou to other cities I was for the most part satisfied. Only two points caused me to feel ashamed. One is that in terms of city size, the other cities are all bigger than Lanzhou. According to the Guilin report, Guilin's total area is 1,060 sq. km. Many surrounding counties are under its jurisdiction.... Our Lanzhou has only sixteen sq. km. That is really too small. Second, there is the problem of finances. Last year our budget for six months was only 900,000 yuan. Guilin's for one year is 6,000,000. Guilin itself only [has to] collect 2,000,000 itself. The rest comes from the provincial government."[15] Cai went on to note that although a third of Lanzhou's budget came from provincial sources, the city should be able to "step forward" to a better fiscal standing. And assuming that new resources were forthcoming, the mayor imagined a future, thriving (and larger) Lanzhou with neatly laid out commercial, industrial, academic, recreational, and residential zones.[16] The epithet "uncivilized" when applied to places like Lanzhou provoked not merely a denial but a plan to steal a march on the competition.

Mayor Cai's actual accomplishments were more modest: under his leadership, the town built a public Resist and Reconstruct Hall (*kang jian tang*) capable of seating a thousand people, added an official municipal guest house, repaired roads, opened public bathhouses, experimented with supplying scientifically tested potable water to residents at reasonable prices, and installed a number of street lamps.[17] These achievements, as well as grander plans to make Lanzhou a fully modern city, were touted with the enthusiasm befitting a local booster. Mayor Cai also succeeded in making Lanzhou bigger. Within a few months of his speech, and in the name of better planning and administration, Cai negotiated a tenfold increase in area for Lanzhou municipality.[18]

Remote Lanzhou's somewhat far-fetched claims to centrality were made more plausible by the unsettled nature of China's urban hierarchy. In contrast to recent Qing times, there was no clear center to look to. In the period from 1900 to 1950, the political capital of China strayed all over the map: Beijing in 1900–1912, 1912–28, 1948 (as "secondary capital"), and 1949–50; Nanjing in 1912, 1927–37, 1940–45 (as "puppet capital"), and 1946–49; Luoyang in 1932 (as "administrative capital"); Xi'an in 1932–43 (as "secondary capital" Xijing); and Chongqing in

1937–46.[19] With a more flexible definition of what constituted a national capital, Guangzhou, Wuhan, and Yan'an might also qualify during the months and years they hosted insurgent Nationalist and Communist regimes. Fixed status as important or unimportant, central or peripheral, was something cities could not count on and needed not necessarily accept. Who was to say where the center of China or a region within China actually was or, indeed, whether China would survive as a single political entity? Lanzhou was obliged to defend its position and importance. But so were Beijing, Shanghai, and Nanjing. In 1927, when the question of which city should be China's capital was debated, one brief in favor of the winner Nanjing acknowledged that Beijing, in addition to its position as current capital and cultural center, had become a railway hub served by four lines. But Nanjing had four rail lines as well and was better situated in the new "Pacific era" by dint of ready access to the ocean.[20] Of course, the author conceded, the argument he had just made against Beijing might also favor Wuhan. But Wuhan, with its three linked cities of Wuchang, Hankou, and Hanyang straddling the Yangzi River, was too vulnerable to flooding. Admirers of Wuhan stressed the tri-cities' struggle against natural forces as a badge of higher modernity. Wuhan rivaled St. Petersburg in the degree of human effort required to construct it in the face of an unpromising physical environment, a quality also shared by Hong Kong and Qingdao.[21] After 1945, this debate was reopened, with many northerners favoring Beijing and southerners Nanjing.[22] Compromise proposals imagined Beijing as a political or "land" capital and Nanjing as a ceremonial or "sea" capital. Other candidates included Wuhan, Xi'an, and Jinan. Even Lanzhou won adherents on the basis of its central geographical location.[23]

The rise and decline of cities based on changing political and economic realities was nothing new in Chinese urban history.[24] The positioning of military garrisons, the licensing of salt monopolies, or the raising or lowering of a city's administrative status could have deep and long-lasting effects on urban commercial and cultural life. What was new in the early twentieth century was the promise of uniform progress made against the reality of unevenness imposed by political upheaval, staggered treaty-port openings, the vagaries of global economic change, and the progressive modernization of transport. The windfall of attention, refugees, and investment Lanzhou received during the war years rapidly diminished after 1945, as people and capital flowed south and east.[25] Lanzhou did not become the Washington, D.C., or Brasilia of China. However, after 1949, in a recentered People's Republic, new political decisions to develop the surrounding region's natural resources led to further bursts of construction and growth.

Objective measures of urban development (or decline) were rarely congruent with the pace and direction of change imagined by planners, politicians, and residents. The real Lanzhou of the 1930s and 1940s lay somewhere between the desolation evoked by Qian Julin—and presumed by skeptical officials from other cities—and the festival of development imagined by Mayor Cai. In Lanzhou, stove beds (*kang*) were heated by horse dung or dung mixed with coal, and yet, lim-

ited electrical service had been installed here before it was available in more developed Xi'an to the east.[26] Drinking water from wells in the surrounding hills was
not always safe, and water taken by carriers from the Yellow River outside of the
city's North Gate was polluted by human and animal waste.[27] Public health problems such as contaminated water contributed to the fact that in December 1934,
in one city hospital alone, 2 percent of Lanzhou's population was treated for disease.[28] And yet, as this statistic proved, Lanzhou did have the beginnings of a
modern medical establishment. The fact that living in Lanzhou could make one ill
was a spur to reform.

Lanzhou was a study in contrasts weighted toward the preindustrial, with city
walls still intact but also abutting a famous iron bridge built across the Yellow
River in 1909.[29] Like Qingdao's 1890 iron pier, the Yellow River bridge both
served transportation needs and staked out a symbolic foothold for the future expansion of a machine-age China.[30] A few official buildings, banks, and hospitals
in Lanzhou were modern style and of two or three stories. But most residences
and shops had dirt floors, mud roofs, and old-style paper windows.[31] Self-
consciously conservative Lanzhou people described their community as one in
which "women's feet are small [bound] and heads [hair-styles] are big." But more
recently, the number of women with natural feet and bobbed hair had seemed to
increase day by day.[32] Despite the existence of a number of struggling factories,
Lanzhou remained dependent on other cities for even simply made goods. For example, mule carts were all manufactured in Xi'an and rickshaws were also imported from there, as well as from Kaifeng and Zhengzhou.[33] But this dependency
also reflected Lanzhou's commercial ties with distant cities and integration into regional and national markets.

Lanzhou was a hub of trade for Gansu as well as Xinjiang, Qinghai, Ningxia,
and Suiyuan. As such, it was a likely location for the reprocessing of goods like
wool and hides. But attempts to build blanket and tanning industries in the area
had faltered by the 1930s.[34] In the mid-1870s, Zuo Zongtang, governor-general of
Gansu and Shaanxi appointed to suppress Muslim rebellions in the northwest,
had ordered construction of a gunpowder plant and a weaving factory in
Lanzhou.[35] The weaving factory, outfitted with equipment purchased in Belgium,
was one of the earliest machine-powered plants in China and so in a class with
comparable mechanized projects like the Tianjin telegraph bureau, the Kaiping
mines, and the first textile plant in Shanghai.[36] However, once Governor-General
Zuo left the local scene for further military and political challenges in Xinjiang
and other corners of the empire, these industrial projects languished.[37] A similar
fate met a tanning factory opened in 1922 in the nearby county seat of Tianshui.[38]
Despite efforts by a former local official who "sent men to buy machinery in
Shanghai and employed technicians from big tanneries in Tianjin and Sichuan,"
the business failed because of "poor management." Lanzhou's backwardness was
both a burden and a provocation to development-minded officials and residents.
The pressure to push the city beyond its current capabilities came from both out-

siders bent on exploiting the region's resources and strategic position, and insiders anxious for their community to reach standards set by sister cities like Shanghai and Guilin.

All this pushing and maneuvering could not in one stroke alter the basic facts of economic and geographic life. Cities in China were deeply affected by their rural surroundings and hinterlands. Lanzhou's money market was closely keyed to the agriculture cycle of planting and harvest.[39] Since much of the city's interurban trade depended on camel trains (to Baotou and then by train to Tianjin), commercial and manufacturing activity peaked in the spring and fall and was idle in late spring and summer to permit replenishing of the camel herds.[40] Lanzhou's urban economy—however modern it might appear when judged by products available in markets, technologies installed in factories and offices, and plans promoted in political meetings—was still captive to the reproductive cycle of the camel (and to the flotilla of inflated goatskin rafts carrying goods downriver to Baotou). In fact, the war-induced growth of the city in the late thirties and forties increased dependency on the camel as demand for transport rose and the availability of fuel for cars and trucks became ever more erratic.[41]

The geographer Clifton Pannell has argued that in China as late as 1937 "not a great deal of progress [had] been made in the emergence of a truly national urban system."[42] Given the documented rise of significant interregional trade in the late imperial period (c. 1550–c. 1920) and the acceleration of trade in the twentieth century, the presence of Zhengzhou-made rickshaws and Shanghai consumer goods in Lanzhou helps sketch a picture of more significant, if incomplete, progress.[43] Uneven rates of development made coastal cities like Shanghai different in both degree and kind from cities of the interior like Lanzhou. But many inland cities, no matter how remote from the coast, were equipped with basic modern institutions and technologies like police forces, telecommunication and rail links, and factories. Militarists, politicians, merchants, and tourists used Chinese cities in systematic ways to win wars, mobilize political supporters, sell products, and pursue pleasure. This conscious, systematic use of urban China was one means by which such a national system took shape. In turn, an urban infrastructure of rail, telegraph, and telephone lines and branching systems of commerce, culture, and politics made the idea of an integrated China more than an imperial afterthought or a modern abstraction.

As embarkation points, entrepôts, and busy producers of goods and services, Shanghai and other large coastal cities dominated industry, foreign trade, and the production of newspapers, films, and magazines. By keeping up with the rest of the world, Shanghai in particular stayed ahead of most places in China. Shanghai's "first textile mills were built before any in the American South, and by 1930 it had . . . the largest mill in the world; its first cinema opened five years after San Francisco got its first large movie house; and by the late 1930s its Commercial Press was publishing each year as many titles as the entire American publishing industry."[44] By 1946, 85 percent of imports to China passed through Shanghai and

60 percent of exports left from the city's docks.[45] And yet, as Susan Mann notes, "up to 80% of China's national product was still being produced outside of Shanghai's developed enclave during the early twentieth century, in the dispersed economies of rural marketing systems that formed the broad base of China's central place pyramid."[46] Citing G. William Skinner's work on China's central place system, Mann emphasizes the likely low general rate of urbanization in China in the first half of the twentieth century, probably far less than the 20 percent often mentioned in contemporary writings, though more than the 6 percent estimated for the late nineteenth century.[47] A more recent estimate places the urban population at 16.1 percent in 1949.[48] However, low overall rates of urbanization were combined with "a *more balanced* pattern of growth . . . than is generally found in other societies during the same period," and one that "favored market towns and villages rather than larger cities."[49]

There is truth in the image of an urban China paced and shaped by messages, goods, models, and technologies from Shanghai. Bits and pieces of Shanghai, like the "modern girls" glimpsed by Qian Julin on Wuquan Mountain, turned up all over, and travelers from Shanghai saw the imprint of their city in surprising places. The geographer Fang Wenpei noted that Chengdu's Chunxi Road East Avenue, "well-ordered and bustling, strangely resembled Shanghai's Nanking Road."[50] Even Lanzhou had silk, cloth, and foreign goods shops "by and large patterned on Shanghai department stores."[51] The trade might be called capital goods (*jinghuo hang*) in Lanzhou, connoting an earlier pattern of obtaining luxury items from Beijing, but the goods themselves came now from metropolitan Shanghai and Tianjin.

This Shanghai model writ large or small reflected more direct, yet subtle, kinds of influence and control. Shanghai and Beijing newspapers tended to dominate journalistic enterprise in other cities. Wuhan had forty newspapers but "most plagiarize Shanghai and Beijing newspapers."[52] News items were in turn copied by other newspapers until the news became more and more out of date as one read copies of copies. Old news in Wuhan and out-of-fashion clothes in Lanzhou thus shared a common point of origin and common standard of backwardness. Local markets were "conquered" by metropolitan papers.[53] Because of advances in communications, Shanghai papers could arrive in Suzhou or Hangzhou in a few hours and Beijing papers in a day or two. Residents learned, according to critics, not to take seriously the pasted together dailies that made claims to be their city's newspapers.[54]

However, the marketing of newspapers from the coast could also promote reciprocal patterns of interaction. The Tianjin feminist newspaper *Funü ribao* (Women's daily), founded in 1923, was one of several newspapers with that name published in different cities by different groups of women activists.[55] The stated purpose of the paper was to provide "a place for women to speak," permit "women in different parts of China to produce powerful propaganda materials," and encourage coordination of a nationwide movement.[56] During a period in

1924, when the question of whether men should head women's schools was being debated in the *Funü ribao,* female students in a women's college in Baoding rebelled against their male headmaster.[57] The Tianjin newspaper sent a special correspondent to Baoding to contact the students and cover the story, with the initial interviews being done by telephone from the reporter's hotel because school authorities had locked the women in the college. Baoding, as a military and warlord center, had a reputation for conservatism. However, Yuan Shikai's use of the city for military training, beginning in 1902 as part of the Qing New Policies reforms, led to the founding of army and police schools and later a law academy and veterinary and medical schools.[58] Unlike Zuo Zongtang's industrial enterprises in Lanzhou, Yuan's educational ventures took hold. In due course, Baoding acquired so many schools and academies that it earned the reputation of being a "student city." Newspapers, libraries, and printing factories underpinned a growing cultural establishment of uncertain political loyalties. In this light, an outbreak of feminism in Baoding is not so surprising.[59] As the protest unfolded over a period of weeks in 1924, women and women's organizations from around the country wrote in to support the Baoding students, demonstrations were held in Tianjin on their behalf, and the students themselves sent a deputation to Tianjin to mobilize support. Through the medium of the feminist press, one could act locally in the presence of a national audience and, from the standpoint of editors in coastal centers, compose the larger meaning implicit in scattered outbreaks of school protests. Provincial cities like Baoding responded to sceming "treaty-port" issues like feminism in distinctive ways. The Baoding women's protests focused less on their school head's maleness than on his incompetence and failure to press ahead with educational reform, a stance very much in line with their city's decades-old New Policies ethos.[60] The site for feminist politics was not just big cities like Tianjin or even smaller towns like Baoding but a network of publishers, writers, readers, and activists linked by subscription, rail, phone, and a shared sense of women's issues.

The diffusion of institutions and technology to cities like Baoding was impressive. By 1918, two-thirds of provincial capitals had libraries.[61] In contrast, half of early-twentieth-century Russian cities "had no library of any kind and 95 percent had no institutions of higher education."[62] By the mid-thirties, most provincial capitals in China had "power plants, electric lights, flour mills, match and soap factories, telegraph and telephone installations, as well as modern schools, colleges, hospitals, hotels, and Christian churches," according to Olga Lang.[63] Lang also noted that "sometimes there are private houses and government buildings inspired by European architecture of Edwardian times. Some streets are paved with asphalt. Many business houses use foreign types of advertising and even neon lights. On street corners loudspeakers broadcast news and music from Shanghai or Nanking, adding a new note to the traditional noises of the Chinese street. Long modern gowns, rare in the hsiens, are frequent. Universities, normal schools, and technical institutes provide the city and its provinces with a modern intelligentsia. Local newspapers print Chinese and foreign news."[64] By midcentury, many cities had majority populations of literate residents, most of whom had some level of formal education.[65] Even places several steps behind Shanghai or Tianjin looked to be budding with promise. Though Chongqing, as late as 1933, had only just begun to replace rattan sedan chairs with automobiles and rickshaws, it was still judged as having the potential to rival "other great Chinese commercial ports" once its streets and roads were rebuilt and widened.[66] Even though Qingdao lacked sufficient freshwater for drinking and industrial purposes, it could be judged by boosters as "not having reached its peak of prosperity" rather than as being simply inferior to Shanghai and Tianjin.[67] Although Lanzhou's conservative reputation in matters of gender was well deserved, the city's rendition of 1919 May Fourth protests included student demands for male-female equality and women's liberation.[68]

The distribution of modern machines and sentiments, though patterned by coastal-interior and core-periphery relationships, was given to unpredictable highs and lows of action and intensity. A "balanced" urban system weighted toward the interior and smaller urban and marketing centers has led scholars like Rhoads Murphey to underline the historic separateness or alien nature of coastal cities based on their inability to complete or even begin the economic and cultural conquest of the rest of the country.[69] And yet this same system, by its market-sensitive nature, facilitated the distribution of Shanghai's economic, institutional, and cultural products. To borrow a term of Certeau's cited by Cochran, Shanghai's enclosure of modernity in such brilliant and tarnished form made it an ideal field for "poaching" by entrepreneurs, activists, and planners from all over China.

In interior cities like Lanzhou, the imprint of Shanghai and other coastal cities, though clear, continued to be limited by a variety of material factors. In addition to the greater weight of agricultural and pastoral realities on urban life, replicating habits of consumption was easier than building whole new modes of production. Industrialization, and the social transformations it wrought, spread more slowly from city to city than industrial products distributed through established and expanding markets. One might put down Lanzhou's difficulties in building an industrial base to its remoteness, but, as William Rowe points out, despite Wuhan's factory boom, nearby middle Yangzi River "commercial and handicraft centers as important as Shashi, Xiangyang, and Changde saw remarkably little industrialization until after the Second World War."[70] Nanjing's 1920s victory in the competition to become China's capital resulted in government-led economic and population growth without the rise of a factory economy. Toward the end of the Nanjing decade, less than 1 percent of the city's population worked in a handful of mechanized factories.[71]

If the influence of Shanghai was broadly but unevenly felt throughout urban China, even Shanghai appears to have been incompletely "Shanghainized" (*Shanghai hua*).[72] Olga Lang noted in the 1930s that in Shanghai, "although modern dress was a common sight, the traditional garb predominated. Many streets were in no way different from those of" Beijing, Hankou, or Baoding.[73] Recent research by Hanchao Lu on shopping habits of the Shanghai population confirms Lang's observation and suggests that the existence of Nanking Road as a central attraction of the modern city did not displace smaller neighborhood stores and shops as centers of residential life.[74] This is not surprising since cities normally cannot urbanize their hinterlands without receiving rural influences in return.[75] The more products Shanghai sent to the interior the more rural dwellers it drew to its factories and industrial slums. The fact that some fashion-minded Chengdu or Lanzhou residents were more attuned to Shanghai's Nanking Road than many "urban villagers" in Shanghai suggests that the borders of modern urban China ran through the coastal metropolis as well as between Shanghai and its near and remote hinterlands.

Shanghai and other coastal cities also felt the influence of interior urban centers. For example, Hankou's financial markets were sufficiently powerful to influence those of Beijing and Shanghai.[76] Cities other than Shanghai might set the standard for building and development projects. When a "greater Shanghai plan" was drawn up in the 1920s, Qingdao was cited by backers as "our model" for the most modern harbor facilities.[77] As Wang Ling has recently pointed out, relationships among cities in terms of relative dominance or subordination could be quite complicated.[78] The weight of treaty-port economic power eventually altered Beijing's long-standing dominance of Tianjin. However, the rise of Tianjin owed a great deal to investments made in military and other industries by the Qing state. Republican-era Beijing politicians like Cao Kun retained large holdings in Tianjin, while Beijing's demand for investment and equipment for projects like its waterworks and electric companies stimulated the growth of suppliers in Tianjin. Political power concentrated in Beijing converted to economic power, and cultural authority in Tianjin revisited the old capital and advanced the project of modern design. The basic construction and interior work for Beijing's new library built in 1934 as a hybrid of Chinese and Western forms were carried out by Tianjin firms.[79]

Travelers, politicians, and journalists saw cities of this period in modular and composite form. One could find Shanghai in most cities in China, and elements of these cities in Shanghai. As Lao She noted with amusement, even elements of a decadent city like Beijing had begun turning up in more modern centers of urban life:[80]

Since Beiping was bequeathed its status as former "ancient capital," its pageantry, its crafts, delicacies, dialect, and policemen, have gradually been dispersed to the four corners, spurred by the search for new places of wealth and men of awe-inspiring demeanor like the emperors of old. And so Westernized Qingdao has Beiping "hot pot"; in bustling Tianjin late at night you can hear the low and mournful cry of peddlers selling Beiping-style delicacies; in Shanghai, Hankou, and Nanjing there are policemen and official messengers who speak Mandarin and eat sesame-flavored pancakes. Scented tea from the south is double-smoked in Beiping and sent south again. Even pallbearers can on occasion be found on trains to Tianjin or Nanjing, bearing the coffins of the high and mighty.[81]

Cities were not only centers of commerce in other things; they themselves could become commodities in whole or part and be dispatched by train or slower form of transport to colonize or embellish the social, economic, and political life of other cities. Influences were reciprocal rather than unidirectional, and unpredictable rather than tightly planned. In the process, the points and lines of urban China grew and thickened in ways that promised an alteration in the role and power of cities as a system. Cities became the object of reflections on the nature of urban and social life and the sites of extensive economic and social change. Critics who took a broader view of China's urban condition and prospects complained that governments only seemed to pay attention to the largest cities and ignored the potential of "interior and ordinary" urban centers.[82] As one sign that cities had come to exist as a separate category of thought, policy, and culture, municipal studies emerged as a scholarly and administrative discourse.[83] Fashions in bobbed hair, hot pot, and municipal reform spread from city to city within a receptive urban culture.

City governments themselves were prey to fashion and the enthusiasms of the moment. In the space of a few months, from the early winter of 1928 to the summer of 1929, nine urban centers selected official city flowers. Cities justified their choices on local and national grounds.[84] In Shanghai, cotton defeated the lotus in a popular poll in an expression of city pride in, and concern for, the troubled textile industry. Ningbo's municipal government picked the lotus on the grounds that the flower could "thrive under a fierce sun [Japan]," and that, since it grew in water, it could represent the reputation of intrepid, sea-going Ningbo residents as the "Norwegians of Asia." Devoting time to choosing official city flowers might suggest misplaced priorities given more pressing urban issues like poverty, drug addiction, and crime. But the event underlines the fact of urban development during this era as both a particular and a general phenomenon. Not every city could support a globally competitive textile industry or tannery, much less an effective municipal government. But every city could, if it wished, join in localism's latest incarnation—civic boosterism—and puzzle over the choices offered by peonies, chrysanthemums, bamboo, and roses as signs of participation in a national movement for a more modern city in China. The airfields, buses, hospitals, and harbors would follow as a matter of developmental logic. To be a modern Chinese was to be proud of one's hometown—native or adopted—and to see local development as a concrete embodiment of the larger, necessarily more abstract reality of China. In the process, the old sentiment of localism, fueling competition and, paradoxically, reinforcing demands for centralized budgets and national standards, helped fabricate new ideologies and policies like nationalism and economic modernization.

CITIES AND SOCIAL CRITICISM:
THE IMPULSE FOR REFORM

Cities like Shanghai, Guangzhou, and Beijing were centers of social criticism and polemic because they were modern. They had the requisite concentrations of newspapers, political parties, universities, labor unions, and publishing houses to support public discussion and action. Even a small cluster of modern institutions in a city like Baoding provided sufficient means for joining a national chorus of critics and advocates. While never famous for political activism, Lanzhou residents participated in the founding of the Republic and early protest movements like the May Fourth Movement in good part because one institution—the Gansu College of Law and Politics, opened in 1909—provided a base for Republican and radical politics.[85] With the further aid of networks of educators, graduates, and students from Lanzhou resident within other cities or involved in national politics, political circles in the city were able to receive information and cues about political and social issues from Beijing or Guangzhou and react accordingly during national movements like the May Fourth protests.[86] Personal networks, hometown ties, and the core of modern institutions characteristic of provincial cities permitted the emergence of an urban political community that was remarkably inclusive and integrated.

Cities were also centers of social and political criticism because they were cities and so presented critics and activists with urban problems to recoil from and react to. Urban life stimulated social criticism directed at gaps between rich and poor classes, clashes between old and new (in areas like fashion, politics, business, and culture), differences in style and function among cities (as in the supposed conflict between commercial Shanghai and cultural Beijing), and the chasm perceived to have opened up between city and village.[87] According to Susan Mann, writers tended to take a systematic approach to the problem of cities based on the assumption that urban problems were part of a larger rural (and small town) context.[88] Some critics rejected the city in nativist fashion and proposed a rerooting of Chinese civilization in the village. Others sought to rebuild or reconstruct rural China by using the wealth and resources of cities. Still others defended urbanization as an engine of growth and accepted urban crisis as a necessary by-product of progress.

Chinese urbanites not only faced each other and compatriots in the countryside but also counterparts in New York, Paris, Tokyo, and Berlin. The kinds of models proposed by reformers were often taken from the global discourse on urban planning. For example, the garden city idea (*tianyuan xinshi*) enjoyed a considerable vogue in the twenties and thirties in China. Dong Xiujia, an acute observer of urban affairs who held positions in the Shanghai and Hankou municipal governments in the 1920s, advocated the creation of garden cities to meet the health and housing needs of both city and village.[89] The filthiness of modern cities and the backwardness of village life might thereby be canceled out by bringing nature into the city and modern conveniences into the countryside. Otherwise, China was fated to sink to a medieval level of "barbarism." Intellectuals just returned from European cities where traditions of municipal planning and management tended to be strong could become incensed at the seeming irrationality of the still-standing city walls, growing rickshaw trade, and shortages of basic services like street paving and cleaning.[90] The presence of treaty ports provided ready access to the particulars of these Western models. The rapid construction of Qingdao by the Germans in 1901–6 left "a little Berlin" of broad streets and neat white buildings with red-tiled roofs that struck visitors as parklike in aspect.[91] These relatively complete, "exported" cities, or cities within cities, of the treaty-port era served as an open kit of modern devices.[92]

The mobility and turbulence that unified and buffeted urban China ensured that reform thinking would penetrate the interior and reach smaller urban centers. When a new municipal government was established in Lanzhou in the summer of 1941, the city's Nationalist newspaper observed that in the past "the construction of our country has mostly been in the east, especially in the great coastal cities."[93] However, the editorial went on, advances in European and North American urban planning directed at garden and satellite cities had shown that smaller cities like Lanzhou constituted the future of urban design. Anticipating the arguments Mao Zedong was later to make about the need for inland industrial alternatives to coastal development, the paper argued that Lanzhou was certainly safer (though not immune) from enemy attack. The recasting of Lanzhou as a Western garden city eventually inspired initiatives in pursuit of this ideal. In the spring of 1942, Mayor Cai Mengjian announced plans to carry out the greening (*luhua*) of the city through a tree-planting campaign.[94] A tree in deforested Gansu was as striking an image as one planted in the slums of Shanghai. A garden city in Lanzhou also fit the ambitions of dislocated administrators and modernizers forced to pick up where Zuo Zongtang had left off. While Lanzhou's flurry of municipal reforms would not have happened when it did without the intervention of the war, urban reform as an idea and policy had been introduced to other interior cities like Chengdu long before the Japanese drove China's national government west.[95]

An eye for the aesthetic possibilities of a new urban China was accompanied by a nose for corruption and decay. Like their contemporaries in Europe and North America, Chinese reformers found the bad smells attending congestion and urbanization a particular outrage. From a scientific perspective, the smell of sewage signaled the threat of disease.[96] In this regard one late imperial legacy—nightsoil collection—provided a ready target and object lesson on the need for reform. Long-standing prejudices directed against nightsoil carriers by city residents made the case for modern sewers or stricter regulation of nightsoil removal easy to make. The fact that human excrement was an urban resource of value to an agricultural society was less important than the need to make Chinese cities smell the same as modern, Western ones (in which, if they were not garden cities, the odor of excrement would presumably be replaced by that of smokestack and combustion-engine pollution).[97] One reformer sardonically reported that Xuanwu Gate in Beijing was also known as "Shit Gate" by local people because of its regular use as a point of conveyance by nightsoil haulers.[98] Another decried the "unsurpassed . . . stink of the nightsoil drying yards outside Anding Gate."[99]

One individual, whose account of development in the Wuhan cities in the 1920s was generally appreciative, did not refrain from noting the "stink" that assailed one when one left the foreign concession area.[100] And since the smell was associated with inadequate sanitation measures by municipal authorities, the bad smell was directly related in this critic's mind to other forms of corruption and inefficiency: "Although there is a police force, they have no idea what sanitation is."[101] The German and Japanese periods of direct municipal administration in Qingdao were marked by a high degree of success in the areas of sanitation and health. After retrocession of control to China in 1922, the city became gradually dirtier. A reform-minded observer noted that "although twice a year, in the spring and fall, police were dispatched to inspect the city, they did this in a perfunctory manner and without any real effect."[102] However, for nativists, cities stank of worse things than raw sewage. According to Zhou Zuoren, all cities had a disagreeable "Shanghai odor" (*Shanghai qi*), a quality the folklorist Tao Xingzhi termed "Shanghainization" and defined as "busyness, vulgarity and selfishness."[103] Cities turned honest men and women into degenerates as a matter of course through activities like rickshaw pulling and prostitution, wherein "uncounted male citizens" were used as "beasts" and their female counterparts as "playthings."[104] Even seemingly harmless practices like leisure hours spent in the parks of Shanghai were suspect. The revolutionary and writer Chen Tianhua believed such idle promenading to be so dangerous to one's personal and patriotic resolve as to justify leaving the city before it was too late.[105] The expansion of the city's leisure industry in the form of public amusement arcades and the selling of lottery tickets threatened to undermine "cultural order" and place city residents in the grip of "carnal desire."[106] Observers fretted that older forms of recreation linked to festivals like those celebrated at the New Year were being replaced by "dog races, roulette, dance halls, massage, and various kinds of improper enterprises."[107] Mao Dun portrays the revulsion of a young activist standing "stupidly at a tram station on the street corner. All around him were perfumed women with gleaming arms and legs, the rumble of vehicles, the noise of people, the arresting green and electric lights. An indescribable disgust arose in him."[108]

When this kind of antimetropolitan critique was developed most fully, technical modernity seemed to matter less than the general idea that the bigger and the more powerful the city, the more terrible the price paid for Western-style progress. And so for one intellectual disillusioned with urban life of the 1920s, commercial Guangzhou, industrial Shanghai, and political Beijing were "the three great centers of Chinese materialism" and, at the same time, the three worst "holes of poverty."[109] The notion that big was bad opened up opportunities for critics in the interior. In 1941, a Lanzhou newspaper, playing on the conventional image of Shanghai as an "island" "orphaned" by the Japanese occupation (discussed in chapter 11 by Paul Pickowicz), printed an article entitled "Shanghai: Poisoned, Orphaned Island" describing a city in the grip of poverty, moral decay, and, now, enemy occupation.[110] The appeal to a Lanzhou readership of a powerful Shanghai cut off and laid low can be easily imagined. But the tables could not have been turned in so neat a fashion without the import of coastal models of urban administration, business, politics, and culture, combined with a reflexive anti-big-city current in contemporary social and political thinking.

Other critics, while aware of the moral and social problems represented by unsanitary conditions and degenerate behavior, also looked to the city for solutions. While cities were often the objects of criticism, they also represented a new standard of remedy. Advocates for cities stressed the importance of a more favorable attitude toward cities in moving beyond the traditional "agriculture-based state."[111] Citing India as a negative example, Dong Xiujia asserted that no country that emphasized agriculture alone could end up in a strong position.[112] Arguing in an undisguised antirural vein for a more balanced approach, Dong pointed out that "cities are the centers of the national economy."[113] Whereas cities can create wealth out of desolate landscapes, as the cases of Hong Kong and Qingdao proved, "China's villages have existed for thousands of years without the slightest improvement."[114] Eventually, city-driven economic growth would raise the standard of living in rural China as urban residents and industries bid up the price of agricultural goods.

Another strong, pro-city statement came from Hu Shi, who, reacting to the reality of rural and urban interpenetration, argued that Chinese cities were not urban enough: "The main reason for the failure of our big cities is that up until now we still have not broken with the customs of rural life. These habits include freedom, doing what one pleases, and being disorganized and passive. The new habits required by urban life [are an] involvement in politics, respect for law, systematic organization, and an active [attitude toward] work. If we cannot rid ourselves of these rural habits and live and work in tune with the city, we will not be able to manage urban affairs."[115] For political liberal Hu Shi, village air made one free and irresponsible, while the modern city was a workshop of industry and citizenship. As long as Chinese cities retained a rural air, they would resist the discipline of modernity. In partial recognition of the power of rural and small-town ways of life in the cities themselves, another writer, who evoked the experience of "stepping back several centuries" when he walked out into the surrounding countryside, agreed that "even within the same city the thinking of some people may range far into the future, beyond the realm of present-day life and experience, while others are stuck fast in the ways of their ancestors and will not deviate from them even a trifle."[116] Chinese cities bordered the fields of rural China and housed residents whose habits remained just as rustic as those who still farmed. The challenge, it seemed, lay in extending the city limits outward to the village and inward to those city people who remained immune or resistant to modern life.

That a liberal like Hu Shi praised the disciplinary value of modern urban life suggests a dilemma faced by those who would use the city as a means of changing China and Chinese. Freedom in the city might belong to a crusading newspaper editor or protesting students seeking to expand the public sphere of debate and

contention. But freedom also belonged to guilds and families screened from public view and official regulation by shop rules, courtyard walls, and traditions of
self-regulation. This had been Sun Yat-sen's famous complaint when he derided
the traditional freedoms held by clan, family, and locality as making Chinese society so much loose "sand" in the hands of revolutionaries and reformers. Reformers took advantage of limited, but significant, freedoms of press, publication, and
assembly to demand cities that were cleaner, safer, more efficient, and more productive. Since these goals required a more disciplined citizenry and a larger state,
reformers embraced administrative solutions to social problems. This sometimes
left the defense of urban freedom to local elites accustomed to commanding apprentices, workers, and other dependents and inclined to support authoritarian
regimes capable of supplying social order. In the search for common ground, the
pluralism encouraged by commercial culture and free public spheres was rivaled
by the elite and popular appeals of order, discipline, and planning.

CITIES, THE STATE, AND CITY PEOPLE

As a result, if many urban reformers imagined cities playing a burgeoning role in
charting China's future, they also assumed that the state would enlarge its presence in urban affairs. As William Kirby shows in chapter 4, the impulse to administer and plan gained strength among elites throughout the Republican era.
Despite the poor reputation of government for solving China's great problems,
administrative initiatives during the late-nineteenth-century self-strengthening
and the post-Boxer, New Policy era gave a strong impetus to the modernizing city.
As late as the 1920s, it was clear to one observer of Wuhan's development as an industrial city that the four factories developed by Zhang Zhidong beginning in 1889
laid the foundation for the hundred or more that existed by 1924.[117] Zhang in 1895
also authorized construction of a modern cotton mill in the small, lower Yangzi
River city of Nantong. As Qin Shao has shown in a new study of Nantong, local
reformer Zhang Jian used this enterprise as a base to build a huge industrial, commercial, and cultural establishment.[118] By the early 1920s, Nantong not only had
several textile factories but also an ironworks, wine factory, flour mill, and even a
movie studio. Even when they failed to measure up to reformers' expectations, late
Qing projects left surprising and subtle legacies. The turn-of-the-century construction of Zuo Zongtang's weaving factory in Lanzhou and the iron bridge
thirty years later not only nudged the city into the machine age but also accomplished a "miracle" in the history of the region's two-wheeled or camel-borne
transport system by encouraging the use of four- or even six-wheeled carts to bear
the weight of the heavy metal equipment that needed to be freighted in.[119] In later
decades, ordinary mule carts were improved by exchanging iron wheels for old automobile wheels and tires.[120] The New Policies also were of decisive importance
in the growth of public utilities in many cities.[121] Cities that pioneered in the development of utilities later provided equipment and expertise for other urban cen-

ters. When officials in Xi'an decided in the 1930s to modernize the city's antique system of two hundred hand-cranked telephones, they managed to obtain cast-off telephone and electrical equipment from Hankou and Nanjing and install a new phone system serving nearly a thousand customers.[122] In addition, the proliferation of new urban organizations like chambers of commerce took place throughout the country within a legal and administrative framework built by late Qing reformers.[123]

Republican-era political failures have obscured successes at the newly defined level of municipal governance. The absence in the late imperial system of a formal place for citywide, municipal government represented a suppressed administrative possibility. Big enough to address problems like local transportation and social order and small enough to avoid responsibility for military security or rural distress, the modernizing Chinese city could exploit advantages of scale that other localities and regions lacked. Therefore, if one is searching for the origins of an interventionist, administrative Chinese state, the city is a good place to look.

However, even when planners and administrators mustered the resources and will to carry out modernization projects, city residents often proved less than enthusiastic about the circumstances under which such public goods were provided. In a wide-ranging essay on local opposition to urban "reconstruction" (*jianshe*), Dong Xiujia identified several reasons why resistance to road-building and other public development efforts was so common. First of all, projects of all sizes disrupted urban life while often failing to convince residents of future benefits like higher property values and better communications.[124] In many cases, compensation for land taken for public purposes was set too low.[125] Attempts to widen streets in Guangzhou stirred the "opposition of private property owners who were [not surprisingly] reluctant . . . to see their property destroyed."[126] The same kind of complaints erupted in Lanzhou when the municipal government tore down buildings as part of a road-repair program.[127] Lanzhou officials claimed that improved communications finally pleased everyone and opined that "destruction is the mother of success" in such enterprises. But not everyone was so easily convinced. When the Beijing waterworks, established in 1908 by Zhou Xuexi, sought to lay pipe into the city, the line of construction happened to cross a sliver of graveyard property belonging to the imperial clan.[128] Zhou expended months of effort to negotiate passage through the parcel in the face of angry attacks by clan officials and accusations that the company had dug up graves in its haste to excavate. Even in cases where the interest at stake lacked such potent social or spiritual connections, customary expectations of compensation for property taken by the state made actions by developers liable to provoke an intense reaction.[129]

One way in which municipal planners and builders were able to avoid extensive conflicts with private property holders was to tear down city walls and construct roads and streetcar lines in their place. The destruction of city walls in the twentieth century has sometimes been seen as an expression of modernist, totalitarian fury directed at tradition and "feudalism."[130] Certainly such emotions existed on the part of planners and builders. Defenders of city walls accused reformers of mindlessly destroying an important cultural and historical legacy.

Shortly before the fall of the Qing, reform-minded officials considered the possibility of demolishing Beijing's massive walls and installing a streetcar system in their place.[131] In 1912, a newspaper editorialist, Leng Wangu, in an article entitled "Beijing's Walls Must Not Be Torn Down," blamed the "mentality of tearing down walls" (*chaicheng de sixiang*) on "great political reformers" who believe that "because a dictatorial form of government has been overthrown, nothing in China that is old may be left standing."[132] Leng attacked what he saw as the shallowness and mindlessness of such actions:

> Although merchants and commoners are not so inclined, political reformers feel they must tear them down. And besides demolishing walls, there is cleaning the streets (*jingjie*). What is this thing called "cleaning the streets"? It is the wholesale knocking down of old houses to open up new, modern roads. In addition, [they] construct colossal foreign buildings which effect a great appearance and may be beneficial and healthy [but really reflect] an immaturity, a temperament [geared toward] managing things, superficiality, a parading of foreign prosperity, a failure to grasp the true nature of China (*guonei*), and a lack of understanding of the difficulty of [finding] resources.

Deeply skeptical of plans made by those he sarcastically referred to as "the new men of purpose and principle" (*xin zhishi*), Leng pleaded for "preservation of ancient relics," especially those in good condition like Beijing's walls, and cutting new gates where they were needed to meet the criticism that city walls were incompatible with modern traffic and communications. Modernity encompassed destruction as well as construction. This connection between tearing down and building up was an article of faith among many revolutionaries, from Sun Yat-sen to Mao Zedong. Whether defacing a temple image in the name of hostility to superstition, tearing down a city wall to build a road, or destroying a class to make room for the people, violent assault on things and people helped define one's modernist credentials. While the first half of the twentieth century in China arguably witnessed more destruction than construction, the two processes were intimately related in the minds of planners, builders, and developers of all ideological stripes.

Leng Wangu was probably correct in claiming that grand and violent forms of developmentalism hostile or indifferent to cultural preservation lay behind the destruction of city walls. However, another, perhaps more practical, reason had to do with choosing the path of least resistance through the maze of individual and corporate property rights embodied in the Chinese city. The massive amounts of tamped earth and brick that had to be cleared out suggests the inertial force of that part of the urban tradition. The removal of Guangzhou's walls took three years, and the result was new, broad avenues suitable for modern transport.[133] But even there, wall demolition excited the opposition of owners of adjacent housing who feared damage to property values.[134]

In explaining resistance to the kind of general program of construction Leng Wangu railed against, Dong Xiujia also pointed to another practical problem: residents feared and resisted the tax increases often levied to finance reform projects.[135] Planners felt obliged to try to accomplish in a few years, through bold, expensive strokes, what took decades or centuries to achieve in European cities. Once built, projects like roads and telephone lines had to be maintained, and in the case of labor-intensive bodies like police forces, supported through large additional budgets for wages. Police levies, in particular, in the form of house or gate taxes, were often regarded as a burden by city residents.[136]

Municipal bureaucracies also insisted on the same, elaborate structure of bureaus and agencies no matter what the size or needs of the city in question.[137] Prestige and developmental ambitions reinforced the notion of big governments even for small cities. As a result, the greater part of municipal budgets went to pay official salaries rather than fund construction and service-oriented projects city people might better appreciate. Dong cited Ningbo, Anjing, and Suzhou as examples of cities too small to justify a full complement of municipal agencies. Nonetheless, residents were called on to support outsized bureaucratic structures with their tax contributions. Poor performance, linked to corruption, insufficient funds, or skewed priorities, further alienated residents.[138]

Finally, the failure to develop self-government institutions prevented emergence of what Dong characterized as proper sentiments (*ganqing*) between officials and residents.[139] Administrators "did not really listen" to city people (*shimin*), and so residents naturally opposed many policies they neither understood nor sympathized with. Chengdu police reformer Zhou Shanpei made an effort to build in such sentiments through a system of police commissioners (*juzheng*) at the subprecinct level who were to be "chosen by the people," but this method of linking police and community did not come to fruition.[140] Where such links emerged, as they did between shopkeepers and precinct stations in Beijing, they formed questionable marriages of convenience between policemen starved for unpaid wages and local merchants seeking to "rent" protection.[141] Even reformers with scant interest in democratic reform acknowledged that the key to successful "municipal reconstruction" (*jianshi*) was providing real "benefits to the people" in order to establish trust and, eventually, a cultural or spiritual reconstruction of the city (*jianxin*).[142]

Dong Xiujia recommended a number of measures designed to slow down the process of government-induced change, lighten the tax burden, educate the public, consult with various circles (*jie*) in the city about government plans and projects, and fight corruption.[143] Such moderation was in sharp contrast with the reformist zeal of leaders of cities like Shanghai or Lanzhou who were eager to commence projects, raise revenues, and defeat opposition to their schemes. Trying to put the brakes on development earned local people the contempt of officials who did not share Dong Xiujia's more balanced perspective and instead regarded such actions as evidence of feudalism, superstition, and selfishness. Remedies of

the kind Dong suggested are interesting, coming as they do from a committed urban reformer. They suggest a measure of common ground with the typical,
though far more piecemeal, reactions of local residents and groups when faced
with ambitious municipal projects.

Public skepticism of government was linked to the basic difficulty that municipal regimes had in distributing services and benefits to publics broad enough to
stand for the *shimin* as a whole. The building of public utilities, for example, tended
to benefit the relative few who could afford electricity, piped-in water, and telephone service.[144] And the dramatic improvements promised did not always represent such a sharp or positive break with past practice. In the port of Yantai, Chinese and foreign merchants contributed funds to finance a number of paved roads
comparable to the best Shanghai had to offer. On the one hand, these new roads
stood in stark contrast to the filthy and often impassable small lanes and alleyways.
On the other, old-style streets made of cobblestone were still serviceable and not
in any obvious need of replacement.[145] Likewise, replacing nightsoil carriers with
modern sewage treatment systems promised to fix something that was not so much
broken as smelly and limited in its capacity to keep pace with the modern city that
reformers idealized. As Leng Wangu observed in his polemic on city walls, if one
finds a wall "hopelessly ruined, an eyesore and an impediment to traffic," by all
means one should tear it down.[146] But if, like the Beijing walls of 1912, they are
"solid and lofty" and help keep out bandits, one should leave them alone. Rational choice was not always on the side of reformers. In the case of tax reform, existing and seemingly corrupt tax-farming schemes might appear relatively fair to
residents when compared with higher, noncustomary rates resulting from a more
"rational" system imposed from above.[147]

A remarkable feature of the development of municipal administration in the
Republican period is the weakness of democratic and representative institutions.[148] The trend lines in urban political participation and state building both
climbed upward in the first half of the century. May Fourth-era students with
their mass protests, and political leaders with their newly built armies and parties,
dramatized the often opposing—but also complementary—poles of popular
movement and political order. The middle ground of an institutionalized public
sphere faltered as electoral institutions and representative assemblies fell flat after
the early Republic. In fact, the peak of institutional commitment to elections and
assemblies in Shanghai may have come in 1909 under Qing reformers.[149] This
was not simply a matter of political intransigence on the part of officials. By the
end of the second and the early part of the third decade of the twentieth century,
many political activists had become "disillusioned with local politics."[150] Late-
Qing- and early-Republican-era enthusiasm for local self-government faded "as local assemblies were seen as instruments of bureaucratic venality and local elite exploitation."[151] Periodic attempts were made to democratize municipal institutions.
But groups critical of government policy often had difficulty agreeing on how to
transform their oppositional stance to bureaucratic or arbitrary rule into institu-

tional reform. Proposals in 1925 to form a special municipal unit in Shanghai with a mayor elected by residents were opposed not only by the national government and militarists but also by self-identified "local gentry and merchant" groups who wanted to handle local affairs themselves in a manner that seemed consistent with the city's "antigovernment" image.[152]

Although municipal reformers continually called for greater citizen participation in city politics and government, the trend in government was toward less accountable, more authoritarian administration. Late Qing initiatives promised municipal assemblies, and the 1911 revolution sparked regional and local suggestions for elected mayors and councils.[153] But Yuan Shikai's suspension of self-government regulations in 1914 cut short the constitutional basis of municipal democracy. Later attempts to reform city government were as likely to address the issue of independence from the central government as direct participation by residents.[154] Decentralization of power, whether based on the conventions of localism or newer federalist principles, had a higher priority than democratization. The southern Nationalist regime borrowed the American commissioner model of city government. But whereas commissioners in places like Galveston, Texas, were elected, the Nationalist plan called for the mayor to be selected by the provincial government.[155] Throughout the early 1920s, provincial governments promulgated revivals of more democratic arrangements. But none was implemented. After national unification in 1928, the dominant thrust in Nationalist administration of cities was what one contemporary nicely termed a "French-style" statism.[156] In Beijing, with many government functions performed by the police, and announced plans for self-government in the early 1920s continually deferred, the city's municipal office functioned as a kind of "public works bureau" with few direct ties to city people.[157]

By the early thirties, despite a raft of plans for democratic self-government in urban areas, the basic structures were still "officially managed" (*guanban*).[158] As a result, as Dong Xiujia complained, "the people, aside from paying taxes, transmit nothing to the government"—except, one might add, their periodic protests, bribes, and extortion payments.[159] A general municipal election took place in Beijing in 1935, but the government in Nanjing quickly nullified the results.[160] This rejection of democratic practice makes the Shanghai municipal government's decision in 1929 to put the question of the city's official flower to a vote in a popular poll all the more poignant. The other eight cities involved made the decision by administrative fiat or, in one case, upon the recommendation of local notables.[161]

The issue of state power in cities of the period is complicated by the fact that nongovernmental bodies like chambers of commerce served variously as agents, partners, or opponents of the regime. One way of looking at the development of municipal government in the twentieth century is to see this as a process whereby earlier structures of informal governance by local elites were formalized in new governmental institutions. But the statist and antidemocratic trends of the earlier

Republic seriously disrupted any such movement and left these often-powerful social groups in an ambiguous position.

Variation in the role of chambers of commerce is particularly striking as another example of broad diffusion of a particular modern form—the professional association (*fatuan*)—and consequent adaptation to local conditions. As in the case of schools, public utilities, and other modern institutions, chambers of commerce spread rapidly from metropolis to city to town, aided by the balanced or bottom-heavy nature of China's urban networks. By way of comparison, the development of chambers in Japan proceeded slowly and deliberately, so that the number of chartered commercial societies increased from 56 in 1900 to 61 by the end of the second decade of the twentieth century.[162] China had nearly 1,000 in 1912 and more than 1,500 registered chambers of commerce in 1919.[163] Since local chambers sometimes failed to register with the government, the actual number was probably even higher. Chambers in larger cities resembled their counterparts in European or North American cities in their range of activities related to improving commerce, mounting exhibitions, and lobbying the government. Chambers in smaller cities and towns might only serve to mediate commercial disputes.[164] Or, as in Nantong, they might play "an indispensable part in ... the creation of schools, transportation facilities, new police forces, and land reclamation companies."[165] All chambers of commerce provided conditional access to the significant wealth of member firms and guilds, thus attracting the attention of government entities bent on constructive activity or simple extortion. In an era when revenues lagged far behind planned expenditures, chamber contributions—for projects like Nantong's schools and police and Lanzhou's new town hall—enabled reform-minded officials to continue to move forward.[166] Qing reformers originally had wanted chambers of commerce to play the role of junior partner in an overall strategy of state-directed and -inspired economic development.[167] Though chambers were granted the role of "protecting commerce," and presumably their interests as merchant bodies, the new organizations were discouraged from having anything to do with politics or public policy. But chambers were soon drawn into such political realms by the very logic of the reforms themselves. Bureaucrats in Beijing in some cases saw local merchants as allies against the foot-dragging exhibited by conservative local officials.[168] The revenue-collecting and regulatory activities of the state also triggered a merchant response. As Nantong's Zhang Jian observed with considerable excitement, "Since chambers of commerce have been established in various places, merchants ... have gradually acquired the mentality of not putting up with the obstructions and extortion of customs officials. When confronted with these old injuries, they now cry out at the injustice instead of keeping silent and bearing them like they did before."[169]

Some merchants were now as impatient with the old proverb that cautions "In business only discuss business" as political reformers were with the presence of city walls, dirty streets, and outmoded municipal administrations. Discussing business led to debating political issues like taxation, legal reform, and foreign competition. Moreover, the key to success in business and in the larger project of build-ing a powerful China seemed to be organization beyond one's firm and beyond one's city. As two Shanghai chamber officials complained in 1909, "Chinese mer-chants are sick! We are in a state of collapse! [Merchant] A and B will not work with each other. This business and that one lack mutual empathy. This port and that port fail to communicate. The situation daily worsens as we find ourselves at loggerheads with each other. Thus weakened we are subject to official oppression and the control of foreigners."[170]

As Yu Heping observes in a recent study of Chinese chambers of commerce, Chinese merchants came to have a national perspective as a result of the influence of New Policy rhetoric and policies and their own involvement in chamber activ-ities. During the period 1907–14, local chambers of commerce, led by merchants in Shanghai and Hankou, gradually began to work in concert, leading to the for-mal establishment of an "All-China Federation of Chambers of Commerce" in Shanghai in 1914.[171] Three hundred protests in seventeen provinces during the spontaneous 1905 anti-American boycott demonstrated the potential power of a mobilized, nationwide merchant community. A journal published in Shanghai beginning in 1909 reported on merchant activities throughout the country and printed the messages, letters, and telegrams of local chambers.[172] Merchants, like political reformers and feminists, found intercity urban China supportive of consciousness-raising and organization building. To be sure, formal links also stim-ulated factional conflict and government oppression. At one point in 1916, a split along north and south, big-city- and county-level chambers threatened to over-turn results of an election for the Federation presidency.[173] In 1914, the central government was forced by merchant protests to redraft new chamber of com-merce laws that would have banned any national organization, required chambers to use language signifying an inferior administrative status in "reporting to superi-ors" (*bing*), and stipulated that chambers must report to and accept the detailed guidance of local officials.[174]

The merchants' remedy of organizing upward to citywide status and outward to other cities closely followed the strategies pursued by other groups, classes, and circles during this period.[175] Politicians ranging from Liang Qichao and Sun Yat-sen to Mao Zedong and Hu Shi agreed that if grouping together was a source of strength, the bigger the group the better. Merchant leaders reasoned that "when merchant and merchant come together[,] that produces a chamber of com-merce.... If chambers unite in a [national] federation (*dahui*), the extent of its ef-fectiveness will be hundreds of times greater than [that of] today's chamber."[176] Being Chinese meant joining and following ever-larger groups and organizations, hitching part of one's identity to membership in unions, chambers, federations, and parties.

The Chinese city supported this process of group formation and integration in a variety of ways. Late imperial cities were already relatively well organized within particular trades and communities of sojourners, examination candidates, and temple goers.[177] In some cases citywide trades or guilds had formed federations to help govern large commercial cities like Hankou.[178] Taking the next step of formalizing intergroup cooperation, while risking factional struggle and other forms of conflict, did not require a huge leap in terms of organizational resources and practices. In addition, the customary mobility of merchants and other sojourners from city to city and city to town and village facilitated the spread and replication of innovations like the chamber of commerce. Provincial hostels (*huiguan*) and hometown associations (*tongxianghui*) played important roles in hosting and undergirding association building.

In the absence of movement toward representative government, democracy—in the sense of election of officers and rule of law—made greater headway within nongovernmental bodies than in the juridical and political space that lay between state and society. Chambers of commerce reinforced established guild practices of holding meetings and elections in ways that made both chambers and member guilds more democratic.[179] The wave of chamber of commerce building in the last years of the Qing and the first decade of the Republic was followed by the reorganization of guilds in many cities along chamber lines. Byrna Goodman has shown how *tongxianghui* in Shanghai were subject to these same kinds of procedural innovations.[180] In Beijing, the practice of rotating leadership positions among the elders of a native-place organization gave way to the election of presidents or boards of directors.[181] In some cases, the government seems to have mandated democratization as a means of opening up autonomous and opaque institutions to government regulation and monitoring. Democratic practice—real enough, if judged by fights for control of local unions and chambers, and assertions of rights to vote for leaders and decide matters of collective importance—coexisted with encroaching state surveillance and continuing paternal hierarchies.

The conservative, order-keeping stance often taken by local organizations like chambers of commerce and other professional associations was a frustrating fact of urban political life for municipal reformers and political agitators alike. Though chambers finally supported and helped finance the 1911 revolution, the initial impulse of the organized merchant community had been moderate rather than revolutionary. During the first years of the Yuan Shikai presidency, chambers typically sided with government as a force of order against the political demands of revolutionary agitators.[182] As Yu Heping concludes in his study of the many progressive and innovative features of chambers of commerce in the late Qing and early Republic, the paramount goal of merchant elites was order. "No matter what kind of government, what kind of doctrine, what kind of party, [merchants] only wanted to maintain social order."[183] Anything else was liable to be seen as "a bad system, bad government, and even the enemy, the 'party of disorder.'"[184] In the aftermath of the turbulent May Thirtieth Movement, a left-wing observer of the Nanjing urban scene made the following analysis: "The bourgeoisie have organized their power in three forms: the chamber of commerce, the satin [trade] association, and [other] local societies. These latter include an agricultural society, a lawyers' association, and various guilds. Their power exceeds that of the chamber of commerce. But aside from ingratiating themselves with officials and militarists, they care nothing for local public or national affairs. Last year during the heat of the May Thirtieth Movement, nothing could stir them."[185] Shorn of polemic, the passage accurately describes some of the key functions of local elite organizations. "Ingratiating themselves" with officialdom and the armies in the neighborhood was often the key to maintaining social order and protecting local interests. In fact, an earlier article on the student movement in Nanjing had complained that this "live and let live" attitude was not confined to merchants of the city, since students also accepted unspoken limits on their protest activities.[186] Such self-restraint was one of the hallmarks of the late imperial urban social order, and the value attached to informal, mutual adjustment had yet to dissolve even in an age of ideological "heat."

In order to act effectively, officials either tried to ignore local notables like chamber of commerce leaders or selectively co-opt them. Activist municipal officials, like Mayor Wu Tiecheng of Shanghai in the early 1930s, succeeded best when they constructed a narrow base of support for their policies among social and economic elites they shared political and native-place connections with.[187] Such tactics of Chinese municipal officials resembled those of U.S. mayors in the early stages of urban renewal in the 1950s who handpicked compliant citizens' action commissions to mobilize public support without disturbing their control of the reform agenda.[188] For example, Mayor Wu's appointed municipal council of 1932 was weighted to include fellow Cantonese and bankers from Zhejiang and Jiangxu who were politically reliable. Later, this council was broadened by the addition of selected educators, journalists, and labor union leaders willing to cooperate with the government (and in a few cases oppose government initiatives on a narrow range of issues).[189] The way the Shanghai municipal council functioned was clearly at odds with the democratic promise embedded in many political reform proposals from 1909 on. However, by working the practice of consultation into the council's operations, the minimum expectations of a narrow range of local elites could be met as they "contributed their opinions on municipal matters" to the government.[190] In cases where elites managed to retain their prestige and broad influence over urban society, such consultations could be binding in ways that suggest that the underdevelopment of democracy was partially offset by the mediating efforts of local notables. Kristin Stapleton cites Chengdu's "Five Elders and Seven Sages" (*wulao qixian*) as examples of late Qing degree holders who remained "arbiters of the public good" into the 1940s.[191]

These two tendencies—administrative absolutism and elite mediation—helped set the stage for the urban reaction to Japanese occupation. After the initial phase of brutal assault, including the terror bombing of Shanghai and the Nanjing massacre, Japanese authorities settled in for a general program of development and order keeping. In north China, in fact, "the overall distribution of productive capacity, the urban character, the communications situation, and the regional economic functions of an urban system produced great changes."[192] Since the Japanese were capable of providing both administrative guidance and social order, a local, urban perspective on the occupation might easily counsel collaboration even at the price of putting aside the national ambitions these local interests had once aligned themselves with. As Frederic Wakeman suggests in chapter 9 of this volume, such tendencies toward treason were strong among opportunists and villains. But there were also systemic and cultural reasons for collaboration, ranging from the persistence of reporting to superiors, whomever they might be, as an element of political and bureaucratic culture to the fielding of a cadre of notables expected to ingratiate themselves with the regime in place. Being a local booster could be an expression of national patriotism. But defending closely allied local interests might also lead to a charge of treason.

The adaptability of late imperial urban traditions is, in retrospect, quite impressive. Byrna Goodman and others have shown how native-place ties so important to Mayor Wu (and practically everyone else in urban China) expanded to serve a broad range of social, political, and economic purposes.[193] These findings seem to conflict with the harsh judgment Hu Shi made about the tendency of urban residents to keep their hometown identities at the expense of a true commitment to the city they actually lived in.[194] As evidence Hu offered the fact that individuals continued to list their native places on their calling cards and inscribe these connections above the gates to their residences. The task ahead, according to Hu, involved changing the attitudes of urban residents so that they would behave more like city people than country people or visitors: "Our first duty today in reforming municipal government is to create *shimin*. The way to create *shimin* is not to scream about overthrowing feudalism by banning the inscribing of native-place on calling cards or on one's front gate but rather to gradually carry out *shimin* participation in government."[195] In fact, Goodman points out that because of the adaptability of native-place solidarities and their role in making abstract notions like "nation" concrete in the defense of family and hometown, we might imagine urban residents of the Republican era skipping the stage or level of *shimin* consciousness.[196] Hu Shi was, perhaps, wrong about the supposed debilitating and narrowing force of native-place sentiments. But he may have been correct in pinpointing the tentativeness of an urban identity "for itself."

There were many exceptions to this tendency to think and act subethnically, sublocally, and nationally rather than in a citywide direction. The threat of physical attack on a city, as happened in many places during the warlord period, instilled in residents a strong, if momentary, sense of the city as a community of fate.[197] Beijing residents who opposed moving the national capital to Nanjing in 1928 made their case on behalf of themselves as *shimin*.[198] Other forces likely to provoke self-conscious actions by *shimin* included contact with the modern city as a technological and institutional entity: a rapid rise in rates of taxation, changes brought on by construction projects, and higher utility rates or fares. The role of urban resident as consumer of public services or even private housing was an important vehicle for raising *shimin* consciousness. The weight of a new tax or the prospect of a new regulatory policy prodded citizens into realizing the dimensions of an urban community of fate and, on occasion, acting on that basis. Hu Shi's argument that *shimin* consciousness required participation in municipal government suggests a dialectical relationship between city people as citizens and consumers, on the one hand, and citywide administration and power, on the other. For example, during the long process in which the Beijing Streetcar Company was proposed, financed, and constructed, all kinds of protestations were made by and on behalf of Beijing's *shimin* concerning issues like the need for public ownership, danger to residents who might be struck by streetcars, harm done to the livelihood of rickshaw pullers, and damage inflicted on historic and cultural sites.[199]

An open letter from "city resident" Qin Zizhuang, dating from the summer of 1923, while construction was in progress, captures the flavor and complexity of the emerging civic and urban consciousness Hu Shi was advocating. Qin begins by sarcastically observing that Beijing is developing streetcars at the very moment cities in Europe and North America are abandoning theirs in favor of buses. However much urban consciousness owed to late imperial civic activism, *shimin* status by the 1920s included an awareness of how city life in China compared to conditions in the larger, global world of cities. Stepping into that world, if only rhetorically, lent critical force to statements of urban concern.

The brunt of Qin's argument against the streetcar was directed against the aesthetic and cultural damage the utility promised to inflict on Beijing, and it is framed by Beijing's ambitions as a world city, ambitions presumably shared by developers of the streetcar and city officials. Qin appealed for a balance between progress and preservation: "Please note that in the future the streetcars will run from Tiananmen out to Xidan and Dongdan Arches and from Tiananmen to Tianqiao. This will wipe out the historical and cultural edifice of Tiananmen in its entirety and cause the heritage of hundreds of years to be cut off and scattered in a moment for the sake of the greed of a few. If we consider the capital cities of other countries, we see that they all have one or two magnificent avenues for natives and foreigners to stroll upon for purposes of edification, like the Champs Elysees in Paris, Unter den Linden in Berlin, and Wellington Street [*sic*] in London." Allowing Beijing "to be covered by the streetcar company's sprawling mess of poles and lines" would ruin the "clean" lines of the city for future generations. Not doing everything to save Beijing's treasures and vistas would be tantamount to giving in to "personal disgrace, the dying out of one's name, and the destruction of one's country." The people of Beijing would face "the censure of generations of our descendants and the ridicule of foreigners." The logic of this argument drives Qin to embrace his fellow city residents and the category of *shimin:* "Why not seize the moment and rise up to force negotiations with the company? At the same time, we should unite the *shimin* to complain to the municipal office and the police with the full force of our opposition and not stop until the [route of the planned] track has been changed. If this company in its perverse pursuit of profit does not adopt the goodwill of our *shimin*, we *shimin* must ourselves make the appropriate response."[200]

On the one hand, Qin's plea that the city's architectural values have the same standing as personal reputation and the survival of family and nation highlights the potential power of the city as an emotive and critical force. While his arguments echo the preservationist sentiments found in Leng Wangu's defense of the city walls in 1912, Qin has found within the modernist reform stance that Leng condemned the grounds for resisting and revising what he saw as bad planning and a poor use of the technologies available globally. Qin's metropolitan sensibility and boosterlike zeal resemble that of the mayor of Lanzhou (and, as Mingzheng Shi reminds us, the Beijing municipal office derided by Qin).[201] On the other hand, the *shimin* identity assumed and celebrated in this open letter risked coming in a poor fourth behind national, group, and individual values and interests.

CONCLUSION

Most cities of this period, despite evidence produced by muckraking critics who saw urban concentrations only as corrupt and evil places, had significant supplies of what Robert Putnam has recently described as "social capital" or "features of social organization, such as trust, norms, and networks, that can improve the efficiency of society by facilitating coordinated actions."[202] In Putnam's book on Italian political development, he contrasts the "feudal autocracy" of the Italian south and the "communal republicanism" of the north.[203] The former made the dynamic and progressive rule of a Frederick II possible but also hastened the decay into clientelism and fragmentation when a strong central power was not present. The latter provided community support and direction for civic action and development, projects twentieth-century Chinese would term *jianshe*. Putting aside the important question of regional differences, Chinese cities of the early twentieth century inherited a late imperial legacy of autocracy that normally pulled its administrative punches (in part by the subtle means of not granting cities special municipal status beyond serving as the centers of larger territorial units) and communal or corporate self-management inclined toward political self-restraint. The balancing act performed by state and city depended on the intermittent exercise of social connections and a stabilizing structure of patronage and clientelism extending through state and society.

The remodeling of the Chinese city through the import of new technologies and organizational forms in the twentieth century presented officials and city people with new opportunities for building from the top down (technocratic and administrative initiatives), the middle out (the realm of *fatuan* and local elite bodies), or the bottom up (the growth of labor unions and other grassroots organizations). From one point of view, the problems lay in the middle where local elites used modern organizational forms and ideologies to prevent administrators from acting decisively and mobilizing the energies of ordinary people. Chambers of commerce, designed to promote growth and reform (and often willing to act on that mandate), just as often tended to function like brakes on municipal reform rather than as engines of civic leadership. But if one is not handed the wheel through democratic enfranchisement, perhaps the brake of passive resistance and retreat is the next best mechanism to take hold of. City people then had to choose between imperious, somewhat alien (or actually foreign) technocrats and bureaucrats, more familiar and often conservative leaders of the circle their group was nested in, and radical activists who typically lacked both administrative and social power.

In order for social capital to be actually spent on civic endeavors, the catalytic or mediating influence of a Zhang Zhidong in Hankou, Zuo Zongtang or Cai Mengjian in Lanzhou, or Zhang Jian in Nantong was extremely important. These leaders helped integrate the pivotal middle level of elites into projects and tap resources available in higher-level administrative budgets or more distant metropolitan centers. Without such leadership, the power, wealth, and status available to support development might remain dormant or devoted solely to private or corporate enterprise.

Such projects were often pursued in a spirit of boosterism. Cai and Zhang Jian were heir to a tradition of localism that celebrated everything from tasty hams and fine pottery to beauty spots, pilgrimage sites, virtuous widows, and brilliant scholars. The test of a locale's value was measured in recognition accorded by elite consumers and imperial edict. The early twentieth century found new standards in the form of production figures, bacteria counts taken from water sources, the size of membership rolls, numbers of tourists, and recognition of a city, building, or person as a national model. As one travels around China today, at the turn of another century, and samples local beers and other liquors touted as superior to those of a neighboring county or province, visits newly developed theme parks and warm-spring resorts, tours sausage plants and pottery factories run as township and village enterprises, and talks to local officials and entrepreneurs about their dreams and schemes for development, echoes of Lanzhou as garden city or Nantong as a little Shanghai are clear and insistent. Broad participation in China's development has long been more than a matter of state control or popular protest. One could become Chinese in the modern sense by joining a demonstration or a party, but also by training for a profession, opening a local museum, or marketing a local resource. These latter, more local and pluralistic enterprises should not be equated with democracy or a localism invariably hostile to national authority. But they do comprise sites where social capital can be invested in ways that foster diversity, criticism, and a measure of autonomy.

In tracing the distribution of technical and institutional modernity, we can with some confidence identify the component parts of an urban China reorienting itself around a recognizably modern city of offices, factories, movie theaters, and public parks. But it is also clear that the more complex reality of urban—and rural—life "away from Nanking Road," Tiananmen, and the iron bridge at Lanzhou needs to be brought into the picture of a developing and decaying urban China.[204] Brave words about garden cities and municipal reconstruction and an impressive collection of new machines and technologies held the high ground of discourse and policy. If the words often rang hollow and the machines sometimes rusted from disuse (or were broken by Luddite rivals), the pattern of development and the pressure for local progress on a national scale endured. Of course, most people still lived in the countryside. But even rural people came to be judged by urban standards of health, productivity, political activism, and knowledge about the world. Most people who finally "became Chinese" were not urbanites. But if they acquired elements of their modern Chineseness by joining a mass organization or militia, learning a propaganda song, pursuing a marriage based on love, buying a national brand of cigarettes, or brushing their teeth as a matter of personal hygiene, the point of origin for such behavior was likely to be someplace like Shanghai or Lanzhou, if not Paris or Tokyo. The process of making such actions and ideas parts of a Chinese identity as adopted values or hybrid constructs traversed a shifting topography of places high and low.

NOTES

1. Xu Xueli, "Tuo ling dingdong yundilai—Lanzhou minjian yunshu shilue" (The tinkling sound of camel bells—an outline history of indigenous forms of shipping in Lanzhou), *Xibei shidi* (Historical geography of the northwest) 3 (1989): 100. A mid-seventeenth-century magistrate listed dangerous or impassable roads as one of the area's major shortcomings.

2. Ren Mei'e, "Lanzhou fujin dizhi yanjiu" (An investigation of the topography of Lanzhou and vicinity), *Fangzhi yuekan* 8, no. 45 (1 April 1935): 18–19. Air connections to Lanzhou were radically curtailed during the war years because of fuel shortages. *Lanzhou shizheng yizhounian* (A year in Lanzhou municipality: July 1941–June 1942), vol. 1 (Lanzhou: Lanzhou shizhengfu mishu chubian, 1942), 10.

3. Ren Mei'e, "Lanzhou fujin dizhi yanjiu," 19.

4. Sherman Cochran and Andrew C. K. Hsieh, with Janis Cochran, trans., eds., and intro., *One Day in China: May 21, 1936* (New Haven: Yale University Press, 1983), 178.

5. Ibid., 179.

6. Ibid. Qian's point may also have been that religious practice was just as tainted by commerce and devoid of devotion in Lanzhou as in Shanghai. The editors of *One Day in China* note that the general purpose of reportage on religious activities was to expose the follies of "superstition," although not all the entries are aggressively antireligious in this sense (141). Qian is content to underline the recreational and mercenary motivations of festivalgoers. He seems more interested in mocking provincialism than in attacking popular religion.

7. Yao Yiyun, *JingHu lu luxing zhinan* (A Nanjing-Shanghai Road travel guide) (Shanghai: Shijie chuban hezuoshe, 1933). However, in some cases building modern roads had little impact on interurban commerce because of a shortage of trucks and the attempts to prevent old-style carts from using (and damaging) pavement. William T. Rowe, "Wuhan and Its Region, 1736–1938" (paper presented at conference on "The Chinese Metropolis in the XXth Century," Lyon, 5–7 May 1993), 21.

8. Wang Wang, ed., *Xin Xi'an* (New Xian) (Shanghai: Zhonghua shuju, 1940), 67–68.

9. Zhou Yirang, "Wuhan sanzhen zhi xianzai ji qi jianglai" (The three Wuhan cities and their future), *Dongfang zazhi* (hereafter *DFZZ*) 21, no. 5 (10 March 1924): 70.

10. The line was finally completed in the late 1940s. (Rowe, "Wuhan," 19–20.)

11. *Year in Lanzhou Municipality*, 2:126–32.

12. Xu Xueli, "Tuo ling dingdong yundilai," 101.

13. Liao Kaitao, ed., *Lanzhou* (Taibei: Zhengzhong shuju, 1957). The recorded population grew from 57,846 in 1937 to 156,948 (pp. 28, 44).

14. *Year in Lanzhou Municipality*, 1:131.

15. Ibid.

16. Ibid., 2:2–3.

17. *Gansu minguo ribao*, 16 March 1942, p. 3; *Year in Lanzhou Municipality*, 1:23–24, 2:11–13.

18. *Year in Lanzhou Municipality*, 2:1–2.

19. Liu Jingkun and Fu Bing, "Minguo shiqi de shoudu, peidu yu xingdu" (Capitals, secondary capitals, and administrative capitals during the Republican era), *Minguo dangan*, no. 1 (1994): 114–17.

20. Zhang Qiyun, "Zhongguo zhi guodu wenti" (The question of China's capital), *DFZZ* 24, no. 9 (10 May 1927): 5–6.

21. Zhou Yirang, "Wuhan sanzhen zhi xianzai ji qi jianglai," 81.

22. Zhang Ji (from Hebei) and Yu Zuoren (Shaanxi) pressed for Beijing. Southerners had the advantage of Nanjing's having been Sun Yat-sen's choice. Liu Jingkun and Fu Bing, "Minguo shiqi de shoudu, peidu yu xingdu," 117.

23. Chen Cheng, a Zhejiang native who had served in military and civilian posts charged with the defense of Wuhan, proposed Wuhan. Shanxi native Liu Guanxun advocated Xi'an. Geologist Weng Wenhao (Zhejiang) suggested Jinan (ibid.).

24. Cycles of boom and decline are intrinsic to G. William Skinner's theory of independent macroregion development. Skinner, ed., *The City in Late Imperial China* (Stanford: Stanford University Press, 1977). A vivid example of a city caught in successive periods of turbulence can be found in Antonia Finnane, "Yangzhou: A Central Place in the Qing Empire," in *Cities of Jiangnan in Late Imperial China*, ed. Linda Cooke Johnson (Albany: State University of New York Press, 1993). See also Rowe on the ups and downs of middle Yangzi cities like Yichang, Changsha, Shashi, and Xiangtan. Rowe, "Wuhan," 18–19.

25. *Xinxing de gongye chengshi—Lanzhou* (A developing industrial city—Lanzhou) (Lanzhou: Gansu renmin chubanshe, 1987), 13.

26. *Year in Lanzhou Municipality*, 1:22; Pan Yimin, *Lanzhou zhi gongshangye yu jinrong* (Industry, commerce, and banking in Lanzhou) (Shanghai: Shangwu yinshuguan, 1936), 5.

27. Pan Yimin, *Lanzhou*, 3–4; *Year in Lanzhou Municipality*, 2:12–13.

28. Pan Yimin, *Lanzhou*, 7.

29. Ren Mei'e, "Lanzhou fujin dizhi yanjiu," 7.

30. Xuan Bo [pseud.], "Qingdao," *Guowen zhoubao* 2, no. 46 (29 November 1925): 5.

31. Pan Yimin, *Lanzhou*, 3.

32. Ibid., 1.

33. Ibid., 23.

34. Ren Mei'e, "Lanzhou fujin dizhi yanjiu," 14–15.

35. *Developing Industrial City*, 12. This source and Ren Mei'e date the factory founding at 1875 and 1877, respectively (Ren Mei'e, "Lanzhou fujin dizhi yanjiu," 14).

36. Ren Mei'e, "Lanzhou fujin dizhi yanjiu," 14.

37. *Developing Industrial City*, 12; Ren Mei'e, "Lanzhou fujin dizhi yanjiu," 14–15.

38. Ren Mei'e, "Lanzhou fujin dizhi yanjiu," 15.

39. Ibid., 8.

40. Ibid., 19.

41. *Year in Lanzhou Municipality*, 1:11.

42. Clifton Pannell, "Recent Growth and Change in China's Urban System," in *Urban Development in Modern China*, ed. Lawrence J. C. Ma and Edward W. Hanten (Boulder: Westview, 1981), 98.

43. See for example William T. Rowe, *Hankow: Commerce and Society in a Chinese City* (Stanford: Stanford University Press, 1984); Lyman P. Van Slyke, "Merchants, Commerce, and Products on the Move," in *Yangtze: Nature, History, and the River* (New York: Addison-Wesley, 1988); and Thomas G. Rawski, *Economic Growth in Prewar China* (Berkeley and Los Angeles: University of California Press, 1989).

44. Lucian W. Pye, foreword in *Shanghai: Revolution and Development in an Asian Metropolis*, ed. Christopher Howe (Cambridge: Cambridge University Press, 1981), xv.

45. Cheng Guangyu, *Zhongguo dushi* (Chinese cities) (Taibei: Zhongguo wenhua chubanshe, 1953), 24.

46. Susan Mann, "Urbanization and Historical Change in China," *Modern China* 10, no. 1 (January 1984): 83.

47. Ibid., 84.

48. Zhang Qingjun, "Minguo shiqi dushi renkou jiegou fenxi" (An analysis of the structure of urban population during the Republican period), *Minguo dangan*, no. 1 (1992): 128.

49. Mann, "Urbanization," 84. Emphasis in the original.

50. Fang Wenpei, "Sichuan kaocha ji" (An investigative account of Sichuan), *Fangzhi yuekan* 6, no. 7 (1 July 1933): 3.

51. Ren Mei'e, "Lanzhou fujin dizhi yanjiu," 7.

52. Zhou Yirang, "Wuhan sanzhen zhi xianzai ji qi jianglai," 79.

53. Ren Baitao, "Difang baozhi bianji" (The editing of local newspapers), *DFZZ* 18, no. 17 (10 September 1921): 98.

54. Ibid.

55. Cities with other *Funu ribao* included Changsha and Nanjing (*Funu ribao* [Tianjin], 12 February 1924, p. 2; 28 March 1924, p. 1). Biographical sketches of Li Zhishan and Deng Yingchao, mentioning their roles in Tianjin women's circles and journalism, can be found in Xu Yuqun, ed., *Minguo renwu dazidian* (A comprehensive biographical dictionary of the Republic) (Shijiazhuang: Hebei renmin chubanshe, 1991), 285–86 and 1505.

56. *Funu ribao*, 1 January 1924, p. 1; 2 January 1924, p. 2; and 12 February 1924, p. 2.

57. For the story of the Baoding Number Two Women's College affair, see *Funu ribao*, 22 March 1924, p. 1; 24 March 1922, p. 2; 28 March 1924, p. 1; 1 April 1924, p. 3. For the general issue of who should run women's schools, see "Women's Schools and Female School Heads," *Funu ribao*, 10 March 1924, p. 1.

58. Wang Ling, *Beijing yu zhouwei chengshi guanxi shi* (A history of Beijing and its relations to nearby cities) (Beijing: Yanshan chubanshe, 1988), 135–36.

59. Wang Ling also notes that Baoding military academy graduates later become the backbone of the radical Whampoa Academy (ibid.).

60. *Funu ribao*, 22 March 1924, p. 1. Like other women in other cities, the Baoding students were angry at the school's fundamentalist, "revive the ancient" (*fugu*) attitude. But

they also complained that their teachers were unqualified and could only babble about such topics as economics.

61. Wan Shaoyuan, "Shiren zhumun de tushuguan shiye" (Undertaking libraries for the common people), in *Minguo shehui daguan* (An omnibus of Republican society), ed. Xin Ping, Hu Zhenghao, and Li Xuechang (Fuzhou: Fujian chubanshe, 1991), 954.

62. Moshe Lewin, *The Gorbachev Phenomenon: An Historical Interpretation* (Berkeley and Los Angeles: University of California Press, 1991), 30.

63. Olga Lang, *Chinese Family and Society* (New Haven: Yale University Press, 1946), 78.

64. Ibid., 78–79.

65. Zhang Qingjun, "Minguo shiqi dushi renkou jiegou fenxi," 134–35. Based on a survey of figures from Nanjing, Shanghai, Beijing, Qingdao, Hankou, and Xi'an, 30.86 percent of men and 60.64 percent of women were illiterate.

66. Fang Wenpei, "Sichuan kaocha ji," 3.

67. Xuan Bo, "Qingdao," 21.

68. *Lanzhou daxue xiaoshi* (A short history of Lanzhou University) (Lanzhou: Gansu renmin chubanshe, 1990), 9. The conduit for these ideas seems to have been a magazine entitled *Xin Long* (New Gansu), which was published in Beijing by Lanzhou students resident in the capital, and sent back home to be read by college and middle-school students.

69. Rhoads Murphey, *The Outsiders: The Western Experience in India and China* (Ann Arbor: University of Michigan Press, 1977).

70. Rowe, "Wuhan," 31. For a Shashi perspective on the problems associated with building an industrial base against the grain, see Wang Kaibing, ed., *Luetan chengshi jingji fazhan lue* (On urban economic development strategies) (Wuhan: Hubei renmin chubanshe, 1990), 17.

71. Tang Wenqi and Lin Gang, "Shilun 1927–1937 nian Nanjing chengshi jingji fazhan yu noncun fudi zhi guanxi" (A discussion of the relationship between urban economic development in Nanjing and the rural hinterland, 1927–1937), *Minguo dangan*, no. 2 (1987): 87. A Reconstruction Commission found 847 industrial firms in the city in 1934 in a tally that included handicraft factories and small firms. Only 18 factories met the stricter definition of *gongchang* used by the Social Welfare Bureau in a 1935 industrial survey.

72. The folklorist Tao Xingzhi used the term in a critical sense. This is discussed in Hung Chang-tai, *Going to the People: Chinese Intellectuals and Folk Literature, 1918–1937* (Cambridge: Harvard University Press, 1985), 14.

73. Lang, *Chinese Family*, 80.

74. Hanchao Lu, "Away from Nanking Road: Small Stores and Neighborhood Life in Modern Shanghai," *Journal of Asian Studies* 53, no. 4 (November 1994).

75. For example, in Africa, despite self-conscious efforts by Europeans to make urban centers "bastion cities" they could "claim to dominate, set apart from the mysterious and dangerous bush," "Africans did as much to ruralize the city as Europeans did to urbanize the countryside. Africans would try to mold urban life to their own ways and in their own neighborhoods." Frederick Cooper, "African Urbanization," in Peter N. Stearns, *Encyclopedia of Social History* (New York: Garland, 1994), 22.

76. Zhou Yirang, "Wuhan sanzhen zhi xianzai ji qi jianglai," 75.

77. Chen Zhenyi, "Da Shanghai jianshe ce" (The greater Shanghai reconstruction plan), *DFZZ* 23, no. 18 (September 1926): 10. The article acknowledged that Qingdao in turn had received its excellent harbor plan from Germany.

78. Wang Ling, *Beijing*, 108–10.

79. Ibid., 110.

80. The theme of decadence and development is explored in David Strand, "Decadence et modernization: Groupes sociaux et action politique a Pekin au debut du XXe siecle," in *Les Metropoles chinoises au XXe siecle,* ed. Christian Henriot and Alain Delissen (Paris: Editions Arguments, 1995), 32–47.

81. Lao She, *Luotou Xiangzi* (Camel Xiangzi) (Hong Kong: Yuelin youxian gongsi, n.d.), 306–7.

82. Dong Xiujia, *Guomin jingji jianshe zhi tujing* (Avenues of national economic reconstruction) (Shanghai: Shenghuo shudian, 1936), 168.

83. One sign of the level of academic and governmental interest in the city as an administrative unit can be found in Lu Danlin, ed., *Shizheng quanshu* (A complete handbook of municipal government) (Shanghai: Daolu yuekan she, 1931). The volume collects essays published elsewhere by municipal reformers like Dong Xiujia and others and reports on municipal reform efforts in a dozen cities as large as Shanghai and as small as Nanchang and Wuzhou. For Dong's career in municipal affairs as an official and writer, see Xu Yuqun, ed., *Minguo renwu dacidian* (A comprehensive biographical dictionary of Republican China), 1273. Prior to holding teaching and government positions in China, Dong studied municipal economics and government in the United States.

84. Lu Weizhen, "Shihua buyi" (An addenda on city flowers), *DFZZ* 27, no. 11 (10 June 1930): 87–90.

85. *A Short History of Lanzhou University.* Upon news of the abdication of the Manchu monarch in February 1912, "several members of Gansu educational circles" affiliated with the college demanded that the loyalist Shaan-Gan governor-general proclaim a republic, cease military action designed to maintain the Qing, and start using a Republican "reign title" (*nianhao*) and a Western calendar (6).

86. Ibid. For example, a graduate of the college met Sun Yat-sen in Guangzhou in 1917 and accepted Sun's charge to return to Lanzhou and spark participation in the "Constitution Protection Movement" Sun was engaged in leading.

87. For the classic statement of an urban-rural gap growing in the 1920s, 1930s, and 1940s, see Fei Hsiao-t'ung, *China's Gentry: Essays on Rural-Urban Relations* (Chicago: University of Chicago Press, 1953). Rowe speculates that this gap represented a sharp break with late-imperial and early-twentieth-century patterns of economic exchange and reciprocity and may have been more the result of political disorder and failure than a consequence of urbanization. Rowe, "Wuhan."

88. Mann, "Urbanization," 94–107.

89. Dong Xiujia, "Tianyuan xinshi yu woguo shizheng" (Garden cities and municipal government in China), *DFZZ* 22, no. 11 (10 June 1925): 44.

90. This is Chen Duxiu's summary of criticisms related to him by a friend, in Chen, "Beijing shida tese" (Ten outstanding features of Beijing), in *Beijing hu: xiandai zuojia bixia de Beijing* (Beijing in the words of modern writers), ed. Jiang Deming, vol. 1 (Beijing: Sanlian shudian, 1992), 4 (dated 1 June 1919).

91. Xuan Bo, "Qingdao," 6.

92. For a comparative perspective on the "city as export," see Mark Girouard, *Cities and People: A Social and Architectural History* (New Haven: Yale University Press, 1985), chapter 11.

93. *Gansu minguo ribao,* 1 July 1941, p. 1.

94. *Gansu minguo ribao,* 8 April 1942, p. 3.

95. See, for example, Kristin Stapleton's discussion of reforms carried out in 1920s Chengdu under the auspices of the warlord Yang Sen: "In the 1920's, new visions of urban

organization and culture developing in eastern China found supporters among a younger generation of Chengdu elites, who briefly looked to Yang Sen as their champion." Stapleton, "Yang Sen in Chengdu: Urban Planning in the Interior," in *Constructing the Modern in Chinese Cities, 1900–1950,* ed. Joseph W. Esherick (Honolulu: University of Hawaii Press, 1999).

96. As Lanzhou officials knew. For official statements about the importance of reform in garbage collection, the cleaning of public toilets, and the like, see *Gansu minguo ribao,* 17 February 1942, p. 4.

97. For a broader appreciation of the urban-rural connections involved in nightsoil collection, see Andrew Morris, "Fight for Fertilizer!: Excrement, Public Health, and Mobilization in New China," *Journal of Unconventional History* (May 1995).

98. Zang Qifang, "Shizheng he cujin shizheng zhi fangfa" (Municipal government and methods of advancing municipal government), in *Shizheng quanshu* (A complete handbook on municipal government), ed. Lu Danlin (Shanghai: Daolu yuekan, 1931), 44–45.

99. Chen Duxiu, "Beijing shida tese," 4.

100. Zhou Yirang, "Wuhan sanzhen zhi xianzai ji qi jianglai," 77.

101. Ibid.

102. Xuan Bo, *Guowen zhoubao* 2, no. 49 (20 December 1925): 19.

103. Chang-tai Hung, *Going to the People: Chinese Intellectuals and Folk Literature, 1918–1937* (Cambridge: Harvard University Press, 1985), 14.

104. Zang Qifang, "Shizheng he cujin shizheng zhi fangfa," 45. Zang was particularly angry not only that were these activities permitted but that they were taxed to support the operations of government.

105. Ernest P. Young, "Problems of a Late Ch'ing Revolutionary: Ch'en T'ien-hua," in *Revolutionary Leaders of Modern China,* ed. Chun-tu Hsueh (New York: Oxford University Press, 1971), 227.

106. Jian Hu, "Dushi shenghuo zhi meihua" (The beautification of metropolitan life), *DFZZ* 18, no. 2 (25 April 1925): 1–2.

107. *Zhongguo yuebao* 3, no. 1 (1 January 1935).

108. Quoted in Frederic Wakeman, *Policing Shanghai, 1927–1937* (Berkeley and Los Angeles: University of California Press, 1995), 11–12.

109. Yi Jiayue, cited and discussed in Mann, "Urbanization," 99.

110. *Gansu minguo ribao,* 3 July 1941, p. 5.

111. Gu Duilu, "Zhongguo shizhi gaiguan" (General survey of the Chinese municipal system), *DFZZ* 26, no. 17 (10 September 1929): 33.

112. Dong Xiujia, *Guomin jingji jianshe zhi tujing,* 3.

113. Ibid., 159.

114. Ibid., 161.

115. Hu Shi, preface no. 3 to *Shizheng juyao* (Essentials of municipal government), by Bai Dunyong (Shanghai: Dadong shudian, 1931), 1.

116. The scholar Qu Xuanying, writing in 1930, cited by Mann, "Urbanization," 88.

117. Zhou Yirang, "Wuhan sanzhen zhi xianzai ji qi jianglai," 75. See also Rowe, "Wuhan," 12, for a discussion of factors leading to "overnight industrialization" in the Wuhan cities.

118. Qin Shao, "Making Political Culture—the Case of Nantong, 1894–1930" (Ph.D. diss., Michigan State University, 1994).

119. Xu Xueli, "Tuo ling dingdong yundilai," 100.

120. *A Year in Lanzhou Municipality*, 1:11–12. The rubber tires persuaded officials to permit the carts to use modern roads, an important concession since iron-wheeled carts were banned and fuel for trucks and cars was in chronic short supply during the war years.

121. For the impact of the New Policies on Beijing, see Mingzheng Shi, "Corporate Interest or Public Good: Public Utility Companies of Early 20th Century Beijing" (paper presented at AAS annual meeting, Chicago, 6–9 April 1995).

122. Wang Wang, *Xin Xi'an*, 27.

123. Yu Heping, *Shanghui yu Zhongguo zaoqi xiandaihua* (Chambers of commerce and China's early modernization) (Shanghai: Shanghai renmin chubanshe, 1993), 23–25, 75–76, 202–3. Yu emphasizes both the importance of the *xinzheng* reforms in stimulating chamber development.

124. Dong Xiujia, *Guomin jingji jianshe zhi tujing*, 170.

125. Ibid., 174.

126. Edward Bing-Shuey Lee, *Modern Canton* (Shanghai: Mercury Press, 1936), v.

127. *Gansu minguo ribao*, 2 July 1942, p. 3.

128. Liu Gengsheng, "Zhou Xuexi yu jingshi zilaishui shiye" (Zhou Xuexi and the metropolitan waterworks business), *Beijing dangan shiliao*, no. 2 (1987–1988): 69.

129. See Rowe's account of the building of the Hankou city wall in 1862–64. Rowe, *Hankow: Conflict and Community in a Chinese City, 1796–1895* (Stanford: Stanford University Press, 1989), 293–94. Rowe concludes that "the state did retain the power of eminent domain, enabling it to condemn and acquire property earmarked for public purposes, for which it usually compensated the owner at a negotiated price" (66).

130. This sentiment can be found, for example, in Simon Leys (Pierre Ryckmans), *Chinese Shadows* (New York: Viking, 1977), 57–60. Ryckmans further traces this modernist fury to a deeper atavism.

131. These plans were reportedly made in 1910. See Naito Konan, "Constitutional Government in China," in "Naito Konan and the Development of the Conception of Modernity in Chinese History," ed. and trans. Joshua Fogel, *Chinese Studies in History* 17, no. 1 (fall 1983): 61.

132. Leng Wangu, "Beijing cheng wanbuke chai" (Beijing's walls must not be torn down), *Aiguo bao* (Beijing), 8 September 1912, p. 1.

133. Lee, *Modern Canton*, 13–14.

134. Ibid., 19. The municipal authorities acted "against the will of narrow-visioned capitalists . . . reluctant to see their property destroyed."

135. Dong Xiujia, *Guomin jingji jianshe zhi tujing*, 171.

136. Bian Nofu, "Nanjing gaikuang" (Survey of Nanjing), *Xiangdao zhoubao* 153 (15 May 1926): 1467.

137. Dong Xiujia, *Guomin jingji jianshe zhi tujing*, 171–72, 179.

138. Ibid., 172, 174.

139. Ibid., 173.

140. Kristin Stapleton, "Police Reform in a Late-Imperial Chinese City: Chengdu, 1902–1911" (Ph.D. diss., Harvard University, 1993), 149–50, 196.

141. David Strand, *Rickshaw Beijing: City People and Politics in the 1920s* (Berkeley and Los Angeles: University of California Press, 1989), 96.

142. *Gansu minguo ribao*, 2 July 1942, p. 3. The point was made in a speech by a local GMD official.

143. Dong Xiujia, *Guomin jingji jianshe zhi tujing*, 176 and 182.

144. Zang Qifang, "Shizheng he cujin shizheng zhi fangfa," 44. Mann also emphasizes this point ("Urbanization," 91).

145. Yang Lihui, "Yantai diaocha" (Investigation of Yantai), *DFZZ* 21, no. 12 (25 June 1924): 81.

146. Leng Wangu, "Beijing," 2.

147. Christian Henriot, *Shanghai, 1927–1937: Municipal Power, Locality, and Modernization* (Berkeley and Los Angeles: University of California Press, 1993), 160. In this case the Shanghai Butchers Guild accepted the new tax system when it was allowed to keep control of a general welfare fund for members.

148. This is a major theme in Henriot, *Shanghai*.

149. Ibid., 36.

150. Hans J. Van De Ven, *From Friend to Comrade: The Founding of the Chinese Communist Party, 1920–1927* (Berkeley and Los Angeles: University of California Press, 1991), 10.

151. Ibid.

152. "Shanghai wenti" (The Shanghai question), *DFZZ* 22, no. 4 (25 February 1925): 6.

153. Gu Duilu, "Zhongguo shizhi gaiguan," 34–35.

154. Ibid., 36. In 1920 Chen Jiongming, as one might expect, emphasized the importance of independence from central control.

155. Ibid., 36–37.

156. Ibid., 39.

157. Bai Dunyong, *Shizheng juyao* (Essentials of municipal government) (Shanghai: Dadong shudian, 1931), 12.

158. Dong Xiujia, "Zhongguo shizhi zhi jinjing" (Frontiers of municipal government) in *Shizheng quanshu*, ed. Lu Danlin (Shanghai: Daolu yuekan she, 1931), 105.

159. Ibid., 106.

160. Henriot, *Shanghai*, 35.

161. Lu Weizhen, "Shihua buyi," 89–90.

162. Yi Guan, "Quanguo shanghui zhi xiankuang yu jianglai zhi xiwang" (The condition and future prospects of chambers of commerce throughout the country), *DFZZ* 16, no. 3 (March 1919): 219.

163. Ibid.; Yu Heping, *Shanghui yu Zhongguo zaoqi xiandaihua*, 75–76.

164. Yu Heping, *Shanghui yu Zhongguo zaoqi xiandaihua*, 220.

165. Qin Shao, "Making Political Culture," 107.

166. *Gansu minguo ribao*, 16 March 1942, p. 3. The Lanzhou chamber contributed a hundred thousand dollars to reconstruction efforts at a time when there was only fifty to sixty thousand in the municipal government's budget for such projects.

167. Yu Heping, *Shanghui yu Zhongguo zaoqi xiandaihua*, 25.

168. Ibid., 23.

169. Ibid., 98.

170. Ibid.

171. Ibid., 100–108.

172. Ibid., 107. The journal was entitled the *Chinese Merchant Federation Magazine* (*Huashang lianhe bao*).

173. Ibid., 184. A candidate from Gaoyang county in Zhili was defeated by the president of the Wuchang chamber. The Gaoyang and northern faction tried to overturn the results but were defeated by threats of nationwide denunciation (through circular telegrams) of alleged corrupt practices by representatives from Shanghai and Hankou.

174. Ibid., 89.

175. For an extended discussion of this tendency toward escalating (and sometimes de-escalating) scales of organization, see David Strand, "Changing Dimensions of Social and Public Life in Early Twentieth Century Chinese Cities," in *La societe civile face a l'Etat: Dans les traditions chinoise, japonaise, coreene et vietnamienne*, ed. Leon Vandermeersch (Paris: Ecole Francaise d'Extreme-Orient, 1994).

176. Yu Heping, *Shanghui yu Zhongguo zaoqi xiandaihua*, 89.

177. David Strand, "Historical Perspectives," in *Urban Spaces in Contemporary China: The Potential for Autonomy and Community in Post-Mao China*, ed. Deborah S. Davis, Richard Kraus, Barry Naughton, and Elizabeth J. Perry (New York: Cambridge University Press, 1995).

178. See Rowe, *Hankow*, on guild federations in Hankou.

179. Yu Heping, *Shanghui yu Zhongguo zaoqi xiandaihua*, 158–72. Yu acknowledges that many guilds were oligarchic and exclusive (along the lines of class or hometown affiliation) but argues that the general trend in chamber and guild development was toward greater democracy and inclusiveness.

180. Byrna Goodman, "New Culture, Old Habits: Native-Place Organization and the May Fourth Movement," in *Shanghai Sojourners*, ed. Frederic Wakeman and Wen-hsin Yeh (Berkeley: Institute of East Asian Studies, 1992), 83.

181. Wu Zhezheng, "Huiguan," in *Beijing wangshi tan* (Talks on past events in Beijing) (Beijing: Beijing chubanshe, 1988), 88.

182. Yu Heping, *Shanghui yu Zhongguo zaoqi xiandaihua*, 280–302. For example, many chambers supported Yuan against the Nationalists in the "Second Revolution" of 1913.

183. Ibid., 382.

184. Ibid.

185. Bian Nofu, "Nanjing gaikuang," 1468.

186. "Nanjing tongxin" (Letter from Nanjing), *Xiangdao zhoubao* 60 (26 March 1924): 482.

187. Henriot, *Shanghai*, 58–59.

188. Robert A. Dahl, *Who Governs?: Democracy and Power in an American City* (New Haven: Yale University Press, 1961), 122–24.

189. Henriot, *Shanghai*, 60–61.

190. Dong Xiujia, *Guomin jingji jianshe zhi tujing*, 183. Dong praised the Chinese Shanghai government for its efforts in this area of limited consultation.

191. Stapleton, "Police Reform," 325.

192. Zhou Junqi, "Guanyu jindai quyu chengshi xitong yanjiu de jige wenti" (Some problems in the study of regional urban systems in the modern period), *Tianjin shehui kexue*, no. 5 (1994): 107.

193. See Goodman, *The Native-Place, the City and the Nation: Social Organization and Regional Identity in Shanghai* (Berkeley and Los Angeles: University of California Press, 1995).

194. Hu Shi, preface no. 3, 2.

195. Ibid.

196. Goodman, "Expansive Practices: Charity, Modern Enterprise, the City and the State," chap. 4 in *Native-Place*.

197. Strand, "City People under Siege," chap. 9 in *Rickshaw Beijing*. The record of Beijing suggests, however, that this protective reaction required the active leadership of local elites to be effective.

198. "Beijing *Shimin* Oppose Moving the Capital to Nanjing," *Yishibao*, 30 June 1928, p. 7.

199. *Beijing dianche gongsi dangan shiliao* (Historical materials from the Beijing Streetcar Company archive) (Beijing: Beijing yanshan chubanshe, 1989), 100–101, 118–19. See also Strand, *Rickshaw Beijing*, chap. 6.

200. *Beijing dianche gongsi dangan shiliao*, 118–19.

201. Mingzheng Shi, "Corporate Interest."

202. Robert Putnam, *Making Democracy Work: Civic Traditions in Modern Italy* (Princeton: Princeton University Press, 1993), 167. Putnam cites James Coleman's use of the term "social capital."

203. Ibid., 130.

204. See again Hanchao Lu's "Away from Nanking Road."

FOUR

Engineering China:
Birth of the Developmental State,
1928–1937

William C. Kirby

1. VISIONS OF MODERN CHINA

In December 1926, the engineer Peter Palchinsky wrote to the prime minister of
the Soviet Union. Science and technology, he argued, did more—even than Communism!—to shape modern society. The twentieth century was "not one of international communism, but of international technology. We need to recognize not a
Komintern, but a 'Tekhintern.' "[1] Ideas like these would get Palchinsky shot in
Stalin's Russia. For the Nationalist movement of China's Guomindang, which
three months later quit the Comintern and purged itself of Communists, they
were at the heart of its conception of modernity.

Shanghai—as Leo Lee has argued so eloquently—may have been the native
place for a new, public culture of private life; but in 1928 Nanjing was the capital
of a "new China" whose aim was as much the physical as the cultural remaking of
the nation. If in Shanghai modernity could be defined as "the material transformation of everyday life,"[2] Nanjing was consumed with the industrial metamor-
phosis of *national* life, planned by a central—and centralizing—government.
China would be industrialized and internationalized (for the two went hand in
hand) through the mediation of the state. This was a quite different vision of the
modern than could be found in Shanghai's kiosks, cafes, and department stores.
At a time of permanent national crisis, it was ultimately a compelling one.

The new government aimed to "reconstruct" China to make it modern. A
gleaming capital would rise out of the mud alleys of Nanjing, a city twice destroyed in the previous century. The cities would be industrialized, the countryside
electrified, and the provinces joined by networks of railroads, motor roads, and—
most exciting of all—air routes to get the "stagnant race" of Chinese (Sun
Yatsen's phrase) on the move.[3] The landscape would be transfigured through electrification, industrialization, and communications. All this would be planned "sci-

entifically" by a government imbued with a technocratic confidence and cooperating with advanced industrial nations.

To some extent these transformations were under way well before 1928, even in the absence of a working central government. China was enjoying a "dynamic and robust" industrial boom that had begun over a decade earlier.[4] Its major cities (Shanghai, Beijing, Canton, and even Chengdu) engaged in rudimentary urban planning.[5] An embryonic rail network had been created with foreign capital. But the National Government came to power with an agenda to do much more. Its late leader had proposed a "second industrial revolution" in which a hundred thousand miles of rail would be laid, the Yangzi tamed and its Three Gorges dammed, and automobiles manufactured so inexpensively that "everyone who wishes it, may have one."[6]

Sun Yatsen's *Industrial Plan* (*Shiye jihua*, published first in English as *The International Development of China* six years before the establishment of the Nationalist regime) was the first attempt to design the integrated economic development of a unified China. One author dates the beginning of "modern China" from its publication.[7] Today, many Three-, Four-, Five-, and Ten-Year Plans later, it remains the most audacious and memorable of national development programs. Sun's strategies to develop "the vast resources of China . . . internationally under a socialistic scheme, for the good of the world in general and the Chinese people in particular" would be shared by his Nationalist and Communist successors.[8] The realization of his *Industrial Plan* became the cardinal goal of Nationalist economic policy. In the People's Republic, Sun's "great legacy" for the management of the modern Chinese economy would be celebrated.[9]

Sun's more concrete plans also left their mark.[10] His sketch of a national Chinese rail network, which emphasized political aspirations (linking provincial capitals) over economic relationships, provided the framework for Nationalist and early Communist routing plans.[11] His two-paragraph proposal to "improve the upper Yangzi" with an enormous dam spawned seventy-five years of effort and debate.[12] When construction finally began in 1994, it moved an unpoetical engineer, P. R. C. Premier Li Peng, to verse:[13]

As we begin to carry out the blueprint
It is a new era
And the tide is high

Sun was the visionary, not the scientist, economist, or engineer. Yet projects of the scale and complexity of those he advocated would bring scientists, economists, and engineers into the center of Chinese governance. The academies, commissions, and ministries created to "reconstruct" China would, in turn, change the mission of the Chinese state. If Sun Yatsen could admire publicly Lenin's New Economic Policy, praising its promotion of state capitalism and "national socialism,"[14] his successors would lay the foundation for a Stalinist state in China, the economic management of which would be the responsibility of the world's largest bureaucracy.

The result would not be "technocracy," a term that has been rendered in Chinese as "the dictatorship of engineers,"[15] for among Sun's other contributions to the modern Chinese polity were the supremacy of the Leninist party-state and the centrality of the military in it.[16] But with Sun began a dream of modernity to be interpreted by a transformative government. Revered by his disciples as the Republic's founding father, or *guofu,* Sun was more precisely the spiritual father of the Chinese developmental state.[17]

2. PARIS OF THE EAST: NANJING AND "RECONSTRUCTION"

The National Government aimed to make its mark on China first in its new national capital, the old "southern capital," or Nanjing. Although a former dynastic capital and, very briefly, the seat of the first government of the Republic, it was better known in modern times for "sieges, sacks, massacres, rapine, conflagration and destruction."[18] During the civil wars of the mid–nineteenth century it had been utterly destroyed, first by the Taiping rebels, who made it their "heavenly capital," and then by vengeful Qing loyalists. It had been a battleground again in 1911 and 1913. The Nationalists' "Nanjing decade" began in 1927, with their military occupation of the city, and it would end in 1937 with the city's conquest and "rape" at the hands of the Japanese;[19] in between, however, the Nationalists tried to build a capital worthy of their dreams.

Their model capital was inherited in a sorry state. Writers could praise Nanjing's scenic qualities because much of the city had become "a veritable *rus in urbe*" in the past century: "One finds inside the city-walls of Nanking waste spaces, ponds, and patches of cultivated land scattered here and there in the same way as they are outside of the walls."[20] Its population was about one-third of what it had been in early Ming times, when more than 1 million inhabited Nanjing.[21] As a modern city it was "notorious for its dim electric light, narrow and uneven roads, and poor telephone service,"[22] not to mention its mud and mosquitoes. There was no sewage system save the infested canals, which served as a source of drinking water for the city's poor.[23] All this was but a challenge. A new Nanjing might be created from nearly nothing: it could become what we might think of today as a Chinese Brasilia.

Within a year of the founding of the regime, the Office of Technical Experts for Planning the National Capital under the leadership of an American-trained engineer had developed a detailed and beautifully illustrated design for a reconstructed Nanjing.[24] The city's boundaries were vastly expanded to house both the new government and (planning rather too conservatively into the next century) an anticipated population of 2 million. Rail connections were to be enhanced and a huge airport built. Detailed plans were drawn for modern sewage, drinking water, and electric power systems. A new government district of nearly ten square kilometers was be erected on the site just west of the old Ming palace, south of the

Ming tombs and an imposing Sun Yatsen Mausoleum. At its center would be a modern palace complex, on a north-south axis, dominated at its northern end by a massive Guomindang headquarters (*Zhongyang dangbu*), an international architectural marvel combining features of Beijing's Temple of Heaven and the U.S. Capitol in Washington, D.C. (The site of the National Government was along similar lines on a smaller, subservient scale.) The Nanjing municipal government would get its own quarter with a large but tasteful yamen compound, in traditional style, near the Bell Tower. A Cultural Center, including an Olympic-sized stadium, would be situated on Wu Tai Mountain.[25] Beyond all this the city would be beautified. Twelve new parks would be constructed. In Parisian style, trees would line the avenues. Electric streetlights would be made in the shape of Chinese lanterns. "Obnoxious and dangerous industries" would be located away from the city center, on the northern bank of the Yangzi. A "comprehensive system of parkways and main arteries" was conceived, dominated by the grand, six-lane *Zhongshan lu*, or Sun Yatsen Road. A "ring boulevard" was to encircle the new capital, but not, as later in Beijing, at the expense of the city wall. The wall would be retained, perhaps with the thought—times being what they were—that it might be needed. So Nanjing's ring road would run *on top* of the old wall, offering its motorists a panorama of city, river, and suburbs.[26]

It will be obvious to a visitor to contemporary Nanjing, which today looks more a provincial than a national capital, that not all these things were built. A few were, some in dramatic fashion: *Zhongshan lu* was bulldozed forty meters wide through the city center to honor the *guofu* and was rushed to completion in time for Sun's interment in his stately mausoleum in June 1929. Residents in the way were given ten days to leave their homes.[27] The new center of the city, Xinjiekou, where *Zhongshan lu* converged with other main arteries, was turned into a large concrete rotary. The central buildings of the party-state were indeed located near an old palace—but in rather more modest quarters in the old Taiping palace grounds. Government ministries, after several years of being housed in borrowed and occupied buildings, were gradually moved to more properly ministerial quarters. And massive numbers of trees were planted. Seedlings imported from France would later shade a Communist Nanjing.

The most telling point about Nanjing's face-lift was that it was *planned*. Nanjing was the first Chinese city to employ comprehensive zoning and planning regulations designed according to international standards.[28] Its Office of Technical Experts drafted the national legislation for municipal planning and zoning. A National Capital Reconstruction Commission was organized in 1929 to carry out a six-year plan to build municipal services, parks, roads, and housing. In this it was led by its engineering division and a force of city planning engineers.[29] If Nanjing today can lay claim to being "one of the most beautiful, clean, and well-planned cities in China," this is due in part to the determined efforts of Nationalist engineers and public works officials—and to the fact that their most outlandish schemes were unrealized.[30]

There is a long history in China of planning capital cities and their official edifices. What distinguished the Nationalist regime was its confidence in its ability to plan, first for the capital and then for the entire country, on an international technological standard. This was a faith so widely shared in the new National Government that the mission of "reconstruction" was undertaken initially by almost every arm of it.

Electrifying China.   A Reconstruction Ministry (*Jianshebu*) was created in January 1928, fittingly enough with Sun Yatsen's son, Sun Ke (Sun Fo), as minister. "Reconstruction," Sun Ke said upon taking his post, "is of course the first and foremost goal of the Revolution."[31] Sun Ke's faith in government planning had been tested in Canton, where as mayor he had presided over the introduction of modern sewers and public utilities. Sun Ke was reconstruction minister for only six days when he undertook a six-month European tour to win foreign investment for his father's plans. His trip was a total flop, and while he was away his ministry was abolished; but he returned to China undeterred and drafted a *fifty-year* plan to construct the railways, harbors, and industries that Sun Yatsen had envisioned. This *Jianshe dagang cao'an* (Draft plan for [realization of] the fundamentals of national reconstruction) became Guomindang policy in November 1928. For a few years Sun Ke could pursue one part of this plan in his new capacity as minister of railways, but the larger task of planning and coordinating "reconstructive" enterprises had fallen to a new National Reconstruction Commission.

Established in February 1928, the National Reconstruction Commission (*Jianshe weiyuanwei*) was composed of some thirty-nine members, including all ministers of cabinet rank, all heads of provincial Reconstruction Bureaux (*jiansheting*), and the mayors of Nanjing and Shanghai municipalities. Although deputed to "research, prepare, and complete a Reconstruction Plan for the Whole Country" in the "spirit" of Sun Yatsen's guidelines, it quickly focused on electrification.[32] It seemed to follow (with the proper political substitutions) Lenin's famous dictum that Communism meant "Soviet Power plus the electrification of the whole country."[33] Sun Yatsen had been almost as eloquent on this subject as Lenin: he had urged electrification in writings and speeches since 1894. Civilization, he later wrote, was defined by the "age of electricity." In 1924 he had told his Guomindang comrades that "if China wants to learn the strong points from foreign counties, it should, first of all, try to use electricity rather than coal as an energy source."[34] (Just how Sun thought electricity would be generated is not clear.) As Yun Zhen, a young engineer in the National Reconstruction Commission who would later direct much of China's electrical industries, recalled: electric power, which would promote industry and commerce, permit the exploitation of natural resources, and increase agricultural production, was considered "the people's salvation."[35]

The National Reconstruction Commission began by drafting a grandiose, Soviet-style plan for lighting up the country. "Super-power" stations linked by high-tension transmission lines would supply large areas, and their substations would gradually replace small local stations.[36] But as in Lenin's Russia, where the unveiling of the national electrification plan in the form of an enormous map, dotted with lightbulbs, took enough of Moscow's meager power supply that the rest of the city had to be blacked out,[37] the National Reconstruction Commission had its hands full illuminating the capital city. Its nationalization and reorganization of the Nanjing Electrical Works would count as one of its major successes.

The commission had to compromise both on the scope of its plans and on principles of ownership of the Chinese electrical power enterprise. It was the first National Government agency to confront directly the ambiguities of Sun Yatsen's economic thought regarding what should be "public" (and government owned) and what should remain in the private sphere. In principle, electrical enterprises of the large scale planned by the commission ought to have been of "strategic" importance and under government ownership. The power works at Nanjing were indeed nationalized. But the large majority of China's 575 electrical power enterprises were privately run and of very small size, and the commission had neither the man- nor, as it turned out, the willpower to take them over. Only seventeen plants were government owned by 1930, and to preclude further nationalizations a National Association of Private Electric Power Enterprises (*Quanguo minying dianye lianhehui*) organized in 1929 to plead its collective case to Nanjing.

The commission faced fiscal reality—the small financial capacity of the new government compared with its large aims—by evolving quickly into a *regulatory* body for what now began to be considered "public utilities": *gongyong shiye* (publicly used enterprises) that would not be *gongying shiye* (publicly run enterprises). The government still had a strong role to play, however. Regulations for electrical enterprises promulgated in 1930 standardized technical systems among electric power firms and required government approval for any new electrical utilities or for the issuance of bonds to expand old ones. In its regulatory capacity the commission authored regulations that covered a broad range of other services and enterprises, including public waterworks, gas companies, trolley and autobus lines, radio stations, shipping companies, and (just being formed) commercial airlines. The government reserved the right to regulate prices and profit margins for twenty (later thirty) years, and could determine how "excess" annual profits (defined as in excess of 25 percent of capital) would be reinvested (e.g., in plant expansion, employee pension funds, etc.).[38]

The commission's regulatory initiatives were symptomatic of one pattern of state intrusion into the economy that marked the early Nationalist years. Before 1927, Chinese industry and commerce had been "comparatively free from legislative and administrative control of a regular nature."[39] The first years of Nationalist rule, however, saw passage of a considerable body of legislation affecting commerce and industry, including a Law of Insurance (1929), Maritime Law (1929), Negotiable Instruments Law (1929), Trademark Law (1930), and a new Company Law (1929), which regulated the organizational structure of private corporations.[40] Private businesses were subjected to a broad range of new taxes, inspections, certifications, export duties, and import tariffs by a government that was now strong enough and close enough to China's industrial and commercial centers to enforce them, when it wished to.

The regulatory approach to economic development was pushed perhaps farthest in the case of government intervention to modernize one of China's oldest industries, that of silk manufacturing, as will be discussed below. But regulation alone could not accomplish the *Industrial Plan* or entice the foreign assistance that was essential to it. As the National Reconstruction Commission withdrew to an oversight and regulatory role, its original mandate, to coordinate all economic development efforts, fell in 1931 to another bureaucratic superbody, the National Economic Council (NEC, *Quanguo jingji weiyuanhui*). The list of its putative powers was impressive and included authority over all publicly financed projects for economic development.[41] But it was above all a vehicle for cooperation with the closest equivalent of Palchinsky's "Tekhintern," the League of Nations.

3. COOPERATION WITH THE TEKHINTERN

The League of Nations had been active in an advisory capacity in China in matters of public health since the early 1920s. The director of the Health Section of the League's Secretariat, Dr. Ludwig Rajchman, was the moving spirit behind the League's involvement with China after the formation of the National Government. After 1927 he assisted in the formation of China's National Quarantine Service, which recaptured one area of Chinese administrative control from the Maritime Customs. He suggested a larger program of cooperation by which the League, as a multilateral agency, could supply technical aid without political risk to the National Government.[42] Politics would in fact never be absent from the League mission, which could not be separated from the League's condemnation of the Japanese seizure of Manchuria in 1931. (Rajchman would be cashiered in 1934 as Technical Agent for China for his pro-Chinese sentiments.) It is accurate to say, however, that the League program in China that developed after 1931 was "one of the most purely disinterested aid programs of the twentieth century."[43]

The League's work through the NEC was multifaceted but also limited to certain domains, reflecting the international organization's own definition of development assistance. It was not a World Bank capable of financing industrial infrastructure. Its work in China was defined by the three main League organizations represented in the founding of the NEC: those for health, economics and finance, and communications and transit. They provided advice, technical training, and, to a small degree, loans for experimental projects. In addition the League's Committee on Intellectual Cooperation supported educational and scholarly exchanges. As a group, however, these were categories broad enough to involve League advisers in matters ranging from silkworms to highways to higher education.[44]

The League's economic and finance section was employed by the NEC to promote fundamental reform of sericulture in order to revive one of China's most important export industries. In Japan, a centralized system of "scientific breeding control," government subsidy, and export promotion had overcome China's former dominance in the world market and produced Japanese silk of a standard quality that was both cheaper and better "than the best Zhejiangese."[45] As the Great Depression took hold in the West between 1928 and 1933, exports of the inferior Chinese product fell by two-thirds. The National Government had promoted reform in the industry since 1927 and had worked with provincial officials to establish a "Commission for the Standardization of Sericulture in Jiangsu and Zhejiang" the following year. In 1932 the national and provincial governments worked with private industrialists to set national quality standards for silk manufacture, with government funding for research, agricultural extension, and inspection. To control a blight affecting Chinese silk larvae and to standardize quality, only silk certified by an official silk control bureau could be sold.[46] That same year, the League's expert, Benito Mari, former chairman of the Italian Association of Sericulture, conducted a survey of the silk industry in five provinces. He gave his international expert's imprimatur to "compulsory Government regulation" of the industry, including "a State monopoly for the control of everything pertaining to the cultivation of mulberry trees, to the preparation of silkworm eggs, to the rearing of silkworm and cocoons and to the price and sale of cocoons."[47] Although the government did not go quite that far, it followed Mari's advice by intruding into the industry in three new ways: the spraying with disinfectant of buildings (mostly private homes) used in silk production; the collectivization of silkworm maturation in temperature-controlled sheds; and, as in Japan, the banning of privately grown silkworm eggs (eggs grown on government-licensed sericultural farms were to be used instead).[48] These regulations were highly unpopular with farmers, who made their feelings known in the Zhejiang Silk Riots of 1933, and were highly effective in improving yield and quality in the counties where they were carried out with determination. Terry M. Weidner, who has studied the effort to regulate the silk industry, concludes that it "went a long way toward righting a troubled industry desperately in need of reform," even if at political cost to the regime.[49]

The most publicized aspect of the League/NEC cooperation was the work of the League of Nations Engineering Mission to China (through the League's Communications and Transit Office) in flood control and water conservancy.[50] Cooperation had begun in principle but not yet in fact when, in the summer of 1931, Yangzi River floods resulted in the deaths of six hundred thousand Chinese. As in the case of the silk industry, the League urged greater centralization and government control of all aspects of water conservancy. (This had been urged, too, by the professional Society of Chinese Water Control Engineers [*Zhongguo shuili gongcheng xuehui*].) Initial work in flood relief and epidemic prevention (70 percent of the deaths were due to disease and starvation)[51] evolved into an integrated approach to national hydraulic engineering under a centralized Water Conservancy Administration. Apart from this administrative coordination, League expertise was focused on specific regional projects, notably dike restoration on the Yangzi and its tributaries and on engineering plans for the management of the Huai River. Here, short-term successes were most obvious in what did not happen: League-assisted flood control projects were "so effective that renewed high water in 1935 did little damage."[52] The long-term impact—for example, on interregional coordination of water management projects, experience in dam construction, and the training of Chinese hydraulic engineers—has yet to be researched.[53]

Perhaps the most impressive, and certainly the most extensive, result of the League's Engineering Mission was in the building of highways. Sun Yatsen's vision of "one million miles of road built in a very short time as if by a magic wand"[54] had not yet to come to pass, but the fast pace of road building in the 1920s by provincial governments and bus companies provided a foundation for the Nationalists' planned national road network. Whereas in 1920 perhaps as little as 100 miles of improved road (theoretically passable by motor vehicle) existed in the entire country outside the foreign concessions, over 20,000 miles had been built by 1928; that number would reach nearly 40,000 in the first two years of the National Government, with a further 35,000 projected. (Beyond this, in more than thirty large cities, city walls were in the process of being torn down for replacement by motor roads.)[55] The majority of this road building took place under provincial Reconstruction Bureaux: in Zhejiang, for example, the Nanjing era saw the construction of a system of all-weather roads "linking every major political and economic center in the province."[56] For provincial and national officials alike, motor roads were the affordable alternative to a major expansion of the rail system, for which capital and investors were lacking in the early 1930s.[57]

Here again NEC and League engineers urged centralization and standardization. Road engineering standards and traffic laws varied enormously from province to province, often from locality to locality. So did road signs and traffic signals, which were mostly "incomprehensible" anyway.[58] Until 1932 cars licensed in one province could not be driven in another. (After extended negotiations, the provinces of Zhejiang, Anhui, and Jiangsu, as well as the cities of Nanjing and Shanghai, agreed to recognize each other's plates; still, thereafter, cars licensed in one province could travel in another only after paying an additional fee.)[59] Integrated planning began under a new Bureau of Roads, while League and Chinese engineers built experimental roads at different locations with local materials.[60]

It was with great fanfare, therefore, that the Shanghai-Hangzhou Motor Road opened on October 10, 1932, as the first section of the Shanghai-Guangxi Trunk Line, itself part of a planned seven-province, eleven-trunk-line project of approximately 14,000 miles. This was a typical "modern" road of this region, with alignment and grades meeting international standards, built on a foundation of broken brick and surfaced with crushed shells and cinders. Some two hundred automobiles motored that day the seven hours from Shanghai to Hangzhou, some completing the return trip the same day. The road was in fact not quite finished (ready or not, it *had* to open on National Day), and there were some problems: farmer resistance to the road was expressed by the building of a stone wall across it; T. V. Soong's party knocked down several confused pedestrians; and in traffic the road proved much dustier than predicted—it would later get a cheap oil coating. But on the whole the venture was declared a great success.[61]

Educating Engineers.   All of the League/NEC endeavors had implications for another sector, that of scientific and technical education. Efforts in water conservancy and road construction competed with each other, and with railroads and private industry, for the services of a prize group of Chinese civil engineers from Shanghai's Jiaotong, or Communications, University and a small number of other institutions. In the Nanjing decade the number of Chinese specialists, educated at home or abroad, in the employment of the rail lines had finally sufficed to meet the (political) demand for Chinese leadership in the technical positions formerly held by foreigners;[62] but for new endeavors such as the road network the shortage was such that the League Engineering Mission proposed that the Bureau of Roads train its own engineers in a new Technical Civil Engineering Station.

The centralizing, rationalizing thrust of the League mission was perhaps best expressed in its proposal for a nationwide Employment Bureau for Intellectual and Technical Workers. It aimed to place university graduates in positions where they could "best serve the nation ... [while supplying] the Chinese central and provincial administrations, as well as public and private undertakings in the country, with the qualified technical persons required." The bureau would have branch offices in Geneva and the United States coordinating the technical studies of Chinese abroad with their future careers in China.[63] Such a comprehensive bureau never materialized, but the "nationalization" of job placement in specific disciplines would begin in the early years of the war.

More immediately influential were League proposals for a fundamental reform of Chinese higher education to meet the needs of economic development. This was the work of the League program on International Intellectual Cooperation, which had been founded with the noble goal of promoting peace by creating a "universal conscience" through the international exchange of scholars.[64] It was a hard-boiled group, however, that the League dispatched to China in 1931, at the outset of its technical assistance program, to propose (as its two-hundred-page report was titled) *The Reorganization of Education in China.*[65]

This "Becker Commission," named for its leader, the former Prussian minister of education C. H. Becker, decried the "alarming consequences of the excessive influence of the American model on Chinese education,"[66] by which was meant, above all, the then-prevalent curriculum of electives and "credits," which enhanced general education at the expense of specialized knowledge, and the organization of faculty in departments and colleges, which worked against centralization and oversight. Although arguing against vulgar utilitarianism in education, the report was harshly critical of the lack of central planning for China's hybrid system of public and private, Chinese and foreign, colleges and universities. Its recommendations aimed to strengthen the state's hand in setting educational agendas. It proposed (not surprisingly, perhaps) a continental-style restructuring—for example, academic chairs in place of departments—to centralize administration, including national-level oversight over chaired appointments; to rationalize geographically and fiscally the system of national (*guoli*) universities; and to establish a nationwide system of entrance examinations that would permit authorities to channel admissions to specific disciplines.[67] Although Chinese officials resented the public criticism, what Ruth Hayhoe calls the Becker Commission's "authoritarian view of knowledge"[68] found a sympathetic hearing in Nanjing.

Many of the commission's recommendations were adopted over the next three years. Chen Guofu, one of the formulators of Guomindang cultural policy, went even further in proposing in 1932 that in order to "train talent to meet society's needs," China's universities should stop admitting students of the humanities and law for a decade.[69] Serious (if not quite so drastic) reform began that same year under Chen's political protégé, Dr. Zhu Jiahua, who was named minister of education. A German-trained geologist long active in Nationalist developmental policy, Zhu brought to his office both strong scientific and political credentials; he began a restructuring of higher education away from the humanities and social sciences—in which enrollment began to be limited—in favor of science, engineering, and, at the secondary level, vocational training.[70] The 1929 organizational law for Chinese higher education had already required that each university have a school of science, engineering, medicine, or agriculture. Government financial support for these areas now increased markedly. Engineering programs at Jiaotong, National Central, and Qinghua Universities, to name the most prominent, were bolstered in areas of existing strength—civil and mechanical engineering—and supported in the expansion of programs in chemical and electrical engineering. From 1931 to 1936, the percentage of students in fields of science and engineering doubled in government-funded institutions. For the decade as a whole (including the early war years) engineering enrollment trebled. In the same period, the numbers of students enrolled in the arts fell by one-third, and those in law and political science by one-half. These curricular priorities were extended beyond the state sector to private and missionary colleges through a process of regulation and registration that had begun in 1929 but was more consistently enforced after 1932.[71] As Wang Shijie, the former chancellor of Wuhan University who succeeded Zhu as minister of education, would argue, knowledge was to be "harnessed to produce results in connection with the economic development of the country."[72]

The League's influence, like its work in China, was spread over the many different areas in which its Technical Advisory Mission was active. League engineers and funds were focused on specific projects of manageable scale. Their efforts had none of the pretense and grandeur of Sun Yatsen's plan. Never was there articulated a developmental philosophy behind all their activities. There was, however,

a consistent pattern of advice regarding economic, technical, and educational development in favor of a state-managed, centralized approach to economic development emphasizing the promise of scientific and engineering expertise. The
League's work could only reinforce the more statist tendencies in the Nanjing
regime.

In the end all the League could offer *was* advice, which the Chinese government could give material form in projects of dam and road construction. The
road-building enterprise, ultimately one of the signal material achievements of
the Nationalist regime, was predicated on further assumptions regarding China's
industrial development, among them—as Sun Yatsen had urged—the creation of
a domestic automobile industry. This would be the role of the state-owned China
Automobile Manufacturing Company (*Zhongguo qiche zhizao gongsi*), which began as
an assembly operation of diesel trucks on a Daimler-Benz model.[73] To knit China
together where roads and railroads could not go would be the task of civil aviation, which by the end of the Nanjing decade, through official joint ventures with
Pan American and Lufthansa, would connect China's major cities on regular
schedules.[74] Airplanes for these routes were ultimately to have been made in
China, by another Sino-foreign joint venture, the China Air Materials Construction Company (*Zhongguo hangkong qicai zhizao gongsi*).[75] To give China the capacity
to produce its own industries, machines, and tools on a world-class scale was the
aim of still more ambitious joint ventures: to build a Central Steel Works, a Central Machine Works, and indeed an entire "new industrial center" of state-owned
firms in central China.[76] These were to be the driving forces of what by the mid-
1930s was increasingly called a "controlled" (*tongzhi*) economy. All this ambition
was in the true spirit of Sun Yatsen. To manage it, however, required a rather different kind of government official than he could have imagined.

4. A GOVERNMENT OF ENGINEERS?

Neither the National Reconstruction Commission, in its emphasis on regulation
and licensing, nor the National Economic Council, whose efforts concentrated almost exclusively on areas of cooperation with the League of Nations mission, had
the independent capacity to lead China's economic development, let alone realize
Sun Yatsen's extravagant plans. The same could be said of the National Research
Institute (*Zhongyang yanjiuyuan*, or Academia Sinica), which had been conceived by
Sun Yatsen as a scientific academy in the service of the state, but which had no
straightforward policy function.[77]

The lack of unified direction did not indicate a lack of talent or expertise. It
may be that the policy confusion so apparent to contemporary observers—and explained by later scholars in terms of the "cliques" and "factions" of a terminally
disorganized regime—was in part the result of a certain degree of success in the
creation of new state institutions to manage a modern economy.[78] Scholars who
have worked in the archives of the Nanjing-era Ministries of Railroads and Fi-

nance, for example, have stressed their high degree of technical professionalism and bureaucratization.[79] The official vocabulary for public officials was reformed to reflect areas of competence and to emphasize the interchangeability of individuals: hence the proliferation of terms such as *xingzheng renyuan* (administrative personnel), *caizheng renyuan* (financial personnel), and *zhiyuan* (professional staff) of all sorts.[80] In the mid-1930s a strong "administrative efficiency" movement in Nanjing's ministries, stressing the "scientificization" (*kexuehua*) of administration and the professionalization of civil service, reflected trends already present in the more technically demanding ministries, such as those of Industry and Finance, which made increasing use of standards set by the Ministry of Personnel and the Examination Yuan in their recruitment procedures.[81] These may have remained, as Julia Strauss has argued, "strong institutions in a weak polity."[82] Indeed their success as professional bureaucracies appears to have been directly related to their degree of insulation from political processes. Among public officials, the perceived gap between political generalists (*wenguan, zhengwuguan*) and technical, or functional, specialists (*gongzhi renyuan, shiwu renyuan*) was very large.[83] It follows, then, that these very "modern" and increasingly specialized institutions were not easily mobilized for priorities set by political leadership and were ill suited to interministerial cooperation. (Perhaps this is one reason that the Ministry of Foreign Affairs, to take a quite different example, which Strauss finds to be "one of the best institutionalized state organizations across the entirety of the Republican period,"[84] earned a high reputation for professionalism while having almost nothing to do with the formulation of foreign policy.)

The growth of specialized bureaucracies reflected the ever greater availability of university and technical school graduates—furthered by the educational reforms of 1932—and their gradual incorporation into government service. It mirrored, too, the participation of professional associations in policy formulation. Take the case of engineers.

A Chinese Society of Engineers (*Zhonghua gongchengshi xuehui*) had been formed in 1912 with 148 members under Zhan Tianyou (Jeme Tien Yau), the daring chief engineer for the Beijing-Zhangjiakou railroad (completed in 1909), which was the most famous and difficult line built entirely under Chinese auspices.[85] The Society's work of establishing the field in China, standardizing engineering education, and promoting a nationalistic agenda was augmented by the activities of the Chinese Engineering Society (*Zhongguo gongcheng xuehui*), founded at Cornell University in 1918 by Chinese pursuing advanced engineering studies in the United States. The merger of these two groups in 1931 formed a new Chinese Society of Engineers (*Zhongguo gongchengshi xuehui*) with some 2,300 members; by 1948 its membership would reach 14,000. The drive toward professional autonomy and self-regulation that had marked the earlier engineering associations gradually gave way to greater cooperation with, and reliance on, the state that now educated and certified engineers.[86] Throughout the period of the National Government, the Society took as its central purposes the development of the Chinese engineering industry and the realization of Sun Yatsen's *Industrial Plan*.[87] Its thirteen research groups were headed by leading engineers mostly already in government, such as Shen Yi, chief of public works for the Shanghai municipality, and Yun Zhen, the head of electrical engineering for the National Reconstruction Commission. Over time their work (and indeed the careers of many of them) would be incorporated in and become indistinguishable from the work of the new National Resources Commission, the engineers' stronghold in the National Government.[88]

From Industrial Policy to War Economy. The National Resources Commission stands out as the most comprehensive attempt to apply science and engineering to government work and the unfinished task of "reconstruction." It can be distinguished from other agencies of its day in that it became a highly professional, bureaucratized, politically insulated institution that *also* served the immediate interests of state leadership. Simply put, the National Resources Commission (NRC) was born of a redefinition of "reconstruction" to favor producer industries and national defense. In the aftermath of the Japanese seizure of Manchuria, industrial policy, which had ranged from electrification to reform in the silk industry, became identical with military-industrial development. China's "international development" came to mean cultivation of the kind of international economic relationships capable of rendering China militarily and industrially self-sufficient—or at least able to defend itself—through the domestic production of steel, machinery, arms, trucks, aircraft, and electrical equipment in the interior.[89]

The aims and methods of the new agency were clear enough in nomenclature: the NRC began in 1932 as a "National Defense Planning Commission" (*Guofang sheji weiyuanhui*), a team of leading scientists and engineers who built on the research of the Society of Engineers to design defense-related industries. It would become a large bureaucracy controlling most of a growing state industrial sector and the trade mechanisms affecting Sino-foreign cooperation, because, as its later renaming (in 1935) indicates, it was empowered to survey and exploit Chinese natural resources, particularly ores and minerals, for national development and international exchange.[90] Through barter-credit exchanges, it was able to import whole plants and provide for the international training of personnel for its Central Steel Works, Central Copper Works, Central Machine Works, and Central Electrical Manufacturing Works, among other state-owned enterprises.[91]

If the managed economies of interwar Europe were to a considerable degree an elaboration of the experience of the "war economies" in the First World War,[92] the reorganization and growth of economic bureaucracy in China in the mid-1930s was above all preparation for the Second. From a longer perspective this should not surprise us, as military agendas were never far removed from industrial plans in the late Qing and early Republic. What is in retrospect astonishing is that they were almost entirely absent as the rationale for Sun Yatsen's *Industrial Plan* and very understated in early Nanjing-era reconstruction efforts. But many of those plans (for example, for roads, railroads, and electrification) had important military dimensions and would be continued under the new industrial bureaucracy. Thus the concept of a massive hydroelectric power station in the Yangzi Gorges—one that might serve a relocated regime in wartime—received its first scientific survey under the Defense Planning Commission in 1932.[93]

The strength and endurance of this bureaucracy over two decades (it became China's largest employer, apart from the army, and outlasted its predecessors, competitors, and even the regime) and the rise of its leaders to high political positions were due to its mission, deemed indispensable to national survival, and to a technocratic arrogance based upon unchallengeable expertise.[94] Led by a respected, incorruptible, and crusty scholar, the geologist Weng Wenhao—who also served as president of the Society of Chinese Engineers—the National Resources Commission was better degreed and otherwise academically certified than any other part of government. In making its first recruits in 1932–33, its National Specialized Talent Investigation Committee compiled data on eighty thousand specialized personnel in China and abroad for potential service in state industry, part of which was later circulated as a "Who's Who of Chinese Engineers." Over the next two decades, as it gained control—through industrial construction and a series of nationalizations—of some 70 percent of all Chinese industry, it would serve as the employer of first choice for a generation of Chinese engineers. It in turn was served by an increasingly complex matrix of science and engineering, recruiting its employees from a science-oriented system of higher education and entering into cooperative research relationships with Beijing, Qinghua, Nankai, and Jiaotong Universities.

In the prewar as in the war years, the NRC was a form of "national service" for Chinese engineers. But quite apart from patriotic motives, in a period of economic depression and government intrusion in the private sector, the NRC was an engineer's salvation. Those hired were paid better (on the same scale as management) and lived under more protected circumstances than employees of any part of the Chinese government. For the NRC was not just a de facto ministry of industry and planning. Its enterprises became comprehensive *danwei*, or work units, and called themselves such. Housing, dining, shopping, schooling (for employees and their children), banking, recreation, and health facilities were provided for engineers and workers alike. Opportunities for study and internships abroad were available, particularly to junior engineers. Engineers would pursue their work in isolation from the "partification" (*danghua*) efforts of the Guomindang party-state. Their enterprises would be without party branches until 1943 and under only nominal party supervision thereafter.[95]

Chinese engineers shared with their professional counterparts in other nations a "configuration of faith in science, technology, nationalism and industrialism."[96] To a certain degree NRC engineers, like their predecessors in the National Reconstruction Commission and National Economic Council, played the role, in the Nationalist state, of the *tekhnicheskaia intelligentsia* of the early Soviet Union, the applied scientists, engineers, and agronomists who comprised the new elite that Kendall Bailes calls the "technostructure" of the state.[97] This was not at the margin of the state but essential to its purposes. In China, the eventual linkage of "reconstruction" with national security promised to strengthen the security of state and nation while broadly promoting the development of economic infrastructure. The achievements of Nationalist engineers and planners (as in the NRC-orchestrated removal of Chinese industry to the interior at the beginning of the war) and even their unrealized ambitions (as in the revival, with much ballyhoo, of the Three Gorges Dam Project in the 1940s) would lend prestige and a certain legitimacy to the government that sponsored them. Above all China's engineers were essential to Nationalist China's survival in an eight-year war against a technologically superior enemy.[98]

5. CONCLUSIONS

The new National Government had sought to control China's progress from the center; one should try sometime to count the extraordinary number of party and government institutions founded in 1927–28 that began with the term *zhongyang*, or "central." But in considering the Nanjing regime as an embryonic "developmental state," there is no pretending that a single or coherent developmental strategy existed until the overwhelming threat of war brought military-economic considerations to the center. Over forty years ago Douglas Paauw summed up, quite accurately, the Nationalist approach as one emphasizing "some aspects of the technological preconditions for economic growth."[99] What also existed, however, was an ethos of optimism, not describable or even rational in economic terms, that China could be remade physically, and indirectly economically, by the planned application of international technology under the leadership of homegrown scientific and technical talent. For the new National Government after 1927, economic planning was not just policy: it was gospel and ritual. All arms of government were believers and practitioners. There was, in Sun Yatsen's *Industrial Plan*, a centrally distributed catechism, but no GOSPLAN. But there was the spirit—captured well in an international textbook of the period—that planning, with its "philosophical faith in the power of scientific research and constructive imagination," offered "a new mode of feeling, life, and living."[100]

"Constructive imagination" was certainly at the heart of Sun's grand project, which proved at once an inspiration and, because it could not possibly be realized, a burden to the National Government. Yet this was a burden undertaken cheerfully by a young and talented (at minimum, well-certified) government that, like Sun, dared to think big: to plan a stunning national capital; to electrify the country and dam the Gorges; to tie the country together in networks of roads; and to build overnight the nation's heavy industries.

The effort to accomplish even part of this required more than Promethean values. It compelled an ideal of professionalism (*zhiye zhuyi*) in the central government of a kind that only recently had asserted itself in municipal and provincial affairs.[101] The Nanjing government's very partial success in its economic development plans should not conceal the fact that, in the effort, the purpose and makeup of China's central government underwent an important change. National economic development was now the responsibility of the government—one it would ultimately take seriously enough that it would regulate, control, and finally nationalize almost all industry. The private sphere of economic life was correspondingly constricted. Within the regime, bureaucratic superagencies created to manage the economy, such as the National Reconstruction Commission, National Economic Council, and National Resources Commission (which over time absorbed the projects and personnel of all the others), would create an enduring civilian government in which engineers—those who wanted to build things, get things done—would prevail over economists, who knew how little the government could afford. These institutional foundations and policy preferences would survive largely intact on both sides of the Taiwan Strait at least until the late 1950s.[102]

Lenin had once looked forward to the "very happy time" when politics would "recede into the background" while engineers and agronomists would "do most of the talking."[103] This would occur in neither Russia nor China. By 1937, however, when the Japanese rolled into Nanjing on the new Shanghai-Nanjing road, the retreating Chinese government was quite different from the party-led army that had marched north from Canton a decade earlier. It still was no "technocracy," if by that term we mean a government under the political rule of technical elites.[104] Yet an army of engineers now moved with the seat of government upriver, to Chongqing.

NOTES

Abbreviations

AH	Academia Historica, Taiwan
AS	Academia Sinica, Taiwan
CASS	Chinese Academy of Social Sciences, Beijing
GYZL	*Zhongguo jindai gongyeshi ziliao* [Materials on the modern history of Chinese industry], ed. Chen Zhen. Beijing: Sanlien shudian, 1961.
IMH	Institute of Modern History
NA	National Archives, Washington, D.C.
NRC	National Resources Commission archives
PAC	Party Archives Commission of the Guomindang, Taiwan
SASS	Shanghai Academy of Social Sciences Documentary Collection
SDN	Société des Nations [League of Nations] archives, Geneva
SHA	Second Historical Archives of China, Nanjing

1. Loren R. Graham, *The Ghost of the Executed Engineer: Technology and the Fall of the Soviet Union* (Cambridge: Harvard University Press, 1993), 43. Friends convinced Palchinsky not to mail this letter, but his ideas became well-known.

2. The quote is from Wen-hsin Yeh's introduction to this volume.

3. Sun Yat-sen, *The International Development of China* (1922; reprint, Taipei: Sino-American Publishing, 1953), 191.

4. Thomas G. Rawski, *Economic Growth in Prewar China* (Berkeley and Los Angeles: University of California Press, 1989), 116.

5. On the culture of urban progressivism in the provinces, see Kristin Stapleton, *Civilizing Chengdu: Chinese Urban Reform, 1895–1937* (Cambridge: Harvard University Asia Center, forthcoming).

6. Sun, *International Development*, 192.

7. T'ang Leang-li, *Reconstruction in China* (Shanghai: China United Press, 1935).

8. The quote is from Sun, preface to *International Development*, v. Generally, see Michael R. Godley, "Socialism with Chinese Characteristics: Sun Yatsen and the International Development of China," *Australian Journal of Chinese Affairs*, no. 18 (July 1987): 109–25.

9. See ibid., 119.

10. For a review of Republican-era research on Sun's plans, see Zhong Shaohua, "Zhongshan shiye jihua yu Zhongguo xiandaihua" [Sun Yatsen's *Industrial Plan* and China's modernization (Sun Yatsen University, Gaoxiong)], *Zhongshan shehui kexue jikan* [Sun Yatsen social science quarterly] 5, no. 4 (December 1990): 134–48.

11. Richard Louis Edmonds, "The Legacy of Sun Yat-sen's Railway Plans," *China Quarterly* 111 (September 1987): 442.

12. Sun, *International Development*, 66–67; Hong Qingyu, "A Review of the Work during the Early Stages of the Three Gorges Project," in *Megaproject: A Case Study of China's Three Gorges Project*, ed. Shiu-hung Luk and Joseph Whitney (New York: M. E. Sharpe, 1993). For contemporary debates see Dai Qing et al., *Yangtze! Yangtze!*, ed. Patricia Adams and John Thibodeau (London: Earthscan, 1994).

13. Li Peng, final lines from his "Qinyuan Chun" [Ode to a great river], presented on the occasion of the formal beginning of work on the Three Gorges Project, quoted in *Xinmin wanbao* (December 15, 1994).

14. Lin Jiayou, "Shilun Sun Zhongshan zhenxing Zhongguo shangyede jingji sixiang ji qi yanbian" [The evolution of Sun Yatsen's economic thought regarding the revitalization of China's commerce], *Minguo yanjiu* [Republican research] 1, no. 1 (1994): 37.

15. Jiang Jiwei, "Jishu yu zhengzhi" [Technology and politics], in *Xuexi* [Study] no. 16 (1957): 12, cited in Li Cheng and Lynn White, "Elite Transformation and Modern Change in Mainland China and Taiwan: Empirical Data and the Theory of Technocracy," *China Quarterly*, no. 121 (March 1990).

16. William C. Kirby, "The Nationalist Regime and the Chinese Party-State, 1928–1958," in *Contemporary East Asia in Historical Perspective*, ed. Merle Goldman and Andrew Gordon (Cambridge: Harvard University Press, 2000).

17. The term "developmental state" is appropriated from Chalmers Johnson's study of Japanese industrial policy of the same and later periods, and is used to stress a common grounding in nineteenth-century continental European neomercantilist conceptions, which, in the Chinese case, combined with inherited traditions of state economic regulation and international models of economic intervention in the 1920s and 1930s to define very broadly the economic purposes of the Nationalist regime. See Johnson, *MITI and the Japanese Miracle: The Growth of Industrial Policy, 1925–1975* (Stanford: Stanford University Press, 1982), 17 ff. This is not to dispute the contention of Douglas Reynolds that the institutional transformation of the Chinese state dates from the *xinzheng* (New Policy) reforms of

the early twentieth century (see his *China, 1898–1912: The Xinzheng Revolution and Japan* [Cambridge, Mass.: Council on East Asian Studies, 1993]), but to suggest a self-conscious, developmental mission on the part of the Nationalist regime that distinguishes it from its predecessors. On the Nationalist party-state as the political precondition of its Communist successor, see Robert E. Bedeski, *State-Building in Modern China: The Kuomintang in the Prewar Period* (Berkeley: Center for Chinese Studies, University of California at Berkeley, 1981).

18. Glenn Babb, "Nanking—a City with a Past and a Future," *Weekly Review* 25, no. 11 (August 11, 1923): 36, cited in Maryruth Coleman, "Municipal Politics in Nationalist China: Nanjing, 1927–1937" (Ph.D. diss., Harvard University, 1984), 1.

19. See Iris Chang, *The Rape of Nanking* (New York: Basic Books, 1997).

20. T'ang Leang-li, *Reconstruction*, 330.

21. Coleman, "Municipal Politics," 252.

22. Ibid.

23. Ibid., 18.

24. Guodu sheji jishu zhuanyuan banshichu [Office of Technical Experts for Planning the National Capital], comp., *Shoudu jihua* [Plan for the capital] (Nanjing: Guodu sheji jishu zhuanyuan banshichu, 1929).

25. Ibid., 25–32.

26. Ibid., passim. The quotations are from Min-Ch'ien T. Z. Tyau, ed., *Two Years of Nationalist China* (Shanghai: Kelly and Walsh, 1930), 389–94; see also Coleman, "Municipal Politics," 252–54. The restoration of the Ming city wall—without a highway atop it— would not begin until 1995. New China News Agency report 16 May 1995.

27. Coleman, "Municipal Politics," 254.

28. As in the case of the Chinese city in Shanghai, which quickly followed Nanjing's model, city planners and public works officials tended to be young university graduates who were "enthusiastic and generally honest." See Christian Henriot, *Shanghai, 1927–1937* (Berkeley and Los Angeles: University of California Press, 1993), 170.

29. Tyau, *Two Years*, 389, 396–98.

30. The quote is from Barry Till, *In Search of Old Nanjing* (Hong Kong: Joint Publishing Company, 1982), 203. Generally, on the physical state of Nanjing and its official structures in the Nanjing decade, see *Xin Nanjing* [New Nanjing] (Nanjing: Nanjing shi zhengfu, 1933); Chen Jimin, ed., *Minguo guanfu* [Republican government offices] (Hong Kong: Jinling shu chubanshe, 1992); and "Nanjing shi zhi jingji jianshe" [Economic development of Nanjing], in *Shinianlai zhi Zhongguo jingji jianshe* [China's economic development in the past ten years], comp. Zhongyang dangbu guomin jingji jihua weiyuanhui [Commission on national economic planning of the Central Committee] (Nanjing, 1937).

31. Wang Shuhuai, "Jianshe weiyuanhui dui Zhongguo dianqi shiye de guihua" [The National Reconstruction Commission's planning for China's electric power industry] (paper presented to the Conference on the Centennial of Sun Yat-sen's Founding of the Kuomintang for Revolution, Taipei, 1994), 5.

32. The quote is from ibid., 5.

33. V. I. Lenin, "Report of the All-Russia Central Executive Committee and the Council of People's Commissars on the Home and Foreign Policy to the Eighth All-Russia Congress of Soviets," 22 December 1920, reprinted in *V. I. Lenin: Selected Works in Three Volumes*, vol. 3 (Moscow: Progress Publishers, 1977), 461.

34. For a selection of Sun's comments on the topic, see Wang Shuhuai, "Jianshe weiyuanhui dui Zhongguo dianqi shiye de guihua," 3–4.

35. Yun Chen, "Dianqi wang" [Electrical power network], *Jianshe yuekan*, no. 9 (October 1930): 37.

36. Tyau, *Two Years*, 289.

37. This map unveiling took place at a party congress in 1920. See Alec Nove, *An Economic History of the U.S.S.R.* (New York: Penguin, 1969), 71.

38. Tyau, *Two Years*, 287; Wang Shuhuai, "Jianshe weiyuanhui dui Zhongguo dianqi shiye de guihua," 10–11; *Jianshe weiyuanhui gongzuo jiyao* [Summary of the work of the National Reconstruction Commission] (Nanjing: Jianshe weiyuanhui, 1929).

39. G. E. Hubbard, *Eastern Industrialization and Its Effect on the West* (London: Oxford University Press, 1938), 209.

40. See William C. Kirby, "China, Unincorporated: Company Law and Business Enterprise in Twentieth-Century China," *Journal of Asian Studies* 54, no. 1 (February 1995): 43–63.

41. SHA 44(2)78, Chin Fen, "The National Economic Council" (March 1935), 1.

42. F. P. Walters, *A History of the League of Nations*, vol. 1 (Oxford: Oxford University Press), 1952.

43. Cheryl Payer, "Western Economic Assistance to Nationalist China, 1927–1937" (Ph.D. diss., Harvard University, 1971), 9.

44. Generally on the League-NEC endeavors, see SHA 44(1719), "Quanguo jingji weiyuanhui gongzuo baogao" [Reports of the work of the National Economic Council], 1934–1937; Zhang Li, "Yijiusanling niandai Zhongguo yu Guolian de jishu hezuo" [China's technical cooperation with the League of Nations during the 1930s], *Zhongyang yanjiuyuan jindaishi yanjiusuo jikan* [Quarterly of the Institute of Modern History of the Academia Sinica], no. 15 (December 1986): 381–414; Tze-hsiun Kuo, "Technical Cooperation between China and Geneva," *Information Bulletin* 1, no. 6 (July 1936); Lau-King Quan, *China's Relations with the League of Nations, 1919–1936* (Hong Kong: Asiatic Litho Press, 1939); Norbert Meienberger, *Entwicklungshilfe under dem Völkerbund. Ein Beitrag zur Geschichte der internationalen Zusammenarbeit in der Zwischenkriegszeit unter besonderer Berücksichtigung der technischen Hilfe an China* (Winterthur, 1965); Jürgen Osterhammel, " 'Technical Co-operation' between the League of Nations and China," *Modern Asian Studies* 13, no. 4 (1979): 661–80; Tao Siu, "L'Oeuvre du Conseil National Economique Chinois" (Ph.D. diss., L'Université de Nancy, 1936).

45. Terry M. Weidner, "Local Political Work under the Nationalists: The 1930's Silk Reform Campaign," *Illinois Papers in Asian Studies*, no. 2 (1983): 67. See also Lillian Li, *China's Silk Trade: Traditional Industry in the Modern World* (Cambridge: Harvard University Press, 1981), 200.

46. Weidner, "Local Political Work," 70.

47. Benito Mari, "Summary Report on an Enquiry on the Re-organization of Chinese Sericulture," annex no. 7 in *Annexes to the Report to the Council of the League of Nations of Its Technical Delegate on His Mission in China from Date of Appointment until April 1, 1934* (Nanjing, 1934), 231.

48. SHA 44(1719), "Quanguo jingji weiyuanhui gongzuo baogao" [Report of the work of the National Economic Council], 1937, 33–40; SHA 44(2)78, Chin Fen, "The National Economic Council," 67–70; Lau-King Quan, *China's Relations*, 219–26; Tao Siu, "L'Oeuvre," 73–77.

49. Weidner, "Local Political Work," 79.

50. See SDN, General 50/R5669–71, Reports of the Engineering Mission of the League of Nations in China, 1932–35.

51. Osterhammel, " 'Technical Co-operation,' " 667; J. L. Buck, *The 1931 Floods in China* (Nanking: Department of Agricultural Economics of the University of Nanking), 1932.

52. Arthur Young, *China's Nation-Building Effort, 1927–1937: The Financial and Economic Record* (Stanford: Stanford University Press, 1971), 347. See also 376–86.

53. On the maze of regional interests involved in water management, see David Pietz, "The Huai River and Statebuilding in 20th-Century China" (Ph.D. diss., Washington University, 1998).

54. Sun, *International Development*, 192.

55. See A. Viola Smith and Anselm Chuh, *Motor Roads in China*, U.S. Department of Commerce Trade Promotion series no. 120 (Washington: U.S. Government Printing Office, 1931), 2–3, 7, 20 ff.

56. Noel Miner, "Chekiang: The Nationalists' Effort in Agrarian Reform and Construction" (Ph.D. diss., Stanford University, 1973), 237. Miner disputes the economic utility of the roads in a curious argument that implies that "passenger traffic," which dominated road use, had no economic value.

57. On the economics of roads vs. railroads in China, see Smith and Chuh, *Motor Roads*, 3–4.

58. SDN, General 50/R5669–71, "Engineering Mission of the League of Nations in China, Report No. 7," 7 September 1932, p. 3.

59. SDN, General 50/R5669–71, "Engineering Mission of the League of Nations in China, Report No. 8," 19 October 1932, p. 4 and appendix.

60. For a review of highway building work through 1935, see SHA 44(1719), "Quanguo jingji weiyuanhui gongzuo baogao" [Report of the work of the National Economic Council], 1935.

61. SDN, General 50/R5669–71, report of 19 October 1932, p. 1; report of 10 December 1932, appendix: "Highway Inspection Trip to Hunan Province"; SHA 44(2)78, Chin Fen, "The National Economic Council," 6–14.

62. On the position of some seven hundred Jiaotong graduates in the railway industry, see Chang Jui-teh, "Technology Transfer in Modern China: The Case of Railway Enterprise (1876–1937)," *Modern Asian Studies* (1992).

63. SDN, General 50/R5721, "Scheme for the Establishment of an Employment Bureau for Intellectual and Technical Workers."

64. "China and International Intellectual Co-operation," *Information Bulletin* [Council of International Affairs, Nanking] 2, no. 1 (11 September 1936): 1–2. For a broader context see Akira Iriye, *Cultural Internationalism and World Order* (Baltimore: Johns Hopkins University Press, 1997), 60–64.

65. C. H. Becker et al., *The Reorganization of Education in China* (Paris: League of Nations Institute of Intellectual Co-operation, 1932).

66. Becker et al., *Reorganization*, 25. Becker was also an orientalist of some note. Other members of the commission were the French Communist Paul Langevin, from the Collège de France; M. Falsky, a Polish specialist in primary education; and R. H. Tawney of the London School of Economics, who used his time in China well, completing the study published as *Land and Labor in China* (London, 1932; reprint, Boston: Beacon Press, 1962).

67. Becker et al., *Reorganization*, passim; Ernst Neugebauer, *Anfänge pädagogische Entwicklungshilfe under dem Völkerbund in China, 1931 bis 1935* (Hamburg: Institut für Asienkunde, 1971); Ruth E. S. Hayhoe, "China's Higher Curricular Reform in Historical Perspective," *China Quarterly*, no. 110 (June 1987): 202–3.

68. Details of the official response are well set out in Stefan Knirsch, "Reformen im chinesischen Erziehungswesen in der Nanjing-Ära" (Magisterarbeit, Albert-Ludwigs-Universität, Freiburg, 1995); Hayhoe, "China's Higher Curricular Reform," 203.

69. Chen Guofu, "Gaige jiaoyu chubu fangan" [Draft plan for the reform of education], in *Chen Guofu xiansheng quanji* (Taipei: Zheng Zhong shuju, 1952), 169.

70. Zhu Jiahua, *Jiuge yue lai jiaoyubu zhengli quanguo jiaoyu zhi shuoming* [Explanation of the Ministry of Education's reform of national education in the past nine months] (Nanjing, 1932).

71. See the excellent discussion of this process in James Reardon-Anderson, *The Study of Change: Chemistry in China, 1840–1949* (Cambridge: Cambridge University Press, 1991), 208–29; Hayhoe, "China's Higher Curricular Reform," 402.

72. Wang Shijie, "Education," in *The Chinese Yearbook, 1937* (Shanghai: Commercial Press, 1937), 1032.

73. Gyzl, 3:1102–3.

74. See William M. Leafy Jr., *The Dragon's Wings: The China National Aviation Corporation and the Development of Commercial Aviation in China* (Athens: University of Georgia Press, 1976), 13–16; Bodo Wiethoff, *Luftverkehr in China, 1928–1949* (Wiesbaden: O. Harrassowitz, 1975), 104–31; Jack C. Young, "Joint Venture and Licensing in Civil Aviation: A Sino-American Perspective," *Stanford Journal of International Studies* 15 (1979): 253.

75. AH, 2–12.02.I, file, "Zhongguo hangkong qicai zhizao gongsi" [China Air Materials Construction Company] (1934–37); GYZL, 3:921.

76. SASS, Ministry of Industry file, "Gongye zhongxin" [Industrial center]: "Guoying gangtiechang" [State-run iron- and steelworks] Ministry of Industry report, August 1932; "Benbu yinianlai choushe guoying gongye gaikuang" [Overview of this ministry's preparations for state-run industry in the past year], March 1933; "Shiyebu chouban guoying gongye" [Ministry of Industry preparations for state-run industries], 1936; GYZL, 3:790–93.

77. *Guoli Zhongyang yanjiuyuan shiqi niandu zong baogao* [Annual report of the Academia Sinica (1928)] (Nanjing: Zhongyang yanjiuyuan, 1929); Lin Wenzhao, "Zhongyang yanjiuyuan de choubei jingguo" [Preparatory process of the establishment of the Academia Sinica], *Zhongguo keji shiliao* [Historical materials of Chinese science and technology] 9, no. 2 (1988): 70–73; Lin Wenzhao, "Zhongyang yanjiuyuan gaishu" [General description of the Academia Sinica] in *Zhongguo keji shiliao* [Historical materials of Chinese science and technology] 6, no. 2 (1985): 21–31. An important new study is Shiwei Chen, "Government and Academy in Republican China: History of the Academia Sinica, 1927–1949" (Ph.D. diss., Harvard University, 1998).

78. On cliques, see, for example, Hung-mao Tien, *Government and Politics in Kuomintang China, 1927–1937* (Stanford: Stanford University Press, 1972), 45–72.

79. Zhang Ruide [Chang Jui-teh], *Zhongguo jindai tielu shiye guanli de yanjiu* [Research on modern Chinese railway management] (Nangang: Zhongyang yanjiuyuan jindaishi suo, 1991); Julia Strauss, *Strong Institutions in Weak Polities: State Building in Republican China, 1927–1940* (Oxford: Clarendon Press, 1998).

80. Julia Strauss, *"Wenguan* ('Lettered Official'), *Gongwuyuan* ('Public Servant') and *Ganbu* ('Cadre'): The Politics of Labelling State Administrators in Republican China," *Indiana East Asian Working Paper Series on Language and Politics in Modern China*, no. 6 (July 1995).

81. Strauss, *Strong Institutions*, 42.

82. Ibid.

83. Strauss, "*Wenguan.*"

84. Strauss, *Strong Institutions,* 167.

85. Zhong Shaohua, "Zhongguo gongchengshi xuehui jianshi" [Brief history of the Chinese Society of Engineers] (manuscript, 1987); Ralph Heunemann, *The Dragon and the Iron Horse* (Cambridge: Council on East Asian Studies, Harvard University, 1984), 69–70.

86. In this, the history of Chinese engineering associations would more closely resemble European than American professional associations. On comparative methodological approaches, see Charles E. McClelland, *The German Experience of Professionalization* (Cambridge: Cambridge University Press, 1991), 21; Magali S. Larson, *The Rise of Professionalism: A Sociological Analysis* (Berkeley and Los Angeles: University of California Press, 1977); and Hans Hesse, *Beruf und Wandel. Ein Beitrag zum Problem der Professionalisierung* (Stuttgart: Enke, 1968).

87. Indeed the first suborganization established by the Society was its "Committee for Carrying Out Sun Yatsen's Industrial Development Plan." See Zhong Shaohua, "Zhongguo gongchengshi xuehui jianshi."

88. Zhong Shaohua, "Zhongshan shiye jihua yu Zhongguo xiandaihua" [SunYatsen's *Industrial Plan* and China's modernization], *Zhongshan shehui kexue jikan* [Sun Yatsen social science quarterly (Sun Yatsen University, Gaoxiong)] 5, no. 4 (1990): 134–48; Zhong Shaohua, "Sanshi zhi sishi niandai dui Zhongshan shiye jihua de zhuanmen yanjiu" [Specialized research on Sun Yatsen's industrial plan in the 1930s and 1940s], *Beijing shehui kexue* [Beijing social science], no. 4 (1986): 107–9.

89. See SHA 28(5965), "Zhonggongye jianshe jihua shuomingshu" [Explanation of the plan for heavy industries] (1936). On individual enterprises see *Ziyuan weiyuanhui yuekan* [NRC monthly] 1, no. 2 (June 1939): 85–100, 158–59, 337; 1, no. 3 (July 1939): 163–66; 2, no. 1 (January 1940): 37 ff; Lianqing zongbu [Combined Services Forces] Library, Taipei, materials on arsenal development filed as "Guofang gongye ji wuqi fazhan" [National defense industries and armaments development] (Taipei, n.d.); CASS, *Ziyuan weiyuanhui zongyang jiqichang jianshi* [Short history of the NRC's Central Machine Works] (NRC internal draft history, November 1940); SHA, 28(5965)3, "Guanyu choushe Xiangtan zhongyang gangtiechang zhi bangyue" [On the agreement to establish the Central Steel Works at Xiangtan], June 1936. On the selection of sites for the "national defense center," see Wang Dezhong, "Lun Woguo kangzhang 'guofang zhongxin' de xuanze yu xingcheng" [On the selection and formation of the "national defense center" during the war of resistance], *Minguo dang'an* [Republican archives], no. 1 (1995): 62–70.

90. SASS, NRC 47 (4) 0007, Weng Wenhao, "Guofang sheji weiyuanhui zhi mudi ji shuoming" [Goals and clarification of the National Defense Planning Commission], December 1932; SASS, NRC 47 (2) 0018, Weng Wenhao, "Guofang gongye chubu jihua caoan, 1933–1934" [Draft preliminary plan for national defense industry]; SHA 47(32) "Canmo benbu Guofang sheji weiyuanhui mishuting gongzuo baogao" [Work report by the secretariat of the National Defense Planning Commission under the general staff (for 1934)].

91. The fullest documentary description is in SHA 28(5965), "Zhonggongye jianshe jihua shuomingshu" [Explanation of the plan for heavy industries] (1936).

92. William McNeill, *The Pursuit of Power: Technology, Armed Force, and Society since A.D. 1000* (Chicago: University of Chicago Press, 1982), 345.

93. Hong Qingyu, "Sanxia gongcheng qianqi gongzuo" [Early stages of the Three Gorges Project], *Zhongguo keji shiliao* [Historical materials of Chinese science and technol-

ogy] 8, no. 3 (1987): 3–10; Huang Shangzuo, "Minguo shiqi kaifa changjiang sanxia shuili ziliao chouhua shimo" [Complete story of planning the Three Gorges project in the Republican era], *Zhongguo keji shiliao* [Historical materials of Chinese science and technology] 5, no. 3 (1984): 19–27.

94. See William Kirby, "Continuity and Change in Modern China: Chinese Economic Planning on the Mainland and on Taiwan, 1943–1958," *Australian Journal of Chinese Affairs* 24 (July 1990).

95. Author's interviews with Qian Changzhao, Cao Liying, Yun Zhen, Sun Yunxuan, Huang Hui, Xie Peihe, 1988–93. See, for example, *Xiangtan dianjichang, 1936–1986* [Xiangtan electrical machinery plant, 1936–1986] (Xiangtan: Yiangtan dianjichang, 1986), 1–5, a fifty-year retrospective; Zheng Youkui et al., *Jiu Zhongguo Ziyuan weiyuanhui* [NRC of Old China] (Shanghai: Shanghai shehui kexueyuan, 1991), 302–15; and also Xue Yuexun, "Ziyuan weiyuanhui de rencai peixun" [NRC's nurturing of talent], *Guoshiguan guankan* [Journal of the Academia Historica], no. 50, 183–214.

96. See Kees Gispen, *New Profession, Old Order: Engineers and German Society* (Cambridge: Cambridge University Press, 1989), 49.

97. Kendall E. Bailes, *Technology and Society under Lenin and Stalin: Origins of the Soviet Technical Intelligentsia, 1917–1941* (Princeton: Princeton University Press, 1978), 15, 418. On engineering and social mobility in the U.S.S.R. (which would make an intriguing study in the Chinese case) see Harley Balzer, "Engineers: The Rise and Decline of a Social Myth," in *Science and the Soviet Social Order,* ed. Loren R. Graham (Cambridge: Harvard University Press, 1990), 141–67.

98. William Kirby, "The Chinese War Economy: Mobilization, Control, and Planning in Nationalist China," in *China's Bitter Victory: The War with Japan, 1937–1945,* ed. Steven I. Levine and James C. Hsiung (New York: M. E. Sharpe, 1992).

99. Douglas S. Paauw, "The KMT and Economic Stagnation, 1928–1937," *Journal of Asian Studies* 16, no. 2 (1957): 214.

100. L. L. Lorin, *The Problem of Economic Planning* (n.p., 1931), 31, cited in G. Chen, "Chinese Government Economic Planning and Reconstruction," in *Problems of the Pacific, 1933,* ed. B. Lasker and W. L. Holland (Chicago: University of Chicago Press, 1934), 382.

101. For example, in the corporatist representation of professional interests in proposed provincial constitutions of the early Republic. See Marie-Claire Bergère, "The Chinese Bourgeoisie," in *The Cambridge History of China,* vol. 12, pt. 1 (Cambridge: Cambridge University Press, 1983), 779–80; Sie Ying-chow, *Le fédéralisme en Chine* (Paris, 1924).

102. See Kirby, "Continuity and Change." If this approach is correct, it of course questions the assumption of Vivienne Shue's stimulating discussion of the modern Chinese state, that the Republican era was "profoundly unstable and hostile to economic and political institutionalization." See Shue, *The Reach of the State: Sketches of the Chinese Body Politic* (Stanford: Stanford University Press, 1988), 104.

103. Bailes, *Technology,* 459.

104. Space precludes an extended discussion of definitions of "technocracy" here. For one approach in a contemporary Chinese context, see Li Cheng and Lynn White, "Elite Transformation and Modern Change in Mainland China and Taiwan: Empirical Data and the Theory of Technocracy," *China Quarterly* 121 (March 1990): 1–35.

FIVE

Hierarchical Modernization: Tianjin's Gong Shang College as a Model for Catholic Community in North China

Richard Madsen

As practiced by ordinary Chinese Catholics today, the Catholic religion in north China abounds in paradoxes. On the one hand, it seems profoundly antimodern, sacralizing and idealizing the values of rural life. Most of the devout Catholics whom my colleague Fan Lizhu and I interviewed in Hebei Province in 1993 expressed their commitment by rejecting not only Marxism but much of modern science, as well as modern commerce. They warned their children against any claims of natural science, especially theories of evolution, that would contradict a literal reading of the Bible. As a thirty-three-year-old priest put it, "The education our youth have received [in government-run schools] is materialistic and atheistic. Where do people come from? Does God create people or do people create God? Do people come from monkeys? Never!"

They are also opposed to many of the values of the modern market economy. Says the leader of a village Catholic association, "I agree with what our bishop said [in his Christmas sermon yesterday]: 'Blessed are the poor.' The purpose of living in the world is not to seek enjoyment.... Catholic teaching is contrary to human desires. I'm not opposed to making money by working hard. But I feel confused about how to reconcile making money with obeying the teaching of God. I always teach my children not to be too greedy." Finally, the "true believers" among the Catholics were often opposed to urbanization. As a woman studying to be a nun put it, "If Catholics live outside the village, they will forget God, because no one will remind them."[1]

In the first half of this century, however, north China was the home of some of the most progressive thinkers in twentieth-century Catholicism. For example, one of the priests attached to the same French Jesuit community that inculcated the conservative ideas quoted above, was Pierre Teilhard de Chardin, the great Jesuit paleontologist and theologian who boldly and controversially attempted to reconcile modern theories of evolution with Catholic theology.[2]

The conservative rural Catholics whom I quoted above lived in Hebei's Xian county, which even today is 97 percent Catholic and the site of one of the greatest concentrations of Catholics in China. Xian county had been evangelized by French Jesuits from the province of Champagne beginning in the mid-1800s. The Catholic vicariate of Xian county was the center of French Jesuit missionary activity in north China. Although most of the French Jesuits were confined to the rural villages of Xian county, the Xian county Jesuit community also ran an institution for higher education, Gong Shang College (College of Industry and Commerce), in Tianjin, about four hours by car from the famous cathedral in Zhangzhuang, which was the spiritual center of Xian county. It was at this college—one of only three Catholic colleges in China—where Teilhard de Chardin resided and where in 1939 he composed his most famous theological essay, *The Phenomenon of Man*. The bishop of Xian county today, Bishop Liu Dinghan, who gave the sermon about the blessedness of the poor cited above, received his vocation while attending that college. Although run by the Jesuits of the Xian county community, that college appears at first glance to have represented a vision of modernity completely opposite to that of the antiurban, antiscientific, and anticommercial vision of the rural Catholics in Xian county.[3]

The college was devoted to educating the sons of the *bonne bourgeoisie* of Tianjin in the subjects of commerce and engineering. In the 1930s, it published a weekly newspaper, *Daoguang*, which propagated popular science and celebrated modern trends around the world. And it was connected with the world renowned, Jesuit-run Beijiang Museum, which was the research base of Frs. Pierre Licent and Pierre Teilhard de Chardin.

In their rural base, then, the Jesuits tried to protect Catholics from modernity, while in their urban outpost they tried to prepare Catholics for modernity. The French Jesuits did not seem to see any inconsistency in the two approaches. But how could such different approaches be part of the same Catholic community?

The answer lies in a traditional European Catholic understanding of community. The kind of European Catholicism brought to China in the early twentieth century shared with most Protestant and even secular Europeans a commitment to modern science, technology, and industry, but it possessed a different conception of community, a conception more consistent with traditional Chinese views than with Protestant or secular views. Built on individualistic assumptions, these latter—which are by and large still the views of modern Western social science— see community as based on common beliefs: a community is a group of individuals who cooperate with one another because they share the same ideas and interests.[4] If one defines community in this way, it would be difficult to see how the rural Catholics of Xian county with their antimodern ideas could be part of the same religious community as the sophisticated urban Catholics connected with the Jesuit college in Tianjin.

But the Counter-Reformation church brought to China by European missionaries in the nineteenth century defined itself less as a community based on shared ideas than as one based on status within a common hierarchical authority. A person could be a Catholic in perfectly good standing without knowing much doctrine, and Catholics from different social levels with different levels of education could have very different ways of understanding their faith. Furthermore, Catholics could in practice adhere to many different moral standards, because the community inevitably contained a wide array of saints and sinners as well as ordinary flawed people with mixtures of good and bad qualities. There were fervent Catholics and lax Catholics, but lax Catholics were still Catholics as long as they did not completely reject the authority of the church. To be a Catholic, then, was not primarily a matter of intellectual belief or even of virtue, but of living under a chain of authority that descended from the pope down through the episcopacy to local parish priests. This was, moreover, a view of hierarchical community that was still imbued with the aspirations of Christendom. The church would make society whole by integrating all social institutions with its divinely constituted hierarchy.[5]

Sociologically, this hierarchically integrated community could take very different forms, depending on the social ecology within which it was implanted. A crucial factor affecting the forms that the Catholic community took was how it maintained its boundaries—what did its leaders think they had to do in order to protect their flock from those parts of the world that the church could no longer control? The ways in which the French Jesuits ran their school in Tianjin were determined, I argue in this essay, by their perceived need to maintain effective boundaries between their school and a rapidly changing, secular urban environment. They perceived this need because they accepted the assumptions of Counter-Reformation European Catholicism that it was the mission of the church to bring as many social institutions as possible under the sway of an ecclesiastical hierarchy—in effect, to re-create medieval Christendom. And insofar as it could not do this, the church should effectively seal off from the non-Catholic world those parts of society under its embrace. The urban environment of the first half of this century posed special challenges to this form of mission. Perhaps unintentionally, this paternalistic, defensive conception of mission reinforced hierarchical and paternalistic tendencies within Chinese culture and thus contributed to a distinctive Chinese way of responding to the challenges of modernity.

In telling this story, I hope to add some complexity to standard accounts of the ways in which Chinese became modern in the twentieth century. Insofar as modernization has meant *some* degree of Westernization, we must recognize that the "West" is enormously diverse, Western culture extremely variegated, and Western visions of modernity often contradictory. Chinese who wanted to modernize by emulating the West had many different Wests to choose from. The religious, cultural, and social models presented by the French Jesuits in north China were clearly different from those presented by, say, liberal Protestant universities like Yanjing. A Chinese alumnus of Beijing's Yanjing University recently remarked, "When we visited the [Catholic] Fu Ren University [which was in fact less conservative than Gong Shang College], we used to say that it was like going from capitalism to feudalism."[6]

Moreover, in the changing contexts of the first half of this century, the Western models evolved in ways that their proponents could not have anticipated, the Chinese reactions to them took forms that neither Chinese nor Westerners could have foreseen, and this led to patterns of meaning and configurations of social structure that no one could have envisioned.

BOUNDARY MAINTENANCE
IN COUNTRYSIDE AND CITY

According to the Counter-Reformation model of Catholic life that was seemingly adhered to by most of the French Jesuits who established Gong Shang College, church authority should ideally be intertwined with all the major social institutions that constituted a Catholic's environment. The church should control the major schools and newspapers, it should patronize the arts, it should be connected with the political authorities, and it should have enough economic power to sustain its cultural institutions and to be the chief source of help for the poor and sick. Catholic missions in rural China tried to realize this "integralist" ecclesiastical vision. It was not enough to convert individuals. The church had to build whole social environments that were under the authority of ecclesiastical hierarchies. So missionaries strove to create whole villages, or at least whole lineages within a village, that were Catholic. And when they were really successful, as the Jesuits were in Xian county, they created a whole region in which all major aspects of life were dominated by the Catholic Church. Even today, in Xian county almost every village is marked by a church spire. Before the Communists took power, almost all elementary schooling was in church-run schools, health care was provided by a Catholic clinic, and economic aid in time of disaster was provided by church-dispensed charity. Local political leaders were Catholics. Local social life revolved around the church. Catholics were under great pressure to marry fellow Catholics. Church festivals provided the most important community activities. To be a Catholic, the people of Xian county say even today, is to live in the "world of God."[7]

In Xian county, the boundaries of that world were fixed by a natural rural social ecology. It was easier to meet most of one's economic, social, and cultural needs by dealing with fellow Catholics than with non-Christians. The major marketing center for the region was in the town of Zhangzhuang, which was also the site of an imposing cathedral.[8] In the compound surrounding this cathedral were concentrated the major cultural and social welfare institutions of the county, all under church control: a seminary, a famous Catholic library, a convent, a clinic, elementary and middle schools, and a Catholic cemetery renowned for its excellent *fengshui*. These physical spaces were infused by the rhythms of religious time, marked by daily prayer and Sunday Sabbath observance, by great periodic community festivals like Christmas, Easter, Pentecost, and the Feast of the Assumption of Mary, and by Catholic life-cycle rituals of baptism, confirmation, matrimony, and burial. Since the county was almost exclusively Catholic, residents could be put under considerable social pressure if they sought to fulfill economic or political ambitions that would be against the interests of the Catholic majority. In such an ecological niche, the boundaries between the world of God and the world of non-Christians were clear and secure.[9]

Inevitably, though, when the church sought a Catholic presence in a city like Tianjin, the boundaries between church and world could not be defined in such a clear way. But for all the surface differences between the Catholic life centered on the Jesuit college in Tianjin and the villages of Xian county, there was a fundamental similarity in understanding of Catholic community. As in the villages of Xian county, the Jesuits strove to build a world of God in which as many aspects of life as possible were assumed under the authority of the church. Catholic students, future leaders of society, would study together in a school controlled by the Fathers, live together in dormitories supervised by the Fathers, worship together in a school chapel at mass celebrated by the Fathers. But the boundaries between this world and the non-Christian world were perforce more ambiguous. The Catholic students would have to attend classes together with non-Christian students, for it was neither economically nor politically possible to construct a college solely for Catholic students. The college itself would have to be part of a larger system of non-Catholic academic institutions. To survive and flourish it had to interact constantly with non-Catholic political authorities and to gain the support of non-Catholic social elites. As a modern institute of higher learning it had to teach about ideas in natural and social science, not to mention literature and philosophy, that had been developed by non-Catholics. The challenge faced by the Jesuits was how to keep this non-Catholic social and cultural environment from loosening the grip of church authority on the fledgling urban Catholic community. In other words, how would they maintain the boundaries between the educated Chinese Catholic community and the non-Catholic community? The nature of this challenge was constantly changing as the political and social environment of the college changed.

The twenty-seven-year history of the Jesuit college in Tianjin can be divided into three periods, each characterized by a different way of maintaining the boundaries between this part of the Chinese Catholic community and the non-Christian world. From internal documents written by the French Jesuits for their superiors and supporters, we get a sense of how they tried to preserve their school's Catholic identity by building different kinds of barriers between church and world to adapt to different circumstances. From school yearbooks and catalogues, we can get a sense of how the Jesuit attempt to preserve a Catholic identity influenced the ways in which both Catholic and non-Catholic members of the school—students, faculty, and alumni—constructed their Chinese identities.[10]

L'INSTITUT DES HAUTES ETUDES INDUSTRIELLES
ET COMMERCIALES DE TIENTSIN

The official name of the school changed in the course of its history. Eventually, in 1933, when it was officially accredited by the Nanjing government's Ministry of Education, it was called *Tianjin gong shang xue yuan,* which in English documents of the time was rendered as "Tientsin Kung Shang College." But in its first years, the school's official name was not a Chinese but a French name, L'Institut des Hautes Etudes Industrielles et Commerciales de Tientsin. The school was a *French* school in China, not a *Chinese* school founded and maintained by French priests. It was by socializing Chinese into French culture—and preparing them for jobs in French-run government or commercial agencies—that the Jesuits hoped to separate them from their non-Christian Chinese world and bring them into the hierarchical embrace of the church.

In 1919, the papal encyclical *Maximum Ilud* had warned missionaries about the dangers of identifying their faith with their country,[11] but the French Jesuits in the 1920s still resisted the warning. Ever since the mid–nineteenth century, the French government had been the official protector of Catholic missions in China, using gunboats if necessary to defend the right of Catholic missionaries to evangelize, and expecting in return missionary support for French imperialistic interests. In the mentality of the French Jesuits, it seemed indeed as if God spoke French. In a publicity statement (probably written for the French press) issued from the school in 1924, its first year of operation, the Jesuits emphasized the role of the French language in their curriculum: "Of six hours of class every day, three are devoted to French. . . . The assignments in the other courses tend gradually to be done in French. Later the courses in the upper division [facultes superieures] are given in French. As a matter of fact, in all of north China, the Institut des Hautes Etudes is the *only* French establishment giving *secondary* education to Chinese students."[12] This was important as a counterweight to the predominant influence of "Anglo-Saxons" in north China. "In the big cities of the North, there are a number of large educational establishments directed by Anglo-Saxons. The American influence is considerable. . . . English is extremely prevalent in the ruling class. A course in English is obligatory in middle schools; in the Universities, teaching is given in English. French is being placed on a lower level."

The press release concluded with an appeal for French government subsidies: "An enterprise like this cannot be crowned with success without the help of the French government. . . . Obviously we do not seek any personal profit. It seems good that this work is to the great benefit of France." The Far Eastern branch of the French Chamber of Commerce stated what kind of benefit was envisioned. French business in China needed Chinese managers and engineers who could speak French and were familiar with French ways of working. And the French commercial attaché in China wrote, "Above all, the best agent of French propaganda in China is a *technical* school of French education," just like the one the Jesuits were establishing (emphasis in the original).

Of course, the ultimate purpose of the school was not supposed to be political or commercial, but religious. As the Jesuits saw it, the main problem with the Anglo-Saxon schools was that they taught Protestantism. The Protestants were making a huge effort in Chinese higher education and had gained a great deal of influence in government establishments. Although they had achieved "minimal success in terms of changing hearts," they had gained "considerable . . . prestige among the learned classes." Unfortunately, however, "among the upper classes, Catholicism seems to be the religion of the poor and ignorant, in spite of its brilliant role under Kangxi. It is essential to demonstrate to people who take legitimate pride in their ancient civilization and who prize new progress that the Catholic religion is capable of surpassing every other religion in the domain of spiritual culture and moral formation." Besides counteracting the unfortunate influence of Anglo-Saxon Protestants, the school was urgently needed to defend against the even more baleful influence of secularism. The state universities were having a "deplorable influence on the future leaders of China." "Atheism, rationalism, Bolshevism—every sort of unfortunate fruit is found in the new education."[13]

As early as 1910, the Jesuit superior of the province of Champagne had visited Xian county and recommended the creation of such a school. Instability in China and the world war in Europe delayed these plans. But by 1919, the Jesuits received a charge from the Vatican's Sacred Congregation for the Propagation of the Faith (Propaganda Fidei) to construct an institution of higher learning in Tianjin for children of the upper classes (*pro filiis nobilium*). The need now seemed urgent. The influence of both Anglo-Saxon Protestants and secularist Chinese had increased since the Great War.[14]

Thus, the Institut des Hautes Etudes was finally established on Tianjin's Racecourse Road in the autumn of 1923. Although commonly called "Hautes Etudes," the school actually began as a college preparatory upper-middle school and then expanded to include genuine higher-level education, housed in a handsome stone building set in a neatly tended, walled-in campus. In the school's first year of operation, the student body consisted of fifty students, all but three coming either from "Mandarin families" or commercial and banking circles. "Our vision," wrote the Jesuits, "is to attend to the intellectual elite of the country."[15] In practice, they seem to have identified "intellectual elite" with "social elite."

Established concurrently was the Institute of Research in Natural Science, staffed by Frs. Licent and Teilhard de Chardin and including the Beijiang Museum of Natural History. (In a conference held to celebrate the establishment, Teilhard lectured on a special research project he was carrying out for the museum in collaboration with French scientific circles.)[16] Although Fr. Licent said that the students of the Institut de Hautes Etudes would be the primary beneficiaries of the museum and research institute, the students in fact seemed to have had rather little direct relationship with the latter. Frs. Licent and Teilhard did not teach classes in the school. Although students who were studying geology could use the library and perhaps some of the lab facilities of the museum, their curriculum did not include much of the pure science that was the museum's specialty.[17] The main benefit that the museum brought to the school was reflected prestige. The museum became world renowned. Frs. Licent and Teilhard both eventually won international honors, including awards from the French and Belgian governments and from the Japanese government. Their fame may have indirectly helped the school by attracting the attention of would-be donors.

The academic structure of the school was thus hierarchical in a way that reflected the logic of the church's religious hierarchy. At the top was a research institute, staffed by committed Jesuit priests, that was engaged in pioneering dialogue with the most advanced levels of secular scientific thought. Under this was a school whose students and faculty had little contact with the potentially heretical ideas being explored by the institute. The Jesuits at the research institute patrolled the boundary between the church and the world and potentially even risked their faith in the process. Underneath them, less advanced students were kept segregated from such dangerous activities while benefiting from the intellectual shelter provided by their superiors.

The "Catholicity" of the Institut des Hautes Etudes was assured by the composition of its faculty—six French priests, one Italian layman, and four Chinese alumni of the Jesuit Aurora University in Shanghai. The initial student body was not so predominantly Catholic, however. Only about one-fourth were members of the church. In accordance with Vatican regulations, the Catholic students lived in a special dormitory and even used a study hall separate from that of the non-Catholics, although Catholics and non-Catholics attended classes together.[18] The school thus protected its Catholics from the world by providing a place where they could be segregated from non-Christian influences under the watchful eye of the Fathers—but one in which they could also be prepared to engage with the world by interacting with a relatively safe buffer population of fellow students who were non-Christian but Francophone and presumably Francophile.

Besides French, the curriculum contained the standard courses of a European-style upper-middle school: mathematics, philosophy, physics, geography, Chinese literature, design, and typing. As the school expanded into higher education, it specialized in business management and a variety of types of engineering. The only place where Catholic teaching might be directly inserted in the curriculum was in the philosophy course, which dealt—it seems in an orthodox, Catholic Thomistic fashion—with "liberty, responsibility, conscience, and moral practice."[19] The view of the French Jesuits seemed to be that what constituted a Catholic education for upper-class Chinese was not mainly the content of the curriculum, but the formal structure of the institution within which the curriculum was enacted. It was hierarchical, with priests at the top. It was French, with people of French nationality in charge and with most of the non-French faculty members having been educated in French universities. Moreover, the French language was at the center of instruction. The Jesuits seemed to assume that even without imparting any formal religious instruction, a hierarchical, clerically controlled, French institution would transmit the true faith because it was the very embodiment of that faith.

The most important sign that students were being receptive to that true faith would be that they converted to Catholicism. Only a relative few did. The first convert was baptized in 1927, three years after the school was established, and after that, even as the numbers of students expanded to over a thousand, only a handful of students were baptized every year. (Overall, however, about 25 percent of the student body was Catholic, mostly from old Catholic families around Tianjin. This was a higher percentage than the percentage of Protestants in typical Protestant universities.)[20] But even though most students remained non-Catholic, the Jesuits still pointed to the school spirit as evidence that students were being influenced for the better by the Catholic faith. One of the most admirable characteristics of the students, the Jesuits thought, was their docility: "The work is serious. Discipline is imposed without difficulty. We like the students' docility, their good spirit, their respectful deference to their teachers."[21]

During the nationalist movement of 1925, the students at the Institut des Hautes Etudes remained calm and refrained from participation in the agitation sweeping intellectuals throughout the country. This quiescence set a standard for the school. Students from the Institut des Hautes Etudes refrained from actively participating in all of the great movements in the Republican era. In college yearbooks, the students themselves expressed pride in this lack of activism. Even for non-Catholic students, it was a mark of the well-disciplined character of their school.

In its very institutional structures, then, the Institut des Hautes Etudes embodied a common early-twentieth-century European understanding of the nature of the Catholic faith and the mission of the church in the world, a vision of faith and mission that was firmly rooted in sixteenth-century Counter-Reformation theology. In that vision, Catholic faith and practice were virtually identified with submission to a clerical hierarchy. To bring people into the Catholic faith was to bring them under the scope of this hierarchy and cultivate within them the virtues that made obedience to hierarchical authorities easy. Furthermore, the faith was deeply identified with national Catholic cultures. In countries like France, where much of the population was abandoning Catholic practice, the Catholic hierarchy often identified the essence of Catholicism with those aspects of national culture that resisted revolution and modern social change.

In this vision, however, not all kinds of revolution and all kinds of modern social change were bad. A revolution such as had occurred in China might be good if it swept away conservative leaders who resisted being influenced by Christianity. Basically, revolution was bad if it diminished the power of ecclesiastical authorities, good if it opened the possibility of extending such power. Social change resulting from advances in science, technology, and industry was by no means bad in itself. The church supported institutions of higher learning such as the

Institut des Hautes Etudes in order to contribute to such advances. But these were potentially bad if they increased human pride, which took the form of decreasing respect for the natural hierarchies of life—which could eventually lead, of course, to disobeying ecclesiastical hierarchies.

Consonant with this vision, it was salutary to offer a clerically supervised higher education to *filiis nobilium*. The scientific parts of this education might enable them to contribute to the progress of their societies; the humanistic parts might enable them to provide sophisticated leadership in complex societies; the moral parts might nurture a spirit of noblesse oblige. But it might not be good to broadly offer lower-class people the same kind of education. The scientific and technological parts of such education might too quickly raise their expectations and make them dissatisfied with their place in life. The humanistic parts might confuse them and render them skeptical about the moral verities that sustained them within their families and communities.

As long as one accepts the hierarchical view of life central to Counter-Reformation European Catholicism, the French Jesuits were not being inconsistent in promoting an antiscientific, unreflexive folk piety in Xian county and a modern scientific education in Tianjin. Different classes of people should have different kinds of knowledge, different levels of sophistication in the understanding of the faith. In fact, these very differences reinforced one of the most important bulwarks of the Catholic faith, a healthy respect for hierarchy.

Catholicism of the kind propagated by the French Jesuits in north China in the 1920s and 1930s was antimodern only in an ambivalent, ironic sense. It in fact helped develop some of the principal institutions of modernization—science, technology, and industry—and it encouraged its believers to contribute to the building of a modern Chinese state. At the same time, though, it maintained an unmodern ideology. Unlike mainline Protestantism or Deweyan liberalism or revolutionary Marxism, it did not encourage, in principle or in practice, a flattening of hierarchies, an approval of social mobility, or a generalized skepticism of traditional authorities. It accepted as natural the deep cultural differences between city and countryside. Its solution to problems posed by such differences was not to try to make everybody the same but to encourage everybody to be satisfied with their station in life. The poor were to be helped by the moral responsibility inculcated in the rich. As long as men were kept aware that they do not live by bread alone, all would be benefited by the material goods made possible through scientific and economic progress.

In the first stage of the existence of the Institut des Hautes Etudes, this traditional, hierarchical vision of Catholicism was seen as virtually inseparable from French culture, at least conservative strands within that culture. By the 1930s, however, a new stage in the life of the school began. The Republic of China was finally gaining enough strength and coherence to set the terms under which foreign educational institutions could work in China. The Institut des Hautes Etudes could no longer be a French institution on Chinese soil. It had to become a Chinese institution, registered with the state and adhering to Chinese government educational standards. Moreover, the influence of French culture steadily declined because of a lack of French priests available to staff the institution and a lack of funds from depression-ridden France to sustain it.

Under these circumstances, the Jesuits had to confront the question of how to preserve the Institut's Catholic character while discarding its French character. This involved refining their view of what were the boundaries between the Catholic community and the world. As they did so, their changing vision interacted with changing aspirations of the Chinese students who were attracted to the school.

GONG SHANG COLLEGE

The first part of the school's French identity to be diminished was its devotion to the French language. Students would be attracted to a school that used French as its principal language of instruction, it had been thought, because they would have special access to jobs as engineers for the French-owned railroads or as managers in the French commercial houses. But in north China, the political and economic power of France was waning. As a "Note on French Influence in the Tianjin Institute" observed in 1933, "Railroads that utilize French-speaking engineers have gone into Chinese hands. As far as commerce is concerned, even in the French houses, there is not much place for people who speak only French and no English." Moreover, in the middle schools that were the primary source of recruitment to the Institut des Hautes Etudes, the primary foreign language was English, not French. Therefore, the primacy of the French language was "paralyzing the development of the school."

For a way out of this problem, the Jesuits solicited the opinions of competent persons, "in particular members of the French colony [*sic*]." They agreed that "English [not Chinese!] was the language of commercial affairs and industry in China." The Jesuits decided, therefore, that they had to adopt English as the school's principal foreign language. "If an evil, this is a necessary evil."[22]

They took great pains, however, to assure their French friends and supporters—and perhaps to assure themselves as well—that, even without the language, the school would still purvey French culture. The school would still use "French methods, French books, translated into English or Chinese[,] . . . Chinese professors trained in France, and a total system of general education completely different from the American system of departments and the Chinese system, which is a copy of the American." The school had a reputation of being French, and the students who came to it demanded, "if not an education in French, at least the education of France."[23]

The school could maintain a French-style education, however, only if it controlled the shape of its curriculum. In 1933, this capacity, too, was taken away. The school was forced to seek accreditation under the Nanjing government's Ministry of Education, and to gain accreditation it had to structure its curriculum in accord with Nanjing's educational system—which was, really, as the French Jesuits noted with displeasure, the "systeme Americain."

At first the Jesuits were reluctant about seeking accreditation from Nanjing. From the beginning they had prided themselves on the independence of their school from Chinese political control—though not from French government approval and support. As a condition for Chinese government approval, they would have to appoint a Chinese president and a Chinese prefect of studies and ensure "equal treatment for Chinese personnel." Furthermore they would have to officially register the school's name—a Chinese name—with the Ministry of Education. The formal control of the school would pass from French to Chinese hands, and the formal identity of the school would become Chinese.[24]

In the long run, though, there was no way to resist the need for accreditation. Without official recognition for their degrees, the students could not get jobs in Chinese organizations. Though they could get jobs in foreign firms, these were gradually being taken over by the Chinese; and it was clear that the days of the foreign concessions were numbered. The French Jesuits would be acting within a world in which they could no longer rely on French culture to provide the buffer separating their Catholic community from the non-Catholic world. Finally, the argument for accreditation was sealed by appeal to political and ecclesiastical authority: "the French foreign ministry recommends it"; and Cardinal Constantini, the Vatican's Apostolic Delegate to China, approved it. Thus in 1934, the school was duly registered in Nanjing under the name Gong Shang College.

In the thinking of the French Jesuit missionaries, however, the school could fulfill its religious mission only if it were at least informally under French clerical control. To facilitate the accreditation, they had named as president a Chinese Jesuit with a doctorate in philosophy from Louvain, Fr. Francis Xavier Zhao Zhensheng. Fr. Zhao was chosen, the official Jesuit history says, "to *legally* represent the Institut in its official relationships."[25] From the tone of their discussion, it seems clear that this talented Chinese priest was only a figurehead. The person really in charge of the college was not the president, but the rector, Fr. Rene Charvet. Once accreditation was granted, Fr. Zhao was replaced as legal president by a Mr. Hua, who had been working in the service of one of the French priests, was "well in the hand" of this priest, had been educated in France, and was a "Francophile."[26] The French Jesuits remained firmly in control of the college.

But their ability to exercise their control gradually waned, not because of anything the Chinese government did, but because of a lack of Jesuit personnel and funds from France. Although the lack of funds caused by the depression in Europe was serious, even more serious was the lack of manpower. Even as the Gong Shang College had expanded in size and complexity—in the 1930s, for instance, it added departments of architecture and chemical engineering—fewer Jesuits were available for the mission in China. Out of fifty faculty members, only six were Jesuits. A report written in 1937 by Fr. Pollet, the vice rector, noted that only 33 out of 323 hours of instruction given weekly was given by Jesuits. All too often, students were "abandoned into the hands of untrustworthy laity."[27] Priests like Fr. Pollet seemed to have the idea that what now made their education Catholic was simply the presence of a French Jesuit giving instruction. Even if a priest taught engineering or some such subject with no direct religious content, his very presence would ensure a significant connection between the ecclesiastical hierarchy and the academic institution.

The attenuation of priestly influence now meant, Fr. Pollet thought, that the school had to be more discriminating in the work that it undertook. When the Jesuits first established their Institut des Hautes Etudes, they were unclear as to their goals. Now they had to define more clearly what they were about. For instance, the college had recently added a department of civil engineering, even though there were no Jesuits trained as civil engineers to be part of such a department. Should they refrain from adding new departments if there were no priests to be part of the staff?

In response, Fr. Charvet, who served several stints as rector of the college, wrote that the addition of new departments should be based on national need rather than simply the availability of a priest. For instance, it was important for the college to have a chemical engineering department, even though there were no Jesuits available who were trained in that field. Chemical engineering was important for the development of Chinese industry—for making Chinese products meet international standards.[28] It seems that Fr. Charvet's view prevailed.

What was going on in this debate was a further shift in the Jesuits' understanding of how they should draw the boundaries between their Catholic academic community and the world. Now that the distinction could no longer be based on French culture, it was based more exclusively on French clerical authority. The school was Catholic not because it formally taught much that was distinctively Catholic and not even because it inculcated a way of life that made its students visibly different from non-Catholics. It was Catholic because it was controlled by priests, who were themselves under the authority of the Catholic hierarchy.

This way of thinking can be understood in terms of the sociological distinction made by Ernst Troeltsch between *church* and *sect*. These two forms of religious life have contrasting styles of origination justified by contrasting ways of thought.[29] The mentality of the French Jesuits in charge of Gong Shang College was typical of that in Troeltsch's model of a church.

Unlike the ideal typical sect, which is an exclusive group of active believers out to change the world, the church is an inclusive institution that conforms to the world. The leaders of a sect would deem themselves successful to the degree that they get all of the members of the sect to fervently believe and practice its common teachings. The leaders of a church would not expect all of the church members to be fervent believers, because the church is inclusive—it embraces good and bad people alike. The success of the church is measured by how many people it brings within its realm. As long as they are within that realm, some bad people will become good, some indifferent people will become faithful. But this will happen in God's own time through the mysterious grace of God. If few people become fervent believers and fewer become saintly, that is not the fault of the leaders of the church. They will have done their part simply by expanding the sphere of influence of the church, even if this entails making compromises with the world. In the mentality of Counter-Reformation Catholicism—which was a typical example of the sociological model of a church—this sphere of influence was conceived of in an even more authoritarian way than before. It was desirable that members of the clergy live exemplary lives and be able to influence the laity by personal inspiration, but it was not essential. What was essential was subsumption under duly constituted ecclesiastical authority. Even when the Gong Shang College could not provide enough priests to exert direct personal influence on its students, it could at least claim that it brought them within the scope of an institution connected at the top to ecclesiastical structures.

But without French cultural or political influence to back up their ecclesiastical authority, the priests had to work harder to patrol the boundary between the Catholic community and world. In the meantime, it became easier for Chinese currents of culture and politics to pour into the school. To an ever greater degree, in other words, Chinese students shaped the school for their own purposes. Nonetheless, they could never completely ignore the boundaries established and still shakily maintained by the Jesuits. The school amplified certain aspects of Chinese culture and dampened others.

Whether they were Catholic or non-Catholic, did the kinds of students attracted to Gong Shang College tend to understand their identity and role in society in ways different from students who attended Protestant or state-run schools? The best available source to consult in order to assess student mentalities is the annual yearbooks issued by the school—I have editions from 1937, 1939, 1940, 1948, and 1950. Like yearbooks in American colleges, these were edited by graduating seniors, under the supervision of some faculty members—usually including, in the case of Gong Shang College, one of the priests. However, the entries have a freshness, a naïveté, a spontaneity that suggest they represent authentic attitudes.

One of the most striking qualities of the yearbooks is what they leave out. There is hardly any mention of religion. Even on the pages of pictures of the school, there is hardly anything—perhaps only a single small picture of a statue of the Blessed Virgin in a campus grotto—that would suggest the college was a religious school. In the 1937 yearbook (published in June, just a month before the outbreak of war with Japan) students each state what person they most admire and wish to emulate. Twenty out of forty-eight students mention Chiang Kai-shek. A half dozen mention Sun Yat-sen. Some invoke foreigners like Thomas Edison and Abraham Lincoln. A few cite Confucius or Zhuangzi. Only one says Jesus.[30]

The yearbooks have more to say about morality, but it is not very profound. They are prefaced with platitudinous moral exhortations from the Jesuits. For example, Fr. Pollet, then serving as dean of studies, urges, "Believe what you think to be true. Do what you think to be right." A commencement speech by one of the Jesuits talks of the need to subordinate the "small self" to the "big self" of the community. Students write that they have learned that having a strong moral character is just as important as having knowledge.[31]

Socially, the students seem naive and sheltered. Consider their accounts of the two months of military training mandated by the Nanjing government, at a military camp near Baoding during the 1936–37 school year. The Jesuits were unhappy with this requirement—concerned about the disruption to the academic year, worried about how the students would suffer from being away from home and living in primitive conditions, and anxious about temptations to the Catholic students' faith and morals. But many of the students seemed to have found this training to be one of the most meaningful experiences of their lives. The yearbook contains a long essay describing one student's experience, and there are a number of shorter references to the training. It is apparent from these accounts that most of the students had never traveled far from home, and certainly not lived in the countryside. They are moved by the poverty and primitive living conditions of the countryside. The long essay describes at great length the barracks, bathing facilities, and meals at the military camp, which were considerably harsher (though probably not nearly as harsh as most peasant accommodations) than anything the writer had experienced before. But the students felt that they gained tremendous benefits from this training. It had toughened their bodies, strengthened their wills, and given them a patriotic way of thinking. One of the students wrote a poem upon reaching a summit after a day's march: "Who says that north China produces traitors and running dogs. / *We* are still the sons of China who will construct China. / Sleep! / We will use our blood and sweat to cleanse away our fatherland's shame. / Don't forget! / This is a day to remember." Several accounts spoke of the students weeping bitterly when the training was over.[32]

In this extracurricular training, the students gained a toughness and a patriotic determination that their college had not provided. When they expressed their aspirations in the 1937 yearbook, the graduating seniors now talked in the nationalistic, patriotic terms that most of their young contemporaries would have used on the eve of the Sino-Japanese War. One difference between the patriotism developed at Gong Shang College and that expressed in places like Yanjing or Beida, however, was that the Gong Shang students were less willing to take matters into their own hands; they did not want to challenge duly constituted government authority.

For instance, according to a student narrative of the principal events of 1936, "the most satisfying part of this year was the attitude of our fellow students. Anybody who knows anything about society knows about the 1936 student movements. What use would it have been to have carried on demonstrations and to have boycotted classes to indirectly express unhappiness because of some unnecessary events? This was simply an opportunity for some leaders to achieve a kind of success. All of the members of our class—more than sixty of us—knew the futility of boycotting classes and demonstrating. We thought that any agitation that kept students from carrying out their work under the leadership of the government was irresponsibly disruptive. Therefore, even though we were in the midst of a great tide of student unrest, we did not move, we calmly attended classes. This is undoubtedly because of the training we received in the slogan 'Seek the truth from facts.' It was also because the students in our class truly understood the direction of today's youth!"[33]

In their own history of the college, the French Jesuits took pride in having discouraged student activism. However much neighboring university campuses like Nankai University might have been convulsed by nationalist movements of 1925, 1931, 1935–36, the Jesuits managed to keep the trouble out of their campus. It seems that the kinds of students who came to Gong Shang College were mostly willing to internalize this Jesuit attitude. The confluence between Jesuit convictions and student aspirations produced an apolitical school atmosphere. It sustained a vision of China in which intelligent elites of good character who worked hard within the established political system would make China into a better place, for the greater glory of God.

It was a vision that did not challenge the prevailing class system. The students of Gong Shang College were a privileged, indeed pampered, elite. Nothing the Jesuits taught suggested that they would have to give up those privileges. The logic of the school's religious orientation was protective rather than socially activist. If the social gospel encouraged students in Protestant universities to enter Chinese history so as to transform it (as suggested by the Yanjing University motto, "Freedom through Truth for Service"), the Counter-Reformation Catholic vision institutionalized in Gong Shang College encouraged students to escape from Chinese history so as to be saved from it. When the Jesuits did encourage the students to engage in social service beyond the walls of the school, they did this only for the school's spiritual elite, a special association of the most devout Catholics among the student body. Members of this association not only attended mass daily but also participated in works of charity, such as visiting prisons, bringing Christmas toys to orphanages, and so on.[34] But it was charity aimed at smoothing the rough edges of a harsh society without challenging the structure of that society and carried out under careful supervision so as to keep its practitioners from being sullied by that society.

In philosophy and social science courses, the Jesuits provided an intellectual rationale for this stance. A course on sociological theory offered in the 1940s was centered on "the social problem: critical examination of the various solutions that have been proposed (liberal, socialistic, Catholic doctrines)."[35] I do not have any more detailed information about the content of this course, or about the content of an article one of the Jesuits wrote in the 1930s—in *Beichen* (Ave Maris Stella), a magazine for Catholic intellectuals established at Gong Shang College in the late 1920s but later moved to Beiping's Fu Ren University—about applying the teaching of the papal encyclical *Rerum Novarum* to Chinese society. We may assume, however, that the Jesuit thinking followed closely the principles promulgated by Pope Leo XIII in his 1891 *Rerum Novarum* and Pope Pius XI in his 1931 encyclical

Quadrigesimo Anno. The social teaching of Leo XIII was against unfettered liberalism and called for the state to intervene to ensure a just wage and decent working conditions and for workers to form voluntary associations to overcome their individualism. Forty (*quadrigesimo*) years later, Pope Pius XI extended Pope Leo XIII's critique of liberalism to the conditions of the Great Depression. The solution to these unprecedented problems, the pope taught, was not in socialism, because of its collectivist, materialistic, and atheistic orientation. The solution lay in a morally motivated cooperation between capital and labor, a kind of corporatism, but one that avoided the suppression of freedom that had come with Mussolini's fascism.[36]

I doubt whether Gong Shang College students, especially the non-Catholics, were deeply influenced by hearing lectures or reading articles on this Catholic social theory. But the ethos of the school, its cultivation of the *bonne bourgeoisie*, its discouragement of political activism, its emphasis on moral character development and ameliorative noblesse oblige, constituted a living instantiation of this teaching. Unfortunately, such a vision of society was of little relevance to the brutal struggle that was about to engulf China as the Sino-Japanese War began.

THE WAR YEARS

With the outbreak of war, the faculties and many of the students of the great state universities of the north fled to southwest China to continue their intellectual work in such a way as to aid in their government's resistance against Japan. Yanjing, the American Protestant university in Beiping, was closed after Pearl Harbor, and its core students and faculty also went to the southwest. But like Fu Ren University, the Catholic University in Beiping, Gong Shang College remained open where it was. The Jesuits seem not to have given any serious thought to moving to the southwest.

Now the challenge of maintaining the boundaries between their urban university and a war-torn world was more difficult than ever. The Jesuit solution was to defend the boundaries more energetically than ever, even if this meant bearing the moral burden of making personal compromises with worldly powers in order to protect the students behind their walls.

There were good Catholic theological reasons for rationalizing that it was more important for the church to be present in the midst of a troubled society, offering its sacraments to Catholics and incorporating as many social institutions as possible under its hierarchy, than for the church to be effective in pursuing any particular human cause. Thus the Jesuits of Gong Shang College focused their attention on the sheer survival of their institution, and were willing to make what compromises were necessary in teaching and behavior in order to ensure that survival. There was a logic, a moral integrity to this position. But to outsiders unsympathetic to the church, it would look dangerously like collaboration with the enemy.

In other Catholic institutions, theological reasons were found for a more active resistance. Notably, behind the walls of Fu Ren University in Beiping, Chinese faculty members organized an underground resistance group that later carried out Guomindang work in the area.[37] But it does not seem that the members of the Gong Shang College community did anything comparable. Some students, at least, did want to participate in the resistance, but the Jesuits seem to have discouraged this. Their strategy for coping with Japanese occupation was first of all to avoid doing anything that would invite Japanese reprisals. As the Jesuit history put it, "The presence in the school of elements capable of inciting incidents and the patriotic imprudence of the young, were able at any instant to cause grave difficulties." When such events occurred, "the Fathers of the house were not capable of giving the Japanese the desirable explanations." So, compromising their long-held position regarding the French character of their community, the Jesuits of Gong Shang College asked their Father General for some outside help: "Can we get a priest from [the Jesuit-run] Sophia University in Tokyo to establish a liaison with the Japanese authorities? . . . a priest knowledgeable in Japanese. Preferably a German."[38]

Thus, in 1938, there arrived from Japan a Fr. Borsch, the first in a series of German Jesuits who would be assigned to the Jesuit community at Gong Shang College to help the Jesuits mediate with the Japanese occupation forces. Fr. Borsch and his successors also ministered to the spiritual needs of Catholics in the Japanese military community. He said mass for them, heard their confessions, and offered spiritual counsel. If the Jesuit educational mission in Tianjin was no longer identified with French culture and politics, it was no longer unambiguously identified with Chinese culture and political aspirations either. Serving China's enemies, as well as Chinese themselves, it projected a vision of Catholicism as standing above all culture and politics. The survival of the church—and the major institutions affiliated with the church—was an end in itself. Even if the church could do nothing, would do nothing, directly to help the Chinese people fulfill their greatest immediate historical need—the need to resist Japan—the church, by surviving, by maintaining a presence through Gong Shang College among the upper classes of Tianjin, could in the long run, in God's mysterious ways, bring them eternal benefits.

In the meantime, the Jesuits did what they could to alleviate some of the misery of the war. They distributed food and clothing to refugees streaming into Tianjin. They continued to carry out baptisms—they rejoiced to report thirty new baptisms in 1938—and to administer the other sacraments. And in Tianjin, they continued their educational enterprise.

In ways the Jesuits could perhaps never have anticipated, that enterprise indeed flourished. Since Gong Shang College was the only institution of higher learning still open in Tianjin, it drew in more students than ever before, students whose affluent families were willing to pay the high tuition necessary to support the college. The number of students in the handsome campus on Racecourse Road went from about six hundred in 1937 to almost two thousand by 1945. In 1943, the expansive tide was running strongly enough that the Jesuits opened a new women's division of the school. Focusing on a liberal arts rather than a commercial or technical education, the women's division reached about two hundred students by 1945.[39] In spite of the disruption of war, the Jesuits were even able to improve their facilities. In 1938, for instance, they installed a handsome new marble altar in their chapel, the gift of some wealthy Tianjin Catholics.[40]

To all external appearances at least, the school atmosphere remained completely apolitical. There is something eerie about reading the school yearbook for 1940. It is full of stories of athletic contests waged, friendships formed, technical skills acquired, eternal verities learned, good traits of character—"honesty, energy, straightforwardness"—developed. But there is almost nothing that would suggest that a war was raging in China, and for that matter in Europe. The closest one gets to a feeling that there is something amiss is a poem written by one of the graduating students: "We are now preparing to enter a dark [*heian*] society. We have to change it—make it glorious. . . . We have to make a new society—or at least not allow ourselves to be corrupted by an evil society. Before you, you see thorns and wild beasts—but this is your chance for glory. Take up sword and spear, and hoe."[41] Whatever agonies such a student would face, however, would come after he left the sheltered walls of the college. Gong Shang College was an island of light and serenity in a dark and storming world.

The Jesuits kept it that way by, among other things, keeping all books "critical of a certain country" out of the parts of the library open to public access.[42] If such books were to be consulted, they could be done so only by specially approved students, and the books could not be taken back to dormitories. Besides suppressing any public criticism of the Japanese, the Jesuits acceded to the Japanese demand that study of the Japanese language be required for graduation. A Japanese teacher sent from Japan was added to the faculty for this purpose. The Jesuits also submitted themselves to regular scrutiny by Japanese inspectors. They seemed to develop good rapport with the inspectors. In 1943, they even received a visit—which "went very well"—by a delegate from the imperial household.[43]

Some students nonetheless carried out anti-Japanese activities, including it seems, in 1944 at least, sabotage against Japanese property. When the Japanese became suspicious of some of the students residing in the school and came to investigate, the Jesuits protected the students by getting rid of any evidence that would have compromised them. If the evidence had been found, "this would have led to the ruin of the University and the condemnation to certain death of the students." Because the Jesuits protected the anti-Japanese students in this way, "some of our students were not willing to accuse us, as they were pressured to do later, of being imperialists and enemies of China."[44]

The Jesuits were indeed eventually accused by the Communists of being Japanese collaborators as well as imperialists. They might claim that they did nothing to advance the Japanese war effort and cooperated with the Japanese only enough to ensure the survival of their college and their mission. They would point to the way that they shielded some anti-Japanese students from prosecution. But they also did their best to discourage such "youthful imprudence," and in their account they seemed concerned about the fate of the students because of its possible effect on the fate of the school. Was passive survival a sufficient goal for a Catholic institution during the Sino-Japanese War?

Protestants such as those who ran Yanjing University might have answered in the negative. They might have thought that no institution is indispensable for conveying God's grace, since God speaks directly to each believer's heart. They could justify moving their institution away from Beiping to Chengdu so that it could carry out its work without compromise. For Catholics, God becomes present through the institution of the church. The church has to be present in all of its essential hierarchical order in every place under every circumstance for sacramental grace to be conveyed. Therefore the fundamental institutions of the church had to be preserved in north China, had to remain available to the faithful no matter what hardships this might cause its ministers, even if this entailed compromising with the principalities and powers of a sinful society. Of course, there is nothing in Catholic theology that says a church-run *college* is a fundamental institution of the church. But it is easy enough for people who have invested their lives in building up such an institution, in a belief that this was part of their God-given vocation, to tell themselves that it was God's will that their school continue at all costs.

If for the French Jesuits the effort to keep the school open sprang from a theologically inspired vision of maintaining the presence of the church, for many of the Chinese who attended the school and taught in the school it presented a practical opportunity for making the best of a bad situation. The college was not as good as, say, Nankai, but it presented an opportunity to continue one's education or to practice one's profession in a hard time. Almost all of the nonclerical foreign teachers who had been at the school during the 1930s left at the outbreak of the war. The school provided job opportunities for an increasing number of talented young Chinese scholars. For its increasing numbers of students, the school provided a good technical education and a living space with some serenity and security. During the war years, Gong Shang College became more Chinese than ever. The proportion of non-Catholic Chinese students to Catholic students increased, as did the proportion of secular Chinese faculty to foreign Jesuits. The school gained a place in the hearts of wealthy Tianjin families who in other times would have sent their students to Nankai or Beiyang Universities. But the school became Chinese in a way that associated it with a particular kind of Chinese identity—a kind that would not fare well in the ideological campaigns of the Maoist era.

Whatever the theological rationale for staying in Tianjin, the paternalistic, protective orientation of Gong Shang College provided Chinese urban middle classes with a model for being Chinese in a time of great stress. If you cannot avoid a situation, then passively accept it, make some compromises to stay close to those family members and colleagues for whom you bear special responsibility, try to escape the vicissitudes of a bad time by dwelling on timeless truths, conceal your true feelings from those hostile to you, keep yourself under control—and wait. While the students and faculty of Gong Shang were waiting, the Communists in Yanan and even the Guomindang in Chongqing were taking a more activist, more heroic posture—striving to change the world, not merely keep it at arm's length.[45] Drawing on the legacy of their most heroic moments, they have represented the true twentieth-century Chinese identity as that of an activist. Over the long run, though, perhaps the wartime stance of the Jesuits of Gong Shang College rings truer to the common sense of the majority of the Chinese people about how best to cope with the calamities visited upon them by the excesses of the activist minority.

THE AGONY OF GONG SHANG COLLEGE

Ironically, the Jesuits' religiously motivated effort to keep the world at bay had brought Gong Shang College its greatest degree of worldly success. During the war, it had more students and faculty than ever before and more influence even among non-Catholic social circles in Tianjin. But that very success compromised its religious mission. The success brought the world into the community. Most of the increasing numbers of students were not in Gong Shang College because they were loyal to its religious principles or even to the priests who were in charge. They were there because the college provided a convenient space to get started on their careers in spite of the war. Once the war was over, and better opportunities for advancing their careers presented themselves, they would leave the school.

Soon after the surrender of Japan, the faculties of Gong Shang's major rival universities, Nankai and Beiyang, returned from their exile in the southwest. In an effort to revive these universities, the government provided subsidies that enabled them to simultaneously provide higher salaries and charge lower tuition than Gong Shang. Large numbers of Gong Shang students deserted the school for Nankai or Beiyang, and most of the faculty did so as well. Gong Shang College was forced to replace its well-credentialed teachers with recent alumni who had no more than an undergraduate degree.

While losing its ability to maintain a loyal student body, the college was also losing its ability to gain outside financial support, especially from war-ravaged France. Then, in the spring of 1946, the last contingent of French soldiers left Tianjin, marking the end of extraterritoriality. The last vestiges of the French protectorate over Catholic missions were gone. The Jesuit who wrote the official history of Gong Shang College did not see this as a victory for the Chinese people. The end of extraterritoriality opened the way to a completely arbitrary form of liberty, he thought: "The Communists were above all the main beneficiaries."[46]

Perhaps it was especially difficult for missionaries steeped in the hierarchical tradition of the Catholic Church to give up a paternalistic sense of control over Chinese Catholic institutions. In any case, the time of the foreign missionaries was coming to an end in China. In response to the Chinese tide of nationalism, the Vatican was finally turning over direction of the Chinese church to a Chinese episcopate. The Chinese church was still extremely hierarchical, but now it was controlled by Chinese who had no special respect for French hierarchy. In 1945, Bishop Thomas Tian Gengxing of Beijing was made the first Chinese cardinal.[47] Chinese Jesuits, and later in the 1940s Chinese diocesan priests, increasingly took control of Gong Shang College.

Cardinal Tian visited Gong Shang College in May of 1946. The priests at Gong Shang held a grand reception for him, attended by all the elite of Tianjin—"all the civil and military authorities, directors of schools and banks, our entire professorial faculty, and two American diplomats."[48] Over two decades, the work of Gong Shang College had indeed established the connections necessary to call upon all of the established leaders of the city. As stated in a mimeographed report issued by the Jesuits at the end of 1946, "Of the seven Bureaux of Public Works in Tianjin, four are directed by our former students. In all important banks and all large commercial enterprises, one finds our alumni. Because of this, we everywhere find people sympathetic to our work."[49] Unfortunately for the Jesuits, most of their prominent alumni worked for an establishment soon to be overthrown by the Communists.

As they had over the years, the Jesuits of Gong Shang strove to keep themselves aloof from Chinese popular politics. At the end of 1946, large, leftist-inspired demonstrations against American troops stationed in the city swept the student communities. Once again, the priests were able to keep most of their students from participating (though to do so they had to close the college for several weeks). In January of 1947 two inspectors sent by the Guomindang government praised the discipline of the Gong Shang students in the face of temptation to participate in such movements. The approval of the government paid off in 1948, when the college was favorably reviewed and reaccredited under the Guomindang government's new educational system. The Jesuit go-between in this process, as in the earlier accreditation application, was Archbishop Yu Bin of Nanjing, who was and would remain extremely closely tied to the Guomindang. In the process of accreditation, the college's name was once again changed—this time to Jingu College.

The Jesuits had worked hard to get this accreditation, and they thought it was good news. But as they looked at the overall context of their work, they could see that it was a useless piece of good news. Communists were advancing into Xian county, and put their superior, Father Charvet (who had once been rector of the college) under arrest. Priests were fleeing from Communist-occupied rural areas and coming to live in the Jesuit residence at the college. A new world of Chinese nationalism was coming into being, and it was overwhelming any barriers the Jesuits could build against it.

In May of 1948, as the "political sky darkened and the storm approached," and practical efforts to barricade against the storm failed, the Jesuits decided to make special recourse to the Blessed Virgin, Our Lady Queen of China. This is what the villagers of Xian county had done a half century before, during the Boxer uprising. Then, the legends said, as frightened Catholics huddled within their church compounds, the Virgin had appeared atop their church steeples in glorious power and broken the Boxer siege.[50] Praying for a similar deliverance, the priests of Gong Shang carried a statue of Our Lady Queen of China in a great procession around the college, accompanied by a fervent crowd of Catholics from throughout the city. But during the Boxer troubles, the Catholic communities of Xian county had been relatively self-sufficient villages surrounded by sturdy mud and brick walls. The Catholic community of Gong Shang was part of a large, complex city and, especially now that the French protectorate was gone, its barriers against the unbelieving world were composed of religious symbols and social connections, not sturdy physical stuff. The political sky continued to darken. On January 15, 1949, the Communists took control of Tianjin, and in the semester that followed, there began, as the Jesuit chronicler puts it, "l'agonie des Hautes Etudes."

The Communist Party established a school "soviet," or administrative committee, composed of Chinese professors, administrators, students, and staff. Under the committee's guidance, the students became what they had never been before—political activists. "Liberated" from the supervision of the Jesuits, the students filled the walls of the college with posters "attacking the Americans, attacking religion, attacking our authority, which was put under the name of imperialism." The Jesuits saw this as an example of what happened when impressionable young people were deprived of proper supervision. More accurately perhaps, it was an example of what the Communists could do by manipulating people through their own more aggressive forms of hierarchical supervision.

By the middle of 1949, the new government of Tianjin had made the teaching of materialism obligatory in all schools. They began a violent campaign against Gong Shang College, and by the end of the year they tried to force the dismissal of all Jesuits from the faculty and administration. Employing the "Chinese way," the Jesuits called upon their friends in the Tianjin elite. They gained a temporary victory: the mayor of Tianjin wrote a long letter praising the Fathers for the success of the college and the help given to its students. This temporarily forestalled the dismissal of the Jesuits. "But this was a 'loss of face' for our adversaries. In China, this is unpardonable, and must eventually be paid for."[51]

The Jesuits held on in spite of great sacrifices because they felt a responsibility to give protection, help, and comfort to their Catholic students as long as possible. But they could no longer erect adequate barriers between their students and the world. They could no longer even protect themselves. In January of 1951, all of the Jesuits were finally dismissed from their jobs. The priests were placed under surveillance and subjected to long, excruciating interrogations. Some were arrested. The others dared have no further contact with Chinese friends, even with the Catholic students, for fear of compromising them. On July 11, 1951, all the Jesuits were expelled from their residences behind the walls of the college, and, soon after, all the French Jesuits were expelled from China.

The yearbook for the class of 1950 contained no pictures of any priests. Written by the "School Administrative Committee," the preface made no mention of Christianity, but it was full of exhortations for students and faculty to become the

People's intellectuals, not the exploitative intellectuals of the old society. If the college's students, faculty, and alumni followed the principles of Marxism-Leninism, served the people, and followed the mass line, it promised, they would lead the motherland to a glorious future.[52]

LEGACIES

In the early 1950s, Gong Shang College was dismantled and its libraries and other resources used to form the basis of the three main institutions of higher education in Hebei Province—Hebei University, which occupied the Gong Shang campus in Tianjin, Hebei Normal University, which was built in Shijiazhuang after 1953, and Hebei Normal School, which is located in Zhangjiakou. During the Cultural Revolution, Hebei University was moved from Tianjin to Baoding. The campus built by the Jesuits is now used by the Tianjin Foreign Language Institute, although a small part is still used to house Hebei University students and faculty who need to do research in Tianjin.[53]

For a few years after the Jesuits left in 1951, the public chapel remained open and one of the Chinese priests came daily to offer mass. Control over the Chinese Catholic Church steadily tightened, however. The government began a movement to force Catholics to renounce foreign ties and to submit to "Catholic reform committees" controlled by the government's Religious Affairs Bureau and the Communist Party's United Front Work Department. Eventually, by the mid-1950s, the government had set up a mass organization called the "Catholic Patriotic Association" to be the liaison between Catholics and the government. The Vatican denounced these arrangements. The government arrested bishops and priests who supported the Vatican, a persecution that reached a high point during the antirightist campaign. At the same time, a small percentage of China's priests and bishops supported the Patriotic Association. One of the most prominent among them was the Jesuit Bishop Francis Xavier Zhao Zhensheng, the first Chinese figurehead president of Gong Shang College, who had in 1937 been ordained a bishop and made the Vicar Apostolic of Xian county. In 1957, several Chinese bishops carried out ordinations of new Chinese bishops, who had been elected by the Catholic Patriotic Association but not approved by the Vatican.[54]

Thus was born a tragic split within the Chinese Catholic Church between those who supported the Patriotic Association and were allowed to continue to worship publicly and those who resisted and were forced to carry out their religious activities underground. Most bishops and priests who supported the underground were put into prison, becoming in the minds of most Chinese Catholics martyrs for the faith.

During the Cultural Revolution all religious activity, even that associated with the Patriotic Association, was suppressed, and all churches were closed. In the post-Mao era of "Reform and Opening," the government allowed public Catholic religious life to resume. This led to an extraordinary resurgence in Catholic life.

Newly opened churches were packed with enthusiastic worshipers, churches destroyed during the Cultural Revolution were rebuilt, seminaries and convents were reestablished, new bishops and priests were ordained. All of this was allowed, however, only as long as it was carried out under the official auspices of the Patriotic Association. At the same time, the underground church revived and became bolder, more vigorous, and better organized than ever. This has led not simply to renewed confrontation with the government, and to the arrest and punishment of many underground clergy, but to a bitter, sometimes even violent, split within the Catholic community between those loyal to priests associated with the "public church" and those loyal to priests in the underground. In Tianjin today, there are currently three men each claiming to be the legitimate bishop of the diocese, one a bishop approved by the Patriotic Association (although he himself began his career as an underground bishop) and two underground bishops. Each has his followers, and this has led to a greatly troubled Catholic community.

The troubles of this new situation are the result of the confrontation between a new political situation and the older forms of community we have seen exemplified in the history of Gong Shang College. Now, as then, Catholic identity is defined in terms of status within a hierarchical structure of authority. Now, as then, an important part of the responsibility of the priests and bishops who occupy higher levels of the hierarchy is to patrol the boundaries between church and world and to protect ordinary Catholics from that world.

In the current political situation, protecting one's Catholic flock confronts Chinese bishops and priests with terrible dilemmas. Should they—as the Jesuits did at Gong Shang College under the Japanese—make compromises with the powers of this world in order to protect a space for Catholics in their charge? Or should they resist heroically, even though this might invite a hostile government to completely suppress their community? Many of the bishops and priests who have cooperated sufficiently with the Catholic Patriotic Association to be allowed to work aboveground are not opportunistic collaborators but simply people who are doing their best to protect the church under difficult and ambiguous conditions.

Because the Chinese Catholic community sees itself in such a hierarchical fashion, enormous responsibility is placed on the shoulders of these clerics. But now it is doubly difficult to fulfill that responsibility, because the authority of many of the clerics is questionable. In the first half of this century, during hard times like the Sino-Japanese War, the difficult decisions made by priests like those at Gong Shang College were not open to debate by those under them. But now the Chinese Catholic community bitterly debates the decisions made by its priests. Still following a Counter-Reformation model of the church, many of the laity might say that they ought to give unquestioning obedience to a legitimate priestly authority. But it is unclear who is legitimate, because the Vatican has no diplomatic relations with the People's Republic and it cannot send a papal delegate to adjudicate between the claims of, say, the three bishops who claim to be the legitimate authority in the Tianjin diocese.

Although one way to solve this problem would be to reestablish a clear chain of command to the Vatican, another way would be to deemphasize the importance of hierarchy in the Catholic Church. This could be done by emphasizing a biblically based vision of the church as a "people of God." If taken seriously, this would lead to a less paternalistic kind of church, one that did not try to protect believers from the world but inspired each believer to take an active, mature responsibility for his or her actions in the world. In line with the principle of Catholic social philosophy called "subsidiarity," which emphasizes the need for responsible authority to be exercised at the lowest practicable levels, this vision of the church would also encourage believers to govern themselves in most matters from the bottom up, rather than wait for authoritative commands from the top down.[55] In the mid-1960s, the Second Vatican Council, inspired in part by the theological vision reached by Teilhard de Chardin while he was in Tianjin, called for just such a new understanding of the church—a Catholic community that would not try to dominate the world or to set itself apart from the world, but would learn God's will by discerning the signs of the times within the history of the world. Because of its long isolation under the Communist regime, the Chinese Catholic Church is only now, very slowly, beginning to assimilate this modern Catholic vision.

The problems of the Chinese Catholic Church are in some ways reflective of problems of contemporary Chinese culture as a whole. Chinese cultural traditions are very complex, and there are strands that could support an open, entrepreneurial modern society as well as strands that would support a relatively closed, static society. In the twentieth century, the Maoist Communists played on the latter, in effect combining some of the worst of East and West into a political culture that, though changing now, still shapes life in Mainland China. There are many strands too in Catholic traditions, some of which are quite compatible with open, pluralistic modern societies. But the version of European Counter-Reformation theology that was propagated in north China in the first half of this century resonated with some of the more defensive, authoritarian strands of Chinese culture—indeed, some of the same strands that Communist ideology resonated with. The Catholic idea that paternalistic authority figures must protect those passive subjects under them has its parallels with Confucian paternalism. The concern about building barriers between the church and the world has its parallel in a Chinese obsession—encouraged also by conservative Communists—with building walls to keep out foreign influences and unsettling thoughts.[56]

And the crisis of China at the end of the twentieth century is parallel with the concurrent crisis of the Chinese Catholic Church. Too much of the population is too oriented to authority, inclined to be politically passive, never having had the opportunity to develop habits of responsible self-governance. But at the same time, they can no longer accept the legitimacy of the authorities governing them. Out of such painful dilemmas, we may hope, might come new forms of religious and political reformation that will combine some of the most forward-looking elements of Chinese humanism with some of the most flexible strands of Western politics and culture.

NOTES

1. These quotes are taken from ethnographic fieldwork conducted by Fan Lizhu and myself in the suburbs of Tianjin and in Xian county, Hebei, in 1993, with the support of a Luce Foundation grant. The results have been published in Richard Madsen, *China's Catholics: Tragedy and Hope in an Emerging Civil Society* (Berkeley and Los Angeles: University of California Press, 1998).

2. Teilhard de Chardin wrote a number of scientific monographs on the excavations of "Peking Man" at Zhoukoudian. He is best known for his theological works, however. The most famous of these, *The Phenomenon of Man* (English trans. by Bernard Wall [New York: Harper and Row, 1959]), was written in 1939 in Tianjin while he was confined to the Jesuit residence and unable to do his scientific research because of the Sino-Japanese War. Like his other theological works, this was deemed heretical and its publication forbidden by the church. It circulated in mimeographed form among a small circle of Teilhard's friends and was finally published in France in 1955, after his death. For biographies in English, see Robert Splaight, *The Life of Teilhard de Chardin* (New York: Harper and Row, 1967); Paul Grenet, *Teilhard de Chardin, the Man and His Theories*, trans. R. A. Rudorff (New York: P. S. Eriksson, 1966); Leon Cristiani, *Pierre Teilhard de Chardin: His Life and Spirit*, trans. Martin Jarrett-Kerr (New York: Macmillan, 1960); Henri de Lubac, *The Religion of Teilhard de Chardin*, trans. Rene Hague (New York: Hawthorn Books, 1966).

There were other important progressive priests and intellectuals who made a base in Tianjin in the first half of this century—people whose work was more directly related than Teilhard's to contemporary Chinese politics. Notable was the Belgian Lazarist Vincent Lebbe, who advocated an identification of Christianity with Chinese nationalism and pressed for the establishment of a church under the direction of a Chinese episcopacy rather than foreign missionaries. Lebbe was controversial, and many Catholic missionaries, especially the French missionaries discussed in this chapter, were not very sympathetic to his approach. Although in the long run Lebbe's vision has been very influential, in the 1920s and 1930s the kind of Catholic vision that I discuss in this chapter represented the mainstream of Catholicism in China. For a good introduction to the life of Lebbe, see Eugenio Menegon, "Catholic Intellectuals in Republican China and Their Search for National Identity" (manuscript, 1995).

3. The other two Catholic institutions were Shanghai's Zhendan (Aurora) University, which was also run by the French Jesuits, and Beijing's Fu Ren University, which was established by the American Benedictines but in the 1930s was taken over by the German-based Society of the Divine Word. Zhendan was similar to Tianjin's Gong Shang College in its use of the French language as a medium of instruction and its adherence to French educational methods with emphasis on professional education rather than liberal arts. Zhendan, in fact, clung to the use of the French language longer than Gong Shang because there were more opportunities for French-speaking Chinese in Shanghai. Fu Ren University placed a greater emphasis on the liberal arts and in practice put more emphasis on integrating Chinese and Western cultural traditions. Although there is an extensive scholarly literature on the sixteen Protestant institutions of higher education in China, the contribu-

tion of Catholic higher education to China's modernization is a neglected topic. One of the few articles on the subject is Ruth Hayhoe, "A Chinese Catholic Philosophy of Higher Education in Republican China," *Tripod* 48 (1988): 49–60.

4. See Robert N. Bellah, Richard Madsen, William M. Sullivan, Ann Swidler, and Steven M. Tipton, *Habits of the Heart: Individualism and Commitment in American Life* (Berkeley and Los Angeles: University of California Press, 1985).

5. For a sociological analysis (as distinguished from theological and historical analyses, of which there are a vast number) of the Counter-Reformation Catholic Church, see Victor M. Perez-Diaz, *The Return of Civil Society* (Cambridge: Harvard University Press, 1993), 109–83. The classic sociological study still remains that of Ernst Troeltsch, *The Social Teaching of the Christian Churches*, trans. Olive Wyon (London: George Allen, 1931).

6. Comment made at the conference "Yanjing University and Chinese Higher Education," Claremont McKenna College, Claremont, Calif., May 22–26, 1996.

7. Madsen, *China's Catholics*, 62.

8. For recent Chinese histories of the Zhangzhuang Cathedral and its associated community, see Zhang Pingyi and Kang Yu, "Xianxian Zhangzhuang Tianzhu Jiao Congjiaotang de Fandong Huodong yu Dai Dongnan Renmin de Fan Di Ai Guo Yundong," in *Hebei Wenshi Cikan Xuanji*, vol. 1 (Shijiazhuang: Hebei Renmin Chubanshe, 1980); and Pei Shulan, ed., "Tianzhutang zai Xianxian deng chude Tianchan," *Jindaishi Cikan* (Review of modern history).

9. See Richard Madsen, "The Catholic Church in China: Cultural Contradictions, Institutional Survival, and Religious Renewal," in *Unofficial China: Popular Culture and Thought in the People's Republic*, ed. Perry Link, Richard Madsen, and Paul G. Pickowicz (Boulder, Colo.: Westview Press, 1989), 103–20.

10. For a complete list of sources, see Edward Malatesta, "Resources at the Jesuit Archives in France Pertaining to L'Institut des Hautes Etudes Industrielles et Commerciales de Tianjin" (paper presented at "International Symposium on Historical Archives of Pre-1949 Christian Higher Education in China," Chinese University of Hong Kong, December 1993). The most important parts of this material were photocopied by Fr. Malatesta and are available at the Ricci Institute of the University of San Francisco. About half the documents are in French, half in Chinese. The French documents include a ninety-five-page typewritten manuscript on the history of the Institut, "L'Universite Tsinkou, Ecole des Hautes-Etudes de Tien-tsin, Histoire d'Un Quart de Siecle," by Paul Bornet, S.J. This manuscript was written between 1949 and 1951 and based on diaries kept by the Jesuits at the school, as well as on the personal memories of Fr. Bornet, who served on the school's faculty. This history was written for internal use, not for external publication. In the archives, there is a letter to Fr. Bornet from his superior telling him to include the shadows as well as the bright spots in his chronicle. The archive also includes internal memos debating school policy, as well as press releases and brochures written to solicit French support. The Chinese documents include yearbooks, several school catalogues, a report written in support of accreditation, copies of the school newspaper *Daoguang* (published weekly between 1930 and 1937), and copies of the tables of contents of the religious journal *Beizhan*, the *Gong Shang Xuezhi*, and academic journals on engineering and on Chinese law published at the Institut. Unless otherwise noted, all translations from the French or Chinese are by myself.

11. Quoted in George Minamiki, S.J., *The Chinese Rites Controversy from Its Beginning to Modern Times* (Chicago: Loyola University Press, 1985), 190. (See also Eugenio Manegon, "Catholic Intellectuals in Republican China" [manuscript, Department of History, Uni-

versity of California at Berkeley, 1995], 3.) Issued by Pope Benedict XV, this encyclical was deeply influenced by the views of Fr. Vincent Lebbe. It represented an attempt by the Vatican to circumvent France's position as protector of Catholic missions. Many French missionaries resisted, as will be apparent from this essay. For the political context of the encyclical, see Jean-Paul Wiest, *Maryknoll in China* (Armonk, N.Y.: M. E. Sharpe, 1988), 45–47.

12. This four-page typewritten document is dated Tianjin, 15 February 1924.

13. Typewritten draft of a brochure about the Institut, 1931.

14. Paul Bornet, "L'Universite Tsinkou," 1–5.

15. Report dated 15 February 1924.

16. Bornet, "L'Universite Tsinkou," 6.2.

17. This is acknowledged in the school catalogue published in May 1935.

18. Typewritten draft for a brochure on the Institut, 1931.

19. French description of school, 15 February 1924; Chinese catalogue, 1935.

20. See Jessie G. Lutz, *China and the Christian Colleges, 1850–1950* (Ithaca: Cornell University Press, 1971).

21. French description of school, 15 February 1924.

22. "Note sur l'Influence Francaise de l'Institut de Tientsin," 13 February 1933, typewritten.

23. "Note sur l'Influence Francaise"; the Chinese catalogue for 1935 speaks of the French influence in terms of a style of education: thorough and practical, proceeding in a methodical manner, and not emphasizing pompous abstractions.

24. Memos concerning a consultation of February 1931 on whether official recognition should be requested. Also, Bornet, "L'Universite Tsinkou," 19–22.

25. Ibid., 21.

26. Ibid., 26.

27. Fr. Pollet, 8 January, 1937.

28. "Extraitades remarques du P. Charvet sur le rapport du P. Pollet," n.d.

29. Troeltsch, *Social Teachings*, vol. 1, 328–82; and vol. 2, conclusion.

30. Yearbook, 1937.

31. Yearbook, 1939.

32. Yearbook, 1937.

33. Ibid.

34. Bornet, "L'Universite Tsinkou," 30–31.

35. Catalogue of the newly established Women's Division, 1943.

36. Jean-Yves Calvez, S.J., "Economic Policy Issues in Roman Catholic Social Teaching: An International Perspective," in *The Catholic Challenge to the American Economy*, ed. Thomas M. Gannon, S.J. (New York: Macmillan, 1987), 15–26.

37. Menegon, "Catholic Intellectuals," 26–28.

38. Bornet, "L'Universite Tsinkou," 42–43.

39. See the enrollment chart presented in a report by Frs. Charvet and Denys, 10 December 1946.

40. Bornet, "L'Universite Tsinkou," 45.

41. Yearbook, 1941.

42. Bornet, "L'Universite Tsinkou," 53.

43. Ibid., 60.

44. Ibid., 74. This section of Fr. Bornet's history, recounting events that took place between 1942 and 1946, is less detailed than the rest of the document. According to a note in

the manuscript, the original fifteen pages dealing with this period were destroyed in June of 1951, just before the French Jesuits were expelled from Tianjin, because they made mention of persons connected with Bishop Yu Bin, who had been declared a traitor by the Communists. The new version was written without benefit of the diaries and reports used in the old version.

45. See David E. Apter and Tony Saich, *Revolutionary Discourse in Mao's Republic* (Cambridge: Harvard University Press, 1994).

46. Bornet, "L'Universite Tsinkou," 76.

47. Before the establishment of a national episcopate, China was considered a mission territory under direct control of Propaganda Fidei in Rome. Its regions were called Vicariate Apostolates and, though headed by bishops, some of whom were Chinese, were not dioceses. With the establishment of a Chinese episcopate, China was now considered to be a national church, governed (under Vatican supervision) by its own conference of bishops, in the same way as, say, the Catholic Church in France or the United States. The conferral of the status of cardinal on Thomas Tian was part of the recognition of this new status for the Chinese church. Eric Hanson notes that the Vatican gave the red hat to Thomas Tian at this time, rather than to Yu Bin, because Yu Bin was considered too closely tied to the Guomindang. Eric O. Hanson, *Catholic Politics in China and Korea* (Maryknoll, N.Y.: Orbis Books, 1980), 95.

48. Bornet, "L'Universite Tsinkou," 78.

49. Report by Frs. Charvet and Denys, 10 December, 1946.

50. Information from ethnographic fieldwork reported in Madsen, *China's Catholics,* 91.

51. Bornet, "L'Universite Tsinkou," 89.

52. Yearbook, 1950.

53. This information was graciously provided to me by Wang Xiaoqing, a graduate of Hebei University who worked on a project to compile its history.

54. See John Tong, "The Catholic Church from 1949 to 1990," in *The Catholic Church in Modern China,* ed. Edmund Tang and Jean-Paul Wiest (Maryknoll, N.Y.: Orbis Books, 1993), 7–27.

55. Such theological issues are thoroughly discussed in Kim-Kwong Chan, *Toward a Contextual Ecclesiology: The Catholic Church in the People's Republic of China (1979–1983): Its Life and Theological Implications* (Hong Kong: Chinese Church Research Center, 1987), 333–412.

56. See the discussion in the 1988 Chinese TV series *Heshang.* For English translation and commentary, see Su Xiaokang and Wang Luxiang, *Deathsong of the River: A Reader's Guide to the Chinese TV Series* Heshang, trans. and ed. Richard W. Bodman and Pin P. Wan (Ithaca: Cornell East Asia series, 1991).

SIX

The Grounding of Cosmopolitans: Merchants and Local Cultures in Guangdong

Helen F. Siu

WHERE WERE THE MERCHANTS?

In his study of Hankou merchants in the eighteenth century, William Rowe points to their institutional significance as an autonomous social force in dialogue with the late imperial state. Their physical presence matured well before the forces of modernization, which were associated with the coming of the West.[1] David Faure, however, stresses the lack of an independent identity for mercantile groups. His study of Foshan focuses on the literati concerns shrewdly pursued by a range of town-based elite a century earlier. There might have been powerful mercantile interests, but he sees no conscious cultural identity apart from state ideology.[2]

Scholars have debated about mercantile groups, their trade organizations, family institutions, lifestyles, outlooks, and networking with literati and state. The maturing of marketing systems from the Song dynasty onward is well demonstrated by studies on Shanxi, Huizhou, Fujian, and Jiangnan.[3] Cycles of commercial growth and decline were interwoven with dynastic fortunes. They also contributed to a regional renaissance of the arts and culture, family institutions, and popular religion.[4] Despite the material and cultural impact of mercantile groups, their identities remained as ambiguous in historical records as in the minds of analysts.

The ambiguity has much to do with the fact that successful merchants cultivated a great deal more than their trades. Huizhou merchants during the Ming invested in academies and literati pursuits. Those in Jiangnan excelled in the craft of garden building and fine arts.[5] In Fujian, they built elaborate temples.[6] In Guangdong, they acquired and developed vast river marshes (*sha*) in the name of ancestral estates. These estates were the backbone of the evolution of an elaborate lineage complex.[7]

If those engaging in mercantile activities subscribed to the cultural forms of the literati and contributed significantly to the making of local society, we should

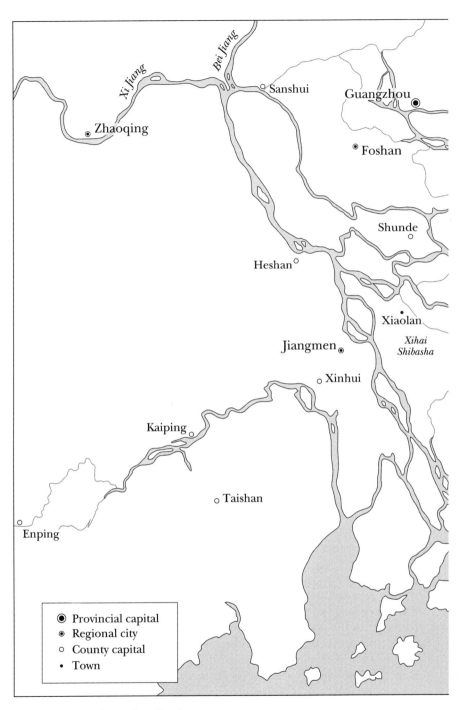

Pearl River Delta, Guangdong Province.

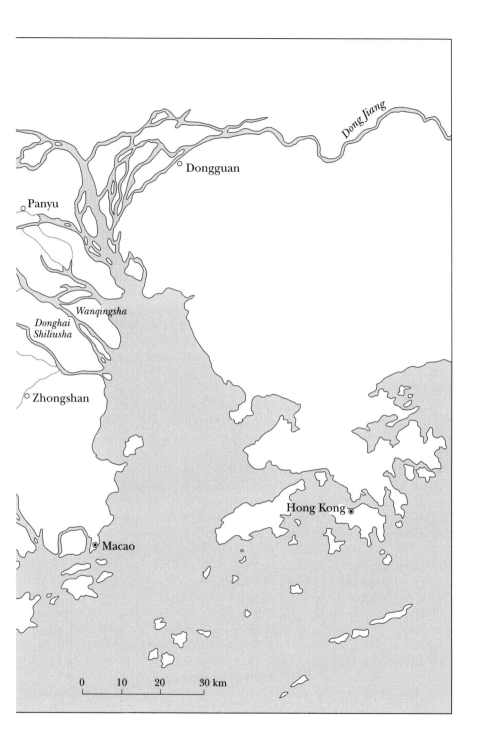

Dong Jiang

Dongguan

Panyu

Wanqingsha

Donghai
Shiliusha

Zhongshan

Hong Kong

Macao

0   10   20   30 km

not assume that merchants were extraneous to agrarian institutions and threatening to state orthodoxy. However, such an assumption often frames research questions and historical explanations: the difference between the studies by William Rowe and David Faure thus becomes one of historical time and place. The Foshan elites would be seen as having emerged from a rural political economy and having borrowed state ideologies to legitimize their operations. The Hankou merchants had another century to develop private urban institutions and regional networks in order to "collude, negotiate, and conflict" with the state on their own terms.

The assumed totalizing impact of the imperial order and its hostility to commercial activities continue to shape scholarly imagination for the Republican period. Chinese historians have agonized over the Qing's failure to modernize China's economy. To them, the culprit was state orthodoxy as much as Western imperialism. In their view, when imperial prerogatives weakened, the new Chinese bourgeoisie emerged from under the shadow of the decaying Qing state. They thrived when the preoccupation of Western powers in Europe during the First World War created competitive opportunities for indigenous businesses. Labeled compradors (*maiban*), capitalists, and national bourgeoisie, depending on the side of the political spectrum they were cast, these groups were seen to have reached a golden age in an emerging metropolitan landscape of treaty ports and coastal cities.[8]

A similar analytical logic is extended to the Chinese diaspora. Wang Gungwu maintains that overseas Chinese merchants thrived due to their distance from imperial control and to their skillful adaptation to colonial and local states in Southeast Asia.[9] Liu Kwang-ching observes the privatization of mercantile activities as reflected in guilds and native-place associations. He chronicles how late Qing compradors used their intimate knowledge of Western institutions to promote new practical philosophies on state and society.[10] New business interests in the early twentieth century were seen as continuing this maneuver between the legacy of tradition and modern Western challenges. Scholarly attention focuses on processes of nation-state building, where an assertive cosmopolitan elite assumed an autonomous identity and public space.[11] Riding on their "marginality," select entrepreneurial groups in Republican Nanjing, Shanghai, and Guangzhou conspicuously positioned themselves as national politics became decentered.

However, one cannot ignore the demise of mercantile groups in other regional cities and towns. The decline of the Huizhou merchants started in the early nineteenth century, when the monopolistic powers of state licenses were eroded. Many *hang* merchants in Guangzhou were bankrupted before the system was finally abolished. The devastation of the long-distance traders of agricultural products in Guangdong in the early twentieth century also stood in sharp contrast to the fortunes of the new militarized bosses in the same region.

It remains difficult to pinpoint the predicaments of the range of entrepreneurs in Chinese history, their membership, the nature of their business, their lifestyles and outlooks, their shifting alliances with power, and their national impact. If the term *merchant* defies definition as a distinct social category vis-à-vis the state in the Ming and Qing, merchants' differing fortunes in the Republican era are also hard to categorize. It may be more fruitful to treat these mercantile experiences as multilayered processes that intertwined with the making of cultural, economic, and political institutions in particular historical junctures. Granted that there are always winners and losers in history, a discussion of what contributed to the fate of mercantile groups in relation to the fluctuating fortunes of state and local society will sharpen our focus on their identities. Instead of subscribing to the mechanical dichotomies of state/market, urban/rural, elite/popular, and public/private, we may focus on the creative linkages forged by merchants in their efforts to excel in the circumstances in which they found themselves. As a result of those efforts, they changed the terms for dialogue and invented new cultural arenas, which integrated local society, the larger political order, and their own identities.

Once local agency and its historical complexities are analyzed, state institutions and agendas appear to have been nuanced and amorphous rather than restrictive and bureaucratic. At a discursive level, the state could be a fluid cultural idea subject to manipulation and contest. In previous articles, I have argued for a decentered view of the Chinese state. Such a view allows us to appreciate more fully the input from various social groups positioned in different parts of the empire. These groups had emulated what they perceived as literati values of the political center. In the process, they contributed to the creative making of regional society as well as the authoritative language of the state. What became recognized as cultural orthodoxy had much to do with the local resourcefulness of these agents, intentional or otherwise.[12]

The ambiguous nature of merchants and their cultural efforts also allows us to rethink the terms of debate on "civil society" in historical and contemporary China. In a study of contemporary urban China, Elizabeth Perry aptly summarizes such rethinking: "Our Western social science habit of viewing state-society relations as a zero-sum game, in which society's gain is the state's loss, does not shed much light on a China where private ties, public associations, and state agents are so thoroughly intertwined."[13]

What follows will be an exploratory essay, a rethinking of historical and ethnographic materials on the Pearl River delta that I have collected over the years. The maneuvers of mercantile groups in the late imperial period will be contrasted with those in the early twentieth century. If there are visible gaps in the data and a conscious rereading of it, this is because my research has not been focused on mercantile experiences or the Republican period. I shall draw upon the works of historians and, in particular, colleagues who have worked on Guangdong. In the past few years, we have tried to fine-tune issues in historical anthropology, reset basic parameters on which the map of Chinese culture was drawn, and uncover voices in crucial moments of history that might not have been given the attention they deserve.[14]

MERCHANTS IN THE MAKING
OF THE LATE IMPERIAL STATE AND SOCIETY

If we do not analytically pose state orthodoxy and agrarian institutions against merchant interests, how do we assess the historical efforts of mercantile groups in bridging state and local identities? Scholars often assume that literati were more important than merchants in creating ideological commitment to the state.[15] They may acknowledge that gentry and merchants often overlapped in membership in the commercial regions during the Ming and Qing, but they seldom give merchants a leading cultural voice.[16] However, Yu Ying-shih in a recent article presents ample evidence, from the sixteenth century on, that merchants were able to create cultural space on their own terms while making every attempt to emulate orthodoxy. In the process, they changed the overall philosophical orientation of Chinese tradition itself.[17]

To give due attention to the interactive impact of merchants' actions on mainstream culture and society, Susan Mann argues that, "like all agrarian societies, China offered merchants ideological sanctions and organizational roles that legitimized their status, incorporating them fully into the workings of the body politic.... The Qing call to 'make people content and facilitate the activities of merchants' (*anmin tongshang*) recognized the integral relationship between a state agrarian order and a regular flow of commerce."[18] Her study minimizes the assumed incompatibility of state orthodoxy and merchant interests, and focuses on liturgical leadership and market town development made possible by a state that recognized the merits of commerce.

David Faure brings attention to another side of the merchants' bridging functions—the merchants' initiative in making local rural society, the cultural foundation of which was shared, if not synonymous, with the Confucian state. He addresses the problem by highlighting new dimensions of being a merchant and making lineage. Stressing that mercantile activities permeated many social arenas, he observes, "Historians of China recognize that, in the Ming and the Qing, merchants contributed to their lineages and drew from them resources that they put into their business activities. While this view of the lineage gives it a place in business history, it nevertheless characterizes lineage institutions as being extraneous to the world of business. In this short note, I wish to argue that the distinction between lineage and business activities can often be misleading, and that the development of the lineage as an institution must be recognized as an intrinsic element in the history of Chinese business."[19] In a political system where commercial law did not exist, Faure argues, patronage was actively sought to ensure business security. From the Ming dynasty on, the territorially based lineages that rose to dominate the landscape of the towns and villages of south China, with their corporate estates, ornate ancestral halls for ritual and worship, and array of literati members, were consciously cultivated to provide the necessary patronage networks for the fledgling commercial interests.[20]

Faure's analytical point is relevant in other aspects of social life as well. Materials from the Pearl River delta in the Ming and Qing periods largely support the view that corporate lineage estates in the sands (*sha*), popular religious beliefs and practices, academies, and strong territorial bonds based on settlement rights in the expanding delta grew with the region's commercialization. Although these cultural features were long recognized as major components of a state agrarian society, their making could not have been possible without crucial input from and impact on mercantile interests.[21]

Historical records from Foshan illustrate the point. Foshan was one of the four prominent market towns (*zhen*) of China. Since the Ming, it had been famous for iron-implements industries, pottery kilns, and dyed-cloth and papermaking businesses. However, it excelled not in industries alone. It was home to the delta's powerful lineages surnamed Xian, Li, Chen, and Huo. From the 1400s to the 1800s, these lineages produced a dazzling array of literati figures and owned extensive river marshes, kilns, lumber farms, ironworks, pawnshops, markets, and river landings. They had mobilized effectively for community defense, especially against the rebellion by Huang Xiaoyang in 1450. They were also promoters of a cult of the ancestral temple (*zu miao*) in Foshan with elaborate annual rituals.

The career of a prominent native of Nanhai county, in which Foshan was located, illustrates a creative fusion of these multiple interests and experiences. Huo Tao's ancestors supposedly started as duck farmers in the river marshes. They later operated iron-casting businesses, pottery kilns, and lumber farms. Huo Tao succeeded in the literati route. In his rise through the ranks of the imperial bureaucracy in the Ming, his family accumulated vast properties in the sands, which formed the backbone of corporate lineages that David Faure described. As minister for the board of rites in the Jiajing reign (1522–66), Huo Tao sided with the emperor against a majority of the ministers in the Great Rituals Controversy (*da liyi*) during the 1520s. According to Faure, the debate was one of the most emotionally charged and divisive in the Ming court. By supporting the emperor's wish to give ritual superiority to his blood ancestor rather than to the person from whom he inherited the throne, Huo sided with two other senior officials of Guangdong to stress the primacy of primordial ties. It was not entirely coincidental that, in 1525, Huo built a hall to honor founding ancestors of his lineage in his native village, Shitou *xiang* near Foshan. After that, there was in Guangdong a proliferation of territorially based lineage formations that stressed blood ties to the focal ancestor, literati achievements, written genealogies, and landed estates.[22]

Faure's observations may lead one to credit Huo Tao with the creation of a literati form of cultural orthodoxy in Guangdong. However, Huo was also known to promote overseas commerce when the Ming court was advocating exclusion. He opposed the court's policy of suppressing sea trade (*haijin*), noting that trade with Southeast Asia could be mutually beneficial and that China should not commit self-imposed closure (*zikun*) by rejecting traders from those areas.[23]

The Foshan materials show that the mercantile activities, the development of the sands, the rise of corporate lineages, and literati achievements intertwined to create a thriving regional culture and society. Mercantile activities did not appear to constitute a social force that arose from a previously undifferentiated rural society, nor did merchants eventually develop autonomous voices challenging the state. Instead merchants seemed to function best during the heyday of imperial fortunes and orthodoxy, and when rural society was intimately linked to merchant operations. Mercantile interests and their cultural maneuvers had allowed local, regional, and state identities to complement and penetrate one another. This historical process is summarized by two Chinese economic historians, Tan Dihua and Ye Xian'en. Although framed in Marxist language, the message is clear:[24]

> Foshan zhen prospered during mid-Ming when iron- and pottery works developed under the general conditions of an increasing social division of labor and commodity production. However, feudal power privileging descent rose with Foshan's economic prosperity and strengthened its control over and interference in the economy. When prominent merchants continued to become feudal gentry, and when lineages invested in scholarly talents with lineage properties, cultivating droves of feudal bureaucrats, Foshan became filled with these literati types, expanding forever the consuming and parasitic population. A productive city gradually became a place of consumption; a specialized industrial and commercial city ended up being a fortress of feudalism. (163)

Social pluralism, competent self-management, a coherent prosperity, and alliance with officials stressing morality and restraint are themes noted by historians in the characterization of merchant-state relationships in the Ming and Qing in many areas of China.[25] Moreover, as the Foshan materials show, the merchants' intrinsic role in local society was by no means a matter of passive accommodation of a lack of alternative investment opportunities. The security of their urban operations depended on the active cultivation of rural bases and the associated cultural repertoire, which the imperial dynasties had promoted as their own civilizing agenda.[26]

COMPARATIVE MATERIALS ON HUIZHOU MERCHANTS

The parallels between Foshan and Huizhou merchants are striking. Despite the span of historical time and space between Anhui province where Huizhou lies, and the Pearl River delta in Guangdong province, which is home to Foshan, some comparisons can be made.[27] First, owners of large private lands in Huizhou were rare. Ye Xian'en observes in his book on the Huizhou merchants in the Ming-Qing period that few private landlords owned over 100 *mu* of land.[28] This form of investment in land was small in proportion to the enormous wealth accumulated in commerce. However, merchant contributions to ancestral estates were substantial, amounting sometimes to thousands of *mu* in wooded hilly land.[29]

Many of the estates were rented out long term to rich households who contracted bond servants (*dian pu*) to manage the wooded lands.[30] These operations assured merchants of a steady supply of products (such as lumber, bamboo, and tea) for their trade, and profits accumulated were often turned into loans for interest collection. The vast sandy land in the Pearl River delta auctioned out by town-based ancestral trusts to tenant contractors for long-term development quite paralleled the cultivation of woods for lumber in the hills of Huizhou.[31] Furthermore, in Guangdong, it was common to find entire villages of particular surnames that were bond servants to established lineages. However numerous their members were, they were treated by their patrons as mixed surnames (*za xing*), that is, as members of lineages without ancestral halls and subject to numerous ritual restrictions.[32]

Economic functions aside, the estates in both Huizhou and Guangdong and the rituals they financed had a cultural-political dimension. They were set up in the name of founding ancestors. With due recognition by state officials, local populations claimed native roots and the associated rights of settlement and use. Furthermore, the estates were managed by those linked to the town merchants with particular social bonds and obligations. Many of the functionaries had become prosperous entrepreneurs themselves, but cultural rules demarcating status remained strong.[33] The merchants' contribution to the estates legitimized their membership in the community despite their prolonged residence in towns and cities. Harriet Zurndorfer's examination of the Fan lineage estates reveals generations of land and other investments by lineage segments whose members became prosperous in commerce.[34] In a word, lineages were more than kinship and rituals: they were cultural inventions with significant economic and political impact.[35] In an emerging status hierarchy of which lineage became a significant component, a merchant could profit as kin and patron.

Cultural strategies extended beyond the local community. Historical materials on Huizhou merchants point to the elaborate political networking created by the merchants' support of education.[36] In the six counties of Huizhou, there existed fifty-one academies of varying sizes and visibility, most of them built during the Ming and early Qing, when the Huizhou merchants were enjoying great prosperity. From village schools to county academies, merchants' support not only prepared their kin for officialdom but the academies also became the arena for activities other than schooling. At times as a result of territorial bonds, at times as a result of kinship, these institutions were where local leaders, merchants, and officials composed the local and regional versions of a literati language for practical politicking. The numbers of graduates are staggering. During the Ming, Huizhou produced 298 *juren* (provincial graduates) and 392 *jinshi* (metropolitan graduates). In the Qing, it produced 698 *juren* and 226 *jinshi*.[37] The importance of the Xin'an school of thought (*Xin'an xuepai*), brandishing leading neo-Confucians as its native sons, can be seen as part of such a process.[38] It may be useful to view the late imperial state as a totalizing cultural idea rather than as political machinery, and as such it allowed local agents to maneuver shrewdly from within.[39]

The Huizhou merchants were also distinguished by their conspicuous elaboration of literati lifestyles, regional drama, and the arts. Major Huizhou opera troupes (*Si da Hui bang*) had prominent merchant patrons.[40] It would be difficult to dismiss their actions as unsophisticated acquisition of "superfluous things."[41] Ironically, in the merchants' eager emulation of the literati and in their subscription to what they perceived as state orthodoxy, they created new social and cultural space within the imperial order that linked city to country. In a word, judging from the development in Huizhou, merchants could be central to the very cultural processes of state making and of incorporation of local society into the imperial order. Hence their liturgical role during the high Qing.

G. William Skinner's work on the hierarchy of markets confirms the importance of economic nodes for cultural integration. The economic importance of the Huizhou merchants in the Yangzi River system is reflected in a saying that "one cannot claim to have a market if there are no Huizhou merchants."[42] Moreover, their influence on mainstream cultural pursuits could hardly be discounted. It is worth noting that out of the four persons who, at the request of Emperor Qianlong, donated over five hundred types of books and manuscripts to the imperial library (*Si ku quan shu guan*), three were merchants of Huizhou origin.[43]

CRISES IN THE LATE QING: A BALANCE DISTURBED

While merchant groups were able to maintain integrative links with both regional society and metropolitan politics during the dynastic heyday in the Ming and Qing, the balance was fundamentally disturbed as the nineteenth century wore on. Philip Kuhn and Susan Mann attribute the late Qing crisis to the intensified attempts by the state to reach society directly, after the growth of regional militaristic interests in the wake of midcentury rebellions. The capacity for merchant groups to meet an increasingly interventionist state depended greatly on how rooted the merchants were in the local community. This is illustrated by Mann's description of reactions by merchant groups in Huicheng (the Xinhui county capital) and neighboring Jiangmen city to the imposition of the transit tax (*lijin*) in mid–nineteenth century. The Xinhui merchants, represented by a locally entrenched fan palm guild and regionally powerful lineage formations, successfully resisted the tax. The Jiangmen merchants, many being transport brokers (and I suspect they had been *dan* fisherfolk in origin, with no local roots), avoided the tax by leaving the area. (The *dan* were a floating population of tenant-farmers, fisherfolk, and transport functionaries.) The historian Luo Yixing observes the similar fate of prosperous merchants a few decades later in Lubao, a river market north of Foshan that had thrived on being a distribution center of regional goods. The merchants met stiff competition from rising local bosses in the surrounding countryside, who used the label *shuiliuchai* (floating twigs, a term for the *dan*, who often were not given settlement rights in local communities) to disenfranchise them.[44] These labels, imposed on the less rooted by landed groups, were a powerful cultural means of exclusion and of defining social hierarchy in the late imperial order.

Paradoxically, merchants also suffered when the state faced its own crisis of legitimacy. Problems began to surface in the early nineteenth century in different guises. When the power of the state to grant trading monopolies diminished, the Huizhou merchants rapidly declined.[45] So did the Fu-Rong salt-yard elite lineages in Sichuan at the end of the century, when the structure of state authority governing salt production could no longer be profitably manipulated. Merchants in the regional cities and market towns of the Pearl River delta did not depend on state licenses. They thrived for another few decades in the nineteenth century by maintaining their own local monopolies and regional networks. With the influx of overseas Chinese capital after the 1911 revolution, fan palm and citrus peel merchants in fact reached the height of their prosperity.

However, the fact that the state lost its authoritative presence eventually caught up with them. They had less to draw on to enforce the terms of their trade in the local and regional environments. There were fewer means to redress contractual and credit arrangements that had been broken, and they were vulnerable to encroachment by marginal groups. They experienced tremendous hardships when they lost territorial control in the rural hinterland to local bosses who did not respect the moral authority and the power play embodied in literati etiquette or communal rituals. In Xinhui county, many large enterprises in the trading of grain, fan palm, and citrus peel closed down. Properties owned by guilds and academies, and town-based ancestral estates, were forcibly taken and sold by local strongmen who rose from the regional fringes. Their troops often occupied communal temples that were made into tax collection stations. At times, when negotiations with local bosses broke down, heads of merchant organizations were held ransom. The demise of the merchants accelerated during the war with Japan when central authority completely eroded. In Xiaolan *zhen* of Zhongshan county, over a hundred of the town's 393 ancestral halls were dismantled by local bosses who maintained a tense truce with the Japanese military and the Nationalist generals.

The merchants' difficulties were partly due to the general disruptions of war and political turmoil that brought great destruction to both villages and cities. In rural north China, Philip Huang has argued, the commercialized areas suffered greatly, especially those where warlord armies passed.[46] Prasenjit Duara stresses the intrusions of the Nationalist state via local agents in regional and county governments.[47] The merchants in the county capitals and market towns of the Pearl River delta, whose businesses provided crucial links between rural and urban areas, were caught at both ends. Some businesses survived, but others declined.[48] While appreciating what Joseph Esherick and Mary Rankin describe as the broad range of strategies available to local elites for maintaining dominance, one wonders if the rise of the new power holders in the Republican era could have been a catalyst for the demise of those who had prospered by traditional means before.

Mercantile groups in general did not face a common enemy—an imperial state clinging to "feudal" traditions. Instead, they were drawn to the political center and local society in vastly different but equally intense ways. New power holders in the early twentieth century, be they mercantile or militaristic, were able to make a new language of the nation and create alternative territorial bonds that attached local regions to the Republican state. Those who depended on the language of the imperial state and its shared cultural assumptions in local community fell by the wayside.

In the sections that follow, I will focus on a less explored factor in the demise of the merchants in the Pearl River delta in the Republican period: their inability to maintain ties to the rural community due to the rise of militaristic local bosses.[49] The cultural resources with which merchants adorned themselves, and which had dovetailed with the imperial order's civilizing enterprise, had been crucial to their social identity and economic prowess in the regional cities and towns during a large part of the late nineteenth century. It seems that the usurpation of a rural base eroded their claim to a legitimate place in the state patronage networks. This correspondingly closed off the arenas for practical networking and political negotiation based on shared assumptions. Moreover, unlike their counterparts in Guangzhou or Shanghai, these merchants were not close enough to the new political centers to develop any alternative cultural arenas to maintain the necessary political dialogues. When the state became less of a malleable cultural idea and more a predatory military power, the predicaments of commercial groups seemed to have become progressively grim. This upset the delicate balance between compliance and resistance that David Strand perceptively describes as the "embrace and foil of state agents" by commercial groups.[50]

If we follow this scenario, we must ask questions different from those already asked: What kind of mercantile groups were major players in the Republican period? How do we disaggregate their access to economic resources and cultural strategies? With regard to partnership in the building of a modern nation-state and cultural identity, whose golden age was it? How do we evaluate the fate of the traditional merchant institutions and arenas in the face of the rise of the new merchant-industrialist groups? Until we remark on their differing local bases and their complicity with imperial orthodoxy or with modern state institutions, it may be difficult to characterize the age of the Chinese bourgeoisie and its part in the restructuring of region, state, and nation, then and now.

GUANGDONG MERCHANTS

To understand how the Guangdong merchants lost to militaristic bosses from the regional fringes, one needs to examine the rural bases of the merchants as they had cultivated them. Since the mid-1980s, I have worked with a team of historians on several sites in the Pearl River delta, which is made up of the West (*Xi*), North (*Bei*), and East (*Dong*) River systems.[51] From the Ming to the late Qing, this part of the delta underwent rapid commercialization.[52] Marketing networks intensified among the towns and villages from the edge of the sands to county capitals. Regional cities emerged as production and distribution centers for local and long-distance trade in specialized agricultural and handicraft products. As described earlier in this essay, the distinguished products in Foshan were iron implements, pottery, dyed cloth, and paper.[53] In Xinhui, the commodities were grain, citrus peel, and fan palm. Over centuries of settlement, identities were constructed with elaborate ritual complexes that allowed local inhabitants to claim significant affiliations with the expanding Chinese imperial order—as migrants from the Central Plains, and as descendants of royal branches and officials. These processes of cultural construction were marked by important turns in local political economy as highlighted below.

The Development of the Sands

In order to elaborate on how merchants in the towns and regional cities anchored themselves in the delta, one cannot ignore the development of the sands, the associated cultural dynamics, and the power relationships that arose. Various elite interests in the towns were intimately tied to the conversion of vast areas of river marshes into cultivable farmland. They also controlled the harvests for a grain trade that grew in importance as the delta became commercialized. Settlers in Xinhui started to reclaim land on the western edge of the delta from the late Song on.[54] Extensive river marshes matured further southeast during the Ming.[55] The reclamation of the sands accelerated to such an extent that officials in the eighteenth century had to intervene due to massive flooding in the upper reaches of the river delta.[56]

Much of the sands was reclaimed in the name of town-based lineage estates during the Ming and Qing. Merchant groups in county capitals and market towns often financed these highly capitalized projects. They acquired river marshes measured in units of *qing* and donated them to ancestral estates.[57] Major tenant contractors for long-term rental of these ancestral estates often were managers of the estates themselves. They parceled out the land to give short-term leases to farmers. Being a tenant contractor of an ancestral trust could be an exclusive business. To qualify for the auctioning of the leases from the ancestral trusts, bidders were required to pay large deposits.[58] From the start, merchant wealth was intimately tied to land development and the subsequent grain trade.

The Language of Lineage and Ethnic Hierarchy

Investment in ancestral estates could be profitable. More important, affiliation with an estate enabled merchants to speak the language of territorial community based on patrilineal descent. The language also marked a clear political geography with an ethnic hierarchy. Town residents on the edge of the sands claimed lineage pedigrees connected with prominent families from the Central Plains, flaunted their wealth and literati connections, and put up severe barriers against those they referred to as *dan*. Backed by official pretensions and often by force, this lineage complex was an effective tool for claiming settlement rights, mobilizing large capital investment for the reclamation of the marshes, excluding potential challengers, and, not least, assuring business terms. Magnate lineages in the Foshan area that rose during the Ming—in Xiaolan town and Shunde county capital in the eighteenth and nineteenth centuries, and in Shawan *xiang* during the late Qing—were remarkable examples.[59] Disputes over the boundaries of properties as they changed with the meandering of the rivers were resolved not only with cultural strategies to demonstrate authority: power was also exerted by semiofficial militia organizations and bureaus set up by an alliance of officials, merchants, and lineage trusts in the urban nodes.[60]

However, the dominance of the merchant-gentry alliances was not assured. The remoteness of the sands allowed rapid social mobility among even those most discriminated against. Local functionaries accumulated enough of their own resources and negotiated with their former patrons. The use of force was not uncommon. They eventually acquired the necessary cultural symbols to establish themselves against a new layer of tenant farmers and *dan* fisherfolk farther out in the expanding marshes. Who could start an ancestral hall in a settled area became a most contentious issue in local life, and led to bloodshed, feuds, and lawsuits among surname groups.

Underlying the intense struggle over the cultural symbol of lineage were shrewd economic claims for rights to control the sands. Community and lineage halls, temples, and academies were public arenas for flexing political muscles. Closer to the county capitals, where one found official bureaus and magistrates, literati institutions and etiquette framed the terms of conflict and negotiation. As one ventured farther into the sands, increasingly control depended on the display of sheer physical might. In these areas, where gentrified rituals ceased to matter and the corresponding political leverage faded, the language of control was mixed with those of popular religious cults, brotherhood, and the outlaw. In a recent essay, Liu Zhiwei and I argue that identities were fluid. In times of peace, some of the floating population who engaged in transport and commerce accumulated enough resources to become respectably "landed." In times of disorder, those who remained in the regional fringes were branded as pirates.[61]

Coastal Trade

The historical circumstances of Guangzhou as a government-designated trading port since the Ming had also encouraged extensive sea-trading networks with Southeast Asia and beyond.[62] The impact of foreign trade along the coast and in the delta was profound. Not only were local agricultural and handicraft production stimulated by tastes and demands outside of the empire, but foreign silver too entered into daily trading transactions as much as temple contributions.[63] Even before the massive import of opium from the late eighteenth century on, foreign trade created powerful merchant gangs with armed fleets, culturally ambiguous brokers, and sophisticated marketing networks linked to river ports and market towns.[64] The tremendous wealth created was quite beyond the government's capacity to supervise. As in the inland rivers, in peaceful times these trading gangs maintained an appearance of respectability as merchants. In times of dynastic closure, they were labeled as crafty barbarians, local bosses, pirates, and smugglers.[65]

In sum, the political ecology of the sands and the coast allowed (and necessitated) the intertwining of dazzling commercial and landed wealth, the juxtaposition of territorial lineage groups, elaborate rituals, literati pretensions, outlaw imagery, and the blurring of boundaries with unorthodox and overseas interests. These had characterized mercantile life in Guangdong from the Ming through the early twentieth century. *Water Margin* (All men are brothers), a classic Ming novel about a group of outlaw heroes, was hardly fictional, nor was the idea of an exclusively town-based merchant elite conceivable. Questions remain. What caused the dramatic reversal of fortunes in the first few decades of the Republican era? Why were the merchants no longer able to perform their integrative functions of bridging state, literati, and rural community, which they had done well since the Ming? I would like to use historical materials centering on Huicheng to explore the questions.

NINETEENTH-CENTURY HUICHENG, XINHUI

Huicheng had been a sizable county capital since the Ming.[66] The four largest lineages in town, the He, Liu, Xu, and Mo, held ownership rights to extensive sands in the south and southeast of the county. The He lineage, numbering over three thousand in population, was particularly powerful because of He Xiongxiang, a minister of revenue in Nanjing during the Wanli reign in the Ming. His family moved from a village at the southern edge of the county capital to the town center at *Shangshu fang*, a neighborhood named after his official position. During his long retirement, he "mingled in the market with fishermen and peddlers," but he emerged to exert great influence whenever local circumstances required.[67] The other lineages also had ancestral halls clustering at the southern gate of the city, mixing with growing merchants' quarters and grain wharves that were connected by numerous waterways to other market towns and county capitals in the delta.[68] However, the processes of growth were periodically disrupted and local populations were dislocated. There were widespread revolts by bond servants against their lineage masters in the delta in the Ming. The coastal evacuations imposed by Emperor Kangxi in the early Qing also caused hardships.[69] New immigrants eventually resettled in the area. They grew into territorial lineages themselves, with demonstrated claims to settlement rights and eventual literati status.[70]

As mentioned earlier, reclaiming the sands became a capitalized commercial undertaking requiring long-term investment of labor and resources as well as the flexing of political muscles. Merchants in Huicheng and Jiangmen continued to invest in the sands in the nineteenth century in the form of trusts and estates. For example, an ancestral estate, the *He Bingru Gong tang*, operated the Zhihe grain shop in the Daoguang period and later opened the Hecheng native bank in Jiangmen. It acquired 140 *mu* of sands.[71] Another record describes a Li surname whose lineage claimed that they once had an ancestral hall at the western gate of the county capital. At the end of the Qing, a site was located at the center of Huicheng. Some members loaned and donated cash for the "rebuilding" of a hall in order to deposit their ancestral tablets. The managers spent 73,000 taels of silver for the building and used the remaining 24,000 taels to acquire river marshes between Xinhui and Xiangshan counties to create an ancestral estate.[72] Vast areas of sands were thus tied to the town through a hierarchy of tenant contractors and functionaries acting as clients and kin.

Grain from the sands was marketed in Huicheng and other towns in the delta. Another dominant commodity for long-distance trading was fan palm. The commodity linked the rural areas to Huicheng in multiple ways. A local historian estimated that by the late nineteenth century, over 250 *qing* of the county's diked fields were devoted to palm growing. The growers were large, some having 20 or so *qing* of palm fields, and many dried the leaves for processing as well.[73] Another group of enterprises made the fans. The large-scale ones took up long-distance trading.

Merchant organizations in Huicheng commanded a powerful presence in the surrounding area. Growers, fan processors, and traders belonged to various guilds, which oversaw an elaborate division of labor, credit arrangements, trading etiquette, and shrewd politicking. The overarching organization for the fan palm trade was the Fan Palm Guild (*Kuishan huiguan*), with its management body the *Yuqing tang*.[74] Smaller guilds further divided the trade, based on the particular grades of fans to be produced, the location of the workshops, and the region to which they transported their goods.[75] A major concern of the trade organization was control of the supply. Unregistered selling of the fan palm by growers caused prices to fluctuate and made it difficult for traders to maintain the standard of products.[76]

The long-distance traders (*chujiang bang*) depended on networks of native-place and guild associations, reaching scores of regional cities such as Hankou, Chongqing, Suzhou, Zhenjiang, and Changsha. They returned to Xinhui with a variety of products from other provinces (such as herbal medicine from Sichuan and cotton cloth and jute from Hunan, Hubei, and the Yangzi River delta) to be sold in the surrounding regions.[77] Since the nineteenth century, water transport through Jiangmen was a convenient channel for reaching Guangzhou, Shanghai, and Hong Kong. Sometimes foreign steamboats were employed. At the turn of the century, those of Butterfield and Swire, a British company, carried an average of two to three hundred tons of fan palm per boat to northern China, among other local agricultural products such as sugar and citrus fruits.[78]

Trades organizations had existed before the formal establishment of the Fan Palm Guild in Huicheng in 1848. With the guild, the production and trading of fan palm became more institutionalized. The guild grew into the most formidable political and economic power by the late nineteenth century. It held only a few hundred *mu* of land, the income of which was used for ritual and politicking purposes. More important, it wielded monopolistic power over the growing, financing, processing, and marketing of the fan palm. *Yuqing tang*, the management body of the guild, consisted of elected representatives from the various organized neighborhoods (*jia*) representing the different stages of producing the fans. With membership dues and income from its landed estate, the guild at the time boasted an annual income of about 30,000 taels of silver. It gave 1,000 taels to each of two local degree holders, who were entrusted to perform the necessary etiquette with officials. It maintained a militia for the collection of rent and surcharges and for the securing of the supply of fans from delinquent contractors.[79] When Nie Ergang was county magistrate in the 1860s, the traders in the guild were led by Liang Chunrong, a member of the Gangzhou public bureau. As Susan Mann observes in her reading of magistrate Nie's public announcements, the guild effectively fended off the magistrate's numerous efforts to impose the *lijin* tax.[80]

Prosperity continued for the dominant members of the guild for at least two decades into the twentieth century. A few of the major fan palm enterprises also traded citrus peel, an equally important commodity produced locally for long-distance trading. Among the enterprises were *Lin hengji* and *Liu yiji*. Both were family businesses that lasted generations and held landed estates. They monopolized the markets in Chongqing and, later, Shanghai.[81] Solidarity of the town merchants was made visible by rituals in the guilds and by the celebrations and parades of the deities at Dilintang, a communal temple in the commercial district at the southern edge of town.

Apart from the networks of relationships based on ancestral estates, temples, and guilds, an important arena in which local gentry, merchants, and officials mingled was the county academies.[82] These academies were organized on a territorial basis. According to a Xinhui county gazetteer (1840), *Gangzhou shuyuan* (academy) was set up by a county magistrate who allocated to the academy 1,100 *mu* of land in 1752. Local elites in Huicheng and some nearby townships took over its administration in 1806. A magistrate in 1760 established the *Jingxian shuyuan* in Jiangmen. He granted to the academy some river marshes that had been subject of a lawsuit. *Xi'nan shuyuan* was set up in 1845 by eight degree holders of different surname groups. Its estate was built through contributions from patrons in two subcounty districts in the southwestern part of the county. The academy forged an alliance of gentry and merchant interests who claimed ties to that region.

Although the academies had explicit goals of promoting education and literati values, their agendas included far more than Confucian schooling. Each of the academies owned between 600 and 1,000 *mu* of river marshes. Rituals for the birthday of Confucius were performed in keeping with the state's explicit educational goals. Grants were given to aspiring scholars. However, literati aspirations were linked to territory and kin. The beneficiaries were members of the home areas represented by the academies. The lineage ideal was reinforced, as patrons from a range of surnames from a particular region donated land to build up the academy's estate; the academy reciprocated by putting up tablets of their ancestors for worship. In turn, the legitimizing concern of ties to land and agriculture (*wuben*) was confirmed in the claims of origin. The question remains: to what extent were these academies reflections of state orthodoxy for social control, and to what extent were they local inventions? The process of mutual appropriation is worth exploring.

I see the academies as visible urban arenas where local nonofficials and, in particular, a growing community of merchants whose economic interests were intertwined with the development of the rural hinterlands shrewdly defined spheres of influence and control by improvising on a repertoire of literati symbols. To borrow Prasenjit Duara's idea for north China, these merchant-gentry institutions were nodes in a visible cultural nexus of power that bridged rural-urban distances, delineated social boundaries, defined statuses and identities, exerted control, and ultimately gave every participant his respective place in an evolving imperial order.[83]

The academies became centers for political mobilization in times of crisis. In the mid-1850s, local rebels associated with the Red Turbans sacked the county capitals of Shunde, Heshan, Jiangmen *zhen,* and besieged Huicheng for two months. They also ravaged the surrounding townships. The Xinhui county magistrate and a handful of local notables made every effort to assemble community leaders at the various academies to coordinate defense.[84] A meeting was first called at the *Gangzhou shuyuan.* When Jiangmen was threatened, members met at *Jingxian shuyuan.* Public bureaus (*gongju*) were formed within the context of the academies. Contributions were solicited from prominent merchants, while lineages in the surrounding townships provided volunteers. However, the leaders were constantly frustrated by unrest within their own camps from "unworthy members" of various surnames as much as by the reluctance of wealthy families to be involved. Most fled the county capital, and those who remained in the city stayed away from the public bureaus. The Fan Palm Guild, a symbol of mercantile interest in Huicheng, was in fact taken over by rebel troops for a short period.[85]

As in other parts of China, the disturbances in the delta changed the power relationships that merchants and landed elites had cultivated in the countryside. The century that began with the Red Turbans in 1854 and ended with the Communists in 1949 saw general militarism in the region. Both state officials and merchant-gentry organizations in the county capital seemed increasingly unable to mediate or supervise local militia units. The militarized bosses at the regional fringes took matters into their own hands. Various sands protection associations (*husha*) rose under their leadership with the explicit aim to collect taxes and protection dues. The notorious *Dongnan ju* (renamed *Dongnan gongyue* after the public bureaus were abolished) was led by local bosses of three townships in the southeast of the county.[86] It used armed fleets in the sands to smuggle salt, to force harvest, and to extract taxes and surcharges. The county magistrate Nie Ergang could only express indignation when gentry members of the *Xi'nan shuyuan* reported to him that farmers within the academy's jurisdiction were arrested, beaten, and jailed by the *Dongnan gongyue's* militia. When the magistrate's men caught the smugglers, the militia claimed them back. In one case, armed guards from the bureau came with a signed statement from their leaders. They forcibly took the boats carrying the seized goods and sailed away.[87]

By the late nineteenth century, the merchants' participation in Huicheng's social-political life shifted to a new institution and arena—the charitable associations (*shantang*). Individual charitable acts by merchants were historically well-known, and they were rewarded with academic and official titles. However, large-scale organizations for philanthropy and relief for the poor mushroomed only during the last decades of the Qing dynasty. They involved visible merchant participation in local society that focused on social problems arising from a changing urban landscape.[88] Their functions ranged from providing relief for the poor in the form of free food, medical care, coffins, and burials to maintaining public calm in times of crisis. In Huicheng, the board members of charitable associations were native bankers and leading traders of grain, fan palm, and citrus peel.

The limited focus of this chapter does not allow a detailed exploration of this new institutional form of merchant involvement in local society during the late Qing. My observation is that, in practice, these associations became urban in orientation, although the charitable acts continued to draw moral authority shrouded in Confucian terms.[89] Future research will determine whether the shift of attention to relief for urban poor was a cause or a consequence of the town-based merchants' loss of moral authority, which they used to share with those in the countryside.

WINNERS AND LOSERS IN THE REPUBLICAN ERA

When the imperial order faded into the background, social groups attached to particular institutions rose and fell with the political turbulence at the national, regional, and local levels. In the towns and cities of the Pearl River delta, merchants' fates seemed to be intimately tied to the structures of power and influence encompassed in the territorial bond—relationships and resources centering on lineage organizations, market hierarchies, popular religion, and political patronage. As the Qing fell, the languages of local dominance and state authority were reworked.

The Demise of Town-Based Ancestral Estates

In a previous essay focused on the Republican period, I compare the sharply different ways local strongmen in three townships transformed lineage institutions from within.[90] In Tianma *xiang* a few miles south of Huicheng, tenant contractors of lineage estates based in the county capital thrived by taking over the land of their patrons and then building ancestral halls in the village to claim settlement rights. The demise of the town-based estates had to do with the structure of land tenancy, rent collection, and the payment of taxes. Cash rents collected from tenant contractors on a long-term basis became worthless in the financial upheavals of the Republican decades. However, the estates were obligated to pay numerous taxes and surcharges imposed on land by local and regional state officials. The tax farmers (who collected taxes for the government but kept any amount they collected beyond the government's quota) happened to be local bosses themselves and often forced or colluded with managers of the estates to "sell" land cheaply. During nearly a decade of war with Japan (1937–45), grain became a precious commodity. The bosses, many of whom sided with the Japanese military that occupied Huicheng, took over palm and citrus fields and grew grain instead. They collected rent in kind from farmers and deposited the grain in the grain mills at Huicheng for speculation.

The changing relationship between the Chens of Tianma and the established lineages based in Huicheng was highlighted in an episode in 1948. At that time, there was a civil war on a national scale. Locally, the political vacuum provided opportunities and economic fluidity. The Mo lineage, landlords with large holdings and merchants in Huicheng, claimed that its ancestors had been settled in the area since the Ming and maintained elaborate ancestral halls. In the first few decades of the twentieth century, local bosses from Tianma, some of whom had been tenant contractors and functionaries of the Mo, had numerous conflicts in and out of court over control of the Mo estates in the sands. In the 1940s, it happened that a landowning family of the Mo lineage in Huicheng ran a county newspaper. The editor, Mo Chaoxiong, was a lawyer and county politician. He published an article written by his father ridiculing the humble cultural origins of the Chens (who were known locally as *dan*). When mediation by other politicians failed, local bosses at Tianma mobilized over a hundred villagers to march to the newspaper office in Huicheng with the intention of beating up Mo Chaoxiong. Mo managed to escape, but they destroyed his office. The county government officials, having been bribed by the Chens, did little to stop the mob and did not legally charge the offenders.[91]

The ancestral estates of major lineages in Xiaolan *zhen* of the neighboring Zhongshan county had a slightly different fate. Since the eighteenth century, the town had been dominated by an alliance of landed interests and grain traders from four major surnames whose ancestral estates held vast areas in the sands. For a town of a few thousand residents, the 393 ancestral halls had a towering presence. However, by the 1930s, they too were losing to the military bosses. Local strongmen from the sands did not build ancestral halls in the sands because there was no sizable village. Instead, they moved into town, took over the temples, and dismantled many of the ancestral halls. In the most important community event for the town in 1934, the chrysanthemum festival—which was held once in sixty years—the surviving ancestral trusts were barely able to keep up appearances. Instead, the active participants were members of mixed surnames who had speculated on financial markets in Shanghai. Their allies were local military officials who were political clients of warlords in Guangzhou.[92]

When the Japanese military occupied the area later in 1939, local bosses in town maintained an uneasy truce with the Japanese unit stationed in Shiqi (the county capital of Zhongshan). Over a hundred of the town's 393 ancestral halls were torn down. A social club, known as the *Siyou tang*, was set up by the head of the town, in which the different bosses could socialize and work out conflicts of interests. They formed "companies" to collect grain and taxes in the sands, very often by a blatant show of force.[93] Their patron was Yuan Dai, former captain of a crop-protection force and current commander of the third regiment under the Nationalist government. His deputy and cousin, Qu Renze, kept troops in the town, while seven of his captains were stationed in the sands.[94]

In Shawan of Panyu county, a smaller market town further southeast toward the sands, a He lineage had accumulated 60,000 *mu* of reclaimed river marshes. Members of this lineage, together with smaller surnames such as Li, Lai, and Huang, had built 116 ancestral halls. Annual rituals involving the founding ancestral hall, the *Liugeng tang*, and the local Beidi temple were formidable spectacles.[95] Residents in town lived off the grain rent. The collection of rent had depended on powerful tenant contractors who were lineage members themselves. In the turbulent decades of the Republican era, auctioning off the land and collecting rent necessitated a show of force. Estate managers and tenant contractors, who were the major participants in these auctions, were escorted by their own entourage of armed guards. The assets of *Liugeng tang*, the positions of its managers, and the vast power networks it commanded became the center of contention. Identification with the ancestral estate continued to be reinforced because of the intense competition. But local residents clearly distinguished the more "legitimate" managers and tenant contractors from the new local bosses, who, like their Zhongshan counterparts, organized collection companies out in the sands to extract protection fees, and who preyed on the rich and poor alike.[96]

In sum, a new generation of local strongmen rose from the regional fringes. Their power was not culturally recognized, but they were able to accumulate vast assets at the expense of the town-based lineages. They sidestepped the traditional arenas of negotiation by linking themselves directly to new regional military figures in a volatile network of patronage and intimidation. A different language of power prevailed over the cultural nexus that had been cultivated by the gentry-merchants for centuries. As rural communities were drawn into the personal orbit of the territorial bosses, the authoritative presence of the imperial order became increasingly remote in the daily lives of the villagers.[97] Militarists in Guangdong and elsewhere did take on various literati trappings and activities, such as building their own ancestral halls, patronizing schools, running for county government offices, and financing community rituals. However, these ritual efforts to gain legitimacy were diluted by the rapidly deepening crisis in the large political order.[98]

The Degentrification of Merchants in Huicheng

Commerce was rapidly "degentrified" as well in the early twentieth century due to rapid changes in the larger political environment. After the 1911 revolution, overseas Chinese investment was sought by various warlord regimes. The influx of capital reached its height during the rule of the warlord Chen Jitang, who held power in Guangdong from 1931 to 1936. His regime made great efforts in building an industrial and trading infrastructure centering on Hong Kong and Guangzhou.[99]

Although located at the western edge of the delta, Huicheng was the capital of a county known for its emigrants to Hong Kong and the United States decades earlier. The calls for nation building and modernization presented opportunities and challenges. Huicheng saw an influx of newcomers in the trading of fan palm and citrus peel, which began to break the monopoly of the elite merchant groups.[100] *Yuqing tang* changed its leadership structure in 1922. The body of representatives from the various *jia* (neighborhoods where fan palm enterprises were located) was renamed *lishi hui* (executive committee).

Until the late 1930s, literati figures connected to the former Gangzhou public bureau continued to play a role in the politics of the guild.[101] But real power was concentrated in the hands of Lu Zuonan, who became chair of the executive committee. His career illuminated the political fluidity of the times faced by merchant leaders and the maneuvers they made in order to thrive. Lu entered the fan-drying trade in 1918 through his former profession as a charcoal merchant. He rapidly expanded into fan making and became an upstart in the long-distance trade group. He represented a neighborhood of fan makers in the Fan Palm Guild. He was appointed a board member of the Xinhui Chamber of Commerce (formed in 1908) soon after. In 1922, when *Yuqing tang* reorganized, he assumed the headship. Two years later, he also took over the chairmanship of the chamber of commerce; its armed militia he transferred to the Fan Palm Guild. The *shangtuan* (merchants' militia) was first organized in the wake of a massive looting of the merchants' quarters in Huicheng by bandits.[102] It grew rapidly, expanding from five small bands in 1919 to eleven bands with nearly five hundred men and eight hundred rifles. Lu himself headed the band based in Sanya, where his enterprise was. He fought and colluded with local bosses who had taken over palm fields and who often sold their fans to the highest bidder rather than to contractors in town.[103] As a member of the executive committee of the Xinhui branch of the Nationalist Party, he used the same militia, which had been renamed *mintuan*, to put down a workers' strike in the late 1920s. He was also chief organizer for the parade of deities at Dilintang in 1930, an event organized once in ten years. His role during the Japanese occupation was not recorded, but his business empire survived into the 1940s. However, none of his networking with the local community saved his life. Branded as a local bully, he was tried in public and shot by the Communists during the land reform.

Similar episodes showed the precarious position of the town merchants, who were sandwiched between the local bosses and new regional military commanders.[104] Soon after the Qing fell, regional warlords rapidly sold various government properties in Guangdong. Huicheng was no exception. A group of merchants of the Yu surname from the neighboring Taishan county had a higher-order ancestral hall next to the old magistrate's office in Huicheng. They offered to buy the property in a secret deal with some officials linked to the warlord Long Jiguang in Guangzhou. A group of local notables learned of the deal and decided to challenge the bid. To claim the property back, they mobilized an odd alliance of the members of the three public bureaus in Huicheng, the chamber of commerce, and a handful of overseas merchants. They activated political networks in Guangzhou and finally bought the property with the backing of He Jintang, a banker and head of the Xinhui Chamber of Commerce in Guangzhou. The group was keenly aware of the need for broader alliances in politically volatile times, hence the idea of an academy for the entire county. The project stressed the solidarity (*hequn*) of the three regionally based groups of gentry-merchants in a spirit of "self-government" (*zizhi*). It took thirteen years, from 1915 to 1928, for the academy to be built. Copying the organization of the older academies, patrons contributed shares in order to place their ancestral tablets in the new hall. A sum of 634,000 taels of silver was quickly collected for the purpose, and the academy was formally established in 1923. However, the resources dazzled the eyes of regional commanders, one of whom in the same year demanded a protection fee of 10,000 taels. Several major gentry-merchants, including the banker He Jintang, were held by the commander until ransom was paid.[105]

The merchants did not subject themselves to the encroachment of the military commanders and the new state officials without a fight. There was the tax resistance incident in 1923. The merchants' quarters in Huicheng were built along a waterway outside the south gate of the city. Over the years, some shops had been built on the dikes. In 1923, during the wave of reassessing government properties by regional warlords in Guangdong, the county government imposed tax surcharges on temples and shops. The shopkeepers were moved to strike when their shops were boarded up by tax collectors. After mediation by the county head, a sum was negotiated, and the government promised never to make another assessment. Yet the bureau for the development of the sands overruled the decision and imposed new taxes. It took repeated petitioning of the provincial government by an alliance of leading merchants in Huicheng before the original decision was upheld.[106]

However, other efforts by the merchants were not as united. When the old city wall was slated to be dismantled so that a new road could be built, four successive county heads had to maneuver skillfully through competing groups of old and new entrepreneurs for two decades. As it was a lucrative channel for extracting contributions, bribes, and surcharges, there were endless debates as to whether it should be a government project (*guanban*), a joint government-merchant enterprise (*guanshang heban*), or a private project (*minban*). The project was only partially finished when the Communists arrived in 1949.[107]

New energies from Chinese merchants overseas boosted the local transformations of power. This had to do with the gradual shifting of political and economic energies to southern China after the imperial order was dismantled. Dr. Sun Yat-sen, himself a native of Guangdong, relied greatly on overseas Chinese in Hong Kong and the United States (where emigrants from the four counties to the west of the Pearl River delta [Siyi] had established themselves). In the name of modernization and nationalism, overseas merchants sought opportunities to reconstruct their "home bases," real or imaginary. Warlords linked with a new generation of self-styled politicians at the provincial and county capitals also tapped merchants abroad for support through charity organizations, chambers of commerce, and native-place and lineage associations. This trend reached a high point when Chen Jitang controlled Guangdong in the early 1930s. There were several years of stability, with active government investment in infrastructure, industry, and commerce.

A few cases in Xinhui illuminate these energies. The idea of a "native place" remained strong. David Faure has reported the reconstruction of an entire lineage community of the Ruan surname in Tanggang (southwest of Huicheng) after its destruction by feuds with other surnames in 1919. The efforts lasted for more than two decades, the 1920s and 1930s, with a board of directors in Hong Kong hiring local managers for the rebuilding. Having gleaned information from an archive of the correspondences between the manager in Huicheng and the board of directors in Hong Kong, Faure points to the continuous frustrations of the board and its ultimate failure to build a lineage community according to the books. A language of authority that the merchants had taken for granted no longer guided local actions. Political dynamics on the ground were quite beyond their imagination.[108]

The port of Gangzhou was a much more elaborate project involving overseas commercial interests. The port was to be located on the southwestern edge of Huicheng. According to the charter drawn up by the initiators, the alliance was broad and forward-looking rather than narrowly territorial. Merchant patrons from other counties and especially Hong Kong were actively invited to the joint venture. It started in 1910 with a few leading merchants in Hong Kong who, through the efforts of the chamber of commerce for Xinhui merchants in Hong Kong, assembled to plan a port. A charter was drawn up, and in the following month the organizers held a meeting with interested merchants in the *Minglun tang* (Confucian temple) in Huicheng. A few months later, seventy board members were recruited from Hong Kong, and some money committed. Architectural plans for the shops were drawn, and a fort on the opposite side of the river was planned as well. The merchants went ahead even though provincial officials refused to grant a subsidy for the fort project. I could not find other documents to explore further, but the building of the port seemed to have stalled afterward.[109]

About the same time, a similar project to develop the port of Xiangzhou at the tip of Zhongshan county in fact proceeded beyond the blueprints. Roads and shops were built, and some merchants started settling in. They banked on the idea that the provincial authorities would grant the port tax-free status. Migrant fisherfolk along the coast of eastern Guangdong began to congregate to fill transport and other labor demands. However, provincial officials never granted the port tax-free status. The merchants finally cut their losses and left the area. Local bosses took over what remained of the facilities and turned Xiangzhou into a thriving place for wartime smuggling.[110]

The last of the grand projects involved the building of the Xinning-Jiangmen railway. Again, the initiative came from an overseas merchant, Chen Yixi, a Taishan native who had emigrated to the United States. However, the building of the railroad was blocked by unlikely alliances of local gentry, merchants, and military bosses along its planned routes. The project, begun in 1907, was completed in fourteen years, but not without desperate networking and negotiating with regional government offices and military commanders. Numerous conflicts with local militia included the kidnapping of engineers and workers being beaten. The railroad was never very profitable, as roads and new bus lines posed increasing competition. The railroad was bombed by the Japanese military during the war, and the remains were dismantled by various local parties.[111]

LINGERING QUESTIONS

The Pearl River delta during the late imperial and Republican periods saw a drastic reconfiguration of power and authority that had been the bases for "merchant" identities. With their own historical specificity, leading mercantile groups in the Ming and Qing were able to create vigorous dialogues with the state by engaging in a language of orthodoxy. The dialogues took place in the local arenas of lineage, temple, guild, and academy.[112]

After the imperial metaphor receded into the background of political discourse, traditional mercantile groups suffered, as illustrated by those in Huicheng. Militaristic bosses colluded with precarious warlord governments and brandished a volatile language of power. As predatory *da tian er* carved out territories for control with their guns, the new business arena was far from cosmopolitan.[113] The demise of local merchants extended somewhat to overseas Chinese groups whose repeated attempts to re-create their home bases in the delta largely failed to materialize because they too had grown marginal within the local power configurations. Cultural strategies that had enabled merchant interests to merge with landed groups and rural community while sharing the moral authority of the imperial state faded from the public arenas long before the Communists made their direct attack in 1949.

Although the local bosses were hounded out during the land reform in the early 1950s, new arenas for mercantile activities did not materialize. Instead, as I have argued in previous publications, the Maoist regime virtually eliminated all private commerce. Market towns in the delta shrank drastically in size and impact as villages increasingly became cell-like units, their links to the outside severed. One saw the destruction of traditional hierarchies of marketing, lineage, and popular religion, and their associated cultural meanings. These relationships had functioned to creatively link villagers to region and state and had given local agents in late imperial Guangdong a relatively prosperous and pluralistic arena in which to maneuver.[114]

The analytical assumptions that fuel the debates about the Republican period are relevant to the present period. Can one assume that the post-Mao era signifies a struggle between state and market, and between the weighty bureaucracy and new entrepreneurial interests? Or must we find a less dichotomous framework in order to interpret commercial energies that are given relatively free rein all over China? Moreover, how do we take into account the decades of Maoist politics that might have fundamentally changed social institutions and cultural values?[115]

The Pearl River delta in particular is bustling with mercantile activities. The question remains as to who these "merchants" are. The prosperous operations are often dominated by a new generation of local cadres who have captured the market through their positions in the state system. A new authoritarianism comes hand in hand with dazzling wealth.[116] Market-town officials now stage community rituals and pursue the language of native place with unprecedented zeal and scale. This is to give a new grounding to overseas capital and business connections.[117] The politics of native roots has been played up in local festivals and lavish banquets. They are theaters of power and influence. Such politics attracts investments for factories, sports stadiums, and schools. In an era when the central government promotes modernization and cautious exposure to Western ways, local officials and residents seize the opportunity to negotiate the status of being China's new middle class.[118] The "local bosses" of the 1990s are cadres who clog the roads with their Mercedes-Benzes, who use their cellular phones to call public security officers in order to get out of traffic jams, and who install karaoke bars in their grossly magnificent villas to entertain business friends and mistresses.

In Guangdong as in other coastal provinces, new urban landscapes have emerged with new consumption patterns and political networking. But there are lingering questions for contemplation and further research. In the county capitals (and municipalities) of the Pearl River delta, where the dominance of local government cannot be discounted, and where state and commercial interests had been so consciously opposed during the previous decades of Maoist politics, what are the nature and identity of these new commercial bosses? Do we assume that mercantile agendas were only repressed in the previous era and are now exploding with a vengeance after the state decided to recede? Or should we expect local officials, armed with state mandate, on the one hand, and strategic control of local resources, on the other, to blossom into new modernizing elites? Using their entrenched power bases, they negotiate with, compete with, and accommodate state authority as much as they reinvent local traditions. Is this their way of being "Chinese" and "modern" when the central government struggles to define a new "socialism with Chinese characteristics"? If that is the case, what must we learn from previous generations of mercantile experience in order to appreciate the ways that the agendas of the larger polity, state agents, entrepreneurs, and localities are energized and reconstituted?

NOTES

1. See William Rowe, *Hankow: Commerce and Society in a Chinese City, 1796–1889* (Stanford: Stanford University Press, 1984).

2. David Faure, "What Made Foshan a Town? The Evolution of Rural-Urban Identities in Ming-Qing China," *Late Imperial China* 11, no. 2 (December 1990): 1–31.

3. See the works of the Chinese economic historian Fu Yiling on Ming-Qing merchant capital; Ye Xian'en and Harriet Zurndorfer on Huizhou; and Shiba Yoshinobu on Jiangnan, among others. For late imperial China, the cycles of regional systems are presented in the works of G. William Skinner.

4. For family institutions and women, see the works of Patricia Ebrey and Dorothy Ko. For popular religion, see those of Atsutoshi Hamashima, Valerie Hansen, and Richard Van Glahn.

5. See the works of Joanna Handlin Smith, Craig Clunas, and Timothy Brook on Ming commerce and culture.

6. See Kenneth Dean and Zheng Zhenman, *Fujian zongjiao beiming huibian: Xinghua fu fence* (Epigraphical materials on the history of religion in Fujian, Xinghua region) (Fuzhou: Fujian renmin chubanshe, 1995).

7. See David Faure, "The Lineage as a Cultural Invention," *Modern China* 15, no. 1 (January 1989): 4–36.

8. Marie-Claire Bergère, *The Golden Age of the Chinese Bourgeoisie, 1911–1937*, trans. Janet Lloyd (Cambridge: Cambridge University Press, 1989). See also Huang Yifeng et al., *Jiu Zhongguo minzu zichan jieji* (The national bourgeoisie in Old China) (n.p.: Jiangsu guji chubanshe, 1990).

9. See Wang Gungwu, "The Culture of Chinese Merchants," University of Toronto–York University Joint Centre for Asia Pacific Studies, working paper series no. 57, 1990. He argues that overseas Chinese merchants thrived within their own culture when they were free from bureaucratic restraints.

10. See Liu Kwang-ching, "Chinese Merchant Guilds: An Historical Inquiry," *Pacific Historical Review* 57, no. 1 (1988): 1–23; see also his book *Jingshi sixiang yu xinxing qiye* (Economic thinking and new enterprises)(Taipei: Lianjing, 1990).

11. See Mary Rankin, *Elite Activism and Political Transformation in China: Zhejiang Province, 1865–1911* (Stanford: Stanford University Press, 1986); Keith Schoppa, *Chinese Elites and Political Change: Zhejiang Province in the Early Twentieth Century* (Cambridge: Harvard University Press, 1982); essays by Keith Schoppa, Lenore Barkan, and David Strand in the volume of essays edited by Joseph Esherick and Mary Rankin, *Chinese Local Elites and Patterns of Dominance* (Berkeley and Los Angeles: University of California Press, 1990); see also Susan

Mann, "Merchant Investment, Commercialization, and Social Change in the Ningpo Area," in *Reform in Nineteenth Century China*, ed. Paul A. Cohen and John Schrecker (Cambridge: Harvard University Press, 1976), 41–48; Joseph Fensmith, "From Guild to Interest Group: The Transformation of Public and Private in Late Qing China," *Comparative Studies in Society and History* 25, no. 4 (October 1983): 617–40; Michael Godley, "Overseas Chinese Entrepreneurs as Reformers: The Case of Chang Pi-Shih," in *Reform in Nineteenth Century China*, ed. Paul Cohen and John Schrecker (Cambridge: Harvard University Press, 1976), 49–62; Hao Yen-p'ing, *The Comprador in Nineteenth-Century China: Bridge between East and West* (Cambridge: Harvard University Press, 1970).

12. See Helen Siu, "Recycling Tradition: Culture, History, and Political Economy in the Chrysanthemum Festivals of South China," *Comparative Studies in Society and History* 32, no. 4 (1990): 765–94; and afterword to *The Culture of Scholarship*, ed. Sally Humphreys (Ann Arbor: University of Michigan Press, 1997), 139–86. See also, "Where Were the Women? Rethinking Marriage Resistance and Regional Culture History," *Late Imperial China* 11, no. 2 (December 1990): 32–62.

13. See Elizabeth Perry, introduction to pt. 3, "Urban Associations," in *Urban Spaces in Contemporary China: The Potential for Autonomy and Community in Post-Mao China*, ed. Deborah Davis, Richard Kraus, Barry Naughton, and Elizabeth Perry (Washington, D.C.: Woodrow Wilson Center Press; Cambridge: Cambridge University Press, 1995), 297–301; also Elizabeth Perry, "Trends in the Study of Chinese Politics: State-Society Relations," *China Quarterly* (September 1994): 704–14. See also *'Public Sphere'/'Civil Society' in China? Paradigmatic Issues in China Studies*, the special symposium volume of *Modern China* 19, no. 2 (April 1993).

14. For the materials on Xinhui county, Guangdong, please refer to chaps. 3–5 of Helen Siu, *Agents and Victims in South China: Accomplices in Rural Revolution* (New Haven: Yale University Press, 1989). For a sample of historical essays on Guangdong produced by our research group, see David Faure and Helen Siu, eds., *Down to Earth: The Territorial Bond in South China* (Stanford: Stanford University Press, 1995).

15. See Hsiao Kung-chuan, *Rural China: Imperial Control in the Nineteenth Century* (Seattle: University of Washington Press, 1960); also Frederic Wakeman Jr. and Caroline Grant, eds., *Conflict and Control in Late Imperial China* (Berkeley: Center for Chinese Studies, University of California, 1975).

16. Boundaries were blurred. Merchants emulated literati lifestyles and unsuccessful literati turned themselves into prosperous entrepreneurs. See historical materials on Huizhou, and Shiba Yoshinobu, "Ningpo and Its Hinterland," in *The City in Late Imperial China*, ed. G. William Skinner (Stanford: Stanford University Press, 1977), 391–440.

17. See Craig Clunas, *Superfluous Things: Material Culture and Social Status in Early Modern China* (Urbana: University of Illinois Press, 1991), and Timothy Brook, *The Confusions of Pleasure: Commerce and Culture in Ming China* (Berkeley and Los Angeles: University of California Press, 1998), on the deeply felt impact of commercial wealth on culture and society during the Ming. See the insightful essay by Yu Ying-shih, "Business Culture and Chinese Traditions—towards a Study of the Evolution of Merchant Culture in Chinese History," in *Dynamic Hong Kong: Business and Culture*, ed. Wang Gungwu and Wong Siu-lun (Hong Kong: Centre of Asian Studies, the University of Hong Kong, 1997), 1–84.

18. Susan Mann, *Local Merchants and the Chinese Bureaucracy, 1750–1950* (Stanford: Stanford University Press, 1987), 27–28.

19. See David Faure, "A Note on the Lineage in Business," *Chinese Business History* 1, no. 2 (April 1991): 1–3. For a longer version of the paper, reprinted from the Second Con-

ference on Modern Chinese Economic History, see David Faure, *The Lineage as a Business Company: Patronage versus Law in the Development of Chinese Business* (Taipei: Institute of Economics, Academia Sinica, 1989).

20. David Faure, "Lineage as a Cultural Invention"; also Faure, "What Made Foshan," 1990.

21. See the introduction to David Faure and Helen Siu, eds., *Down to Earth.*

22. See also David Faure, "The Emperor in the Village: Representing the State in South China," in *State and Court Ritual in China,* ed. Joseph McDermott (Cambridge: Cambridge University Press, 1999).

23. On the industries and lineages of Foshan, see a series of articles in Guangdong lishi xuehui, ed., *Ming Qing Guangdong shehui jingji xingtai yanjiu* (Research on the society and economy of Guangdong in the Ming and Qing) (Guangzhou: Guangdong renmin chubanshe, 1985), in particular, the following articles: Luo Yixing, "Ming Qing shiqi Foshan yetieye yanjiu" (Research on the iron industries of Foshan during the Ming and Qing); Ye Xian'en and Tan Dihua, "Lun Zhujiang sanjiao zhou de zutian" (On the ancestral estates of the Pearl River delta); Cao Tengfei and Tan Dihua, "Guanyu Ming Qing Guangdong yetie ye de jige wenti" (On several issues of the iron industries in Ming-Qing Guangdong); Tan Dihua and Ye Xian'en, "Fengjian zongfa shili dui Foshan jingji de kongzhi ji qi chansheng de yingxiang" (Feudal lineage power and the impact of its control over Foshan's economy); Zheng Kecheng, "Huo Tao de zhengzhi zhuzhang he jingji sixiang—du *Ming shi. Huo Tao juan* zaji" (Huo Tao's political views and economic thinking—on reading *Ming History, the Biography of Huo Tao*). See also documents from *Ming Qing Foshan beike wenxian jingji ziliao* (Economic historical materials from stone inscriptions of Ming-Qing Foshan), ed. Guangdong sheng Foshan shi bowuguan et al. (Guangzhou: Guangdong renmin chubanshe, 1987).

24. See Tan Dihua and Ye Xian'en, "Fengjian zongfa shili dui Foshan jingji de kongzhi ji qi chansheng de yingxiang," ed. Guangdong lishi xuehui, 144–64.

25. For Jiangnan, see the works of Yoshinobu Shiba, Susan Mann, and Mark Elvin, among others.

26. The magnificent mansions of the Huizhou merchants, their lineage organizations, and their academies were public testimonies. In order to secure a solid grounding for their mercantile operations, merchants had tried to cultivate patronage and territorial bonds through native associations, trade guilds, charity, the buying of degrees, and support of popular religion. See the works of Ye Xian'en, Tan Dihua, and Luo Yi-xing in *Ming Qing Guangdong shehui jingji xingtai yanjiu,* ed. Guangdong lishi xuehui, 1985. For the relationship between popular religion and commercialization, see Valerie Hansen, *Changing Gods in Medieval China* (Princeton: Princeton University Press, 1990); Richard Van Glahn, "The Enchantment of Wealth: The God Wutong in the Social History of Jiangnan," *Harvard Journal of Asian Studies* (1991): 651–714; see also Atsutoshi Hamashima on the Chenghuang temples in Jiangnan. For the late Qing, see Madeleine Zelin, "The Rise and Fall of the Fu-Rong Salt-Yard Elite: Merchant Dominance in Late Qing China," in *Chinese Local Elites and Patterns of Dominance,* ed. Joseph Esherick and Mary Rankin (Berkeley and Los Angeles: University of California Press, 1990), 82–112; see also Lynda Bell, "From Comprador to County Magnate: Bourgeois Practice in the Wuxi County Silk Industry," 113–39, in the same volume.

27. See Ye Xian'en, *Ming-Qing Huizhou nongcun shehui yu dianpu zhi* (Rural society and the system of bond servants in Huizhou during the Ming and Qing) (Anhui: Anhui renmin

chubanshe, 1983); Zhang Haipeng and Wang Tingyuan, eds., *Ming-Qing Huishang ziliao xuanbian* (Selected materials on Huizhou merchants during the Ming and Qing) (Hefei: Huangshan shushe, 1985); Liu Shen, ed., *Huizhou shehui jingji shi yanjiu yiwenji* (Translated essays on the socioeconomic history of Huizhou) (Hefei: Huangshan shushe, 1987).

28. See Ye Xian'en, *Ming-Qing Huizhou nongcun shehui yu dianpu zhi*, 43.

29. See ibid., 42–56, on the small amount of privately owned land and the vast lineage estates in Huizhou.

30. See Harriet Zurndorfer, *Change and Continuity in Chinese Local History: The Development of Hui-Chou Prefecture, 800–1800* (Leiden: Brill, 1989); see also essays in Liu Shen, ed., *Huizhou shehui jingji shi yanjiu yiwenji*. Ye Xian'en asserts that apart from bond servants, migrant laborers—known locally as the shed people (*pengmin*)—were also a source of labor in the lumber, salt, and tea enterprises for which the Huizhou merchants were known (*Ming-Qing Huizhou nongcun shehui yu dianpu zhi*, 84–85, 110–16).

31. See Helen Siu, *Agents and Victims*, chap. 4.

32. The Yuan village (*Yuan jia cun*) next to Chakang, the native village of Liang Qichao in Xinhui, was one such village of bond servants. In Chaolian, an island off the coast of Jiangmen, the established lineages all had bond servants. See also Tan Dihua, "Ming Qing shiqi Zhujiang sanjiao zhou de shipu" (The bond servants of the Pearl River delta in the Ming-Qing period), in *Guangdong lishi wenti lunwen ji* (Selected essays on issues of Guangdong history) (Taipei: Daohe chubanshe, 1993), 45–72.

33. Ye Xian'en, *Ming-Qing Huizhou nongcun shehui yu dianpu zhi*; see also Fu Yiling's work on Fujian, where there had been numerous challenges and conflicts over former bond servants who became prosperous and who tried to establish their own ancestral halls. For similar cases in the Pearl River delta, see Liu Zhiwei's chapter, "Shawan of Panyu County," in *Down to Earth*, ed. David Faure and Helen Siu, 21–43.

34. Her study focuses on the Fan lineage of Xiuning county in Huizhou prefecture. Xiuning and Xi counties are the two regions that produced numerous literati and merchants. See Harriet Zurndorfer, "Local Lineages and Local Development: A Case Study of the Fan Lineage, Hsiu-ning Hsien, Hui-chou, 800–1500," in *Change and Development in Chinese Local History* (Leiden: E.J. Brill, 1989). She argues that the investments in lineage land and charity might not be large, but through financing the compilation of lineage genealogies and occasional charity, merchants were able to confirm their native roots and maintain ties in Xiuning. She uses the example of a Fan Huo, who lived lavishly as a salt merchant in Yangzhou. During serious floods and famine (in 1539 and 1542), he gave huge donations to the victims. However, Zurndorfer argues that these were public acts with political and commercial agendas, just like his giving expensive gifts to friends and officials. He showed no interest in relieving the everyday needs of his kin.

35. See David Faure, "Lineage as a Cultural Invention"; Helen Siu, "Recycling Tradition."

36. See Ye Xian'en, *Ming-Qing Huizhou nongcun shehui yu dianpu zhi*, chaps. 3–5.

37. See ibid., 187–92. It is important to note that some of the degree holders had had urban residences for generations but claimed various rural counties in Huizhou as their places of origin.

38. The neo-Confucians Cheng Hao, Cheng Yi, and Zhu Xi were claimed to be natives of Xi county, one of the six counties within the Huizhou prefecture (also known as Xin'an). See Ye Xian'en, *Ming-Qing Huizhou nongcun shehui yu dianpu zhi*, chap. 5.

39. This runs counter to a top-down approach on state ideology and political control by Hsiao Kung-chuan.

40. For example, the grandson of Zheng Jinglian, a salt merchant who resided in Yangzhou, and Jiang Heting were famous patrons of these operas. See Ye Xian'en, *Ming-Qing Huizhou nongcun shehui yu dianpu zhi*, 227.

41. See ibid., chap. 5 on Huizhou. On the elaborate gardens in Jiangnan in the late Ming where interests of merchants and literati mingled, see Joanna Handlin-Smith, "Gardens in Ch'i Piao-chia's Social World: Wealth and Values in Late-Ming Kiangnan," *Journal of Asian Studies* 51, no. 1 (February 1992): 55–81.

42. See Ye Xian'en, *Ming-Qing Huizhou nongcun shehui yu dianpu zhi*, 78.

43. See Keith Hazelton, "Ming Qing Huizhou de zongzu yu shehui liudong sheng" (Lineages and social mobility in Huizhou during the Ming and Qing), in *Huizhou shehui jingji shi yanjiu yiwenji*, ed. Liu Shen, 76–96, fn. 27 (the article was translated by Liu Zhiwei and Chen Chunsheng). The original reference can be found in Yong Rong et al., *Sifu chuanshu zongmu*, vol. 1, *Shengyu* (Imperial edicts) (Beijing: Zhonghua shuju, 1965), 2.

44. See Luo Yixing, "Territorial Community at the Town of Lubao, Sanshui County, for the Ming Dynasty," in *Down to Earth*, ed. David Faure and Helen Siu, 44–64.

45. See Ye Xian'en, *Ming-Qing Huizhou nongcun shehui yu dianpu zhi*, chap. 3, sec. 6.

46. See Philip Huang, *The Peasant Economy and Social Change in North China* (Stanford: Stanford University Press, 1985).

47. See Prasenjit Duara, "State Involution: A Study of Local Finances in North China, 1911–1935," *Comparative Studies in Society and History* 29, no. 1 (1987); *Culture, Power, and the State: Rural North China, 1900–1940* (Stanford: Stanford University Press, 1988).

48. See *Guangzhou gongshang jingji shiliao* (Historical materials on business and economy in Guangzhou), a special volume on commercial and industrial enterprises in Guangzhou during the early decades of the Republic, *Guangzhou wenshi ziliao* 36 (1986).

49. See Helen Siu, *Agents and Victims*, chaps. 4–5.

50. See David Strand, "Mediation, Representation, and Repression: Local Elites in 1920s Beijing," in *Chinese Local Elites and Patterns of Dominance*, ed. Joseph Esherick and Mary Rankin (Berkeley and Los Angeles: University of California Press, 1990), 218.

51. Our sites were Huicheng (Xinhui county capital) and Jiangmen on the Xi River system at the western edge of the delta, Xiaolan town of Xiangshan county, the settlements (*xiang*) of Shawan in Panyu county further southeast. There are also Foshan City, and Lubao of Sanshui county where North River joined the delta.

52. See Ye Xian'en and Tan Dihua, "Ming Qing Zhujiang sanjiao zhou nongye shangye hua yu xushi de fazhan" (The commercialization of agriculture and the development of markets and towns in the Pearl River delta during the Ming and Qing), in *Ming Qing Guangdong shehui jingji xingtai yanjiu*, ed. Guangdong lishi xuehui, 57–97. See also Tan Dihua, "Qingdai Zhujiang sanjiao zhou shangpin jingji de fazhan yu tudi wenti" (Commodity production and land tenure in the Pearl River delta during the Qing), in *Guangdong lishi wenti lunwen ji*, 81–98.

53. See Luo Yixing "Ming Qing shiqi Foshan yetieye yanjiu," 75–116. See also Tan Dihua, "Cong 'Foshan jieli' kan Ming Qing shiqi Foshan gongshanye de fazhan" (To view the development of commerce and industry in Foshan during the Ming and Qing from reading 'Neighborhoods in Foshan'), in *Guangdong lishi wenti lunwen ji*, 225–42.

54. See Zhao Shisong, comp., *Sanjiang Zhaoshi zupu* (The Zhao lineage genealogy of Sanjiang) (Hong Kong: n.p., 1937). The Zhao lineage of Sanjiang *xiang* (village), which owned extensive diked fields to its southeast, claimed to have descended from the entourage of the last Song emperor, who was defeated by the Mongols in the area. Another record in-

volved the Chens of Waihai *xiang*, south of Jiangmen City, where a Chen Xiang claimed 40 *qing* of sands that yielded a rent of 9,600 *shi* of grain. See Tan Dihua, *Qingdai zhujiang san-jiaozhou de shatian* (The sands of the Pearl River delta during the Qing dynasty) (Guangzhou: Guangdong renmin chubanshe, 1993), 76.

55. The sands reclaimed were situated in the eastern part of Xinhui county, the north-ern part of Xiangshan (after 1925 renamed Zhongshan) county, and the southern part of Panyu county. These sands were eventually known as the *Xihai shiba sha, Donghai shiliu sha,* and *Wanqing sha.*

56. See Kikuko Nishigawa, "Qingdai Zhujiang sanjiao zhou shatian kao" (An exami-nation of the sands of the Pearl River delta during the Qing), trans. Cao Lei, *Lingnan wen-shi* 2 (1986): 11–22, originally published in *Tōyō gakuho* 63, nos. 1 and 2 (1981): 93–136. See also Tan Dihua, "Qing dai Zhujiang sanjiao zhou shangpin jingji de fazhan yu tudi wenti," in *Guangdong lishi wenti lunwen ji,* 81–98.

57. See Huang Qichen, "Ming Qing Zhujiang sanjiao zhou de shangye yu shangye ziben cutan" (An initial exploration of commerce and commercial capital in the Pearl River delta during the Ming and Qing), in *Ming Qing Guangdong shehui jingji xingtai yanjiu,* ed. Guangdong lishi xuehui, 187–236.

58. See Ye Xian'en and Tan Dihua, "Lun Zhujiang sanjiao zhou de zutian," 22–64.

59. See David Faure and Helen Siu, eds., *Down to Earth,* on the evolution of the lineage complex in the Pearl River delta.

60. See the works on Kikuko Nishigawa on the local bureau for protecting the sands in Shunde county; see also Tan Dihua, "Xiangzu dizhu dui Zhujiang sanjiao zhou diqu de kongzhi yu husha de yuanhui" (The control of the Pearl River delta by lineage landlordism and the rise of the sands protection apparatus), in *Guangdong lishi wenti lunwen ji,* 155–74.

61. See Helen Siu and Liu Zhiwei, "Lineage, Market, Pirate, and Dan—Ethnicity in the Pearl River Delta" (manuscript under review).

62. The prohibition of sea trade (*haijin*) was relaxed in 1685, but the Qing government in 1757 closed the coastal ports, except Guangzhou, to foreign trade. See Huang Qichen, Deng Kaisong, Xiao Maosheng, "Guangdong shang bang" (The Guangdong merchant group), chap. 5 of *Zhongguo shida shang bang* (The ten dominant merchant groups of China), ed. Zhang Haipeng and Zhang Haiying (Hefei: Huangshan shushe, 1993); see also Li Longqian, "Ming Qing Guangdong duiwai maoyi ji qi dui shehui jingji de yingxiang" (For-eign trade in Guangdong during the Ming and Qing and its impact on society and the economy), in *Ming Qing Guangdong shehui jingji xingtai yanjiu,* ed. Guangdong lishi xuehui, 279–312.

63. On the circulation of silver in Guangdong during the Ming-Qing period, see Chen Chunsheng, "Qing dai Guangdong de yin yuan liutong" (The circulation of silver dollars in Guangdong in the Qing), in *Ming Qing Guangdong shehui jingji yanjiu,* ed. Ming Qing Guang-dong sheng shehui jingji yanjiu hui (Guangzhou: Guangdong renmin chubanshe, 1987), 206–36.

64. For comparison, see Fu Yiling, *Ming Qing shidai shangren ji shangye ziben* (Merchants and merchant capital in the Ming and Qing) (Beijing: Renmin chubanshe, 1956), on the sea trad-ing groups from Fujian; and Ye Xian'en, *Guangdong hangyun shi (Gudai bian)* (The history of sea transport—volume on the premodern period) (Beijing: Remin jiaotong chubanshe, 1989), on the merchant groups from the port of Zhanglin near Shantou in eastern Guangdong.

65. See Zhang Wenyin, "Ming Qing Guangdong zhongxi maoyi yu Zhongguo jindai maiban de qiyuan" (The East-West trade in Guangdong during the Ming and Qing and

the rise of the modern comprador), in *Ming Qing Guangdong shehui jingji xingtai yanjiu*, ed. Guangdong lishi xuehui, 313–48.

66. Some material on Huicheng is drawn from Helen Siu, *Agents and Victims*, chaps. 2–5. When the chapters were written, they were not focused on the issues I am now exploring. I have also done a conscious rereading of the research materials for this essay.

67. See Tan Dihua, *Guangdong lishi wenti lunwen ji*, 95. Also, according to a local saying, He Xiongxiang accumulated 350 *qing* of sands in his lifetime, which he divided among his sons before his death. Jiuzisha, a strip of river marshes he nonchalantly gave to his newborn ninth son after he had divided his estate, grew in value to 6,000 *mu*. While other properties were taken over or sold over the centuries, Jiuzisha remained the property of the ancestral estate *He Wenyi Gong tang* until the twentieth century. It was a testimony to the power of the He lineage in Huicheng. See He Zhuojian, "Shangshufang He shi fengjian zuzhi" (The feudal organization of the He lineage in Shangshufang), *Xinhui wenshi ziliao* 1 (1963): 51–56.

68. There were the Tan lineage in Chengnan, the Mos of Nanmen, and the Xu of Nanbiantang. According to a document on the rules for the Xu lineage, the author lamented that "for a hundred years or so after the founding ancestor moved from Kaiping to Xinhui, the lineage was prosperous, with literati honors and commercial achievements; but in the last few decades, the lineage has sadly declined." See "Xinhui xiancheng Nanbiantang Xu xing zugang" (The lineage charter of the Xu in Nanbiantang of Xinhui county capital) (manuscript, Huicheng, 1936). In the late 1970s, the ancestral halls of the Mo lineage at the southern edge of Huicheng were still standing.

69. For example, two lineage genealogies in the area recorded these events: *Xinhui Sanjiang Zhaoshi zupu* (The lineage genealogy of the Zhao surname of Sanjiang), and the *Chaolian Lubian Lushi zupu* (The lineage genealogy of the Lu surname in Lubian neighborhood of Chaolian). A Liang lineage genealogy in the neighboring Zhongshan county also recorded similar hardships. See *(Zhongshan) Kanxi Liangshi zupu*, 5a-5b, "Qianmu zupu xu" written in the twelfth year of Kangxi (1673), Zhongshan 1927 edition.

70. For example, the founders of a Chen surname group settled in Tianma village (*xiang*) a few miles south of Huicheng during the Ming. A member of a seventh generation who was a degree holder moved to Wufuli, a neighborhood outside the southern gate of Huicheng. An ancestral hall was built for him in the fifteenth year of Jiaqing's reign (1711) in Wufuli. In the nineteenth century, his tablet was deposited in the *Xi'nan shuyuan* (academy) of Huicheng and in the higher-order lineage hall of the Chens at Xiguan, the merchants' quarter in Guangzhou. See *Chen zu shi pu* (The lineage genealogy of the Chen surname) (Huicheng, 1923).

71. See Tan Dihua, *Qingdai zhujiang sanjiaozhou de shatian* (1991), 79.

72. See "Zhiqing zuci luocheng gongding cigui fu zhengxin lu" (The hall regulations at the establishment of the Zhiqing ancestral hall, with a directory of donors attached) (n.p., 1901).

73. Guan Xiekuang estimated that the fifteen largest grower-dryers of fan palms monopolized about 90 percent of the business; see Guan, "Jiefangqian Xinhui kuiye jingying gaikuang" (The fan palm business in Xinhui before liberation), *Xinhui wenshi ziliao* 12 (1983): 1–28.

74. Under it were these guilds: the *Lianxing gongzhan* for the growers, *Lianxing tang* for the palm-drying fields, *Tongren tang* for fan-making shops, and *Guangshun tang* for the long-distance traders.

75. According to a document of *Jimei tang*, a guild for palm-drying and fan-making businesses, 693 signed on as members between 1713 and 1845.

76. See "Jimei tang huigui bu" (The rules of Jimei tang) (manuscript, Huicheng, n.d.).

77. See Guan Xiekuang, "Jiefangqian Xinhui kuiye jingying gaikuang."

78. See Mo Yinggui, "Ying shang Taigu yangheng jin bainian zai Huanan de yewu huodong yu Mo shi jiazu de guanxi" (The activities of the British company Butterfield and Swire in south China for the last hundred years and the relationship with the Mo lineage), *Guangdong wenshi ziliao* 44 (1985): 77–131.

79. Members often advanced credit for growers with the expectation of a specific supply of fans at a set price. It was difficult to collect during harvest, when growers were tempted to sell to higher bidders.

80. See Susan Mann, *Local Merchants*, chap. 7. See also Nie Ergang, *Gangzhou gongdu* (Public announcements while in office in Gangzhou) (n.p., 1863).

81. See Guan, "Jiefangqian Xinhui kuiye jingying gaikuang"; *Lin hengji* folded before the Japanese war, and *Liu yiji* continued into the early years of the People's Republic. Land reform documents from the Xinhui Records Office (*dang'an guan*) reveal vast estates owned by *Liu yiji*. Members of these enterprises were powerful representatives in the guild and later in the Xinhui Chamber of Commerce; for the citrus peel enterprises, see He Zhuojian, "Jiefangqian de Xinhui chengpiye" (The citrus peel business in Xinhui before liberation), *Xinhui wenshi ziliao* 20 (1965): 111–21.

82. For more detailed descriptions of the academies, please see Helen Siu, *Agents and Victims*, chap. 4.

83. See also Helen Siu, "Recycling Tradition."

84. The Red Turbans disturbance broke out in 1854 and spread to various parts of the Pearl River delta in 1855. The group was put down in the 1860s.

85. For a general documentary history of the Red Turbans in Guangdong, see Guangdong sheng wenshi yanjiu guan and Zhongshan daxue lishi xi, comp., *Guangdong hongbing qiyi shiliao* (The just uprisings of the Red Turbans in Guangdong), vol. 1 (Guangzhou: Guangdong renmin chubanshe, 1992). For events around Huicheng, see Chen Xiangpu, *Gangcheng zhenge ji* (A chronicle of preparing for battle in Gangcheng) (n.p., 1855); Tan Zu'en, *Xinhui jingbian shilue* (An account of rebel suppression in Xinhui) (1855; reprint, Guangzhou: Zhongshan tushuguan, 1960). A record in Tan's accounts mentioned that the Fan Palm Guild was taken over by some rebel troops for a moment.

86. The three townships were Chaolian (with established lineages of the Lu, Chen, Ou, and Pan surnames), Hetang (with the Rong and Li surnames), and Waihai (the Chens). Some notorious rebel leaders during the Red Turbans attacks also came from these townships.

87. See Tan Dihua, *Guangdong lishi wenti lunwen ji*, 155–74, who quoted from "Yan chi Dongnan gongyue geshen lun" (On putting the gentry of the Dongnan alliance under strict order), in *Gangzhou gongdu* by Nie Ergang.

88. In Guangzhou, for example, there were the *jiu da shantang* (Nine Great Charitable Associations). Apart from offering the usual relief for the poor, they diversified quickly into promoting new technologies, women's education, training for local self-government (*difang zizhi*), and maintaining public order. See Tang Yusheng, comp., *Chuan Yue shehui shilu chupian* (The initial compilation of social records of all Guangdong) (Guangzhou: Diaocha chuan Yue shehui chu, 1909). For a detailed analysis of the cultural and political impact of merchants in Hong Kong in the late nineteenth century, see a study of the Tung Wah Hospital by Elizabeth Sinn, *Power and Charity* (Hong Kong: Oxford University Press, 1989). A summary of her argument is found in "Philanthropy and the Business World," in *Dynamic Hong*

Kong: Business and Culture, ed. Wang Gungwu and Wong Siu-lun (Hong Kong: Centre of Asian Studies, the University of Hong Kong, 1997), 230–52.

89. See "Xinhui cheng Tongshen shantang Renji yihui Taoze yihui Zequn yihui xizi shicha zhimai baigu ershiwu qi zhengxinlu" (The twenty-fifth directory of donations for Tonshen, Renji, Taoze, Zequn charity associations for welfare and burial in Xinhui) (Huicheng: Yixing, 1936).

90. See Helen Siu, "Subverting Lineage Power: Local Bosses and Territorial Control in the 1940s," in *Down to Earth*, ed. David Faure and Helen Siu.

91. See Lun Haibin, "Mani ren daohui 'Minhui ribao' " (People from Mani ransacked 'Minhui daily') *Xinhui wenshi ziliao* 6 (1983): 47–50.

92. The opening ceremonies of the festival were officiated by Liang Bingyun, head of the third district and an appointee of the Nationalist government, and He Naizhong, a local resident and onetime adviser to the warlord Feng Yuxiang. A trade fair was organized in Hefeng Shuyaun (academy), which had been built by lesser surnames in town to compete with the established lineages.

93. See *Zhongshan wenshi ziliao*, nos. 1–3, for descriptions of the local bosses in the sands of Zhongshan county. The most powerful companies were the *Minsheng gongsi* (company), based in Xiaolan, and the *Minli gongsi*, based in Minzong, an outpost in the sands.

94. He Yanggao, formerly a large landlord in Xiaolan and a local historian, estimated that in Sisha, a strip of sands southwest of Xiaolan, the area held by these bosses increased from 400 *mu* to about 7,500 after the war (personal interview, 1986).

95. On a detailed analysis of the rise of the He lineage in Shawan, see Liu Zhiwei, "Lineage on the Sands: The Case of Shawan," in *Down to Earth*, ed. David Faure and Helen Siu, 21–43. Beidi was a popular deity in south China. In Shawan, local inhabitants had made it to symbolize the authority of the first emperor of the Ming dynasty. His temple, together with the *Liugeng tang* of the He lineage, was the cultural and political center of Shawan.

96. The former were referred to as "female guns." They used force for defense. The latter were branded as "male guns." They supposedly used force to prey on others.

97. I see this as the beginning of the cellularization of the villages in the twentieth century. The process reached its height in the Maoist period, when the administrative machinery of the Communist Party reigned supreme. See Siu, *Agents and Victims*.

98. Ibid., chap. 5. See also chapter by Siu in *Down to Earth*, ed. David Faure and Helen Siu, on the reworking of the lineage tradition in three communities in the Pearl River delta. For the ritual efforts of militarists in other areas, see Edward McCord, *The Power of the Gun: The Emergence of Modern Chinese Warlordism* (Berkeley and Los Angeles: University of California Press, 1993).

99. See *Nantian suiyue* (The times under the southern sky), a special volume of *Guangdong wenshi ziliao* 37 (1987), on the warlord Chen Jitang in Guangdong during the 1930s.

100. See Guan, "Jiefangqian Xinhui kuiye jingying gaikuang."

101. There was Liang Hongye, whose father was a juror and who himself bought a minor degree. The other gentry leader was from the old He family of Huicheng, a He Ruoshan, who was head of the Xinhui Chamber of Commerce.

102. See Mai Bingkun and Huang Xiaonan, "Xinhui cheng shangtuan shimuo" (The entire account of the merchant militia in Xinhui), *Xinhui wenshi ziliao* 3 (1965): 1–19.

103. A document in 1948 listed members of the guild and their contracted growers. Among the growers were known local bosses. The documents also showed that many grow-

ers did not deliver the contracted amount to the traders. See Xinhui xian kuishan shangye tongye gonghui, ed., *Benhui huiyuan shanghao damai cewei yedian sanqi boli changbing shengbi shengshan laokui yi qingqi wei qingqi yi lan biao* (A survey list of varying types of fan palm delivered [or not yet delivered] by the growers at Damai Cewei to member enterprises of our association) (Xinhui: n.p., 1948).

104. See Siu, *Agents and Victims*, chaps. 4–5. See also Xinhui shuyuan dongshi licaiyuan, comp., "Choujian Xinhui shuyuan zhengxin lu" (The directory of donations for building the Xinhui Academy) (Huicheng: Yixing, 1927); and "Xinhui shuyuan gongding changji ji guanli zhangcheng" (The estate rituals of Xinhui Academy and its operating regulations) (Huicheng: Yixing, 1927).

105. See "Xingjian Xinhui shuyuan de jingguo" (An account of the building of Xinhui Academy), *Xinhui wenshi ziliao* 2 (1964): 30–36, compiled by the journal's editors.

106. See Xinhui cheng yuanhe shanghu weichi tuan, comp., "Chenghui Huihe lian'an puwei shimuo ji" (An account of redeeming the land attached to shops along the banks of Huicheng) (Huicheng: n.p., 1924).

107. See Mo Rongfang and Xu Zhongtao, "Xinhui xian caicheng zulu de jingguo" (The account of tearing down the city and building roads in Xinhui county), *Xinhui wenshi zilaio* 2 (1964): 20–30.

108. See David Faure, "Lineage Socialism and Community Control: Tanggang *xiang* in the 1920s," in *Down to Earth*, ed. David Faure and Helen Siu, 161–87.

109. See *Guangdong Gangzhou shangbu zhangcheng quanjuan* (The complete constitution of the Gangzhou commercial port in Guangdong) (Hong Kong, 1911). See also an account of the planning of the port in *Zhongguo shangye xinshi* (New knowledge on China's commerce) (n.p., n.d.), 178–82.

110. See He Zhiyi, "Xiangzhou kaibu jiqi shengshuai" (The opening of Xiangzhou port and its rise and decline), *Guangdong wenshi ziliao* 46 (1985): 87–97.

111. See Liu Bogao, "Xinning tielu xingjian shi zai Xinhui yudao de difang shili de zunao ji qita" (The obstacles from local power groups met by the building of the Xinning Railway in Xinhui), *Xinhui wenshi zilaio* 9 (1983): 9–11. See also Zheng Dehua and Lucy Cheng, *Taishan qiaoxiang yu Xinning tielu* (Taishan, a land of emigrants and the Xinning Railway) (Guangzhou: Zhongshan daxue chubanshe, 1991).

112. In *Down to Earth*, the contributors argue that local society in the delta was integrated into the Chinese imperial order through constant redefinitions of lineage, territory, ethnic identity, and religious rituals. They focus on the symbolic and instrumental means used by local inhabitants to position themselves within an evolving Chinese culture and polity.

113. The term *da tian er* came from the Chinese domino game. It was used locally to describe local bosses who exerted dominance over a territory.

114. This is the main argument in *Agents and Victims*, a historical account based on my ethnographic fieldwork in Xinhui.

115. I have tried to deal with this question in previous publications: see Helen Siu, "Socialist Peddlers and Princes in a Chinese Market Town," *American Ethnologist* 16, no. 2 (May 1989): 195–212; "The Politics of Migration in a Market Town," in *China on the Eve of Tiananmen*, ed. Deborah Davis and Ezra Vogel (Harvard University Press, 1990), 61–82; and "The Reconstitution of Brideprice and Dowry in South China," in *Chinese Families in the Post-Mao Era*, ed. Deborah Davis and Stevan Harrell (Berkeley and Los Angeles: University of California Press 1993), 165–88.

116. There may be conflicts of interest among levels of government and between center and region, but the connections with the state bureaucracy remain important for good business. See Elizabeth Perry, "China in 1992: An Experiment in Neo-authoritarianism," *Asian Survey* 33, no. 1 (January 1993): 12–22; see Dorothy Solinger, *Chinese Transition from Socialism: Statist Legacies and Marketing Reforms, 1980–1990* (New York: Sharpe, 1993); see also Jean Oi, "The Role of the Local State in China's Transitional Economy," *China Quarterly* 144 (December 1995): 1132–49, on local state corporatism.

117. See Siu, "Community Festivals in South China: Economic Transformation and Cultural Improvisations," in *China Review*, ed. Lo Chi-kin et al. (Hong Kong: Chinese University Press, 1995), chap. 16, 1–17.

118. See Helen Siu, "Redefining the Market Town through Festivals in Contemporary South China," in *Town and Country in China: Identity and Perception*, ed. David Faure and Tao Tao Liu (Basingstoke, England: Macmillan, forthcoming).

PART TWO

The Nation and the Self

SEVEN

Zhang Taiyan's Concept of the Individual and Modern Chinese Identity

Wang Hui

Concepts of the self and the individual are often seen to be at the heart of issues of identity and its crisis in the modern West.[1] Whether this is also the case in the context of Chinese modernity, however, is a matter of question. Lucian Pye argues, for example, that the shock sustained by the modern Chinese psyche has very little to do with issues of identity. Chinese anxieties and uncertainties, in fact, "have a distinctive overtone that can be traced back to the peculiar sensitivity of traditional Chinese culture to the importance of authority for the potentially destructive character of human emotions. The intimate psychic relationships between authority, order, ritual, and the repression of passion all point to a deep Chinese cultural awareness that man finds his only significance as a social being."[2]

This link between the individual and his or her sense of belonging to the collectivity has received just as much emphasis in the writings of Fredric Jameson. Jameson argues that Third World texts, even those that are seemingly private and invested with a properly libidinal dynamic, necessarily project a political dimension in the form of a national allegory. "The story of individual destiny," according to Jameson, "is always an allegory of the embattled situation of the public third-world culture and society."[3] "Third-world psyche" in that context is denied subjectivity and is seen as situational and materialistic despite itself. This accounts for the allegorical nature of Third World culture, "where the telling of the individual story and the individual experience cannot but ultimately involve the whole laborious telling of the experience of the collectivity itself."[4]

Jameson, unlike Pye, does not attribute this allegorical relation between the individual and the collectivity to the unique nature of Chinese cultural tradition. He sees it, instead, as a universal characteristic determined by that tradition's position in the opposition between the Third and First Worlds. Still, if we follow Jameson, the Chinese concept of the individual and the individual's experience implicitly contains the experience of the collectivity. The narrative of individual experiences is at the same time the narrative of group experiences.

Jameson, like Pye, does not at all touch on if or how the relationship between the individual and the national collective experience is mediated. However, we must ask whether using a concept especially linked with psychologism (which must be seen as a tool unique to the modern West) to depict issues regarding the individual and the self within modern Chinese thought has any significance. Moreover, is modern China's cultural shock tied only to the individual's sense of belonging to the group? Before pursuing this further we must define the term "identity."

The problem of identity is linked with its significance and value, that is, the fundamental relationship between "identity" and "orientation." Orientation, however, emerges only within a specific context, because we can express our attitude toward and evaluation of matters only within a range of concrete choices. If we accept these premises, then we see that the problem of identity for the Chinese in the modern time is extremely complicated and multifaceted because it involves concrete sociopolitical and cultural choices. One cannot discuss issues regarding the individual and the self in modern Chinese thought within the abstract framework of First and Third World relations. Nor can one base discussion on the abstract notion of a unique cultural sense of belonging to a collectivity, which leads to nothing but an essentialization of the Chinese "national character."

I argue that, from the late Qing onward, many different concepts of the individual and the self emerged. Each has a particular sociopolitical and cultural content, thereby defying holistic explanations under a single system. Drawing on the work of Zhang Taiyan, this essay will examine the constitution of a major Chinese conception of the individual within the late Qing context. Zhang is the focus of this analysis not only because the concept of the individual is central to his thinking but also because his ideas were uniquely different from those of other major late Qing liberal thinkers, such as Yan Fu and Liang Qichao. Zhang Taiyan was, furthermore, one of the most important thinkers at the turn of the century. During the critical period of 1906–10, Zhang and his intellectual followers, such as Lu Xun, put forward the notion that universal terms such as "government," "settlement," "mankind," "grouping," "the world," "public principles" (*gongli*), "evolution," "materialism," "nature," "duty," and "responsibility" refer in fact to things that lack "self-nature" (*zixing*).[5] By arguing through a mode of negation, they raised the question of individual subjectivity. In other words, Zhang Taiyan and his disciples, unlike Yan Fu and others—including Zhang himself in an earlier time—did not proceed to constitute the individual within the framework of the grouping and society. They employed instead a logic of negation and established the concept of the individual as an opposite to the concepts of the public and the grouping. Zhang formulated the self, the individual, and morality as an opposition to universalistic concepts that were devoid of subjectivity.

With respect to the concepts of the individual and the self and their ramifications in modern Chinese thought, I am particularly interested in the historical constitution of the individual, that is to say, its genealogy. Nietzsche once asked, "What light does the science of linguistics, especially the science of etymology, throw on the evolution of moral ideas?"[6] This question inspires us to begin from the perspective of etymology and its application without employing preconceived notions of human behavior. The approach permits us to show the conditions under which moral (or immoral) concepts produce nature, society, principles of life, and even illness. These investigations reveal the primitive dynamism with which people produce value judgments under different sorts of circumstances over time.

According to Zhang Taiyan, concepts of the individual and the self, in contrast to those of the public and the grouping, had emerged as counterdirectional actions in search of moral value. Zhang's concept of the individual is formulated in opposition to universalistic concepts such as public principle (*gongli*), the nation, and the grouping. This concept is further formulated in order to delineate the limitations of the universal terms. These universals, as we know, had arisen in intellectual circles in response to social problems and political concerns. The self and the individual, as they had been conceptualized both in tandem and in opposition to the universals, are inevitably implicated in this process, and they become political concepts.

I. THE PROVISIONAL CONCEPT OF INDIVIDUALITY

On June 29, 1906, Zhang Taiyan was released from prison upon completing his term, and he left for Japan, where he became managing editor of the revolutionary organ *Minbao*. Between September 9, 1906, and October 10, 1908, when the paper ceased publication, Zhang published, apart from numerous political essays, a series of essays on philosophy and religion that spelled out the theoretical basis of his sociopolitical concepts. These essays were well circulated at the time, and they elicited considerable response in the printed media of the day. Zhang used these essays both to launch attacks on major contemporary thinkers such as Kang Youwei, Liang Qichao, and Yan Fu and to articulate an alternative worldview that was sharply different from a modernist one based on concepts of publicness (*gong*), grouping, and evolution.

Among the core concepts of Zhang's worldview were "the individual" and "self-nature." Zhang Taiyan developed concepts about individuality (*geti*), subjectivity, and other terms to attack contemporary constructions of the nation, the government, the family, the society, and humankind. In doing so, he sought to establish a new ethical revolutionary morality that drew upon a Yogacaric interpretation of Zhuangzi's *Qiwu lun* (On the equality of all things).[7] This is the most complicated and difficult period in Zhang Taiyan's thought, not only because his prose is archaic and obscure but also because he employed a difficult Buddhist vocabulary to express his social thought. To add to the difficulty, the relationship between his intellectual system—in which self-nature and the individual were positive concepts—and his politics contained elements of contradiction. There are two points to this contradiction. First, the concept of the individual, as developed by intellectuals of his day, has served as an important foundation for modern moral and political thinking; this was especially true in the modernist critique of tradition. In the case of Zhang, however, there is a critical dimension to his conception of the individual that was aimed at the denial of the self in modern political thought. Furthermore, Zhang's concepts of self-nature and the individual are opposed to the universal and the collective. They are ostensibly anticollective. But in truth, in Zhang's thinking there was no more important practical mission than construction of a collective national identity.

Many have tried to explain this contrariness of Zhang Taiyan's thought as a contradiction between practical missions and future ideals. They have also pointed to sudden changes and confusion in Zhang's own thinking. But in the interpretation of modern Chinese identity and its multifaceted nature, these explanations are less than useful. Zhang's criticisms of modernity (especially his criticism of the modern concept of time, which leads directly to notions of progress and evolution) became the core ideas for modern morality and literary theory for his students, including Lu Xun. The concept of the individual has, of course, become a key element of modern thought within May Fourth literature, and its rationality is built on a progressive notion of time. How did Zhang Taiyan's concept of the individual, which denies the self and opposes modernity, become an intellectual fountainhead of modern identity (as it did for Lu Xun)?

Before analyzing the sociopolitical import of Zhang Taiyan's concept of the individual, I would like to outline the various nuances of Zhang's concept of this key subject and spell out its implications. To begin with, Zhang's individual is an absolute, subjective entity: "[The individual] does not come into being because of the world, the society, the nation, or other people. Thus the individual fundamentally has no responsibility toward the world, the society, the nation, and toward people."[8] In other words, the individual is not a constituent of the world, a member of society, a citizen of the nation, a follower of a religion, or a relative or friend of others. The condition of being an individual is, in fact, an "absolute" standing above and beyond all commands or external discipline, whether legal, political, social, or economic.[9]

Second, the limit of individual freedom lies in the proscription against harming others. The basic meaning of individual freedom is a freedom of refusal; aided by this freedom, individuals are able to resist the claims of things that assume the form of the suprapersonal, whether social, historical, or natural. Conservative, reclusive, or suicidal behavior is the highest expression of individual subjectivity, because it is a behavior of refusal. It expresses the individual's freedom to refuse all the things that "even the gods cannot interfere with," such as responsibility and duty. Zhang compares public principle (*gongli*) to heavenly principle (*tianli*) and sees both as the antithesis of individual freedom.[10]

Unlike *tianli*, which is grounded in metaphysics, *gongli* is societal and "uses the society's ever-abiding power to suppress the individual." In this regard the ruthlessness and mercilessness of *gongli* even surpass the heavenly principle.[11] In other words, modern society and its organizational ideology are far more suppressive than the traditional authoritarian society, which grounded its ethical system in the concept of heavenly principle.

Third, Zhang Taiyan regards this absolute concept of the individual as a cosmic principle that is intended to make all things equal. In Zhang's thinking, the concept of the individual provides the foundation of a mode of knowledge as well as a system of ethics for coping with the world. This means that his concept of the individual, just like the concept of the individual embedded in a modern worldview, was intended to solve basic problems of social identity. However, Zhang does not take universalistic concepts as true social law; he accepts instead an absolute individual subjectivity. Zhang quotes Zhuangzi, especially the *qiwu* ("making all things equal") chapter, and praises the Daoist philosopher's teaching that all beings should be allowed to follow their preferences. This teaching, according to Zhang, is far superior to the theory of public principle (*gongli*). Furthermore, Zhang draws attention to Hegel's notion that "all matters accord with reason; all things are beautiful." Zhang points out that the two positions, by Zhuangzi and Hegel, seem comparable. The former, however, takes the human mind as the root of difference and an obstacle in making things equal, while the latter takes common purpose as the ultimate destination and sees the multitude as a passage toward that destination. There is an immense distance, then, between Zhuangzi and Hegel, according to Zhang.[12] By underscoring the differences between the two, Zhang Taiyan shaped his concepts of *qiwu* and the individual into a cosmic view that is antideterministic and antiteleological.

In the same fashion, Zhang attacks evolution, materialism, and naturalism by calling attention to his conception of the individual, and reveals the absurdity and falsehood of public principle (*gongli*). Evolution, materialism, and naturalism were key concepts that lay the foundation of modern notions of science and its publicness (*gong*), which in turn became the basis of a theory of social change. Zhang argues, however, that natural law, such as the principle of evolution, does not in itself bear relevance to human affairs: "To follow natural law offers no merit and to oppose it is no crime." But those who subscribe to evolution hate those who do not and accuse them of violating the laws of nature.[13] In the eyes of Zhang Taiyan, the modern worldview was composed of public principle (*gongli*), evolution, materialism, naturalism, and similar "fundamental intellectual delusions." If one allowed these delusions to create a moral order, then the *gongli* of these delusions would provide a foundation for a dangerous despotism, for they would not only eliminate human intelligence but would also take away human happiness and freedom, especially those of the individual. Only by completely wiping out these delusive concepts could the natural order be saved from the interference and intimidation of the supranatural world formed by these concepts and names.

Zhang's criticism of a worldview of *gongli* was derived from the Buddhist theory of cosmic "truth," especially its ideas regarding dependent causation and impermanence. It was not, however, a simple extension of Buddhist thought. When Zhang opposed individual subjectivity against the various kinds of *gongli*, as seen above, he perceived this *gongli* as merely a repressive power surrounding and op-pressing the individual. Although the individual had no self-nature to speak of, the individual was a relatively real entity, even an adequate foundation of morality for "the restoration of all Chinese."[14]

However, the connection between the individual and morality as discussed above should not be seen too simplistically. The individual took precedence over *gongli*, evolution, materialism, and nature, on the one hand, and government, na-tion, society, and family, on the other. This priority, however, derived from the indi-vidual's proximity to, rather than true possession of, self-nature. Furthermore, the link between the individual and morality was established within the complex rela-tionship between the individual and the Buddhist "nonself." What the Buddhists called the self meant governance and substance: "The eternal is called the self; the unmoving is called the self; and the indestructible is called the self."[15] The concept of nonself entails that nothing that exists is an independent, unchanging, self-existent, and self-determining substance, and nothing possesses a self-governing principle or capacity. Because of this dependent causation, all phenomena arise within the conditions of interdependence and thus are relative and provisional.

If the concept of the individual—which opposed that of publicness (*gong*) and the consequent "impartial" modern worldview and ethics of the family, nation, and society—was to be reduced to nonself, might this not lead to moral nihilism? Or, if the individual had no self, then did a true self exist? If it did, then how did the true self relate to the individual? Using suicide as an example, Zhang argued that the person who undertook suicide to "save the self" did not "take the form as the self." Thus outside the form there must be something called the self. Suicide could be explained as a means of escaping the self-form that is shackled by the world and of attaining the true self. The self that committed suicide was thus the *alayavijnana* in an illusory form.[16] Compared with the self-form, which lacked sub-stance, universality, and eternity, only *alayavijnana* was the true self: it was a univer-sal, eternal, subjective, and "completely free self." On the one hand, it was the source of the self, the other, and all phenomena; on the other hand, it abided amid all phenomena.[17] Zhang thus treated the true self, *alayavijnana*, and suchness as a single substance possessed by all things: it was permanent and immutable. Since he believed that *alayavijnana* was not limited to the individual, what he called the "eternal," "unmoving," and "indestructible" "self" was in fact a "greater self," a universal substance that transcended the world of phenomena, much like the Kantian notion of the "thing-in-itself." The moral implications of this would be: "If we can substantiate the nonself, then the world will begin to possess the great compassion of equality."[18] Thus, Zhang regarded the principle of equality not as an ethical rule but an ontological state. This was the basis of the linkages that he identified between Yogacaric thought and Zhuangzi's concept of *qiwu*. It was also the intellectual bridge that led him from the concept of the individual—advanced as the antithesis of the impartial and grouping—to the concept of a supreme pub-licness (*dagong*) that transcended the individual.

Zhang's criticism of the worldview of *gongli* begins with a defense of subjectivity and concludes with a negation of the individual and the individual's subjectivity. His ultimate goal, therefore, is not the absolute, subjective individuality, but universality in the ontological sense. This kind of universality is the origin of the cosmos and of the ethics and morality that society should adhere to. This suggests that Zhang did not make the individual's subjectivity the ultimate moral foundation: it only serves as the premise of his criticism of "public principle" and a worldview associated with it. His concept of the self as nonself actually approximated those "public" ideals (*gong*) from an ontological perspective. His universal principle, however, certainly did not impose on the individual restrictive demands in the name of *gong*, particularly the restrictive moral codes formed within a hierarchical social structure.[19]

Through the negation of the universal (*gongli*) Zhang arrives at an affirmation of the universal (*dagong*), and the new foundation of identity is confirmed. This peculiar thinking process is constructed in the language of the Buddhist Yogacara school and the thought of Laozi and Zhuangzi. We will see that these apparently difficult, self-contradictory, abstract ideas were closely tied with Zhang Taiyan's direct engagement with sociopolitical issues.

II. THE MODERN NATION-STATE
AND THE CONCEPT OF THE INDIVIDUATED SELF

1. Antistate and Antigovernmental Significance in the Concept of Individuality

Zhang Taiyan's concept of individuality was not only a philosophical or moral idea but also a political one. It was developed in opposition to a worldview rooted in the concept of "publicness (*gong*)–grouping (*qun*)," which, in the context of the late Qing, was not merely an abstract moral idea but a substitute term for (and moral foundation of) the modern nation-state and its many modes of social organization. These organizations include the chambers of commerce, learned societies, national assemblies, political parties, and gentry-village communities. The modern concepts such as public principle, evolution, materialism, and naturalism were the most important and dynamic elements in the modern Chinese discourse of the nation-state. The question I pose here: What was the relationship between Zhang's concept of the individual and the discursive network of the nation-state? To put it more directly, as a founding figure of the concept of the modern nation-state and a theorist for the late Qing racial revolution, Zhang made nationalism an especially significant theme during his entire writing career and revolutionary praxis. His provisional concept of the individual was not only a critique and negation of the nation, the government, and social groups—all collectives aimed at the creation of a modern nation-state and at social mobilization—but also a rejection of the very concept of the "nation." If the concept of the individual was a key element in the discourse of the modern nation-state, then how and in what way did this concept constitute a negation of the discourse? How did this contrariety come about? The political use of the concept of the individual formed a social context for the construction of this concept. If this concept and those of race, nation, social group, and community involved different aspects and constructive modes of the modern Chinese worldview, why did Zhang's concept of the individual, which was characterized by denial of the universal, still return to it?

The political significance of Zhang's concept of the individual can be seen, first, in the concept's negation of the nation and the state. In several of his treatises—including "On the Nation" and "On Politics of Representation"—Zhang applied his analytical reasoning to political questions and developed his concepts of individuality and self-nature into a critique of the modern nation-state. In "On the State" Zhang writes, "The 'subjectivity' of the state, first, is artificially ascribed rather than substantively endowed. The construction of the state, furthermore, is the outcome of external power dynamics rather than the extension of inherent, natural principles. The business of the state, above all, is base and sullied, rather than pure and sacred."[20] The first point above is clearly the most important: it establishes the foundation for the two ensuing points. It is precisely in the discussion of whether the state possesses "subjectivity" that Zhang posits the individual and the nation as fundamentally opposed to each other. Invoking the atomistic view of the Buddhist Yogacara school, he argues that "all entities are composed of myriad constituents and thus do not possess their own being. The individuated entities that form the composite, however, can be said to have true being. In contrast, the composite has false being. Since the nation is composed of the people, each person provisionally can be said to be a true being. But the nation has no true being."[21] By drawing an analogy between the atomistic model of matter and the composition of society and nation, Zhang refutes all theories that regard the nation as the subject and the people as object: "Some have said, 'The nation itself has its institutions and laws. Although the people from time to time will be renewed, the institutions and laws cannot be renewed. These being so, [the nation] is thus called a subject.' But this is not true. Institutions and laws change of themselves and do not necessarily follow the old principles. Even if they do not change, they are only the 'expressive appearances' bestowed by previous generations."[22]

What deserves attention is the fact that when he touches on the relationship between the nation and the individual, Zhang discusses the issue of who is the subject; but he does not believe that the subjectivity of the individual is absolute. It has only relative priority within its relations to the nation and other social groups. Since it is merely "nearer to reality than the composite" but is itself still a "false phenomenon," then the conclusion that the nation is a "false being" is not only an extrapolation but follows naturally upon the position of nation in the order of things.[23] Zhang did not elaborate on the relationship between subjectivity and that of "differentiated positions." In principle, the concept of self-nature precluded any hierarchical order or discriminating relationship.

Why did he argue that the world had certain hierarchical order? On the one hand, the assumption of hierarchical order is necessitated by his stress on the priority of the individual; on the other, the issues discussed by Zhang were not ontological but political ones dealing with political regimes and social structures. This testified again to the immediate political significance of the concept of the individual.

The argument concerning the individual's priority over the group aimed at the idea of national sovereignty, which, in the formulations of Zou Rong, Chen Tianhua, Sun Yat-sen, Liang Qichao, and Yan Fu, accentuated the freedom of the totality above that of the individual. The fact that Zhang argued against the sovereignty of the nation from the perspective of Yogacaric thought regarding self-nature means that his discussion of sovereignty did not involve relations between nations—in which case, he was a firm nationalist (and not a statist). Zhang's second criticism of the nation denies the actual significance of the nation's geographical establishment (national boundaries) and its hierarchical construction. It follows upon his idea that all distinctions among things lacking self-nature are the product of "false thoughts." His analysis of the illusory nature of national sovereignty, boundaries, and hierarchical structure leads to the third criticism, that the nation was not a moral wellspring but a lair of iniquity. Only the individual—each and every individual—was a creator of value. Collective activities were not the achievements of abstract groups or the fame of the group's leader but were the individual's creation.[24] Implicit in this conclusion were doubts regarding the right of collective cause to command the lives of individuals and interpret their significance. Viewed from the perspective of modern revolutionary history, this pertains to the rationale of revolution, the ethicality of the call to revolution, the validity of the modernist tendency to link the self with the macroprocess of history, and the natural legitimacy of the modern nation-state and its enterprises. Whereas a religious cause, which calls for the dedication of the lives of those who pursue it, often does not sacrifice anyone else, "the cause of the nation is different. Is it racial revolution? Political revolution? Social revolution? At any rate, it is not to be accomplished by dint of the individual going through hell and high water. If I advocate [the revolution's] commencement, then hundreds of millions of people will follow me and go through hell and high water. . . . If one can only speak of corpses and regard it as something worthy of lofty fame, then how is [carrying out revolution] different from banditry?"[25] In the eyes of Zhang, those such as Yao, Shun, Washington, Napoleon, Bahktin, and Kropotkin, who saw their calling as working for social change and the national project, could not be compared with those such as Sakyamuni, Epicurus, Chen Zhongzi, and Guan Ying, who risked their lives for all humankind, because the former had made their names as a result of the sacrifice of others.

2. *The Relationship between the Individual and the People*

Another aspect of the oppositional duality between the nation and the individual was Zhang Taiyan's radical nationalism. One set of questions related to this is: what is the relationship between the nation and the people, what is the historical context in which Zhang denied the nation, and more important, why was Zhang's mode of discourse an individual/nation duality, and not the more complex one of individual/society/nation?

In the various discussions of modern Chinese nationalism, the nation, national sovereignty, and national institutions (establishment of the constitution, the parliament, and bureaucratic systems) are the most important themes. They are also the primary indicators of the differences between Chinese nationalism and traditional (cultural) Sinocentrism. As forms of group-identity consciousness, concepts of nationality and culture developed very early in Chinese thought. This is seen in the classical texts *Zuo zhuan* ("If they are not of our kin, their minds must be different"), the *Li ji* ("Those who have this knowledge always know to love their own kind"), and the *Xunzi* ("The ancestors are the basis of our kind").[26] According to Wang Ermin's studies, many of the nations of the Spring and Autumn period were clan factions, but many were groups formed as a result of racial or ethnic self-intuition. This is the Chinese/non-Chinese distinction found in the *Zuo zhuan* and the *Analects*. This sort of orthodox racial consciousness achieved a cultural self-identity, as testified by Confucius's remark, "Were it not for Guan Zhong, we might now be wearing our hair loose and folding our clothes to the left."[27] However, as many scholars have already pointed out, in the process of struggle and assimilation within the Chinese people, the idea of nationality did not penetrate people's minds as much as the concept of culture, even to the point where one can say that "eliminating distinctions through culture has been a tradition of political ideals since the pre-Qin era."[28] As seen from the relationship between the Chinese core and outlying foreigners, assimilation did not primarily take the form of establishing military garrisons and general viceroys. The criterion was often merely the observation of the Chinese calendar. The core of ancient China was reflected in the king's capital and five concentric domains of governance, a hierarchical ideal that posed the sovereign as the center and extended outward.[29] In institutional form, relations with outlying non-Chinese were chiefly controlled by the Board of Rites and not agencies responsible for foreign relations or colonization. This shows clearly that the center that preserved the kingly way was the person of the emperor—who combined the political and moral lines of succession—and not the nation. Within this extensive structure, equal relations between nations were extremely difficult to create. In this sense, although the traditional notion of "China" had its complex and multifaceted implications, it was chiefly an "intuition of cultural place," and not a nation-state. In other words, the concept of China and the concept of all Chinese were identical. China does not entail the reality of political unity, but primarily that of cultural and racial unity.[30]

The formation of Chinese nationalism in the late Qing started with the concept of strengthening the barriers between outlying non-Chinese and Chinese. After the Opium War, however, Chinese nationalism gradually absorbed the ideas of national sovereignty and interests. During the period of the Sino-Japanese War and the rise of the reform movement, the Western concept of the nation not only had already become the most prominent characteristic of Chinese nationalism but also was a central idea permeating the political discourse of different political groups. In other words, "the people equals the nation" formula was established by the court's plan of political reform (as seen in memorials and edicts), the propaganda of nonofficial intellectuals (as seen in essays and publications), and the theory and practice of revolutionaries (as seen in speeches, essays, publications, and overseas activities). At the beginning of the Hundred Days Reform, Kang Youwei said, "We should use the power of various kingdoms to rule all under heaven and not use the power of the unified trailing gowns."[31] Liang Qichao directly pitted the concept of the nation against the concepts of "great unity" and "Earthly Realm": "We Chinese do not lack patriotic character. As for those who do not know to love their country, it is because they do not know what a country is. China has been unified since ancient times. . . . [It was] called the Earthly Realm and was not called a country. . . . For several thousand years, we lived together in a small Earthly Realm and never met an equal country, to the effect that we know no country other than our own."[32] In a series of essays, Liang also pitted the individual or the self against the nation (or grouping). His stance, however, was just the opposite of Zhang's, as he declared that the cause of the nation's weakness was the fact that "within everyone's mind and eye there is only the I of his own self and not the I of the collective.[33] . . . What is the idea of the nation-state all about? The nation-state comes into being, first, in opposition (and as an antithesis) to the individuated self. It arises, second, in opposition to the functioning of the imperial court. It exists in opposition, third, to foreign people and an alien nation. It is defined, fourth, in opposition to the global order and larger universe."[34] The concept of the nation comes about through the relationships of the individual, the family, foreign peoples, and the world. Here, however, Liang left out the relationship between race and nation. The political implications of this omission were perfectly clear: its purpose was to dampen the ethnic conflicts between Han Chinese and Manchus and strengthen the unified nature of China as a nation of many peoples. The nation, not the race, became the true subject and source of modern identity and constituted the imaginative structure of the Chinese people within the world order. Sun Yat-sen believed that China since the Qin and Han dynasties had been a nation-state because "nationalism is national-people-ism." Like Liang Qichao, Sun also posed the nation against the clan or lineage.[35] The vision of "nation-state" implied in his national-people-ism may thus be viewed as that of a political leader who had already established the predominance of the Han. Thus the idea of a single nation with many peoples was directly tied to the legitimacy of safeguarding Han Chinese sovereignty. Although these modern thinkers held different views of the state, the nation-state as the most important consequence of Western modernity had already remolded their mental framework. The demands of national identity implied that the nation itself was the true unit of sovereignty: this kind of national sovereignty was defined not only in regard to other nations but also in regard to individuals, families, clans, races, and other social groups within the nation. In other words, to achieve effective social mobilization, the nation's subjectivity implied the loss or partial loss of the subjectivity of the individual, the family, and other social units.

In the context of the nation-state construction, what was the significance of Zhang Taiyan's denial of the nation? We must first observe that from a cultural perspective, Zhang did not reject the concept of the nation. As a prime advocate for modern Chinese "national studies," he saw "national essence"—that is to say, the reworking and exegesis of language, institutions, and personal biography—as an important part of the entire constructive process of the concept of the Chinese nation-state. In February 1902, when the organ of the Guoxue baocun hui (Society for the Preservation of National Learning), *Guocui xuebao* (National essence studies report), was founded in Shanghai, Zhang Taiyan, still in prison, published in it four letters written before incarceration, as well as his prison "random jottings," in which he claimed that "heaven bestowed the national essence on me."[36] In 1906, when Zhang managed *Minbao*, the anti-Manchu, pro-Han thinking of the national essence group could be found in abundance in this publication. When *Guoxue jianghua* (Talks on national learning), edited by Wang Sichen, discussed national learning, it said, "The term 'national learning' was not to be found in ancient times. There must be nations facing nations for the concept of the nation to begin. Then the study of one's own nation as national learning begins."[37] This explained in general the relationship between national learning and the idea of the nation. In "Guocui xuebaoxu" (preface to *Guocui xuebao*), Huang Jie spoke of national substance and national learning together: "Our nation's national substance is the national substance of foreign people's despotism; our nation's theory is the theory of foreign people's despotism."[38] The "nation" of the "national learning" referred to here was the nation of Han Chinese. The "learning" was Han Chinese learning, which was in direct opposition to the despotism of "foreign people" and their "foreign learning."[39] Thus the nation, within the notions of "national essence" and "national learning," primarily was meant in regard to foreign peoples, especially Manchu rulers. It gave rise to racial and cultural ideas and was not the political concept of the nation found in modern international relations. In his "Yanshuo lu" (Record of speeches), Zhang Taiyan summarized his nationalist agenda in two sentences: "The first task is to employ religion to arouse faith and improve the nation's morality; the second task is to use the dynamism of national essence to improve patriotic fervor." The purpose of advocating national essence "was only to have people cherish our Han people's history."[40] Although advocacy of "national essence" was linked with the motive of resisting Western and Japanese influences, its primary meaning derived from the necessity of opposing the Manchus on a cultural level. What he emphasized was the subjectivity and purity of race and culture, the logical conclusion of which was necessarily an "anti-Manchu revolution."

3. Late Qing Statism and the Relationship between Individual and Nation

Clearly, Zhang's denial of the nation was inextricably linked with his anti-Manchu nationalism.[41] This cannot explain, however, why his criticism of the nation adopted the nation/individual duality mode of discourse. On this point, we must analyze from the opposite perspective the position of his opponent Liang Qichao. After he returned from his visit to the United States (1903–6), Liang expressed deep reservations about American democratic government and the Western liberalism he had formerly believed in. He turned to German statist political theory, especially that of Johann Bluntschli and Gustav Bornhak. Liang introduced Bluntschli's criticism of Rousseau's theory of the social contract, which claimed that the theory of the social contract muddled the distinctions between the people and society. Liang said, "The national people are a fixed, unmovable entirety. Society is only a changing, unfixed collectivity. The national people have a single character by law, and society does not. Thus to term them 'the national people' is to associate them always with the country without allowing the slightest permissible separation. To term them 'society' is to make them only an assembly of many individuals."[42]

In addition to the relationship between the "national people" and the ethnic group discussed above, Liang cited the statist ideas of Bluntschli and Bornhak. First, unlike the society composed of individuals, the nation was an organic entity with a spiritual purpose, a physical structure, untrammeled movement, and a developmental process. Liang approved of Bluntschli's criticisms of Rousseau's theory of civil rights and social contract, believing that "national sovereignty" could not be shared with any individual.[43] Second, regarding the political entity, Bluntschli believed that constitutional monarchy was superior to other polities, especially that of the republic. This was not only because the establishment of republican polities depended on specific historical conditions but also because the separation of legislative powers (where the majority ruled) and administrative powers could weaken national sovereignty. Republican polities boasted freedom and equality, but in truth, because their social elite despised the lower ranks of the people, they also were suspicious of excellence. According to Bornhak, republican polities mixed the ruling subject and ruling object, and outside of the people there was no place for the nation. Considering the immediate relevance of this theory, Liang decided: "Our China today is weakest, and what it most urgently needs is organic unity and coercive order. Freedom and equality are secondary."[44] Third, sovereignty belonged neither to the sovereign nor to the society; the nation and its constitutional law were the source of sovereignty. Liang especially condemned the view that the sovereign was the collective authority of individuals but could not be the sovereign of a corporate nationality. He believed that with sovereignty there was the nation, and without it there was no nation.[45] Fourth, regarding the purpose of the nation, although Bluntschli attempted to maintain a rough balance between the nation for itself and the nation as an instrument of the people, "composed of each individual," fundamentally his tendency was toward a clear concept of the nation for itself. "The national purpose occupies the first place, and each individual is a tool to accomplish that purpose."[46] These views of the nation in the end led to Liang's shift toward believing that for China's concrete situation, "enlightened despotism" was even more suitable than constitutional monarchy.[47]

We can clearly see now that the true reason that Zhang Taiyan criticized the nation from the perspective of the individual was his thorough denial of the view that the nation was of supreme political value. The nation did not have its own characteristics and certainly did not have its own dynamic organic quality. Nor did it have sovereignty: only the individual—"each person"—could possess sovereignty. For the individual, the nation was an instrument of despotism and a lair of iniquity. All discriminating relations were the source of inequality, for the cosmos and the world in the ontological sense were equal and without distinction. On the level of politics, the most important political aspect of Zhang's concept of the individual was its complete rejection of the ideals of enlightened despotism and constitutional monarchy. The key issue, however, was still the nationalist question of whether or not one desired Manchu rule. As Zhu Zhixin said in his essay "Xinli guojiazhuyi" (Psychological statism), the nation referred to in Liang Qichao's *Xinmin baoshu* (New citizen report letter), Yang Du's *Zhongguo xinbao* (China new report), and *Dongfang zazhi* (Eastern miscellany) "was nothing other than the Manchu government."[48] On the contrary, Zhang's "Zhonghua minguo jie" (Explaining the Republic of China) repeatedly discussed the unity of the Chinese nation and people. "If one establishes the Han name as a people, then the meaning of the nation resides there. If one establishes the name of China [Hua] as a country, then the meaning of the race also abides there. This is why the Republic of China flourishes." In clearly rejecting a territorial definition in favor of a cultural one, he emphasized the racial character of the concept of China.[49] He also emphasized national sovereignty, but his notion of sovereignty was completely racial, not political. "As well as [the reason] for expelling the Manchus mentioned above, there is the fact that they ruin our country and usurp our sovereignty."[50]

It is worth noting that the debate between Liang Qichao and Zhang Taiyan over nationalism began as early as 1903. In 1907, when Zhang returned to the issue of the nation, the issue of nationalism had even more immediate political implications. This occurred not only because the debate between *Minbao* and the reformist newspapers *Xinmin congbao* and *Zhongguo xinbao* involved acute conflicts between the political groups advocating revolution and reform; it occurred also because during the period between 1905 and 1907 the preparations for constitutional reform were no longer matters for debate among intellectuals or social groups, but matters of practical decision for the Qing government. At the end of 1905, the Qing government sent five high officials, Dai Ze, Duan Fang, Dai Hongzi, Li Shengduo, and Shang Qiheng, to Japan, Europe, and the United States to study constitutional government. Liang Qichao, then in exile, drafted a memorial of over two hundred thousand characters. In 1906 the Qing court announced its program for constitutional preparation: "Supreme power will be centralized at the court. The affairs of the state will be made public in popular discussion. In this manner a new and enduring foundation will be established for a new nation.... At present, however, the laws and institutions are not yet comprehensive, and the people's sagacity awaits enlightenment," and so the government would have to first lend a hand.

Archival materials on late Qing constitutional movement show that preparatory work for the initiation of a constitutional government was carried out extensively in many aspects of society. These include the creation of new state offices, parliamentary assemblies, consultative agencies, local self-governments, legal and judicial bodies, educational and financial associations, and official newspapers, and an adjustment of the Manchu-Han relationship. The overall vision that emerged was one with the Qing court at the center, presiding over the establishment of a hierarchical administrative system resembling that of modern American and European nations, and implementing effective social mobilization from above. An imperial edict announced, "We have great hopes that each will understand the righteousness of loyalty to the monarch and love for the country, and the principle of joining with the collective to advance moral transformation. Individuals will be forbidden to harm the public interest with private opinions or damage the greater plan with petty grudges. They will revere order and preserve peace while preparing themselves to be people of a constitutional nation."[51] Thus the constitutional movement was a shared product of the Qing court and exiled intellectuals; and statism and its values, with the Qing court's legitimacy at its core, defined political discussion during the reform era.

4. The Omission of Societal Space in the Binary Formulation of Individual and Nation

Within the particular nationalist atmosphere of the late Qing, Zhang Taiyan employed the "reality" of the individual to negate the "falsity" of the nation, and used the negative freedom of the individual to critique the freedom of the nation-state. Thus the provisional concept of the individual had profound political implications. Instead of posing a three-way, nation/society/individual relation in discussing the problem of the individual, Zhang elided society, configuring it together with nation in opposition to the individual. In this way, the relationship of mutual stimulation and restraint between nonnational and nongovernmental social organizations, and the nation or government, did not fall within the sphere of discussion.

One of the primary motifs of modern Chinese thought is the formation of the concept of the society, and the popularity of concepts of *gong* (public) and *qun* (grouping) that was directly related to the influx of Western thought and learning regarding "society." Kang Youwei and Liang Qichao's theoretical investigation and political practice concerning "learned groups" (learned societies), "commercial groups" (chambers of commerce), and "national groups" (national associations) developed around the pivot of the relationship between society and the nation (primarily the imperial court). This was how the power of a morally constituted society could check imperial authority and complete the reconstruction of the social and political systems. For Liang Qichao and Yan Fu, the individual's autonomy was inseparable from the establishment of social contract groups and modern state systems. On the one hand, the autonomous social grouping could mediate the process of social mobilization necessary for the establishment of the modern nation-state. On the other, the restraint imposed on the state by the autonomous social grouping provided a public space for individual freedom, hence the fact that so many Western scholars used the designations "civil society" and "public sphere" to explain the theory and practice of the modern Chinese "grouping." In other words, Liang and Yan's individual was a concept within the category of the grouping and the nation-state. According to Liang Qichao, "The reason why our China does not establish an independent nation is only because our people lack the virtue of independence."[52] Liang's formulation of the individual's independence used the establishment of national morality as its means and the establishment of an independent nation-state as its end, and the formation of the social group was a mediating stage.

However, Zhang's concept of the individual not only opposed the nation but was asocial. As he said in "Sihuo lun," "What mankind commonly acknowledges is that one cannot encroach on society for the sake of the individual, nor encroach on the individual for the sake of society." What was referred to here as society included the nation, the government, and all social groups organized by people as individual units. The individual did not come into being because of the nation, society, or other people, and thus did not acknowledge laws, responsibilities, or duties.[53] Within the entire order of phenomena, no phenomenon composed of other constituents had self-nature—"not only the nation, but all of its villages, settlements, groups, and assemblies." It was only each person who truly possessed self-nature.[54] "Wuwu lun" fully expressed the various aspects of Zhang's social thought: that is, there was no government, no settlements, no humankind, no groupings, and no world. The development of the Five Nonexistences involved three stages. At the first stage, there was no government and no settlements; at the second, no humankind and no groupings; at the third, no world. Zhang first treated the individual as an element within all social organizations. These organizations structured discriminating relations, all of which had no self-nature. Thus on the social level, the denial of the nation and other social groups originated in the demand that the individual be liberated from all discriminating relationships. This suggests that Zhang's social thought not only was anarchist but also antisocial. Thus the individual as social atom could also be divided, because, "speaking of the atom, at root it has no space, but later takes shape through mutual contact. Since it has no space, it is amassed into a unity. How could there have been mutual contact? This shows that all talk about the atom is nonsense."[55] This is why he denied humankind, the living beings, and the world altogether.

One particularly important aspect of Zhang's denial of social collectivities is his idea of "no-settlement." Why did Zhang reject the autonomous social group so valued by Liang Qichao and others? According to the Western historical experience, especially that of western Europe, were not civil society and the public it engendered the base conditions for the limitation of state power and the formation of democratic society? The key to an answer to these questions is the fact that society, in Zhang's definition, comprised all kinds of nonindividual collectivities, including the nation, which is quite different from the Habermasian civil society standing outside the state and bearing special relation to the individual's private domain. More important, within the late Qing context, both the dynamism of urban charter associations and the practice of forming them, and the reinterpreta-tion and utilization of the social functions of kin and gentry-based communities, aimed to establish the modern nation-state and carry out social mobilization. The formation of western European civil society took place in the context of the de-velopment of the nation-state. In late Qing China, however, various social groups were formed against the background of the decline of the state apparatus. Euro-pean civil society, and the public sphere built on it, played a crucial role in restricting the despotic state and became a social foundation of the democratic system. In the Chinese case, the civic groups and gentry-village communities em-ployed by the Qing government and a sector of intellectuals had a completely dif-ferent significance. These groups not only aimed primarily to establish a nation-state but were state or quasi-state organs in their very conception, establishment, and social functioning. Founders and members of late Qing learned societies, chambers of commerce, and other social organizations were usually gentry and intellectuals with close ties to the government, and some were officials themselves. The appearance of these social organizations was part of the top-down national reform movement of the late Qing. This demonstrates the lack of a clear division between the activities of these social groups and those of the state. Civic organi-zations themselves were important means for state making, especially the means for the state authority to penetrate grassroots society and strengthen its political and economic control. The state was at the center of all societal activities. This helped to explain the ambiguity of the concept of "the groupings" in the late Qing: most social organizations used the grouping as a rubric, and the highest level of grouping was the "great grouping," which referred to the nation-state. Once we see this, we recognize that Zhang's critique of "the settlement" and all kinds of social grouping was an integral part of his critique of the nation.

5. A Critique of the Parliamentary System

Against the backdrop of late Qing reformist state building, which used the Western nation-state as its blueprint, Zhang held a sharply critical attitude toward the gov-ernment's use of parliaments and local self-governing bodies to expand state power into grassroots society. Many scholars have analyzed in detail Zhang's critique of the parliamentary system; I will not repeat their findings here.[56] What I do wish to emphasize is that Zhang's criticisms of the parliamentary system were directed against the state's use of the system to carry out social mobilization. First, he pointed out that parliamentary polities were another form of feudalism; their most important defect was that they employed status hierarchies to organize society.[57] Second, Zhang perceptively realized that the consultative bodies established in dis-tricts at all levels in China not only would be extremely difficult to operate (espe-cially because of the contrast between the large population and limited numbers of representatives, the huge territory, and the voters' educational level), but even more important, the purpose of establishing parliaments was to exercise control at the grassroots level in an economic sense, especially in solving the central government's difficult problem of tax collection.[58] The parliamentary system originally was intended to expand the people's rights, but in reality, because of economic inequality, it would increase political inequality and create a new social hierarchy.

Third, Zhang believed that the parliamentary system legitimized the special privileges of representatives (local magnates), which clashed with the principle of economic equality within the principle of the people's livelihood. Zhang offered a series of idealistic political proposals that would "check official [power] and extend [that of] the people."[59] On the surface, his proposals resemble Sun Yat-sen's "Principle of the People's Livelihood." In content, however, they were considerably different, as they were rooted in Zhang's critical stance toward capitalism. For example, his plan for "equal distribution of land" was not limited to paddies and swamps but also included mountain and forest preserves and even cattle, clearly indicating his seriousness in attacking the movement of capital. This was precisely the opposite of Sun's proposal of developing state capital in order to develop a capitalist economy.[60] In *Wuchao falü suoyin* (Index to the laws of the five dynasties) and other works, Zhang expressed particular admiration for the traditional idea of "revering agriculture and restraining commerce." He advocated "universal laws" debasing trade and attributed social disorder to "the esteem for merchants."[61] Seen alongside his opposition to new industries and technology expressed in "Wuwu lun," such views clearly betray antimodern sentiments.

It will be recalled that Zhang's denial of the nation emerged from the perspective of the individual. This perspective, however, did not develop at all the economic idea of private property. On the contrary, whether on the level of political rights or economic rights, the individual was closely linked with the concept of equality and not the concept of rights. In the area of economic property rights, his proposals for "equal distribution" of land and the "public establishment" of factories both embodied a principle of "publicness" (*gong*). If we consider that the particular characteristics of his concept of the individual developed in opposition to the worldview of public principle (*gongli*), then on the concrete sociopolitical and economic levels the links between the concept of the individual and the value of publicness (*gong*) deserve special attention. This aids us in understanding why his critique of universality was also rooted in universality.

6. A Critique of Merchants as a Special Interest Group

Zhang Taiyan's critique of political groups also focused on the operation of state power in these organizations and its moral consequences. Learned societies and political parties, as well as chambers of commerce, were the most important among urban groups. Since creation of the Self-Strengthening Learned Society (*Ziqiang xuehui*), most late imperial learned societies were political groups; these were also the precursors of modern Chinese political parties. The most forceful promoter of learned societies was Liang Qichao. He used the term "grouping" for all sorts of social and political organizations. Their most important function was to bring together the Chinese people as a unified nation. In "Lun xuehui" (On learned societies), in *Bianfa tongyi* (The general significance of the reform movement), Liang divided social groups into three types: "National groupings are the parliaments, commercial groupings are companies, and academic groupings are learned societies. Parliaments and companies know and discuss their vocations. Both derive from learning, so learned societies are the mother of those two."[62] As Hao Chang has pointed out, Liang Qichao granted learned societies such an important position because he believed that they formed an integral link in China's state making. Learned societies not only undertook the mission of teaching the people but also provided a way of shaping a certain political identity. Thus they constituted an indispensable bond in transforming China's complex and unorganized society into a unified, cohesive nation.[63] During the constitutionalist movement of the late Qing, political parties had a close relationship with learned societies. Zhang criticized these political groups primarily because of their ties with state power. He said that "if the state has political parties, then not only are most political matters corrupt, but the virtue of the scholar-gentry also declines. It turns the government into a red-light district, and national affairs into a peep show." This, he explained, followed from the election of representatives from political parties, who "ascended overnight to the king's road, sitting to discuss the Way. They seek to express their parties' views, not the will of the people. As for the various craft and commercial parties, all submit to their own private circles."[64] Hence his denial of political groups was twofold: on the one hand, they were self-interested social collectivities that obstructed the rationalization of state making; on the other hand, the activities of Chinese political groups were part of the state's workings. This also was the foundation of his post–1911 revolution theory: "Raise revolutionary armies and eliminate revolutionary parties."

7. The Rejection of Urban Political Organizations

Urban political organizations, including study societies and political parties, were seen as both sources of corruption and instruments of state power and were rejected.

8. The Rejection of Communities Based on Connections

In "Wuwu lun," Zhang advanced his ideal of abolishing the "settlement" (*juluo*), which primarily meant locally based or kin-based clans and tribes. What deserves attention is the fact that this ideal follows the ideal of abolishing the government. "The reason that all clans contend with each other is because the government sustains their separation. If political authority were to disappear, then human beings would still tame and treat generously dogs, horses, and different species. How much more generously would they treat other people?"[65] Zhang's aversion for governments, however, was by no means unconditional anarchism. In his view, the roots of government lay in war. If war did not cease, then the government could not be dispensed with for a single day. "Thus governments are not established to order the people, but in reality are established to deal with governments of other nations. If other countries have governments, then one country cannot unilaterally be without one."[66] Thus the implication of anarchism was that it would eliminate national boundaries, unify languages, and end conflict completely. The so-called no-settlement was mentioned in the sense of ending conflict, since even with the elimination of national boundaries and government, natural differences in environment would remain, leading to conflict and alliances between natural settlements formed according to race, language, or regional differences, and the emergence of new countries and governments. "Thus if we wish to dispense with governments, we must also dispense with settlements. Farmers will be itinerant farmers, craftsmen itinerant craftsmen, and women itinerant women.... They will settle as they change dwellings and move continuously.... This is why government and settlement must be eliminated at the same time."[67]

Zhang Taiyan's "Farmers will be itinerant farmers, craftsmen itinerant craftsmen" emphasized the shedding of land and family ties. This reflected his understanding of the Chinese patriarchal clan system. In *Shehui tongquan* shangdui (A discussion of *A History of Politics*), he commented on Edward Jenks's idea that patriarchal societies "emphasize the people, not the land," pointing out that China's patriarchal society had deep bonds with the land, these bonds being in fact the combination of ancestor worship and the system of land division. It must be noted that Zhang's critique of the patriarchal system was inextricably linked to his political anti-Manchu stance, since, as he saw it, China's patriarchal society accepted the rule of foreign ethnicity. However, within the late Qing context, his assault on the patriarchal system was also based on his antagonism toward the state and the expansion of its power. During the reform period, the national officials' and constitutionalist intellectuals' proposal for local self-government was in essence an attempt to use the gentry-village community to strengthen state power. *Qingmo choubei lixian dang'an shiliao* includes many memorials relating to local self-government. Their central concern was how the nation might employ the gentry, clans, and the system of natural villages to carry out the exploitation, organization, mobilization, and control of society. At the end of the Qing, the reform government requested villages to establish a set of financial institutions to finance the opening of new schools and administrative and self-defense organizations. In addition, the state pressed rural villages unceasingly for tax levies (the amount exceeded by several times the land tax) to finance colossal indemnities and subsequent wars. According to Prasenjit Duara's study of rural north China, levies imposed between 1900 and 1942 were fundamentally different from the land tax and other forms of taxes collected in the past. The levies were not assessed according to population or individual wealth, but were imposed with the village serving as a unit of taxation. Because the villages were allowed to divide up their own tax burdens, the state granted the villages their own powers of taxation and thereby control over their communal budget. After the establishment of new-style schools and public enterprises, these new-style village organizations were empowered to supervise these new enterprises and to assess and collect taxes.[68] On the one hand, the Qing government needed to nurture a group of local leaders to carry out social organization and mobilization and to realize the state's objectives. On the other hand, it had to avoid a social and judicial crisis and respect traditional authority and its institutions. However, the effort of the Manchu Qing government to use local self-government to expand its power was not entirely successful. State revenue and local disorder increased simultaneously, because the ability of the state to control rural society did not match its ability to exploit it. Formal state political authority could rely on informal structures to carry out its own policies. However, it had no means of controlling these structures. As a result, the legitimacy of state structures was checked by the corruption of local officials. Moreover, the extension of state power suggested heightened oppression and bankruptcy within the society. Duara uses Clifford Geertz's concept of involution to describe this characteristic of the expansion of late Qing state authority: "As the state grows in the involutionary mode, the informal groups become an uncontrollable power in local society, replacing a host of traditional arrangements of local governance."[69] Under these conditions, the involution of state authority means that the state bureaucracy did not rely on improving the efficiency of the existing or new establishments (personal or other administrative resources), but on reviving or expanding old state-society ties. For example, when China's old profit-based brokerage system gained in its powers of control, it not only brought about an increase in the number of brokers but also led the brokerage system to penetrate into the society's lowest level—the village. Zhang Taiyan's views toward local elections and rich families have already shown how perceptive he was about this process. At the time, however, he paid perhaps even more attention to the fact that local self-government organizations and their activities, based on local or kin-based ties, were part of the state's activities.

9. Conclusion

Let us turn to the historical significance of Zhang's proposition that "the individuated is the real; the collective is the illusory."

First, in Zhang Taiyan's writing, there is little mention of society, and the individual is set up in opposition to the state in a binary relationship. This has much to do with the historical circumstances in which the notion of society was articulated. Late Qing societal organizations such as chambers of commerce, urban guilds, and so forth often functioned as the entities in between state and society and were organized to help with the tasks of state building, society making, and individual making. As an anti-Manchu nationalist, Zhang rejected all social action in this form as attempts to help consolidate and even enhance the power of the

Manchu court. The opposition between the individuated self and the state thus developed into an opposition between the individual and a state that included all nonstate organizations. Thus, rather than saying that Zhang omitted the sphere of the society, one should say that he understood society as being "statified." This mode of discourse, with its dualistic formulation of individual and state in opposition, profoundly influenced contemporary Chinese political thought. One manifestation has been the custom of enlightened intellectuals finding political identity within the individual/nation duality (regardless of whether one is adopting an oppositional or conservative political stance). Relatively few have explored the social space that might exist between the individual and the state or in the public sphere.

Second, within the individual/state mode of discourse, the individual would never again be an abstract philosophical concept, but would be imbued with a complex structure of meaning. The meaning of the individual, with its absolute sovereignty and absolute equality in existence, had emerged in a concrete social context. Zhang's concept of the individual contained fierce negation of all "coercive" boundaries, such as nationalism, statism, and notions of village and patriarchy.[70] With regard to the state, since the individual was the basis of anarchistic thought, the individual also functioned as the basis for the declaration of popular sovereignty (with the people as individuals). With regard to modern bureaucratic structures, since the concept of the individual eliminated all rationalized social hierarchies, the concept also carried an inherent demand for political equality. With regard to economic structures, since the individual was a rationale for equal rights to the land, the individual was also a source of state socialist thought. With regard to urban groups, since the concept of the individual denied contractual relations, the concept was also the rejection of the individual/society/state mode of discourse. With regard to the patriarchal system and village associations, since the concept of the individual critiqued the gentry-village community (especially that composed of kin and local ties) as an instrument for the expansion of state power, the individual, thus conceptualized, also completely denied the traditional Chinese ethical structure. With this last point, I want to remark on the fact that although on the cultural and intellectual level Zhang promoted the "national essence" and the Chinese tradition, he rejected the clan and other traditional social groups as he developed his concept of the individual. This rejection provided an intellectual logic for modern Chinese antitraditionalism.

One of the central issues in May Fourth antitraditional thought was, as we know, the opposition between the individual, on the one hand, and the family system and traditional ethics, on the other. What deserves particular mention is the fact that Zhang's strong concept of the individual was not yet an intellectual source for capitalist rights to private property or an ethical precondition for a modern state system characterized by democracy. In other words, the individual and its related discourse certainly did not foster a Western-style individualistic culture. On the contrary, within the political, economic, and social sphere, the concept of the individual developed a politically anarchistic, economically socialist, and socially antihierarchical intellectual orientation. The inherent relationship between the individual and universal equality in Zhang's conception contained the promise of a new relationship between the individual and the ideal of *gong* (the public).[71]

Third, on the level of politics, Zhang's radical negation of the nation and all social groups, as developed in his concept of the individual, had deep links with his anti-Manchu nationalism. This was because concepts of nation and social groups, as developed by Zhang's contemporaries at the turn of the century, had been predicated upon an acceptance of the legitimate authority of the Qing government. In this fashion, the radical opposition between the individual and the people (which is also a group) in Zhang's thinking had an immediate, practical consequence. The establishment of the Chinese people as a nation meant seizure of political power from the Manchus by the Han people. Moreover, the concept of the individual in principle underscored the hollowness of official state-making endeavors launched by the Qing court. In this sense, the concept of the individual was an integral part of the discursive structure of the modern Chinese people and nation.

Fourth, the concept of the individual is both self-negating and self-transcending. Zhang had argued that, within the opposition of the individual and the state, collective entities lacked subjectivity. In the end, he asserted that entities without subjectivity were but human artifices, thereby bringing up the concept of no-mankind. Furthermore, in consideration of the history of human evolution, he raised the concept of no-organisms, in order to evade the possibility that microorganisms reconstruct humankind and its society through evolution. Finally, based on the Buddhist doctrine of nonbeing, he raised the concept of the nonworld. Actually, all these arcane concepts drew from the Buddhist principles of "man without self" and "dharma without self." The concept of the individual, then, was self-negating because the individual "always took clinging to *alayavijnana* to be the self, clinging to self-as-real as presented in consciousness, and thoughts of good and evil arose." Moreover, this sort of self and self-as-real were biases and illusory realizations born out of discriminating relations.[72] In other words, what Zhang called the individual and the true (eternal, real, and universal) self were separate. This kind of individual was one without substance, and thus the individual itself was not a phenomenon possessing self-nature and could not become a final source of moral identity. The self thus became a concept of self-transcendence: it had to look elsewhere for substance or self-nature. The separation between the individual and self-nature (ego) was the most prominent characteristic of Zhang's provisional concept of the self. This kind of separation determined that the self would not have its own depth or inherence and could not become a foundation for value or identity. It also determined the inherent logic of Zhang's thought: his emphasis on the individual in the end led to the denial of the individual itself and toward a cosmic type of pursuit for religion, faith, and universality. This was the intellectual dynamic that gave rise to the cosmic vision in his "theory of establishing religion" and "theory of making all things equal."

Fifth, within the framework of the three-natures theory and the "theory of making all things equal," Zhang discussed the question of the individual on the ontological and cosmological levels. In other words, at least in form, the concept of the individual and the concepts of the society and collectivity were unrelated. This means that the concept has nothing to do with what Lucian Pye called "sense of belonging to a collectivity," but rather concerns the problem of the individual's identity—the position and modes of existence—within the cosmos. Whether it be Zhang's demonstration of the individual's subjectivity or his doubts with regard to the real existence of the individual, neither lay within the relationship of individual and society, individual and collectivity, or even individual and self. This special rhetoric concerning the individual and his or her substance determined that Zhang's concepts of freedom and equality would be suprasocial. Thus the relationship of equality among phenomena (including people and things, people and people, and things and things) was a principle of cosmic existence and original (natural) condition, and freedom was another form of expression for this principle and condition. Even though Zhang hinted that this should also be a political and moral principle regulating relations among nations and peoples, this freedom and equality involved no concepts of rights or duty; they did not belong to the spheres of law or morality, much less to the sphere of property. We know already that within the context of "taking the uneven as even," all phenomena have their own character and principles; but we do not know if adjustment or moderation are needed between self and self, or between principle and principle. In other words, in Zhang's mode of discourse, between the individual and the individual there was no mediator of any sort, especially with respect to society.

Zhang's concept of freedom and equality did not contain the principle that the individual precedes the social structure. Nor did it contain the principle that the social structure precedes the appearance of the individual. This was because the term "social" implied a kind of order, an apprehensible entity, a discriminating relationship, a universality, and a despotic and violent potentiality. Zhang's concept of the individual and its related discourse here involved political and social applications, but not political or social science. The political nature of Zhang's social philosophy not only led to differences in his ideas about the individual and its mode of discourse and set them apart from those articulated by Liang Qichao and Yan Fu, but it also led to differences in related ideas developed in modern Western social thought. Zhang's emphasis on self-reliance and the destruction of *gongli* did not lead to an argument in favor of an individual's absolute subjectivity, but to a case for the supremacy of cosmic principle and the idea of *gong*. This *gong* stemmed neither from a ritual system nor from a society, but from a natural principle of absolute equality. The reason Zhang's concept of the individual was fundamentally provisional was because only the *gong* had an eternal, natural condition. Although Zhang's use of the individual to oppose the nation was apparently an extreme case of individualism, he did not see the individual as a source of value or a basis of identity. On the contrary, the source of value and the basis for morality was rooted in a unique condition, a condition of selfless publicness (*gong*).

NOTES

This article has been translated from Chinese by Mark Halperin and condensed and revised by Zhang Qiong.

1. Translators' note: In this essay, the Chinese term *geti* has been translated alternately as "the individual," "the individuated," and "the individuated entity," depending on the context. The term *geren* has been rendered consistently as "the individual."

2. Lucian W. Pye, *The Spirit of Chinese Politics* (Cambridge: MIT Press, 1968), xviii. Wang Hui's reading is based upon a Chinese version of this work.

3. Fredric Jameson, "Third World Literature in the Era of Multinational Capitalism," *Social Text* 15 (1986): 69. Wang Hui's reading is based on a Chinese translation of this text.

4. Ibid., 85–86.

5. Translators' note: We have used Hao Chang's translation of *qun*. See his *Liang Ch'i-ch'ao and Intellectual Transition in China, 1890–1907* (Cambridge: Harvard University Press, 1971), 95. The Chinese term *zixing* is translated alternately as "self-nature" and "subjectivity" in this essay. In Wang Hui's interpretive reading of Zhang Taiyan, a key distinction is maintained between two different kinds of entities: those that are natural and thereby endowed with an authentic *xing* (nature, attributes) residing within the individuated unit (*zi*); and those that are socially constituted, often of a collective nature, to which this *xing* is ascribed. The most prominent significance of *zixing* thus lies with subjectivity but sometimes goes beyond it.

6. Friedrich Nietzsche, "The Genealogy of Morals," in *The Birth of Tragedy and the Genealogy of Morals*, trans. Francis Golffing (New York: Anchor Books, 1956), 188. Wang Hui's reading was based upon a Chinese version of this text.

7. Translators' note: This translation adopts Hao Chang's view of Zhang Taiyan's interpretation of Zhuangzi. See his *Chinese Intellectuals in Crisis* (Berkeley and Los Angeles: University of California Press, 1987), 121–22.

8. Zhang Taiyan, "Sihuo lun" (On the four delusions), in *Zhang Taiyan quanji* (Shanghai: Shanghai renmin chubanshe, 1984), 4th fasc., 444.

9. Ibid., 446.

10. Translators' note: *Gongli*, as Wang Hui explains in the text, is a normative principle (*li*) recognized and accepted by all members of the society and is therefore impartial and public in the sense that it is equally accessible to all (*gong*). In this essay we use "public principle" to translate *gongli* in the hope of differentiating it from *tianli* (heavenly principle), a key concept in Neo-Confucian social philosophy. *Gongli* and *tianli* in Zhang Taiyan's conception appear to share attributes but differ significantly in philosophical foundation.

11. *Zhang Taiyan quanji*, 4th fasc., 449.

12. Ibid. The quote from Zhuangzi is taken from A. C. Graham, *Chuang-tzu*, 53.

13. *Zhang Taiyan quanji*, 4th fasc., 456–57.

14. "Da Tiezheng" (Responding to the iron gong), in *Zhang Taiyan quanji*, 4th fasc., 374–75.

15. "Ren wuwo lun" (On the nonexistence of the human self), in *Zhang Taiyan quanji*, 4th fasc., 419.

16. Translators' note: Peter Gregory defines *alayavijnana* as "the key Yogacara doctrine of 'store consciousness,' the eighth consciousness that operates as the underlying continuum in mental life and functions as the underlying projective consciousness on which delusion is ultimately based. The *alayavijnana* stores the seeds out of which the mental and physical elements that comprise the phenomenal world develop; it stores all experiences as karmically charged seeds, which, under the proper conditions, ripen as actions (whether mental, verbal, or physical), which in turn create new seeds." See his *Inquiry into the Origin of Humanity: An Annotated Translation of Tsung-mi's* Yüan jen lun, *with a Modern Commentary* (Honolulu: Kuroda Institute, 1995), 207 and passim.

17. "Jianshe Zongjiao lun" (On the establishment of religion), in *Zhang Taiyan quanji*, 4th fasc., 414. The same sort of view is also seen in "Ren wuwo lun," in *Zhang Taiyan quanji*, 4th fasc., 427.

18. "Ren wuwo lun," in *Zhang Taiyan quanji*, 4th fasc., 427.

19. The stress on the impartial and the collective in modern thought exhibits a significant parallel to the ritualistic political ideals of Xunzi, whereas Zhang's conception of the "impartial," articulated in Buddhist language, is inherently similar to the ideas of natural publicness (*gong*) and cosmic equality expressed in the Zhuangzi: "Heaven is impartial to everything it covers, earth to everything it carries; why would heaven and earth discriminate to make me poor?" A. C. Graham, *Chuang-tzu*, 93.

20. "Guojia lun" (On the state), in *Zhang Taiyan quanji*, 4th fasc., 457.

21. Ibid., 457–58.

22. Ibid., 459. Zhang explains the so-called expressive appearances as follows: "What most people call appearance can be divided into three parts. Green, yellow, red, and white name manifest appearances. Crooked, straight, square, and round name formal appearances. Taking, giving, contracting, and expanding name expressive appearances. All things belong to manifest and formal appearances, and all matters belong to expressive appearances. The expressive appearances pass away, and with the functions they leave behind, their shape and its boundaries are not yet extinguished, and are named nonexpressive appearances."

23. Ibid., 459.

24. Ibid., 461–62.

25. Ibid., 462

26. Fourth year of the Duke of Cheng, *Zuo zhuan, Shisanjing zhushu*, vol. 6 (Taipei: Yiwen yinshuguan, 1976), 439; "Sannianjian" (Three-year period), *Li ji, Shisanjing zhushu*, vol. 5 (Taipei: Yiwen yinshuguan, 1976), 961; "Lilun" (The discourse on ritual), *Xunzi jijie*, ed. Wang Xianqian, vol. 3 (Shanghai: Shangwu yinshuguan, 1936), 80.

27. *Shisanjing zhushu*, 8:127. Translators' note: We have used the translation by Arthur Waley. See *The Analects* (London: George Allen and Unwin, 1938), 185.

28. Wang Ermin, *Zhongguo jindai sixiang shigao* (A draft history of modern Chinese thought) (Taibei: Huashi chubanshe, 1977), 209–10.

29. See, for example, the description of *wufu* in "Basic Annals of Xia," in *Shiji* (Beijing: Zhonghua shuju, 1982), 75.

30. See Wang Ermin's two articles, " 'Zhongguo' mingcheng suyuan ji qi jindai quanshi" (Tracing the origins of the term "China" and its modern interpretation) and "Qingji xuehui yu jindai minzuzhuyi di xingcheng" (Qing learned societies and the formation of

modern nationalism), in *Zhongguo jindai sixiang shigao* (Taibei: Huashi chubanshe, 1977), 209–32, 441–80.

31. Kang Youwei, "Shang Qingdi disanchu" (The third letter to the Qing emperor [May 29, 1895]), in *Kang Youwei shenglunji*, ed. Tang Zhijun (Beijing: Zhonghua shuju, 1981), 140. "Trailing gowns" refers to how the Yellow Emperor, Yao, and Shun ruled the world by merely donning proper garments. See Zhou Yi, "Xici zhuan," *Shisanjing zhushu*, vol. 1 (Taipei: Yiwen yinshuguan, 1976), 167.

32. Liang Qichao, "Aiguo lun" (On patriotism), in *Yinbingshi heji, wenji* (Collected works and essays from the *Ice-Drinker's Studio*), vol. 3 (Shanghai: Shanghai Zhonghua shuju, 1947), 47.

33. Liang Qichao, "Zhongguo jiruo suyuan lun" (On tracing the origins of China's extreme weakness), in *Yinbingshi heji, wenji*, vol. 5, 15–16, 22–23.

34. Liang Qichao, "Xinmin shuo" (New citizen), in *Yinbingshi heji*. Translators' note: The author does not indicate which part of *Yinbingshi heji* he refers to and gives no volume or page number.

35. For the view that nationalism meant "national-people-ism," see "Sanmin zhuyi" (The three principles of the people), in *Sun Zhongshan quanji* (The collected works of Sun Yat-sen), 9th fasc. (Beijing: Zhonghua shuju, 1981), 184–185.

36. Zhang Taiyan, "Zhang Taiyan guimao yuzhong manbi" (Zhang Taiyan's random jottings from prison in 1903), *Guocui xuebao* (Shanghai), no. 8 (1905): 5.

37. Wang Sichen, *Guoxue jianghua* (Shanghai: Shijie shuju, 1935), 1–3.

38. Huang Jie, "Guocui xuebaoshu," *Guocui xuebao* (Shanghai), no. 1 (March 23, 1905): 3.

39. Ibid.

40. Zhang Taiyan, "Yanshuo lu," in *Minbao*, no. 6 (January 1907): 4. See *Xinhai geming qian shinian jianshi lun xuanji*, 2d fasc., pt. A (Beijing: Sanlian shudian, 1978), 448–52.

41. Translators' note: To distinguish *minzu zhuyi* and *guojia zhuyi*, we translate the former as "nationalism" and the latter as "statism."

42. Liang Qichao, "Zhengzhixue dajia Bolunzhili zhi xueshuo" (The ideas of the great political scientist Bluntschli), in *Yinbingshi heji, wenji*, vol. 13, 68. Behind Liang's view was the major turn in his political attitudes and faith in politics. *Liang Rengong xiansheng nianpu changbian chugao* (A first draft of the long version of Master Liang Rengong's chronological history) has the following note: "The nihilism of his previous deeply felt beliefs and his advocacy of revolutionary anti-Manchuism were completely abandoned. This was a great turn in the master's political thought. His speech and ideas of the next few years were based completely on this foundation." Cited from *Xinhai geming shiqi qikan jieshao* (An introduction to periodicals of the 1911 revolution era), vol. 1 (Beijing: Renmin chubanshe, 1982), 162.

43. Liang Qichao, "Zhengzhixue dajia Bolunzhili zhi xueshuo," 70–71.

44. Ibid., 69, 77–86.

45. Ibid., 86–88.

46. Ibid., 88–89.

47. See Liang Qichao, "Kaiming zhuanzhi lun" (On enlightened despotism), *Yinbingshi heji, wenji*, vol. 17. Hao Chang points out that "his central concern was not with 'enlightened despotism' per se, but with a much broader underlying problem, namely, 'reason of the state.'" In other words, Liang's political orientation was identical to that of Western political thinkers from Machiavelli to Hegel, whose "paramount concern was the rational conduct of government to ensure the survival and security of the state irrespective of its moral

and ideological consequences. Specifically, 'reason of state' consists in the justification of such rational conduct of government as the supreme political end." See his *Liang Ch'i-ch'ao*, 255–56. Liang's interest in "enlightened despotism" was a natural development of his interest in "reason of state." What must be pointed out here, however, is that he had no interest in enlightened despotism itself, but found it an ideal and effective means to solve the problem of the Chinese nation's security and survival during an age of imperialism. This in general also explains Liang's contradictory feelings toward constitutional monarchy and enlightened despotism.

48. Zhu Zhixin, "Xinli de guojiazhuyi," *Minbao* 21 (June 1906): 22–34.

49. Zhang Taiyan, "Zhonghua minguo jie," in *Zhang Taiyan quanji*, 4th fasc., 253. The targets of his criticism were "economic-military theorists," meaning actually Yang Du's essay "Jintie zhuyi shuo" (The theory of economic militarism), published in *Zhongguo xinbao* (China new report) 2 (February 1907): 4. Yang Du believed in enriching the country and strengthening the military, establishing the nation through the military "only toward the outside, but not toward the inside," and carrying out an "economic militarism." During the constitutional monarchy period, he touched on the Manchu-Han Chinese problem. "Between the monarch and the people, those who say that there has been no Manchu-Han Chinese problem for a long time cannot extend this to the imperial house. The imperial house directly stands outside the Manchu-Han Chinese problem." His view was that the monarch was an agency of the nation; the problem was one of whether he is the monarch of the enlightened despotic polity or that of the constitutional monarchical polity, and not one of whether he is a Manchu or Han Chinese. "The monarch is the representative of the entire nation, not that of an entire people." Behind his slogan that "the monarch and people are one, and Manchu and Han have equal rights" was his use of the national problem to obscure the racial problem.

50. Zhang Taiyan, "Zhonghua minguo jie," in *Zhang Taiyan quanji*, 4th fasc., 256.

51. "Xuanshi yule lixian xianxing liding guanzhi yu" (Edict announcing that constitutional preparation will begin by carrying out the formulation of rules for official institutions), in *Qingmo choubei lixian dang'an shiliao*, ed. Gugong bowuguan Ming-Qing dang'anbu (Ming-Qing archives of the National Palace Museum), vol. 1 (Beijing: Zhonghua shuju, 1979), 44.

52. Liang Qichao, "Shizhong dexing xiangfan xiangcheng yi" (The contradictory and complementary meaning of ten kinds of virtuous conduct), published originally in *Qingyi bao* (Pure discussion reports) 82 (June 16, 1901) and 84 (July 6, 1901), later included in *Yinbingshi heji*, *wenji*, 5th vol. See also Liang Qichao, *Liang Qichao zhexue sixiang lunwen xuan* (A selection of Liang Qichao's essays on philosophical thought) (Beijing: Beijing Daxue chubanshe, 1984), 49.

53. Zhang Taiyan, "Sihuo lun," in *Zhang Taiyan quanji*, 4th fasc., 446–48.

54. Zhang Taiyan, "Guojia lun," in *Zhang Taiyan quanji*, 4th fasc., 458.

55. Zhang Taiyan, "Wuwu lun," in *Zhang Taiyan quanji*, 4th fasc., 435.

56. See, for example, Wang Fansen, *Zhang Taiyan ti sixiang ji qi dui Ruxue chuantong di chongji* (Zhang Taiyan's thought and its attack on Confucian tradition) (Taipei: Shibao wenhua chuban youxian gongsi, 1985), chap. 5, sec. 3. See also *Qingmo choubei lixian dang'an shiliao*, vol. 2 (Beijing: Zhonghua shuju, 1979), 603–4.

57. Zhang believed that China's despotic system made for a more egalitarian society than the constitutional systems of the West and Japan. See Zhang Taiyan, "Daiyi ranfou lun," *Zhang Taiyan quanji*, 4th fasc., 300.

58. Ibid., 303.

59. Ibid., 307–8; and "Wuwu lun," *Zhang Taiyan quanji*, 4th fasc., 430–31.

60. See Zhao Jing and Yi Menghong, eds., *Zhongguo jindai jingji sixiang shi* (The history of modern Chinese economic thought), vol. 2 (Beijing: Zhonghua shuju, 1985), 488–502.

61. Zhang Taiyan, "Wuchao falü suoyin," *Zhang Taiyan quanji*, 4th fasc., 84. This work originally appeared in issue 23 of *Minbao*, and was changed somewhat when incorporated into *Taiyan wenlu* (Record of Taiyan's writings).

62. Liang Qichao, "Bianfa tongyi—lun xuehui," *Yinbingshi heji, wenji*, 1st fasc., 31.

63. Hao Chang, *Liang Ch'i-ch'ao*, 108–9.

64. Zhang Taiyan, "Daiyi ranfou lun," *Zhang Taiyan quanji*, 4th fasc., 309. See also Zhang Taiyan's October 1911 essay, "Zhu zhengdang" (Eliminating political parties), in Tang Zhijun, ed., *Zhang Taiyan nianpu changbian* (The long version of Zhang Taiyan's chronology), vol. 1 (Beijing: Zhonghua shuju, 1979), 352–60.

65. *Zhang Taiyan quanji*, 4th fasc., 432.

66. Ibid., 432.

67. Ibid., 434.

68. Prasenjit Duara, *Culture, Power, and the State: Rural North China, 1900–1942* (Stanford: Stanford University Press, 1988), 4.

69. Ibid., 74–77.

70. "Wuwu lun," *Zhang Taiyan quanji*, 4th fasc., 429–30.

71. The manifestation of this notion of publicness (*gong*) in nationalism is the extension of Mozi's "impartial" ethics, in which "undifferentiated love begins its practice with kin," to the relationships between peoples. Zhang said, "What we propose is not limited to the Han people. For other weak peoples who have been conquered by strong peoples, whose government has been usurped and people enslaved, if they have any remaining strength they must unite and recover [their sovereignty and freedom]. . . . If we want to fulfill our nationalism, then we should extend our 'hearts of a child' to rescue others in similar distress and allow them to live in land that is completely independent." Ibid., 430.

72. Ibid., 436–37.

EIGHT

Crime or Punishment?
On the Forensic Discourse
of Modern Chinese Literature

David Der-wei Wang

This essay approaches the subject of "violence and modern China" by examining the dialogical representation of violence and justice in modern Chinese literature. The corpus of Chinese literature from the turn of the century up to the Chinese Communist takeover of the mainland is one replete with horrific natural and humanmade disasters, such as foreign aggressions, civil wars, revolutions, local riots, clan conflicts, famines, and floods, to say nothing of the cataclysmic collapse of established values. While these various forms of violence have engendered a "literature of tears and blood" commemorating the physical and emotional pain of the Chinese people, they have given rise to an equally compelling if not so famous discourse on "crime and punishment."[1]

The entangled relations between violence and justice can be found in the legal-literary discourse of earlier eras.[2] What concerns me here is the way in which modern Chinese writers' inquiries into the terms of violence and justice have served as a poignant index to the rise (and premature decline?) of a new consciousness called Chinese modernity. I consider justice to be a social institution that is implemented in many ways—from legal codes to administrative norms, from consensual conventions to "mythical" taboos—so as to define and curb natural and human forms of violence.[3] By corollary, violence is understood as a demonstration of natural, social, or individual power that crosses the consensual boundary of the rational and results in physical or psychological damage to the victim.[4] These are working definitions and are admittedly provisional. As will be demonstrated by the following examples, these two definitions tend to collapse into each other in a way that is dramatized in some of the most intriguing moments in modern Chinese legal-literary representation.

A high-strung, contentious call for justice permeated modern Chinese literature from the start; it obliged writers to write in order to indict social evils, right wrongs, and prefigure a world of equality and order. This discourse originated in the late Qing and May Fourth eras, when literati promulgated the "new literature" as a total rejection of the old, and it reached its first climax in the forties, in the wake of Mao's Yan'an talks. Chen Duxiu's advocacy of "a literature for the common people" and the leftist writers' slogan "literature for the insulted and the injured" are but the most blatant examples.[5] Under the pens of modern Chinese writers, traditional norms, from imperial mandate to familial patriarchy, are shown as having lost their claims to legitimacy and, worse, as having revealed themselves to be nothing but excuses for systematic coercion. In Lu Xun's words, the Chinese had been attending a spectacular banquet that was nothing but "cannibalism."[6] In revulsion, modern Chinese literature set about to demolish an obsolete system in which oppression had been invisible, even if it took acts of representational violence to stop the old "cannibalism" and make the Chinese see the horrible truth. As critics such as Liu Zaifu have pointed out, Chinese literature under the auspices of leftist aesthetics starts out as "a literature against violence" but becomes a "violence of literature."[7]

After all, in understanding modern China, one sees that violence is not just a theoretical issue.[8] The mutual implication of violence and justice can never be understood as simply what happened "out there" and why some activity had to be punished.[9] One must understand justice as a discourse under which some forms of violence are condemned while others are taken for granted. Insofar as it constituted a major cultural premise in modern China, "violence of representation" presented literature as the meeting ground where poetic justice contested with legal justice, where ink demanded blood. Instead of merely reflecting external instances of violence, literature would demand to be appreciated and enlisted as a radical agency of change. In other words, writing and reading were to be taken as juridical events capable of transforming symbolic victims into social rebels and figurative humiliations into moral passions.

Long before politically correct scholars began to trumpet the power of language and rhetoric, Chinese literary discourse emphasized the politics of literature, and the late Qing had only to substitute European terms in the traditional discourse of the Way. The changing images of the modern Chinese writer, from the "scholarly knight-errant" (*ruxia*), as promoted by Zhang Taiyan (1869–1936) in the late Qing, to the "revolutionary vanguard," as sanctioned by the Communist Party in the late forties, bespoke the writers' persistent attempts to retain their traditional role as arbiters of social order and moral chaos.[10] But Chinese literary history from the Literary Revolution to revolutionary literature has left ample evidence of how such representational claims might backfire. By this I do not mean merely that language might "instigate" criminal activity or that literature might be the victim of false "indictments." I mean that the Way may be rendered mute, due either to self-censorship or to external coercion; and when the name of injustice should be spoken, literature is silent, thereby betraying its complicitous relations with all master narratives, old and new. This, I argue, is the worst form of "the violence of representation."[11]

To further my argument, I will describe how a forensic discourse—a discourse formed by an open debate, in the courtroom or in any other public space, regarding the legal consequences of a narrated event—has arisen and evolved in modern Chinese literature. With examples drawn from four historical moments, the late Qing era, the post–May Fourth era, the thirties, and the Yan'an era, I will show how, at a time when the old political, judicial, and moral order had collapsed and the new orders were yet to be established, literature provided a textual space in which legal cases were presented for debate and deliberation. In each of the examples to be discussed, a certain crime has been committed, followed by a call for a due punishment as a form of revenge, retribution, or discipline. But closer reading suggests that the narrated crime and punishment may have penetrated each other's realms, violating rather than vindicating each other's legal or moral presumptions. These examples reveal a practice of justice that is as vulnerable as it is violent. Meanwhile, as a transmitter of these debatable cases of crime and punishment, the position of literature itself comes to be questioned as an accomplice of criminals or of executioners.

1. JUSTICE UNDONE

For readers of late Qing fiction, one of the most memorable scenes is perhaps the intrusion of Lao Can into the hall of justice in Liu E's (1857–1909) *Lao Can youji* (The travels of Lao Can, 1907). In chapter 16 of *The Travels of Lao Can,* prefect Gangbi is cross-examining a woman prisoner named Jia Wei, who had been wrongly indicted as murderer of the whole family of her father-in-law—a total of thirteen lives—after her alleged adultery was exposed. Exasperated by the woman's response that she could not give the name of her lover-accomplice because she had never had one, Gangbi orders thumbscrews placed on her. One attendant grasps the woman's hair and lifts up her head and another two are pushing her hands into the thumbscrews, and at this crucial moment Lao Can walks into the middle of the courtroom and stops the torture.

Lao Can had learned of the misjudged case from a friend. Outraged by Gangbi's bigotry and cruelty, Lao Can volunteered to draft a letter of impeachment to Governor Zhuang and Judge Bai, Gangbi's superiors, so as to save the innocent defendant. He receives positive responses from Zhuang and Bai. As there is no time to deliver Zhuang's and Bai's letters to Gangbi through the normal channels, in the crucial scene described above, Lao Can is carrying the letters and has walked into the hall of justice without permission.

The illegal intrusion of Lao Can into the hall of justice brings together two strands from contesting themes that have been manifested from the beginning of the novel. The confrontation between Lao Can and Gangbi is not merely a showdown between a chivalrous traveling doctor and a haughty judge-investigator regarding a misjudged case. Rather, it represents the dramatic moment in which the incipient issues of legal praxis and its transgression, governmental mandate and individual agency, social justice and poetic justice, are finally laid on the table for negotiation. As its preface suggests, *The Travels of Lao Can* is a novel written, and expected to be read, in tears.[12] Through Lao Can's travels, the novel introduces a China caught in an array of crises from the Boxer Rebellion to local riots, from natural disaster to impending revolutions. But in his diagnosis of the national malaise, what troubles Liu E (and Lao Can) most is the injustice that prevails throughout the governmental system, a condition that Lao Can believes symptomizes the final sickness of the dynasty.

Despite conventional wisdom, however, Liu E does not hold corrupt officials responsible for the collapse of law and justice. As many scholars have pointed out, what makes the novel polemic is that it condemns apparently good or incorruptible judges, not the corruptible ones, as the real source of evil. In the episode cited above, Judge Gangbi is not a classically "bad" judge but one famous for his sense of integrity. In a judicial system in which buying oneself out of indictments has become the norm, Gangbi is known for taking no bribes, and to that extent he has reason to be proud of himself. But as he tries hard to maintain his clean image, he turns this virtue into a vice. He is so proud of his reputation for virtue that he has become an intolerant puritan, as his Chinese name, homophonous with "bigotry" (*gangbi*), indicates.

When the woman Jia Wei was put in jail, her family had followed the normal rules of the game by paying a sizable sum of money to the court. Instead of returning the money right away, however, Gangbi keeps it, to use as new evidence against Jia Wei; he believes that the family of an innocent defendant would not bribe a judge. He tortures the woman with all kinds of penal instruments, forcing her to confess in accordance with a scenario that jumps to the worst of conclusions. Gangbi's behavior leads Liu E to make the famous commentary at the end of chapter 16: "All men know that corrupt officials are bad, but few know that incorruptible officials are even worse. Whereas a corrupt official knows his own faults and dares not play the tyrant openly, an incorruptible official imagines that since he never takes bribes he is free to do whatever he likes. Then self-confidence and personal prejudice may lead him to kill the innocent or even endanger the state."[13]

Gangbi's perpetration of "pious violence" posits an uncanny challenge to the conventional practice of justice. To scare people away from transgressing the law, or to demonstrate the absolute power of justice over evil, Gangbi can impose a punishment that is crueler and more spectacular than the crime for which the punishment is executed. The effect of Gangbi's law resorts to a penal technology that comes from the very transgression it aims to eliminate. Liu E has described earlier in the novel this paradox of justice in the form of another incorruptible judge, Yuxian.[14] Under his rule, a part of Shandong has become a model region free of crime. But Yuxian has achieved this temporary miracle by setting up a regime of horror; he mercilessly kills not only bandits but also innocent suspects misidentified as bandits. The citizens under Yuxian's governorship enjoy a communal life safe from bandits, their lives saved until they themselves are accused of banditry. That the justice system is legalized violence, so to speak, becomes apparent when the state, in a moment of fanatical self-affirmation, decides that it can eliminate crime.

By exposing the violence concealed behind the facade of "benevolent" governorship, Liu E means to do more than criticize local judicial errors. He sees this hidden injustice as a most dangerous malady that, left unchecked, would eventually jeopardize national well-being. In Lao Can's words, "With so great a reputation as an administrator, . . . within a few years [Yuxian] will become provincial governor. The greater the official position such a man holds, the greater the harm he will do. If he controls a prefecture, then a prefecture suffers; if he governs a province, then a province is maimed; if he [administers the affairs of] the Empire, then the Empire dies!"[15] Liu E has a good reason to make such a radical comment. A historically verifiable figure, Yuxian was later promoted to high position thanks to his judicial impartiality. He turned out nevertheless to be one of the most vehement voices in support of the Boxer Rebellion, which led to national disaster. The final irony is that, in the wake of the invasion of the eight foreign allied armies, Yuxian found himself being indicted by his own government as a war criminal, for having instigated a rebellion aimed at "punishing" foreigners. The incorruptible judge was finally sentenced as a traitor and beheaded.[16]

Back to the episode of Gangbi and the woman Jia Wei. When he is planning to save the woman, Lao Can at the same time involves himself in ransoming a prostitute named Cuihuan, who otherwise would be resold to a lower-class brothel. The girl was a survivor of a massive Yellow River flood in Shandong Province. She had come from a rich farm family in the fertile land between the governmental dikes against the Yellow River.[17] As the Yellow River was about to flood one year, Shandong governor Zhuang took the advice of a scholar to give up areas outside the governmental dikes so as to widen the river and ease the peak of the flood. But the area between the governmental dikes was densely populated and rimmed with smaller dikes built by farmers to protect their land. For fear that these people would fiercely object to his policy, Zhuang was urged to keep it a secret till the last moment. Governor Zhuang was an official well known for his benevolence and fair-mindedness: a "good judge" in other words.[18] In the case of the Yellow River flood, nevertheless, he knowingly let thousands of people be drowned and their properties washed away, as the wisest and most effective policy mechanism.

Governor Zhuang, it will be recalled, is the fictional force whose last-minute interference rescues the woman Jia Wei from the hands of Gangbi. He serves as the deus ex machina whose power sponsors Lao Can in his intrusion in the above-cited courtroom scene. But Lao Can is not unaware of the fact that it is this same Governor Zhuang who has indirectly killed thousands. One innocent has been saved by a merciful man, the governor; thousands of innocents have been killed by that same merciful man. If the criminal in the mystery of thirteen deaths is guilty of murder, how about a "good" judge like Gangbi or Yuxian who has administered so many wrong convictions and unjust capital punishments before this single case? If a small-scale "good judge" (Gangbi or Yuxian) is to be condemned for harming dozens, how about a higher-ranking "good judge" (Governor Zhuang), who is responsible for annulling thousands of innocent lives? No Lao Can turns up to "expose" the governor; indeed, all Lao Can does is salvage a few victims from the thousands sacrificed to the public good and manipulate a small "good judge" with the help of a grand "good judge," whose crimes are also on a much grander scale.

In volume two of *The Travels of Lao Can*, Lao Can has a dream. He travels to Hell and witnesses thousands of condemned souls undergoing various forms of punishment: they are scourged by nail-studded clubs till their flesh falls off their bones, deep-fried in a huge cauldron full of boiling oil, or ground into powder by grindstones.[19] These souls are paying the price for their misdeeds, however trivial, during their lifetimes. As for those who were virtuous when alive, they have been rewarded with a smooth transmigration into their next lives. The dream visit to Hell reinforces Lao Can's belief that some supernatural agency is at work handing out proper retribution.

One wonders if Lao Can's dream visit to Hell in volume two is not to be taken as a belated act of poetic justice, written to counterbalance the numerous episodes of misjudged cases and undeserved sufferings in volume one. Though the secular judicial system fails, Liu E tells us, a higher judicial system still works. The eternal wheel of fortune still turns, at least in Lao Can's dreams.

But for a reader alerted by the first volume of Liu E's novel to the fact that incorruptible judges can be more dangerous than corruptible ones, and that justice on earthly China is only an expensive fantasy, questions remain. Given the way that Hell is visualized as a gigantic, rigid bureaucracy handing out gory punishments according to the book, one can only see it as an extension of, rather than a contrast to, human courtrooms. When the earthly "incorruptible" judge is seen as culpable of abusing justice, one cannot help questioning the "incorruptibility" of the judge of judges, Yama, the ruler of Hell. And the other side of a rigid and abacus-like system of rewards and punishments in Heaven and Hell can be the corrupt and careless system of divine whims and tantrums.[20]

Whereas Liu E takes pains to distinguish the divine and human agencies of justice and their violent consequences, only to call attention to the collusive relation between them, Li Boyuan (1857–1906), Liu's contemporary, approaches the issue from a different angle. Li tells his readers that Hell is neither worse nor better than this world; as a matter of fact, Hell *is* this world. In his preface to his *Huo Diyu* (Living hell, 1906), he says:

> At the trial in the Grand Hall of Justice, the magistrate is the king of Hades; the clerks and underlings are the judges who demand the death penalty; the runners and servants, all three ranks of them, are like the ox-headed and horse-faced demon messengers from purgatory; and the flat bamboo canes and instruments of torture designed to hurt people are like the two edged sword-leaf trees and the hill of knives in Hell. Before the prisoner has been assigned to his quarters or incarcerated in prison, he has suffered more than enough! Alas! Heaven is above us and Hell is be-

low! Although I have never seen this Hell of "judges of Hell," I am afraid there is nowhere one will not find such a hell on earth.[21]

Living Hell is a novel featuring fourteen misjudged cases and cruel tortures presided over by corrupt judges. It has never been a popular work from Li's oeuvre.[22] Among the few critics who appreciated it, the novel was regarded as "the first book written in Chinese which sought to expose malpractice and corruption in the Chinese penal system and to describe in detail a variety of techniques employed to extract information from prisoners."[23] In terms of unveiling the most inhuman aspects of the Chinese legal system, the novel is indeed a chilling success. Such a reading, however, overlooks the real "virtue" of *Living Hell* by making it merely another example of late Qing exposé fiction.

Artistic flaws—the crude language, contrived plotting, and flat characterization typical of late Qing fiction—notwithstanding, *Living Hell* distinguishes itself. A relentless parody of the genre of chivalric and court-case fiction, it also questions the concept of justice and its violation (most exposé novels assume or reaffirm a concept of it). *Justice*, as I am using the word, is not just the implementation of a humanmade or heaven-given law by human or divine judges; it is also the process of questioning and remaking the laws themselves.[24] It contains a dimension in which narrative praxis figures importantly, because there it does not assume an originary concept of justice by which human or celestial laws can be evaluated. Liu E in *The Travels of Lao Can* still betrays a lingering nostalgia about the lost world of chivalry and justice; with all his cynical observations on contemporary society, Li Boyuan makes the abuses of law and order the *pretext* of his novel; his is a world in which chivalry is nullified and justice turned upside down, but there is still a perspective from which abuse is clearly *abuse*. If Liu E still worries about why justice can be so generally violated, Li Boyuan is surprised to see any justice being done anywhere.

What kinds of cases does Li Boyuan examine in his novel? In one story, local officers provoke two feuding families in Shanxi to sue each other. As more and more of their members are put in jail, both families are forced to spend thousands of dollars buying the magistrate's favor; the case comes to a sudden halt as the magistrate moves to a new position (chapters 1–8). In another, a highway robber known for his capacity to endure any form of punishment finally succumbs to the tools of torture invented by a cruel judge (chapter 12). More than half of the episodes in the novel deal with sufferings of the innocent, however. A chaste woman turns down the sexual advances of a local official, only to find herself being charged with murdering her husband, who is actually away on business. The woman suffers horribly in jail and has to be acquitted only because her husband returns from his trip (chapters 13–18). In a similar case, a man who loses all his property in an accidental fire is accused of arson. Without money to buy himself out of the charge and unable to stand police torture, he drowns himself (chapter 33).

In Li Boyuan's world, corruptible judges and incorruptible judges are alike in administering inhuman punishments; innocent people and bandits are tortured equally once they fall into the hands of the judges. In sharp contrast to Liu E, who doggedly searches against all odds for a way of rectifying the social order, Li Boyuan tells us that any effort to amend the way things are will prove too little and too late. If good judges never exist, neither do "good" outlaws. As if ridiculing such popular late Qing chivalric novels as *Sanxia wuyi* (Three knights-errant and five sworn brothers, 1878), in which former lawbreakers are persuaded by loyal judges to serve the emperor, Li Boyuan introduces in *Living Hell* bandits and officials cooperating like business partners in setting up innocent people and cheating them of their money. Business is so good that, since he has made a fortune, one highway robber buys himself a position as county magistrate. This bandit-judge appoints his cohorts as officers and attendants in his court and runs a lucrative business taking bribes from the innocent and the guilty alike (chapters 38–39). All the fourteen cases narrated in the novel end with a nonending, the narrator's moral commentary at the end of each case being at best perfunctory. No justice, not even a dream of divine justice, appears in the novel.

This is where Li Boyuan shows that his novel can at the same time be more conservative and radical than *The Travels of Lao Can*. Like A Ying, Zhao Jingshen, and other critics, one may conclude that Li Boyuan views the total breakdown of a judicial system from a conventional perspective, that of the dynastic cycle. By comparing the world to Hell, he reveals a reliance on conventional wisdom without either questioning its premises or stating a resolution in traditional terms. His cynicism partakes less of skeptical rigor, such as Liu E's, than of noncommittal play. Nonetheless, the way Li Boyuan portrays the late Qing courtroom as a bloody circus marks a radical departure from the traditional aesthetics of spectatorhood. So, just as Liu E's narrative innovations shed an ambiguous light on his politics of writing, Li Boyuan's relentless narratives of bodily torture seize new ground in the morality of reading.

One cannot overlook the possibility that Li Boyuan (and his intended readers) may actually enjoy the blood and pain, in a kind of philosophical schadenfreude. What he ultimately provides in the novel is not an account of misjudged cases but, rather, a *spectacle* of punishments. Few readers will fail to be impressed by Li's meticulous descriptions of the tools and paraphernalia used to torture the indicted. Women are often among the first group of victims in this circus of cruelty. A woman charged with adultery is treated with a "nippled iron": stripped of her clothes, she is "ironed" by a burning-hot metal instrument with nipplelike points.[25] Another woman culprit with tender bound feet is forced to stand barefoot for hours on bricks. As her feet are already deformed thanks to foot binding, she can hardly stand straight for a moment.

Unpleasant as they are, these punishments are only for beginners. Some penal devices are so ingenious that they are even given patent names. "Red embroidered shoes" are shoes made from iron. Prisoners put on the shoes only when they are red hot. "Big red gown" refers to a kind of glue as thick as ox hide. When heated to a liquid, it is applied to the prisoner's body. The courtroom attendants wait till

it dries and then peel it off, together with the prisoner's skin. Judged by the ingenuity of these devices, one may well imagine what other punishments hide behind
such euphemisms as "Dragon flying amid mountains," "Five sons pass the civil
service examination," and "Three immortals make a visit to a cave."[26]

Li Boyuan scrupulously catalogues the variety of courtroom punishments, so
much so that the report acquires an aesthetic of its own. A mock-encyclopedic
form of narrative, of course, is a main trait of late Qing exposé novels. *Living Hell*
stands out as the exposé that relates social justice to bodily pain in the most direct
and systematic way (like the judges it exposes). It features a penal technology that
resorts heavily to the presentation of a bloody corporeal theater, and in this sense
it is almost a textbook illustration of Michel Foucault's notion of the relation between disciplining and punishing, power and law, in premodern society.[27] Pain
and confession are supposed to come together; fragments of information can be
pieced together at the cost of torn limbs. Through performing physical torture
and mutilation in public, the authorities make sure that the law has been literally
implicated into the body politic.

Besides offering lip service to the institution of justice, Li shows little sympathy
for his victims. No matter how he justifies his narrative stance, he cannot hide his
thirst for sensationalism. Following the Foucauldian argument, one can say that
Li's elaborate description of punishment betrays a sadomasochistic penchant,
something that upsets the solemnity of justice and turns it into an excuse for a
macabre carnival. Parading the penal devices used in the courtroom and overex-
posing the pain of the indicted, Li Boyuan imbues his narrative with a cynical subtext, thereby intimating the final stage of the decadent inclination in late Qing fiction. In a similar manner, the novel anticipates a reader who may be as much
provoked as he or she is excited by the bloody cases. Twice removed from the
scene of punishments, the implied reader occupies a safe position and may atten-
tively observe limbs torn apart and bodies charred into pieces. With a quivering
sigh, the reader may experience a quick catharsis, accompanied by a puff of reas-
suring indignation.

These Foucauldian observations lead us back to the question: how can justice
be represented as such? One remembers that, in *The Travels of Lao Can*, Liu E scan-
dalizes his readers by declaring that incorruptible judges are more dangerous than
corruptible judges. While it blurs the distinction between good and bad judges
sanctioned by conventional wisdom, Liu E's discovery is nevertheless based on a
belief that there is an essential system for judging the goodness of a "good" judge;
hence he experiments with various forms of poetic justice, from appropriating the
new Sherlock Holmes techniques of investigation to invoking the old Buddhist
consolations of Heaven and Hell.[28]

Li Boyuan answers the question by telling us that there is no distinction between good and bad judges, because there are no good judges. Li envisions in *Living Hell* a state of legal and bureaucratic anarchy, one that celebrates the complicity between the corruptible and incorruptible judges and shows no sympathy for

the fate of either the innocent or the criminal in custody of the law. Li Boyuan does not solve the dilemma generated by this vision. If Earth is merely Hell, then Li Boyuan is plainly one of the cruel, incompetent, and greedy inhabitants. As an earthly devil, he enjoys staging punishments, the bloodier the better. And as a minion of Yama, his opinions on justice are those of a devil: they question nothing of the divine order. If Earth is Hell, then judges are devils, and writers who judge the judges are also devils. Liu E puts institutions into question; Li Boyuan puts intuitions into question.

2. MISOGYNY AND MISANDRY, FILICIDE AND PARRICIDE

Questions arising in *Living Hell,* as in *The Travels of Lao Can,* about the equivocal relationship between law and violence, between crime and punishment, between the cynical and the carnivalesque response to judicial anarchy, continue to occupy the minds of Chinese writers of the post–May Fourth era. As a matter of fact, modern Chinese literature has been described as originating with a bloody scene. According to his own account, in 1906, Lu Xun (1881–1936), initiator of modern Chinese literature, saw a slide show of decapitation as he was studying medicine in Japan. In the slide, a Chinese is about to be beheaded by Japanese soldiers for serving as spy for the Russians during the Russo-Japanese war, while a surrounding Chinese crowd waits to see the bloody spectacle. Lu Xun was allegedly so traumatized by the slide show that he gave up medical school to become a writer.[29]

As I have discussed elsewhere, violence and "modern" literature erupted at the same time, as Chinese literati set out to gaze at the bloody consequences of their cultural heritage.[30] Modern Chinese literature is not a medium employed passively to reflect extant social abuses; as implied by the dramatic case of Lu Xun, it was instead provoked into existence by a drastic jolt at both the emotive and ideological level, when the author confronted his national status symbolized by a decapitated body. This literature arose as part of the radical Lu Xun's and his contemporaries' search for the cause of the Chinese "original sin," which is projected by the spectacle of decapitation. Lu Xun asks, why did Russia and Japan wage a war against each other yet choose China as their battleground? Why is a Chinese willing to work for one foreign army to spy on the other? Why does the Chinese crowd look on so callously as one of their compatriots is beheaded?

For Lu Xun, the Chinese spy may as well be killed for collaborating in a war that nominally had nothing to do with China. Moreover, just as the spy deserves his capital punishment, so are his fellow Chinese spectators unworthy of mercy.[31] Lu Xun sees in these Chinese a readiness to transform themselves from spectators to practitioners at every cannibalistic rite, though the cost is everyone's blood. Lu Xun's charge could have extended even further, to the Japanese and Russians, who had manipulated the Chinese into humiliating themselves. Finally, Lu Xun must have tortured himself with this question: if all Chinese are culpable for bringing shame upon their nation, what about Lu Xun, the spectator who stands gaping at a slide show of Chinese being humiliated? Is he the last conscience of China, privileged with a superhuman vision and voice? Or does he after all share in this collective Chinese original sin?

Lu Xun's "Kuangren riji" (Diary of a madman, 1918), usually regarded as the harbinger of modern Chinese fiction, invites one more reading. Insofar as his Madman launches a one-man investigation of social evils, only to discover that Chinese society as a whole is guilty of cannibalism, Lu Xun has told a story about justice lost and refound, the most cynical version. The origin of social evil—cannibalism—can be named by the Madman only at the cost of his being confined, censored, clinically (mal)treated, imprisoned, and finally "eaten up" by his closest family members. The story is full of penal and carceral imagery, such as quarantine, persecution, rehabilitation, a stifling iron house, and so on. All these forms of punishment, as the ending of the story tells us, prove to be nothing but preludes to yet another round of cannibalistic banqueting.

If Lu Xun is pessimistic about the retrievability of justice, he is just as equivocal about the consequences of finally bringing that desired justice into practice. Consider his famous allegory of the iron house, in which a crowd is jailed and suffocates from lack of air. Should a sole waker among the crowd wake up his fellow inmates (which might result in a panicked and useless attempt to escape)? Or should he let them die "peacefully" (and therefore become a reluctant witness to mass murder)?[32] In other words, faced with a hopelessly suffocating China, should an intellectual watch the final collapse as a spectator, or should this person come to its rescue, however unworthy it is of the risk? In either case, Lu Xun and his Madman have incarcerated themselves in a dilemma.

Lu Xun's predicament as a justice seeker, together with the cynical, self-deprecating bent of his imagination, may not be completely original, however. An apparently "modern" writer, Lu Xun has a temperament that betrays many fixations inherited from "premodern" writers; what comes to mind are Liu E's elite yearning for justice in *The Travels of Lao Can* and Li Boyuan's cynical spectatorship in *Living Hell*. One recalls that, in the imagined hell of Lao Can's dream, Liu E can still see justice done in another world; in the realistic hell that is contemporary China, Li Boyuan simply scoffs at any attempt at restoring justice. Lu Xun appears as the self-imposed tragic fighter standing at the threshold of Hell, unable, or unwilling, to cross over to either side. As T. A. Hsia speculates, one of the most prominent images Lu Xun takes up as a modern writer is that of a chivalric hero in a dynastic cycle, a hero who holds open the "gate of darkness" to let his comrades and other innocent people flee disaster, only to be crushed by the gate when he falls exhausted.[33]

Straddling the threshold of the "gate of darkness," Lu Xun, as a "scholarly knight-errant," must have sensed the uncertainties in his re-visioning of justice. Like Liu E, Lu Xun wishes to imagine himself as a chivalrous literatus, standing alone against the "gate of darkness" while dreaming a late Qing dream of the true justice on the other side; and like Li Boyuan, Lu Xun cannot take his gaze away from the nightmarish injustice on this side of the gate. Lu Xun must also have known from his predecessors that the "gate of darkness" may not stand between the old and the new China, between injustice and justice. It may instead join the world of institutionalized cannibalism on this side to its phantom replica on the other. Lu Xun cannot indict the "living hell" of China without demonstrating that his power derives from the hell of which he is a part. A Liu E–like champion protesting against social injustice, Lu Xun was no less a connoisseur, à la Li Boyuan, of the dark aspect of humanity, a fact well attested by the ghastly imagery of his essays, memoirs, and stories. Though it is said to be savored in the modern world, the new justice conceived by Lu Xun already has a taste of blood from the old, cannibalistic world.[34]

Two more examples can be cited from Lu Xun's short stories to illuminate the uncanny affinity between the concept of justice and its denial. For instance, the climax of "Zhufu" (New year sacrifice, 1921) is preceded by none other than an argument about the innocent suffering in this world and its redress in the other. In that episode, the ill-fated wife of Xianglin, now reduced to a beggar, stops the homecoming narrator Lu Xun and asks him if the soul survives death. Earlier on, Xianglin's wife was told that, since she had been twice widowed and now deprived of her only son, her body would be sentenced to be torn apart by her dead husbands in Hell. She was advised to donate a threshold at a nearby Buddhist temple, to be trampled on as her substitute so that her sin would be atoned for. In their encounter, the dying woman intends to seek from the narrator Lu Xun a reason for her plight in this life. To her question, the narrator responds, "It is hard to say" (*shuo bu qing*).

The reference to Hell and afterlife brings to mind, again, the dialectic formed by two of the late Qing novels discussed in the last section. Hell, in Lu Xun's narrative, may suggest the underworld courtroom of Liu E's *Travels of Lao Can*, in which retribution is carried out in the most fastidious way; at the same time it may also correspond to the secular judicial institutions of *Living Hell*, which prove to be hideous replicas of the other world. After her donation of the threshold, Xianglin's wife was still treated by her fellow villagers as if under a curse. Neither the justice of this world nor the justice of Hell applies to her. With her question never answered, Xianglin's wife dies, presumably in the fear that she will be eternally tortured in Hell.

But as she dies, Xianglin's wife leaves behind another "hell," so to speak, in which our narrator-author will be eternally tortured. In his failure to either stand by the poor woman or deny collusion with society, the narrator Lu Xun would carry with himself an everlasting sense of guilt. One question remains to be asked, however. Given his obsession with crime and punishment, could it be possible that his vision of Hell is that which Lu Xun fears *and* desires? Not unlike Xianglin's wife who resigns herself to her imagined perpetual condemnation, Lu Xun may have created and inhabited a literary hell of his own from which he was unable, and perhaps unwilling, to escape. The psychological drama of self-imposed crime and punishment constitutes the most treacherous aspect of Lu Xun's, and his followers', image of justice. As will be argued later, this psychological mechanism would eventually be appropriated by the Communists in forming their discourse of crime and punishment.

At the other end of Lu Xun's gallery of characters stands the ne'er-do-well A Q. One may remember how, in "A Q zhengzhuan" (The true story of A Q, 1921), A Q is created as a clown starring in a series of country turmoils, from bullying, attempted rape, robbery, riot, and revolution to his own execution. Throughout the earlier part of the story, A Q dreams of becoming a bandit-hero who, even arrested and sentenced to capital punishment, would die a fearless man. This dream is reinforced after he has watched the spectacle of a beheading at a city theater. For A Q and his rustic fellow villagers alike, the bloody punishment has been romanticized into an exotic event. A Q's imagined "death wish" is finally realized, only in the most ironic manner. A Q believes that he is being executed for a charge of which he is largely innocent; for the crowd coming to see the show of his execution, the much-awaited decapitation turns out to be an anticlimax. Thanks to advances in modern technology, A Q is not ceremoniously beheaded, just shot.

As a parody of a society nurtured on an insatiable cannibalistic desire, the story easily impresses one with its violent potential. At issue here is how the violence and its punishment are described in such a way as to become a fatal comedy of errors. A Q is both the victim and the victimizer of his society. While he has previously committed crimes that result in no legal punishment, he is now executed for a felony he did not commit. A Q is transformed from an enthusiastic onlooker at a bloody spectacle to the devastated scapegoat in that spectacle; his tragedy, if there is one at all, lies in his complacency as a cruel but empathetic watcher. But if A Q's bloody desire was aroused by his watching the beheading scene in the folk theater, cannot one describe the same arousal in Lu Xun's writing about Chinese cannibalism, as a result of his watching of the legendary slide show? As a chronicler-watcher of A Q's tragicomedy, does Lu Xun hide a cannibalistic impulse behind his indign███████uring? If so, has Lu Xun truly done justice to A Q in the literary world?

For the revolution-minded writers of the post–May Fourth era, next to fiction, drama became an important venue in which the debate over justice versus violence was presented. With its mandate to be "acted" out in a public space peopled with viewers, drama appeared more readily to approximate the locus of the courtroom, prodding its implied audience to deliberate over a human case reenacted on the stage. Courtroom drama, just like its fictional counterpart, had been one of the major genres of traditional Chinese literature since the Yuan dynasty.[35] For centuries, Chinese audiences have watched judge-investigators preside over difficult cases on stage, with the denunciation of the villain and the rehabilitation of justice as the climax of the play. In what sense has the modern theater opened up a new horizon in this old genre?

Two early modern plays, *Pan Jinlian* (Pan Jinlian, 1928) by Ouyang Yuqian (1889–1962) and *Dachu youling ta* (Breaking out of the tower of ghosts, 1928) by Bai Wei (1894–1987), can be discussed as examples. As its title indicates, *Pan Jinlian* is a play based on the life and death of Pan Jinlian, one of the most notorious femmes fatales in classical Chinese literature. As one of the earliest modern efforts at rewriting the "bad woman," Ouyang Yuqian's play holds a sympathetic view of Jinlian's motives for committing adultery and murder. Instead of being a blood-thirsty villainess and licentious shrew, Pan Jinlian is cast in Ouyang Yuqian's version as the archetype of the free-spirited Chinese woman sacrificed to a rigid male-centered social system. After having been humiliated and sold by her first master, married to an impotent dwarf, and spurned by the brother-in-law she had fallen in love with, Pan Jinlian turns to adultery and murder, as if these extreme deeds were the only remaining means by which she could express her desire.

A feminist might very well follow up on this theme and develop a reading of Pan Jinlian's sexual politics. At stake here is nevertheless the extent to which Ouyang Yuqian has introduced a dynamic, critical dramaturgy representing traditional justice held at bay. By this I have in mind particularly the final act, in which Pan Jinlian and Wu Song come face to face at the funerary meal in memory of the dwarf Wu Da. Cross-examined by Wu Song as to the murderer of his brother, Pan Jinlian retorts that, while she may be the person who poisoned her husband, the genuine murderers are none other than Wu Song and the other men in her life. As for Ximen Qing, the archvillain of the play and Jinlian's lover, Jinlian defiantly argues that she "has been willing to serve as his plaything," since, unlike other men, Ximen Qing "would treat [her] as nothing less than a plaything."[36] Doubly infuriated by Jinlian's confession, Wu Song demands Jinlian's heart as a compensation for the death of his brother. To the murderous demand, Jinlian responds, "I gave you my heart a long time ago."[37]

Pan Jinlian sounds more like the victim than the principal suspect, whereas Wu Song is less the avenger than the perpetrator of the whole family tragedy. As Wu Song thrusts his sword into the chest of his sister-in-law, justice *seems* to have been done, with Jinlian's protesting words still lingering in the air. Rarely has one seen in traditional court-case drama such a gripping debate between two parties to a murder case, to say nothing of the alleged murderer rising to lay charges against the prosecutor. Crime and punishment threaten to switch roles. Ouyang Yuqian scores one more point, by having the killing of Pan Jinlian take place right at the funerary banquet table. Appetite, passion, and death wish are mixed, invoking the ambiguous undercurrent of Lu Xun's cannibalistic banquet.

Still, what distinguishes Ouyang Yuqian's *Pan Jinlian* most is that he has turned a play *about* a court case into a play *as* a court case. In a conventional courtroom play, the courtroom provides the central chronotope in which evidence is presented, testimonies are heard, and conviction is delivered. None of these elements is to be found in *Pan Jinlian;* missing from the stage is not only the courtroom but also the judge-investigator in charge of the courtroom. A different dramatic effect is thus generated. One is given to feel that, as Pan Jinlian delivers her testimony on the stage, she cannot mean to persuade those unsympathetic characters around her; rather, she argues as if she were addressing across space and time an audience ready to renegotiate moral and legal conventions. Ouyang Yuqian has turned the theater into a substitute courtroom and the audience into the jury-judge.

This implied forensic scene must have indicated a significant moment in regard to the way modern Chinese writers and audience *imagined* justice at the time. Ouyang Yuqian's play is as much a violation of the law of verisimilitude constituted by conventional court-case drama as it is a defiant rewriting of the law sanctioned by moral and political authorities. As will be argued in the following sections, this new "theatrics" of justice and violence would eventually become a major trope in Chinese Communist revolutionary discourse. When the function of the formal courtroom has been handicapped by wayward political and legal forces, a public space like the stage can be used as its phantom substitute; the stage reenacts cases denied access to the courtroom, thus challenging the monolithic institutionalization of judicial procedure.

In Bai Wei's *Breaking out of the Tower of Ghosts,* a different kind of family tragedy bears witness to the tyranny of Chinese cannibalism. In the play, a cruel landlord cum opium dealer, Master Rongsheng, is about to marry Yuelin, a servant girl whom Rongsheng bought years before and adopted later as his foster daughter. This plan is under way despite the fact that Rongsheng has seven concubines and Yuelin has fallen in love with Rongsheng's own son, Qiaoming. In the meantime, Rongsheng has to cope with his rebellious tenants, whose recent riots have been reinforced by the support of local revolutionaries. The plot is further compounded by the appearance of a woman revolutionary named Xiao Sen, who was once impregnated by Rongsheng. On a visit to the mansion of Rongsheng, Xiao Sen is shocked to discover that Yuelin is her long-lost illegitimate daughter, and so the real father of Yuelin is none other than Rongsheng!

One can easily point out the problems of the play. Loaded with creaking plots, improbable characters, and sentimental tears, *Breaking out of the Tower of Ghosts* may well be an example of bad melodrama, indicating the immaturity of the playwright. However, I argue that precisely because these dramatic elements are so "unnaturally" blended, they call attention to the play's contesting ideological powers. A rebellious daughter in her own right, Bai Wei wrote her play on behalf of both modern and traditional Chinese women trapped in the aftermath of the first Chinese Communist revolution, during the course of critiquing the eclipse of justice in the name of revolution.[38] Relentless ethical aberration and physical violence thrive at every level of the play, in the form of rape, incest, child desertion, bribery, riot, murder, revolution, and antirevolution, all the while anticipating the cataclysm of the final disaster.

The play's central symbolism develops around the so-called tower of ghosts (*youling ta*), referring to the site of an old tower taken by Master Rongsheng from a widow. The site has since been deserted amid rumors that it is haunted by ghosts; the only building that remains in the vicinity is a small house, used by Rongsheng to cage women who dare to defy his lust. Shrouded in a deadly atmosphere, the tower site may be a "living hell" where many young females have been tortured. The tower of ghosts also reminds us of the famous essay by Lu Xun, "Lun leifeng ta de daodiao" (On the collapse of the Leifeng Tower, 1926).[39] As the legend goes, the monk Fahai incarcerated the beautiful White Snake under the formidable Leifeng Tower for good—an eternal condemnation of the snake for having fallen in love with a human. The collapse of the tower, after having stood for hundreds of years, represents for Lu Xun a belated natural justice overthrowing the punishment meted out by a male-centered justice system.

Bai Wei makes clear reference to the collapse of Leifeng Tower in her play and adds to it an ironic, bitter note. Although the tower of ghosts no longer physically exists, the old, male power still rules women by invoking the coercive system of the tower. At one point in the play, Bai Wei has one woman servant articulate the fact that the tower site is not haunted by ghosts; it is Master Rongsheng who fakes ghostly sounds from time to time to sustain the old, terrifying myth. Moreover, Bai Wei suggests that the "ghosts" of the tower not only persecute women but also their own young, male descendants. Hence, "the tower of ghosts is referred to by the young master as the [patriarchal tyranny of the] old master. Master Rongsheng may not look like a ghost, but in view of the way he oppresses his young male descendants, isn't he comparable to the Leifeng Tower that crushed the White Snake spirit?"[40]

The archvillain of the play, Master Rongsheng is described as a fiendish landlord, an unscrupulous merchant, a heartless father, and a sex maniac. His evil forces have undermined the political, economic, ethical, and sexual foundations of Chinese society and could let it fall into anarchy at any time. Yet before his final moment comes, Master Rongsheng manages to hold on to his power, as a pillar of his society. As the play develops, when Master Rongsheng's son, Qiaoming, comes forward to challenge his father's wish to marry Yuelin, the father takes out his pistol and slays his son. Not content with that, Rongsheng goes on to trap the leader of the rioting tenants, jailing him under the false charge of being the murderer, and to kill an old servant, who at the last minute reveals that he has been Rongsheng's best friend and romantic rival.

For Bai Wei, crime on such a horrific scale goes beyond the control of imaginable legality. It can only be put down by even more outrageous deeds of violence. In the final moment of the play, when the woman revolutionary Xiao Sen returns and reveals to Master Rongsheng that she was the girl once seduced by him and that Yuelin is their daughter out of wedlock, Rongsheng, in fury, shoots at her. To protect her mother, Yuelin rushes to Xiao Sen with another pistol, which happens to be close to hand, and fires back at her father; father/rapist and daughter/victim thus manage to kill each other. The attempted incest-plus-rape ends with the concomitant crime of patricide-plus-filicide. We last see Yuelin dying in the arms of her mother, deliriously singing celebrations of her pathetic life: a baby deserted by both parents, a child-servant abused by her master, a foster daughter almost raped by her foster father, and a daughter killed by her own father.

What strikes us is that when she is delivering her crazy, dying remarks, Yuelin is made to address directly the implied audience, as if the plethora of anger, madness, and pathos can no longer be contained by the enclosure of the stage but must spill over onto the audience. As in the case of Ouyang Yuqian's *Pan Jinlian*, the theater is turned into a site where a different kind of justice is being sought. To her audience, Yuelin cries, "Shame, shame, ... unbearable shame, revenge, revenge, only to be acknowledged by the sea. Ah! What a world it would be like! (*addressed to the audience*) Red, yellow, green, ... all colors! (crazier, driven to dance) Hahaha! ... Upside down! ... All is upside down! The world has been turned over! ... Fresh, beautiful! ... Hahaha, all is upside down—this is the gift of death."[41] (Stage directions in parentheses; emphasis mine.)

Critics in the Communist camp have praised *Breaking out of the Tower of Ghosts* as a model drama for women's liberation. The theme of class struggle has been highlighted in view of the deadly conflict between the landlord and the proletariat, father and children, man and woman.[42] A feminist of the fundamentalist persuasion would praise the play for its focus on misandry and its celebration of sisterhood and mother-daughter coalition.[43] These critics may have underestimated the (self-) destructive power embedded in the play. Close reading shows that in Bai Wei's world, revolutionary leaders turn out to be either burdened by their dark past or disabled by unforeseeable contingencies. The woman revolutionary Xiao Sen has been so busy with her adventures that she has had no time for the baby, which she left in the hands of cruel and rapacious foster parents; hence the daughter's protest that she never had a real mother. The peasant protest does triumph in the end, but only as the result of landlord Rongsheng's death at the hands of his own daughter. Moreover, Yuelin is never portrayed as a feminist heroine; she appears instead as a girl troubled by a chronic, manic-depressive syndrome, and the root of her psychological instability is traced to her being deserted by her mother. Whereas the incestuous conjugation between father and daughter is stopped by the timely death of the father, the much-expected reunion between mother and daughter comes only at the cost of the daughter's life. Finally, Yuelin is presented as having fallen in love with her own half brother, so that if she had had her (unnatural) way, she would still have committed incest.

The political, ethical, and emotional irrationalities in the play, once unleashed among the characters, never really settle as the curtain drops. These irrationalities, which manifest themselves in the expedient form of madness, I argue, constitute the most equivocal force of the play. As Yuelin is trying to address her listeners beyond the stage, she is said, by other characters and by "stage direction," to have gone mad. Bai Wei may never have achieved the kind of self-irony attained by Lu

Xun in his story about an equally confused mind, "Diary of a Madman." Given her own frustrated biographical experience, however, she manages to showcase a gendered, compulsive soul in desperate quest of a just way out, both within and without the play.

The play takes on another dimension if one looks into its "life" in the extratextual context. As Bai Wei writes in her postscript to the play, the extant version of *Breaking out of the Tower of Ghosts* is actually a rewrite based on an original that had been rudely "taken away" by a male colleague, to be published as his own. This violence in the literary world adds yet another dimension to the risks that a writing woman has to face, while she is writing about the risks her female characters encounter in the male world. Finally, Bai Wei's play lends itself to a parallel reading with Cao Yu's *Leiyu* (Thunderstorm, 1932), a melodrama also dealing with incestuous marriage, forbidden love, mistaken identity, murder, and revolution. Cao Yu's play was an immediate success when premiered in 1932, and would be staged numerous times in the years to come. Bai Wei may not be the playwright that Cao Yu was, but the eclipse of her play, despite its striking resemblance to *Thunderstorm*, serves as one more depressing example of a woman writer's vulnerability when competing for literary power in a male-dominated world.

3. A LITERATURE OF BLOOD AND TEARS

I have described the way in which the concepts of justice and violence evolved along with the development of the genres of fiction and drama. With a series of short stories and sketches, Lu Xun launched a narrative inquiry into the ambiguous terms of crime and punishment in a society bereft of political and ethical order. In a new dramatic form, Ouyang Yuqian and Bai Wei dealt with the polemic of justice by staging the crime scene in such a way as to stimulate a debate among not only characters but theater audiences. In this way, both genres challenged established legal and literary order in a rapidly changing historical context.

By the beginning of the thirties, these two, the narrative deliberation and the theatrical reenactment of crimes and punishments, had converged to become a powerful discourse demanding and instantiating a new definition of social and poetic justice. This discourse was further consolidated as the Communist trope of "mass revolution" gained currency. To show their solidarity with the "insulted and the injured" and to promote a body politic of revolutionary writing, progressive writers united under the banner of a "literature of blood and tears" (*xue he lei de wenxue*).

What is to be noticed is that the slogan, as well as the works produced in its name, derives its power from a renegotiation of the arts of telling and of showing. The literature of blood and tears is believed to possess such demonstrative force as to both *evoke* the blood and tears repressed in the objects of narration and to *induce* blood and tears at the site of writing and representing. Instead of catharsis, as would have been expected of these Europeanized intellectuals, the new poetics aims at inciting action (blood) and indignation (tears). Hence Marston Anderson's sarcastic comment, "The new fiction was to possess the palpable reality of fluids exuded by the body. But significantly the fluids to which the expression refers are released only when the body is physically wounded (blood) or when the spirit is bruised by empathy (tears)."[44]

What Anderson does not mention is that, in the name of displaying blood and tears, this literature offers a discursive format akin to the forensic debate over the nature of violence and its containment. Tears and blood are corporeal clues that need to be reconstituted so as to testify for or against a given defendant. Its performative inclination is expected to be the first step leading toward the final call to justice. As such, the works of "blood and tears" are really not too far away from the two late Qing court-case novels discussed above, in the sense that the realization of crime and justice presupposes a staging in a corporeal theater.

There are, nevertheless, moments in which tears and blood are called on, only to confuse an issue instead of settle one. These moments give rise to the theoretical double bind in legal or ethical disputes. In *Paoxiao lede tudi* (The roaring earth, 1931) by Jiang Guangci (1901–31), for example, the young leftist revolutionary, Li Jie, is forced to make a painful decision as his comrades propose to burn down the properties of local landlord families. As a leader of the local proletariat organization, Li Jie is obliged to see to the implementation of this plan. He is, however, beset by several worries. Li happens to be the son of the richest landlord in town; should the peasants' riot take place in the proposed form of burning and looting, it would mean a total devastation of the Li family estate. Moreover, even though he could not care less about his father's life and fortune, Li is worried about the well-being of his bedridden mother and his younger sister, still a mere child. Should these two females be sacrificed to the cause of justice as part of the peasant rebellion?

Throughout his short career, Jiang Guangci had been known as a tendentious Communist writer with a corpus of works addressing contemporary revolutionism of the most sentimental kind. Jiang's narcissism and romantic eccentricities, nevertheless, compelled in him a literary imagination germane to Communist literature despite its superficial call for altruism and scientific historicism. It is the romantic yearning for a lost, originary, and communal state that makes it easy for a writer like Jiang Guangci to be taken in by Communist myths about return to the lost origin. There is a good reason that he has been regarded as the forerunner of the "revolution plus romance" formula of Chinese leftist fiction. This fact, ironically, may very well be one of the reasons for his ejection from the party in 1930.[45] One is now supposed to read Jiang Guangci's work in a pejorative way, treating it as a "historical phenomenon."[46] But in the above-cited episode of *The Roaring Earth*, Jiang demonstrates an acute sensitivity when dramatizing the personal dilemma of a revolutionary.

A landlord's son, Li Jie had nevertheless fought against his father's oppression of the tenants. After a series of confrontations between father and son, Li Jie leaves

home to pursue his own goals. When he returns, he has become a Communist revolutionary. Li Jie shows no qualms in response to the plan to kill his father and burn
down his family properties. Insofar as Li's father embodies the meanest of the local
reactionary forces, patricide is necessary as a young revolutionary's clearest act of
defiance against a feudal patriarchal system. But Li cherishes a deep feeling for his
mother and is much troubled by the likelihood of her death in the proposed riots.
At one of the most gripping moments in his interior monologue, Li cries:

> I have no father now. I have only an enemy. It is only on the battlefield that I can
> meet the enemy, but I hear that my mother is at home, sick. . . . Mother! Please for-
> give your rebellious son! . . . There is a duty much more important, much greater
> than filial piety. To live up to this duty, I am willing to bear the bad name of rebel.
> Mother, you have lost your son! . . .
>   Alas! A man after all has his feelings. You know how distressed I am! I love my in-
> nocent, darling little sister.[47]

In pain and despair, Li Jie falls unconscious. When he comes to, the burning and
killing have taken place.

After years under the tyrannical rule of Li Jie's father, the rioting tenants finally
prove that they have the will and the capacity to overthrow a landlord. Insofar as
it endorses "rebel justice" at the expense of an existing social order, *The Roaring
Earth* must be regarded as one of the most important models for Chinese Communist fiction of the forties and fifties, a model that celebrates a "spontaneous"
uprising of the proletariat against the ruling class. By forgoing personal and familial attachments, Li Jie has passed the harsh test of his Communist convictions.
He may be guilty of a family murder, but for the advancement of revolution and
history, he understands that the end justifies the means.

There are irksome factors, however, looming behind such a (self-)righteous reading of this episode. Even before the fire starts, we are told, Li's father, the archvillain of the novel, has run away to a nearby town. To revenge their suffering, the
peasants should presumably have tracked him down and punished him in person.
Instead, they choose to set fire to the Li family compound *in the absence* of the villain.
The fire thus works more like a symbol, or "staged" effect, signaling the end of
landlord rule. Moreover, by burning to death a very ill woman and her child, for the
reason that they are immediate family members of the villain, these peasant heroes
show a decided preference for justice in the form of theater, for acts of symbolic
terrorism. By *theater*, I do not mean that the riot or killing is unreal, but that it is
"acted out" in such a way as to gesture toward a revolution that does not actually
happen; instead, the revolutionaries appropriate to themselves the landlord's power
to oppress, punish, and destroy at will. At its best, the symbolic justice mimics the
peasants' desire to throw off oppression; at its worst, the theatrical terror enacts the
peasants' desire to replace and imitate their oppressors. By *terrorism*, I mean that a
ritual asserting loyalty and brotherhood *within* the group of revolutionaries has
been established, one in which the test is the ability to live with terror.[48]

By pushing Li Jie to the center of the stage of terrorism, the tenants wait and watch to see whether their leader will play his role the right way. Li Jie could have prevented the murder from happening, as he well understood that his sick mother and weak sister should not have been held responsible for his father's misdeeds. But he lets the fire engulf his family compound so as to "make a point," to his fellow revolutionaries as well as to himself, that he can relinquish all his ties to the past. Li Jie's mother and sister thus die an undeserved and cruel death, ultimately for the sake of Li Jie's accreditation as one who is a revolutionary more than a son. By killing them for crimes they never committed, Li Jie can purge his own crime, that of being a descendant of a landlord family, though it is a crime Li Jie never committed. Only in feudalism are individuals held guilty of the sins of their ancestors; here, Li Jie offers a feudal proof that he no longer is the property of his father, by destroying the father's other feudal property, buildings, women, and children, allowing himself to think that he has rid himself of feudal consciousness.

Only in feudalism can one purge oneself of the guilt acquired from one's original clan by submitting utterly to the will of one's new clan. The ultimate proof of new cult loyalty is always the capability to destroy the old clan, to put aside one's individual feelings and become as one with the new clan. Jiang Guangci could not have been unaware of the ironies underlying this violent code of self-abnegation. This is most emphatically indicated by Li Jie's monologue: "I have read Turgenev's *Fathers and Sons* and always felt the conflict between the fathers and sons in the novel is too commonplace. It is far less exciting than the antagonism between my father and me. I wonder if there will be a writer who can write out this father-son struggle of mine. I truly hope that such a writer exists."[49] Even before the crime has been committed, the hero of the patricide is already contemplating his status in comparison to famous examples. This is the narcissistic, romantic side of the would-be revolutionary hero, the side that makes him more than ordinarily vulnerable to group shame and group praise.

T. A. Hsia doubts Jiang Guangci's sincerity even at Jiang's seemingly most pained moment. Having seen too many melodramatic gestures in Jiang's works and life, Hsia rightly suspects the veracity of *The Roaring Earth*. My argument is that, given his indulgence in role playing, Jiang's mannerism as a writer and as a revolutionary may have given rise to a crucial trope in Chinese Communist poetics and politics alike. When theater and violence, mutual spectatorship, and reciprocal surveillance are mixed, a dangerous discourse—of romanticism but not of revolution—is born. The question has to be whether this discourse has significantly rewritten the discourse of feudalism or is merely its reiteration, disguised by its romantic, European clothing. One suspects the killing is performed as a bloody public spectacle so as to renew, rather than subvert, the kind of hell of crime and punishment these romantic revolutionaries wish to overthrow.

As one of the best interpreters of Lu Xun's ethics of writing, Wu Zuxiang (1908–94) may well have intended in his stories a thirties' version of cannibalism, indicting a society devoid of any moral and legal resources. Indeed, in the famous

"Guanguan de bupin" (Young master gets his tonic, 1932), Wu takes on cannibal-ism literally, by writing how the young master of a landlord family is nurtured on the milk and blood of a peasant couple during his recovery from a recent car crash. The story ends by recapitulating another of Lu Xun's favorite images, as the peasant husband is sentenced to decapitation, convicted as a bandit courier. Few readers of the story can forget the gory execution scene at the climax, where the dying convict "suddenly struggles and stands up, raising his hands and scream-ing like a demon."[50]

The scene of execution can be treated as a neat reversal of the ending of "The True Story of A Q," in which A Q is quickly shot to death while the crowd looks on. For Wu Zuxiang, a proletarian convict of the thirties would struggle against his oppressors right up to the moment of extinction, registering one last protest against the injustices done to him. Still, "Young Master Gets His Tonic" is a story couched in the rhetoric of "victimology" that marked Lu Xun's tributes to the in-sulted and the injured. It is in novellas such as "Fanjia pu" (Fan family village, 1934), and "Yiqian babai dan" (Eighteen hundred piculs of rice, 1934) that the terms of crime and punishment are polemically reexamined.

In "Fan Family Village," a village woman named Xianzi is subject to increas-ing humiliations and pains as her village is beset by drought, civil war, and changes in rural economic structure. The final blow comes when Xianzi's husband, Gouzi, whose love is her only remaining source of stability, is arrested on a charge of rob-bing and murdering a nun, and a cunning intermediary for the local magistrate comes to demand a bribe. Xianzi turns for help to her mother, who has recently won a considerable amount of money at a lottery, but she is refused. In despera-tion, Xianzi kills her mother by braining the old woman with a sacrificial candle-stick.[51]

I need not belabor the multiple layers of plight surrounding the woman: drought, civil war, religious fraud, superstition, judicial malpractice, murder, rob-bery, parental cruelty, and burgeoning capitalism, each making its contribution to the matricide. Critics from C. T. Hsia to Philip Williams have had a lot to say about the ethical dilemma involved in the final bloody scene of the novella.[52] What used to be considered a quintessential taboo of humanity, matricide, finds it-self justified in given historical circumstances. Xianzi's mother used to be a rustic peasant woman. After working for years as servant to a rich family in the city, she has developed a monstrous desire for money. Ironically, this old woman's acquisi-tive consciousness, which makes her value money more than kinship, augments in equal proportion to her Buddhist convictions about spiritual transcendence. In-stead of helping her daughter out, she would prefer to donate money to the nun-nery run by the nun who would later be accidentally killed by Xianzi's husband.

Xianzi's mother intends to purge her sins from this and previous lives by do-nating money to the nunnery, money which she has made by participating in the new mode of production in the city. Xianzi's husband robs the nunnery with a be-lief that gods may as well pay back part of their worshipers' donation so as to redeem the pain these worshipers are undergoing. In either case, one notices a mounting conflict between different systems of justice. The law of the human world and the ordinance of supernatural beings, the imperative of blood kinship and the rule of monetary ownership, the God of Mercy and the God of Mammon, all are presented in a radical clash, with each axis of the contested values demanding a new judgment. Caught right in the middle of these conflicts, Xianzi is driven to maintain her own "moral sanity," in C. T. Hsia's words, by committing matricide.[53]

Just as in *The Roaring Earth*, a horrific crime has to be done in "Fan Family Village" so as to suppress the inhuman quality of life as it was and underline the necessity of revolution. Whereas the young, educated, landlord-turned-revolutionary Li Jie completes his initiation into revolution by countenancing the killing of his mother and younger sister, an illiterate peasant woman such as Xianzi is now made to go through a similar ordeal of parricide so as to reach her moment of political awakening. Bai Wei's *Breaking out of the Tower of Ghosts* can be regarded as predecessor of both works in terms of parricide, but her play differs in trying to exonerate its patricidal heroine by recourse to the old device of hysteria and madness. However, for Jiang Guangci as for Wu Zuxiang, at a time when the whole world verges on moral and economic bankruptcy, nobody can have clean hands.

It is in this sense that Lu Xun's vision of cannibalism has to be subjected to a new interpretation. Lu Xun sees in Chinese an instinctual need for mutual persecution, which will drive them to final catastrophe. Violence, in the form of parricide, is treated by Wu Zuxiang, Jiang Guangci, and like-minded leftist writers as something capable of generating positive consequences. Revolution is nothing if not a justifiable form of violence, enacted to subvert the traditional form of tyranny. Chinese political theory, from the Zhou dynasty to the Qing, justifies popular violence—if it overthrows a cruel and decadent dynasty and replaces it with the dynasty that is historically anointed to loot, kill, and defy authority until it secures the imperial power. The morbid impulse of cannibalism inherent in the Chinese character that upset Lu Xun is once more legitimated, so to speak, in the hands of writers like Jiang Guangci and Wu Zuxiang. As either would have agreed, at the right historical moment, for the right ideological cause, even the most victimized social being can be, and should be, motivated to walk over any remnants of social and moral law. What distinguishes Jiang and Wu from their fellow writers, at least as far as the examples being discussed here are concerned, is that they are not unaware of the terrible freedom implied in the form of group violence newly sanctioned in the name of revolution. These two writers have dramatized in their works criminal cases so as to warrant not a hasty verdict but a prolonged legal debate.

This leads us to the juxtaposition of two forensic scenes in Wu's acclaimed novella "Eighteen Hundred Piculs of Rice." As the novella opens, representatives of the various houses of the powerful Song clan meet, after a recent drought, to determine what to do with the eighteen hundred piculs of rice they have reserved from the last harvest. The meeting soon deteriorates into a series of squabbles indicative of the conflicting interests among the houses. It is suggested that the rice be sold to pay for irrigation construction, local militia reinforcement, or educational upgrading; or that the proceeds be used to pay off outstanding loans or be given to charity. Behind all these noble causes, however, are generations of corruption and self-interest that have driven the houses farther and farther apart. As the debate continues on endlessly, one important factor has been neglected: the starving tenants who have *produced* the rice. These tenants are waiting outside the clan temple to demand their share of the rice so as to survive.

The central scene of the novella is the clan temple where the meeting is being held. Its refurbishment long overdue, the clan temple stands in dreadful dilapidation, a most telling sign of the decline of the Song clan. The clan temple used to be the site where social functions were performed, most important of which was the executing of familial justice and order. Thus, this meeting is being held at the temple. But as Wu Zuxiang tells us, just as the temple can no longer properly accommodate a family meeting, the continued squabble under the leaking roof of the temple signals the disintegration of the doomed houses. Meanwhile, the angry peasants have run out of patience. They break into the clan temple, grab the representatives, and pillage all the rice.

The novella does not stop here, however. In the uprising, the peasants carry gongs and drums, wear devil masks, and "shriek, jump, and whistle like demons."[54] They drag the district head to an abandoned platform, where the community had once prayed to the rain deity for relief from the drought, and use the site to act out a ritualized destruction of the old order and its superstitions. For a writer as careful as Wu Zuxiang, that the mock trial is performed on a ritual stage cannot be coincidence. Taking justice in their own hands, the peasants still need to return to the site of clan ritual to enact the destruction of the old order.

The eerie carnivalesque atmosphere of the uprising, with all the audiovisual cacophony of peasants dressed as demons and devils, suggests not so much the beginning of a new historical moment—in which a different or at least reinvigorated practice of justice will be hailed—as a return to the mood of late Qing novels such as *The Travels of Lao Can* and *Living Hell*, where the image of Hell is paraded. And as such, violence perpetrated in the name of "modern" justice is tellingly reinstated in its premodern, even prefeudal form. Wu Zuxiang may have attempted to record realistically the way that peasants conceive of justice; but his realistic representation of the revolutionary scene betrays no less a romantic longing for the fiendish and brutal pleasures of originary communal life.

4. LIVING HELL REVISITED

The year 1942 marks a turning point in both the Nationalist and Communist versions of modern Chinese literary history. In response to the increasingly recalcitrant postures among the writers in the "liberation area," Mao gave a series of talks that prescribed the format of Communist literature for the next four decades.[55] Much has been written about the hegemonic status of Mao's talks as well as their disastrous consequences. Two things come to our attention at this juncture. First, as the call for justice expanded to become a national campaign, on behalf either of a regime or a class, the debate about crime and punishment entered into a more tendentious stage. For Communist writers, two wars had to be fought at the same time, the war against the national enemy, the Japanese, and the war against the class enemy, the Nationalist regime. Mutilated bodies and broken families became regular themes of the time; but they were treated in such a way as to be subsumed into the national, or Nationalist, symbolism of a China ravished and lacerated by both external and internal wounds. As I have argued elsewhere, a corporeal typology of "the scarred" was inaugurated at this time, as a climax to the tears and blood flowing through Chinese literature from previous ages, and as an (unfortunate) anticipation of more tears and blood to come in the next few decades.[56]

Second, as far as leftist literature was concerned, there appeared a decisive inward turn, so to speak, as writers came to terms with the new definition of violence. The quarrel between Hu Feng (1902–85) and Mao Zedong as to how reality was to be represented, for all its *ideological* turmoil, mirrors the disturbed *etiological* state of Chinese Communist discourse. Hu Feng and his followers picture in their critical treatise a humanity seriously maimed by the atrocities of inhuman history, so much so that it cannot be rehabilitated until the primitive, individual power inherent in it is called forth. Mao and his cohorts acknowledge the suffering of humanity, but argue that to do justice to "the insulted and the injured," they first have to subordinate individual subjectivity—which seemed to have gone out of control in Hu Feng's hands—to a collective, historical subjectivity.[57]

The debate cannot be adequately characterized in an essay of this scope. But let it be said that the two sides concurred in a diagnosis of the self as beset by *storms*. As will be discussed, whereas Lu Ling (1923–94), Hu Feng's protégé, features a gallery of grotesques trapped in a losing war against their own ferocious ressentiment, Ding Ling (1904–86), one of Mao's grudging followers, moves her drama of revolution toward a portrait of individual passion that has submitted itself to the will of the mass and found its true vocation in self-discipline.[58] If Lu Ling aims at a negative dialectic of the soul caught in its libidinous desire to be free, Ding Ling intends to show how that soul can truly liberate itself through intense acts of continual submission. Set side by side, the two form an unexpected dialogue pointing to how, before the final revolution happens, the mindscape of China has already become the battleground of opposite furious impulses.

This changing configuration of national, international, and "intentional" factors results in a significant reform of the discourse of justice and violence. My first case in point is the well-known short story by Ding Ling, "Wozai xiacun de shihou" (When I was in Xia village, 1941). In the story, a girl named Zhenzhen (literally meaning "chastity-chastity"), who had been known to have defiantly rejected an arranged marriage, was raped when the Japanese invaded her village. To revenge herself,

Zhenzhen secretly signs up for a Communist antiaggressor mission, which requires her to spy on the Japanese army while serving as prostitute. As the story opens, Zhenzhen has returned from the front lines to cure her venereal disease, which she contracted while "serving" the Japanese and, to that extent, China. Her situation, nevertheless, induces more contempt than sympathy among her fellow villagers.

Zhenzhen's rape embodies only the fear any Chinese woman might entertain during wartime; her mission as a prostitute-spy exemplifies total patriotism. But as Ding Ling has it, Zhenzhen's fellow villagers, who mostly remain ignorant of her mission, think of her otherwise. For these villagers, a girl like Zhenzhen who defied an arranged marriage and then failed to safeguard her virginity is already quite detestable; that she should have capitalized on her misfortune and become a prostitute *and* traitor amounts to nothing less than outrage. Meanwhile, Zhenzhen suffers submissively, her venereal disease becoming a physical token of both her patriotic fervor and her unredeemable shame.

Feminist critics have argued forcefully that Zhenzhen's story indicates as much the cruelty of the Japanese invaders as the callousness of Chinese defense forces. As Yi-tsi Mei Feuerwerker puts it, the sufferings of Zhenzhen are "fully 'available' only to women: arranged marriage, rape by enemy soldiers, exploitation of her body by both armies and, after her return to the village, ostracism for violating the chastity code."[59] Zhenzhen's story is built on a paradox, that she can derive self-esteem only through willful self-abandon. For her patriotic contribution, she is rewarded with the most humiliating of diseases. To this one may add one more point. Zhenzhen joins the secret mission supposedly at the call of the Communist United Front. In the cause of liberating the collective body of the Chinese, first her own body must be taken and ruined by the enemies. But when she returns home, it is those "people" that she has vowed to save that ostracize her, in accordance with a most unliberated code of chastity.

But more striking is the fact that, for all the physical illness and tortures she has suffered, Zhenzhen "appears" in the story as a rather healthy-looking person. As the I-narrator puts it, "There was no outward sign of her disease. Her complexion was ruddy. Her voice was clear. She showed no signs of inhibition or rudeness. She did not exaggerate. She gave the impression that she had never had any complaints or sad thoughts."[60] That Zhenzhen appears undisturbed by her painful experience would have indicated, to a romantic reader, a personality of nunlike goodness as well as saintly self-control. Her ideological (or religious?) commitment is stronger than her still-hidden physical degeneration. But I wonder if one can take Ding Ling's narrative merely at face value. Zhenzhen's natural, healthy look is, after all, a front, hiding a body that is rapidly deteriorating. The contrast between how Zhenzhen's body *looks* and how it *feels* invites an allegorical reading; it is symptomatic of a reality or realism that turns against itself. As such, it may very well point to the dilemma that beset Ding Ling as a writer in the "liberated area."[61]

For Ding Ling, to write a story like "When I Was in Xia Village" would have meant to indict the evil forces of reality: the Nationalist regime, the feudal forces, the class enemies, and the Japanese invaders. But as her narrative develops, she cannot celebrate the power of justice represented by the party without pondering its newly installed system of coercion and discipline. Zhenzhen's "crime" of being a free-spirited girl opposing a prearranged marriage should be treated as a virtue in the new society; this virtue is, nevertheless, later rewarded and punished at the same time. Zhenzhen is persuaded to sacrifice for her party and nation on account of the fact that she had already been raped by the Japanese anyway and belittled by her fellow villagers. Later, she proclaims that she did so out of her own free will and that she harbors neither hatred nor regret. Zhenzhen's total submission to the party reveals a revolutionary zeal tantamount to religious fanaticism, her "healthy appearance" a suspicious sign of her deteriorating capacity to judge.

As expected, the story has a bright, formulaic ending. Zhenzhen will go to another city, presumably Yan'an, for medical treatment and rehabilitation. But with all her inglorious past, as a raped woman and a Japanese army prostitute, will Zhenzhen be treated fairly by the puritanical-minded party cadres? Knowing that "illness" and "rehabilitation" are characteristic of Chinese Communist literary and political discourse, one wonders whether Zhenzhen's disease can be cured, even in medical terms.[62] One recalls how the story starts with the frame in which the narrator Ding Ling is sent down to Xia Village for her "rehabilitation, . . . because of the turmoil of the department of politics."[63] Even if she could recover from her physical ailment, chances are that Zhenzhen might end up being like her creator, Ding Ling, spending the rest of her life undergoing the cycle of political illness and rehabilitation.

"When I Was in Xia Village" thus appears as a Communist retelling of Christian-Buddhist hagiography, while it provides a chilling subtext regarding the usefulness and disposability of the female body under the new regime just as under the old one. It is at this point that a dimension of violence and justice in modern Chinese literature has been touched on by a woman cadre author. The case of Zhenzhen demonstrates the advent of an intricate technology of violence that inflicts pain on its victim, only to win the victim's wholehearted support. By writing her story as such, Ding Ling proves that she is not as naive as Zhenzhen. Allegedly thanks to publications such as "When I Was in Xia Village," Mao put forth his literary policy in 1942, followed by the first *zhengfeng* (rectification) movement.[64] In the next few years, Ding Ling, together with some other outspoken fellow writers, would disappear from the scene for "rehabilitation." Given the nostalgic mood of its narrative, "When I Was in Xia Village" turns out to be both a nostalgic posture and an ominous outlook, indicating the end of an age of innocence.

Far away from Yan'an, a young writer named Lu Ling wrote *Ji'e de Guo Su'e* (Hungry Guo Su'e, 1943) in Chongqing, Sichuan, to bear witness to the atrocities of the war. Instead of ordinary patriotic themes, Lu Ling exhibits the primitive psychological landscape of a group of people who have been condemned to the pit of life. At the center of the novel is Guo Su'e, a woman who was driven out of her hometown by famine and banditry, only to be taken by a sleazy opium addict, Liu Chunshou, as his wife. Ever discontented with her circumstances, Guo carries on sexual liaisons with local miners, of whom Wei Haiqing and Zhang Zhenshan have become her favorites. Her adulterous behavior finally results in her death at the hands of her husband and his clan.

For our purposes, *Hungry Guo Su'e* impresses by radically shedding light on an internalized form of violence. In the case of "When I Was in Xia Village," Ding Ling witnesses the transformation of the village girl Zhenzhen into an obedient servant of the people. By contrast, Lu Ling sees in the life and death of Guo Su'e a (self-)destructive impulse that calls for vehement rebellion—against reality itself, if necessary. Guo Su'e's tortured soul can never find peace with itself, let alone submit to discipline.

As the protégé of Hu Feng, the feisty spokesman of a humanist brand of Chinese Marxism, Lu Ling writes of the "spiritual scars" that have in every way distorted Chinese humanity. Guo Su'e's hunger is seen as caused both by her need for food and sex and by her innate yearning for spiritual redemption, which will not happen unless there is a Communist revolution. But just as in the case of Ding Ling, Lu Ling can hardly find a viable way to convey the gospel of revolution without first questioning, however involuntarily, the "hygienic" preoccupation of that gospel. Moreover, given his own obsession with the sadomasochistic forces propelling human desire, Lu Ling sees in the downfall of Guo Su'e a strange mixture of creation and destruction, a libidinous chasm that cannot be filled by sociopolitical institutions.

Thus enters the crucial but ambiguous moment of the novel, in which the adulterous Guo Su'e is caught by her husband and relatives and put on private trial in the back room of a Daoist temple. Guo Su'e is forced to one corner of the room, her clothes torn to pieces but her look ever defiant. As one of the female clan members approaches her, "a devil suddenly comes out [of Guo Su'e]. This devil dishevels her hair, spits saliva, and jumps fiendishly onto the old woman, strangling the old woman [by seizing her] weak throat."[65] Infuriated by this unexpected move, Guo's husband and others tie her to a board and grill her thighs with red-hot pokers, till she loses consciousness in excruciating pain. Guo Su'e is left alone and dies three days later, from lack of food and medical care.

If the scene of the punishment of Guo Su'e seems familiar to us, it is perhaps because it first appears to be a parody of courtroom scenes from late Qing novels such as *Living Hell* and *The Travels of Lao Can*. Nevertheless, while the bloody punishments in the two late Qing novels are attributed to officials, Guo Su'e's death is a spectacle put on strictly under the direction of the masses. The predictable charges against the evil of the male-centered feudalism notwithstanding, the scene reveals how cruelly the social underdogs can be to *each other*, before they unite to stand against their class enemy. As Lu Ling puts it, there is almost a sense of festivity as Guo Su'e's torturers engage in mutilating her body, as if their own repressed desire had found a final, vicarious consummation.[66] Nurtured on the tradition of the "literature of blood and tears," *Hungry Guo Su'e* presents a series of scenes resulting in an overabundance of blood and tears, and it is hard to identify the instigator of the scenes as being squarely from any definite social class.

This leads us to reconsider the crime Guo Su'e committed. As a deserted child, a beggar, an abused wife, and a sexual object, Guo Su'e starts out being a repeat of the stereotypical suffering woman of socialist fiction. As the story develops, her vulgar, militant manners and her seemingly insatiable sexual desire appear to be her new front, which must have raised the eyebrows of many Communists. Compared with Zhenzhen in "When I Was in Xia Village," who willingly donates her soiled body to her country while managing to look healthier than ever, Guo Su'e commits adultery for a much humbler reason: after her body, she has nothing to lose. Guo appears even less pitiable than Pan Jinlian in Ouyang Yuqian's *Pan Jinlian,* who at least has clear motives of love and vengeance as she transgresses all ethical boundaries.

In somewhat dated mid-twentieth-century jargon, Guo Su'e's hunger is driven either by a "lack," a loss of physical and spiritual plenitude, or by an excess of carnivalesque desire, relentlessly demanding fulfillment. In any case, if Communist critics had found it irksome to diagnose Zhenzhen's dubious health, it must have been more difficult for them to explain Guo Su'e's eternal hunger. In the most ironic sense, the death of Guo Su'e might well be the solution to her problem: eternally "repressed," Guo Su'e can no longer stir up trouble and, perhaps thanks to this fact, her corpse can be safely displayed in the gallery of victims in the Communist hall of justice.

In the year 1948, seven years after her visit to "Xia Village," Ding Ling re-emerged with a novel about another village experience. Titled *Taiyang zhaozai Sanggan heshang* (The sun shines over the Sanggan River), the novel deals with the land reform movement in a village of northwestern China, Nuanshuitun. The transformation of Ding Ling in terms of authorial status, subject matter, plotting, character, and even tonality is clearly indicated in the new book. In a humble, almost self-effacing manner, Ding Ling narrates the drastically changing ethical and economic structure of the village after the arrival of a land reform team. Though winner of a Stalin Literary Prize in the early fifties, the novel suffered a sudden eclipse when its author was purged in 1956.[67]

Ding Ling's own ups and downs notwithstanding, the novel represents in many ways the climax of the dialectic of violence and justice discussed in this article. Given all its economic initiatives, the land reform movement as Ding Ling describes it was never a mere attempt at overhauling the infrastructure of rural China; rather it had a superstructural dimension, as its implementing land reform contributed to, and was conditioned by, changes in traditional Chinese ethical, cultural, and legal systems. To that extent, Yi-tsi Mei Feuerwerker has made a significant point when she calls the novel a *historical* novel.[68]

With such built-in epic implications, *The Sun Shines over the Sanggan River* can no longer be treated as a mere account of the transfer of land ownership from landlords to poor peasants. Instead, it wants to capture an apocalyptic moment of history, when a new moral machinery has been activated: the revolution finally has begun. When Ding Ling's peasants demand justice accordingly, they are uttering

outrage stored up in the Chinese soul for hundreds of years; and when the villain—the landlord—is captured, he must be indicted as a *lishi de zuiren* or a "criminal of History."[69] Real "people" have finally seized the power from those inhuman beings who have always oppressed the "people"; the transfer of power over
justice from the ruling class to the ruled is said to have been completed.

Liu Zaifu observes, in a novel like *The Sun Shines over the Sanggan River,* the rise of
a new dialectic of violence and justice. Based on Roland Barthes's typological approach to the forms of revolution, Liu argues that the Chinese Communist revolution appeared as a hybrid, one inspired by both the "bloody ritual" of the
French Revolution and the teleological imperative of the Stalinist Revolution.[70] In
other words, the Chinese Communist revolution as manifested in Ding Ling's
novel takes on a doubly grandiose form, combining both spectacular purgation
and predestined fulfillment.[71]

While acknowledging Liu Zaifu's observation, I would call attention to an indigenous dimension to the Chinese form of revolution. The legal motifs of Ding
Ling's novel, from public trial to communal ostracism, from the theater of blood
to the invention of penal technology, could hardly have been new to twentieth-
century Chinese readers and writers. When class enemies are judged by the arbitrary will of the newly empowered and when punishments are performed with an
aim to arouse bloody festivity, even actual cannibalism, one cannot help recalling
how "Chinese" these modes of imagining justice are. After almost half a century
of debate over the feasibility of justice and its manifestation, one sees in a novel
such as *The Sun Shines over the Sanggan River* not a leap over, but an uncanny return
to, the premodern discourse of crime and punishment.

Take the prosecution of Qian Wengui, the archvillain of Ding Ling's novel, for
example. For years Qian has joined with other local notables to persecute tenants.
Upon hearing of the impending land reform movement, Qian sends his son to the
Communist army and marries his daughter to the local cadre, with the hope of
forestalling possible charges. Qian's wonderful scheme fails. In the climax of the
novel, appropriately subtitled "The Final Combat" (*juezhan*), Qian and his wife are
paraded before the public, humiliated, beaten, and almost clawed to death by the
angry masses. Even the cannibalistic impulse comes close to the edge of consciousness, as the peasants converge to punish the hated landlord: "One feeling animated
them all—vengeance! They wanted vengeance! They wanted to give vent to their
hatred, the sufferings of the oppressed since their ancestors' times, the hatred and
loathing of thousands of years; all this resentment they directed against him. *They
would have liked to tear him with their teeth*"[72] (italics mine). It is not coincidental that
such a ferocious scene appears in Communist fiction of this time. Zhou Libo's
Baofeng zouyu (Hurricane, 1948), another novel on the land reform movement, which
was published about the same time as *The Sun Shines over the Sanggan River,* features a
similar scene with a similar suggestion of cannibalism. At the public trial of the
landlord Hang Laoliu, the angry masses raise clubs and sticks to beat the villain.
Widow Zhang, a weak old woman, raises her club too and cries to Han Laoliu,

"You, you killed my son!"

Her elm stick falls on Han Laoliu's shoulders. As she is about to hit Han Laoliu again, she finds herself short of energy. She drops the stick, jumps over to Han Laoliu, biting his shoulders and arms with her teeth. Nothing else can relieve the hatred in her mind.[73]

If the two public trial scenes are still startling to us today, it is perhaps not due to the questionable modes of popular justice but to the capacity of humans to be so possessed by bloodlust that they jump about and bite, like beasts. The sensational language and bloody descriptions that permeate the texts are reminiscent of the revolutionary works of the earlier generation, such as Jiang Guangci's *The Roaring Earth* and Wu Zuxiang's "Fan Family Village" and "Eighteen Hundred Piculs of Rice." But Ding Ling's work differs in that it programs all the motivations that Wu's and Jiang's peasants would have felt in such a way as to present the animality as a *logical* outcome rather than a momentary human reversion to the bestial. The public trial is made to happen as if in accordance with a court procedure, the difference being that this court scene takes place in an open space that demands *everybody's* attendance and, ostensibly, everybody's judgment. The fusion of the theater, the courtroom, and the site of punishment, long embedded in the early revolutionary plays and fiction such as *Pan Jinlian* and "The True Story of A Q," are finally officialized as an integral part of ultimate Communist legality.

The old questions regarding the way the late Qing novel *Living Hell* represents justice prove to be still pertinent. Whereas *Living Hell* presents a closed courtroom in which all suspects are punished and paraded about as if in a variety show, a novel like *The Sun Shines over the Sanggan River* introduces an open courtroom wherein suspects are served up in a mock cannibalistic feast. Lu Xun's and Lu Ling's cynical vision of the cruel human capacity to humiliate and persecute is enthusiastically endorsed in a model Communist novel. One perhaps would argue that the Communist masses are not the corrupt judges of the late Qing, and that they inflict punishment on the wicked as a necessary step toward long-awaited social justice. Liu E's paradoxical warning in *The Travels of Lao Can* is relevant: self-righteous, incorruptible judges are far more dangerous than corruptible ones.[74] Believing that they are acting at the behest of a new mandate, the Communist masses are more dangerous—when they torture the villains and their families indiscriminately—than the self-righteous, incorruptible judges of the Qing dynasty, not because the technology of torture has advanced but because there is now a vast number of self-righteous, incorruptible judges.

I would further argue that the discourse of violence and justice demonstrated in a novel like *The Sun Shines over the Sanggan River* can also be more cruel than that offered in the two late Qing novels. Liu E and Li Boyuan describe in one way or another the corruption of the late Qing judicial system, pointing out or insinuating that there are cracks between what the law means to achieve and what it really achieves. Despite their righteous or cynical undertones, the two novels contain a dimension of self-reflection, one that compels the writers and their implied readers to renegotiate a judicial and penal system *other than* what is practiced in the novels. By contrast, *The Sun Shines over the Sanggan River* celebrates the mixture of rites of torture and rites of cannibalism and sees it as the *final solution* to the problem of justice; Ding Ling takes for granted what Liu E and Li Boyuan would have either condemned or parodied, if they had not died first.

There is another aspect of violence in a Communist novel like *The Sun Shines over the Sanggan River* that has been less discussed by critics. The land reform movement does not end in the redistribution of the land and properties that used to belong to the rural ruling class. Reform of the Chinese landscape prefigures the reform of the Chinese mindscape. Behind the confrontation between the landlords and the peasants stand the land reformers; their task is to mobilize the long-oppressed peasants to rise against local authorities. Throughout the novel, one witnesses how the reformers plan carefully to arouse anger among the peasants and channel that anger into action. The peasants, at the opening of the novel, are shown as so inhibited by the power of Qian Wengui that they cannot talk about their suffering in public. After they have been "worked on" by the reformers, however, they cannot talk enough about their hatred and vengeful desire. Insofar as they undergo group-therapeutic personality changes designed and initiated by the reformers, the peasants' liberation inaugurates a new, advanced form of serfdom; land reform is the outward form of mind reform.[75]

This psychological reeducation of the peasants is closely related to the so-called violence of language imposed on them. Tang Xiaobing has argued, with Zhou Libo's *Hurricane* as an example, that the function of language in Communist literature at this time has been reduced to the most primitive level, which can "make sense" only in recourse to the invocation of physical scars.[76] Tang sees a dangerous reduction of a symbolic system of linguistic signs to that of bodily spectacle.[77]

One should, however, never take the apparent Communist vulgarization of language for simplification of figural symbolism. The obsession with the reciprocity of ink and blood is not the invention of Communist writers. Lu Xun's "decapitation complex" still has to be regarded as one of the origins of the "scarred" discourse that later prevails in leftist and rightist literature. As argued above, the new violent language can be a well-orchestrated linguistic system, couched in a deep cultural and literary subtext traceable as far back as to late Qing literature. While evoking an immediate, bodily spectacle, this language functions not as a means to do away with but to revitalize a richly encoded discourse of violence. Thus, as David Apter and Tony Saich observe, the violence of language is an intricate, figural mechanism rather than a raw abuse of words, which manages to evoke an exegetical bonding among the party members.[78]

My final point is about the way in which some forms of suffering and punishment, horrific as they are, have been written *as a result of* the new Communist discourse of justice. I have in mind cases where the debate over crime and punishment is least expected, such as the love affair between Heini, Qian Wengui's niece, and Cheng Ren, the newly appointed local leader of the land reform. Before the land reform took place, the two were lovers despite their class difference. Now, under the new legal terms that distinguish the lawful from the unlawful, they have to redefine their relations.

Though closely related to Qian Wengui by family ties, Heini has been treated as a free laborer by Qian and his wife. Now that they have learned Cheng Ren's position in the new power structure, the shrewd couple suddenly change their attitude toward their niece, hoping to use her to win Cheng Ren's favor. Heini is despised by the villagers for a scheme she is innocent of. Although she is accepted later as part of the oppressed class and enlisted to join the rally against her uncle, her romance with Cheng Ren has been indefinitely suspended by public will as well as by self-abnegation.

Cheng Ren is no better off. That Cheng Ren should have transgressed social taboos and fallen in love with a landlord's niece *before* the land reform seems to one a sign of his genuine courage and revolutionary consciousness. But in the new society, Cheng Ren becomes self-conscious of his newly won class status, which carries with it a new taboo as severe as the old one. The romance proves even more trying than before. As he finally decides to pick out Qian Wengui as the chief target of a public trial, Cheng Ren recognizes that he has been less than resolute in facing up to that reality: "He felt as if *he had committed a crime*, and *done something wrong to others, and could not hold up his head.* This was something he had never felt before. . . . He had forgiven [Qian Wengui] everything for the sake of his niece. . . . In his heart he had been secretly protecting her, that is, protecting them, the interests of the landowning class"[79] (italics mine).

Torn between his dedication to the party and his love for Qian Wengui's niece, Cheng Ren finally sacrifices all personal feelings for the sake of the revolution. And the motive that compels him to do so is a deeply embedded sense of prohibition and guilt.

In Cheng Ren's self-sacrifice there lurks a gender politics, one that is crucial to the Chinese Communist way of disciplining the "new" citizen. In "When I Was in Xia Village," Zhenzhen suffered under the old regime because she had lost her virginity, but she was allowed to prove her worth by sacrificing her body again, as a prostitute. Now, under Communist rule, Cheng Ren has lost his ideological purity by falling in love with a class enemy, and to prove his worth he must dedicate himself physically and emotionally to the party. As such, the *man* of the new era has been reduced to playing the role of the *woman* of the prerevolutionary era. Men *and* women will take up the old "feminine" role, so to speak, in the new society, a role in which the taint of evil can be acquired by rape or by association, and can be removed only by continual acts of selfless penitence, if at all. The emasculation of Cheng Ren thus completes the dialectic of gender already started in "When I Was in Xia Village."

Above all, as the homonym of his name suggests, "Cheng Ren" means both "becoming a man" and "dying as a martyr." Humanity can be attained only through a self-willed nullification of separate humanity. Lu Xun-esque cannibalism—institutionalized oppression in the name of social virtue—has reappeared on a grander scale. If Qian Wengui is condemned for his lack of humanity, Cheng Ren is honored because he has chosen to lose his humanity. Qian Wengui tries to bribe his way out of punishment; Cheng Ren condemns himself and carries out his own punishment.

The case of Ding Ling brings us back to where this article started. Late Qing writers like Liu E and Li Boyuan modernized conventional court-case literature by providing venues in which the terms of justice and violence were radically renegotiated. What had seemed complete, divine law and human law, was revealed in its incapacity to address either morality or equity. Their indictments of legal justice led to restatements of poetic justice; hence the beginnings of a new, forensic discourse.

While they look into social abuses and political atrocities, writers since Lu Xun's generation have excoriated social evil and called for the implementation of individual punishment; and they have usually come to the conclusion that justice cannot be done without violence—in the form of a revolution in the self. The consummation of the Qing desire for true forensic discourse was a massive network of self-censorship and mutual surveillance, and the Communist scene of justice shifted from the physical courthouse to the interior monologue. This inward turn of policing would prove to be far more "advanced" than any moment illustrated in the late Qing novels, both in penal technology and juridical efficacy. Violence finally stabilized in the form of self-imposed crimes and self-inflicted punishments, and the moral and legal machinery of a new justice was in full operation.

NOTES

1. Zheng Zhenduo, "Xue he lei de wenxue" (Literature of blood and tears), in *Zheng Zhenduo xuanji* (Works of Zheng Zhenduo) (Fuzhou: Fujian renmin chubanshe, 1984), 1097.

2. The most blatant example in this regard is perhaps the continued invention of cruel penal forms throughout Chinese history. See Wang Yongkuan, *Zhongguo gudai kuxing* (Cruel forms of punishment) (Taipei: Yunlong chubanshe, 1991). Also see Jonathan N. Lipman and Steven Havrell, eds., *Violence in China: Essays in Culture and Counterculture* (Albany: State University of New York Press, 1990).

3. See, for example, *Law in Imperial China: Exemplified by 190 Ch'ing Dynasty Cases* (Philadelphia: University of Pennsylvania Press, 1973); Hugh T. Scogin Jr., "Civil Law in Traditional China: History and Theory," in *Civil Law in Qing and Republican China*, ed. Kathryn Bernheart and Philip C. Huang (Stanford: Stanford University Press, 1994), 13–41; Clifford Geertz, "Local Knowledge: Fact and Law in Comparative Perspective," in *Local Knowledge* (New York: Basic Books, 1983), 167–235.

4. I am referring in particular to the book edited by Nancy Armstrong and Leonard Tennenhouse, *The Violence of Representation: Literature and the History of Violence* (New York: Routledge, 1989). See their introduction, 1–26.

5. Chen Duxiu, "Wenxue geming lun" (On literary revolution), in *Duxiu wencun* (Writings of Chen Duxiu), vol. 1 (Shanghai: Yadong tushuguan, 1931), 135–40.

6. Lu Xun, "Kuangren riji" (Diary of a madman), in *Lu Xun Quanji*, vol. 1 (Complete works of Lu Xun) (Beijing: Renmin wenxue chubanshe, 1981), 420.

7. Liu Zaifu, "Zhongguo xiandai xiaoshuo de zhengzhishi xiezuo: cong 'Chuncan' dao *Taiyang zhaozai Sanggan heshang*" (The politics of writing in modern Chinese literature: From "Spring Silkworms" to *The Sun Shines over the Sanggan River*), in *Fangzhu zhushen: Wenlun tigang he wenxueshe chongping* (Exiling gods: Outlines of literary theory and rereadings of literary history) (Hong Kong: Tiandi tushu gongsi, 1994), 133–34, 140.

8. See Armstrong and Tennenhouse, *Violence*, 1–26.

9. Ibid., 9

10. Zhang Taiyan published "Ruxia pian" (On the scholarly knight) in *Yadong shibao* (East Asian times) in 1899, arguing that the concept and practice of traditional chivalric knight-errantry, or *xia*, is derived from the Confucian scholarly tradition. See Wang Yue's discussion in "Zhang Taiyan de ruxia guan jiqi lishi yiyi" (Zhang Taiyan's concept of the scholarly knight and its historical significance), in *Xia yu Zhongguo wenhua* (Knight-errantry and Chinese culture), ed. Department of Chinese, Tamkang University (Taipei: Xuesheng shuju, 1993), 269–86. See Wendy Larson's discussion in *Literary Authority and the Modern Chinese Writer: Ambivalence and Autobiography* (Durham: Duke University Press, 1991), 31–59.

11. Literature, of course, babbles on about injustice and revolution, but these are just terms in the new master-narrative. The silences are about actual cruelties and actual repetitions, and the worst silence is the one about literary complicity, because it does representational violence to representation itself.

12. Liu E, *Lao Can youji* (The travels of Lao Can) (Taipei: Lianjing chuban gongsi, 1983), 2.

13. Ibid., 245. Throughout my essay I will use the term "incorruptible" to mean specifically "not bribable."

14. This appears in chapter 6 of *Laocan youji*. See C. T. Hsia's discussion in "The Travels of Lao Ts'an: An Exploration of Its Arts and Meaning," *Ts'ing Hua Journal of Chinese Studies* 7, no. 2 (1969): 40–66.

15. Liu E, *The Travels of Lao Ts'an*, trans. Harold Shadick (Ithaca: Cornell University Press, 1952), 70.

16. See C. T. Hsia, "Travels," 50–52 and n. 31.

17. The Yellow River in this area is less than a mile wide and is rimmed by small dikes built and maintained by the farmers whose land they protect. The government-built dikes are massive embankments twenty feet high and are up to three miles away from the water. The land between the two dikes is fertile and thickly populated. See Harold Shadick's note in his translation of Li, *Travels*, 262.

18. See Liu E's commentary at the end of chapter 13 of *Travels*, 124.

19. Ibid., 259–66.

20. Liu E may not have been aware of the potential for this ironic reading. Schematically, however, his novel encourages us to apply on the celestial level the same rules he has been applying to terrestrial justice. By mentioning the bureaucracy of Hell in the context of the failures of human bureaucracy, Liu E sets up the comparison.

21. Li Boyuan, *Huo diyu* (Living hell) (Taipei: Guangya shuju, 1984), 1. I am using Douglas Lancashire's translation, quoted from Lancashire, *Li Po-yuan* (Boston: Twayne, 1978), 64–65.

22. It was the second of Li Boyuan's novels serialized in his magazine *Xiuxiang xiaoshuo* (Illustrated fiction). The novel comprises forty-three chapters; like most of other novels by Li Boyuan, it remains incomplete. Li died when he had finished chapter 39. Chapters 40 to 42 were added by his friend, the novelist Wu Jianren. The last chapter is said to have been written by Ouyang Juyuan, Li's friend and the assistant editor of *Illustrated Fiction*. The novel was not published in book form till 1956 in Shanghai, under the auspices of the well-known scholar Zhao Jingshen.

MODERN CHINESE LITERATURE   *295*

23. Lancashire, *Li Po-yuan*, 63.

24. Here, I am partially indebted to Lyotard's concept of justice. See Jean-Francois Lyotard and Jean-Loup Thebaud, *Just Gaming* (Minneapolis: University of Minnesota Press, 1979), 25–26.

25. Li Boyuan, *Huo diyu*, 72.

26. The first is a long aluminum pipe circled all around the prisoner's body. The attendants inject boiling water at one end of the pipe and let it flow slowly to the other end. The second is a form of capital punishment, meaning to put five nails into the four limbs and the chest of the prisoner. The third is three iron sticks used to beat the prisoner. By pressing one iron stick on the prisoner's chest and the other on his legs, the courtroom attendants check the prisoner's breath at the two ends of his body and force it to accumulate in his stomach. They then use the third stick to beat the prisoner's stomach, and with one loud sound, all the intestines will burst out.

27. Michel Foucault, *Discipline and Punish: The Birth of the Prison*, trans. Alan Sheridan (New York: Pantheon, 1977), 24–85.

28. Lao Can is compared to Sherlock Holmes in chapter 18 for his investigation of the aforementioned murder case.

29. Lu Xun, preface to *Nahan* (A call to arms), in *Lu Xun quanji* (Complete works of Lu Xun), vol. 1 (Beijing: Renmin wenxue chubanshe, 1981), 417.

30. David Der-wei Wang, "Lu Xun, Shen Congwen, and Decapitation," in *Politics, Ideology, and Literary Discourse in Modern China: Theoretical Interventions and Cultural Critique*, ed. Liu Kang and Tang Xiaobing (Durham: Duke University Press, 1993), 174–87.

31. Lun Xun, preface to *Nahan*, 417.

32. Ibid.

33. T. A. Hsia, *The Gate of Darkness* (Seattle: University of Washington Press, 1968), 146.

34. Lu Xun seems to have understood the full meaning of late Qing intellectual chivalry; one cannot always say this for the writers after him, who too often thought they had passed through the gate and left the late Qing far behind them.

35. For a discussion of the rise and development of Chinese court-case drama, see Zeng Yongyi, *Zhongguo gudian xiju de renshi yu xinshang* (An introduction to and appraisal of classical Chinese drama) (Taipei: Zhengzhong shuju, 1991), 55.

36. Ouyang Yuqian, *Pan Jinlian* (Pan Jinlian), in vol. 1 of *Ouyang Yuqian wenji* (Works of Ouyang Yuqian) (Beijing: Renmin wenxue chubanshe, 1984), 90.

37. Ibid., 93.

38. See Bai Wei, afterword to *Dachu youling ta* (Breaking out of the tower of ghosts), in *Bai Wei zuopinji* (Works of Bai Wei) (Changsha: Hunan renmin chubanshe, 1985), 77.

39. Lu Xun, "Lun Leifeng ta de daodiao," in *Lu Xun Quanji*, vol. 1 (Beijing: Renmin wenxue chubanshe, 1981), 174–77.

40. Bai Wei, *Dachu youling ta*, 64.

41. Ibid., 75.

42. Zhu Yiqui, *Zhongguo xiandai xijushi* (History of modern Chinese drama) (Guilin: Guanxi renmin chubanshe, 1981), 234–36.

43. See, for example, Meng Yue and Dai Jinhua, *Fuchu lishi dibiao: Zhongguo xiandai nuxing wenxue yanjiu* (Voices emerging from the foreground of history: A study of contemporary Chinese women's literature) (Taipei: Shibao chuban gongsi, 1993), 227–30.

44. Marston Anderson, *The Limits of Realism: Chinese Fiction in the Revolutionary Period* (Berkeley and Los Angeles: University of California Press, 1990), 44.

45. T. A. Hsia, *Gate of Darkness*, 55–59.

46. Ibid. Also see Leo Ou-fan Lee, *The Romantic Generation of Modern Chinese Writers* (Cambridge: Harvard University Press, 1973), 201–21.

47. Jiang Guangci, *Paoxiao de tudi* (The roaring earth), vol. 2 of *Jiang Guangci wenji* (Selected works of Jiang Guangci) (Shanghai: Shanghai wenyi chubanshe, 1982), 374.

48. See Anthony Kubiak, *Stages of Terror, Terrorism, Ideology, and Coercion as Theater History* (Bloomington: Indiana University Press, 1991), 148. One way to live with terror is to repress it, to survive it by choosing to be unconscious of it, as Li Jie does literally.

49. Jiang Guangci, *Paoxiao de tudi*, 374.

50. Wu Zuxiang, "Young Master Gets His Tonic," trans. Cyril Birch, in *Modern Chinese Short Stories and Novellas: 1919–1949*, ed. C. T. Hsia, Joseph Lau, and Leo Ou-fan Lee (New York: Columbia Press, 1981), 381.

51. Part of the plot summary is derived from that of Marston Anderson, *Limits*, 198.

52. C. T. Hsia, *A History of Modern Chinese Fiction* (New Haven: Yale University Press, 1971), 284–85; Philip Williams, *Village Echoes: The Fiction of Wu Zuxiang* (Boulder: Westview Press, 1993), 82–84.

53. C. T. Hsia, *History*, 286.

54. Wu Zuxiang, "Yiqian babai dan" (Eighteen hundred piculs of rice), in *Wu Zuxiang* (Taipei: Haifeng chubanshe, 1990), 158–59.

55. See, for example, Merle Goldman, *Literary Dissent in Communist China* (Cambridge: Harvard University Press, 1967), 1–50. Few literary historians have noticed that, right after Mao delivered his talks, the Nationalist Party retaliated by commissioning Zhang Daofan, a playwright and literary propagandist, to advocate a literature based on Sun Yat-sen's *Three Principles of the People*. This policy would eventually become the backbone of the anti-Communist literature that the Nationalist Party promoted in Taiwan of the fifties and sixties. A comparative reading of both Nationalist and Communist literary policies indicates, ironically, a parallel between them in theory and practice, despite the fact that they were meant as antagonistic discourses. See Cheng Ming-lee, "Dangdai Taiwan wenyi zhengce de fazhan, yingxiang, yu jiaotao" (On the development, impact, and consequences of the literary policy in contemporary Taiwan), in *Dangdai Taiwan zhengzhi wenxue lun* (Politics and contemporary Taiwanese literature), ed. Cheng Ming-lee (Taipei: Shibao chuban gongsi, 1994), 1–20. Also see my article "Reinventing National History: Communist and Anti-Communist Fiction from 1946 to 1955," in *China in the Transitional Period: 1946–1955*, ed. William Kirby (Cambridge: Harvard University Press), forthcoming.

56. See my article "Reinventing National History," in *China in the Transnational Period,* ed. Kirby.

57. C. T. Hsia, *History*, 326–60. Also see Theodore Huters, "Hu Feng and the Critical Legacy of Lu Xun," in *Lu Xun and His Legacy*, ed. Leo Ou-fan Lee (Berkeley and Los Angeles: University of California Press, 1985), 129–52.

58. See David E. Apter and Tony Saich's discussion in *Revolutionary Discourse in Mao's Republic* (Cambridge: Harvard University Press, 1994), 243–92.

59. Yi-tsi Mei Feuerwerker, *The Fiction of Ding Ling* (Cambridge: Harvard University Press, 1982), 114. Also see Tani Barlow, with Gary Bjorge, ed., *I Myself Am a Woman* (Boston: Beacon Press, 1989), 34–45.

60. Ding Ling, "When I Was in Hsia Village," trans. Gary Bjorge, in *Modern Chinese Stories and Novellas: 1919–1949*, ed. Joseph Lau, C. T. Hsia, and Leo Ou-fan Lee (New York: Columbia Press, 1981), 274.

61. This argument can be read in light of Apter and Saich's recent discussion where they borrow Baudrillard's theory to describe an effect of simulacrum in the production of the revolutionary discourse and revolutionary site, *Revolutionary Discourse*, 224–62.

62. See Huang Ziping's succinct discussion in "Bing de yinyu yu wenxue shengchan: Ding Ling de 'Zai yiyuan zhong' ji qita" (The metaphor of illness and literary production: Ding Ling's "In the Hospital" and other works), in *Zai jiedu: Dazhong wenyi yu yishi xingtai* (Rereading: Mass literature and ideology), ed. Tang Xiaobing (Hong Kong: Oxford University Press, 1993), 51–67.

63. Ding Ling, "When I Was in Hsia Village," 268.

64. Merle Goldman, *Literary Dissent*, 67–86.

65. Lu Ling, *Ji'e de Guo Su'e* (Hungry Guo Su'e) (Beijing: Beijing renmin chubanshe, 1988), 103.

66. Ibid., 104.

67. See Feuerwerker, *Fiction*, 136–46.

68. Ibid., 139–40. Also see Apter and Saich, *Revolutionary Discourse* 263–332.

69. Liu Zaifu and Lin Gang, *Fangzhu zhushen: Wenlun tigang he wenxueshi chongping* (Exiling the gods: Outlines of literary theory and reappraisal of literary history) (Hong Kong: Tiandi tushu, 1994), 130

70. Ibid., 124–25.

71. Roland Barthes, *Writing Degree Zero*, trans. Annete Lavers and Colin Smith (New York: Hill and Wang, 1978), 71.

72. Ding Ling, *Taiyang zhaozai Sanggan heshang* (The sun shines over the Sanggan River), vol. 1 of *Ding Ling xuanji* (Selected works of Ding Ling) (Chengdu: Sichuan renmin chubanshe, 1984), 300. English translation from C. T. Hsia, *History*, 486.

73. Zhou Libo, *Baofeng zouyu* (Hurricane) (Changsha: Hunan renmin chubanshe, 1983), 174. See Tang Xiaobing's discussion in "Baoli de bianzheng fa" (The dialectic of violence), in *Zai Jiedu: Dazhong wenyi yu yishi xingtai* (Rereading: Mass literature and ideology), ed. Tang Xiaobing (Hong Kong: Oxford University Press, 1993), 122.

74. Writers like Liu E criticize the way incorruptible judges abuse their power, torturing innocent people, but they rarely criticize the habit of torturing people who are not innocent. Lao Can the dreamer acquiesces in the most horrible punishments imposed on condemned souls in Hell as much as Liu E acquiesces in the edifying power of horrible punishments imposed on condemned criminals on Earth.

75. See Apter and Saich's description of the so-called Foucault's paradox involved here: "The inversionary discourse that appears offers an unlimited prospect of freedom and proposes to free people from constraints of power, to break the hegemony of the discourse through which it is represented; but it, in turn, becomes hegemonic, all the more as it cleaves to its original intent," *Revolutionary Discourse*, 331.

76. Tang, "Baoli de bianzheng fa," 120.

77. Ibid., 121.

78. Apter and Saich, *Revolutionary Discourse*, chapters 8, 9.

79. Ding Ling, *Taiyang zhaozai Sanggan heshagn*, 247–48.

NINE

Hanjian (Traitor)! Collaboration and Retribution in Wartime Shanghai

Frederic Wakeman Jr.

You young fellows must love your country and not assist the Japanese or be a traitor. Now in Nandao they are in need of a number of young plainclothes soldiers. If you wish to join us, you must follow me.

SPECIAL ACTION CORPS RECRUITER, SHANGHAI, SEPTEMBER 1937

One of the most commonly used epithets in the Chinese popular press of the 1930s and early 1940s was the term *hanjian*, which meant "traitor" or "traitor to the Han." According to the *Hanyu da cidian*, the term "originally indicated the scum of the Han people [*Hanzu bailei*]. Later it generally came to allude to someone who throws in his or her lot with a foreign people [*waizu*] or with foreign invaders, willingly serves at their beck and call, and sells out the interests of the ancestral land and the people [*zuguo minzu*]."[1]

TRANSGRESSING BOUNDARIES

The key word, *jian*, exists in two forms (Mathews 817 and Mathews 818). The first form, which is a character composed of three *nü* (women), primarily means "private, selfish, secret" and "heterodox, depraved, vicious, evil, wicked, demonic." The ancient lexicon *Shuowen* derives these meanings from the notion of doting on or being attached to three women. Secondary meanings include "foul things; scoundrels, ruffians and robbers; spurious, fake; external and internal chaos; crafty, perverse, cunning, treacherous; illicit sexual intercourse; secret communication with the enemy; rape."[2] The second version, which is most often used in the binomial compound, *Hanjian*, has, among other significances, the additional meaning of "transgression."[3] This *jian* is more like a transitive verb: "to commit adultery, to have sex; to break the law; to oppose someone; to trespass, violate, and encroach."[4]

There are behind all these various signifiers three deeply connected meanings of *jian* that eventually adhere to the term "traitor." The first is the notion of illicitly crossing boundaries, of transgressing norms by, in a sense, "going over to them." The second is the notion that this transgression invites, produces, and results in *luan*, or "chaos." And third is the connection between illicit transgression and sexual excess or lust.

The compound *hanjian* came into general usage during the Song dynasty when it described Han (that is, Chinese) officials who spied for the Jurchen Jin dynasty. According to the most authoritative dictionary in use in the People's Republic of China at present, a *hanjian*, then, "is someone who helps a different race [*yizhong*] harm his or her own race [*tongzhong*]."[5] Needless to say the term is more particularistic than such a definition properly would allow: that is, you have to be Han in order to be a *hanjian*. Semantically, in other words, it is difficult to separate political treason from ethnic transgression.[6]

GOING OVER

The two iniquities—betraying universal cultural norms and joining exclusive ethnic enemies—coincided during foreign invasions of China, when the term *hanjian* was hung as a crude label of infamy around the necks of collaborators. At the time of the Ming-Qing transition, the greatest traitors in Ming officials' eyes were *hanjian* who crossed over to the Manchus just before they "entered the pass" in 1644 and occupied the Central Plains. Earlier boundary crossers, or transfrontiersmen, had ambiguous ethnic identities, but their loyalties to the new Qing dynasty were squarely centered on the person of the Manchu khan-emperor to whom they had declared allegiance. It was the later adherents, such as Hong Chengchou and Wu Sangui, who earned historians' opprobrium, though the notion of betraying the Han *ethnie* was intentionally muffled by the time of the Qianlong literary inquisition, when Confucian treachery was identified with the label of "twice-serving ministers" (*er chen*) for those who had been Ming officials before joining the Qing. Of course, the tension nonetheless persisted between Qing culturalism, with its universalistic monarchic pretensions, and the ethnic particularisms of both holders and subjects of the throne.[7]

Even prior to Qianlong's reign (1736–95), despite this late-cultural/early-national tension, the term *hanjian* was widely used within the Qing bureaucracy to designate Chinese who had "gone over" to the tribal peoples of southwestern China.[8] On the part of Qing viceroys and governors there were two impulses along the Miao frontier. One, which was associated with ascriptive officials (Manchu or Han Martial bannermen), was to prevent intermarriage and blame "undependable Han traitors" (*wulai hanjian*) for bringing about difficulties with the Miao. The second was to acculturate the Miao, not segregate them, even if this meant widespread intermarriage across ethnic boundaries. In the early eighteenth century, the Qing government attempted to enforce a quarantine legislated in 1707. Han residence was forbidden in Miao hamlets, and the Miao were prohibited from travel into the interior. *Hanjian* were those Chinese who crossed over the demarcation line, which by the Yongzheng period (1722–35) was becoming impossible to rigidly maintain.[9]

Under the Qianlong emperor, who ruled over a society much more integrated than the formations of the early 1700s, the acculturalists gradually won out. "As the segregationists lost the argument, their tendency to see Han traitors behind every thicket was discredited," and it was not until the Western aggressions of the nineteenth century that the figure of the *hanjian* widely reappeared.[10]

TRAITORS AND TRANSGRESSION

The Opium War brought traitors—*neiying* (fifth columnists), *maiguozhe* (sellouts or collaborators), *jianshang* (treacherous merchants), and *hanjian*—back as primary scapegoats for the Manchu dynasty's defeat by the British Empire. Whether as unscrupulous lictors working for the Pomeranian missionary Gutzlaff when he assumed a local magistracy under English guns, or as a local prefect ransoming Canton from the H.M.S. *Nemesis,* "traitors" were blamed for selling out the country.[11] My purpose is not to dwell upon this rich historical theme in the nineteenth century, however, but rather to note again the connection between ethnocultural treachery and the crossing of boundaries by collusion with foreigners, linked in turn with bestiality, sexual violation, and demonic behavior.[12]

One way of diminishing the cognitive friction between universal and particular identities was to equate humankind-ness with Han-ness. To be read out of the corporate group was to become "other," to lose one's ability to be genuinely human, to leave behind or "transgress" (*jian*) being Chinese (Han) or even being just a man (*han*).[13] In this sense, the ethnic condition of Han-ness was a human state, which governed the trajectory one traced in the course of "crossing over" (*jian*) into nonhumanness. And leaving that state meant associating with demons or animals, such as the "pigs" (*zhu*), or Catholic missionaries depicted in the anti-Christian posters of that period.[14]

In the popular mentality of the twentieth century, treachery (or being a *hanjian*) was also an alienation, an act of madness, that could cut one off from other Chinese people. In a 1938 article entitled "School Principal Becomes a Traitor" ("Xiaozhang zuo hanjian"), it was reported, "Former elementary school principal, Chen Qibai, lost all capacity for self-respect after the War of Resistance began. When the capital was occupied, he took his family from the Yong [River, near Ningbo], and ended by losing his conscience and being stricken with madness [*sangxin bingkuang*]. He changed his name to Chen Daoliang and publicly accepted a post as a secretary in the puppet Executive Yuan in Nanjing."[15] Thus, to be a *hanjian* was to lose the capacity for moral judgment, along with one's primal identity and bestowed name.

After the collapse of the First United Front in 1927 and the commencement of the White Terror, the Communist Party formed a special assassination team under Zhou Enlai's Special Services Committee (*Tewu weiyuanhui*). The group was formally known as the Red Brigade, but its members called themselves the "dog-killers squad" (*dagou tuan*) because they were devoted to murdering deviants (*yiji*), renegades (*pantu*), and traitors (*hanjian*) to their cause. The term *hanjian* was not always applied to those who had "betrayed Marxism" (*beipan Makesizhuyi*) or who had "betrayed their original class background" (*beipan yuanlai de jieji*). But insofar as political "renegades" had left the fold of the party, which was a family of its own, they were also designated as *hanjian*.[16] On their part, right-wing Nationalists regarded the Communists as *hanjian* as well.[17] The secret service chief Dai Li eventually hunted down the "dog-killers squad" in its Shanghai jewelry-store hideout and had its members executed by the Guomindang government in Nanjing.[18]

TREACHERY AND APPEASEMENT

The stronghold of the Chiang Kai-shek régime's campaign against national traitors was a circle of Chiang's own students—Whampoa cadets who founded the Lixingshe (Vigorous Action Society) in February 1932 after Chiang resumed power. Although they were devoutly anti-Communist cadres, these members of the Lixingshe, which formed the core of the Blue Shirts, or Lanyishe, were aroused by Japan's aggression in China. Many of them had been studying in military or police academies in Japan at the time of the Manchurian Railway Incident (September 1931), and after they organized a demonstration in Tokyo that was broken up by the police, they returned to China and joined the Anti-Japanese National Salvation Association of Returned Students from Japan (*Liu-Ri xuesheng kang-Ri jiuguo hui*), formed by Gong Debo and others under the leadership of He Zhonghan's friend and classmate Xiao Zanyu. Gong Debo's newspaper, *Jiuguo ribao* (National salvation daily), printed editorial after editorial calling for the Chinese to "resist the Japanese and root out traitors" (*kang Ri chu jian*), and although Gong himself took no part in the activities of the Lixingshe, many members of that secret organization's "preparations department" used the newspaper as a cover for their own work, pretending to be editors or reporters.[19]

The Blue Shirts who belonged to the Lixingshe were fanatically dedicated to supporting their "leader" (*lingxiu*), Chiang Kai-shek, and to extirpating traitors (*hanjian*).[20] The Lixingshe's "backbone cadres" believed that *hanjian* were both a manifestation and a cause of the weakness of China, reflecting the absence of a national spirit or people's will such as animated the Japanese race. They believed that

> the racial will [*minzu yizhi*] of the Chinese masses is extremely weak, which can be confirmed by the multitudinous numbers of Chinese traitors [*hanjian*] and thieves who have sold out their country [*maiguozei*]. . . . One can almost say that there is absolutely no parallel to this ugly phenomenon in all the other countries of the world. In the Northeast [i.e., Manchuria] and in the Yangzi Valley they shamelessly seek power and wealth by selling out their country. You could say that the interior of China is carpeted with *hanjian*. This is because as modern China suffered one defeat

after another in foreign wars, the psychology of the people changed from deprecation and rejection of outsiders to an attitude of awe and admiration for foreigners. There thus emerged the curious "sight" [*jingguan*] of Chinese hating Chinese but not hating foreigners.... [We] believe that the people who indirectly assist the enemy in destroying China are just as despicable as the *hanjian* and *maiguozei*. They all belong to [the same] category of people who are completely irresponsible and dishonorable. At the same time that the *hanjian* and *maiguozei* are being exterminated, we will also eradicate those elements that lend an indirect hand to the enemy bent upon destroying China.[21]

In other words, not only were outright collaborators—whose motives had, in many cases, to be mixed—simply to be labeled *hanjian* and marked for execution; "indirect" or passive onlookers were designated potential targets as well. Moreover, this indiscriminate persecution by terrorist elements of the Guomindang right wing was to be justified as a means of addressing the humiliation suffered by the nation at the hands of foreign aggressors during the previous century. This marked loss of national self-confidence in the Chinese, seen now as an "inferior race" (*liedeng minzu*), which the late Lloyd Eastman explored in his pioneering study of the Nanjing decade, was a far cry from the culturalist self-confidence of the Qianlong period—though the term *hanjian* was used in both cases.

URBAN COLLABORATION

To be sure, the Blue Shirts had already witnessed the sorry spectacle of Chinese collaborators working closely with the enemy during the Japanese Occupation of Shanghai's northern Zhabei district from January to May 1932. During the attack on Zhabei, the term *hanjian* was applied to Chinese who looted in the wake of the assault by Japanese marines and soldiers on Shanghai's North Station. It was quickly extended to cover collaborators who were said to have gone into the combat zones to "make trouble" by working for the Japanese. Two hundred of these *hanjian* were believed to be Chinese secret agents from northern Jiangsu (Jiangbei or Subei) and Anhui, and a number of them were rounded up and shot by the Shanghai Public Security Bureau and the Nationalist Army.[22]

Once the Japanese drove the Nineteenth Route Army out of Shanghai and established a military occupation, a group of Chinese collaborators formed the Zhabei Citizens Maintenance Association, which was also known as the Shanghai Northern District Citizens Maintenance Association. It began as a street-cleaning operation at a time when Zhabei's thoroughfares were littered with corpses. On March 24, 1932, the Japanese army engaged 150 Chinese coolies to sweep the streets from Suzhou Creek all the way up to North Station. They were supervised by Chinese foremen, probably Subei gangsters, and paid with funds generated by a monthly tax levied on all of the street traders in Zhabei. The operation was run out of the former Zhabei municipal finance office by an organization called the Great Japan New Political Affairs Bureau, which was a puppet "municipal organ" guarded by Japanese soldiers but manned, after April 1, by Chinese collaborators.[23]

The identification of these collaborators with natives of Subei—an ethnic subgroup already treated with negative prejudice by other Shanghainese sojourners—reinforced the connection between *hanjian* and outsiders beyond the pale.[24] Three prominent racketeers were involved in the puppet organization: Gu Zhuxuan, his brother Gu Sungmao, and Wei Zhongxiu. Gu Zhuxuan, the "emperor of Subei," was one of the most infamous gangsters in Shanghai. His brother Gu Sungmao was a former rickshaw coolie who now worked as a foreman in the Star Rickshaw Company and owned a theater that featured Subei dialect performances. Wei Zhongxiu, also a native of Subei, was the former chief detective of the Public Safety Bureau and a disciple of the Green Gang boss Du Yuesheng. Shanghainese and foreigners alike, then, spoke of "Jiangbei traitors" as if their corrupt collaboration with the Japanese Military Police could be explained by the men's dark-skinned faces and hillbilly manners.[25] The public had by April 10 become so "dissatisfied with the foul tactics of these traitors" that the Japanese decided to dissolve the Maintenance Association while they prepared to return Zhabei to the Chinese Nationalist régime.[26]

BLUE SHIRTS

While the Japanese gave up their occupied sectors of Shanghai under international pressure, they moved ahead in north China, consolidating their occupation of Rehe and attacking Zhahar (Chahar). The Christian warlord Feng Yuxiang decided to make a bid for national leadership by mobilizing a resistance movement. Coming out of his self-imposed retirement at Zhangjiakou, Feng announced the formation of the People's Allied Anti-Japanese Army (*Minzhong kang-Ri tongmeng jun*) on May 26, 1933, and began gathering troops.[27] Chiang Kai-shek, however, was thoroughly convinced of the importance of appeasing Japan in order to buy time to exterminate the Communists.[28] On May 31, five days after General Feng's announcement, Chiang's representative, Huang Fu, negotiated a cease-fire with the Japanese. But public opinion seemed to support Feng. The Tanggu Truce was decried as a sellout and Huang Fu denounced as a pro-Japanese *hanjian*.[29]

Chiang's Blue Shirts, fully accepting the generalissimo's policy of *annei rangwai* (first pacify the interior, then expel the external aggressor), shifted their attention to another sort of traitor: those who might collaborate with the Japanese by taking the role of puppet governor under the Occupation. By then, Dai Li, the future head of Juntong (Military Statistics, which was a euphemism for the secret police), was fully in charge of the Blue Shirts' intelligence and covert operations. Under his orders to assail internal rather than external enemies (a redirection that sometimes smacked of scapegoating), secret agent Zheng Jiemin arranged the assassination of Zhang Jingyao, the Hunanese warlord then negotiating with the Japanese.[30] Zhang's demise was meant to scare other *hanjian* out of collaborating with the Japanese.

For there was a significant stratum of political figures, many of them former Beiyang militarists and bureaucrats, who bore a deep antipathy toward the party of Sun Yat-sen and other southerners who had adopted a radical agenda of revolutionary nationalism. Culturally conservative and often trained in Japanese military academies and universities in the last years of the Qing, these northern Chinese leaders saw little harm in cooperating with victorious Japanese generals in the name of a new order in East Asia that would repel Anglo-American imperialism on the one hand, and Soviet Bolshevism on the other. And even if they did not want to venture as far as outright collaboration, they could easily see that it was to their advantage to create a gray zone of complex and ambiguous loyalties that left them some room for maneuver.

Dai Li's strategy, however, was to force these political actors to choose between being live heroes or dead *hanjian*. Gan Guoxun, one of the Lixingshe's founders, later said that the assassination of Zhang Jingyao "aroused and excited the heroes [*haojie*] of Yan and Zhao[,] ... completely changing the social atmosphere of northern China, which was feudal and self-indulgent. All those *hanjian*, such as Wang Kemin, Wang Jitang, and Gao Wenyue, went into hiding. Squirming like worms, they were afraid to make any move whatsoever. Representative northern warlord figures such as Duan Qirui and Wu Peifu bowed to public opinion and pledged loyalty to the center."[31]

Zhang Jingyao's assassination also convinced the Japanese that the Blue Shirts were responsible for most of the terrorism directed against *hanjian* in north China during the period 1934–35, and at their insistence the Lanyishe was supposedly disbanded. In fact, it continued to operate under other guises, partly as an agency engaged in anti-Japanese activities commanded by General Dai Li and partly as a rubric for numerous patriotic and terrorist activities directed against *hanjian* throughout China.[32]

WAR AND NATIONAL SALVATION

War broke out between China and Japan after the Marco Polo Bridge Incident outside Beiping on the night of July 7, 1937. Even before then, a Shanghai "merchants militia" (*shangtuan*) had been formed by the Chinese Chamber of Commerce, which had taken out advertisements in the Shanghai press offering free courses in civic training to shop assistants.[33] During the six weeks between the onset of fighting in north China and the eruption of conflict in the Yangzi delta on August 13, more citizen volunteer groups were formed in Shanghai under the loose supervision of the Nationalist general Zhang Jizhong.[34]

On July 15, for example, the Chinese Youth National Salvation Association was formally inaugurated at the Guandi Temple, where a depot had been established. More than a thousand people showed up to hear speeches by the head of the association, Zhao Gangyi, and by the chief of its execution department, Sun Yaxing.[35] A number of those who came then or later in answer to advertisements in *Zhongyang ribao* (Central daily news) were taken aside and interviewed by Sun Yaxing, who asked them to write about their reasons for joining. Three of these young men later became members of Sun Yaxing's antitraitor assassination group: Wang Zhigu, a twenty-three-year-old factory apprentice; Jiang Haisheng, a nineteen-year-old student; and Zhou Shougang, a twenty-five-year-old printer.[36] A fourth, Sun Jinghao, was the bomber killed on December 3, 1937, at the Japanese victory parade on Nanjing Road.[37]

These new members of the National Salvation Association—all students, apprentices, or shop assistants—attended lectures on the current political situation, and then were asked on July 21 to volunteer to dig fortifications outside Shanghai. About two hundred men, mostly between eighteen and twenty-one years old, volunteered, and under Sun Yaxing's command they proceeded to Nanxiang, where they were attached to the Eighty-seventh Nationalist Division. For the next month, supplied with food but not pay, they dug trenches, working mostly at night to avoid Japanese bombers.[38]

CO-OPTATION

After war broke out in Zhabei on August 13, the Nationalist secret service began to take over these paramilitary operations. General Dai Li met with the Green Gang leader Du Yuesheng in the French Concession to discuss the formation of a Pudong Guerrilla Brigade, a Lake Tai Special Action Command, the Loyal and Patriotic Army (*Zhongyi jiuguo jun*), and eventually the Jiangsu-Zhejiang Operations Committee.[39] And at the beginning of September Chiang Kai-shek's Military Affairs Commission approved the organization of an "emergency period service group" (*feichang shiqi fuwutuan*) to deal with traitors and spies in Shanghai. The Military Affairs Commission subsequently put this group under the orders of General Wang Jingjiu, commander of the Eighty-seventh Nationalist Division, housing its Special Services Squad (*Tewutuan*) in the Shaoxing guild hall in Nandao.[40]

The Special Services Squad also had an investigation section, which was charged with collecting evidence on *hanjian* so that the police could arrest the collaborators and turn them over to the Special Services Squad headquarters for questioning.[41] So deputized, members of the investigation group and other such patriotic volunteers had ample opportunities to form "antitraitor societies" to extort money from merchants dealing in Japanese goods.[42]

The Su-Zhe Operations Committee (*Junshi weiyuanhui Su-Zhe xingdong weiyuanhui*), which was formed in late September to transform "gangland" (*banghui*) members into paramilitary cadres, was nominally chaired by Chiang Kai-shek. Its members included Du Yuesheng, Huang Jinrong, Wang Xiaolai, Yu Xiaqing, Zhang Xiaolin, Yang Hu, Mei Guangpei, Xiang Songpo, and Lu Jingshi. The secretary-general (*shujizhang*) was Dai Li, who used the authority of the committee to organize a General Command Headquarters for the Special Action Army (*Biedong jun zongzhihui bu*) located at Number 1 Shenjiazhai near Fenglinqiao opposite Route Ghisi in South Market. This became the command post of what would be known as the *Song-Hu biedong zongdui* (Song-Hu Chief Special Action Corps), nominally directed by Du Yuesheng, but really run by Dai Li and his secret service agents.[43]

The corpsmen themselves consisted mainly of retail clerks (*dianyuan*) from the Shanghai Shopkeepers Association, local ruffians (*dipi* and *liumang*) from the gangs, routed Guomindang soldiers, laborers thrown out of work by the closing of the factories and shops during the Japanese attack, and organized labor union members.[44] Once trained and armed with Mauser pistols, these units' primary purpose was "solely to locate traitors [*hanjian*]" and turn them over to the nearest Chinese police bureau.[45]

Others were former members of the Chinese Youth National Salvation Association. Toward the end of August, Sun Yaxing's group, for instance, had been renamed a Special Services Corps and transferred to Longhua for military training. In late September, after being provided grenades, pistols, and rifles, they were assigned to patrol the area surrounding the martial law commander's headquarters at West Gate. The corpsmen were authorized to take whatever measures they deemed necessary "to suppress traitors": if they arrested persons "for perpetrating traitorous acts," the suspects were tried by a military court within the headquarters and summarily executed when found guilty.[46]

Naysayers later described the Special Services Corps as "a motley rabble" (*wu he zhi zhong*) that had very little military effectiveness against the Japanese.[47] The units that were supposed to defend the zone from the south bank of Suzhou Creek along Fanwangdu and Caojiadu across to Rihuigang did quickly retreat once the Japanese launched an attack across Suzhou Creek.[48] But Sun Yaxing's company, which was dispatched to the police station on the Nandao Bund in late October 1937 to help the police reserve unit defend the area from attack by the Japanese from the Huangpu River, held its ground. This was where the last stand of the Chinese Nationalist forces took place on November 11, the final day of the Battle of Shanghai.[49] Some Special Services corpsmen fought valiantly and died at the water's edge. Others made their way into the French Concession and International Settlement, where the authorities rounded them up and interned them in special camps—camps that became breeding grounds for the urban terrorists who would continue the war against *hanjian* long after the last contingent of Special Services Corps formally withdrew from Shanghai on February 1, 1938, after issuing a farewell letter to the Chinese press stating that they were leaving the concessions "for the safety of the residents of the foreign settlements." One newspaper commented, "The death of most of the Chinese traitors may have been the work of the corps."[50]

PUPPETS

On December 5, 1937, Su Xiwen, a Waseda-educated philosopher, inaugurated "the Great Way" (the Dadao) puppet municipal government of Shanghai.[51] Su had taught political theory at the private Chizhi University in Jiangwan.[52] His Buddhist-Daoist syncretism ("All under heaven one family / Myriad laws revert to one" [*tianxia yi jia, wanfa gui yi*]) influenced the Great Way government's choice of flag, which was a *taiji* symbol on a yellow background.[53] The Su régime's collaborationist conservatism was reflected in the dating of its documents, which used both the old Chinese lunar and the Japanese Showa reign calendars, as the new administration set out to remove corpses from the Chinese city's streets after the Battle of Shanghai was over.[54] The Dadao régime's immediate task, according to orders issued to police chief Zhu Yuzhen, was to "establish local order" (*chengli difang zhixu*).[55] This meant ideologically stressing that "all under heaven is one family, within the four seas we are all brothers: the Way of the sun and moon, myriad laws reverting to one, great harmony [Datong] throughout the world, and using the Way to establish a state."[56] In political terms, the Dadao government promised to eliminate Communists and Nationalists alike, to extirpate the warlord scourge, and to lay a sound foundation for peace in East Asia.[57]

In truth, the Dadao puppet government was short-lived, at least in nomenclature.[58] The malodorous characteristics of its leading members, a potpourri of Venerable Mother religious cultists, smugglers, gamblers, narcotics dealers, panderers, and former rickshaw pullers, were liability enough.[59] But just as damaging was the Japanese handlers' contempt for Su Xiwen, whose philosophizing was not taken very seriously after the Special Services brought in a tough north China *hanjian* named Wang Zihui to run their Shanghai operations.[60]

Meanwhile, the poet Liang Hongzhi, a former Beiyang bureaucrat, had been "casting romantic glances" (*song qiubo*) at the Japanese, making known his availability as a collaborator.[61] Consequently, after the puppet administrations in north China were incorporated in January 1938 into a single provisional government (*Linshi zhengfu, Rinji seifu*) under Wang Kemin in Beiping, in south China a reform government (*Weixin zhengfu, Ishin seifu*) was set up in March 1938 in Nanjing headed by Liang Hongzhi.[62]

The puppet régime announced that it would establish a constitutional government, wipe out single-party dictatorship, exterminate the Communists, safeguard East Asia from "red-ification" (*chihua*), consolidate peaceful cooperation between China and Japan, return refugees to their homes, establish peace-preservation organizations (*baoan zuzhi*) to exterminate bandits and "cleanse the villages" (*qingxiang*), stimulate industrial and agricultural production with the help of foreign capital from "friendly countries" (*you bang*), revamp education to combine traditional moral values and international scientific learning, abolish excessive taxes, encourage men of talent to come forward and freely criticize the government, and severely restrict the corrupt tyranny of petty officials and clerks.[63]

Shanghai sympathizers, together with members of the Special Services Department of the Japanese Central China Area Army garrison in Nandao, tepidly celebrated the establishment of the new reform government on March 28, 1938. The puppet Self-Government Committee held one meeting in the Confucian

Temple where, under the old five-bar national flag of the Beiyang warlords, the collaborators bowed to the image of Confucius.[64] Another group, which included several hundred "loafers" (*liumang*) and coolies trucked in from Hongkou, gathered at Great China University to hear a speech by the editor of *Xin shenbao* (the Chinese edition of the Japanese daily *Shanghai godo*), followed by huzzahs of "Long live the new government" in unison with the popping of firecrackers and the blaring of a brass band.[65]

Within a month, on April 28, 1938, the reform government had commissioned a new Supervisory Yamen (*duban gongshu*) to take over the functions of municipal administration formerly wielded by the Dadao puppet régime.[66] Su Xiwen formally recognized the superior legitimacy of the reform government by adopting its flag on May 3, but he continued as head of the Supervisory Yamen until October 15, 1938, when Fu Xiaoan assumed office as mayor of the Shanghai Special Municipality (*Shanghai tebie shi*).[67] Once ousted, Su Xiwen was named puppet mayor of Hankou but actually repaired to Tokyo—perhaps to evade assassination.[68]

FU XIAOAN'S PERFIDY

Fu Xiaoan, director of the Chinese Bank of Commerce (*Shangtong yinhang*) and head of the General Chamber of Commerce, was a bitter enemy of Chiang Kai-shek, who had thrown him in prison in 1927.[69] After serving out his sentence and spending a period of exile in Japanese-controlled Manchuria, Fu returned to Shanghai determined to take revenge upon the generalissimo ("I am worth fifty million dollars, but I will spend every dollar I have to get even with Chiang"). In the eyes of most Shanghainese it was Fu's vindictiveness that led him to run the risk to his reputation and eventually to his life by becoming Shanghai's most nefarious *hanjian*.[70]

The damage to Fu's reputation was immediate. In the press of the time, his was just another "puppet show" manipulated by his Japanese masters.[71] At best, he and the poetaster Liang Hongzhi were compared to literati collaborators of the early Qing, such as Hou Fangyu, who pretended to be "recluses" (*yimin*) but were actually "adherents" (*shunmin*) of the Manchu invaders. One journalist remarked that when a country seems about to be destroyed, one sees spilled blood, broken heads, and "brave heroes" who refuse to submit, knowing that their honor will be recorded later in the pages of history. But one also sees a lot of people losing heart and becoming "treacherous elements." These "traitors" (*hanjian*) and "sellouts" (*guozei*) pass their lives well, perhaps even dedicating poems to the "brave heroes," comforting themselves with the thought that they are "managing the peace," and pretending to make a sacrifice as "unsung heroes" themselves.[72]

To such critics of hypocrisy, Fu Xiaoan himself would answer that he was merely being a "realist" (*xianshizhuyizhe*), working with the conquerors for the sake of the Chinese people. But it was hard to maintain that position when, like so many collaborators with access to food supplies when there was such scarcity, with the power to levy taxes backed up by Japanese troops, and with special economic privileges denied to those whose businesses were being expropriated, Fu Xiaoan clearly flourished by governing as a puppet official.

His "realism," in other words was too self-serving to be plausible. Left-wing columnist Ding San insisted that the true "realism" was the vision of China's warriors struggling to gaze ahead to the clarity of absolute truth, siding with the peoples of the world against aggression and invasion in places like Abyssinia and Czechoslovakia. Fu's "realism," however, was nearsighted and self-interested; it characterized those in China who had elected to join the anti-Communist federation and the movement to compromise for peace. By so doing these "realists" had become "quasi traitors" (*zhunhanjian*) or "traitors" (*hanjian*) to that higher global cause.[73]

POLARIZATION

In France, when divisions sharpened after the November 1942 Allied invasion of North Africa, *collabo* became a general term of opprobrium. Occupied China began during 1938 to witness a similar polarization between the "warriors" of resistance and the "traitors" of collaboration—a polarization that reinforced a spirit of mass national unity by blaming collaboration on a small group of misbegotten traitors.[74] This can be seen, for example, in a lengthy series of letters supposedly written by a young woman, "the daughter of a traitor," to her lover, "a warrior of the resistance."[75]

Lying in bed in the moonlight she repeatedly calls out his name, "Jian," to tell him of her pain and grief.[76] "Even though I am the daughter of a traitor, I am certainly not a traitor myself." Who could have thought that this quiet place would fall into enemy hands? How could she have possibly foreseen that her father would "passively" become the head of the puppet Maintenance Association (*Weichihui*)?[77]

By the time she realized that she was in the lair of the Japanese "demons" (*emo*), it was too late: she had already been seized by the god of misfortune. She had thought of committing suicide, but instead she had coped by pretending to be happy and sympathetic whenever she had to talk with "them." How could they ever possibly know the internal pain she was suffering? In this bitter environment, she secreted her three years with Jian, when they promised each other to be forever like two stars twinkling in the summer sky, never to be extinguished unless the heavens themselves perished. The memory of that love kept her alive, ready to seek an escape. "I don't blame you," she tells Jian, for despising her as a Japanese soldier's mistress. "No one could understand the circumstances I have been in." She constantly thinks of his life as a warrior. When "they" lament guerrilla victories, she secretly exults, happy that "you are one of our awe-inspiring Chinese men." When she hears that "our armies increase in strength," her heart is entirely soothed.[78]

At one time, she thought of running away and joining Jian, but she is watched too closely. And even if she could join the guerrillas, she is not sure that Jian would forgive her. Besides, she can use her position in the enemy's camp to do more effective work than she could as a guerrilla.[79] "You don't believe that?" Does Jian think that "the weak daughter of a *hanjian*" couldn't possibly have the strength to do significant work? The truth is, she already has accomplished something that no one—not even her father—knows about. Because the "demons" *banzhang* (Japanese *hanchō*, squad leader) believed that the deputy Maintenance Association chief was extorting too much from the people, the "demons" had him shot in order to maintain their reputation. But it was really she who "exterminated the traitor with a borrowed knife" (*jie dao chu jian*) by tricking the "demons."[80]

She has to confess that ever since the deputy chief was killed, she has been afraid that his ghost would return, especially on nights like this in the moonlight, which makes her hair stand on end. But then she loses her fear of that "thing" (*dongxi*), because she knows the souls of "our brave warriors" of the resistance are striking down his ghost in the underworld. He is to be abominated, not feared. When you are full of zealous hatred, fear is gone.

Now she has reached a critical phase, which is also her greatest opportunity. She wants to use the last, minute fraction of her life to fulfill this soul-satisfying task.[81] Three times "demons" have wanted to "eat me up," but she survived each time: "If I were a weakling—Jian! Before, I often told you that I was a weakling, that I was an absolutely helpless and absolutely passive weakling. But now I have to deny it. I believe that I'm not only not a weakling, I'm not one of those ordinary, backward women weaklings. Rather I am a strong-willed and determined person, a bold and imposing Chinese person. Don't you see? If I were still a weakling, how could I have been eaten up, invaded, and yet not have committed suicide? But I am still alive today, and I will not be eaten up, I will not be invaded."[82] Her plan is to kill the Japanese squad leader who has ravished her; for "demons always will be demons—they lack the rational ability of civilized human beings."[83]

The metaphor of the ravished or "eaten" woman applied to an invaded China is not, of course, new. Even before Zou Rong's *Revolutionary Army* (*Geming jun*), it appears in variant in the poetry of Wu Weiye and the dramaturgy of Kong Shangren. And it was certainly a common symbol, as numerous scholars have recently pointed out, during the 1930s and '40s. Here, however, it gives form to feelings about the Japanese, who have literally raped their way up the Yangzi River, that spill over onto their collaborators. The Japanese are "demons" who "eat up" Chinese women; they are beings without souls or reason. The *hanjian*, fit to be denounced by their own daughters, are turned into hungry ghosts, "things," who deserve to be slaughtered in life as in death.[84] Indeed, to renounce them and to kill the enemy is to cease being a "backward" weak woman and to become an "imposing" and virile Chinese warrior.[85]

In her last letter to Jian, the "daughter of a *hanjian*" reveals her final plan. The *emo* has asked her to marry him. She consents, telling the Japanese "demon" that "for the sake of his and my reputation, for the sake of my father's face, and in order to demonstrate our local area's peaceful qualities, we should hold a lavish banquet to start off on our joyful life together." All of the Japanese officers are invited to attend the banquet three days thence, and she plans to come to the party herself tarted up like a prostitute to raise her glass in toasts with the *emo* until they are drunk. Then, asking Jian to be prepared to bring his guerrillas in to strike, she plans to pull out the pistol her "demon" has given her and taught her to use, and strike down the Japanese *emo* like the soldier she now is. "Bearing a pure white body and soul, I am prepared to set out on the glorious road back home [*guisu*]." Certain to die, she wants her lover to know that "I may be the daughter of a *hanjian*, Jian, but I am not a perverse and demented [*sangxin bingkuang*] traitor myself!"[86]

The polarization of "heroes" and "traitors" served the United Front well. Candidly admitting that after the retreat from Wuhan in December there were numerous "wavering elements" (*dongyao fenzi*) among the Chinese, the resistance press stressed the importance of "sharing a bitter hatred of the enemy" (*tongchou dikai*)—that is, hatred of both the Japanese occupiers and their *hanjian* puppets— in order to close ranks around a United Front that had brought the Communist Party back into national politics.[87] On January 1, 1939, the Nationalist government in Chongqing issued an announcement "strictly dealing with *hanjian*":

> Since the beginning of all-out war with Japan, there is not a single one of the soldiers and civilians of the entire country who does not share a bitter hatred for the enemy. Taking the nation and the people as the foundation, they steadfastly resist and vow never to waver. Now, there is a small number of perverse and demented [*sangxin bingkuang*] followers who are willing to be used by the enemy invaders and to slavishly serve the foe like a ghost [seeking out victims] for the tiger [*weihu zuochang*] in an utterly loathsome way.[88] The government has already explicitly ordered the Military Affairs Commission to investigate, order the arrest of, and severely punish according to the law those [who] have participated in each area's puppet organizations. Moreover, it has already promulgated regulations regarding the punishment of *hanjian* and clearly designated each of the criminal sanctions for collaborationist acts, issuing orders that they be implemented in order to clean out the traitors. Now, just as the circumstances of the War of Resistance take a turn for the better, the Japanese invaders have one layer of crafty schemes after another. If we don't root out the scoundrels, then how are we going to maintain social order?[89]

The Nationalist government was willing to forgive those former traitors who "washed their hearts" (*xixin*), because it believed in the possibility of self-renewal. But those who continued to be traitors to the people (*minzu pantu*), who continued to act publicly as puppets or to behave clandestinely as *hanjian*, not only risked the wrath of Heaven, but they also faced public elimination by their fellow citizens.[90]

The increasing polarization of Nationalist heroes and puppet traitors was one result of the defection of Wang Jingwei from the Chongqing régime and his launching of a "peace movement" (*heping yundong*) to hold talks with the Japanese.[91] Yet even as his enemies styled him a *hanjian* in increasingly absolutist terms, Wang and his followers—many of them "romantic revolutionaries" in the second and third decades of the century known for their political "wavering" as self-doubting intellectuals—grew ever more conscious of the ambiguousness of their position.[92]

According to Zhou Fohai's diary, on May 13, 1940, Wang Jingwei remarked outside the Japanese military headquarters in Hankou that back in Chongqing people called each other "national heroes" (*minzu yingxiong*), while he was being styled a *hanjian* even though he and his allies thought of themselves as "national heroes" too.[93] The fact of the matter was that whether or not one ended by being a *minzu yingxiong* depended on whether one ended by "saving the country" (*jiuguo*). Wang and his friends believed that the only sure way to "save the country" was to seek a peaceful solution: "If I end up as a national hero, then there will forever be peace between China and Japan. If I end up as a traitor, then we will never be able to resolve the discord between China and Japan."[94]

Later that year, on September 2, Wang said in Beiping: "One group of Chinese wants to kill me. One group of Japanese also wants to kill me. Each has their own evidence [to justify this]. This proves my position correct. The Chinese wanting to kill me proves that I am not advocating a War of Resistance. The Japanese wanting to kill me proves that I am not a traitor [*hanjian*]."[95] According to Zhu Zijia, this same attitude colored the thinking and behavior of Wang Jingwei's entourage. They tried to hold fast to the notion of their being "national heroes," but the environment around them finally convinced them that they might well end up being vilified as "traitors."[96]

Wang's brother-in-law, Chu Minyi, initially believed that there were two aspects to the war against Japan: one was military resistance, which was Chiang Kai-shek's task, and the other was peace negotiations, which was Wang Jingwei's assignment. After all, Chiang himself had said that "resistance was easy, peace was hard." That was why Chu had decided to join the peace movement and "compromise out of consideration for the general interest" (*weiqu qiu quan*): "If I don't descend into hell, then who else will descend into hell?"[97] Li Shengwu, minister of education for Wang, declared during his trial in 1946, "At that time most men of resolve [*zhishi*] said that if Mr. Wang really could protect the nation's position, penetrating deep into the enemy's rear area, pursuing the task of saving the country, it could well be of modest benefit to the War of Resistance."[98]

The ambiguity—and ambivalence—of collaboration was explored twenty years after Pearl Harbor by Zhu Zijia in the preface to the fourth volume of his memoirs on the Nanjing régime. In a complex culturalist response to the stigmatization of *hanjian*, he wrote:

> One other objective in writing this book is to speak to all of the descendants of the Yellow Emperor[99] and let them know that this group of people called *hanjian* are not the demons portrayed in propaganda or in their imaginations. Chen Gongbo said, "It is right to resist, but there is no alternative to peace." Zhou Fohai also said, "The War of Resistance is meant to save the nation. Peace is also meant to save the nation." Consequently, in this entire book I have absolutely never found fault with the

War of Resistance. Nor have I gone so far as to look after my own narrow self and betray my conscience to bare my left shoulder in mourning for the *hanjian.* I want to use the facts to tell all of the descendants of the Yellow Emperor that if a nation has so many *hanjian* selling out their country, then this would be a disgrace never to be washed clean in the history of the Chinese people. Even though you could not possibly have been a *hanjian,* if 10 million *hanjian* appear among the people, then it is still a disgrace to which not a single person can claim exception.[100]

But all of that complex cultural equivocation was wiped away at the time by the direct and simple issue of national betrayal. On January 5, 1939, Li Zongren described Wang Jingwei as someone who "betrayed his party and country" (*beipan dangguo*). Others accused him of selling out his country for personal gain, of becoming the Franco of the Far East, and of being a Japanese "yes-man vermin" (*yingshengchong*).[101] So many Chinese had compromised with the Japanese in north China because they had lacked self-esteem, because they had thought they were an inferior race (*liedeng minzu*), because they had been told they were the "sick man of Asia" (*dongya bingfu*). The Chinese had to cast aside such self-doubt and prove they were humankind's "most excellent race" (*youxiu minzu*) by repudiating the traitors in their midst—even if they were members of one's own family.[102]

The attack on *hanjian* would not only restore self-esteem; it would also corroborate the patriotic identity that Chinese shared under the Occupation. Shanghai newspaper editors declared in December 1938, "Coexisting on an isolated island, we feel all the more that we are Chinese, and that our responsibility to be Chinese citizens is all the heavier. We also feel that, with the exception of shameless *hanjian,* we are all the more cordial and kind to each other."[103] Although "Chinese do not attack Chinese," the people must also understand that the "big traitors" (*da hanjian*) had to be brought to justice.[104]

The editors of *Yibao* wrote in May 1939, "Ever since Wang Jingwei betrayed the country and fled into exile, all of the country's people have come to recognize the face of a *hanjian* in his communicating with the enemy and seeking to surrender, and they have unanimously supported the central [government's] sanctions upon him, as the struggle to oppose Traitor Wang is centrally linked to the struggle against *hanjian.*" That same editorial called upon the central government to purge all Wang Jingwei elements, to punish those who suggested compromise with the enemy, to mobilize forces to attack Wang elements in Shanghai, to make Wang the theoretical center of the attack against *hanjian,* to expose his treacherous activities, and to use the campaign to elevate the morale-building drives then going on in Free China to mobilize support against the Japanese.[105]

By then, the lines were clearly drawn. However sensitive the "peace party" collaborators were to their own ambivalence, word had gone out to one and all that *hanjian* were simply traitors to be read out of the Chinese race. Solidarity and resistance demanded the traitors be eliminated. *Hanjian* did not deserve to be killed only because they were "treacherous merchants" smuggling black market rice and driving up the price for decent Chinese;[106] or because they opened up opium supply bureaus to "poison" (*duhua*) their compatriots;[107] or because they heedlessly "extorted" (*sougua*) higher and higher taxes from the farmers the Japanese permitted them to govern; or because they sold out Chinese economic interests to their masters in Tokyo.[108] They deserved to be killed just because they were *hanjian*, and that was all there was to it.

Beginning in October 1938, the resistance newspaper *Wenxian* began to publish lists of puppet officials and local police chiefs, entitled "Investigation Charts to Root Out Traitors [*chujian*]."[109] In November, the entire roster of Liang Hongzhi's "flocks" (*qunchou*) of puppets at all levels of the reform government was printed, and that was followed by further lists of the "betrayers of the masses" (*qunjian*) in north China, Zhejiang, Anhui, Shanxi, and Jiangsu.[110] By January and February of 1939, the newspaper was publishing the local Shanghai office and residence addresses of reform government officials, including bureau and department chiefs of the Shanghai municipal puppet government.[111] In April, *Wenxian* printed a list of local district chiefs (*qugongshuzhang*), along with their salaries from the puppet régime, for Pudong, Nanshi, Huxi, Zhabei, Baoshan, Chuansha, and Nanhui. And that was followed in turn by lists of addresses of the managing editors of thirty *hanjian* newspapers in the Jiang delta and of the owners of fourteen opium shops (and their revenues, which totaled 225,000 yuan per month) in the Caojiadu badlands.[112] Each of these designations amounted to disgrace at best, death at worst—even to those puppets under the tightest protection and in the highest places.[113]

Shortly before dawn on October 11, 1940, the puppet mayor Fu Xiaoan's cook, Zhu Shengyuan, stole silently by the *hanjian*'s bodyguards to slash the sleeping mayor to death with a butcher's cleaver.[114] Zhu had worked for Fu for twelve years, but he had set aside personal loyalty for a higher cause when he was secretly recruited for the Nationalist secret service by General Dai Li.[115]

TARGETING *HANJIAN*

With the Second United Front agreement reasonably secure, Dai Li's men turned their attention to the Japanese and their collaborators. By 1938, the Military Statistics Bureau, or Juntong, had been formally separated from the civilian secret police and placed under Dai Li's direction. One of its primary missions was to prevent any of Chiang Kai-shek's rivals from opening peace talks with the Japanese and forming a plausible puppet government. The key to this effort was Shanghai, where Nationalist agents could use the safe haven of the concessions to mount terrorist operations against *hanjian*.[116]

The Shanghai station of Juntong was quickly disabled after the Japanese took over the Chinese sectors of the city. However, Dai Li managed to maintain two special operations units through the period of "island Shanghai" (November 1937 to December 1941). Because of Chiang Kai-shek's fury over the "treacherous activities" of collaborators in the city, these two covert action units under Zhao Lijun and

Lin Zhijiang received the government's backing even though their operations threatened to draw the Japanese into seizing the International Settlement with force majeure—a move, by the way, that ultimately might not have disserved Chiang's long-term strategy of drawing America into the war against Japan.[117] These units, and especially Zhao Lijun's squad, were thus responsible for many of the major assassinations of the time, including the deaths of Zhou Fengqi and Zhang Xiaolin.[118] According to one estimate, Dai Li's men carried out over 150 assassinations in Shanghai between August 1937 and October 1941, when even the operations units were penetrated by the puppet secret service at 76 Jessfield Road.[119]

It is important to recognize the special place accorded to assassins in ancient Chinese history, as well as in the rise of revolutionary nationalism during the twentieth century.[120] In the second-century Wu family shrine, celebrated as a quintessential expression of the Confucian culture of Eastern Han, there are engraved thirty-three picture stories exemplifying the virtues of filial sons, wise ministers, eminent wives, virtuous rulers, and so forth, of the past. Six of those thirty-three wall carvings are "stories" of loyal assassin-retainers: Cao Mei seizing Duke Huan of Qi, Zhuan Zhu assassinating King Liao of Wu, Jing Ke's attempt to assassinate the king of Qin, Yao Li's assassination of Prince Qing Ji of Wu, Yu Rang's attempt to kill Xiang Zi of Zhao, and Nie Zheng's assassination of the uncle of the king of Han.[121] Each of these commoners was regarded as a hero because he sacrificed his own life without hesitation to kill his master's enemy out of a divine anger animated by loyalty rather than personal rancor. As Liu Xiang put it in the *Shuo yuan* (A garden of talks), "When Zhuan Zhu assassinated King Liao, [his movement] was like a comet attacking the moon and like a falling star shining in bright daylight. When Yao Li assassinated Prince Qing Ji [his movement] was like a dark eagle striking a tower terrace. When Nie Zheng assassinated the uncle of the king of Han [his movement] was like a white rainbow crossing the sun. These three people were all commoners[,] . . . but when they were still nursing their anger, their power could even terrorize great kings."[122]

The first Chinese revolutionary to attempt political assassination was Shi Jianru, who tried, as a "man of determination" (*zhishi*), to kill the Manchu governor of Guangdong in October 1900.[123] Although Shi had no developed rationale of his own for this suicidal effort, his attempt marked a transition from the personal loyalty of feudal assassins to the political commitment of revolutionary nationalists, mediated by a certain purity of motive dedicated to a just cause. Other Chinese radicals influenced by Japanese anarchism and Russian nihilism began to enunciate a doctrine of sacrificial terrorism beginning in 1902. Yang Dusheng, a Chinese student at Waseda, learned of Russian revolutionary assassination efforts through the work of Kemuyama Sentaro, whose *Modern Anarchism (Kinsei museifushugi)* was translated into Chinese under the title *Freedom's Blood (Ziyou xue)*; and Yang subsequently helped Huang Xing, the Hunanese student leader, to found the first of several assassination corps that culminated in the formation of the Northern Assassination Corps (*beifang wansha tuan*) in 1905.[124]

The Northern Assassination Corps was best known for its member Wu Yue, who tried to annihilate a delegation of five government political reform commissioners at the Beijing Railroad Station in September 1905. Wu Yue blew himself up instead, but he left behind a tract called *Heaven's Vengeance* (*Tian tao*) that was published in April 1907 in the Revolutionary Alliance organ, *Min bao*. The tract called for "assassinationism," quoting the reform movement martyr Tan Sitong; and it cited with admiration the conscripts' revolt led by Chen She against the tyrant of Qin as an example of the inspirational righteousness of the romantic *xia*, or medieval knight.[125]

Early on, then, the figure of the revolutionary assassin was cast with molds that originated in both the new world of international revolutionaries and the traditional realm of self-sacrificing knights-errant and loyal retainers pledged to avenge their masters' lives and honor. Although particular motivations varied from case to case, the assassinations of Enling, governor of Zhejiang, in 1907 by Xu Xiling; of Fuqi and Fenshan in Guangdong in 1911; and of Liang Bi by Peng Jiazhen in January 1912 partook of these two traditions that converged most dramatically on the eve of the Xinhai Revolution in the famed effort by Wang Jingwei to blow up the Manchu regent Zaifeng (Prince Chun).[126]

Political assassination did not cease once the Qing dynasty was overthrown, but—as in the infamous conspiracy of Yuan Shikai to murder Song Jiaoren in 1913—revolutionary pretexts were often absent. Moreover, during this period of political fragmentation, when boundless ambitions flourished, adventurers in the *haohan* (tough guy) tradition were not slow to present themselves as the leaders of armed men, mercenaries to some and loyal followers to others, willing and ready to serve as the "claws and teeth" of competing claimants to power. Dai Li was just such a leader himself, and he was by no means unique.

Personal heroism aside, the special operations of Dai Li's Juntong were facilitated by a large population of veterans and former members of the various citizens' volunteers corps and Special Services Corps that had sprung up during the first few months after the Marco Polo Bridge Incident. We have observed how Sun Yaxing recruited followers and served in the Special Services Corps during the Battle of Shanghai. As a section leader with formal military training and as former head of the Chinese Youth National Salvation Association, he was a leading "warrior" (*zhanshi*) in the urban strife against collaborators after the city fell to the Japanese.

THE SUN YAXING TERRORIST GROUP

When Shanghai fell, Sun Yaxing managed to escape to Hangzhou, where the chairman of the provincial government instructed him to serve as a police officer in Shaoxing county. At the end of February 1938, possibly already under secret service control, he returned to Shanghai "with a view to bring[ing] all the former members of the Third Company of Special Services Corps, who were in Shanghai, to Hankou to further [the] National Salvation Movement in the latter city."[127]

Two of the future members of his assassination team, Jiang Haisheng and Zhao Liang, remembered signing up and leaving for Hong Kong by boat and reaching Hankou by late February 1938.[128]

By then Sun was already waiting for them, having precipitately left Shanghai when he saw a report in one of the newspapers that the leader of the Chinese Youth National Salvation Association—that is, Sun himself—was in the city.[129] Others, including Wang Zhigu, nephew of Wang Shihe, Chiang Kai-shek's chief bodyguard and executioner, joined Sun Yaxing on the spot.[130] The entire group was assigned different tasks. Ten were detailed for "special duty" in Changsha. Thirteen were told on April 25, 1938, that they had been chosen for urban guerrilla work in Shanghai "to suppress traitors."[131] This was the assassination group's one point of contact with General Dai Li, who told its members that they were under the direct orders of Sun Yaxing.[132] Joined by Wang Zhigu, the group was divided into three- or four-man teams, which proceeded via Jiujiang, Nanchang, Jinhua, and Ningbo to Shanghai on May 1–2.[133]

Zhou Shougang, a printer from Chongming, had returned to Shanghai in February 1938, where he was completely dependent on relatives. One day in late June, Zhou bumped into Wang Zhigu and told him he was "practically destitute." Wang said that "he might be able to find [Zhou] work, should [he] care to participate in the assassination of 'traitors.'" Zhou was willing to do so, and he repeated this when Wang Zhigu brought Sun Yaxing to his residence at 13 Rue du Weikwei. On July 3, Sun Yaxing told him to move his residence to 62 Route Vallon, where his job would be to function as Sun's courier.[134]

The same combination of circumstances—unemployment, a need for comrades, patriotism, a hatred of *hanjian*—drew in Chen Kaiguang, a teenager unable to find work since graduating from primary school.[135] Chen was approached by Zhao Liang, who invited him to join the Chinese Youth National Salvation Association. Out of patriotism Chen Kaiguang expressed his "willingness to help in the extermination of traitors." Zhao acknowledged the young man's idealism, but he told him that to prove his ultimate loyalty he would have to perform a special duty on July 7, 1938. Chen agreed to serve.[136]

Chen's duty was to commemorate the anniversary of the Marco Polo Bridge Incident by setting off explosives in public places. The group had already wounded one of the commissioners of the puppet Shanghai Citizens Society, tried to kill racketeer Zhang Xiaolin, murdered two law clerks working for a collaborationist lawyer, and shot a Chinese who had adopted Japanese citizenship. On July 7, the group prepared to discharge a much more indiscriminate attack—as though the crusade against *hanjian* justified any measures whatsoever. Together, the teams launched eighteen grenade attacks, killing two Japanese mill employees and two Chinese, and wounding eight Chinese after tossing a bomb into a floating restaurant along the Shanghai Bund.[137]

During the ensuing uproar, the police rounded up more than a thousand suspects, the Japanese issued formal protests, and British and U.S. diplomats attempted to persuade Chiang Kai-shek to call off his special operations teams. But Chiang insisted that he had no connection with these crimes.[138] Later the Chinese minister of foreign affairs told the American chargé d'affaires, in Chongqing, "Where the victims were 'puppet' Chinese officials, the assassinations were probably perpetrated by persons acting spontaneously from patriotic motives or in revenge for wrongs suffered at the hands of the Japanese.... The Japanese themselves had instigated murders of political opponents, and he [the minister of foreign affairs] did not exclude the possibility of their killing their own partisans as well in order to discredit the Municipal Council."[139] In Shanghai, meanwhile, the International Settlement police managed to wring a confession out of one of Sun Yaxing's accomplices, and thus broke the band up, arresting twenty-four of the young *shimin* (urbanites) who had pledged themselves to eradicate *hanjian*.

TERRORISM CONTINUES

Sun Yaxing's arrest failed to stop the attacks on *hanjian* simply because—as Sun admitted under interrogation—"[there is] more than one assassination group working on a line similar to that adopted by my squad."[140] On February 19, 1939, one of these other groups astonished the public by assassinating the heavily guarded foreign minister of the reform government, Chen Lu, in his own living room in the French Concession.[141] Liu Geqing led a team of Juntong assassins who shot down Chen Lu in front of his family and two guests.[142] As Chen Lu's body fell to the floor, Liu Geqing drew out a scroll and threw it over the traitor's body. It read in large black characters: "Death to the Collaborators. Long Live Generalissimo Chiang Kai-shek!" Another sheet, unrolled across the sofa, read: "Resistance Will Result in Victory. Construction of the Country Will Succeed. Keep China's Property Forever!" Both were signed by the "Chinese Iron and Blood Army."[143]

Ten days later, the "Blood and Soul Traitor Extermination Corps" set off bombs simultaneously outside four Chinese dancing establishments: the Oriental Hotel, Ciro's, the Café and Paradise Ballroom, and the Great Eastern Ballroom. The terrorists left behind "A Warning to Our Dancing Friends" in the form of leaflets that read:

> Dancing friends: some of you can dance the fox-trot, others the waltz. Why don't you go up to the front to kill? Some of you spend lavishly on brandy and whiskey. Why don't you give the money to our troops so that they can buy more munitions to kill the enemy?
>
> Dancing friends: why spend your money for cosmetics when your bodies smell of the odor of a conquered people? The only way to remove that smell is to give your warm blood to the nation. You have been amusing yourselves over the Lunar New Year. Our meager gift tonight—bombs—will help to give you added pleasure.[144]

This mixed animus against the new bourgeoisie and political *hanjian* reflected the Blue Shirts' distaste for Westernized Shanghai. Clearly, the terrorists were enlarging their range of targets to include "semitraitors" and the kind of "indirect assistants" that the Lixingshe propagandists had promised to wipe out in the first place. In other words, class hatred and xenophobia were converging—a nativist and Jacobin phenomenon that emerged most dramatically during the Cultural Revolution a little more than two decades later. As the late Lloyd Eastman once pointed out, in the eyes of Nationalist Blue Shirts and Communist Red Guards alike, Western styles of life rendered the treaty-port bourgeoisie "traitors" (*jian*) to the rural "Chinese" (Han) values of the Volk just as much as their capitalist exploitation of the masses.[145]

In early March 1939 the Shanghai branch of the Nationalist Party formed a People's Mobilization Society "to develop a wide-spread mass movement in Shanghai to carry on military, political, [and] all anti-Japanese and National Salvation work provided they are [*sic*] not contrary to the laws and ordinances of the Government." The society's manifesto read, "We swear [that] hereafter we will not live with the enemy robbers under the same sky, and will demonstrate the strength of the various classes of the people. Not only will the obstinate enemy in the suburbs be caused to shrink and to conceal themselves and to return Chinese territory to us, but also in the foreign concessions we should make known the heroic and unyielding spirit of descendants of our Chinese ancestors.... Some may assume responsibility for detection and secret service work; some may undertake the work of assaulting and killing the traitors."[146] A few days later terrorists tried to kill Zhu Ganting, the head of the puppet tax bureau in Pudong.[147] Though that attempt failed, the Nationalist "heroes" did succeed in their next major attack on a prominent *hanjian:* Xi Shitai, chief secretary (*mishu zhuren*) of the puppet police force in Shanghai.[148]

THE XI SHITAI ASSASSINATION

Xi Shitai, a Japanese-trained physician, practiced medicine in his own Shitai Hospital.[149] After the Nationalists withdrew from Shanghai, Dr. Xi joined the Japanese military press section and became Police Commissioner Lu Ying's principal secretary.[150] Xi Shitai was thus a prime target for assassination by Chongqing agents.[151]

The leader of the three-man assassination squad was a twenty-two-year-old Songjiang native named Yuan Dechang.[152] His two coconspirators were Peng Fulin, a slim twenty-year-old waiter, and a clothing salesman named Zhao Zhixiang.[153]

Zhao Zhixiang, a typical Shanghai *xiao shimin* (petty urbanite), was also twenty-two years old. After an apprenticeship in a French Concession tailor's shop, he had worked for five years as a sales clerk in two other "foreign dress shops." He had earned enough to marry the daughter of a villager back home in Pudong, but at the height of the depression in 1937, Zhao was laid off and had to go back to live with his brother. His wife returned to her mother's home, and they remained apart because Zhao had to live hand-to-mouth while war raged across the river in South Market.[154]

On March 5, 1939, Zhao Zhixiang decided to cross the river to try to find a job once again in the unoccupied International Settlement. After searching in vain, he recalled once meeting Yuan Dechang, a man with Pudong guerrilla connections, who often used to book rooms in the Nanjing Hotel on Shanxi Road.[155] When Zhao Zhixiang approached the Nanjing Hotel telephone operator, Yuan Dechang immediately emerged from a back room.[156]

Yuan Dechang recognized Zhao, and told him to rendezvous on the afternoon of March 14 in front of the Great World amusement center.[157] Zhao Zhixiang duly showed up and was immediately taken by Yuan to a boardinghouse off of Rue Lafayette, where Yuan rented an attic room. That same day, the third member of the team, Peng Fulin, moved in with them. Thereafter the three lived together as "bosom friends." The attic was even large enough for Zhao Zhixiang to bring his wife into the city to stay for a week before going back home to Pudong.[158]

On the afternoon of April 4, 1939, Yuan Dechang sent Zhao Zhixiang out to buy food. Zhao returned to find Yuan and Peng cleaning a couple of pistols. Five days later, the three men moved to the Nanjing Hotel. Yuan and Peng came and went. Returning late on the night of April 10, the two agents told Zhao that the following morning they were going to "assassinate a traitor."[159] Their secret mission was confirmed by a letter signed by one Zhou Jianhua and supposedly sent to Zhao Zhixiang at a Ningbo address.[160] Yuan read the letter aloud to the other two semiliterate men. It spoke about three men carrying out the duties entrusted to them by the "four hundred million citizens" of China, and enjoined them to be "brave, steady, enthusiastic, [and] clever," and to "take exercises to make [their] bodies strong." It urged them to lead their lives "in accordance with the principles of the New Life Movement laid down by General Chiang": piety (as comrades they should love each other), righteousness (as citizens they should be dutiful toward the nation by crushing "the traitors who are . . . betraying their mother country"), integrity (as heroes they should punish corrupt officials and traitors), and conscientiousness (as patriots they should take steps against not only those traitors who "aimed at securing high positions for themselves and obtaining money for their own pockets" but also those who enjoyed themselves "in dancing, gambling, and other amusements"). The letter concluded: "Kill the enemy and annihilate the traitor!"[161]

The next morning, April 11, the three men reassembled at the head of Juyili Alley, Lloyd Road. Yuan Dechang assigned Peng Fulin to take care of the watchman inside the lane.[162] Zhao Zhixiang was to keep an eye out for police patrolmen.[163] None of them knew that the watchman had already invited the beat patrolman inside his guard post for a cup of tea.[164]

At 9:15, Dr. Xi stepped out of his back door and started down the alley. Yuan Dechang waited in the shadows. As the doctor approached, Yuan stepped in front of him and started firing .38-caliber dumdum bullets. Peng Fulin simultaneously rushed toward the guard post. When he saw the police constable at the watchman's side he fired his weapon, striking the policeman in the right arm. The watchman drew his own gun and fired back, hitting Peng in the chest. Peng ran back out the alley, fleeing through the rear door of a tea shop. Behind him the mortally wounded Xi Shitai fell into the arms of family members who helped him back into the house where he died on the living room floor.[165]

Meanwhile, Yuan Dechang and Zhao Zhixiang escaped in separate directions. Zhao Zhixiang made the mistake of returning to the Nanjing Hotel on Shanxi Road, where he stood helplessly by as the badly wounded Peng Fulin stumbled into the hotel lobby supported by a fellow waiter Peng had appealed to for help.[166] Zhao had no choice but to rent three rickshaws and ask to be taken to nearby Paulun (Baolun) Hospital.[167]

When the hospital staff admitted Peng Fulin, they also phoned a gunshot report to Louza Station. By 11 A.M. Shanghai Municipal Police detectives were at Paulun Hospital. Peng Fulin had too deep a chest wound to be interrogated formally, but he did tell the investigators that he had been mysteriously struck by a stray shot along Lloyd Road. Zhao Zhixiang corroborated this fanciful tale at Peng's bedside, and was instantly detained and taken to Louza Road for questioning. Members of the Japanese Military Police attended the interrogation.[168]

While Zhao Zhixiang was being questioned, other Shanghai Municipal Police detectives searched Peng and Zhao's room at 11 Wenxian li, where they found the letter from Zhou Jianhua that incriminated them as members of a Nationalist secret service assassination squad.[169] Confronted with this evidence, Zhao Zhixiang broke down and confessed. At 2:30 that same afternoon the officers took him in handcuffs to Peng Fulin's hospital room, and when Peng—who was in "a very weakened condition"—heard Zhao's confession, he too admitted his complicity. At 3:00 the next morning Peng gave up the struggle and died. For Zhao Zhixiang, a greater ordeal lay ahead.[170]

On April 19, 1939, the Shanghai Municipal Police escorted Zhao Zhixiang across the boundary line at Suzhou Creek and, as a token of their "sincerity," handed Zhao over to the Japanese Military Police. The former tailor's apprentice was never to be seen again.[171]

COLLUSION

There were many more deaths to come—*hanjian* to be exterminated—in 1940 and 1941, but patriotic terrorism and civil resistance ceased in Shanghai after the Japanese attack on Pearl Harbor. The polarized clarity of mutual opposition had by then been blurred by the Nationalist intelligence services' strategy of *quxian jiuguo* ("saving the nation in a devious way"): that is, of both overtly working with the enemy's intelligence services and covertly infiltrating thousands of lower-ranking double agents into the puppet Special Work organization.[172] This policy of entwinement, according to mainland Chinese sources, was secretly adopted by

Chiang Kai-shek and Dai Li sometime between March 30, 1940 (when Wang Jing-wei was formally installed as the leader of a unified puppet government), and before January 1941 (when the New Fourth Army Incident occurred in southern Anhui).[173]

Wang Jingwei's puppet régime was roundly detested.[174]

> Wang Kemin's provisional government and Liang Hongzhi's reform government were the senior generation that had formerly operated under the sign "traitor" [*jian*]. In the occupied zone everyone called them the "former Han traitors" [*qianhan*]. Naturally enough, Wang Jingwei's collaborationist régime was called the "latter Han traitors" [*houhan*]. Many of these treacherous scoundrels verbally acknowledged that they were "latter Han traitors" but quite unabashedly saw no cause for shame. But ever since the "latter Han traitors" took the "former Han traitors' " place as Japanese puppets, the people gnashed their teeth and hated them bitterly. This was because the "former" were actually no match for the "latter" in heinousness, especially since the "latter" had their den of monsters at No. 76 (the puppet secret service organ)—the mere mention of which turned one pale—where people were mowed down like fields of hemp.[175]

But Chiang Kai-shek's secret service units colluded with them nonetheless.

For Chiang Kai-shek had given the same orders to the civilian secret service under Chen Lifu and Xu Enzeng (director of Zhongtong, the Central Statistics Bureau). Xu was in direct and personal communication with Ding Mocun, former Zhongtong agent and now one of the heads of the Special Work Headquarters of the Nanjing régime. Whenever clerks in the Zhongtong Code Section in Nationalist Chongqing received a wireless message from Ding's transmitter, they hand-carried it immediately to Director Xu, who deciphered it for his and Chiang Kai-shek's "eyes only."[176]

Dai Li had an identical arrangement with Zhou Fohai, Nanjing's arch *hanjian* by all Guomindang public accounts. Dai also placed key agents such as Mao Sen (who was captured by the Japanese in occupied Shanghai) in the security services of the Nanjing administration, where their deeds sometimes served Juntong ends, and sometimes served the puppet government—including the arrest, torture, and execution of Chinese patriotic "warriors."[177] Meantime, puppet agents were also infiltrating Juntong on behalf of the Japanese, while Communist spies simultaneously cooperated with the puppets, the Japanese, and the American Office of Strategic Services, just as they also tried to place agents within Military Statistics. As a consequence of this fractured clandestine politics, most of which was totally impenetrable to the public, their ultimate loyalty remained very much in question throughout the war; and despite the extreme polarization between "warriors" and "traitors" there was not quite the same clarity of choice as one could imagine in the case of the French resistance to the Nazis.[178]

For, even though the resistancialist myth was quickly exposed in postwar France, certain fundamental polarities remained. "Whenever any party refers to the Occupation [in France], it invariably touches on the century's central issues:

society or nation, equality or hierarchy, state or individual, morality or efficiency, segregation or integration of alien cultures and ethnicities."[179] In postwar China, such stark binaries were often befogged by compromise and expediency. Mao Sen, for example, was redeemed by Dai Li and went on to become director of the Second Department of the Third Front Army.[180] Even more egregiously, the "four great traitors" (*si da hanjian*) of Guangdong—Guo Weimin, Zhao Guizhang, Xu Tingjie, and Li Fuqun—who together were responsible for so many patriots' deaths, received favorable treatment in the protective custody of General He Yingqin and Dai Li despite the outcries of the Guangdong provincial assembly.[181]

Historians in China have never fully explored the issue of wartime *hanjian*.[182] But when Chinese historians do address the subject, they will have to confront the question of clearness of choice, if only to show how motley people's aims were at the time, and how muddled were the distinctions between friend and foe when the agents of at least three seats of government—the Nationalist party-state in Chongqing, the Reform puppet-state in Nanjing, and the Communist rebel-state in Yan'an—competed among themselves for positional advantage in whatever settlement was likely to fall out after the Japanese were defeated.[183]

CONCLUSION

The postwar settlement further clouded the issue, if only because of the carpetbagging of the Nationalists who took coastal China back from the Japanese. While Chiang Kai-shek assigned the task of *sujian* (eradicating traitors) to Dai Li, and while many leading "traitors" were tried and killed, a number of prominent collaborators were able to buy their way out of *hanjian* status on the spurious grounds of, say, having been secret members of Dai Li's Loyal and Patriotic Army (*Zhongyi jiuguo jun*).[184] Conversely, because of Dai Li's death in an airplane crash in the spring of 1946, those puppets who actually had been in secret communication with Juntong could not call upon General Dai as a witness to their ultimate loyalty when they were tried and sentenced to death for treason.[185]

The truth was that matters were never quite so distinctly drawn as implied by the polarization between "warriors" and "traitors." Many figures, including prominent Communists such as Pan Hannian and Nationalists such as Miao Bin occupied deeply ambiguous positions as they navigated the mined shoals of the wartime period.[186]

Miao, for example, was one of the founders of the Sun Yat-sen Study Society at Whampoa in December 1925. Dismissed on corruption charges as Jiangsu chief of police, he returned to his hometown, Wuxi, married the niece of Rong Zongjing (whose son is now vice president of the People's Republic of China), and became chief manager of the magnate's flour mills. In 1937, Miao Bin joined the puppet régime in Beijing, directed the training unit of Wang Jingwei's Youth League (*Qingnian xunliansuo*), and organized the pro-Japanese New People's Society (*Xinminhui*). In 1940 he became president of Wang Jingwei's Examination Yuan, vice president of the Legislative Yuan, and a vice director of the East Asia League, which promoted the Greater East Asia Co-Prosperity Sphere. According to his later testimony before the Jiangsu Higher Court, however, he had by January 1943 been in contact with Dai Li's intelligence organs, passing funds and information to Nationalist agents in Shanghai; and by August he had, he contended, become a regular working agent or officer (*gongzuo renyuan*) of Juntong. In March 1945, Miao Bin went to Tokyo to hold talks with Premier Koiso Kuniaki, passing himself off as a representative of the Nationalist government. Because he accepted this dubious claim, Koiso was overthrown in April 1945, and Miao returned to China.[187]

After VJ day, Miao Bin was at first not treated as a war crimes prisoner but rather was placed in protective custody. In April 1946, after clamorous public censure, Miao Bin was put on trial before the Jiangsu Higher Court. About to be judged guilty and sentenced, Miao was suddenly spared when a letter reached the court from Juntong, confirming that Miao had indeed become a special agent of the Military Statistics Bureau in August 1943. Yet, shortly after his release by the Higher Court, Miao Bin was just as suddenly taken back into custody, transported to Suzhou, rushed to trial, and executed as a traitor for reasons that will probably never be fully known.[188]

Such political murkiness is certainly not peculiar to the *hanjian* of the War of Resistance. What is specific, in a way that may help us understand what it means to become Chinese, is the paradoxical rigidity and flexibility of the boundary between embracing and renouncing allegiance or loyalty to "Chineseness."

Recognizing the problematical nature of allegiance to the Chinese nation-state after eight years of competing wartime régimes plus the civil war's legacy of divided sovereign entities, we can still roughly distinguish between three different modes of disloyalty: betraying one's primal "natural" identity ("you're a traitor to your race"), betraying one's vocation ("you're a traitor to your calling"), and betraying one's cause ("you're a traitor to your word").

Under the Qing dynasty, elite loyalty was mixed: the dynasty could claim primal allegiance from bannermen and demand vocational loyalty from Confucian officials. There was a degree of personalism, of course: the Qianlong emperor could reward loyal bureaucrats and posthumously punish disloyal ministers. But this discrimination publicly eschewed the issue of primal loyalties. The rise of the Tongmenghui revolutionary movement was about just that, though its ideological solution was insufficient to hold a polity together. In Republican China, a different dissolution formed: the strain between loyalty to one's cause and loyalty to one's identity. This was why Wang Jingwei was in such an excruciating position when he lamented the way in which "popular clamor" killed the "true patriots" of the Ming. "High sounding words are anathema, pride kills victory, modesty averts defeat."[189]

A quisling's lament, Wang's words were only persuasive if one ignored the full implications of what it meant to be a *hanjian* in the mid–twentieth century, a time in Chinese history in which once-universal cultural loyalty retained a central place, along with a particularly contemporary allegiance to folk and race. Identity—the primal meaning—mattered above all. If you "stepped out," you lost your connectedness; but if you came back in, you could, in most cases, reassume it. More than "traitor" to a cause, *hanjian* meant betraying one's ethnocultural identity. The cost of exclusion was intolerably high, but the price of readmission was lower than a punishment based upon dishonor.

In other words, Han-ness could get you back in, and the slate might be wiped clean. During and after the War of Resistance, it was the Chinese Communist Party's ability to take over the issue of identity—that is, adopt the cloak of Chinese ethnocultural centrality—that helped it win the hearts and minds of the people. The collaboration issue was thereby muted (though it emerged again in the spy scares and witch hunts of the Cultural Revolution), because all one had to do to remain within the vast mass of *limin* (black-haired people) was to acknowledge Chinese identity and make amends for past lapses "among ourselves": be it departure for abroad, life under a colonial régime, or service to a government in exile.

If the base meaning of treachery, of being a traitor or *hanjian*, is cultural and ethnic transgression, then political betrayal can be mitigated by primal loyalties, reasserted through cultural and ethnic integration. Outsiders may be put off by thinly veiled hints of this "we-they" division, but members of the Chinese ecumene can take heart in their capacity to let political bygones be bygones. That is why, in the most down-to-earth and current of ways, the authorities in mainland China continue so obdurately to expect, nay demand, eventual reunification with Taiwan. And that is also why Taiwanese exclusiveness—a refusal, in effect, to admit to being "just" Chinese—is viewed by those same mainland authorities as such a baneful threat to the One China that the two major political parties conjure on both sides of the Taiwan Strait.

NOTES

Abbreviations

CWR   *China Weekly Review.*
RDS   Records of the Department of State Relating to the Internal Affairs of
          China, 1930–1939. Government Documents Library, microfilm 31217, U.S.
          National Archives, College Park, Maryland.
RWSSZ   Shanghai shi dang'an guan, comp. *Ri wei Shanghai shi zhengfu* (The Japanese
          puppet government of Shanghai). Shanghai: Dang'an chubanshe, 1986.
SB   *Shen bao.*
SMA   Shanghai Municipal Archives.
SMP   Shanghai Municipal Police (International Settlement) Files. Microfilms from
          the U.S. National Archives.
WX   *Wenxian* (Documents). 8 fasc., 2 suppl. Shanghai: Zhonghua daxue tushu
          youxian gongsi, October 1938 to May 1939.

I owe thanks to members of the "Becoming Chinese Conference," and especially to Prasenjit Duara and Hsü Ying-shih, and to Jonathan Spence, who served as commentator on the paper. I also want to acknowledge the critical help proffered by members of the Center for Chinese Studies Colloquium, including Lowell Dittmer, David Johnson, Lydia Liu, and above all Wen-hsin Yeh, whose remarks as discussant of the paper helped me to explore several dimensions neglected in the original essay. Research on this paper was conducted with the help of the Center for Chinese Studies, the Committee on Research of the University of California, and the Walter and Elise Haas Chair Endowment for Asian Studies. Research assistance was provided by Elinor Levine, Jen Ling Liu, and Douglas Stiffler.

1. Luo Zhufeng, ed., *Hanyu da cidian* [The comprehensive Chinese dictionary], vol. 6 (Hong Kong: Sanlian shudian, 1990), 49. The verbally less flamboyant *Zhongwen da cidian* [The encyclopedic dictionary of the Chinese language] (Taibei: Zhongguo wenhua xueyuan chuban bu, 1967) compiled on Taiwan, whose editor in chief is Zhang Qiyun, defines it as a "term for someone who willingly harms his own country for the benefit of a foreigner" (20:79).

2. Zhang, *Zhongwen da cidian*, 9:143; Luo, *Hanyu da cidian*, 4:349.

3. Other related compounds include *jianren* (artful villain), *jianqiao* (double-faced, deceptive), *jianxi* (spy), *jianmou* (treacherous plot; to plot against), and *zuojian* (to act the spy). Like *hanjian*, the term *jianxi* (with the first form of the character) was first employed widely in the Song dynasty (though the usage can be found in the *Jiu Tang shu*) to mean a spy employed by the barbarian Jin dynasty. Zhang, *Zhongwen da cidian*, 9:145.

4. Luo, *Hanyu da cidian*, 4:268–69. Pronounced *gan*, it was used in *Zuo zhuan* as a verb for usurping a king's throne. See also Zhang, *Zhongwen da cidian*, 9:53.

5. Luo, *Hanyu da cidian*, 6:49.

6. The ethnic component can be shifted. On Taiwan, one hears the term *taijian* applied to Taiwanese who do not favor independence.

7. Pamela Kyle Crossley, "An Introduction to the Qing Foundation Myth," *Late Imperial China* 6, no. 1 (December 1985): 3–24; "Manzhou yuanliu kao and Formalization of the Manchu Heritage," *Journal of Asian Studies* 46, no. 4 (November 1987): 761–90; and *Orphan Warriors: Three Manchu Generations and the End of the Qing World* (Princeton: Princeton University Press, 1990); Joseph Richmond Levenson, *Confucian China and Its Modern Fate: A Trilogy* (Berkeley and Los Angeles: University of California Press, 1968); Frederic Wakeman Jr., *The Great Enterprise: The Manchu Reconstruction of Imperial Order in Seventeenth-Century China*, 2 vols. (Berkeley and Los Angeles: University of California Press, 1985), all passim.

8. In the early fifteenth century, during the Ming, "the battle line [along the southwestern frontier] was drawn not only between barbarians and civilians (*min*), but also between collaborators and other law-abiding residents." Leo K. Shin, "Contracting Chieftaincy: Political Tribalization of the Southwest in Ming China" (paper presented at the Center for Chinese Studies Annual Symposium, "Empire, Nation, and Region: The Chinese World Order Reconsidered," Berkeley, California, March 3–4, 1995), 37.

9. Usually intermarrying with the Miao, *hanjian* acted as intermediaries in Miao contacts with Han officials and merchants. *Jianmin* (treacherous people), however, were the staff members, sergeants, and runners who served as advisors to the hereditary chieftains along the frontier. Donald Sutton, "Sinicizing and Signifying in the Eighteenth Century: Ordering the World of the Ethnic Frontier" (paper presented at the Center for Chinese Studies Annual Symposium, "Empire, Nation, and Region: The Chinese World Order Reconsidered," Berkeley, California, March 3–4, 1995; long version of the paper March 2, 1995, p. 12).

10. Donald Sutton, "Sinicizing and Signifying in the Eighteenth Century: Ordering the World of the Ethnic Frontier" (paper presented at the Center for Chinese Studies Annual Symposium, "Empire, Nation, and Region: The Chinese World Order Reconsidered," Berkeley, California, March 3–4, 1995; short version of the paper March 2, 1995, p. 19). The most interesting aspect of this progression was the latitude afforded to ascriptive officials to deem transgressors as being traitors to the Han.

11. Arthur Waley, *The Opium War through Chinese Eyes* (London: Allen and Unwin, 1958); Frederic Wakeman Jr., *Strangers at the Gate: Social Disorder in South China, 1839–1861* (Berkeley and Los Angeles: University of California Press, 1966).

12. Paul A. Cohen, *China and Christianity: The Missionary Movement and the Growth of Chinese Antiforeignism, 1860–1870* (Cambridge: Harvard University Press, 1963); Mark Elvin, "Tales of *Shen* and *Xin*: Body-Person and Heart-Mind in China during the Last One Hundred and Fifty Years," in *Zone: Fragments for a History of the Human Body*, ed. Michel Feher, with Ramona Naddaff, pt. 2 (New York: Zone, 1989), 267–349; Frank Dikötter, *The Discourse of Race in Modern China* (Stanford: Stanford University Press, 1992); Wakeman, *Strangers at the Gate*, all passim. There was, to be sure, a "functional" side to this linkage between native treachery and foreign collusion. William C. Kirby has noted, "Efforts to control the internal effects of foreign penetration could take the form of castigating Chinese with foreign connections as traitors." Kirby, "Intercultural Connections and Chinese Development: External and Internal Spheres of Modern China's Foreign Relations," in *China's Quest for Modernization: A Historical Perspective*, ed. Frederic Wakeman Jr. and Wang Xi (Berkeley: Institute of East Asian Studies, University of California, 1997), 208–33, citation on 215.

13. In vernacular Chinese, *han* also means "man" and is gendered masculine, as in *laohan* (old man), *hanzi* (he-man, brave fellow), *dahan* (big man), and *haohan* (brave man).

14. Cohen, *China and Christianity*.

15. *SB*, 24 December 1938, p. 2:6.

16. Zhongyang zuzhi bu, tewuzu, diaocha ke, ed., "Zhou Enlai cansha Gu Shunzhang jiashu ji yiji fenzi sanshi yu ren maicang Shanghai zujie quyu zhi faxian" [Zhou Enlai's slaughter of Gu Shunzhang's dependents and the discovery of more than thirty deviate elements buried in the Shanghai concession region], Bureau of Investigation Archives document D112(276/7435B/19933), pp. 10 and 336–37; Li Tianmin, *Zhou Enlai pingzhuan* [A critical biography of Zhou Enlai] (Hong Kong: Youlian yanjiusuo, 1975), 104; Li Zhaochun, "Shenfen fuza de Pan Hannian" [The complicated identities of Pan Hannian], *Gongdang wenti yanjiu* 9, no. 3 (n.d.): 114–18, citation on 115; Roger Faligot and Remi Kauffer, *Kang Sheng et les services secrets chinois (1927–1987)* (Paris: Robert Laffont, 1987), 105; SMP, D-9319, 1939, pp. 2–3; Shen Zui, *Juntong neimu* [The inside story of the Military Statistics (Bureau)] (Beijing: Wenshi ziliao chubanshe, 1984), 64.

17. Shen Zui, *Juntong neimu*, 92.

18. Ibid., 63–64; Concession Française de Changhai, Direction des Services de Police, Service Politique, Document No. 237/S. *Étude—le mouvement communiste en Chine, 1920–1933*, Shanghai, December 15, 1933, pp. 40–41.

19. Deng Yuanzhong, *Sanminzhuyi Lixingshe shi* [A history of the Sanminzhuyi Lixingshe] (Taibei: Sixian chubanshe, 1984), 110.

20. Xu Youwei, "Lixingshe yu Riben (1932–1938 nian)" [The Vigorous Revival Society and Japan, 1932–1938] (paper presented at the Thirteenth International Association of Historians of Asia Conference, Sophia University, Tokyo, September 5–9, 1994), 5; T'ien-

wei Wu, "Contending Political Forces during the War of Resistance," in *China's Bitter Victory: The War with Japan 1937–1945*, ed. James C. Hsiung and Steven I. Levine (Armonk, N.Y.: M. E. Sharpe, 1992), 51–78, citation on 55–56; Taiheiyō sensō gen'in kenkyū-bu, eds., *Taiheiyō sensō e no michi* [The road to the Pacific war], 8 vols. (Tokyo: Nihon kokusai seiji gakkai, 1962–63), citation in 3:250; Frederic Wakeman Jr., "Confucian Fascism" (paper given at the Modern China Seminar, Columbia University, April 1989); and Maria Hsia Chang, *The Chinese Blue Shirt Society: Fascism and Developmental Nationalism* (Berkeley: Institute of East Asian Studies, University of California, 1985), passim.

21. Xu Youwei, "Lixingshe yu Riben," 5. This is the author's synopsis and condensations of a half dozen Lixingshe tracts.

22. Shanghai Municipality Public Security Bureau, *Shanghai shi gong'anju yewu baogao* [Shanghai Municipality Public Security Bureau report of affairs], vol. 5 (Shanghai: Shanghai Municipality Public Security Bureau, July 1931–June 1932), 54, 84–85, 214.

23. Article translated from *Xin wan bao* (April 5, 1932), in SMP, D-3445, 5/4/32. See also Tan Shaoliang's April 5 report in the same file.

24. Then, and later in 1937, hundreds of Koreans and Taiwanese came to work for the Japanese special services units in Shanghai. More than a thousand Koreans were settled in surrounding farmlands. Again, the linkage between *hanjian* and the alien was reinforced.

25. Tan Shaoliang's report, "Citizen's Maintenance Association," SMP, D3445, 5/4/32, pp. 4–5; and D. S. Golder to Special Branch, SMP, D-3445, 7/4/32; Emily Honig, "The Politics of Prejudice: Subei People in Republican-Era Shanghai," *Modern China* 15, no. 3 (July 1989): 243–274; Emily Honig, "Creating Ethnicity: Subei People in Shanghai," *Modern China* 15, no. 3 (July 1989): 26; Emily Honig, "Migrant Culture in Shanghai: In Search of a Subei Identity" (n.p., n.d.), p. 10.

26. Article translated from *Xin wan bao* in SMP, D-3445, 27/4/32.

27. Feng denounced Chiang Kai-shek's government for failing to resist the Japanese. Howard L. Boorman, *Biographical Dictionary of Republican China*, vol. 2 (New York: Columbia University Press, 1967–1971, 1979), 42.

28. Deng Yuanzhong, *Sanminzhuyi Lixingshe shi*, 110. Chiang actually declared domestic pacification the priority in a speech on July 23, 1931, after the Guangdong-Guangxi clique denounced Party Center. Ibid., 126–27.

29. Parks M. Coble, "Super-Patriots and Secret Agents: The Blue Shirts and Japanese Secret Services in North China" (paper presented at the Center for Chinese Studies Regional Seminar, Berkeley, 21 March 1987), 18.

30. Zhang Weihan, "Dai Li yu 'Juntong ju,'" [Dai Li and the Military Statistics Bureau], in *Zhejiang wenshi ziliao xuanji*, ed. Wenshi ziliao yanjiu weiyuanhui, fasc. 23, *Neibu* publication (Zhejiang: Renmin chubanshe, 1982), 137.

31. Gan Guoxun, "Guanyu suowei 'Fuxingshe' de zhenqing shikuang" [The true conditions and actual circumstances of the so-called Fuxingshe], *Zhuanji wenxue, xia*, 35, no. 5 (November 1979): 83.

32. Haruke Keiin [Yasutane], *Shanghai tero kōsaku 76 gō* [Working it out in Shanghai's Number 76] (Tokyo: Mainichi shimbun sha, 1980), 33–35; Parks M. Coble, *Facing Japan: Chinese Politics and Japanese Imperialism, 1931–1937* (Cambridge: Council on East Asian Studies, Harvard University, 1991), 228. According to Thomas Chao, a State Department informant, the Blue Shirts had gained control of "municipal and provincial police organizations in the capital and in important places throughout the country.... They practically dominate the armed forces of the government." "Blueshirts Organization," report from

Nelson Trusler Johnson, Nanking Legation, to secretary of state, May 8, 1937, in *RDS*, no. 00/14121, 10 June 1937, pp. 3–4. *Shanghai Nichinichi* reported that the Blue Shirts' twelve thousand members were mostly young officers. "'Blue Shirts' to Suspend Anti-Japan Activities," *Shanghai Times*, January 21, 1936, p. 1.

33. The *shangtuan* was formed in February 1937.

34. "Shanghai Special Service Corps Arrest," report by Detective Sergeant Pitt, in SMP, D-8039a, 25/10/37, p. 1.

35. "Deposition of Sung Yah Shing," in SMP, D-8635, 24/7/38, p. 7. The deputy chief was Liang Tongfang.

36. Wang, born outside Ningbo, was the son of a captain in the Republican Army. After primary school in his village, he attended Nanjing Middle School for three years. Then, through an uncle's introduction, he was apprenticed to a machine factory in Pudong, where he had lived and worked until the Marco Polo Bridge Incident. He went to the Guandi Temple in response to the newspaper notice, and was posted to Sun Yaxing's section. "Deposition of Wong Tz Koo," in SMP, D-8635, 27/7/38, p. 1. Jiang, born in Nanjing, was the son of a Jinjiang shop assistant. He attended primary school in Jinjiang and then boarded at Shanghai Middle School (Nandao) where he studied Chinese literature from March 1936 to June 1937. The day he left school to move in with a friend of his father, he bought a copy of *Central Daily News* and saw the advertisement. He enrolled in the association without telling his mother. SMP, D-8597, 22/7/38, pp. 1–2. Zhou, a native of Chongming, where he received an elementary education, came to Shanghai by himself at the age of fourteen (fifteen *sui*) to serve an apprenticeship at a printing press in the French Concession. He worked in four different printing shops before becoming a printer at the *Zhongguo dabao* (China herald). "Deposition of Tsou Sue Kong," in SMP, D-8635, 26/7/38, p. 1.

37. *CWR*, 19 February 1938, p. 321.

38. "Deposition of Sung Yah Shing," 8–9; SMP, D-8597, 2–3; "Deposition of Wong Tz Koo," 1–2; "Deposition of Tsou Sue Kong," 2.

39. Wang Fangnan, "Wo zai Juntong shisinian de qinli he jianwen" [What I experienced and learned about during my fourteen years in the MSB], in Chinese People's Political Consultative Conference Editorial Committee, ed., *Wenshi ziliao xuanji* [Selections of historical materials], fasc. 107 (*zong*) (Beijing: Zhongguo wenshi chubanshe, 1987), 144–45; Xu Zhucheng, *Du Yuesheng zhengzhuan* [A straightforward biography of Du Yuesheng] (Hangzhou: Zhejiang sheng xinhua shudian, 1982), 95; Zhu Zuotong and Mei Yi, eds., *Shanghai yi ri* [One day in Shanghai], vol. 1 (Shanghai: Huamei chuban gongsi, 1938), 133–36.

40. "Emergency Period Service Group Report," SMP, D-8039a, 23/9/37, pp. 1–2; SMP, D-8039A, 10/9/37, p. 1, and D-8615, 22/9/39, p. 1; Xu Zhucheng, *Du Yuesheng zhengzhuan*, 100.

41. Fu Duoma, twenty-seven years old and a native of Dinghai, joined the Special Action Corps on August 20, 1937—the very day the Public Security Bureau requested help from the Shanghai Municipal Police in arresting Chinese "traitors" believed to have poisoned public tea urns (a belief that aroused mobs on August 17 to beat several suspects to death). After hostilities had broken out on August 13, Fu Duoma had moved into the closed-down Xinguang Primary School (of which he was the former principal) at Changxingli in Zhabei. Fu was arrested by the police on September 16, 1937. SMP, D-8039A, 22/8/37, 26/8/37, and 10/9/37, passim. "[After the August 1937 bombings] patriotism in its most drastic guise ran through the city like fire in the form of 'traitor hunts'; any poor wretch

who loitered about for no more nefarious reason that he had nowhere to go was liable to be trampled or beaten to death. For several days tea vendors were in peril because there was a wild rumor that traitors were poisoning the tea." Vanya Oakes, *White Man's Folly* (Boston: Houghton Mifflin, 1943), 174.

42. "Deposition of Sung Yah Shing," 3–4; Emily Hahn, *China to Me: A Partial Autobiography* (Philadelphia: Blakiston, 1944), 54–55.

43. Zhang Weihan, "Dai Li yu 'Juntong ju,'" 100–101; Shen Zui, "Wo suo zhidao de Dai Li" [The Dai Li I knew], in Shen Zui and Wen Qiang, *Dai Li qi ren* [Dai Li the man] (Beijing: Wenshi ziliao chubanshe, 1980), 21–22; "Special Service Corps Arrest," 3; Xu Zhucheng, *Du Yuesheng zhengzhuan*, 99; Haruke Keiin, *Shanghai tero kōsaku 76 gō*, 48–50.

44. Zhang Weihan, "Dai Li yu 'Juntong ju,'" 100–101.

45. SMP, D-8039a, 10/9/37.

46. "Deposition of Wong Tz Koo," 1–2; "Deposition of Tsou Sue Kong," 1–2; "Deposition of Sung Yah Shing," 9–10.

47. Xu Zhucheng, *Du Yuesheng zhengzhuan*, 100.

48. Ibid., 100–101.

49. Edgar Snow, *The Battle for Asia* (Cleveland: World Publishing, 1942), 52. See also Zhu Zuotong and Mei Yi, *Shanghai yi ri*, 1:101–11.

50. "Woosung-Shanghai Special Chinese Corps Leaves Shanghai," *Da mei wanbao*, 1 February 1938. Translated in SMP, D-8039A, 4/2/38, pp. 6.

51. *RWSSZ*, 1–2 (see also the first illustration in the frontispiece, a photographic copy of the founding announcement); Lynn White, "Non-governmentalism in the Historical Development of Modern Shanghai," in *Urban Development in Modern China*, ed. Laurence J. C. Ma and Edward W. Hanten (Boulder, Colo.: Westview Press, 1981), 48.

52. Su Xiwen, forty-seven years old, was originally from Amoy and had been head of the Fujian Finance Bureau. *RWSSZ*, 13. Note, however, that Boyle and Zhu Zijia identify him as being brought over to Shanghai from Taiwan by the Japanese army. John Hunter Boyle, *China and Japan at War, 1937–1945: The Politics of Collaboration* (Stanford: Stanford University Press, 1972), 112; Zhu Zijia [Jin Xiongbai], *Wang Zhengquan de kaichang yu shouchang* [The beginning and end of the drama of the Wang régime], vol. 4 (Hong Kong: Chunqiu zazhi she, 1961), 32; Robert Barnett, *Economic Shanghai: Hostage to Politics, 1937–1941* (New York: International Secretariat, Institute of Pacific Relations, 1941), 19.

53. This was also the symbol on the flag of the Xinminhui (New People's Society), which trained cadres and promoted the "kingly way" (*ōdō* or *wangdao*) of Confucianism on behalf of the provisional government in north China. The Xinminhui was patterned after the Manchurian Xiehehui (Concordia Society), used by General Kita Seiichi (the foremost "puppeteer" in north China) as part of the *baojia* of the North China Area Army's special services units and the system of local control by the Peace Preservation Committees. The Xinminhui's president, Miao Bin, also emphasized Buddhism as the common heritage of China and Japan. Boyle, *China and Japan at War*, 85, 91–94; George Edward Taylor, *The Struggle for North China* (New York: International Secretariat, Institute of Pacific Relations, 1940), 72–74. As Prasenjit Duara shows, some of these "modern redemptive societies" dated back to the second decade of the twentieth century and drew upon gentry syncretism. Others, such as the Yellow Way Society (*Huangdaohui*), enrolled former gangsters and engaged in assassinations and bombings on behalf of the Japanese. Prasenjit Duara, "Of Authenticity and Woman: Personal Narratives of Middle-Class Women in Modern China" (paper prepared for the conference "Becoming Chinese: Passages to Modernity

and Beyond, 1900–1950," University of California at Berkeley, June 2–4, 1995) 2–3; *WX*, fasc. 1 (10 October 1938): D45.

54. SMA, Wang 1.1.10—Dadao file, cover sheet dated in both lunar and solar (24 February 1938) figures—"Jingchaju xiang zhangze" [Rules and regulations of the Police Bureau], pp. 2, 5–7. Cleaning up bodies and debris after the Japanese invasion was how the puppet régime of "traitors" (*hanjian*) commenced as well in 1932 in Shanghai. Zhu Zijia, *Wang Zhengquan de kaichang yu shouchang*, 4:32; Frederic Wakeman Jr., *Policing Shanghai, 1927–1937* (Berkeley and Los Angeles: University of California Press, 1995), 197. See also *RDS*, 893.00 P.R. Shanghai/117 June 1938, p. 15. Photographs of the flag are to be found in the frontispiece photographs in *RWSSZ*, and in *CWR*, 8 January 1938, p. 152. To justify its rule, the puppet government accused both the GMD and Chinese Communist Party of spreading civil war across the country and promised to restore peace and tranquillity. *RWSSZ*, 6.

55. SMA, Wang 1.1.10, pp. 5, 9b, 18, 24a. The head of the public health section was Fan Jimin, thirty-six *sui*, who had a degree in medicine from the Zhejiang Specialized Medical School (*yiyao zhuanmen xuexiao*). He had been head of the Songjiang county hospital. SMA, Wang 1.1.58—Dadao file (April 1938)—"Guanyu jingju neiwai yuanjing" [Long-term perspectives for the police], pp. 2b. The chief advisor for the detective squad was Li Jinbiao, a gangster who had been a detective in the Song-Hu police department (*Song-Hu jingcha ting*). Li was later assassinated by Nationalist agents on October 28, 1939. *SB*, 29 October 1939, p. 9. For an organizational chart of the Dadao government, see *RWSSZ* 3–5.

56. *RWSSZ*, 12.

57. Ibid.

58. SMA, Wang 1.1.58—Dadao file—"Guanyu jingju neiwai yuanjing," pp. 19. There is a complete roster of the Dadao police bureau for March 1938 in SMA, Wang 1.1.226—Dadao file—"Jingchaju sanyuefen qingce" [Police roster in March]. The inspectorate (including Chief Inspector Liu Wanqing and Chief Investigator Xu Wenbing) is listed in SMA, Wang 1.1.34—Dadao file—"Jingchaju weiren ji renmian" [Police department appointments and dismissals], pp. 66a; and other important positions (Hu Zhenggu, head of the Detective Brigade, and his deputy, Huo Liangchen) are noted in SMA, Wang 1.1.29—Dadao file—"Jingchaju cunren" [Police department personnel assignments], pp. 2b–3b. When people heard the term "Dadao Municipal Government" (*Dadao shi zhengfu*), they invariably smiled, because *dao4* (way) was a homophone for the character *dao4* (robber), making the phrase mean "the Municipal Government of the Big Robbers." Zhu Zijia, *Wang Zhengquan de kaichang yu shouchang*, 4:32.

59. For lists of these municipal officials, along with records of their turpitudes, see *WX*, vol. 2 (10 November 1938): E42–E44.

60. Wang Zihui later served as minister of industry (*shiye buzhang*) in the reform government. Qin Xiaoyi, *Zhonghua minguo zhongyao shiliao chubian—Dui Ri zhanzheng shiqi* [Initial compilation of important historical documents of the Republic of China—The period of the war with Japan], *Di liu bian: Kuilei zuzhi* [pt. 6: Puppet organizations] (Taibei: Zhongguo Guomindang dangshi weiyuanhui, 1981), 139.

61. Cao Zhenwei, "Liang Hongzhi," in *Wang wei shi hanjian* [Ten Wang puppet traitors], ed. Huang Meizhen (Shanghai: Shanghai renmin chubanshe, 1986), 406–7; Zhu Zijia, *Wang Zhengquan de kaichang yu shouchang*, 5:108–9. For an intimate and artfully written portrait of Liang, see Zhu Zijia, *Wang Zhengquan de kaichang yu shouchang*, 4:36–37. Liang Hongzhi was born in Changle (Fujian) in 1881. His grandfather, the eminent scholar Liang Zhangju (*jin-*

shi, 1802), served as governor of Guangxi during the Opium War and helped defend Canton against the British. Liang Hongzhi got his own *juren* degree in 1903, but when he went to the capital for the metropolitan exams, they were abolished. He entered the *jingshi daxue tang* (Imperial University) instead. During the second decade of the twentieth century, he was a leading member of the Anfu clique. When the Anfu clique was overthrown in August 1920, Liang sought refuge in the Japanese legation. He returned to the government in 1924 when Duan Qirui resumed power. In 1925, the Duan régime fell, and Liang spent the next ten years in Tianjin, Shanghai, and Dalian. Zhu Zijia, *Wang Zhengquan de kaichang yu shouchang*, 6:108; Hummel, *Eminent Chinese of the Ch'ing Period (1644–1912)*, vol. 1 (Washington, D.C.: United States Government Printing Office, 1943), 499.

62. "Weixin zhengfu zuzhi xitong ji zhongyao zhiyuan biao" [Table of organization and important personnel of the reform government], in *Zhonghua minguo weixin zhengfu zhenggang* [Political program of the Chinese National Reform Government] (Nanjing: Zhonghua lianhe Tongxun she, 10 September 1939), attachment to p. 311; Qin Xiaoyi, *Zhonghua minguo zhongyao shiliao chubian*, 127–28, 132–38; Nashimoto Yūhei, *Chūgoku no naka no Nihonjin* [The Japanese in China], vol. 2 (Tokyo: Heibonsha, 1958), 65–74; Liu Qikui, "Wang Kemin," in *Wang wei shi hanjian* [Ten Wang puppet traitors], ed. Huang Meizhen (Shanghai: Shanghai renmin chubanshe, 1986), 342–43; Israel Epstein, *The Unfinished Revolution in China* (Boston: Little, Brown and Company, 1947), 315; T. K. Koo, "Some Economic Documents Relating to the Genesis of the Japanese-Sponsored Régime in North China," *Far Eastern Quarterly* 6, no. 1 (November 1946): 66; Boyle, *China and Japan at War*, 88–89 and 110–11; F. C. Jones, *Japan's New Order in East Asia: Its Rise and Fall, 1937–45* (London: Oxford University Press, 1954), 72; Imai Takeo, *Shina jihen no kaisō* [Reminiscences of the China Incident] (Tokyo: Misuzu shobo, 1964), 282–83. Wang Kemin's government, it was said, was composed of "tired retired old scoundrels, forgotten petty warlords, people who have been smoking opium for the past ten years." Emily Hahn, *The Soong Sisters* (New York: Doubleday, Doran, and Company, 1941), 306.

63. *Zhonghua minguo weixin zhengfu zhenggang*, 1. See also Qin Xiaoyi, *Zhonghua minguo zhongyao shiliao chubian*, 140–41. For the "cleansing of villages" policy, see Qin Xiaoyi, *Zhonghua minguo zhongyao shiliao chubian*, 142–43; Huang Meizhen, ed., *Wei ting yin ying lu—Dui Wang wei zhengquan de huiyi jishi* [Chronicles of the secret shadows of the puppet court—records of the memoirs of the puppet Wang régime] (Beijing: Zhongguo wenshi chubanshe, 1991), 52–53.

64. Zhu Zijia, *Wang Zhengquan de kaichang yu shouchang*, 4:33. The reform government initially operated out of the New Asia Hotel in Hongkou because the Japanese army had commandeered most important government buildings in Nanjing. Boyle, *China and Japan at War*, 112.

65. SMP, D-8155D, 30/3/38, p. 1. "The real masters," Franz Michael has pointed out, "are the Japanese Special Service Bureau and the Military Police." Michael, "The Significance of Puppet Governments," *Pacific Affairs Pro* 4 (December 1939): 400–412.

66. *RWSSZ*, 18–20. For the regulations governing the relationship between the Nanjing central government and the Shanghai Special Municipality (*Shanghai tebie shi*), see *Zhonghua minguo weixin zhengfu zhenggang*, 79–80; and *RWSSZ*, 18–19. The Supervisory Yamen was not even powerful enough to find office quarters in Shanghai. In October 1938 its representatives were still hunting, having discovered that "the most suitable accommodations [had] already been preempted by the Japanese authorities." *RDS*, 893.00 P.R. Shanghai/121, October 1938, p. 15.

67. *RWSSZ,* 31, 38. For the organization of the Shanghai Special Municipality government, see ibid., 43–45; and *SB,* 15 October 1938, p. 10.

68. *Shanghai Evening Post and Mercury,* 25 November 1938, p. 1, in SMP, D-8870, 25/11/38. Su Xiwen led a delegation of ten puppet officials, accompanied by ten Japanese military and special services officers, to Tokyo. *WX,* vol. 3 (10 December 1938): F40.

69. Fu's original name was Zongyao. He was from Zhenhai (Zhejiang), and had been a client of the warlord Sun Chuanfang. He was also head of the board of directors of the Shanghai French Commercial Tramway Company (*Shanghai Fashang dianche gongsi*). Zhang Weihan, "Dai Li yu 'Juntong ju,' " 138.

70. Percy Finch, *Shanghai and Beyond* (New York: Charles Scribner's Sons, 1953), 312.

71. See, for an example of this puppet master imagery, "Wan kuilei ju kaimu" [Puppet show opens in Anhui], describing the Japanese ensconcement of a puppet government in Anhui on October 28, 1938. *SB,* 4 November 1938, p. 2b. When the resistance press reported that such-and-such a puppet had "taken power," the term invariably used was *dengchang* (coming on stage). See, for example, *WX,* vol. 6 (10 March 1939): D80.

72. Wen Jingdao, "Saochu yimin qi" [Sweeping out the energy of the recluses], *SB,* 12 October, 1938, p. 4:16. Elsewhere in this volume, Pickowicz points out that most collaborators were presented as being "foreign" in terms of their dress and behavior. They participated in "an alien, capitalist culture of merchants" that denied people "their essential Chineseness."

73. Ding San, "Xianshizhuyizhe" [Realists], *SB,* 19 November 1938, p. 4:16.

74. Stanley Hoffman's foreword to Henry Rousso's *The Vichy Syndrome* is relevant in this regard. "What [Rousso] shows, explicitly and vividly, is how the French chose to believe that Vichy had been the creation of a small group of rather wicked (but still more misguided than evil) men, that the crimes committed were crimes of the Germans and of very small bands of collaborationists, and that most of the population had resisted the Occupation in some degree." Stanley Hoffmann, foreword to *The Vichy Syndrome: History and Memory in France since 1944,* by Henry Rousso, trans. Arthur Goldhammer (Cambridge: Harvard University Press, 1991), viii.

75. The letters appeared a little more than a month after the United Front journal *Wenxian* reported that Wang Zuntong and her sisters had failed to keep their father, Wang Kemin, from serving as the head of the Beiping puppet régime. Subsequently, Zuntong had fled from the side of "this *hanjian,*" abandoning the "spiritual prison" of her father's household to seek refuge in Hong Kong, where she planned to devote her energies to the nation and the people. *WX,* vol. 1 (10 October 1938): D69. Wartime propaganda repeatedly adjured wives and daughters to keep their menfolk from becoming collaborators: "Not only do we personally swear not to be *hanjian,* we also want to exhort our parents and brothers, our husbands and sons, our relatives and our friends not to do work that is harmful to our progeny and our people. We want to do [whatever is needed to make sure that] all around us there is not a single trace of *hanjian.*" *Funü wenxian* supplement to *WX,* vol. 7 (April 1939): 3.

76. *Jian* means "hard, firm, steadfast, determined."

77. The Maintenance Association, which was usually congruent with the Self-Government Association (*Zizhihui*), was the local collaborationist law-and-order entity. For lists of local Maintenance Association members in a dozen Jiangsu counties—a presentation that invited assassination—see *WX,* vol. 2 (10 November 1938): E44–E45.

78. Ye Shan, "Wo shi yige zhanshi le" [I'm a warrior now], *SB,* 18 November 1938, p. 4:14.

79. The resistance press vaunted examples of "heroines" (*nü yingxiong*) such as Cai Yifei, the Lake Tai woman warrior who was killed in battle by Japanese bayonets. *WX*, vol. 3 (10 December 1938): F47. See also the supplement, *Funü wenxian*, vol. 7 (April 1939): 18–19, 23–24.

80. This is a variant of the saying, "Murder someone with a borrowed knife" (*jie dao sha ren*)—that is, use someone else to kill an adversary.

81. The term for this minute fraction is *chana*, a Buddhist term from the Sanskrit *kshana*.

82. Ye Shan, "Wo shi yige zhanshi le," *SB*, 19 November 1938, p. 4:16.

83. Ibid.

84. The theme of ghosts and demons, or of tigers and their attendant *chang*, was prevalent in anti-Japanese and antipuppet propaganda. In a poster put up by the *Guoji fan qinglüe yundong dahui Zhongguo fenhui* (Chinese Branch of the International Anti-Aggression Movement Society) in 1938, there is a portrayal of a Chinese avenger thrusting a torch in the face of a tiger-monster thrown back against a heap of its victims' skeletons. Frontispiece to *WX*, vol. 3 (10 December 1938).

85. The resistance press published as many examples it could find of sons renouncing their fathers for "turning traitor for personal gain" (*maiguo qiurong*). This was called "extinguishing family relationships for a greater cause" (*dayi mieqin*). *WX*, vol. 3 (10 December 1938): F47.

86. Ye Shan, "Wo shi yige zhanshi le," p. 4:14.

87. *WX*, vol. 3 (10 December 1938): F11. "Wavering elements" could be kept in place in occupied China and used as informants or secret agents by the United Front. Ibid., vol. 5, 10 February 1939, B38.

88. A *chang* is the hungry ghost of a person eaten by a tiger who urges the tiger to eat others so that his or her soul may be freed.

89. *WX*, vol. 5 (10 February 1939): D11. The repetition in this announcement of phrases such as *sangxin bingkuang* could be a matter of the government picking up then-current phrases to describe traitors, or it could suggest that the letters to Jian were actually written by government propagandists, who were probably men. Although the authenticity of the "Jian letters" is dubious, the movement of these stock phrases from government to populace and back again—a characteristic of good propaganda—is certain.

90. Ibid.

91. Wang's followers invariably described their becoming collaborators as "joining the peace movement" (*canjia heping yundong*). During his October 21, 1946, war crimes trial, Zhou Fohai told the court: "At that time we exerted ourselves to carry out the peace movement because we wanted to help the people out of their suffering in the Occupied Zones. It was not to conspire with the enemy or to oppose our country." *SW*, 156.

92. For a sensitive portrait of Wang Jingwei as an ambivalent collaborator hoping to be a patriot to the end, see Boyle, *China and Japan at War*, 350–51.

93. Wang Jingwei detested *hanjian*. In March 1937, after seeing Chinese puppet troops in action in Suiyuan, Wang declared, "When China was invaded in the past, it often happened that the despicable acts of traitors rather than the aggression of aliens inflicted the most deadly blow upon the country. That Chinese should be unfaithful to their own people is a disgraceful stain on the pages of our history, and if such humiliating acts should be repeated China would suffer early extinction." Lawrence K. Rosinger, "Wang Ching-wei— the Technique of a Traitor," *Amerasia* 4, no. 6 (August 1940): 271.

94. Zhu Zijia, *Wang Zhengquan de kaichang yu shouchang*, 1:91.

95. Ibid., 92.

96. Ibid.

97. *SW,* 277. Chu's altruism, however, has to be placed alongside the financial killing this popular health promoter made after his stint as foreign minister when his sister, Chen Bijun (Mme. Wang), got him appointed governor of Guangdong. Boyle, *China and Japan at War,* 279–80.

98. *SW,* 583.

99. Lit. Yan Huang—Emperors Yan and Huang.

100. Zhu Zijia, *Wang Zhengquan de kaichang yu shouchang,* 4:ii–iii.

101. *WX,* vol. 5 (10 February 1939): D11; vol. 8 (10 May 1939): B17.

102. *WX,* vol. 5 (10 February 1939): B38. Fang Renzhi's father, Yanchu, was secretary of the puppet Self-Government Association (*Zizhihui*) of Qingpu. In July 1938, Renzhi ran the following notice in the Hankou *Dagong bao:* "My father returned to Qingpu after the National Army left Shanghai for the west, and occupied an important post in the Maintenance Association [*Weichihui*]. Renzhi has repeatedly reproved him to no avail.... This kind of behavior is shameless. Not only does it harm the country, it also brings disgrace upon the family. Now, because Renzhi is unwilling to be the descendant of a *hanjian,* he is placing in the newspaper this respectful warning to relatives and friends. From this day on Renzhi completely breaks off father-son relations (this does not extend to his mother). He is willing as well to contribute his service to the country in order to wipe away this oppressive humiliation." Ibid., vol. 1, 10 October 1938, D69.

103. Ibid., vol. 3, 10 December 1938, H14.

104. Ibid., vol. 5 10 February 1939, B38.

105. Ibid., vol. 8, 10 May 1939, E23–E24.

106. *Hanjian* and "treacherous merchants" (*jianshang*) were engaged in smuggling rice along the coast of Zhejiang and Jiangsu. *SB,* 3 December 1938, p. 2:7. High rice prices were blamed upon "underhanded control of the rice market by certain traitorous merchants who, in conspiracy with the Japanese and puppet authorities, are making handsome profits." SMP, D-8039, 7/3/39, p. 1.

107. Contemporaries frequently used the term *duhua* to refer to the poisoning of China with heroin and opium as part of a Japanese and puppet plot to weaken the Chinese race. See, for example, the article, "Duhua Jiashan" (Poisoning Jiashan), which describes the opium sales bureau set up by the Japanese and the puppet magistrate in the county seat. *SB,* 22 November 1938, p. 2:7; M. S. Bates, "The Narcotics Situation in Nanking and Other Occupied Areas," *Amerasia* 3, no. 11 (January 1940): 525–27; *WX,* vol. 1 (20 October 1938): D43; vol. 2 (10 November 1938): E40; and vol. 3 (10 December 1938): F43. The Chongqing authorities accused the Japanese of encouraging this drug abuse for three reasons: (1) revenue; (2) maintaining the livelihoods of undesirable Japanese and Korean elements, thereby keeping them out of Japan; and (3) weakening Chinese wartime resistance by poisoning the people. Joyce Ann Madancy, "Propaganda versus Practice: Official Involvement in the Opium Trade in China, 1927–1945" (master's thesis, Cornell University, 1983), 29–30, 33. The connection between drugs and treachery was obvious to the Japanese. "Spies were generally gangsters. Bright gangsters. Paper money had no value for them. They wanted opium. In big cities or large villages there were always pariahs. We'd find them and train them, threaten them, cajole them. We'd tell them, 'If you take the wrong course we'll kill you, but if you do what you're told you'll have to build warehouses to hold your fortune.' Then we'd bring out the opium. 'I'll do it!' they'd say in a minute." Statement by Uno Shin-

tarō, in Haruko Taya Cook and Theodore F. Cook, comp., *Japan at War: An Oral History* (New York: New Press, 1992), 154.

108. *Hanjian*, serving as district officials in Songjiang, were described as increasing taxes, collecting all the white rice, and extorting money and goods from the peasants and townsfolk. *SB*, 26 November 1938, p. 2:7. When Wang Zihui, the reform government's minister of trade and industry (*shiye buzhang*), returned from an economics conference in Tokyo, he was described in the Shanghai press as having gone "to sell out the people's interests" (*chu mai minzu liyi*). *SB*, 6 December 1938, p. 3:10.

109. *WX*, vol. 1 (10 October 1938): D51.

110. Ibid., D49–D50; and vol. 2 (10 November 1938): E41–E42. The newspaper also published a list of the "excesses" committed by these "dogs" in order to ridicule them: the governor of Jiangsu ordering everyone to worship Confucius on the grounds that Confucius was the teacher of "Oriental culture" (*dongfang wenhua*), the mayor of Haining conducting a lantern procession and shouting, "Long live great Japan! Long live the reform government!" and so forth. Ibid., vol. 2 (10 November 1938): E44–E46.

111. Ibid., vol. 5 (10 February 1939): D59, and vol. 7 (10 April 1939): D82.

112. Ibid., vol. 6 (10 March 1939): D80, and vol. 7 (10 April 1939): D83–D86. D88–D89.

113. At the same time, *Wenxian* published lists of "eliminated traitors" (*chujian*), who were typically local Maintenance Association heads assassinated by Nationalist death squads. See ibid., vol. 2 (10 November 1938): E46; vol. 3 (10 December 1938): F41–F42; vol. 5 (10 February 1939): D59–D60; vol. 6 (10 March 1939): D80; and vol. 7 (10 April 1939): D84.

114. *RWSSZ*, 63–64.

115. British Foreign Office Records, Her Majesty's Public Record Office, London, FO371–24663; Zhang Weihan, "Dai Li yu 'Juntong ju,'" 138–39; Confidential U.S. State Department Central Files, China: Internal Affairs, 1940–1944, 893.00 P.R. (Political Reports)/Shanghai, 145, October 1940, p. 15; *CWR*, 11 October 1940, p. 168. A fifty thousand dollar reward was put on Zhu's head, and the Japanese launched a manhunt throughout all of occupied China, but Zhu was never caught. *RWSSZ*, 64–65; Cheng Shuwei and Liu Fuxiang, *Daoguang jianying: Minguo ansha jishi* [The glint and flash of cold steel: An actual record of assassinations during the Republic] (Beijing: Tuanjie chubanshe, 1989), 168–74.

116. The impact of terrorism on collaborators living in Shanghai was severe. Zhou Fohai compared the fear of air raids in Chongqing with the dread of terrorism in Shanghai: "Plainly speaking, a man of my standing would have been safe anywhere [in Chongqing] in case of air raids, being provided with the strongest of bomb-proof dugouts.... My life [in Shanghai in 1939] is constantly being threatened by the Communists and the 'special service' element of the Chongqing régime. As there is no warning of an approaching assassination..., I think the danger to life created by these terrorists is much more serious than a Japanese air raid." Boyle, *China and Japan at War*, 261.

117. For the same reason, Chen Lifu and Chen Guofu also ordered Wu Kaixian, in the summer of 1939, to clear up the party "underground organization" in Shanghai. Wu established the Shanghai Party Political Unification Committee (*Shanghai dang zheng tongyi weiyuanhui*), and through Du Yuesheng secured the help of the racketeer Huang Jinrong to curb or eliminate collaborationist elements. Jiang Shaozhen, "Du Yuesheng," in *Minguo renwu zhuan* [Biographies of Republican personages], ed. Li Xin and Sun Sibai, vol. 1 (Beijing: Zhonghua shuju, 1978), 317.

118. Wang Fangnan, "Wo zai Juntong shisinian de qinli he jianwen" [What I experienced and learned during my fourteen years in the MSB]. In Chinese People's Political Consultative

Conference Editorial Committee, ed., *Wenshi ziliao xuanji* [Selections of historical materials], fasc. 107 (*zong*) (Beijing: Zhongguo wenshi chubanshe, 1987), 144. General Zhou Fengqi was slated to become minister of defense in the reform government when he was killed in the French Concession by two Juntong agents on March 7, 1938. *RDS*, 893.00/14214, report of assistant naval attaché, Shanghai, 7 March 1938. Lu Bohong was killed on December 30, 1937, after forming the collaborationist South Market Local Self-Government Committee.

119. More than forty Japanese military officers were also shot down. Chen Gongshu, *Yingxiong wuming: Beiguo chujian* [Anonymous heroes: Weeding out traitors in north China], pt. 1 (Taibei: Zhuanji wenxue chubanshe, 1941), 10. There were other operations conducted by the Guomindang's civilian secret service, the Central Statistics Bureau, or Zhongtong, quite apart from Dai Li's organization. Huang Meizhen and Zhang Yun, *Wang Jingwei guomin zhengfu chengli* [The establishment of the Wang Jingwei National Government] (Shanghai: Shanghai renmin chubanshe, 1984), 297. "Was Juntong more active than Zhongtong in occupied areas? They were both active. Was there more coordination between Juntong and Zhongtong in occupied areas than in free areas? We did not want them to know one another. In case one system was exposed, the other would be exposed also [if there were coordination]. In underground work in enemy areas it is better to keep two systems separate." "Ting Mo-ts'un, Chün-t'ung, and Chung-t'ung during the War," 1, in *Ch'en Li-fu Materials* (Materials relating to the oral history of Mr. Ch'en Li-fu, done with Miss Julie Lien-ying How as part of the Chinese Oral History Project of the East Asian Institute of Columbia University between December 1958 and July 2, 1968).

120. Jonathan Spence, "Goodfellas in Shanghai," *New York Review of Books* 45, no. 9 (May 28, 1998): 36–38 passim.

121. Hung Wu, *The Wu Liang Shrine: The Ideology of Early Chinese Pictorial Art* (Stanford: Stanford University Press, 1989), 168–69.

122. Transl. in ibid., 190.

123. After joining Sun Yat-sen's group, Shi—who was from Panyu—made three attempts to blow Deshou up. He was caught and executed on the third try. Edward S. Krebs, "Assassination in the Republican Revolutionary Movement," *Ch'ing-shih wen-t'i* 4, no. 6 (December 1981): 49–50. "Political assassination is a form of death that occurs suddenly to an individual who is involved in politics as the result of *covert* planning by one or more individuals." Daniel Tretiak, "Political Assassinations in China, 1600–1968," in *Assassination and Political Violence: A Report to the National Commission on the Causes and Prevention of Violence*, ed. James F. Kirkham, Sheldon G. Levy, and William J. Crotty (New York: Praeger Publishers, 1970), 637.

124. Yang, who wrote *Xin Hunan* (New Hunan), the chief manifesto of Huang Xing's China Revival Society (*Huaxing hui*), believed, "In reconstructing society, we cannot simply reorganize the old society. We must destroy the old society and cleanse it." Krebs, "Assassination in the Republican Revolutionary Movement," 53–54.

125. Ibid., 45, 55.

126. Tretiak, "Political Assassinations in China," 644. Although rumor had it that Wang Jingwei was spared execution because his handsome looks captivated the empress, a likelier explanation is that the Japanese secretly intervened to prevent his death. As far as the public knew, Prince Su, president of the Board of Civil Administration, was moved by Wang's passionate statement of his motives to reduce the sentence to life imprisonment. Prince Su subsequently visited the prisoner in his cell. Boyle, *China and Japan at War*, 17–18; Barbara Brooks, "Spies and Adventurers: Kawashima Yoshiko" (paper presented at the Center for Chinese Studies Regional Seminar, Berkeley, 21 March 1987), 2–3.

127. "Deposition of Sung Yah Shing," 13.

128. Zhao Liang, thirty-four years old, was a native of Hangzhou. He had worked as a cardboard box maker for twelve years in Nandao before war broke out in 1937, and he volunteered to serve under Sun Yaxing. "Deposition of Zau Liang," in SMP, D-8635, 26/7/38. Microfilms from the U.S. National Archives, p. 1.

129. "Deposition of Sung Yah Shing," 13–14.

130. Zhang Weihan, "Dai Li yu 'Juntong ju,'" 132; "Deposition of Wong Tz Koo," 2.

131. SMP, D-8597, 22/7/38, pp. 7–8; "Deposition of Sung Yah Shing," 15.

132. "Deposition of Zau Liang," 2. Jiang Haisheng said that they were explicitly told that they had to carry out Sun's assassination orders directly. SMP, D-8597, 22/7/38, p. 8.

133. "Deposition of Sung Yah Shing," 15–16.

134. "Deposition of Tsou Sue Kong," 1–2; "Deposition of Zau Liang," 2–3.

135. Alias Chen Yuanliang, he was a native of Shanghai whose parents came from Guangdong. His father was a private watchman in the French Concession. "Deposition of Zong Kwei Kong," in SMP, D-8635, 25/7/38. p. 1.

136. Ibid., 2.

137. Ibid., 3; "Deposition of Zau Liang," 3–5.

138. *RDS*, 893.102 S/1654, 11 July 1938.

139. Ibid., 9–10.

140. "Deposition of Sung Yah Shing," 27.

141. *WX*, fasc. 6 (March 10, 1939): D-81.

142. "Further Assistance to Japanese Military Police," report by D. S. I. Crighton, in SMP, D-9037, 18/3/39, pp. 5–7.

143. "Deposition of Dan Pau Nyi," in SMP, D-9037, 3/11/39, pp. 3–4; "Deposition of Ping Foh Chang," in SMP, D-9037, 3/11/39, pp. 3–4; "Further Assistance to Japanese Military Police," 7–8; "Assassination of Reformed Government Official," Miscellaneous Report no. 89/39, dated February 19, 1939, in SMP (International Settlement) Files, D-9037, 9/11/39, pp. 4–6; "How the Foreign Minister Was Assassinated,"*Xin shenbao*, November 9, 1939, translated in SMP, D-9037, 9/11/39; Wen-hsin Yeh, "Dai Li and the Liu Geqing Affair: Heroism in the Chinese Secret Service during the War of Resistance," *Journal of Asian Studies* 48, no. 3 (August 1989): 551; Yeh, "The Liu Geqing Affair: Heroism in the Chinese Secret Service during the War of Resistance" (paper presented to the Regional Seminar, Center for Chinese Studies, University of California at Berkeley, 21 March 1987), 23; *China Post*, 21 February 1939, p. 1; *North China Daily News*, 21 February 1939, p. 1; *Shanghai Times*, 21 February 1939, p. 1; *CWR*, 25 February 1939, p. 3.

144. *CWR*, 4 March 1939, p. 12. See also *WX*, vol. 7 (10 April 1939): D90.

145. Lloyd E. Eastman, *The Abortive Revolution: China under Nationalist Rule, 1927–1937* (Cambridge: Harvard University Press, 1974).

146. Regulations of the Shanghai People's Mobilization Society enclosed in *Foreign Relations of the United States. Diplomatic Papers, 1939, Volume 4, the Far East, the Near East, and Africa* (16 May 1939) U.S. Department of State. (Washington, D.C.: U.S. Government Printing Office, 1955), pp. 50–51.

147. *CWR*, 11 March 1939, p. 48; *SB*, 28 February 1939, p. 11; and 7 March 1939, p. 11. Zhu, a graduate of the Baoding Military Academy who had served the Beiyang warlords, was one of the leading officials in the Finance Bureau (*Caizheng ju*) of the Dadao régime. Members of the Liang Hongzhi reform government had been promised generous payments to their family survivors should they fall prey to terrorists' guns. *CWR*, 4 March 1939, pp. 10, 47.

148. *SB*, 12 April 1939, p. 10.

149. He was a native of Suzhou. During his period of study at the Tokyo Ika Daigaku, Dr. Xi had taken a Japanese wife. In Shanghai she became the senior of his two concubines, the principal wife and other concubine being Chinese. Ibid.; SMP, D-9122, 4/11/39.

150. According to *Shen bao*, Dr. Xi's eldest son, Xingzhi, was in charge of a special radio broadcasting station "engaged in spreading strange reports" and acting as an agent on behalf of Japan. *SB*, 12 April 39, p. 10.

151. *Tairiku shimpo*, 12 April 1939, translated in SMP, D-9122, 13/4/39.

152. Yuan's native place was either Songjiang or Kunshan. He was described as being about five and a half feet tall with "thin build, thin face, pale complexion, long hair brushed back, wears foreign clothes, no hat, speaks Shanghai dialect." SMP, D-9122, 15/4/39, pp. 2–3.

153. Peng, who was from Liyang, recalled first meeting Yuan and Zhao at the Wing On (Yongan) Department Store roof garden. Ibid., 12/4/39. Zhao Zhixiang later told the police, however, that he had known Peng before the war broke out in Shanghai, and that Peng (who was then a waiter at the *Dadong xin lüguan*) and he would often rent a room with a couple of friends to play mah-jongg. Ibid., 11/4/39. Peng, who most likely was a trained Juntong agent, also later told the police that he had just happened to bump into Yuan Dechang outside a Chinese movie theater on Avenue Edward VII on April 7, and that he had told Yuan that he had no interest in participating in "patriotic activities."

154. Ibid., 11/4/39.

155. Zhao had met Yuan in the first place through a Pudong guerrilla section chief surnamed Zhang, who had defected to the Japanese in January 1939. Ibid., 11/4/39.

156. Ibid. The telephone operator was probably an agent of Juntong, which had an excellent telephone and telegraph monitoring section, and which often used Shanghai hotels as listening posts. Shen Zui, *Juntong neimu* [The inside story of the Military Statistics (Bureau)] (Beijing: Wenshi ziliao chubanshe, 1984), 46–47. The operator in this case, one Pu Fuxin, was interrogated by the Shanghai Municipal Police after the assassination and released. The Japanese Consular Police later claimed that he was a key figure in the assassination ring, but even with the help of the Shanghai Municipal Police they were unable to run him down. SMP, D-9122, 13/4/39, p. 1, and 12/5/39, p. 1.

157. Zhao's account of this haphazard encounter is dubious. The letter from Zhou Jianhua (see below), later found by the police in Peng Fulin's hotel room at the Nanjing Hotel, referred to an earlier "matter" that Yuan, Peng, and Zhao had successfully carried out, strongly suggesting that Zhao had worked together with the other two Juntong agents in an earlier operation. Ibid., 11/4/39.

158. Ibid., 11/4/39 and 12/4/39.

159. Ibid.

160. The envelope had part of a three-cent stamp, which Zhao noticed was not postmarked. This was corroborated later by the police when they found the letter in Peng Fulin's hotel room. Ibid., 15/4/39. The name reads "Zhou [the dynasty] Sword China." The return address on the envelope was the Guansheng yuan shop at 416 Rue du Consulat. When Shanghai Municipal Police detectives later visited this store, they were not surprised to find no one named Zhou on the premises. Ibid., 11/4/39 and 15/4/39.

161. Cited in ibid., 11/4/39. See also the testimony dated 14/4/39.

162. Xi Shitai's house was located at No. 12, Lane 127, Lloyd Road, but the back door opened onto Lane 139. Ibid., 11/4/39.

163. One of the interrogations suggests there may have been a third lookout, Peng Fulin's younger brother, Jinyi, who escaped with Yuan Dechang. Ibid., 13/4/39.

164. The forty-year-old Shandong guard, Song Jiangrong, was a police watchman, Chinese police watchman no. 277, licensed to bear firearms. Zhao, the Chinese beat policeman, Chinese police constable no. 730, was armed only with his whistle. Ibid., 11/4/39.

165. Ibid., 11/4/39.

166. The twenty-three-year-old waiter, a tea boy at the *Dadong xin lüguan* (94 rue Palikao), was named Li Xinghe. The police initially mistook him to be Peng Jinyi, Peng Fulin's brother; but they soon discovered his real identity. Li Xinghe claimed to have met the wounded man along Lloyd Road, where he had hired two rickshaws to take them to the Nanjing Hotel. On the way, however, the two had stopped by Yuan Dechang's place where Peng Fulin had given him back his pistol. Ibid., 11/4/39. 12/4/39, 15/4/39.

167. Ibid., 11/4/39.

168. Ibid.

169. One of the men must have returned to the boardinghouse with their luggage after checking out of the hotel.

170. Ibid., 11/4/39, 15/4/39

171. Ibid., 20/4/39. This was two days after a Nationalist assassin "executed" Wang Xianming, a section chief (*kezhang*) in the puppet municipal government, in the French Concession, and on the very day that Yang Qiguan, chief of the municipal Department of Statistics and Taxes (*tongshui chu*), was repeatedly stabbed by a "heroic Han" (*zhuang Han*). *SB*, 18 April 1939, p. 12, and 21 April 1939, p. 11. On July 21, 1939, the Japanese Military Police informed the Shanghai Municipal Police, who had handed Zhao over to them, that the prisoner had been sentenced to death on July 10. SMP, D-9122, 22/7/39, p. 1.

172. Cheng Yiming, "Juntong tewu zuzhi de zhenxiang" [The truth about the special services organization of Juntong], in *Guangdong ziliao*, vol. 29 (Guangzhou: Wenshi ziliao chubanshe, 1980), 231–33; Shen Zui, *Juntong neimu*, 83; Zhang Weihan, "Dai Li yu 'Juntong ju,'" 146. Emily Hahn poked fun at the public rumors in the 1940s that Chiang Kai-shek was "in constant secret communication with Wang Ching-wei [Jingwei]" as an emblem of the Chinese obsession with espionage, but the truth was not far removed insofar as Dai Li was concerned. Emily Hahn, *China to Me: A Partial Autobiography* (Philadelphia: Blakiston, 1944), 96.

173. Xianggang qunzhong chubanshe, ed., *Dai Li zhi si* [The death of Dai Li] (Hong Kong: Xianggang qunzhong chubanshe, n.d.), 16.

174. One letter to the editor of *China Weekly Review* read: "Since the occupation of the Shanghai outskirts by the Japanese invaders and their 'running dogs,' headed by Wang Ching-wei [Jingwei], this city, which was formerly known as a metropolis of peace and order, has now become a place of horror." *CWR*, 29 March 1941, p. 109.

175. Tao Juyin, *Tianliang qian de gudao* [The isolated island before daybreak] (Shanghai: Zhonghua shuju, 1947), 1.

176. The messages were thereafter kept in a special file numbered 0042 (42 being the multiplication of 7 times 6 or "76") in a green safe in his office. Liu Gong, "Wo suo zhidao de Zhongtong" [The Central Committee Statistics Bureau that I knew], *Wenshi ziliao xuanji*, no. 36 (Beijing: Wenshi ziliao chubanshe, December 1962), 79; Zhu Zijia, *Wang Zhengquan de kaichang yu shouchang*, 2:68–74.

177. Xu Zongyao, "Zuzhi Juntong Beiping zhan heping qiyi de qianqian houhou," *Wenshi ziliao xuanji*, no. 68 (Beijing: Zhonghua shuju, 1980), 206; Xu Zhaoming, "Hanjian Zhou Fohai goujie Juntong ji qi xiachang" [Chinese traitor Zhou Fohai's unsavory alliance

with the BIS and his final outcome], *Wenshi ziliao xuanji*, no. 64 (Beijing: Zhonghua shuju, 1979), 204–8; Poshek Fu, *Passivity, Resistance, and Collaboration: Intellectual Choices in Occupied Shanghai, 1937–1945* (Stanford: Stanford University Press, 1993), 152–53; Cheng Yiming, "Dui Shen Zui 'Wo suo zhidao de Dai Li' de buchong, dingzheng," in *Guangdong wenshi ziliao*, vol. 22 (Guangzhou: Wenshi ziliao chubanshe, 1979), 248.

178. Mao Dun [Shen Yanbing], *Fushi* [Corrosion] (Chengdu: Sichuan renmin chubanshe, 1981), passim; Henry Rousso, *The Vichy Syndrome: History and Memory in France since 1944*, trans. Arthur Goldhammer (Cambridge: Harvard University Press, 1991), 114. But see also Ralph Hewins, *Quisling: Prophet without Honor* (London: W. H. Allen, 1965), 20; and H. R. Kedward, *Occupied France: Collaboration and Resistance, 1940–1944* (London: Basil Blackwell, 1985), 32–33.

179. Rousso, *Vichy Syndrome*, 300.

180. Cheng Yiming, "Dui Shen Zui 'Wo suo zhidao de Dai Li' de buchong, dingzheng," 249.

181. Xianggang qunzhong chubanshe, ed., *Dai Li zhi si*, 13–14.

182. Collaboration, however, was the main subject of a long-running television series in mainland China in the 1980s about wartime Beiping. The series, based upon a work by Lao She, was called *Four Generations under the Same Roof* (*sishi tongtang*). One major exception is the research group under Professor Huang Meizhen at Fudan University. See, e.g., Huang Meizhen and Zhang Yun, *Wang Jingwei guomin zhengfu chengli*, passim.

183. This discussion owes much to Poshek Fu's subtle analysis in Fu, *Passivity, Resistance, and Collaboration*, 162–65; and in Poshek Fu, "Intellectual Resistance in Shanghai: Wang Tongzhao and a Concept of Resistance Enlightenment, 1937–1939" (paper delivered at the Association for Asian Studies meetings, San Francisco, March 24, 1988), 7.

184. Cheng Yiming, "Dui Shen Zui 'Wo suo zhidao de Dai Li' de buchong, dingzheng," 247. For an example of an "arch traitor" escaping capital punishment after turning over five tons of gold and silver, see the case of Wang Shijing. *Wenhui bao*, 16 October 1946, p. 1.

185. This ambiguity is present throughout the war crimes cases detailed in Nanjing shi dang'an guan, ed., *Shenxun Wang wei hanjian bilu* [Records of the interrogations of the Wang puppet traitors] (Jiangsu: Jiangsu guji chubanshe, 1992).

186. Li Zhaochun, "Shenfen fuza de Pan Hannian" [The complicated identities of Pan Hannian], *Gongdang wenti yanjiu* 9, no. 3 (March 15, 1983): 114–18.

187. Cheng Yiming, "Dui Shen Zui 'Wo suo zhidao de Dai Li' de buchong, dingzheng," 16; Howard L. Boorman, *Biographical Dictionary of Republican China*, 3:36. Koiso Kuniaki, a member of the Tasei (Control) faction and former commander of the Japanese military forces in Korea, was trying to wrest control of the army from the militarists then in command. The Miao Bin affair provided his enemies in the cabinet with a pretext to call for his dismissal. Information supplied by Dr. Irwin Scheiner.

188. Cheng Yiming, "Dui Shen Zui 'Wo suo zhidao de Dai Li' de buchong, dingzheng," 17; Howard L. Boorman, *Biographical Dictionary of Republican China*, 3:37. Though there is no evidence to support the hunch, Dai Li's accidental death after Miao Bin's release may have had more than a little to do with his rearrest.

189. Cited in Boyle, *China and Japan at War*, 33.

TEN

Of Authenticity and Woman: Personal Narratives of Middle-Class Women in Modern China

Prasenjit Duara

The iconoclastic modernism of the May Fourth Movement was scarcely the only vision of modernity in Republican China. While the intellectual history of these alternative views has received some attention in the scholarship, the social history of these views has not.[1] Urban, middle-class social forms in the Republic—from charitable societies to the family—were dominated by models of modernity that have been obscured by the narrative of radical emancipation, which found little place for "tradition" in its ideal of the emancipated individual. At about the same time that May Fourth ideals were galvanizing a certain segment of the intelligentsia, a new, much more broadly based type of association was emerging in urban China with ties that linked it (to a greater or lesser degree, depending upon the particular association) organically to rural and popular culture. In this essay I shall discuss the construction of women's identities within this middle-class milieu. I will argue that the reconceptualization of morality and spirituality in this milieu had profound implications for the identities of women. In the second part of the essay, I will focus on the gap between the pedagogy of the leadership and the life stories of the women themselves in one of these associations, the Daodehui, or Morality Society.

I call these associations modern, *redemptive* societies. The most well known of these, apart from the Morality Society, were the Dao Yuan (Society of the Way) and its partner, the Hongwanzihui (Red Swastika Society), the Tongshanshe (Fellowship of Goodness), the Zailijiao (Teaching of the Abiding Principle), the Shijie Zongjiao Datonghui (Society for the Great Unity of World Religions, first organized in Sichuan in 1915 as the Wushanshe), and the Yiguandao (Way of Pervading Unity), among many others. To be sure, these societies were significantly different from one another, but what they had in common was a remarkable indicator of the new milieu of urban life across China. A distinctive feature of these societies was their division of the civilized world into the East and the West, where the West represented science and material culture, and East Asian civilization represented the hope for the spiritual and moral regeneration of the world. In many ways these societies represented a development of the late imperial syncretist tradition (*sanjiao heyi*)—which first gained popularity among the Confucian gentry as well as the Buddhist and Daoist laity in the sixteenth and seventeenth centuries—particularly in their emphasis on a redemptive universalism and moral self-transformation.[2]

However, the new global context of the twentieth century significantly transformed the meaning of their project. Many of these societies were established, or flourished, during World War I, when a discourse criticizing Western civilization as being overly materialist and violent began to emerge globally. These societies sought to supplement and correct the material civilization of the West with the spiritual civilization of the East. This supplement took the shape of a religious universalism in which Confucianism, Daoism, Buddhism, Islam, and Christianity all supposedly embodied the same universal spirituality. Like other modern religious and morality societies the world over, these societies were outfitted with charters and bylaws, and their goal of world redemption was matched by a strong this-worldly orientation, exemplified perhaps best of all by the Red Swastika Society. While the name of this society referred to a Buddhist symbol, it should also be seen as an Eastern equivalent of the Red Cross Society, which it was modeled upon.[3] Discursively, the older conceptions of time embodied in Buddhism and Confucianism were exchanged for an evolutionary vision of history (*jinhua*). Indeed, these societies justified their raison d'être in the language of evolutionary history, arguing that without the moral and spiritual regeneration that they promised, not only would human evolution stall but it would turn still more hedonistic and violent.[4] In their conception, human society was expected to evolve to moral perfection, but only by way of Eastern spirituality.

The pervasive nature of this symbiotic formulation of modernity in China does not need much demonstration. The Kuomintang (KMT) regime of the 1930s subscribed precisely to such a dualistic formulation, and the New Life Movement exemplified the urge to revitalize the material conditions of modernity through a muscular, or rather, ascetic, Confucian moralism. This conception is most strikingly identified with a modernist, evolutionary framework in Chen Lifu's philosophy of a parallel material and spiritual evolutionism. Chen's parallelism also represents one of the more creative means of accommodating the nation's past in a modern future so characteristic of nationalist ideology the world over. Chen argues that the evolution of material civilization without spiritual progress inevitably leads to the enslavement of humankind by things.[5] Even while it recognizes the livelihood of the people as the supreme goal, the New Life Movement will inject moral qualities from the essence of Chinese civilization into this effort so that history can be propelled into civilizational perfection—Datong, or the Great Unity.[6]

Given the discursive affinities between many of these societies and the KMT, it is surprising to find that from 1927 on, the KMT outlawed and persecuted many of these societies, including the Morality Society.[7] The KMT regime condemned these societies as riddled by superstition and dominated by local bullies and warlords. Central to understanding this hostility, I believe, is the way in which the

KMT devised its representation of tradition to exclude popular religious practices—in part at least to excise and contain the power of religious heterodoxy. Thus, I have argued elsewhere that the KMT characterization of the spiritual as part of China's national essence incorporated modern, licensed religions, while it proscribed as superstition a range of religious societies from the heterodox to those it suspected of political opposition.[8] Included among these were not only sectarian and several secret societies but also most of the modern, redemptive societies. In keeping with their syncretist heritage, many of the religious practices of these redemptive societies were, in fact, drawn from popular culture; for instance, the popularity of the Daoyuan, or the Red Swastika Society, was often attributed to its practice of divination and planchette.[9] Thus several of these societies drew from late imperial syncretism not only by synthesizing different religious teachings but also by accommodating popular gods and practices, which made them a much more organic part of Chinese society.[10] In contrast, the KMT appears to have espoused a more elitist variant of the dualistic formulation of modernity.

Apart from the East versus West, or spiritual-moral versus material, duality, these societies were also premised upon another duality: the outer versus the inner. In the outer realm, these societies not only conducted philanthropic activities associated with traditional charities (*cishan shiye*), such as establishing and managing soup kitchens and poorhouses, but expanded their sphere to include modern hospitals, schools, and contributions to international relief works. Thus, for instance, the Hongwanzihui, which had professors of Esperanto among its members and branches in Paris, London, and Tokyo, contributed substantially to relief works in China and abroad, such as those conducted after the Tokyo earthquake and natural disasters in the Soviet Union.[11] The Zailijiao, which may have had a membership of between three hundred thousand and several million (it had forty-eight centers in Tianjin alone) developed drug rehabilitation centers using herbal medicines and self-cultivation techniques (*zhengshen*), which were said to fully cure over two hundred opium addicts a year.[12] As we shall see below, external or "public" service was not only significant in itself, but the discourse of "public service" would generate new possibilities of selfhood, which was so important to most of these societies.

This inner realm of selfhood was focused on producing the self-cultivating subject. Such self-cultivation practices (*ziji xiuyang, xiushen*) ranged from the exercise of a strict disciplinary regimen to cultivating the habit of close moral and spiritual introspection designed to produce the self-cultivating subject as the moral citizen of the new world. Some societies emphasized strict vows of abstinence from drugs, meats, and alcohol; others, quasi renunciation of the family; and still others, detailed codes of moral behavior and bodily comportment.[13] Most societies combined all three.

THE SPACE OF AUTHENTICITY IN MODERNITY

In this essay, I am centrally concerned with the production of this interior space in which the self is constituted, or interpellated, in Louis Althusser's terms.[14] Interpellation is the act by which the individual recognizes himself or herself in the appellation pronounced by the other, as when we turn around upon hearing the policeman call out "Hey, you." How do social powers authorize themselves to pronounce that name, to define that representation with which the individual is prepared to identify or to negotiate her identification? Thus my first concern is with the manner in which a space of inviolability is created that authorizes certain powers to define a representation of the self and render it immune to challenges from alternative discourses.

The inviolability of this space is secured by the symbolization of certain activities or practices—such as the rites of a nation, the vanishing festivals of a village, the self-sacrifices of women—as sacred or authentic. Within this space, social power can be cloaked in the robes of a pure and inner authenticity, the sacred space of (or in) the secular and modern. While this space exists in all societies, modern and premodern, it serves a rather special function in modern societies dominated by the discourse on evolutionary history and the conception of linear time it embodies. The anxiety produced by a conception of time that has potentially no end, goal, or moral purpose generates as much a need for faith in the future (progress), as for a secure identity symbolized by the unchanging essence. The space of inviolable authenticity is equivalent to the unchanging essence. Like the national flag, it is the sacred core of identity.[15]

What nationalists and others refer to as the unchanging essence of a nation or civilization is a repeatedly reconstituted representation whose historicity is concealed by its pace of change, which is not synchronous with change in other spheres.[16] In locating this sphere of authenticity within the problematic of linear history, I wish to separate it from a purely or primarily psychologistic reading of these essences and traditions. Thus, while Joseph Levenson's interpretation of the re-creations and manipulations of "tradition"—as being psychologically comforting to modern Chinese intellectuals who needed to assert the particularity of Chinese history in the face of the overwhelming superiority of scientific civilization and values—may have been true for some intellectuals at some time and place, the reconstruction of tradition had other meanings and functions not reducible to salving the inferiority complex of Chinese intellectuals. All nations and societies that see themselves as subjects progressing or evolving through linear time need to constitute an "unchanging core" in order to recognize themselves in their ever-changing circumstances. Hence the role of tradition or sacred national symbols or core values in Britain or France or America. What is interesting about the Chinese and other non-Western cases is that the aporia of having to be of the past and also not of it is presented as having to be both Eastern and Western. Thus there is an imbrication between Easternness, national or cultural essence, and the space of authenticity, each functionally different, but each authorizing the other.

The homology between East versus West and essential versus evolving was characteristic of much non-Western modern thought in the first half of the twentieth century, and typically it authorized the space of authenticity in several Asian societies of the time. Partha Chatterjee's work on the colonized middle class in Bengal shows us how nationalist ideology in late-nineteenth-century India appropriated the middle-class production of a sphere that he calls the inner domain of sovereignty of nationalist ideology. Like so much Chinese nationalism discussed above, Indian nationalism was built upon a duality of the scientific and material versus the spiritual and cultural. Thus, while the Indian nation had much to learn from the material and scientific civilization of the West, in spiritual matters India had the upper hand and a contribution to make to world civilization.[17]

Chatterjee's particular contribution is to show how this dualism was organized in a way that created an inner realm of national life that could not be contested by the colonial power. Nineteenth-century Bengali middle-class intellectuals had reworked certain historical texts to define the ideal "woman" and distinguish her from depictions of the "traditional" (i.e., recent historical, rather than the quintessential) Bengali woman, from depictions of contemporary lower-class women, and from the figure of the Western, materialist, and masculinized woman. Modern Indian nationalism found this trope of the enlightened but "traditional" woman to be highly congenial and appropriated it as the core of the essential nation. Tradition thus came to mark a realm of inner sovereignty that was simultaneously demarcated as domestic, spiritual, and feminine. The Hindu nationalist representation of woman—educated and educating, but personifying the spiritual virtues of domesticity—gave body to this national essence. While on the one hand, this lofty idealization of the Hindu woman provided new aspirations for some women, it also represented a new nationalist patriarchy and produced a sense of failure for women whose real lives could not match this idealization.[18]

The creation of an inner realm of authenticity in the modern discourses of Republican China was important in authorizing a space that was off-limits, less to colonial powers than to Westernizing forces within China—most significantly the social forces spawned by the May Fourth Movement. It is hardly a coincidence that many of these redemptive modern societies emerged in the last years of the second decade of the twentieth century or in the early 1920s, and that Sun Yat-sen's valorization of Chinese traditional virtues within nationalist rhetoric took place at around the same time as the May Fourth Movement. As a result, two very different representations of women emerged in China. On the one hand, there was the May Fourth representation of the radically anti-Confucian, indeed, anti-familial, nationalist woman, and on the other, the variety of more conservative constructions of woman as the representative of the soul of tradition, with which we are concerned here. These two conceptions tended to be deeply inimical to each other, and after the KMT-Communist split in 1927, thousands of "modern" women were killed because they were accused of participating in free love or simply because they had bobbed hair and unbound feet.[19] Throughout the Republic, the image of the modern Westernized woman was associated at various different levels of society with promiscuity and impurity, an image conveyed effectively in the stories of Mao Dun and others.[20] Lu Xun also wrote bitter denunciations of modern Confucianists such as Kang Youwei who insisted on reifying the traditional image of the self-sacrificing woman, and who thereby sought to perpetuate their domination over women.[21] In the short story "Soap" (1924), Lu satirizes such middle-class Confucianists who were disturbed by modern, Westernizing influences in Chinese life. Lu's protagonist is particularly agitated by the mixing of gender roles—girls sporting short hair, attending schools with boys, and the like. He finds in a beggar girl on the street the means to revive Confucian values, not by addressing her poverty, but by elevating her to serve as a model of self-sacrificing, filial piety.[22]

The conservative view of women was by no means simply a throwback or a resistance to modernity. Nationalists and social reformers of all stripes sought to bring about reform of the traditional social order in which women were seen to have been oppressed. The need for women's education, the abolition of foot binding, and the urgency of prenatal care were espoused by Kang Youwei and others who were considered conservative.[23] Rather, what was being constructed here was a trope of woman as embodying "tradition within modernity." Women were to participate as modern citizens in the public sphere of the nation, but they were also expected to personify the essence of the nation or civilization. Wang Jingwei's lecture in a girls' school in 1924 expresses this conception aptly. Wang exhorts the girl students not to give in to the demands of the family but rather to use their education to rid society of its evil customs and build a progressive nation in China.[24] Wang next goes on to suggest, however, that although the Chinese tradition is rife with noxious customs, the women of China have an admirable and long tradition of self-sacrifice (*xisheng*), whether in their natal home where they willingly sacrifice their happiness for the sake of their parents, or in marriage for the sake of their husband, or in old age for the sake of their sons. Wang is aware that many in the old society often exploited this tradition to deprive women of their freedom, but he also believes, he says, that women sacrificed their desires from a voluntary and deeply felt conviction (*zhenzhende qinggan*) for the good of the community: "Chinese women are rich in the spirit of self-sacrifice. If we can properly direct this spirit toward . . . [the collectivity] and use it, then we can, on the one hand, perhaps preserve a little of the essence [*jingsui*] of the teachings of several thousand years and, on the other, still plant the roots of modern liberatory thought. In seeking education for girls, I hope we can uphold our mission to inherit the past in order to enlighten posterity [*chengxian qihou*]."[25] Thus Wang identifies woman as the locus of unchanging authenticity not by sanctifying the home and domesticity—as in India—but by redirecting the virtue of self-sacrifice to the nation.

THE MORALITY SOCIETY AND MANZHOUGUO

I shall examine here the views of the Morality Society (the Daodehui) about women and the narratives of its women lecturers during the early 1930s in the

Japanese puppet state of Manzhouguo. The Society was founded in Shandong in 1918, and Kang Youwei served as its president in the 1920s, until he died in 1928.[26] The Society had a strong syncretic religious character through much of the 1920s (presumably when Kang was alive), but the religious component seemed to have waned by the 1930s, when its focus on morality and charity gained salience. Nonetheless, in identifying its source of moral inspiration, the founder of the Society, Wang Fengyi, declared that all three historical religions in China pointed to the permanence of the moral: Confucianism holds that without righteousness, wealth and nobility are like passing clouds; Buddhism, that that which has form must die; Daoism, that only good and evil are without form and so have a long existence. Thus morality persists and gives meaning to the universe, and it is the morality of the East that will save the universe from the materialism and destructiveness of the West.[27]

The Morality Society flourished in Manzhouguo—as did other similar organizations—because of state support and patronage of its activities. As organizations that promoted a civilizational ideal, these redemptive societies, as well as many secret societies that valued traditional Confucian ideals like *zhong* and *yi*, were attractive to the Japanese imperialists from the early 1930s, when they developed the ideology of pan-Asianism and Eastern civilizational values versus Western materialism. According to Japanese researchers and officials of the puppet administrations in north China, these societies claimed to command enormous followings. Thus the Fellowship of Goodness claimed a following of 30 million in 1929, and the Red Swastika Society, a following of 7 to 10 million in 1937.[28] However, Chinese nationalist intellectuals and scholars have tended to ignore them, and those who do care to mention them cite lower figures. Thus Wing-tsit Chan cites a figure of thirty thousand members (not followers) for the Red Swastika Society in 1927.[29] Further he dismisses these societies as "negative in outlook, utilitarian in purpose, and superstitious in belief."[30]

Given the paucity of Chinese data on these societies, the best we can do is to interrogate the Japanese records. While we can assume that the Japanese researchers may have wanted to exaggerate the numbers in these groups, there was also a concern for accuracy since these surveys were conducted principally to assess the potential for support for and opposition to their rule. The figures cited above refer to the spread of these societies all over China largely before the Japanese Occupation. A cursory glance at materials in the Number Two Historical Archives in Nanjing originally compiled at the county and city level during the Japanese Occupation of north China reveals an enormous number of these and other religious societies registered with the local government during this period; the total figure for participants or followers of all societies within a single county or city often reached beyond tens of thousands. Given that many of these were first registered only after 1937, it is not clear to what extent they may have emerged in response to the Occupation itself; but many, especially the many religious societies, clearly predated the Occupation.

Although a fuller analysis of this problem is the subject of another essay, my provisional interpretation of these materials is that a good number of traditional religious societies—secret societies as well as modern redemptive societies—existed and flourished during the Republic; but because of nationalist disapproval and governmental repression, they were forced into clandestine or semiclandestine status. As we shall see below, the Japanese regime in both Manzhouguo and north China sought to utilize these societies selectively, but I do not think that this should, ipso facto, disqualify these societies from being considered seriously.[31] As societies with civilizational or religious ideals, they may have considered the issue of a national government as less important than the ability to pursue their vision of a transnational community. However disingenuous the Occupation regime may have been, these societies must have seized the opportunity to operate openly in public, often for the first time. To disregard or condemn them would testify to our complicity with a nationalist narrative that imposes the stark choice of collaborator or patriot upon those who sought to live their lives as they might in any society.

At the time the Morality Society encountered the Manzhouguo regime, there was a remarkable convergence of ideological interests between it and certain currents in Japan. Similar "redemptive" societies in Japan, such as the Shibunkai, offering Confucianism and Shinto as the spiritual alternative to excessive materialism and individualism had begun to grow in strength during the 1920s, particularly as economic conditions worsened and social unrest grew. Asiatic moral systems emphasizing ethical responsibilities were celebrated as alternatives to capitalism and Marxism, both Western doctrines.[32] In the 1930s, the redemptive rhetoric of elite Confucian societies and the right-wing nationalists and militarists not only began to come together but was also assimilated in an active political and educational program by the Japanese government.[33]

By the 1930s, the Manzhouguo state, which drew its real power from the Japanese military, inherited an ideology and language with which to forge an alliance with the redemptive societies in northeast China. Like the KMT government in Nanjing, the Manzhouguo government censured the "superstitious" character of the redemptive societies, but instead of seeking to eradicate the societies themselves it saw the potential for their transformation into state-controlled civic organizations.[34] In this new political framework, the Manzhouguo branch of the Morality Society, which severed ties with its headquarters in Beijing in 1932, became, under the supervision of the Manzhouguo government, a *jiaohua* (*kyōka* in Japanese) organization—an agency engaged in the welfare and enlightenment of the people.[35] Indeed the transition from a more religious orientation to morality and charity in this Society is probably attributable to its closer supervision by the state.[36]

The Morality Society was perhaps the most elite Chinese organization among all such societies in Manzhouguo. Its membership and officeholders boasted top officials, merchants, and landowners at all levels of Manzhouguo society, from the major cities to the subcounty townships. The message of peace, morality, and spiritual salvation of the world by the East befitted these successors of the old gentry elite. As a *jiaohua* agency it revealed a strong propagandist urge. It put great stock by its cadres or activists (*shi*), who were characterized as benevolent and resolute.[37] Through their activities in schools, their lectures, their spreading of *baihua* (vernacular) commentaries of classical morality, and through establishing popular enlightenment societies to "reform popular customs and rectify the people's minds and hearts," the Society propounded a strong rhetoric of reaching out to all—rich and poor, men and women.[38] By 1934, the 312 branches of the Manzhouguo Society operated 235 "righteous" or "virtuous" schools, 226 lecture halls, and 124 clinics.[39]

The records of this Society allow us to see how it evolved historically from the gentry culture of the late empire. In the biographies of model figures honored in the 1930s for their virtuous and moral actions frequently undertaken in the first two decades of the twentieth century, before the Society was founded, filiality and loyalty are often cited.[40] But the bulk of such honors are granted to men and women who established, managed, or contributed money for "virtuous and chaste girls' schools" (*zhennü yixue; baonü yixueyuan*). Moreover, while the biographies of model individuals traceable in these records to the late nineteenth century indicate that temple building and repairs were common activities in the last years of that century, by the Republican period the establishment of these schools may have become a more common virtuous activity than contributions to building temples or arches dedicated to chaste widows. Doubtless, the emphasis upon virtuous girls' schools developed with the spread of female education in public institutions. The pages of the journal *Funü zazhi* in the early 1920s are filled with essays about the problem of having boys and girls in the same class, and Lu Xun both records and satirizes this anxiety among gentry men in "Soap."[41] Virtuous girls' schools represented a core institutional means to manage a generalized anxiety about the loosening of morals and fundamental values, an anxiety that became increasingly focused upon the bodies of females. Thus, one woman claimed that she only really understood what it meant to read after her father transferred her from a regular school to a virtuous school. Learning to read was not true learning unless reading could shape the body and its conduct (*xing dao shenshang, na jiao shizi*).[42]

The twentieth-century discourse on female virtue found here is clearly continuous with the cult of chaste widows and virtuous wives of late imperial times.[43] Descriptions of the establishment of the virtuous schools are couched in the language of this tradition: model men and women who had established virtuous schools were inspired by chaste women's biographies in the *Lienü zhuan* (Records of Chaste Women), as well as by the personal examples of chaste widows and virgins in the family. But inevitably, there was also a shift in the meaning of female virtue. Just as nationalists like Wang Jingwei in the KMT reorganized the role and meaning of the ideal women, so too in the Morality Society; as the figure of woman pervaded the space of authenticity, it became the site for reconstructing tradition. It is hardly possible to characterize the attitude of this Society as an expression of nationalism, since the Society operated under a puppet regime, but many of these modern re-demptive societies in Manzhouguo developed an authenticity derived from the same sources as did KMT nationalism or the kind of conservative middle-class ide-ology that Lu Xun satirized. While nationalists sought to preserve a *national* essence in the evolutionary process, the Morality Society sought to preserve an East Asian essence while acknowledging the necessity of material evolution.[44]

Among the records of the Society, the Oral Records of Morality Seminars of the Third Manzhouguo Morality Society, held in 1936 in Xinjing (Changchun), comprise an extraordinarily revealing text of over three hundred pages of per-sonal narratives and testimonials of the leaders and teachers of the Society, who taught in its righteous schools and went around the country giving lectures on morality. The bulk of these narratives is organized around five categories drawn from the classical tradition: *zhiming* (to know your fate), *zhixing* (to know your na-ture), *jinxin* (to devote your heart and mind, to devote yourself), and *lishen* (to es-tablish your self or body); in turn *lishen* is often divided into *lizhi* (to resolve your will) and *liye* (to fulfill an enterprise or profession). Finally, there is the category *zhizhi* (to know your limits).[45] Participants in the seminar made presentations about how their lives were guided by the appropriate morality within each of these categories. We hear the life stories of about twenty-five women and an equal num-ber of men, although the total number of speaking men was greater because of the many introductory speeches made by Manzhouguo civil and military officials. From the speeches and narratives of both the men and the women, I shall try to construct an image of how woman is constituted as a subject. From the personal narratives of the women I will try to demonstrate the gap between the constituted subject and the enunciating subject. The enunciating subject seeks to negotiate this interpellative gap in a variety of ways, even as she derives meaning and spiri-tual sustenance—identity—from the constituting ideology or pedagogy.[46]

The introductory lectures by officials inevitably stressed the mediating role of the Society between the state and the family. The Manzhouguo police were closely associated with the project for moral renewal of the citizenry. The head of the Capital Police Bureau declared that in order to attain national goals and renew the people, it was first necessary to cleanse the people's hearts. While this was the in-direct responsibility of the nation-state, it was more directly the responsibility of such agencies as the Morality Society. Such societies should bond the people to the state (*guanmin yizhi*) by nourishing ethical attitudes and duties toward the family, society, and the nation.[47] Employing an orthodox Confucian rhetoric, these offi-cials repeatedly emphasized the central importance of the five ethical relation-ships in constructing a chain of loyalty to the state.[48] This is how Tachibana Shi-raaki formulated the logic: "Morality is the basis of belief, whereas superstition has no basis in morality. The youth at home must believe in the elders, the wife in the husband, and the husband in the wife. If there is no harmony within the fam-ily, then there will be no harmony in society and no harmony in the nation. The Morality Society thus represents the progress [*jinbu*] of morality."[49]

The goals of the nation-state could be fulfilled only when the family was strong, when husbands were righteous and wives obedient. Within the family, the ideal moral roles for men and women were very different. Masculine virtues were represented by loyalty, incorruptibility, bravery, and self-restraint. On several occasions in their narratives, men recounted as virtue the self-control by which they restrained the urge to beat their wives. One of them indicated that in showing restraint he was expressing his filiality because both of his marriages had been arranged by his mother.[50] Director Feng (Feng *zhuren*) was once faced with a serious moral crisis when his youngest wife threw his baby son on the floor: seized by a desire to avenge his progeny, he was about to strike her when he recognized the virtue of self-restraint.[51] Female virtue often entailed following the three obediences (*sancong*). The locus classicus of this doctrine is the Book of Rituals (*Yili sangfu zhuan*), which says that a woman should obey her father before marriage, her husband upon marriage, and her son upon the husband's death. But in the pedagogy of the Society, as we shall see, obedience on the part of women did not necessarily entail confinement to the household. It was more that the ideal woman was shaped (or regulated) by the virtues of the family and by the reproduction of these virtues in the righteous schools and the Morality Society itself.

It was thus in the representation of the family, and the special role of women within it as repositories of the essence of (all that was good in) tradition, that the new middle-class patriarchy made common cause with the Manzhouguo state. Woman became the upholder of the "new family" that was the basis of citizenship.[52] The new family was morally pure, selfless, and committed to moral regeneration of the world by adhering to the "kingly way" (*wangdao*).[53] Thus weddings were to be frugal and unostentatious since the goal was for the couple to achieve love and righteousness.[54] Women (and, to a lesser extent, men) were encouraged to rid themselves of jewelry and other accoutrements so that they could come to know their inner selves.[55] The Morality Society not only conducted lectures and ran schools but also organized many family research groups (*jiating yanjiushe*) in which the role of model wives and mothers was investigated. It was from these research societies that the righteous girls' schools received the knowledge necessary to improve women's service to the family and nation without their having to leave the home.[56]

The pedagogy of the Morality Society by no means merely reproduced the historical image of the ideal Confucian woman—whatever that may have been. It involved a representation of woman that was neither abject nor liberated in the way of the "Western woman." Wang Fengyi reported a conversation with a Christian pastor in which Wang reveals the inadequacy of historical religions. Wang declared that he believed in all religions since they all pointed to the same Way (*dao*), but he protested that these religions neglected or demeaned women in the education of the Way. He insisted that women should be educated and independent (*liye*) so that they could understand the Way.[57] Thus women's education was necessary both from the state's perspective of improving the family and home and from the Society's perspective of having them understand morality. The reconstructed tradition here mobilized an image of woman that redefined her in accordance with modern discourse even while claiming a pristine traditionalism—East Asianism at the heart of the culture- and nation-building project.

WOMEN AS ENUNCIATING SUBJECTS

Who were the women who joined these societies, particularly the lecturers? As lecturers, they must, at some level, have believed in the pedagogy. Like teachers everywhere, they expressed demoralization when few attended their lectures, and were gratified by a large turnout. Many of them were women with much grief in their lives. There were, among many others, those whose children had died young, those locked in loveless marriages, those who sought solace because a younger wife or concubine had been brought in to replace them, and those who were younger wives bullied by older wives and in-laws. Many were devout Buddhists and found the Society to be basically compatible with their Buddhist faith. These were women for whom the Morality Society offered a rationalization or justification of their fate, a means of coping with their difficult lives, and, often, spiritual solace. A woman named Tu declares that hers is the fate (*ming*) of a stepmother. At first neither the old nor the children treated her well no matter how hard she tried. But she has now come to understand her fate and has resolved her will (*lizhi*). Whereas earlier she had been addicted to drugs, now she is a vegetarian and feels no need for drugs. Indeed, she has acquired such strength and influence in her household that no one in her household takes drugs. A Mrs. Zhao states simply that earlier she would be sad when people called her "wife number two" (*er taitai*). Now she has learned to live with her fate (*tianming*), and she is happy. Mrs. Liu's in-laws got a "little sister" (a concubine) for her who was filial and sisterly, and so she had to learn to be a good elder sister. She decided to make up to her in-laws and husband by performing service to society, which she has done for the past ten years.[58]

But resignation, coping, and solace from grief and mistreatment were not the only meanings that women derived from their participation in the Morality Society. These narratives also reveal various strategies whereby women were able to maneuver the goals of the Society to secure advantage for themselves and for other women. This was hardly easy, because many women must have experienced the interpellative or constituting activity as a form of objectification. Counterrepresentations of the modern, Westernized woman were readily available to these women. Newspapers in Manzhouguo debated the issue of women's liberation, and until 1941 at least, often carried positive images of liberated, Western, and Westernized women. Indeed, it was the often unacknowledged irruption of elements of this discourse of the liberated woman into their own that enabled some of their maneuvers. Yet it is also clear that they accepted the virtue of filiality and even obedience to patriarchs. Most of all, they appeared to derive their inspiration and strength from the spirit of devotion and self-sacrifice—from that space of authenticity carved out by the pedagogy of the Society. For us, the challenge is to see how they could be true to their subjectivity inscribed by the Morality Society while recovering some agency as enunciating subjects.

The first and perhaps most important difference between the discourse of these redemptive societies and the historical Confucian or patrilineal discourse on women was that the rhetoric of confining women to the home in these societies was balanced or countered by a valorization of public or social service.[59] Not only did these societies have an ideology of public service, but they were themselves part of the public sphere. As such, women who participated in them as members, whether as audience or lecturers, were, ipso facto, involved in activities outside the home. Recall that, even in the official articulations of the duty of the Society to create a nested hierarchy of moral obligation linking the individual to the state, the family was not directly linked to the state. This relationship was mediated by the need to fulfill a moral obligation to society. The view of society, or *shehui*, as a positively evaluated sphere of human—male and female—interaction represented a significant, though not necessarily recognized, departure from earlier historical discourses containing women within the domestic sphere.[60] Mrs. Zhao was one who did recognize the significant difference: "Those of you under the age of forty have had the benefit of a modern education and may work outside the home. Those of us over forty are barely literate and we know little about affairs outside the home. Now this [Morality] society allows us to exchange knowledge: I can go to your home and you to mine; we are not restricted by being rich or poor.... From this it is clear that the future of women is bright. We can come and hear lectures everyday; we can obtain morality: the young can be filial to the old and the old can be kind. I hope my sisters will strive to build the future."[61]

The realm of the social, however, was rife with ambiguity and was emerging as an object of contestation. Even in Mrs. Zhao's comments, which reveal a deeply felt sense of liberation, moral development afforded by the emergence of the social was ultimately brought to bear to restore filiality. While many of the men acknowledged the importance of service to society, they believed that confining women, though not necessarily to the home, was the best possible way for society to develop. Just as the virtuous girls' school was the way to regulate the behavior of girls who were exposed to society, so too, for some of these men, women's participation in the Morality Society was itself an ideal way to control their activities outside the home. The director of the Society, Mr. Feng, had four wives, all of whom, he claimed, were happily involved with the Morality Society, and who regularly *ketou* (kowtowed) to its teachers.[62] Not everybody in the Society accepted this pattern of containment. Indeed, even among the leadership Wang was prominent in espousing women's education and independence. Girls and women sometimes reacted against efforts at containment. The investigator of a survey of social welfare organizations in Manzhouguo reported an episode at one of the virtuous schools that he witnessed in 1937 in Liaoyuan county.

The investigator, Takizawa Toshihiro, reported that the school and its dormitories were basically well maintained. It derived its income from a wool-weaving workshop and a grain store. It had separate lecture halls for women citizens (*funü shimin*) appointed with a picture of the emperor Puyi and an altar to Confucius. On one of the days he was there, a vigorous discussion on the subject of "the spirit of nation-building and women in the family" (*jianguo jingshen he jiating funü*) followed a talk given by a lecturer from Fengtian (Shenyang). Takizawa was impressed by the dedication of the students and teachers to popular enlightenment and the way in which they criticized the old-fashioned attitude of the lecturer. Takizawa recommended that rather than preach homilies to these children, the Society should emphasize the teaching of practical life skills. In this way, they would learn from the scientization (*kagakuka*) of everyday life.[63]

Such reactions to the discursive and institutional efforts to channel women's behavior are less visible in the personal narratives. Nonetheless, the positive evaluation of the realm of the social or public in modern discourse, together with the ambivalence of the leaders (contrast Feng's behavior with Wang's comment on religions denying women), created opportunities that these women seized and utilized to the fullest extent.[64] A Mrs. Bai decided to give up the life of the inner quarters because she realized that the world of women was a very grasping one in which one could not be ethical. By giving lectures in society she can make a living, which permits her to support both her mother and mother-in-law. Thus she can be filial and moral without being dependent upon anyone, neither husband nor children.[65] A recently married woman accepted the foreordained role of the daughter-in-law to be like water: to serve all in the family with devotion—to be filial to her in-laws, help her husband attain a Buddhist nation, be kind to her children—and rid herself of vain desire. At the same time, women can follow the men and devote themselves to social good. Indeed, once one has satisfactorily served the in-laws, it is incumbent in the next phase to serve the world.[66]

Mrs. Chen reveals the significance of public service and the independence that it can bring to women. She emphasizes the utility and value of women in the family and the importance of these qualities in purifying the world and resolving to do good for society. She begins her narrative with an account of how her father-in-law brought her into the household because the education she received from her mother would bring good values into their home. These were the qualities that permitted *lishen*, the ability to establish oneself. In earlier periods, *lishen*, to the extent that it referred to women, referred to feminine bodily comportment within the domestic sphere. In a booklet of moral instruction for women that circulated in the late imperial period, *lishen* is described as a "way of being tranquil [*qing*] and chaste [*zhen*]. Tranquillity brings purity [*jie*] and chastity brings honor [*rong*]. While walking do not turn back your head; while speaking do not expose your teeth; while sitting, do not move your knees; while standing, do not raise your voice.... When of necessity you have to go out, be sure to veil your face.... Only when you establish your body in such proper and upright ways [*lishen duanzheng*] can you be a person [*fang ke weiren*]."[67]

The close connection between personhood and bodily comportment did not disappear during the Republic. Recall the comment of the woman who had learned the true meaning of reading only after applying it to her bodily conduct. But this is not how Mrs. Chen uses *lishen*. Personhood for her depends on material independence. According to her, the best route to *lishen* is to set up a livelihood of one's own (*liye*). Now that Manzhouguo has entered the era of Datong, or the Great Unity, Mrs. Chen avers, women have plenty of opportunity to make a livelihood. Once they have set up a living, they can then devote themselves to the task of purifying the world (*huozhe neng sheshen shujie*). In this way, because one would not be working for money or fame, one could rid oneself of greed. Was this not the best way to *lishen*?[68]

Several points in this personal narrative deserve attention. First, observe the ease with which the meaning of *lishen* in one context (home) is transferred to another (society), where it may be subversive of the original context. Crucial to this transfer (and subversiveness) is not simply the valorization of social service but the corollary notion of financial autonomy. The notion of *liye*, often treated in these narratives as a subset of *lishen*, becomes one of the most important concerns of these women as they seek to establish a material base to enable their role as moral citizens of the Society and the world. Second, note the appropriation of the rhetoric of the Manzhouguo state. Many women were purposeful in their use of state rhetoric and tended to seize any rhetorical openings to advance the condition of women. Finally, there is the conflation of service in the outside world and moral purification of this world. It suggests that participation in the social world is subordinated to ethical and religious goals. These goals occupy the space of authenticity and inner meaning for the individual woman, but it is a space framed by the new patriarchy of the middle class and the state.

The interweaving of these three elements—appropriation of the rhetoric; the act of carving out a space, role, and basis for independent social action; and the employment of this autonomy to achieve the moral and religious goals of the Society—is, adjusting for individual details, a recurring pattern in the women's narratives. Note how Grandmother Cai elides over her unfiliality in an era when universal education has become an unquestioned value: at the age of thirty-three, Grandmother Cai confesses, she defied the wishes of the elders and went off to study. Now she is a grandmother and it is her responsibility to devote herself (*jinxin*) to the education of her children and grandchildren. She closes with the comment that she is a vegetarian, is deeply religious, and has tried to rid herself of vain desires. Here the value of women's education in wider society, in the modernist rhetoric of the Manzhouguo state as well as in strains within the Morality Society, allows her to justify an earlier act of unfilial behavior. She finesses filiality, however, not only with the superior card of universal education but also with the end play of devotion to spiritual virtues.[69]

The strategy, if it can be called such, is to detach oneself from one kind of pedagogical value but continue to derive meaning from the constitutive representation by emphasizing another of its qualities or values. Thus, while Grandmother Cai concluded her game by leaving the antagonist with the finessed filial card in his hands, Mrs. Li, like several others, uses filiality to trump unquestioned obedience to her husband. Ever since she heard a leader of the Society talk about caring for his own mother, Mrs. Li determined to set up her own source of livelihood (*liye*) to care for her ailing mother. Since she had to go out of the home, her husband yelled at her and accused her of being unfaithful. She says that she has never loved any man other than her husband. But now her loving heart has set.[70] Mrs. Sun has had to care for her sick father and student brother. Her husband has had problems at work and cannot provide for all of them. She has been inspired by these wise words of the leader (*shanren*): "In devoting herself, the woman must not weary the husband; rather she should be able to help the husband obtain virtue," to set up an independent means of livelihood.[71]

The ideal of moral autonomy within *lishen* is sometimes interpreted in such a radical way that it subverts the very basis of the pedagogy: family values. Thus one Ms. Liu declares that her understanding of *lishen* includes the philosophy of single living—the merits of remaining unmarried (*dushen zhuyi sixiang*). We also see a kind of feminist filiality overcoming patriarchy. A Mrs. Liu recalls that her mother was ordered back to her natal home. She and her brother were not permitted to visit her. Later she and her brother devoted themselves to restoring the family and she established a source of livelihood for her mother. This woman goes on to challenge the sages. She says, "The sages ask us to follow the three male figures [*sancong*] and learn from our husbands. We listen to our husbands, but they do not hear us. My husband eats meat and is not very virtuous, whereas I have only eaten meat once and I am a filial daughter-in-law. Should I not be the one from whom he should learn the Way? But he was formed early, and I am incapable of helping him. Anyway, I am not much concerned about my marriage."[72] Note, however, even in this last episode, the filial link to the mother appears to be the driving sentiment for Mrs. Liu.

Perhaps the episode that best reveals the inseparability of the search for autonomy and the commitment to the moral values of the Society is narrated by the same Mrs. Chen who urged women to take advantage of the job opportunities for them in Manzhouguo. "I was once sent to Beijing to lecture, but my husband followed me and insisted that I return home. Why is it that men can bully women so? I asked the teacher [*shanren*] if I should return. He replied, 'You may return. What do you have to fear? All you have to know is whether or not you have the will.' I returned. In Tianjin I was asked whether I returned of my own will. I nearly wept. I had resolved to return because I remembered that I could not violate my parents' will [*ming*]. The next time I left, I went away for four years. And so I am what I am today. The important thing is to know your own will [*zhi*]. It is how and why people make up their minds that is important, not the decision itself. I believe it is important to be filial. . . . When you have an independent income you are not only, as the teacher says, the iron master [*tie caizhu*], you become the golden master [*jin caizhu*]."[73]

I want to dwell on this moving and complex narrative not because of the way this woman, like so many others, has grasped the importance of outside service and financial independence, or because of her perception of the continued importance of filiality. Rather I am struck by the thought that the source of strength and resolve for this last woman derives precisely from the very ideology that constrains her in so many other ways. It is by knowing her mind and cultivating her resolve (*lizhi*) that she is able to establish her independence from her husband despite the constraints. The ideas in the proceedings of the conference that most restrict women are contained in the segment entitled *zhizhi*, to know the limits. The doctrine invoked most often as a constraint, and indeed, as self-constraint, is that of the three obediences, or *sancong*. When faced by such constraints, one as strong and gifted as Mrs. Chen can still pick her way around them, but that is not necessarily true for many other women. Mrs. Chen acknowledges the importance of these obediences but does not dwell upon them at length. From our fathers, she says, we can know our nature, from our husbands our fate, and through our sons we can establish ourselves (*lishen*). She does not elaborate upon what she means by *lishen* here, but moves immediately to the differences in the ways in which her parents were "good people" and the way she can be a morally pure person. Her parents were good people of a village or county; she is a good citizen of the entire nation, and indeed the world.[74] Once again she invokes the expanded community of moral service to elude these constraints.

But not all the women were as skillful as Mrs. Chen. Mrs. Zhao says that her greatest aspiration is to be a man, so much so that she sometimes forgets that she is a woman. But her nature is that of a woman, her mind is that of a woman, and her body is that of a woman. She needs to remind herself constantly about these constraints. Another woman cites the sages to acknowledge to herself that a woman, in her duty to observe the three obediences, must recognize the limits of her freedom. Mrs. Liu believes that having a woman's heart, she was not filial to her in-laws and did not obey her husband (*congfu*). Consequently, they brought a "sister" into the household. Now she tries to be a good wife and obeys her husband dutifully. Although they are poor, they are pure inside.[75] Thus we are returned to the pedagogy of authenticity.

CONCLUSIONS

What difference does it make that the alternative vision of modernity and modern subjectivity espoused by the redemptive societies flowered under a Japanese rule that conducted brutal military experiments and engaged in horrifying violence in its occupation of China? While we ourselves may not be particularly sympathetic to their redemptive vision, to tar these people with the brush of collaborationism is to slip into an easy nationalist moralism that was immoral to them. The goal of these societies was to attain a level of moral and spiritual commitment that would enable the individual to transcend the walls of nationality and ethnicity. The Manzhouguo government constructed a space for them—for the first time—in which to operate and flourish, and they responded, I believe, with considerable enthusiasm. Indeed, the nationalist condemnation forces the question: can a Chineseness be denied to those who seek their identity in their own cosmopolitan traditions? At the same time, it is undeniably true that this regime often subverted these ideals for its own imperialist or militarist purposes. But how far can we go in holding a people responsible for the state's manipulation of their ideals? Does this responsibility authorize our dismissal or condemnation of the varied, and even mixed, motives behind a mostly ordinary people's pursuit of their goals and ideals?

Similarly undeniable is the reality of women's subjugation within the Morality Society. I have cited the constraints on the women toward the end of my essay in order to remind myself of the limits of interpretation, to acknowledge the extent to which the pedagogy did shape the women's subjectivity. Yet just as I believe that an abstract master narrative of the nation cannot deliver the full or final judgment on a person's sense of value, I am impressed by the extent to which the enunciating woman was able to carve out an autonomy within the modern patriarchy.

To be sure, there were divisions of opinion among the men of the Morality Society itself that gifted women were able to exploit. But I would like to propose that discourses and representations that structure the reality of the individual are unable to prevent the irruption of elements from alternative or ambient discourses into their language, in this case the irruption of elements from the discourse of the modern woman and, even more, from the discourse of the ideal of universal public service and economic independence. This transformation is often disguised metaleptically—by the continued usage of an older language that has come to signify a different, newer meaning—as with the transformation of *lishen* and *liye*, which accompanied the emergence of the social realm. Discursive irruption into the interior space of authenticity from alternative discourses did not occur only among conservative or traditionalizing societies. While the May Fourth view of the nation had little place for the tropes of the past, there was a discursive split in its imagery of woman. In the wartime writings and propaganda of many May Fourth activists, the nation was depicted in the historical figure of a chaste woman raped by an aggressor—an irruption of both past and contemporary, conservative representations of woman and nation into the May Fourth Movement's vision of modernity.[76]

At the same time, the women's enunciation of the rhetoric of the Morality Society should not be mistaken as purely instrumental manipulation. These women were not one-dimensional rational actors who manipulated language to maximize their utility. Some critiques of the idea of hegemony come dangerously close to such a position. James Scott's interesting work on subaltern groups who pay lip service to or use the "hegemonic" ideology to pursue practices from a hidden transcript suggests a flexible view of ideology that is welcome, but its instrumentality is overdrawn.[77] The women lecturers of the Morality Society were people who maneuvered the language in the same moment in which they were constituted by it. The moral and spiritual goals that pervaded the space of authenticity enabled a defiance of pedagogy even while they limited the behavior and identities of these women. As spirituality and filiality were reinforced in deeply personal ways, the authentic space continued to both inspire and constrain subjects, and its inviolability itself was not challenged. But its meaning was changed.

NOTES

I am particularly thankful to Li Haiyan for her superb help as a research assistant on this project. I am also thankful to the participants of the conference on "Becoming Chinese" who commented on the paper I presented, which became this chapter. Thanks are also due Susan Mann, Thomas Pixely, Joan Scott, Mayfair Yang, and others who gave me valuable comments. Some of the materials in this paper have also appeared in Prasenjit Duara, "The Regime of Authenticity: Timelessness, Gender, and National History in Modern China," *History and Theory* 37 (October 1998), 287–308; and in Duara, "Transnationalism and the Predicament of Sovereignty: China, 1900–1945," *American Historical Review* (October 1997): 1030–51.

1. On the intellectual history, see Charlotte Furth, *The Limits of Change: Essays on Conservative Alternatives in Republican China* (Cambridge, Mass., 1976).

2. Kai-wing Chow, *The Rise of Confucian Ritualism in Late Imperial China: Ethics, Classics, and Lineage Discourse* (Stanford, Calif., 1994), 21–25.

3. Takayoshi Suemitsu, *Shina no mimi kaisha to jishan kaisha* (China's secret societies and charitable societies) (Dalian, 1932), 354.

4. Wanguo Daodehui Manzhouguo zonghui bianjike, ed., *Manzhouguo Daodehui nianjian* (Yearbook of the Manzhouguo Morality Society), vol. 4 (Xinjing: Wanguo Daodehui Manzhouguo zonghui bianjike, 1934), 1. Hereafter known as *MDNJ*. See also Takizawa Toshihirō, *Shūkyō chōsa shiryo* (Materials from the survey of religions), vol. 3: *Minkan shinyō chōsa hokokusho* (Report on the survey of popular beliefs) (Xinjing, 1937), 67.

5. Chen Lifu, *Xin shenghuo yu minsheng shiguan* (New Life and the Minsheng conception of history), Geming wenxian, vol. 68: *Xin shenghuo yundong shiliao* (Taipei, 1976), 128.

6. Ibid., 133.

7. Ōtani Komme, *Shyūkyō chōsa shiryo* (Materials from the survey of religions), vol. 2: *Kirin, Kento, Binko, kakosho shūkyō chōsa hōkoku* (Report on religious surveys of the various provinces of Jilin, Jiandao, and Binjiang) (Xinjing, 1937), 69, 123; Suemitsu, *Shina no mimi kaisha*, 251, 255.

8. Prasenjit Duara, *Rescuing History from the Nation: Questioning Narratives of Modern China* (Chicago, 1995), chap. 3.

9. Suemitsu, *Shina no mimi kaisha*, 302.

10. See Chow, *Rise*, 22–24, for late imperial syncretism.

11. Suemitsu, *Shina no mimi kaisha*, 292–305.

12. Ibid., 262–63.

13. Ibid., 266, 326–28; Takizawa, *Shūkyō chōsa shiryo*, 76–78; Wing-tsit Chan, *Religious Trends in Modern China* (New York, 1953), 164–67.

14. Louis Althusser, "Ideology and Ideological State Apparatuses (Notes towards an Investigation)," in *Lenin and Philosophy* (New York, 1971).

15. The anxiety associated with the linear representation of phenomenological time—time as a succession of instants, of nows—seeks resolution through structures of continuity.

This is the role of the unchanging in evolution or what Derrida has called the "intemporal kernel of time." In Derrida, this intemporal kernel is the elusive "now," which is related to other categories of presence such as being, essence, and substance. Yet like them, the now can never truly escape time, that is, cannot escape being-past or being-future, rather than being-present (Jacques Derrida, "*Ousia* and *Gramme:* Note on a Note from *Being and Time,*" in *Margins of Philosophy,* trans. Alan Bass [Chicago, 1982], 40). Linear history, which recapitulates the aporia of linear time, has to develop an artifice that allows it to narrate over the succession of "nows," to negotiate or conceal the gap between the deadness of the past and the need for it (Paul Ricoeur, *Time and Narrative* [Chicago, 1984, 1988], 1 [1984]: 1–30; 3 [1988]: 138–41). For linear histories this artifice is the *subject* of history—the nation, race, or class. At the same time that the subject enables history as the living essence of the past, it also enables a freedom from the past: that which evolves is that which remains even as it changes. For a more detailed examination of the relationship between authenticity and time, see Duara, "Regime."

16. Similarly, by "tradition" I refer not to some abiding essence or primordial inheritance, a view found both in nationalist and modernization paradigms of our times. I see it rather as a discursive production, an inheritance that is resignified in the inheriting process—a re-presentation (See Duara, *Rescuing History,* chap. 3). It is precisely because the past is reproduced or coproduced by the present that there is so much diversity and contestation over tradition, and that characterizations of this tradition are so changeable over time.

17. Partha Chatterjee, *The Nation and Its Fragments: Colonial and Postcolonial Histories* (Princeton, 1993), chap. 6.

18. Ibid., chaps. 6–7.

19. Norma Diamond, "Women under Kuomintang Rule: Variations on the Feminine Mystique" *Modern China* 1, no. 1 (1975): 6–7.

20. Mao Dun, "Mud," in *Furrows: Peasants, Intellectuals, and the State: Stories and Histories from Modern China,* comp. and ed. Helen F. Siu (Stanford, 1990), 33–39.

21. Lu Xun, "Wozhi jielieguan" (My views on chastity), in *Fen,* in *Lu Xun Quanji,* vol. 1 (1918; reprint, Taipei, 1989), 101–13.

22. Lu Xun, "Feizao" (Soap), in *Panghuang,* in *Lu Xun Quanji,* vol. 2 (1924; reprint, n.p., Lu Xun Quanji chubanshe, 1927), 189–207. For a fuller interpretation of Lu Xun's writings on this subject, see Prasenjit Duara, "Regime."

23. Kazuko Ono, *Chinese Women in a Century of Revolution, 1850–1950,* trans. and ed. Joshua Fogel (Stanford, 1989), 27.

24. Wang Jingwei, "Duiyu nüjiede ganxiang" (Reflections on women's world), *Funü zazhi* 10, no. 1 (1924): 106–7.

25. Ibid., 108.

26. *MDNJ,* 1:1.

27. Hailing from Chaoyang county in Rehe, Wang Fengyi (1864–1937) was a self-educated, rural intellectual who synthesized the theory of the five conducts (based on the five elements) and yinyang cosmology with the teachings of the three religions into a single doctrine. The careers of Wang and intellectuals like him (and the adoption and promotion of Wang and others by metropolitan elites) need to be studied much more fully (see Lin Anwu, "Yin dao yi li jiao—yi Wang Fengyi 'shierzi xinchuan' wei gaixin zhankai" [Establishing the "way" as religion—explorations of Wang Fengyi's "twelve character teachings"], in *Zhonghua minzu zongjiao xueshu huiyi lunwen fabiao* [Publication of the conference on

the study of Chinese religion] [Taipei, 1989], 11–19). See also Manzhouguo Daodehui bianjike (Manzhouguo Morality Society editorial department), ed., *Disanjie Manzhouguo Daodehui daode jiangxi yulu* (Oral records of morality seminars of the third Manzhouguo Morality Society), pt. 3 (Xinjing, 1936), 1. Hereafter known as *DMDY*.

28. The membership figure for the Fellowship of Goodness comes from Suemitsu, *Shina no mimi kaisha*, 252. The figure for the Red Swastika Society comes from Takizawa, *Shūkyō chōsa shiryo*, 67.

29. Chan, *Religious Trends*, 164. However Wing-tsit Chan does note that the Fellowship of Goodness claimed more than a thousand branches in all parts of China proper and Manchuria in 1923 (165). Suemitsu believes that the Red Swastika had a following of 3 million in 1932 (Suemitsu, *Shina no mimi kaisha*, 302).

30. Chan, *Religious Trends*, 167.

31. To be sure, many of these societies—especially the religious societies—were also militarily opposed to Japanese rule. See especially Takizawa, *Shūkyō chōsa shiryo*, on the Zaijiali.

32. Warren H. Smith Jr., *Confucianism in Modern Japan: A Study of Conservatism in Japan's Intellectual History* (Tokyo, 1959), 123–26.

33. Ibid., 154–66. To be sure, this was a synthetic rhetoric that not only sought to combine Eastern spirituality with Western civilization but also Confucianism with native Japanese traditions. Japan was depicted, especially after the Chinese Republican revolution, as the true leader and champion of Confucianism and Eastern morality—a depiction used to justify intervention in China (145).

34. Takizawa, *Shūkyō chōsa shiryo*, 82–86, 100–102.

35. Carol Gluck, *Japan's Modern Myths: Ideology in the Late Meiji Period* (Princeton, 1985), 103; and Sheldon Garon, "Women's Groups and the Japanese State: Contending Approaches to Political Integration, 1890–1945," *Journal of Japanese Studies* 19, no. 1 (1993): 5–41.

36. The story of the tensions between the Society and the Manzhouguo government over religious worship, account-keeping, school curricula, and ties with secret societies, as well as ideological clashes with progressive groups within Manzhouguo, is a very revealing one and belongs to another history (*MDNJ*, 2:14–16, 25–35, 42–45).

37. Ibid., 4:2.

38. Ibid., 2:36–42; 4:117, 118; 8:22–23.

39. Ibid., 1:21.

40. *DMDY*, 1:10–58.

41. Lu, "Feizao"; Kang Baiqing, "Du Wang jun Zhuomin daxue buyi nannü tongxiao lun shangdui" (A response to Mr. Wang Zhuomin's essay on the inappropriateness of co-education in our universities), *Funü zazhi* 4 (1918): 11; Wang Zhuomin, "Lun wuguo daxue shang buyi nannü tongxiao" (On the inappropriateness of coeducation in our universities), *Funu zazhi* 4 (1918): 5; Yan Shi, "Nannü tongxue yu lian'ai shang de zhidao" (Coeducation and guidance on amorous relationships), *Funu zazhi* 9 (1923): 10.

42. *DMDY*, 4:142.

43. Mark Elvin, "Female Virtue and the State in China," *Past and Present* 104 (1984); Charlotte Furth, "The Patriarch's Legacy: Household Instructions and the Transmission of Orthodox Values," in *Orthodoxy in Late Imperial China*, ed. Kwang-ching Liu (Berkeley, Calif., 1984); Dorothy Ko, *Teachers of the Inner Chambers: Women and Culture in Seventeenth Century China* (Stanford, 1994). See also Chow, *Rise*.

44. *MDNJ,* 1:1; 4:1–2. Although we do not think of Manzhouguo as a nation-state, it did, in fact, possess a highly developed rhetoric of a new type of nation unifying the different races of the area (*xiehe guojia*). However, since its rhetoric had to balance the assertion of national independence with its political dependence upon Japan, the nation was only one of the "ultimate" communities that it emphasized; the other was East Asia.

45. *Hanyu da cidian* quotes passages from the representative texts in which these categories occur: *zhiming* can be found in the text *Yijing, zhixing* and *jinxin* in *Mengzi, zhizhi* in *Liji, lishen* in *Xiaojing, lizhi* in *Hou Hanshu,* and *liye* in *Hanji.*

46. See Homi Bhabha on enunciation: "The reason a cultural text or system of meaning cannot be sufficient unto itself is that the act of cultural enunciation—the *place of utterance*—is crossed by the difference of writing.... It is this difference in the process of language that is crucial to the production of meaning and ensures, at the same time, that meaning is never simply mimetic or transparent." See Bhabha, *The Location of Culture* (London, 1994), 36.

47. *DMDY,* 3:4–5, 38.

48. Three of these relationships—between father and son, older and younger brothers, husband and wife—concern stabilizing family ties; the fourth relationship between friends connects horizontally across families; and the fifth between subject and monarch links the family to the state.

49. *MDNJ,* 11:29.

50. *DMDY,* 4:221–23.

51. Ibid., 4:97.

52. It is interesting to explore the extent to which this discourse on family and the nation-state in Manzhouguo, especially before 1941, paralleled or was influenced by other midcentury nationalist and fascist discourses in Europe and Asia.

53. *DMDY,* 4:134.

54. *MDNJ,* 10:6; 12:24.

55. *DMDY,* 4:151.

56. *MDNJ,* 2:41; 4:27. Thus, the weekly curriculum of the virtuous girls' schools was standardized to devote 2 hours for self-cultivation; 3 for the study of the classics; 5 for art, needlework, and music; 8 for Chinese; 2 for Japanese; 2 for history; 2 for geography; 6 for math; and 2 for nature study (*MDNJ,* 2:1–3).

57. *DMDY,* 4:207. Note, however, that Wang's household was probably very patriarchal. When his daughter-in-law was brought in marriage into their home, she fell into a depression and returned to her uncle's home. Wang claims that after he spoke to her, she happily returned to their home (4:157).

58. Ibid., 4:90, 94, 138.

59. See Furth, "Patriarch's Legacy"; Chow, *Rise;* Elvin, "Female Virtue"; and Susan Mann, *Precious Records: Women in China's Long Eighteenth Century* (Stanford, 1997).

60. Furth, "Patriarch's Legacy."

61. *MDNJ,* 11:30. To be sure, the recent work of Susan Mann and others has shown that the high moralism confining women to the home was a consequence of the Confucian "classical revival" of the eighteenth century and should not be viewed as an eternal feature of imperial Chinese society (Mann, *Precious Records,* 22–31). These writers have also shown that despite all the rhetoric and measures designed to confine women to the home, there was still a great deal of physical mobility among women in late imperial society.

62. *DMDY,* 4:53.

63. Takizawa, *Shūkyō chōsa shiryo,* 94–95.

64. In some ways, the realm of the social functioned like the nation as a legitimating force in providing alternative roles for women. As the sphere of collective activity it was certainly a most important component or building block of nationalist discourse.

65. *DMDY,* 4:185.

66. Ibid., 4:134–35.

67. Song Ruohua, *Nü Lunyu* (The analects of women) (Shanghai, [780?]), 3–5.

68. *DMDY,* 4:181.

69. Ibid., 4:137.

70. Ibid., 4:140.

71. Ibid., 4:139. A Mrs. Zhu recalled being so driven by anxiety when her stepmother arrived after her mother died, that she wore out fifteen pairs of shoes. Later she realized that her stepmother was not unkind and she herself had been unfilial. So, in order to make up for it, she set up a business for the two of them, and her selfish feelings dissolved (4:130).

72. Ibid., 4:132, 188, 231.

73. Ibid., 4:181–82.

74. Ibid., 4:227–28.

75. Ibid., 4:219, 220, 236.

76. In many ways, we may consider the simultaneously alternative and ambient discourses on women in Buddhism and Daoism in the late imperial period to have played a similar role in relation to the Confucian orthodoxy. Thus, despite the heavy rhetoric of "familial moralism" that redefined the position of the wife and marginalized the courtesan in the eighteenth century, women continued to find in Buddhism and Daoism an alternative sphere and the means to escape confinement to the home and patriarchy (Mann, *Precious Records,* 224–25).

77. James C. Scott, *Domination and the Arts of Resistance: Hidden Transcripts* (New Haven, 1990).

ELEVEN

Victory as Defeat: Postwar Visualizations of China's War of Resistance

Paul G. Pickowicz

There was an extraordinary amount of violence in China during the first fifty years of the twentieth century, but the War of Resistance was by far the worst instance. Tens of millions experienced that conflict as nothing less than a holocaust. Death, destruction, privation, and persecution were daily occurrences. Communities were ripped apart. Individual incidents of terror and agony were reported in the press, but, so long as the struggle was still unfolding, it was difficult for participants to evaluate the devastating impact of the war on Chinese society. Not until the defeat of Japan was it possible to craft epic narratives that reflected critically on the "national" meaning of the endless nightmare.

Elite nation builders had their own grand interpretations of the "meaning of the war." Their views, embodied in a variety of official mythologies, have been studied quite carefully. One wonders, however, how ordinary people, including those who lived in the vast areas under direct Japanese occupation and who were cut off from detailed news about the course of the war, thought about the hardships they had suffered during the long ordeal. Once the struggle was over, many prominent Chinese, including politicians, historians, novelists, and journalists, were eager to tell the people about the ultimate meaning of their sufferings. But few were as successful in the role of "voice of the people" as the leading filmmakers. In a word, they captured the imagination of the urban population. Visual images produced at this time were so potent that many decades later, elderly and middle-aged Chinese still remembered the holocaust in the vivid terms spelled out in highly popular postwar film epics.

THE POSTWAR FILM SCENE

In the mid-1930s the Chinese film industry was flourishing. Everything changed when the war spread to Shanghai in August 1937. Many film personalities fled into the interior to aid the resistance. Those who stayed behind did the best they could to make "Orphan Island" films in Shanghai in the foreign concessions, which were beyond direct Japanese control, from 1937 to late 1941. For obvious reasons, however, these works did not deal explicitly with war-related themes.

Throughout the war, and particularly after the attack on Pearl Harbor, Chinese films were made under Japanese auspices in Shanghai and elsewhere. This work had entertainment value but was incapable of considering the impact of the war on ordinary citizens. By late 1944 and early 1945, as the Allies closed in on Japanese forces, relatively few Japanese-sponsored works were produced. Chinese who worked in that sector of the film industry were afraid of being accused of collaboration when the war was over. During the war the Nationalist government tried to encourage filmmaking in the interior. Due to poor production environments and inadequate means of distribution, however, these works, almost all of which fell into the category of patriotic mobilization propaganda, attracted little attention.[1] In short, none of the films made in China between 1937 and 1945 took a comprehensive look at the war and its social consequences. By the end of the conflict, Chinese filmmakers in both the interior and the occupied zones were almost completely idle.

Once victory was in hand, there was an enormous demand for new Chinese-made films, especially works that talked about the war. But the film world responded very slowly. In the twelve months that followed the Japanese surrender on August 14, 1945, not a single Chinese film was completed. Consumers demanded, but did not get, new Chinese productions. Instead, they got old Chinese films and American films.

The situation was so tense that in early June 1946 a riot broke out at the Strand Theater (*Xinguang da xiyuan*) on Ningbo Road in Shanghai, when patrons violently protested yet another screening of an old Charlie Chaplin movie.[2] Consumers looked forward to seeing *new* Hollywood films, but ticket prices were exceedingly high and lines unbearably long. As a result, there was a booming black market for tickets to the most popular American movies.[3] Local papers demanded to know why there were no new Chinese films.

The lack of new film production activity was related to the threat of full-scale civil war and frustrating delays in the takeover of Shanghai and other Japanese-occupied cities. It is sometimes forgotten that the government did not make an official return to its prewar capital in Nanjing until May 5, 1946.

Ordinary film fans had no way of knowing that both the state and private sectors had ambitious agendas for the postwar film industry. For the state, the first step involved nationalizing the Japanese-controlled film studios in Shanghai and Beijing and confiscating their equipment, by far the best moviemaking hardware available in China. By nationalizing these units and refusing to make the equipment available to private sector filmmakers, the state was declaring its intention of going into the postwar motion picture business. This was a first for China. The Nationalist state had been largely uninvolved in the sprawling prewar film industry. When the state began taking over Japanese studios in late 1945, its filmmaking experience was limited to a few crude and highly forgettable wartime propaganda works turned out in Wuhan and Chongqing.

Two of the new state-owned units, China Film No. 1 and China Film No. 2, were located in Shanghai, and one studio, China Film No. 3, was set up in Beijing. To increase its chances of success, the state retained (and thus monopolized) the services of the Chinese technicians and production crews of the former Japanese studios.[4] Lists of Chinese stars who had worked with the Japanese were published, and a few high-profile arrests were made, but no one was tried for treason. Film workers who had cooperated with the Japanese were spared after the war.

The new state studios also offered employment to the many stage and film workers who had served the resistance so valiantly in the interior. With the war at an end, these people now needed jobs. As a rule, however, directors and film workers who had served in the interior were kept apart from those who had remained in Shanghai.

Filmmakers who desperately wanted to revive the private sector after the war had a hard time competing with the state. They had difficulty attracting investors, they had to order new equipment from abroad, and they were unable to offer immediate employment to film workers, most of whom had families to support.[5]

Well before any state or private-sector films were actually produced, there was a good deal of discussion in the popular press about the hopes of postwar filmmakers. Using time-honored neo-Confucian standards, some commentators argued that both state and private filmmakers had a moral obligation to play an uplifting role in the postwar industry. In general, there was a greater awareness of the extraordinary power of the film image than there had been before the war. In May 1946, for instance, one film writer asserted that there was "no agency in the world so capable of being used for adult education as the motion picture." The "propaganda possibilities" of film, he solemnly concluded, "make it one of the strongest and most penetrative influences in human history."[6]

Those who emphasized educational goals (and there were both conservatives and liberals in this camp) tended to be critical of the purely commercial orientation of most prewar private-sector filmmakers. When the overriding concern was moneymaking, critics said, the result was often worthless trash that weakened public morals. It was necessary to look upon films "as something aside from a means of entertainment."[7] In a word, filmmaking was too important to be left exclusively in the hands of greedy merchants and capitalists.

Although the rhetoric was high-minded, the first few postwar films, almost all produced in the new state-owned studios, failed to offer anything new or innovative. Disillusionment and despair were already facts of postwar life, but none of the new works confronted the problem of urban malaise and its connection to the dislocations of war. The very first state-funded postwar production, *Loyal and Virtuous Family* (*Zhong yi zhi jia*), released on August 27, 1946, was written and directed by Wu Yonggang (1907–82), a well-known leftist whose prewar work had been praised by Communist critics. A one-dimensional story of the wartime sacrifices of a patriotic Shanghai family, it differed in no significant way from the simplistic pro-Guomindang and pro-American propaganda films produced by the state during the war. Another early postwar state project was *Songbird on Earth* (*Ying fei renjian*), directed by Fang Peilin and released on November 7. It was precisely the sort of formulaic entertainment musical churned out in large quantities by prewar commercial studios.

The box office success of some of these early postwar films was due, in large part, to their novelty. They were advertised in the newspapers as the "first" postwar this or the "first" postwar that, and people naturally turned out to take a look. Some critics complained that the films were poorly made imitations of Hollywood originals, but the film-hungry audience was understandably curious.

Only a relative handful of film-world insiders knew that, even as these disappointing early postwar movies were making the rounds, startlingly different works were already in production in the state-owned studios and, shortly thereafter, in the private studios. These stunning works, fashioned without exception by filmmakers who had worked in leading Nationalist cultural organizations during the war, boldly asserted that the social disruptions caused by the war were so severe that victory felt like defeat. Despite the depressing nature of these postwar epic narratives, the films were phenomenally popular. Indeed, they caused a sensation that propelled the film industry to the forefront of the Chinese cultural world in early 1947.

PREWAR CONNECTIONS, WARTIME PASSAGES, AND POSTWAR NETWORKS

Chen Liting, Shi Dongshan, Cai Chusheng, and Zheng Junli were especially prominent among the screenwriters and directors responsible for the astonishing surge of creativity that swept through the Chinese film world in late 1946 and early 1947. The four men shared much in common. All four were veterans of the robust stage and screen worlds of prewar Shanghai. Chen Liting and Zheng Junli were leaders of the Shanghai Amateur Experimental Drama Troupe (*Shanghai yeyu shiyan ju tuan*) in the late 1930s, while Shi Dongshan, Cai Chusheng, and Zheng Junli were well-known film personalities associated with Shanghai's glamorous Lianhua Film Studio (*Lianhua dianying zhipianchang*) in the prewar years. All four had contacts in Nationalist government offices, in the business world, and in left-wing cultural circles. All four held moderate political views and refrained from joining political parties. All four fled Shanghai prior to the Japanese occupation in November 1937 and passed many difficult years in the interior working for various Nationalist cultural organizations engaged in resistance activities. All four spent considerable time in wartime Chongqing, returning to Shanghai by early 1946 to breathe life into a postwar reincarnation of the old Lianhua Film Studio called Kunlun (*Kunlun yingye gongsi*).[8] Most important, all four had ambitious plans to film unsettling accounts of the holocaust experience.

A native of Shanghai, Chen Liting (1910–), the most intellectual of the group, was swept up by the post–May Fourth surge of interest in modern drama. In 1931, while attending Daxia University in Shanghai, Chen translated *The Rising of the Moon*, a highly influential early-twentieth-century play by the noted Irish dramatist Lady Gregory.[9] This famous work helped launch a renaissance in Irish drama; it featured lively, direct, and powerful dialogue that was rooted in Ireland's rural folklore. Chen directed and acted in the first Chinese production of *The Rising of the Moon*.

In late 1931 and early 1932 Chen worked as an elementary schoolteacher in rural Nanhui county, east of central Shanghai. Chen began at once directing experimental "street theater" (*jietou ju*) that dispensed with stages, sets, artificial lighting, and other conventions. Actors and audience were in direct contact. Inspired by Lady Gregory's example, Chen emphasized simplicity and clarity of message. His most famous production, *Lay Down Your Whip* (*Fang xia ni de bianzi*), caused an immediate uproar. Years later, during the War of Resistance, it was performed countless times throughout China.[10]

Back in Shanghai by mid-1932, Chen worked for several years organizing and directing amateur theater groups that were loosely affiliated with the League of Left-Wing Dramatists. He also wrote film reviews for *Chen bao* and *Ming bao*, and translated a number of Soviet books on filmmaking, including Vsevolod Pudovkin's *On Film Acting* (*Dianying yanyuan lun*).[11] It was in the mid-1930s that Soviet films began to be screened in China.

When the war erupted, Chen was one of the primary leaders of the Shanghai Amateur Experimental Drama Troupe. His company immediately joined the resistance by breaking into two groups to form the third and fourth brigades of the Shanghai Salvation Drama Troupe (*Shanghai jiuwang yanju*). Chen served as the leader of the fourth brigade. After putting on numerous street performances, including *Lay Down Your Whip*, the troupe fled Shanghai before it fell, in September. For the next three years Chen and his compatriots traveled under harsh conditions through central and southwest China, performing innumerable patriotic plays.

In 1941 Chen arrived in Chongqing and was immediately invited by the Nationalist authorities to join the state-run China Film Studio (*Zhongguo dianying zhipianchang*) and the Central Cinematography Studio (*Zhongyang sheying chang*). But Chen's main contribution continued to be in the theater world. As a member of such state-sponsored groups as the China Art Theater Society (*Zhongguo yishu ju she*), Chen directed leading plays by Wu Zuguang (1917–), Xia Yan (1900–1995), and Chen Baichen (1908–). Chen Liting's most impressive wartime effort was his staging of Guo Moruo's (1892–1978) famous 1942 play, *Qu Yuan*.

Chen Liting was back in Shanghai by early 1946. He was invited to join the state's new China Film No. 2 Studio, and began at once to write and then direct *Far Away Love* (*Yaoyuan de ai*), the first in a series of controversial epics on the social dislocations caused by the holocaust. The premiere, held in Shanghai's well-known Huanghou Theater on January 18, 1947, was a landmark event in postwar filmmaking. Such prominent actors and actresses as Zhao Dan (1915–80), Qin Yi (1922–), and Wu Yin (1909–91), all of whom had worked with Chen before or during the war, were recruited by the state-run studio to play leading roles. The Ministry of Defense supported the production by putting units of uniformed soldiers at Chen's disposal.

Chen Liting made a second film at China Film No. 2 Studio, Chen Baichen's *A Rhapsody of Happiness* (*Xingfu kuangxiangqu*), in late 1947, before moving on to Kunlun, the new private studio, to direct *Women Side-by-Side* (*Liren xing*) in early 1949, a work based on a screenplay cowritten by Chen and the noted dramatist Tian Han (1898–1968). After 1949 Chen served the new socialist regime in many capacities, including a long stint as director of the Haiyan Film Studio in Shanghai from 1957 to 1966. There is no evidence that Chen Liting ever joined the Communist Party, even though many leading film personalities did so in the 1950s.

Shi Dongshan (1902–55), whose original name was Shi Kuangshao, was raised in Hangzhou. His father was an accomplished local artist and musician, but the family was of modest means. Shi left Hangzhou in 1922, finding work as a set designer at the Shanghai Yingxi Film Company (*Shanghai yingxi gongsi*).[12] He directed his first film for Yingxi in 1925, at the age of twenty-three, and in 1930 Shi began working for the legendary Lianhua Film Studio, one of the two most important film companies of the 1930s. Prior to the Japanese occupation of Manchuria, Shi's finely crafted works did not have a particular political orientation. On the contrary, one of Shi's specialties was directing the sort of flashy martial arts thriller that was so popular in the late 1920s.

Beginning in 1931, however, his films took on a more pronounced patriotic tone as the Japanese threat intensified. In 1937 he fled Shanghai for Wuhan and later Chongqing, where he, like Chen Liting, worked for the China Film Studio, an arm of the Political Bureau of the Nationalist government's Military Affairs Commission (*Junshi weiyuanhui zhengzhi bu*). Shi produced a number of highly patriotic wartime propaganda films and directed a few stage plays.

In 1946 he returned to Shanghai and helped found the Kunlun Film Studio. In August 1946 he completed the controversial screenplay *Eight Thousand Miles of Clouds and Moon* (*Ba qian li lu yun he yue*), a narrative thematically consistent with Chen Liting's *Far Away Love*. It was Kunlun's first postwar production. This film, directed by Shi himself, was released simultaneously at the Carlton, Huguang, and Huanghou theaters in Shanghai on February 21, 1947, a month after the triumphant appearance of *Far Away Love*.

Shi Dongshan resided in Hong Kong in 1948, but returned to Beijing in 1949 after the revolution, and was appointed head of the Technology Committee of the Ministry of Culture's Film Bureau (*Wenhua bu dianying ju jishu weiyuanhui*).[13] After 1949 Shi's directorial activities were limited. Shi never joined the Communist Party, and by late 1951 he became the target of political criticism. On February 23, 1955, at the age of fifty-three, Shi Dongshan committed suicide. According to one of his sons, his farewell note was confiscated on the orders of Zhou Enlai, and news of the suicide was suppressed.

Cai Chusheng (1906–68) was born in Shanghai, but returned with his parents to their native place, Chaoyang, Guangdong, when he was six. His formal education was limited to four years in an old-style private school. At age twelve Cai was sent by his father to Shantou to learn a trade, first in an old-style bank (*qian zhuang*) and then in a small shop. Cai was far more interested, however, in amateur theater activities. In 1926 he helped make local arrangements for a Shanghai film company that was shooting a movie in Shantou. In 1929 he moved to Shanghai and, like Shi Dongshan before him, worked at a number of odd jobs in the film industry. Cai's big break came in 1929, when at the age of twenty-three he met the famous actor and director Zheng Zhengqiu (1888–1935), who was also a native of Chaoyang. Zheng immediately brought his compatriot into the well-known Star Film Company (*Mingxing yingpian gongsi*), where Cai directed six pictures. In summer 1931 Cai Chusheng began working at the Lianhua Film Studio, where he met Shi Dongshan.[14] Like Shi, Cai's films of the early 1930s had no pronounced political characteristics. Works like *A Dream in Pink* (*Fenhongse de meng*, 1932) were the sort of mainstream butterfly works that Cai's mentor, Zheng Zhengqiu, had mastered years before. Some of his films were criticized by leftist writers.

It was only after the Japanese attack on Shanghai in 1932 that Cai's films became overtly patriotic. By the mid-1930s he was making a greater impact on the film world than Shi Dongshan was. Cai's masterpiece, *Fisherman's Ballad* (*Yu guang qu*, 1934), written and directed when he was twenty-eight, was the first Chinese film to win an international award.[15]

In 1937 Cai fled the occupation of Shanghai and spent more than four years making Cantonese-language resistance films in Hong Kong. Following the occupation of Hong Kong he fled to Guilin, and finally to Chongqing in late 1944, where he met up with his old friend Shi Dongshan. Cai was seriously weakened by tuberculosis following his departure from Hong Kong, but by February 1945 he was able to serve as a member of the committee on writing and directing of the Nationalist's Central Cinematography Studio. Chen Liting also served on that committee.

In January 1946 Cai returned to Shanghai to help organize the privately run Kunlun branch of the old Lianhua Film Studio. Kunlun's second film, *A Spring River Flows East* (*Yi jiang chun shui xiang dong liu*, 1947), a spectacular two-part account of holocaust dislocation released in three Shanghai theaters (Lidu, Huguang, and Meiqi) on October 9, 1947, on the eve of National Day, was written primarily by Cai Chusheng. The film was so popular it played continuously in Shanghai for almost a year.

Like Shi Dongshan, Cai Chusheng went to Beijing in 1949 and assumed a number of leadership positions in the new cultural organizations, including the vice directorship of the Film Bureau under the Ministry of Culture (*Wenhua bu dianying ju*). Cai did not join the Communist Party until 1956. Owing to harsh treatment during the Cultural Revolution, Cai Chusheng died on July 15, 1968, at the age of sixty-two.

Zheng Junli (1911–69), whose family hailed from Zhongshan county, Guangdong, was born in Shanghai. Fond of art in his early years, Zheng dropped out of middle school during his second year and eventually enrolled in the theater department of the famous Southern Art Institute (*Nanguo yishu xueyuan*). In the 1930s Zheng established himself as one of China's leading stage and screen actors. In 1932 he joined the Lianhua Film Studio, came into close contact with Shi Dongshan and Cai Chusheng, and appeared in many outstanding films. Some films, like *The Big Road* (*Da lu*, 1934, d. Sun Yu), were associated with the left, while others, like *Filial Piety* (*Tian lun*, 1935, d. Fei Mu), were associated with neoconservative causes. There can be no doubt, however, that Zheng was ardently patriotic. On the eve of the war Zheng, like Chen Liting, was a leader of the Shanghai Amateur Experimental Drama Troupe, which formed the third and fourth brigades of the Shanghai Salvation Drama Troupe once the war was under way. Zheng Junli was leader of the third brigade, which also included the well-known actor Zhao Dan. Chen Liting was in charge of the fourth brigade. After doing considerable propaganda work in Shanghai proper, these groups moved into the interior to do long-term resistance work once Shanghai fell.

At Guo Moruo's urging, Zheng served in Chongqing as director of China's wartime Children's Theater Troupe (*Haizi jutuan*). From 1940 to 1942 he worked outside the wartime capital on a documentary film project for the Nationalist government's China Film Studio, returning to Chongqing and the stage as a director and actor in the last few years of the war.[16]

Zheng Junli returned to Shanghai in 1946, joining immediately in the effort to establish the Kunlun branch of the old Lianhua Film Studio. There he worked with Cai Chusheng on the epic film *A Spring River Flows East*. The screenplay, written primarily by Cai, was finished in the summer of 1946. The direction of the film was left primarily to Zheng.

After 1949 Zheng Junli continued making films at the Kunlun Studio. In 1951 his movie *Between Husband and Wife* (*Women fufu zhi jian*) was severely criticized for presenting a "distorted view of life in the liberated areas" after 1949, and Zheng was forced to write a self-criticism entitled "With Deep Remorse I Must Reform Myself" (*Wo bixu tongqie gaizao ziji*). Zheng was allowed to continue working, and he eventually joined the Communist Party in 1958. In 1961, however, his film on the life of Lu Xun was banned before its release, and in 1967, at the outset of the Cultural Revolution, Zheng was jailed. Owing to mistreatment, he died in prison in 1969 at the age of fifty-eight.

FAR AWAY LOVE: A MEANINGFUL FABRICATION

The remarkable postwar works of Chen Liting, Shi Dongshan, Cai Chusheng, and Zheng Junli pose a major question. How was it possible for films that treated victory as defeat to be so popular? To answer this question, it is extremely important to go over almost every detail of their elaborate narrative reconstructions of the war years. This method allows us to appreciate patterns of appeal that link the texts to the popular audience. As Robert Darnton has pointed out, reconstructions of this sort are not objective, historically accurate, or "true" in any strict sense.[17] We study them because they are "meaningful fabrications" that often reveal much about popular perceptions. The point about these works is not that they were historically accurate accounts of the holocaust years, but rather that they were extremely influential and came to be accepted as valid representations by millions of ordinary urbanites in the postwar period. In a word, the films captured a psychological reality that was pervasive in urban society after the war.

The first narrative, an amusing satire called *Far Away Love*, opens in Shanghai in late 1927. Chen Liting believed that a full understanding of the disruptive social dynamics of the war years required a grasp of prewar conditions. As the account opens, the audience sees a respected young professor named Xiao Yuanxi lecturing on the subject of "women and society." Xiao presents himself as a modern-minded intellectual who supports the cause of women's rights.

One day Xiao catches a female servant named Yu Zhen taking a book from his study. She claims she is only borrowing it. Given her rural background, Xiao is amazed the young woman can read. Later he tells a female colleague named Wu Ya'nan that he has a grand experiment in mind. Xiao proposes to take personal charge of the servant's reeducation. He is confident he can mold such fine raw material into a "modern young lady" (*modeng xiaojie*). At first Yu Zhen misunderstands. When she was still in her village, a landlord's son wanted to convert her into a *xiaojie*, that is, his concubine. The two intellectuals convince her that Xiao has nothing but the best intentions.

Yu Zhen finally agrees, and Professor Xiao lectures her on the role of women in modern society. Since "modern" is defined as "Western," the servant is taught Western table manners and the correct way to shake hands with men. Her peasant garb is exchanged for modern, urban clothes. Still, throughout her rigorous training, Yu Zhen continues to function as a servant. For example, Xiao insists that Yu Zhen sit with him at the breakfast table, but he still expects her to serve the meal.

The professor eventually writes a book entitled *On New Women* (*Xin funü lun*) about his experiment, and his fame spreads. He confesses to Yu Zhen, however, that her progress has not been totally satisfactory. She is not an "ideal" woman, he proclaims, because she is insufficiently "independent." Xiao complains that she obeys his commands a bit too mechanically. That problem is addressed, however, when Wu Ya'nan, known throughout the picture as Big Sister Wu, convinces Yu Zhen to go to a public meeting (on the Japanese threat) that the busy professor has no time to attend. Yu Zhen goes in order to show more "independence."

The narrative leaps ahead to 1931. Xiao has married his "ideal" woman and a son is born. Unfortunately, their domestic tranquillity is disturbed by the Mukden Incident. Influenced by Big Sister Wu, Yu Zhen attends ever more meetings. She also enrolls in a class that provides her with some leadership training. Xiao begins to resent the fact that his wife is never home. She justifies her absences by referring to his own remarks about the need for women to show "independence." When Japanese forces attack Shanghai in January 1932, Yu Zhen's father is killed in a bombing raid. Her brother joins the Nationalist army and is killed in the fierce fighting. Throughout the struggle Yu Zhen works as a volunteer nurse. When an armistice brings the fighting to an end in May, the professor is delighted that Yu Zhen will be returning home. But Yu Zhen is depressed because there was no clear victory. She says her brother "died for nothing." Eager to regain control of his wife, Xiao orders Big Sister Wu to keep away from the family.

The narrative leaps ahead to July 1937. The couple has another son and war threatens once again. And once again Wu Ya'nan shows up to recruit Yu Zhen for war preparation. Xiao claims that the war will never reach Shanghai, and when it does he is shaken to the core. When a friend offers him a comfortable military desk job in Hankou, Xiao agrees to flee the city. Yu Zhen insists on staying in Shanghai as long as possible to do dangerous work at the front. Husband and wife separate, but Xiao refuses to take either of the children, even though he is headed for a safe rear area.

Xiao lives a life of great comfort in Hankou. He wears a fancy Nationalist uniform and lives in a spacious home once occupied by Japanese residents. He has servants and an expense account. When he is not attending meaningless meetings, he plays cards in his office. Enthusiastic young people plead for a chance to go to the front, but Xiao urges them to be "logical" and refuses to process their papers. At night Xiao spends his time in Hankou's best nightclubs.

When the Japanese occupy Shanghai, Yu Zhen retreats with other resistance activists. Along the way her infant child is killed in a Japanese strafing assault. Yu Zhen later joins a Nationalist military unit and puts on the crude uniform of infantry regulars. Every day she hikes along with the troops, helping wounded soldiers, refugees, and orphans.

One of the most visually interesting sequences in the film involves the reunion in Hankou between Xiao and Yu Zhen. The gap that now separates them is apparent in everything that happens. She is wearing rough straw sandals and a tattered uniform; he has expensive leather shoes and a full cape. He wants to pay for a rickshaw; she prefers to walk. He wants her to wear women's clothing; she insists on staying in her battle fatigues. He takes her to Hankou's most elegant restaurant; she says she is not hungry. (See figure 11.1.)

The restaurant scene is especially effective. Xiao spends a small fortune on a wasteful dinner while starving children gape through the window. Yu Zhen is appalled by the decadence of the restaurant culture. She asks Xiao when he started smoking and drinking so much. When the bill comes, Yu Zhen says that a soldier at the front could live for a month on what Xiao has spent.

Back in his lavish home, Xiao tries to tell Yu Zhen that life in the rear is different from life at the front and urges her to adjust. But even Xiao's pet dog does not like Yu Zhen. The dog smells Yu Zhen's feet and immediately begins an angry bark before jumping up on Xiao's lap. One evening they go out to a dazzling nightclub for an evening of drinking and dancing to Western music. The party ends abruptly when Yu Zhen slaps a man who is harassing her.

Figure 11.1. Wearing battle fatigues and straw sandals, an embarrassed Yu Zhen (left) enters an elegant Hankou restaurant with her corrupt husband (center), in *Far Away Love* (d. Chen Liting, China Film No. 2, 1947). Courtesy of the Film Archive of China, Beijing.

As the war gets closer to Hankou, Yu Zhen wants to return to the front. Xiao is opposed to her plan. Late one night her thoughts return to the warm feelings of community she enjoyed with her comrades in the army. Before dawn she slips out and returns to the "women's work brigade" at the front, leaving a note that tells Xiao she will return whenever she can.

The war drags on and the paths of husband and wife do not cross. With the fall of Hankou, Xiao drifts to Guilin, where he takes up a minor teaching post. Xiao's dignity continues to slip away. Students sneak out of his meaningless lectures, and a new article of his, entitled "Women's Heaven and Earth Is Still in the Family," is severely criticized in the press.

Yu Zhen, it seems, has a new family. She is working feverishly on the outskirts of Guilin with Big Sister Wu and many others who comprise a wartime National-ist military collective. The group treats the elderly like parents, soldiers like broth-ers, and orphans like their own children.

The film ends when a Japanese assault on Guilin leads to a mass exodus of ter-rified refugees, including Professor Xiao, who looks quite pathetic. His clothes are

disheveled, his glasses are broken, and he has lost almost all his personal posses-
sions. Worst of all, he is not getting the respect he thinks he deserves. He complains that being in a refugee column is like being in the army: "There is no individual freedom!" Actually, the column consists primarily of women, children, and
the elderly. Xiao is one of the few adult males in the group.

The refugees finally make it to an evacuation center where Yu Zhen's women's
brigade has arranged for a caravan of trucks to take the women and children to
safety. It is here that Big Sister Wu spots the wretched Professor Xiao among the
women and children. She then brings Yu Zhen and Xiao together in the final
scene of the movie.

Xiao wants to get back together with Yu Zhen. He says he needs her and cannot understand how she can get along without her husband and family. He wants
her to go to Chongqing with him. When she declines, he asks if she has another
man. She answers that she "loves all of those who have died and all who are still
fighting." She pities him because he "loves only himself." His is a "selfish love."
Still, she promises to talk to him about their relationship once the war is over. Xiao
then jumps on a truck and goes off with the women and children.

EIGHT THOUSAND MILES OF CLOUDS AND MOON: THE ILLUSION OF REALITY

The second narrative, *Eight Thousand Miles of Clouds and Moon*, begins in Shanghai
in the summer of 1937, immediately following the Japanese invasion.[18] Like *Far
Away Love*, this account of the holocaust is particularly interesting because it dwells
on the experiences of a young woman, this time a seventeen-year-old college student named Jiang Lingyu. Inspired by the patriotic appeals of actors who visit her
campus, she wants to join a mobile drama troupe being put together by resistance
organizers. She is both innocent and idealistic, and never asks how she can gain by
actively supporting the war effort.[19]

Lingyu, a native of Jiangxi, lives in Shanghai with her aunt (her mother's sister), uncle, and two cousins (one is a female, a bit younger than Lingyu, and the
other, Zhou Jiarong, a male, is older). The problem for Lingyu, played by the famous actress Bai Yang (1920–96), who spent the war doing cultural work in the interior, is that her relatives firmly oppose her plan to join the troupe and leave
Shanghai. Lingyu's uncle expresses negative stereotypes of actors and stage people. He protests that it is immoral for young men and women to be thrown together in this fashion beyond the supervision of their families, and sternly warns
that "good people will be transformed into bad people" in such circumstances.
Lingyu's aunt asserts that the theater people have unacceptably low social and cultural status. Lingyu insists that they are people of "learning" (*xuewen*) and "standing" (*diwei*). Even her cousin, Jiarong, is opposed. He says the issue is not patriotism ("We are all patriotic"), but rather the illogic of running off with a bunch of
"stars" (*mingxing*).

VICTORY AS DEFEAT 377

But the narrative strongly suggests that the issue is, in fact, patriotism. The choice seems to be between family and country, an extremely complicated choice for most people. In this blatantly manipulative account, as in *Far Away Love*, the characterizations of the family members are so uniformly negative that the choice is easy. The narrative applauds Lingyu, a teenage female, when, to the shock and dismay of her relatives, she sneaks out to run away with the troupe of actors, a group that is clearly linked to the Nationalist government and military. Indeed, during much of the story troupe members wear Nationalist military uniforms. They regard themselves as "cultural soldiers" (*wenhua zhanshi*).

The story follows the troupe as they move from Shanghai to Suzhou, Wuxi, Changzhou, and Wuhan. Although the material living conditions of the troupe are austere, its sense of solidarity is great. In a word, the troupe is Lingyu's new family, a family born of wartime privation. The group tirelessly performs outdoor skits (including a fascinating production of Chen Liting's *Lay Down Your Whip*) to arouse the anti-Japanese indignation of the masses. They also do indoor patriotic plays for the enjoyment of infantry soldiers. Great pains are taken to show that the actors are not at all like the stereotypes imagined by Lingyu's relatives. They are cultured, disciplined, and selflessly dedicated to national salvation.

During the course of the struggle a love relationship develops between Lingyu and a classmate named Gao Libin, who also joined the drama troupe. It is a special love, born of war and sacrifice. Their bond is based on mutual respect and their united contributions to the resistance. As they move farther inland the couple experience every imaginable war-related hardship. One time they see a member of their troupe shot dead by the enemy. Another time Lingyu falls ill and is cared for by Libin and the group.

After the troupe arrives in Chongqing, Lingyu receives a letter from her father in rural Jiangxi. In sharp contrast to the maternal relatives in Shanghai, her father writes approvingly of her patriotic activities and her relationship with Libin. He agrees that they should marry, but urges them to wait until the war is over. The couple accepts his view. "China's victory will be our victory!" they say. Libin, played by the popular actor Tao Jin (1916–86), who spent most of the war doing cultural work in Chongqing, fantasizes about what China will be like when victory is achieved. The country, he predicts, will be peaceful (*heping*), democratic (*minzhu*), and free (*ziyou*), and the people will be happy (*xingfu*). Filial to the core, they plan to invite her father to live with them, and to produce a grandson for his enjoyment.

Suddenly Lingyu's cousin, Jiarong, played by the young actor Gao Zheng, shows up in Chongqing.[20] He claims that he, too, is participating in the resistance, but it is clear from his comments that he is enriching himself by engaging in war profiteering. He even offers to supply Lingyu with coffee, powdered milk, candy, and other delicacies. Jiarong is shocked to find that Lingyu and Libin are not benefiting personally from the war. He cannot understand their selfless dedication. For her part, Lingyu is repulsed by Jiarong's animated description of Chongqing's lively (*renao*) dance and party scene. Interestingly, the growing gap between the two cousins has pronounced "national" and cultural dimensions. The filmmakers take pains to show that Jiarong and his corrupted friends (like Professor Xiao and his cronies in *Far Away Love*) live, dress, and socialize in what is portrayed as the Western manner, while the members of the Nationalist drama troupe (like Yu Zhen's medical team in *Far Away Love*) live and work in ways that are shown to be consistent with essentialistic Chinese customs and morality.

As soon as Japan surrenders in August 1945, Lingyu and Libin get married in a ceremony attended by all their resistance-war comrades. Jiarong stumbles, uninvited, into the wedding party, dressed in a Western suit and tie. Disappointed to learn that Lingyu has married Libin, he invites Lingyu to join him on a special early flight back to liberated Shanghai, where new "postwar" business opportunities await. Needless to say, Lingyu declines.

But the end of the war brings nothing but difficulties for the newlyweds. First, dressed in simple Nationalist military uniforms, they travel to Jiangxi to see Lingyu's father. The couple is shocked to discover that Lingyu's father is dead and the family property has been sold. Morale in her native village is low.

Later, in Shanghai, they visit her aunt and uncle, who now live with Lingyu's cousins in a splendid foreign-style house that Jiarong got from a German national whom he protected just after the war. The reunion does not go well. Jiarong is now dressed in a fancy Western-style military uniform that suggests he is an officer involved in the postwar government takeover of Shanghai. His new girlfriend, shallow and stupid, spends most of her time applying makeup. Lingyu's female cousin has married a well-dressed businessman.

Lingyu and Libin are embarrassed by the comments of their relatives. During a *majiang* game, Lingyu's aunt asks how much money they made during the war performing plays. Jiarong says that people like them who got nothing for "serving the people" (*wei renmin fuwu*) were fools. The uncle adds that many people who lived in the interior (*houfang*) made money. The couple missed one golden opportunity during the war, he points out, but they should not miss another one in postwar Shanghai. Jobless and without the means to secure housing of their own, Lingyu and Libin are forced to live with their relatives for a time, but their relations with the family steadily decline.

One of the most interesting aspects of this film is its perspective on the lives of people who remained in Japanese-occupied areas during the war. With the important exception of Lingyu's relatives and their circle of friends, the portrayal of those who lived under the occupation is surprisingly sympathetic. For instance, Lingyu and Libin are thrilled when they reestablish contact with a group of former classmates who remained in Shanghai during the war. A number of them now work as respected journalists and teachers. Indeed, their close relations with this group of people who suffered under the occupation reminds one of the intimate collectivistic bonds that united resistance activists in the interior. In the end, Lingyu takes a job as a journalist and Libin works as a primary school teacher. (See figure 11.2.)

Figure 11.2. Lingyu (center right) and Libin (center left) are among disillusioned youth who experience hopelessness in postwar Shanghai, in *Eight Thousand Miles of Clouds and Moon* (d. Shi Dongshan, Kunlun Film Studio, 1947). Courtesy of the Film Archive of China, Beijing.

In an especially graphic episode, Lingyu shows great compassion for a desperate widow whose home and property have been confiscated by Lingyu's cousin, Jiarong, in the postwar takeover. Because the widow's husband died at the end of the war, she is now easy prey for people like Jiarong, who use any excuse to charge that people who lived in Shanghai during the occupation are traitors *(hanjian)* who deserve punishment. The homeless widow insists that her husband was not a collaborator. "You think that anyone who remained in Shanghai must have been a traitor!" she cries. Jiarong responds that the old man sold goods to Japanese consumers in his shop and rented rooms to Japanese tenants. The issue in the narrative is not so much the innocence or guilt of the accused traitor's family, but the perspective that the audience is being encouraged to accept. The morally upright Lingyu and Libin show compassion for the plight of the woman. They seem to be saying that ordinary people who remained in Shanghai and who encountered the Japanese every day ought to be viewed sympathetically, while those like Jiarong who pretended to "participate in the resistance" in the interior deserve to be scorned.[21]

Lingyu and Libin decide to move from their relative's luxurious home to a dilapidated one-room flat. Still, their postwar difficulties mount. Lingyu's work as a journalist gets her involved in the effort to expose people like Jiarong and, thus, intensifies family conflict. At one point she confronts her cousin: "Even though you are a relative, I'll write about all your activities unless you return the things you took." Libin works hard as a teacher, but, weakened by years of wartime hardship and postwar scarcity, he contracts tuberculosis.

Toward the end of the narrative Lingyu discovers she is pregnant. Normally this would be a joyous way to begin postwar life. But given the unexpected circumstances, she wonders whether it is a good thing. For a time, their spirits are buoyed by the return to Shanghai of the rest of their comrades in the drama troupe.

The narrative ends months later when Lingyu, alone at night, collapses on a rain-soaked street. Libin panics when she fails to return, and mobilizes the wartime veterans, most of whom are still wearing rough military garb, to fan out through the city to find her. They finally locate her and bring her to a hospital. The cost for her care and the delivery of the baby is five hundred thousand yuan. The leader of the troupe has two hundred thousand yuan, and the rest of the members contribute the remainder. Libin finally arrives at the hospital as a healthy baby is born. But the story closes on a highly ambiguous note. It is not at all clear that Lingyu will survive. The doctor says her only hope is to rest for a year in "a place where the air is clean." The group resolves to care for the baby. "This child is our child," they pledge. Still, the final image is a huge question mark on an otherwise blank screen, followed by a text that invites the audience to participate in the resolution of the problem. It asserts that the actions of the audience will determine whether people like Lingyu live or die.

A SPRING RIVER FLOWS EAST: COMMUNITIES AND IDENTITIES IN FLUX

The third and most powerful narrative, a two-part film entitled *A Spring River Flows East,* features many of the same lead actors and actresses, but this account of the holocaust experience heads in a number of new directions.[22] The first part, "Eight Years of Separation and Chaos" (*Ba nian li luan*), begins not in 1937, but on National Day, October 10, 1931, in the immediate aftermath of the Japanese occupation of Manchuria. As in *Far Away Love,* a serious effort is made to locate war-related issues in the broader context of prewar conditions. In this story the protagonist is a young man named Zhang Zhongliang, who works as a night-school teacher in a class attended by female textile workers in Shanghai.

Zhang, an ardent patriot who advocates immediate resistance to Japanese aggression, has organized a gala National Day talent show in a factory union hall. At the end of the show he is urged by young workers to make some patriotic remarks. His passionate anti-Japanese speech elicits two different responses. The majority applauds wildly and throws money on the stage; one female worker, Sufen, idolizes the dashing and heroic teacher. But a small minority seated at the front, consisting of management and staff, is alarmed by the spontaneous political demonstration. Zhang (played by Tao Jin) is summoned by the factory's manager, who claims to be as patriotic as the next fellow. He insists, however, that Zhang's political activities will irritate the Japanese and bring unwanted attention to the factory, thus threatening the livelihood of the workers.

After this opening tone is set, the narrative turns to the romantic relationship between Zhang Zhongliang and Sufen. Showing the utmost respect for the family matriarch, Zhang invites Sufen to come home for dinner one night to meet his mother. Naturally, the mother takes an immediate liking to the shy and highly "traditionalistic" young woman (played by Bai Yang). Zhang proposes marriage to Sufen later that night and, as he presents her with a ring, is heard promising that the couple will "be together forever" (*yongyuan zai yiqi*). The couple get married and before long a son is born.

Unfortunately for them, full-scale war breaks out in mid-1937, and Japanese forces are fast approaching Shanghai. Their dreams of family unity are smashed. Determined to join a Red Cross unit, Zhang tells his mother and wife that they should stay behind in Shanghai, but that if the situation becomes intolerable, they should flee to their native village in the countryside, where Zhang's father and younger brother, Zhongmin, are living. "I'm leaving you only because of the resistance war," Zhang tells Sufen.

Zhang's Red Cross group gets caught in the middle of the bloody struggle for Shanghai and then retreats west when the city is lost. His family flees to the countryside and links up with Zhongmin and his fiancée, who belong to a guerrilla unit based in the hills. Zhongmin, played by Gao Zheng (the evil cousin in *Eight Thousand Miles of Clouds and Moon!*), is a paragon of Confucian virtue. When the Japanese close in on the village, Zhongmin respectfully asks his father's permission before escaping with his fiancée to the guerrilla base.

In 1938–39 Zhongliang travels with Nationalist units to Hankou and then Nanchang, all the while doing exhausting and dangerous Red Cross work. But life is much worse for his family under the Japanese occupation. Japanese forces confiscate grain, property, and livestock and require the people to do backbreaking forced labor. When a merciless new grain tax is announced, villagers plead with Zhongliang's father, the village school principal, to appeal to the enemy. Instead of reconsidering, the Japanese execute the old man. The local guerrilla unit gets revenge by wiping out the Japanese post in the village, but Sufen, her son, and mother-in-law decide to return to Shanghai to wait out the war.

Meanwhile, Zhang Zhongliang has been captured by the Japanese in the interior and forced to do slave labor. He escapes, however, and, dressed in rags and penniless, arrives in Chongqing in 1941. He tries to find resistance-related work, but fails. He is also frustrated in an attempt to secure factory work in one of the war industries. In a deep depression, he looks up an acquaintance from Shanghai by the name of Wang Lizhen, played by the famous actress Shu Xiuwen (1915–69), who made resistance movies in Chongqing during the war. Wang offers to let Zhang live in her spacious house and promises to use her influence with a wealthy businessman named Pang Haogong to get him a meaningful job.

Zhang is shocked to discover, however, that Pang's company is not helping the resistance at all. Pang is a war profiteer. His employees hang around all day, while his lieutenants enjoy a carefree life of dancing, partying, eating, drinking, and romancing. Zhang complains to Wang Lizhen that "there's not an iota of resistance spirit at the company." Wang laughs hysterically and tells him he needs to relax and adjust to life in Chongqing. His spirit weakened, Zhang finally gives in to temptation. Not only does he accept her advice, he also succumbs to her seductions. After several rounds of heavy drinking, Zhang ends up in Wang's bed. Wang is unaware that Zhang is married.

At the end of part one the story returns briefly to Shanghai, where Sufen and Zhang's son and mother are struggling to survive under a cruel occupation. Even though they live in a simple shack and have barely enough to eat, Sufen and her mother-in-law help out at a school that tends to war orphans. One night, at a moment when Zhang is in bed with Wang in Chongqing, Sufen wonders why the family has not heard anything from him for years.

Unlike the first part of this epic narrative, which covers the period from 1931 to 1944, the second part, entitled "Before and after Dawn" (*Tian liang qian hou*), takes place almost entirely in the summer and autumn months of 1945. The beginning of this segment is dominated by the story of Zhang Zhongliang's meteoric rise in the ranks of Pang Haogong's elaborate business organization. Before long he becomes Pang's chief aide, fully complicitous in a web of corrupt wartime profiteering and influence peddling. While Zhang and his new friends and cohorts feast on lobsters and crabs flown into Chongqing from occupied Shanghai, Zhang's mother, wife, and son are barely managing to make ends meet under the Japanese occupation. To make matters worse, toward the end of the war Zhang decides to marry Wang Lizhen at a lavish wedding ceremony in Chongqing. During the wedding feast a letter addressed to Zhang arrives from his wife. Fearful that his prewar past will be revealed, he destroys the letter.

In his capacity as Pang's most trusted assistant, Zhang is among the first to fly back to Shanghai when the war ends. Pang has used his influence to get Zhang designated as a "takeover official" (*jieshou dayuan*). Their goal is to get off to a fast start in exploiting postwar economic opportunities. In liberated Shanghai, arrangements have been made for Zhang to live in the home of Wang Lizhen's cousin (*biaojie*) He Wenyan, played by the well-known actress Shangguan Yunzhu (1920–68). At first, He Wenyan courts Zhang's favor because she wants him to help get her husband, who has been arrested for collaborating with the Japanese, released from jail. Later she discovers that her husband has been seeing other women, so she allows him to languish in prison while she focuses on yet another seduction of Zhang, the rich newcomer from Chongqing. Zhang instantly agrees to the new arrangement but asks Wenyan what they will do when Lizhen arrives from Chongqing. Wenyan says it will be no problem: Lizhen will be his "resistance-war wife" (*kangzhan furen*); she will be his "secret wife" (*mimi furen*).

Zhang's first wife, Sufen, and his mother and son are worried sick because they have heard nothing from him in the first few weeks of the postwar period. Although the war is over, the family's economic situation steadily worsens. Desperate for work, Sufen looks for a job as a domestic servant. As fate would have it, she gains employment as a day worker in the large house run by He Wenyan. Indeed, her husband is in bed with Wenyan on the morning Sufen arrives to be interviewed for the job. The lipstick-stained bed clothes she will have to hand wash belong to her own husband, who once promised her that they would be together for eternity.

Soon thereafter Wang Lizhen arrives from Chongqing and takes up residence with Zhang at Wenyan's house. Now, for the first time, all three of Zhang's women are under the same roof. Wenyan knows about Lizhen, but not about Sufen. Lizhen knows nothing of Zhang's connections to Sufen or Wenyan. Sufen knows nothing about her husband's presence in the house. Zhang, of course, is unaware of Sufen's work in the servants' quarters.

A major crisis explodes at a sumptuous National Day banquet held at the house on October 10, 1945. The guest of honor is Pang Haogong. Just as Pang is about to force Zhang and Lizhen to do a tango for everyone, Sufen, who is serving drinks to the guests, spots Zhang. A major scandal then erupts in front of all the guests. Sufen collapses on the dance floor, Lizhen screams hysterically, and Wenyan cracks a wicked smile when it becomes clear that Zhang is indeed married to the servant. Lizhen runs upstairs, threatening suicide if Zhang does not divorce Sufen. Zhang promises her he will get a divorce. Sufen runs home to break the bad news to her son and mother-in-law. The mother is numbed by Sufen's disclosures. By coincidence, the old lady has just received a letter from her younger son, Zhongmin, the upright guerrilla fighter who sacrificed for the nation throughout the war. He has written to announce his marriage to his prewar sweetheart, who worked alongside him throughout the difficult years of national struggle. Zhang's mother pulls her grandson over and tearfully tells him to learn from the example of his uncle Zhongmin rather than his father. (See figure 11.3.)

In a highly emotional final sequence, the old lady takes Sufen and the young boy to a confrontational meeting with Zhongliang, who is now caught in the middle; his mother, wife, and son are downstairs, while his second wife and mistress are upstairs. At this point the narrative centers on the issue of Zhang's choice. Will he go back to his old life or continue to embrace his new life?

Disgraced by her husband's conduct, Sufen commits suicide by jumping into a nearby river. The old lady and the young boy rush to the waterfront, but it is too late. A distraught Zhongliang arrives on the scene, but seems incapable of assuming responsibility for his grieving family members. Before long, Lizhen and Wenyan arrive in a fancy American automobile to urge Zhongliang to leave with them. Viewers are not allowed to learn what Zhongliang decides to do. As the

Figure 11.3. Postwar dreams are shattered when Zhang Zhongliang's "wartime" wife (right) contemplates suicide after discovering that he has a "prewar" family, in *A Spring River Flows East* (d. Cai Chusheng and Zheng Junli, Kunlun Film Studio, 1947). Courtesy of the Film Archive of China, Beijing.

story ends, his mother looks into the camera, as if addressing the audience, and wails, "In times like these, decent people can't survive, while villains live for a thousand years!"

FAMILY NARRATIVES AS NATIONAL ALLEGORIES

One of the first (and rather odd) things one notices about these popular resistance-war narratives is that very little is said about the massive violence of the war itself. The enemy is almost never seen. No Japanese appear in either *Far Away Love* or *Eight Thousand Miles*. In *A Spring River*, Japanese atrocities are shown in detail only in the relatively brief episodes involving Zhang Zhongliang's capture, the occupation of his native village, and the closing of the school for orphans in Shanghai. Postwar Japanese films like *The Human Condition* (*Ningen no joken*, d. Masaki Kobayashi, 1959) contain many more details about the brutality of Japanese forces in China.

The most obvious explanation for such an omission is that postwar filmmakers simply did not have the budgets or the technical means to re-create the sort of large-scale battle scenes one normally associates with war epics. Instead, the directors of these works skillfully inserted bits of wartime documentary footage in a few strategic places to give a graphic sense of the terror that engulfed combatants and noncombatants alike. But it is not these explicit treatments of violence that make the three films successful and convincing as holocaust narratives.

Rather than focus on violence, these directors, and the many who followed their lead in 1947 and 1948, decided to emphasize the social consequences of protracted war. This appears to be what the postwar audience wanted. More specifically, all three films dwell almost exclusively on the fate of the family unit in the holocaust environment. Telling the story of the war in the form of family histories made sense in basic production terms. Postwar filmmakers had the means of executing such a plan. More important, however, the decision resonated with a long family-centered tradition of Chinese cinema.[23] Nothing was more important in the mid-twentieth-century social structure of China than the family unit. And, more than anything else, ordinary people experienced the war as members of family groups.

All three films adopt the view that in experiential terms it was not the nation as a whole that suffered during the war, it was Chinese families that suffered. And the losses were staggering. Families were ripped apart and then reconfigured in a variety of unfamiliar ways. In *Far Away Love*, Yu Zhen loses her father, her brother, and her son. Morover, the war forces her to confront issues of legitimate and illegitimate authority in family life. In the end her marriage is destroyed. In *Eight Thousand Miles*, Jiang Lingyu's family disintegrates before her eyes. When she returns to her native village, her father is dead and the family dwelling has been sold. During the course of the war she loses all respect for her relatives in Shanghai, who fail to support her plan to join the resistance. Her cousin Jiarong becomes a war profiteer.

Wartime dreams about reuniting families are dashed when the war is over. Lingyu's family exists in name only. When Lingyu learns of her family's corrupt and exploitative postwar activities, she moves out and rejects her relatives. Indeed, when she turns to journalistic work, her own family becomes a target of her scathing investigative reporting.

Lingyu's attempt to start a family of her own is frustrated. She has a child, but it is by no means clear that she will live to see the child grow up. The prewar Chinese family seems to have no future. For people like Yu Zhen (in *Far Away Love*), Lingyu, and Libin, its role has been assumed by the collective surrogate family of friends and comrades that evolved in the interior during the war. It is this group that plays the nurturing and support roles normally associated with the consanguine family, and that commands the loyalty and respect of people like Yu Zhen, Lingyu, and Libin.

The account of wartime family breakup in *A Spring River* is even more devastating. This is because the fascinating protagonist, Zhang Zhongliang, is markedly different from the positive characters (Lingyu and Libin) that one encounters in

Eight Thousand Miles. The story of Zhang Zhongliang and his family is more interesting and more painful precisely because Zhang appears first in "Eight Years of Separation and Chaos" as a heroic figure. His heroism has two interrelated dimensions. First, he is an ardent patriot, willing to sacrifice to defend the nation from Japanese aggression. Second, despite his youth, he is an old-fashioned, Confucian-style family man. He is devoted to his equally traditionalistic wife and son (promising that they will be together "forever") and profoundly filial in his interactions with his kindly mother. Zhang's excellent relations with his family are central to the subsequent development of the narrative. He is willing to sacrifice for the nation-state because, by doing so, he will be protecting and defending his family way of life. In this film (and in *Eight Thousand Miles*) the dominant vision that positive characters have of postwar life entails a "great reunion" that will bring decent families back to where they were in the prewar period. Victory meant family restoration.

One of the greatest tragedies of the war is that for millions of people the "great reunion" never happened. There was no return to prewar modes. Indeed, in *Far Away Love,* hopes for a family reunion are dashed well before the end of the war. The case of Zhang Zhongliang in *A Spring River* is particularly poignant (and more complex than the cases of Lingyu and Libin in *Eight Thousand Miles*) because he is a "good" man who went "bad" during the war itself. The visions he had of a "great reunion" are not simply denied to him (as they were to Lingyu and Libin), but he abandons them once he becomes entangled in a web of wartime corruption, greed, and moral depravity. Most disturbing of all, it is by no means clear at the end of the narrative that the corrupted hero can be reformed and returned "home" to his mother and son. The whole meaning of the term "family" has been distorted beyond recognition when Zhang, confused and panicky, is shown together on (of all days) National Day with his prewar wife, his wartime wife, and his postwar "secret" wife.

DEFINING THE AUDIENCE AND ITS NEEDS

These three family narratives, and especially *Eight Thousand Miles,* were clearly inspired by the personal wartime experiences of the screenwriters and directors who had joined the resistance. Shi Dongshan, for instance, worked in a traveling theater troupe during the early years of the war and eventually reached Chongqing, just like the characters in his movie.[24] It does not follow, however, that the primary audience for these films was people like themselves who had traveled to the interior.

By failing to ask questions about the audience, scholars have failed to note the obvious. The primary target audience for these films was people who stayed behind and endured the harsh Japanese occupation. In large cities like Shanghai, most people had stayed behind. After the war they were by far the largest potential audience for the new epic accounts of the war. They may not have participated in the resistance, but they too experienced the war as separation and deprivation. They too experienced the immediate postwar period as disappointment and disillusionment.[25] Victory did not feel like victory when families remained fragmented and when innocent people were accused of collaboration.

People returning from the interior had much to learn about how ordinary citizens had suffered under the occupation, and the movies under review provided such information. But it appears that these films primarily addressed the needs of the people who had stayed behind. Cut off from reliable news during the war, they had many questions about events that had unfolded "out of view" in the interior. Therefore, they were strongly attracted to epic narratives that "re-created" the war and, thus, allowed them to "see" the disorienting social forces that it had unleashed. They needed answers to nagging questions about family defeats that followed national victory.

After the war many ordinary Shanghai residents felt stigmatized by their decision to remain in Shanghai during the years of conflict. Many were defensive about their personal histories. Some of the people who returned from the interior felt superior and treated those who had remained behind in condescending fashion. One of the most striking things about the grand holocaust narratives under review here, and especially *Eight Thousand Miles* and *A Spring River*, is that they view the ordinary people who lived under the Japanese (the very same people who made up the audience for these films) in a sympathetic light. These narratives firmly rejected the view that people who had stayed behind were unpatriotic collaborators. It is easy to understand why such films were so popular.

This is not to say that these films contained no criticism of those who lived under the occupation. In *Eight Thousand Miles* the portrait of Lingyu's aunt and uncle is most unflattering. They are clearly greedy war profiteers. But more important are the sympathetic characterizations of the old woman (whose property is seized by Jiarong on the pretext that her husband was a traitor) and the patriotic classmates who are reunited with Lingyu and Libin after the war.

In *A Spring River* the brief representations of traitors like He Wenyan's husband are striking, but far more vivid are the visual portraits of those who were victimized by the foreign aggressors. Zhongliang's father and the other patriotic villagers are exploited mercilessly by the Japanese, and his mother and wife suffer unspeakably in urban Shanghai. They have atrocious housing, they lack adequate food supplies, and they are humiliated by the enemy time and again. These compassionate accounts of the misery of Sufen and her mother-in-law were warmly welcomed by postwar moviegoers. It was gratifying to "see" their own story on screen.

But postwar film fans saw much more on the screen than sympathetic images of their own wartime sufferings in occupied Shanghai. They also learned from these powerful narratives that not all the people who traveled to the interior were motivated by selfless patriotism. Professor Xiao Yuanxi is presented in *Far Away Love* as a cowardly man whose acceptance of a government desk job in Hankou is motivated more by fear than patriotism. The detailed accounts of the activities of

Pang Haogong and his corrupt associates in *A Spring River* revealed a disgraceful life of wartime comfort and privilege. The tales of the moral decline of people like Zhang Zhongliang in *A Spring River* and Xiao Yuanxi in *Far Away Love* are particularly gripping because they make it clear that many well-regarded citizens who traveled to the interior did not behave patriotically. One of the most effective editing techniques used in *A Spring River* to accentuate the failings of people like Zhang Zhongliang in the interior involved a constant cutting back and forth from scenes of brutality and hardship in occupied Shanghai to scenes of luxury and decadence in Chongqing. This allowed the audience to "see" what was blocked from view during the war. After viewing these movies it was easy to conclude that people who lived in the occupied areas sacrificed more than those who sat out the war in the interior.

ISSUES OF CLASS AND GENDER

Characterizations such as good and evil, strong and weak, selfless and selfish had definite class and gender dimensions in these popular family narratives. In terms of social class, intellectuals (with the important exception of Professor Xiao), artists, factory workers, and peasants are cast in an exceedingly positive light in all three films. The urban bourgeoisie, however, is treated very harshly in all three narratives. It is to this class that Professor Xiao is assigned. In *Far Away Love* he is cast as a self-centered, petty bourgeois snob. In *Eight Thousand Miles,* Jiarong, his parents, and friends are revealed as wartime and postwar profiteers who have no patriotic inclinations whatsoever. In *A Spring River,* the factory owner who is upset by Zhongliang's patriotic speech on National Day, the businessman Pang Haogong, and, finally, Zhang Zhongliang himself are portrayed as greedy and heartless opportunists who prey on the poor and defenseless. None of the films offers even one example of a patriotic capitalist. Most interesting of all, the bourgeoisie is indicted as a class not because it is incompetent in professional terms, but rather because of its moral failings. In the end, the problem of the bourgeoisie in Chinese society is treated more as a moral problem than as an economic or political problem. The individualism of businessmen and petty bourgeois professors prevents them from behaving patriotically. These sorts of representations of class are, of course, quite familiar. Prewar films and fiction were filled with similar images of upright working people, patriotic students, and selfish bourgeois elements.

A far more provocative aspect of these grand narratives is their treatment of gender issues. Indeed, the characterizations of men, and particularly men in the prime of life, are highly critical. The narratives seem to hold men responsible for China's plight: men were not able to prevent the Japanese invasion and, after the war, were not able to reunite the nation. The failings of China, in this controversial reading, are the failings of its men. Some men, like Jiarong, the young businessman, are greedy and corrupt. Some, like Pang Haogong, are crude bullies. Some, like Professor Xiao, are shameless hypocrites. Others, like Zhang Zhongliang are simply weak, indecisive, and ineffectual until they link up with people like Pang. They value a social life that stresses the pleasures of wine, women, and song. According to patriarchal norms, men are ultimately responsible for the well-being of the family, and by extension, the nation. But in these family narratives most of the males who are central to the stories are not seen in such time-honored roles. Very little information is supplied about their family life: nothing is known about Professor Xiao's background, Jiarong has no wife or children, nothing is known about Pan Haogong's family, and Zhang Zhongliang's relations with women are motivated primarily by lust once he leaves his family. In short, the viewer is led to believe that wartime conditions brought out the worst in China's men. There are positive portrayals of men in these narratives, including the characterizations of Libin in *Eight Thousand Miles* and Zhang Zhongmin in *A Spring River*, but in both films these attractive male figures are of secondary importance.

If war brought out the worst in men, it appears to have brought out the best in Chinese women, at least according to these popular postwar visualizations. On the whole, women seem stronger and more capable than men under wartime circumstances. In *Far Away Love*, Yu Zhen, a rural servant "trained" to be a middle-class housewife, sacrifices everything for the resistance while her cowardly husband runs away. In *Eight Thousand Miles* the entire story of the holocaust and its social consequences is seen from the perspective of a remarkably resilient and persistent young intellectual woman, Jiang Lingyu. In *A Spring River*, the most important women, Sufen and her mother-in-law, are not at all like the modern and progressive-thinking Lingyu, but, like Lingyu, they have a remarkable ability to endure hardship and survive without the help of their husbands and adult sons. These images of strong, independent, and patriotic women are among the most intriguing aspects of postwar cinema. Characters like Yu Zhen, Lingyu, and Sufen stand in sharp contrast to the negative and threatening images of the femme fatale that were so prevalent in prewar cinema.

Even the negative female figures, the bourgeois women, are not exactly a recycled version of the 1930s screen vamp. They too seem stunningly independent and resourceful in the harsh wartime environment. Confused and weak, Zhang Zhongliang is no match for the tough-minded Wang Lizhen. Similarly, He Wenyan proves to be unusually capable of adjusting and adapting to a wartime and postwar world in which relations with men are fleeting and unreliable.

Given the highly patriarchal norms of Chinese society in the mid-twentieth century, it is striking to see the extent to which cultural decency, wartime strength, and anticolonialism are gendered female in these films, all of which were written and directed by men. Similarly, it is surprising to see the extent to which cultural degeneration, weakness under wartime conditions, and the failure to resist colonialism are gendered male. This picture of wartime China shows patriarchal norms and the family institution itself to be in serious disarray. With a couple of important exceptions (Libin and Zhang Zhongmin), men are irresponsible and unpredictable, while women are strong and capable.

THE CULTURAL POLITICS
OF POSTWAR HOLOCAUST EPICS

For decades the classic films *Far Away Love, Eight Thousand Miles of Clouds and Moon,* and *A Spring River Flows East* have been thought of as "leftist" works fashioned by filmmakers who supposedly were under the control of the Communist Party. Critics close to the Nationalist Party accepted this view and, thus, questioned the credibility of the filmmakers and dismissed the films.[26] They never attempted to explain the astounding popularity of the movies or, more important, to appreciate the extent to which the filmmakers had close links to the Nationalist state and party during and after the war. Critics close to the Communist Party accepted the view that the films were "leftist" and celebrated the "progressivism" of the artists, thereby claiming these important artifacts as their own.[27]

In fact, the cultural politics of these holocaust narratives are not so clear-cut. The political and cultural content of the films is neither as pro-Communist nor as anti-Nationalist as most observers would have us believe. The films have a highly critical tone, but the social criticism is consistent with perspectives associated with both the Nationalist and Communist Parties. *Far Away Love* was made by the Nationalists themselves in a state-run studio. All three movies were officially reviewed and approved by Nationalist state censors.[28] In recent years, industry personalities familiar with these films have asserted that state censors had been bribed. But this is not a very convincing explanation of why they were passed by the censors. Daily advertising in local newspapers reveals that all three films had extremely long runs in Shanghai and other major cities. The state certainly had the means to shut down theaters that showed offensive films, but no serious effort was made to discourage repeated screenings of the three epics under review here.

Communist and Nationalist cultural historians have failed, each for their own reasons, to mention that *Far Away Love, Eight Thousand Miles,* and *A Spring River* were among the ten films made in 1947 that received the coveted Zhongzheng Culture Prize named in honor of Chiang Kai-shek himself. All recipients got a cash award and a handsome Oscar-like trophy. *A Spring River,* the most critical of the three films discussed here, was listed first among the ten "glorious" winners by *Shen bao,* hardly an antigovernment newspaper.[29] Actress Bai Yang, who joined the Communist Party in 1958, won the first Chiang Kai-shek best actress award in 1947 for her performances in *Eight Thousand Miles* and *A Spring River.* For nearly fifty years the two sides in the civil war have been too embarrassed to acknowledge this unsettling fact.

Scholars in the People's Republic account for the production and public release of these films by emphasizing the ability of the filmmakers to outsmart Nationalist bureaucrats who were eager to crush works critical of wartime and postwar social disarray. Actually, the critical thrust of these movies was well known. There was no revolutionary conspiracy. Spectacular newspaper advertising that appeared long before the films were first shown was remarkably explicit. Ads for *Far*

Away Love, a government-made movie, proclaimed, "All men are selfish; women struggle for liberation!" (*nanren dou shi zisi; nuzi lizheng jiefang*), "How will women of today find a way out?" (*shidai nuxing chulu hezai*), and "The ideal wife turns out to be more than anyone imagined!" (*lixiang taitai chuchu chaochu lixiang*). Ads for *Eight Thousand Miles* declared, "So many sorrows and tears before and after victory!" (*shengli qianhou xing suan lei*) and "See never-ending waves of ugliness; curse never-ending and ferocious corruption!" (*kan wuwan de jieshou choutai; ma wuwan de tanwu ezhuang*). Ads for *A Spring River* stated, "An epic production that shakes the Chinese film world" (*zhenhan Zhongguo yingtan de wenyi ju zhi*) and "A beacon that can be seen for ten thousand miles; eight years of separation and chaos; heaven is in distress, earth is in misery; ghosts and spirits are moaning!" (*fengyan wanli; ba nian li luan; tian cho di can; gui shen wu yan*).[30] Advertising campaigns, some of which were funded with government money, underscored rather than concealed the critical thrust of these painful narratives.

The praise heaped on these films by the mainstream popular film press suggests that the community was acutely aware of the critical and controversial approach to the war taken by Chen Liting and other postwar directors. For instance, the April 1947 edition of the popular film magazine *Dianying*, a nonpolitical publication that normally concerned itself with the divorces of film stars, the number of kissing scenes in American movies, the shape of Bai Guang's legs, and the kinds of cosmetics used by Hollywood matinee idols, boldly asserted that *Far Away Love, Eight Thousand Miles,* and *Heavenly Spring Dream (Tiantang chun meng,* d. Tang Xiaodan, March 1947), another controversial war-related film produced in a state-run studio, were fine examples of postwar films that "illustrated reality and gave voice to the people."[31]

The *Dianying* article, which appeared before the release of *A Spring River,* asserted that these films were popular because the screenwriters were attuned to "the inner feelings" of the film audience. By contrast, many veteran screenwriters were said to be out of touch. They had the "connections" to get their stories made into films, but they were interested in cinema only as "a tool to make a fortune." They exploited the postwar demand for films, but their scripts were "terrible." The magazine called explicitly for more films like *Eight Thousand Miles,* which it claimed was the "first postwar Chinese film" purchased by foreign buyers for distribution in Europe. As for the money-grubbers whose films failed to deal with the real concerns of the audience: "These scum who hurt the Chinese film industry should be sent to the gallows that has been set up by the people. They should be purged!"[32]

Nationalist authorities allowed the films to be screened in part because they were consistent with critical perspectives held within the Nationalist Party and government.[33] Disillusioned elements within the Nationalist movement realized that the cultural and political messages of the films struck a responsive chord among the millions who had resided in enemy-occupied areas during the war. This was an audience that desperately wanted to "see," and thereby "experience," events that had taken place in the interior. These were people who wanted to understand the connection between wartime dislocations and the bitter disappointments that ordinary people experienced immediately following victory. The films ask the questions: Why did victory not feel like victory? Why did the people who sacrificed the most seem to benefit the least? And why did those who sacrificed the least seem to benefit the most?

It is time to look at such works not solely in terms of the highly polarized politics of the civil war era and after, but also in terms of the complex relationship between commercial filmmakers working in the state and private sectors and their vast film audience. When the films are analyzed from this perspective, is it possible to see that the cultural politics of these epic narratives were far from radical or "progressive." They were decidedly conservative. All three films argue that certain core Chinese values, especially those governing social relations within the family, were broken down and forgotten during the long years of wartime separation and dislocation.

Without exception the positive characters in all the films (Yu Zhen, Lingyu, Libin, Sufen, Zhongmin, and even Zhongliang before his moral decline) were people who cherished "traditional" family values: respect for parents and devotion to spouse and children. Their patriotism and unselfish public-spiritedness were natural extensions of their old-fashioned, neo-Confucian cultural orientation. There is nothing left wing about the mores of these people.

The negative characters (Professor Xiao, Jiarong, Pang Haogong, Lizhen, Wenyan, and Zhongliang after his moral demise) are people who betrayed time-honored family values and adopted alien ways that make them decadent, irresponsible, and greedy. Their wartime behavior, according to the logic of these narratives, was also an extension of their immoral family relations. They are incapable of acting patriotically, it seems, because they do not accept "real" Chinese cultural values. Some are cowards, and some actually betray the nation, while others participate in the resistance only because they are motivated by personal gain.

The audience is being told that people who had been faithful to traditional Chinese family values sacrificed selflessly in the interior or suffered unjustly in the occupied territories. People who had abandoned old-style family values were hedonistic profiteers, shameless collaborators, or cowards. After viewing narratives of this sort, the audience, comprised essentially of ordinary people who suffered under the occupation, knew who to blame for their wartime and postwar miseries. The underlying argument of these films, one usually not associated with "leftists," is that the erosion of traditional family values during the war was a destructive phenomenon that weakened the entire society. Nowhere is the state or Nationalist Party blamed for the moral decline. Still, it is hard to avoid the conclusion that these films eroded public confidence in the postwar state nevertheless.

It is not enough, however, merely to point out that the family values embraced by the negative characters are simply "untraditional." They are foreign. Every effort is made in these works to show that the negative characters responsible for much of the wartime and postwar misery of common people behave, look, and even dress in a "Western," "bourgeois" manner. Their culture is an alien, capitalist culture of merchants. The narratives seek to deny these people their essential Chineseness. Stripped of their Chinese identity, these personalities behave, not surprisingly, in ways that are incompatible with the national interest. The films, therefore, are anticolonial in two senses: they resist Japanese imperialism and they reject Western bourgeois culture.

It is inadequate, however, simply to dismiss these characterizations as so much Marxist anticapitalism. There is something very Confucian and culturally conservative about the antimerchant thrust of these popular visualizations. When it comes to denouncing capitalism and the bourgeoisie, there is much that Chinese Marxism of the 1930s and 1940s shared in common with the neoconservative approaches that surfaced in urban China in the 1930s.[34] In August 1948, ten months after the release of *A Spring River*, Jiang Jingguo himself blasted Shanghai's big-money interests: "Their wealth and their foreign-style homes are built on the skeletons of the people. How is their conduct any different from that of armed robbers?"[35]

But what about the image of the collective family that emerges so prominently throughout *Far Away Love* and at the end of *Eight Thousand Miles?* Surely this a revolutionary vision of the new socialist society that awaited China. Surely it justifies the view that these films are the work of leftists. The problem is that while the image is definitely "collective," it is far from revolutionary. The "collective" or surrogate family espouses most of the old family values advocated by the positive and patriotic characters! The audience is told there is a need for drastic social change, but it should be a transformation that will restore real Chinese family values rather than reject them.[36] It will be a change that eradicates the pernicious influence of the alien culture of greedy merchants.

Women appear in these films as remarkably strong and independent survivors of the holocaust experience. These images were undoubtedly welcomed by women viewers, said to comprise a majority of the audience for postwar Chinese films.[37] Yu Zhen and Lingyu are "liberated" from oppressive families, and find happiness and fulfillment in wartime Nationalist collectives. But their liberation is from the unpatriotic, bourgeois, foreign-style family, not from patriarchal authority in general. The new surrogate families to which they bond allow for an active role for women, but they remain essentially patriarchal. Women who liberate themselves from alien bourgeois families have only one option: to resubmit to the "Chinese-style" patriarchal authority of the patriotic collectives. These collective groupings embrace what are viewed as essentialistic Chinese family values. They are values linked to the rural pasts of Yu Zhen, Lingyu, and Sufen.

China won the war. China defeated Japan. But the social consequences of the holocaust were most profound. When the war was over, victory felt like defeat, not only for many of those who joined the resistance, but especially for those millions who endured the hardships of enemy occupation. *Far Away Love, Eight Thousand Miles,* and *A Spring River* were early postwar attempts to explain that feeling.

DEFEAT AS VICTORY AND VICTORY AS DEFEAT

During the early phases of the war there was a tactical need for a popular culture that mobilized people and showed how defeat could be turned into victory. As Chang-tai Hung has pointed out, wartime popular culture made a significant contribution to the resistance effort.[38] Personal and family losses were staggering, but millions of people were determined to sacrifice for national salvation. Of course, most wartime popular culture was state-directed propaganda. It resisted Japanese imperialism quite effectively by building a strong sense of community, but its approach to Chinese society was largely uncritical.

The popular culture of the immediate postwar period discussed in this chapter headed in new directions because it was responding to different needs. Now the challenge was to explain why victory felt like defeat. Even though cultural workers in the state sector were among those who addressed this question, the most vibrant postwar popular culture can hardly be characterized as state-directed propaganda. In fact, those who produced the new popular culture took pride in their relative independence from the state. Some directors accepted state financial support but continued to function as independent-minded and critical artists nevertheless.

One is tempted to say that controversial postwar films are better characterized as an example of popular culture directed by intellectual elites who had close ties to the literary world. But the story of postwar popular culture is more complex (and more interesting) than that. Most popular postwar films, including state and private-sector productions, are interesting examples of top-down and bottom-up cultural cross-fertilization. Intellectual elites like Chen Liting and Shi Dongshan definitely did not pull the victory-as-defeat theme out of thin air and then impose it on a politically docile public in a top-down manner. The popular culture they produced fed on discontent that was already a pronounced fact of postwar life. The filmmakers did not create the disaffection.

But just because postwar filmmaking was not a clear case of top-down cultural imposition by the state or by independent cultural elites does not mean that it was a matter of filmmakers blindly chasing public opinion. That is to say, the most popular postwar productions cannot be regarded as instances of purely commercial activity in which filmmakers contribute little or nothing of their own, preferring instead to give the masses whatever they seem to want. Postwar filmmaking involved an intersecting of elite and mass cultural currents. The ideas and concerns one finds expressed in these works are a combination of elite and popular views.

The Guomindang claimed in the immediate postwar period that it wanted a high-minded, morally engaged, and educational film industry. It wanted a curtailing of what it viewed as degenerate pulp filmmaking. Ironically, the response to this plea was *Far Away Love, Eight Thousand Miles of Clouds and Moon,* and *A Spring River Flows East,* films that destabilized Chinese society.

The movies discussed here were surprisingly independent and critical, but they were not intended to be revolutionary. Their original purpose was to address injustices and stimulate reform. But as the political situation in China spun out of control, these films had the longer-term, but unintended, effect of being oppositional and even subversive.

The case of postwar filmmaking is more complicated and ambivalent than writings by Nationalist and Communist scholars allow, because there was a clear connection between the Nationalist state and the production and distribution of controversial films. Some of the most disturbing films made in 1947, pictures like *Far Away Love, Heavenly Spring Dream,* and *Diary of a Homecoming (Huan xiang riji,* d. Zhang Junxiang), were produced in government studios, funded with government monies, and distributed with government support.

The state had ample means of cracking down on these and the most disturbing private-sector films. But the fact is that the state did little or nothing to prevent production and distribution, and its failure to get tough had little to do with bureaucratic inefficiency or corruption. A more convincing explanation, but one that has been resisted by Nationalist and Communist scholars alike, is that the sentiments of despair and disillusionment conveyed by the films were consistent with the views of many state and Nationalist Party insiders. Clearly, in early 1947 there were state cultural elites who regarded these works as constructive calls for reform, rather than as conscious attempts to subvert state and party authority. Like the filmmakers themselves, they had no idea that these popular films would serve to deepen the mood of disillusionment and cynicism and thus further undermine government credibility.

In brief, the case of popular culture under review here does not fit into any ready-made analytical paradigm. The lines between official and unofficial, state and private, elite and popular, commerce and art, and loyalty and disloyalty are too blurry here to be accounted for by any ready-made theory of popular culture, including that of the influential Frankfurt school. As Chandra Mukerji and Michael Shudson have observed, Frankfurt school thinkers "perceived mass culture as aesthetically and politically debilitating, reducing the capacities of audiences to think critically and functioning as an ideological tool to manipulate the political sentiments of the mass public."[39] Postwar Chinese films definitely fall into the category of commercial mass culture, but their critical/democratic essence cannot be accounted for by the Frankfurt school model.

These popular films also fail to fit into any single aesthetic format. Chen Liting called *Far Away Love* a "tragicomedy" (*bei xi ju*), but it is better characterized as a rare example of film satire. *Eight Thousand Miles of Clouds and Moon, A Spring River Flows East,* and *Heavenly Spring Dream* were classic melodramas (*tongsu ju*), and *Diary of a Homecoming* was a playful farce. But, in sharp contrast to what Chinese Marxist scholars say, none of these works had much to do with cinematic "realism."

They distorted, collapsed, and simplified events in a variety of highly sensational ways. They are the "meaningful fabrications" referred to by Darnton. But while the images may not have been "realistic," they were incredibly powerful. In the end, it is their power that intrigues. The filmmakers discussed here were successful (in ways they could not be after 1949) because they knew the anxieties and concerns of their audience (that is, they were in touch with the psychological realities of those troubled times), they knew how to distill, process, and package the information that was "coming up from below," and they knew how to "sell" the final product.[40] Their epic holocaust narratives were not a mirror reflection of popular opinion, but neither were they unconnected to the mood of postwar bitterness and despair.

Alfred Hitchcock supposedly said, "Movies are life with the boring parts cut out." This is another way of saying that movies are not real life at all. The popular films under review here may not have been "realistic," but they clearly captured the public imagination. They created the illusion of reality. They were powerful and, ultimately, subversive because they explained why ordinary people felt defeated after the victory over Japan. In late 1946 the director Shi Dongshan referred explicitly to the new challenges of postwar filmmaking when he wrote that he and his friends found "reason and justification" for the hardships suffered during the war. "It was more difficult," Shi confessed, "for us to understand why, in the months after victory, we felt defeated."[41]

NOTES

1. Some important wartime films produced in the interior include *The Light of East Asia* (*Dongya zhi guang*, d. He Feiguang, 1940), *Young China* (*Qingnian Zhongguo*, d. Su Yi, 1940), *Storm on the Border* (*Saishang fengyun*, d. Ying Yunwei, 1940), and *Japanese Spy* (*Riben jiandie*, d. Yuan Congmei, 1943), all completed at the China Film Studio (*Zhongguo dianying zhipianchang*) in Chongqing.

2. "Strand Theater Incident," *China Weekly Review* 102, no. 3 (June 15, 1946): 51–52.

3. *Dianying* 1, no. 6 (October 20, 1946): 19.

4. Ibid.

5. Ibid.

6. V. L. Wong, "Motion Pictures Today Important Agency in Education—of Old and Young," *China Weekly Review* 101, no. 11 (May 11, 1946): 230.

7. Ibid., 231.

8. For an account of the Lianhua Studio in the early postwar period, see You Ming, "Lianhua dianying zhipianchang xunli" (A tour of the Lianhua Film Studio), *Dianyi huabao* (December 1, 1946): 8.

9. Zhongguo dianyingjia xiehui, Dianying shi yanjiu bu, ed., *Zhongguo dianyingjia liezhuan* (Biographies of Chinese filmmakers), vol. 2 (Beijing: Zhongguo dianying chuban she, 1982), 237–44.

10. Chang-tai Hung, *War and Popular Culture: Resistance in Modern China, 1937–1945* (Berkeley and Los Angeles: University of California Press, 1994), 55–64.

11. *Zhongguo da baike quanshu: dianying* (The great encyclopedia of China: Cinema) (Beijing, Shanghai: Zhongguo da baike quanshu chuban she, 1991), 51.

12. Ibid., 357–58.

13. Zhongguo dianyingjia xiehui, Dianying shi yanjiu bu, eds., *Zhongguo dianyingjia liezhuan*, 1:15–23.

14. Ibid., 1:338–49.

15. *Zhongguo da baike quanshu: dianying*, 44.

16. Zhongguo dianyingjia xiehui, Dianying shi yanjiu bu, eds., *Zhongguo dianyingjia liezhuan*, 2:286–97; *Zhongguo da baike quanshu: dianying*, 482.

17. Robert Darnton, "Workers Revolt: The Great Cat Massacre of the Rue Saint-Severin," in *Rethinking Popular Culture: Contemporary Perspectives in Cultural Studies*, ed. Chandra Mukerji and Michael Schudson (Berkeley and Los Angeles: University of California Press, 1991), 100.

18. A published text of *Eight Thousand Miles of Clouds and Moon* can be found in Zhongguo dianying gongzuozhe xiehui, ed., *Wusi yilai dianying juben xuanji* (An anthology of screenplays of the post–May Fourth era), vol. 2 (Hong Kong: Wenhua ziliao gongying she, 1979), 1–81. The dialogue in the film itself does not always follow the text of the screenplay. The title of the film is taken from a line in the famous poem entitled "Man jiang hong," by Yue Fei (1103–41).

19. For a contemporary review of the film, see Man Jianghong, "Ba qian li lu yun he yue" (Eight thousand miles of clouds and moon), *Dianyi huabao* (December 1, 1946): 2–3.

20. For a sketch of the young actor Gao Zheng, see Xi Zi, "Lianhua wu xin ren" (Five new faces at Lianhua), *Dianyi huabao* (December 1, 1946): 14–15.

21. For a sensitive and sympathetic portrait of people who lived under the Japanese occupation of Shanghai, see Poshek Fu, *Passivity, Resistance, and Collaboration: Intellectual Choice in Occupied Shanghai, 1937–1945* (Stanford: Stanford University Press, 1993).

22. A published text of *A Spring River Flows East* can be found in Zhongguo dianying gongzuozhe xiehui, ed., *Wusi yilai dianying juben xuanji*, 2:85–230. The dialogue in the film does not always follow the text of the screenplay, especially in the concluding scenes. The title of the film is taken from a line of a poem by the famous Tang poet Li Bai.

23. Zheng Junli's own lengthy discussion of *A Spring River Flows East* is contained in his book *Hua wai yin* (Sound beyond the image) (Beijing: Zhongguo dianying chuban she, 1979), 1–18.

24. See Jay Leyda, *Dianying: An Account of Films and the Film Audience in China* (Cambridge: MIT Press, 1972), 166.

25. One of the best studies of the immediate postwar mood of Shanghai is Suzanne Pepper, *Civil War in China: The Political Struggle, 1945–1949* (Berkeley and Los Angeles: University of California Press, 1978).

26. See Du Yunzhi, *Zhongguo dianying shi* (A history of Chinese cinema), vol. 2 (Taibei: Taiwan shangwuyin shuguan, 1978), 96–101.

27. See Cheng Jihua, Li Shaobai, and Xing Zuwen, eds., *Zhongguo dianying fazhan shi* (A history of the development of Chinese cinema), vol. 2 (Beijing: Zhongguo dianying chuban she, 1963), 210–14, 217–23.

28. For a new study that sheds light on the complexities of the censorship institution, see Xiao Zhiwei, "Film Censorship in China, 1927–1937" (Ph.D. diss., Department of History, University of California, San Diego, 1994).

29. *Shen bao,* February 15, 1948. See the Sunday supplement entitled *Mei zhou huakan* (Weekly pictorial).

30. All of these advertising texts can be found in the film advertising sections of *Shen bao* in 1947, especially in the January, February, and October issues.

31. *Dianying* 1, no. 8 (April 1, 1947): 16–18.

32. Ibid.

33. For a fascinating discussion of the antimerchant, antibourgeois sentiments of both Chiang Kai-shek (Jiang Jieshi) and Chiang Ching-kuo (Jiang Jingguo) in the postwar period, see Lloyd Eastman, *Seeds of Destruction: Nationalist China in War and Revolution, 1937–1949* (Stanford: Stanford University Press, 1984), 172–215.

34. For a discussion of similarities between leftist, centrist, and rightist films of the prewar 1930s, see Paul G. Pickowicz, "The Theme of Spiritual Pollution in Chinese Films of the 1930s," *Modern China* 17, no. 1 (January 1991): 38–75.

35. Quoted in Eastman, *Seeds of Destruction,* 182.

36. Leftists in the Chinese countryside in the 1940s also espoused traditionalistic cultural criticism of postwar society. See Edward Friedman, Paul G. Pickowicz, and Mark Selden, *Chinese Village, Socialist State* (New Haven: Yale University Press, 1991).

37. *Dianying* 1, no. 9 (June 1, 1947): 3.

38. Hung, *War and Popular Culture,* 270–85.

39. Chandra Mukerji and Michael Schudson, eds., *Rethinking Popular Culture: Contemporary Perspectives in Cultural Studies* (Berkeley and Los Angeles: University of California Press, 1991), 38.

40. I would like to thank Professor Tu Wei-ming for suggesting the use of the term "psychological reality."

41. This statement by Shi Dongshan is contained in a handout distributed to all ticket holders when they entered the theater to see *Eight Thousand Miles of Clouds and Moon* in 1947. An original copy of the handout survives in the Film Archive of China (*Zhongguo dianying ziliao guan*) in Beijing.

GLOSSARY

Ailuo bunaozhi　艾羅補腦汁
anmin tongshang　安民通商
annei rangwai　安內攘外
an-shen　安身

Ba nian li luan　八年離亂
Ba qian li lu yun he yue　八千里路雲
　和月
Bai Chongxi　白崇禧
Bai Wei　白薇
Bai Yang　白楊
baihua　白話
Baike xiaocongshu　百科小叢書
baike zhi xue　百科之學
Bailing huabao　百齡畫報
bailingji　百齡機
banghui　幫會
baoan zuzhi　保安組織
baofeng zouyu　暴風驟雨
baonü yixueyuan　堡女義學院
baoxiao hetong　包銷合同
Baxian　巴縣
Beichen　北辰
Beijiang bowuguan　北疆博物館
Beiyang　北洋
benpai chanpin　本牌產品
biaojie　表姐
Biedong jun zongzhihui bu　別動軍總
　指揮部

bing　稟
bisuan　筆算

cabi dancai　擦筆淡彩
cabi dancai hua　擦筆淡彩畫
Cai Chusheng　蔡楚生
Cai Mengjian　蔡孟堅
Cai Yuanpei　蔡元培
caizheng renyuan　財政人員
chaicheng de sixiang　拆城的思想
chang shi　常識
Chaoyang, Guangdong　潮陽，廣東
Chen Baichen　陳白塵
Chen bao　晨報
Chen Duxiu　陳獨秀
Chen Guofu　陳果夫
Chen Kaiguang　陳開光
Chen Lifu　陳立夫
Chen Liting　陳鯉庭
Chen Tianhua　陳天華
Cheng Jihua　程季華
chenghuang miao　城隍廟
chengli difang zhixu　成立地方秩序
chengxian qihou　承先啓後
Chiang Kai-shek　蔣介石
chihua　赤化
Chu Minyi　褚民誼
chujian　鋤奸
chujiang bang　出江幫

399

chu-shen   出身
Chushi zhexue   出世哲學
cishan shiye   慈善事業
congfu   從夫
congshu   叢書

da liyi   大禮議
Da lu   大路
Da shijie   大世界
da tian er   大天二
da tou meinü hua   大頭美女畫
Da yitong   大一統
da zongtongfu ziyi   大總統府諮議
Dachu youling ta   打出幽靈塔
dagou tuan   打狗團
dahui   大會
Dai Hongci   戴鴻慈
Dai Ze   戴澤
dajia guixiu   大家閨秀
Dalu diantai   大陸電台
dan   蛋
danbang fanyun jituan   單幫販運集團
dao   道
Daodehui   道德會
Daoguang   道光
Daoyuan   道院
Datong   大同
dian   電
dian pu   佃僕
Dianshizhai huabao   點石齋畫報
Dianyi huabao   電藝畫報
Dianying shi yanjiu bu   電影史研究部
Dianying yanyuan lun   電影演員論
difang zizhi   地方自治
dili   地理
Ding Ling   丁玲
dipi   地痞
diwei   地位
Dong Xiujia   董修甲
Dong ya zhi guang   東亞之光
Dongfang wenku   東方文庫
Dongfang zazhi   東方雜誌
Dongnan gongyue   東南公約
Dongya bingfu   東亞病夫
dongyao fenzi   動搖分子
Du Yaquan   杜亞泉

Du Yuesheng   杜月笙
Du Yunzhi   杜雲之
Duan Fang   端方
duban gongshu   督辦公署
Duhui de ciji   都會的刺激
dushen zhuyi sixiang   獨身主義思想
Dushu   讀書

e dan lian   鵝蛋臉
er taitai   二太太

fang ke weiren   方可為人
Fang xia ni de bianzi   放下你的鞭子
fatuan   法團
Fenhongse de meng   粉紅色的夢
fenzhi   分支
Fu Ren   輔仁
Fu Xiaoan   傅筱庵
Fu Yanchang   傅彥長
Funü ribao   婦女日報
funü shimin   婦女市民
Funü zazhi   婦女雜誌

Gan Guoxun   干國勛
ganqing   感情
Gao Libin   高禮彬
Gao Zheng   高正
geti   個體
gong   公
Gong Debo   龔德柏
Gong shang xueyuan   工商學院
Gonghe guomin duben   共和國民
    讀本
Gongheguo jiaokeshu   共和國教科書
gongju   公局
gongli   公理
gongsi   公司
gongsi heying   公私合營
gongying shiye   公營實業
gongyong shiye   公用實業
gu   古
Gu Songmao   顧松茂
Gu Zhuxuan   顧竹軒
guanban   官辦
guang   光
guanggao da wang   廣告大王

guanggao ke 廣告科

Guangzhi 廣智

guanmin yizhi 官民一致

guanshang heban 官商合辦

Guifei chuyu 貴妃出浴

guinü 閨女

guo 國

Guo Moruo 郭沫若

Guocui xuebao 國粹學報

Guofang sheji weiyuanhui 國防設計委
員會

Guofu 國父

guojia 國家

guomin 國民

Guomindang 國民黨

guonei 國內

guowen 國文

Guoxue jiben congshu 國學基本叢書

haijin 海禁

Haizi jutuan 孩子劇團

Hang Zhiying 杭稚英

hanjian 漢奸

He Feiguang 何非光

He Wenyan 何文艷

He Zhonghan 賀衷寒

helihua 合理化

heping 和平

hequn 合群

hang 行

houfang 後方

houfang chengshi 後方城市

Hu Feng 胡風

Hu Shi 胡適

hua 化

Hua wai yin 畫外音

Huang Chujiu 黃楚九

Huang Jinrong 黃金榮

Huang Kewu 黃克武

Huang Liushuang (Anna May Wong)
黃柳霜

huatou 滑頭

Huazhong yiyaopin tongzhi lianhehui
華中醫藥品統制聯合會

huiguan 會館

Huo diyu 活地獄

huozhe neng sheshen shujie 活者能捨
身淑界

husha 護沙

Ji e de Guo Su'e 饑餓的郭素娥

jia 甲

Jiang Guangci 蔣光慈

Jiang Haisheng 江海生

Jiang Jieshi (Chiang Kai-shek) 蔣介石

Jiang Jingguo (Chiang Ching-kuo) 蔣經國

Jiang Lingyu 江玲玉

Jiang Weiqiao 蔣維喬

jianguo jingshen he jiating funü 建國精
神和家庭婦女

Jianming guowen jiaokeshu 簡明國文
教科書

jiannao 健腦

jianshe 建設

Jianshe weiyuanhui 建設委員會

Jianshebu 建設部

Jiansheting 建設廳

jianshi 建市

jianxin 建心

jiaohua (kyoka) 教化

jiaoyu bu shending 教育部審定

Jiaoyu zazhi 教育雜誌

jiaozheng xisu 教正習俗

jiating yanjiushe 家庭研究社

jie 界

jie 潔

jieshou dayuan 接收大員

jietou ju 街頭劇

jihua jingji 計劃經濟

jin 今

jin caizhu 金財主

Jin Xuechen 金雪塵

jinbu 進步

Jindai funü 近代婦女

Jing'an 靜安

jinghuo hang 京貨行

jingjie 淨街

jingsui 精髓

Jingu 津沽

jinhua 進化

jinshi 進士

Jintan (rendan) (Chinese-made) 人丹

Jintan (rendan) (Japanese-made)　仁丹
jinxin　盡心
ju jiazhe　居家者
juluo　聚落
Junshi weiyuanhui Su-Zhe Xingdong wei-
　yuanhui　軍事委員會蘇浙行動委
　員會
Junshi weiyuanhui zhengzhi bu　軍事委
　員會政治部
juren　舉人
juzheng　局正

kagakuka　科學化
kang　炕
kang jian tang　抗建堂
kangzhan furen　抗戰夫人
kanpo　漢方
ketou　磕頭
Kexue xiaocongshu　科學小叢書
kexuehua　科學化
Kuangren riji　狂人日記
Kuishan huiguan　葵扇會館
Kunlun yingye gongsi　崑崙影業公司

Lao Can youji　老殘遊記
Leng Wangu　冷頑固
Li Bai　李白
Li Boyuan　李伯元
Li Fuqun　李輔群
Li Lihua　李麗華
Li Mubai　李慕白
Li Shaobai　李少白
Li Shengduo　李盛鐸
Li Shizeng　李石曾
Li Zehou　李澤厚
Liang　兩
Liang Hongzhi　梁鴻志
Liang Qichao　梁啓超
liangyou　良友
Liangyou huabao　良友畫報
Liangyou tushu gongsi　良友圖書公司
Liangyou wenku　良友文庫
Liangyou wenxue congshu　良友文學
　叢書
Liangyou zhi shen　良友之神
Lianhua dianying zhipianchang　聯華電
　影製片廠

Lianhua dianying zhipianchang xunli
　聯華電影片廠巡禮
Lianhua wu xin ren　聯華五新人
Lienü zhuan　烈女傳
lijin　厘金
Lin Shu　林紓
Lin Yutang　林語堂
Lin Zhijiang　林之江
lingpai lianhao　領牌聯號
Linshi zhengfu　臨時政府
Liren xing　麗人行
lishen duanzheng　立身端正
lishi　歷史
lishi hui　理事會
Liu Dinghan (Bishop)　劉定漢
Liu E　劉鶚
Liu Geqing　劉戈青
Liu Ruiheng　劉瑞恆
Liu Zaifu　劉再復
liu zang liu fu　六臟六腑
liumang　流氓
Lixian guomin duben　立憲國民讀本
liye　立業
lizhi　立志
Longhu gongsi　龍虎公司
louzhi　漏卮
Lu Fei Bohong　陸費伯鴻
Lu Jingshi　陸京士
Lu Ling　路翎
Lu Xiaoman　陸小曼
Lu Xun　魯迅
lühua　綠化

Ma Guoliang　馬國亮
maiban　買辦
maiguozhe　賣國者
Man jiang hong　滿江紅
manhua　漫畫
Mao Dun　茅盾
Mao Sen　毛森
Mei Guangpei　梅光培
Meiguo xiao wulai　美國小無賴
meinü　美女
meiren　美人
Meng Sen　孟森
mengxue duben　蒙學讀本
Miao Bin　繆斌

miaoling nülang　妙齡女郎
mimi furen　秘密夫人
minban　民辦
ming　命
Ming bao　明報
mingxing　明星
Mingxing yingpian gongsi　明星影片
　公司
mintuan　民團
minzhu　民主
minzu　民族
modeng　摩登
modeng xiaojie　摩登小姐
Morishita Hiroshi　森下博
mu　畝

Nakajima Seiichi　中島精一
nanguo yishu xueyuan　南國藝術學院
Nanhui xian　南匯縣
Nankai　南開
naozi　腦子
Nongxue zazhi　農學雜誌
nüxue　女學

Ouyang Yuqian　歐陽予倩

Pan Jinlian　潘金蓮
Pang Haogong　龐浩公
pantu　叛徒
Paoxiao le de tudi　咆哮了的土地
Peng Fulin　彭福林
pengmin　棚民

Qian chuan weiyuanhui　遷川委員會
Qian Rulin　錢茹林
qian zhuang　錢莊
qifa mengmei　啓發蒙昧
qifa sixiang　啓發思想
qimeng　啓蒙
Qin Yi　秦怡
Qing　清
qing　清
qing　頃
Qingnian Zhongguo　青年中國
qingxiang　清鄉
Qingxin shuyuan　清心書院
qipao　旗袍

qiwu　齊物
Qu Yuan　屈原
Quan yong guohuo hui　勸用國貨會
Quanguo jingji weiyuanhui　全國經
　濟委員會
Quanguo minying dianye lianhehui
　全國民營電業聯合會
qun　群

renao　熱鬧
Rendan (Japanese-made)　仁丹
Rendan (Jintan) (Chinese-made)　人丹
rendan huzi　仁丹鬍子
Riben jiandie　日本間諜
rong　榮
Rong Zongjing　榮宗敬
Ruan Lingyu　阮玲玉
ruo bu jinfeng　弱不禁風

Saishang fengyun　塞上風雲
sancong　三從
sangxin bingkuang　喪心病狂
sanjiao heyi　三教合一
sha　沙
sha　傻
Shang Qiheng　尚其亨
Shangguan Yunzhu　上官雲珠
Shanghai hua　上海化
Shanghai jiuwang yanju　上海救亡演劇
Shanghai qi　上海氣
Shanghai shangye lianhehui　上海商業
　聯合會
Shanghai xinyaoye gonghui　上海新藥
　業公會
Shanghai xinyaoye shangye gonghui
　上海新藥業商業公會
Shanghai yeyu shiyan ju tuan　上海業餘
　實驗劇團
Shanghai yingxi gongsi　上海影戲公司
Shangpin shijie　商品世界
Shangshu fang　尚書坊
shangtuan　商團
Shangwu yinshu guan　商務印書館
shanren　善人
shantang　善堂
Shantou　汕頭
Shaonian zazhi　少年雜誌

shehui 社會
shen 身
Shen bao 申報
Shen Zhifang 沈芝芳
shen-fen 身分
sheng 聲
sheng, guang, dian, hua 聲, 光, 電, 化
shi 士
Shi Dezhi 施得之
Shi Dongshan 史東山
Shi Kuangshao 史匡韶
shibunkai 斯文會
shidai (jidai) 時代
Shijie Zongjiao Datonghui 世界宗教
　大同會
shimin 市民
shinü hua 仕女畫
Shiye jihua 實業計劃
shizhuang shinü tu 時裝仕女圖
Shu Xiuwen 舒繡文
shuiliuchai 水流柴
shuyuan 書院
si 私
Si da Hui bang 四大徽幫
Si ku quan shu guan 四庫全書館
Sihuo lun 四惑論
sishu 私塾
Su Xiwen 蘇錫文
Su Yi 蘇怡
Sufen 素芬
Sun Ke 孫科

Taiyang zhaozai sanggan heshang 太陽
　照在桑乾河上
Takeda 武田
Tan Sitong 譚嗣同
Tao Jin 陶金
Tewu weiyuanhui 特務委員會
teyue jingxiao hetong 特約經銷合同
Tian Gengxin (Cardinal) 田耕莘
Tian liang qian hou 天亮前後
Tian lun 天倫
tianli 天理
tianming 天命
tianru yundong 天乳運動
tianxia yi jia, wanfa gui yi 天下一家萬
　法歸一

tianyuan xinshi 田園新市
tianzu yundong 天足運動
tie caizhu 鐵財主
Tiyu shijie 體育世界
Toa 東亞
tongmeng 童蒙
Tongshanshe 同善社
tongxianghui 同鄉會

waihuo 外貨
Wan Laiming 萬籟鳴
Wan you wenku 萬有文庫
Wang Fengyi 王鳳儀
Wang Hui 汪暉
Wang Jingwei 汪精衛
Wang Kemin 王克敏
Wang Lizhen 王麗珍
Wang Ruoshui 王若水
Wang Xiaolai 王曉籟
Wang Yunwu 王雲五
Wang Zhigu 王志固
Wang Zihui 王子惠
wangdao 王道
wanhui liquan 挽回利權
wanquan guohuo 完全國貨
wei renmin fuwu 為人民服務
Wei Zhongxiu 韋鍾秀
Weixin yundong 維新運動
Weixin zhengfu 維新政府
Weng Wenhao 翁文灝
wenguan 文官
Wenhua bu dianying ju 文化部電影局
Wenhua bu dianying ju jishu weiyuanhui
　文化部電影局技術委員會
wenhua zhanshi 文化戰士
Wenhua ziliao gongying she 文化資料
　供應社
wenku 文庫
wenming (bunmei) 文明
Wo bixu tongqie gaizao ziji 我必須痛
　切改造自己
Women fufu zhi jian 我們夫婦之間
Wozai Xiacun de shihou 我在霞村的
　時侯
Wu Kunrong 吳坤榮
Wu Liande 吳連德
Wu Tiecheng 吳鐵成

Wu Ya'nan　吳亞南
Wu Yin　吳茵
wu zang liu fu　五臟六腑
Wu Zhihui　吳稚暉
Wu Zuguang　吳祖光
Wu Zuxiang　吳組緗
wuben　務本
Wujiang　吳江
wulao qixian　五老七賢
Wuquan　五泉
Wushanshe　悟善社
Wusi yilai dianyiang juben xuanji　五四
　以來電影劇本選集
Wuwu lun　五無論
Wuzhou da yaofang　五洲大药房

Xi Zi　系子
Xia Yan　夏衍
xian　縣
Xian xian　獻縣
Xiandai wenti congshu　現代問題叢書
Xiang Songpo　向松坡
Xiao Yuanxi　肖元熙
Xiao Zhiwei　肖志偉
Xiaoshuo yuebao　小説月報
xie　邪
xifang　西方
Xin funü lun　新婦女論
xin wenhua　新文化
xin wenxue　新文學
xin zhishi　新知識
Xin'an xuepai　新安學派
xing dao shenshang, na jiao shizi　行到
　身上那叫識字
xing yan　杏眼
Xing Zuwen　邢祖文
xingfu　幸福
Xingfu kuangxiang qu　幸福狂想曲
xingzheng rengyuan　行政人員
xinmin　新民
Xinshidai shidi congshu　新時代史地
　叢書
xinxue　新學
xinyao　新药
xinzheng　新政
xinzhi　新知
xinzhishi　新志士

xisheng　犧牲
xiucai　秀才
xiushen　修身
Xixiangji　西廂記
xiyi　西醫
Xu Enzeng　徐恩曾
Xu Weinan　徐蔚南
Xu Xiaochu　許曉初
Xu Zhimo　徐志摩
Xu Zhuodai　許卓呆
xuesheng　學生
Xuesheng zazhi　學生雜誌
xuetang　學堂
xuewen　學文
xuexiao　學校
xuxurusheng　栩栩如生

Yan Fu　嚴復
Yang Aili　楊愛麗
Yang Guifei　楊貴妃
Yang Hu　楊虎
Yang Xingfo　楊杏佛
yanggu　洋鼓
yanghao　洋號
Yangyao gongsuo　洋药公所
Yanjing　燕京
yanjiu xueli　研究學理
yanzhuang shaofu　艷裝少婦
Yao yuan de ai　遙遠的愛
yaofang　药房
yi　義
Yi jiang chen shui xiang dong liu　一江
　春水向東流
Yiguandao　一貫道
yiji　異己
Yili sangfu zhuan　儀禮喪服傳
yindanshilin bu　陰丹士林布
ying chun　櫻唇
Ying Yunwei　應雲為
Yingmei yancao gongsi　英美菸草公司
Yingwen zazhi　英文雜誌
Yingyu zhoukan　英語週刊
Yinxing　銀星
Yiqian babaidan　一千八百擔
Yishou tang　頤壽堂
Yishu jie　藝術界
yizhi hua　一枝花

Yizhi lihua chun dai yu 一枝梨花春帶雨
yongyuan zai yiqi 永遠在一起
you bang 友邦
You Ming 幽明
Yu Bin (Bishop) 于斌
Yu Xiaqing 虞洽卿
Yu Zhen 余珍
Yuan Congmei 袁叢美
Yuan Dechang 袁德昌 (袁得昌)
Yuan Shikai 袁世凱
Yue Fei 岳飛
Yuguang qu 漁光曲
Yuying xueyuan 育英學院

za xing 雜姓
zahuo dian 雜貨店
Zailijiao 在理教
zang 臟
Zhang 張
Zhang Jian 張謇
Zhang Jingyao 張敬堯
Zhang Ruogu 張若谷
Zhang Taiyan 章太炎
Zhang Xiaolin 張嘯林
Zhang Zhidong 張之洞
Zhang Zhongliang 張忠良
Zhang Zhongmin 張忠民
Zhang Ziping 張資平
Zhangzhuang 張莊
Zhao Dan 趙丹
Zhao Dihua 趙棣華
Zhao Gangyi 趙剛義
Zhao Guizhang 趙桂章
Zhao Jiabi 趙家璧
Zhao Zhensheng (Bishop) 趙振聲
Zhao Zhixiang 趙志祥
zhen 貞
zhen 鎮
Zhendan 震旦
zheng 正
Zheng Boqi 鄭伯奇
Zheng Junli 鄭君里
Zheng Mantuo 鄭曼陀
Zheng Zhengqiu 鄭正秋
zhengshen 正身

zhengwuguan 政務官
zhennü yixue 貞女義學
zhenzhende qinggan 真真的情感
zhi 志
zhiming 知命
zhixing 知性
zhiye zhuyi 職業主義
Zhiying 稚英
zhiyuan 職員
zhizhi 知止
zhong 中
zhong 忠
Zhongfa da yaofang 中法大药房
Zhongfa Huaxi qu fen gongsi 中法華西區分公司
Zhongguo da baike quanshu: dianying 中國大百科全書: 電影
Zhongguo dianying chuban she 中國電影出版社
Zhongguo dianying fazhan shi 中國電影發展史
Zhongguo dianying gongzuozhe xiehui 中國電影工作者協會
Zhongguo dianying shi 中國電影史
Zhongguo dianying zhipianchang 中國電影製片廠
Zhongguo dianying ziliao guan 中國電影資料館
Zhongguo dianyingjia liezhuan 中國電影家列傳
Zhongguo dianyingjia xiehui 中國電影家協會
Zhongguo gongcheng xuehui 中國工程學會
Zhongguo gongchengshi xuehui 中國工程師學會
Zhongguo xinwenxue daxi 中國新文學大系
Zhongguo yishu jushe 中國藝術劇社
Zhonghua 中華
Zhonghua gongchengshi xuehui 中華工程師學會
Zhonghua guohuo 中華國貨
Zhonghua jingxiang 中華景像
Zhonghua shuju 中華書局
Zhonghua yishu daxue 中華藝術大學

Zhonghua zhiyao chang　中華製藥廠
Zhongshan xian　中山縣
Zhongyang sheying chang　中央攝影廠
Zhongyi　中醫
Zhou Fengqi　周鳳岐
Zhou Jianren　周建人
Zhou Jiarong　周家榮
Zhou Libo　周立波
Zhou Minggang　周鳴崗
Zhou Shougang　周守剛
Zhou Shoujuan　周瘦鵑
Zhu Hu Binxia　朱胡彬夏

Zhu Yingpeng　朱應鵬
zhufan dianlu　煮飯電爐
Zhufu　祝福
zhuren　主任
ziji xiuyang　自己修養
zikun　自困
zilai huolu　自來火爐
zixing　自性
ziyou　自由
Ziyuan weiyuanhui　資源委員會
zu miao　祖廟
Zuo Zongtang　左宗棠

CONTRIBUTORS

Sherman Cochran is professor of history at Cornell University. His new book is *Encountering Chinese Networks: Western, Japanese, and Chinese Corporations in China, 1880–1937* (Berkeley and Los Angeles: University of California Press, forthcoming). His current research is on consumer culture in Chinese history.

Prasenjit Duara is professor of history at the University of Chicago. His most recent book is *Rescuing History from the Nation: Questioning Narratives of Modern China* (Chicago: University of Chicago Press, 1995). He is currently working on a project on Sino-Japanese discursive relations, tentatively entitled "Manchukuo and the Frontiers of the East Asian Modern."

William C. Kirby is professor and chair in the Department of History and director of the Asia Center at Harvard University. A historian of modern China, he studies China's economic and political development in an international context. He is the author of *Germany and Republican China* (Stanford: Stanford University Press, 1984) and coeditor of *State and Economy in Republican China: A Handbook for Scholars* (Cambridge: Harvard University Asia Center, 1999). His current projects include studies of the international development of China in the twentieth century, the history of modern Chinese capitalism, and the international socialist economy of the 1950s and China's role in it.

Leo Ou-fan Lee is professor of Chinese literature at Harvard University. He is the author of *The Romantic Generation of Modern Chinese Writers* (Cambridge: Harvard University Press, 1973) and *Voices from the Iron House: A Study of Lu Xun* (Bloomington: Indiana University Press, 1987). His new book is *Shanghai Modern: The Flowering of New Urban Culture in China, 1930–1945* (Cambridge: Harvard University Press, 1999).

Richard Madsen is professor of sociology at the University of California at San Diego. He is coauthor (with Anita Chan and Jonathan Unger) of *Chen Village* (1984; second edition 1992) and author of *Morality and Power in a Chinese Village* (1984), *China and the American Dream* (1995), and *China's Catholics: Tragedy and Hope in an Emerging Civil Society* (1998), all published by the University of California Press.

Paul G. Pickowicz is professor of history and Chinese studies at the University of California at San Diego. He is author of *Marxist Literary Thought in China: The Influence of Ch'ü Ch'iu-pai* (Berkeley and Los Angeles: University of California Press, 1981), coeditor of *Unofficial China: Popular Culture and Thought in the People's Republic* (Boulder: Westview, 1989), coauthor of *Chinese Village, Socialist State* (New Haven: Yale University Press, 1991), and coeditor of *New Chinese Cinemas* (Cambridge: Cambridge University Press, 1994).

Helen F. Siu is professor of anthropology at Yale University. She is the author of *Agents and Victims in South China: Accomplices in Rural Revolution* (New Haven: Yale University Press, 1989), editor of *Furrows: Peasants, Intellectuals and the State* (Stanford: Stanford University Press, 1990), and coeditor (with David Faure) of *Down to Earth: The Territorial Bond in South China* (Stanford: Stanford University Press, 1995).

David Strand is professor of political science and history at Dickinson College. He is the author of *Rickshaw Beijing: City People and Politics in the 1920s* (Berkeley and Los Angeles: University of California Press, 1989) and coeditor (with Kjeld Erik Brødsgaard) of *Reconstructing Twentieth Century China: State Control, Civil Society, and National Identity* (Oxford: Oxford University Press, 1998).

Frederic Wakeman Jr. is the Haas Professor of Asian Studies and director of the Institute of East Asian Studies at the University of California at Berkeley. His most recent book is *The Shanghai Badlands: Political Terrorism and Urban Crime, 1937–1941* (Cambridge: Cambridge University Press, 1996).

David Der-wei Wang is professor of Chinese literature at Columbia University. His recent publications include *Fictional Realism in 20th Century China: Mao Dun, Lao She, Shen Congwen* (New York: Columbia University Press, 1992), *Narrating China: Chinese Fiction from the Late Qing to the Contemporary Era* (Xiaoshuo Zhongguo: Wangqing dao dangdai de Zhongwen xiaoshuo) (Taipei: Ryefield Publication Company, 1993), and *Fin-de-Siècle Splendor: Repressed Modernities of Late Qing Fiction, 1849–1911* (Stanford: Stanford University Press, 1997).

Wang Hui, a senior research fellow of the Chinese Academy of Social Sciences, is one of the founders and chief editors of the journal *Xueren* (Scholar) and is editor in chief of *Dushu* (Reading) magazine. He has been pursuing research in Chinese intellectual history and Chinese literature since the 1980s. He is the author of *Fankang juewang* (Fighting despair: A study of Lu Xun and his literary world) (Taibei: Jiuda wenhua gufeng youxian gongsi, 1990; Shanghai: Shanghai renmin chubanshe, 1991), *Wudi panghuang* (Hesitating on nothingness: "May Fourth" and its echoes in modern Chinese history) (Hangzhou: Zhejiang wenyi chubanshe, 1994), *Wang Hui zixuanji* (A self-selected collection of works of Wang Hui: Paradox of modern Chinese thought) (Guilin: Guangxi shifan daxue chubanshe, 1997), and *Xiandai Zhongguo sixiang de xingqi* (The emergence of modern Chinese thinking) (Beijing: Sanlian shudian, forthcoming).

Wen-hsin Yeh is professor of history and chair of the Center for Chinese Studies at the University of California at Berkeley. She is the author of *The Alienated Academy: Culture and Politics in Republican China* (Cambridge: Harvard University Press, 1990) and *Provincial Passages: Culture, Space, and the Origins of Chinese Communism* (Berkeley and Los Angeles: University of California Press, 1996). Her current research is focused on the urban history of modern Shanghai.

INDEX

A Q (fictional character), 272, 281
A Ying, 267
Academia Sinica, 148
academies, 199, 207–8, 213, 219n26
advertisements: children in, 50; cigarette, 49,
54; for Commercial Press publications, 34,
35–36, 38, 39; domesticity portrayed in,
48–49, 52; drugstore, 82; for films, 368,
390–91, 398n30; and mass culture, 83–84;
medical, 49, 54, 66, 67, 68–69, 70, 78,
84–86; nationalism and, 67, 70; newspaper,
69, 70, 80, 81, 86; recruiting assassins,
304–5, 329n36; in *Shen bao,* 69, 86; and social reality, 62; for textbooks, 34, 36–37, 38,
39; Western and Chinese imagery in, 72–73;
women in, 48, 73–75. *See also* Huang Chujiu,
advertising by
Africa, 130n75, 309
Ailuo Brain Tonic, 7, 65, 71; advertising for, 64,
69, 71–72; packaging of, 63, 64
airports, 139
alayavijnana (true self), 236, 253, 256n16
All-China Federation of Chambers of
Commerce, 120, 134n173
Althusser, Louis, 344
American Brewer and Company, 49
American Medical Association, 67
American Tobacco Company, 53
Analects, 240
anarchism, 315
ancestor worship, 250

ancestral estates, 191, 198–99, 210–11. *See also*
lineage estates
ancestral halls, 201, 204, 223n70
Anderson, Benedict, 2, 32–33, 55–57
Anderson, Marston, 278
Anfu clique, 332n61
Anjing, 116
annei rangwai (first pacify the interior, then expel
the external aggressor) policy, 303
Anti-Japanese National Salvation Association of
Returned Students from Japan, 301
anti-Japanese propaganda, 334nn84,89
anti-Manchu sentiment, 242, 250, 251, 257n42
antirightist campaign, 184
Apter, David, 291, 297n61
archival materials, 1–2
Aristotle, 41, 42
assassinations, 17, 317–18, 336n113; of Chen Lu,
318; of Fu Xiaoan, 314; late Qing, 315–16; of
Li Jinbiao, 331n55; of Lu Bohong, 337n118;
of Wang Xianming, 340n171; of Xi Shitai,
319–21; of Zhang Jingyao, 303–4; of Zhou
Fengqi and Zhang Xiaolin, 315, 337n118
assassins, 17, 20, 305, 315, 317
Aurora University, 187n3
authoritarianism, 9, 14, 16, 28n13
automobile industry, 148
Automobile Manufacturing Company, 148

Bagehot, W., 41
Bai, Judge (fictional character), 262

Bai, Mrs. (Morality Society lecturer), 355
Bai Chongxi, 89
Bai Wei, *Breaking out of the Tower of Ghosts*, 273,
274–77, 282
Bai Yang, 376, 381, 390
Baike xiaocongshu (Mini collection of encyclopedic
knowledge), 40
Bailes, Kendall, 152
Bailing huabao (Long Life Pictorial), 80
Baoding, 105, 109; military academy, 129n59,
175; women's movement in, 105, 129–30n60
Baolun Hospital, 321
Baotou, 103
baptisms, 178
Barat, D., 86
Barlow, Tani, 90
Barthes, Roland, 2, 289
Basic Collectanea of National Learning (*Guoxue
jiben congshu*), 40
Battle of Shanghai, 306, 307, 316
Baudrillard, Jean, 297
Becker, C. H., 146, 157n66
Becker Commission, 146–47, 157n66, 158n68
Beichen (Catholic magazine), 176
Beidi temple, 211, 225n95
Beijiang Museum of Natural History, 162,
167–68
Beijing: as Chinese capital, 100, 101, 123, 128n22;
city walls of, 115, 117; criticism of, 111; drug-
stores in, 89; influence on other cities, 107;
and May Fourth Movement, 7; railroad con-
nections to, 99, 128n10; streetcars in, 124
Beijing Streetcar Company, 124
Beijing University, 36, 151, 175
Beijing waterworks, 114
Beijing-Zhangjiakou railroad, 149
Beiyang militarists, 304, 308, 338n147
Beiyang University, 180, 181
Benedict XV, 189n111
Benedictines, 187n3
Bengal, women in, 346
Bentham, Jeremy, 41
Bergson, Henri, 40, 41
Bhabha, Homi, 33, 363n46
biographies, 42
Bjørnson, B., 42
Blue Shirts, 301, 303–4, 318, 319, 328–29n32
Bluntschli, Johann, 243
Board of Civil Administration, 337n126
Board of Rites, 240
body, 50–51, 77–78. *See also* female body

bond servants, 199, 205, 220n32
Book of Rituals, 352
Bornet, Fr., 188n10, 189–90n44
Bornhak, Gustav, 243
Borsch, Fr., 178
Bowley, A. L., 41
Boxer Rebellion, 182–83, 263, 264
boycotts, 70, 71, 72, 120
Brasilia, 139
British-American Tobacco Company, 76
Buddhism, 330n53, 343; and Morality Society,
348, 353; in social thought of Zhang Taiyan,
15, 233, 235–36, 238, 253, 256n19; women in,
364n76
Bureau of Roads, 145, 146
Butterfield and Swire, 206
Butterfly fiction, 35, 36, 54

cabi dancai (rub-and-paint), 73, 94n50
Café and Paradise Ballroom, 318
Cai, Grandmother (Morality Society member),
356
Cai Chusheng, 368, 371, 372; *A Dream in Pink*,
371; *Fisherman's Ballad*, 371. See also *A Spring
River Flows East*
Cai Mengjian, 99, 100, 101, 126
Cai Yifei, 334n79
Cai Yuanpei, 40
calendar: Chinese, 240; Japanese, 307; Western,
6, 32, 56
calendar posters: advertising medicines, 7, 74; as
commercial art, 53–54, 82; Lu Xun on, 62,
76–77; 1930 example of, 55; origins of, 32;
painters of, 7, 61n50, 62, 73, 77–78; in rural
China, 82; and Western calendar, use of, 6,
56; Western influence on, 77–78; and
women, as portrayed on, 7, 54–56, 61n50,
62, 73, 76
camel trains, 103, 113
"cannibalism" (Lu Xun), 261, 270, 271, 272, 273,
274, 280–81, 282, 289, 290, 292
Cao Kun, 107
Cao Mei, 315
Cao Yu, *Thunderstorm*, 277
capital cities, 100–101, 123, 124, 128n22, 141
Capital Police Bureau, 351
Carlton Theater, 370
Carnegie, Andrew, 42
categorization of knowledge, 5, 40–44
Catholic colleges, 162, 168–69, 187–88n3. *See
also* Gong Shang College

Catholic community, 162–63, 165, 174, 186
Catholic Patriotic Association, 184, 185
Catholicism: under Chinese episcopate, 181–82, 190n47; conversion to, 169; Counter-Reformation model, 162–63, 164, 169–70, 174, 185, 186; after cultural revolution, 161, 184–85; as depicted in posters, 300; European, 162, 163; and hierarchical authority, 163, 164, 169–70, 173–74, 185, 186; and modernity, 162, 170; in rural and urban settings, 162, 165, 170; social theory in, 176–77, 186; values of, 161. *See also* French Jesuits; Jesuits
cellularization of villages, 216, 225n97
Central China Area Army (Japanese), 307
Central China Commission for Control of Medicine (*Huazhong yiyaopin tongzhi lianhehui*), 88
Central Cinematography Studio (*Zhongyang sheying chang*), 369, 371
Central Copper Works, 150
Central Daily News, 329n36
Central Electrical Manufacturing Works, 150
Central Machine Works, 148, 150
Central Steel Works, 148, 150
Certeau, Michel de, 2, 106
Cervantes, Miguel de, 42
Chakang (Xinhui), 220n32
chambers of commerce: governance of, 120, 121, 134n173, 135n179; in Japan, 119; late Qing framework for, 114; mentioned, 308; and merchant militia, 304; as mode of social organization, 237, 245, 247, 248; and municipal governance, 118–20; and municipal reform, 125–26; as source of revenue, 119, 134n166
Chan, Wing-tsit, 348, 362n29
Chang, Hao, 249, 255n7, 257n47
Chang Chien Wen, 50
Changde, 106
Changsha, 129n55
Chao, Thomas, 328n32
Chaolian, 220, 224n86
charitable associations, 209, 224n88
charity, 220n34
Charvet, Fr. Rene, 172, 173, 182
Chatterjee, Partha, 2, 346
Chen, Mrs. (Morality Society member), 355–56, 357–58
Chen, P. C., 50
Chen Baichen, 369; *A Rhapsody of Happiness*, 370
Chen bao, 369
Chen Bijun, 335n97

Chen Cheng, 128n23
Chen Duxiu, 32, 44, 131n90, 261
Chen Gongbo, 312
Chen Guofu, 89, 147, 336n117
Chen Jiongming, 134n154
Chen Jitang, 212, 214, 225n99
Chen Kaiguang (Chen Yuanliang), 317, 338n135
Chen Lifu, 322, 336n117, 343
Chen lineage, 197, 223n70; of Tianma, 210, 223n70; of Waihai *xiang*, 222n54, 224n86
Chen Liting, 368, 369–70, 371, 372, 391, 394; *Lay Down Your Whip*, 369, 377; *A Rhapsody of Happiness*, 370; *Women Side-by-Side*, 370. See also *Far Away Love*
Chen Lu, 318
Chen Qibai (Chen Daoliang), 300
Chen She, 316
Chen Tianhua, 111, 239
Chen Xiang, 222n54
Chen Yixi, 215
Chen Yuanliang (Chen Kaiguang), 317, 338n135
Cheng Hao, 220n38
Cheng Ren (fictional character), 291–93
Cheng Yi, 220n38
Chengdu, 104, 110, 116, 122, 131–32n95
Chiang Kai-shek: antibourgeois sentiment of, 398n33; and Blue Shirts, 301; and Dai Li, 314, 323; and Fu Xiaoan, 308; mentioned, 61n55, 174, 390; and regulation of new medicine, 85; and special operations, 89, 304, 318, 322; and Wang Jingwei, 340n172; and war against Japan, 303, 314. *See also* Blue Shirts; Dai Li
children, 39, 50
Children's Theater Troupe, 372
China Air Materials Construction Company, 148
China Art Theater Society (*Zhongguo yishu ju she*), 369
China Bookstore, 33, 37
China Film No. 1, 367
China Film No. 2, 367, 369, 370
China Film No. 3, 367
China Film Studio (*Zhongguo dianying zhipianchang*), 369, 370, 372, 396n1
China Medical Journal, 85
China Revival Society (*Huaxing hui*), 337n124
China Weekly Review, 340n174
China-France Company of the Western Region, 87
Chinese Bank of Commerce, 308

Guoxue jiben congshu (Basic collectanea of national learning), 40
Gutzlaff (missionary), 300

Habermas, Jurgen, 2, 33, 58n8, 246
Hahn, Emily, 340n172
Haiyan Film Studio, 370
Hang Laoliu (fictional character), 289–90
Hang Zhiying, 7, 73, 74, 75–76, 78
hanjian: and betrayal of ethnocultural identity, 19, 299, 324–25, 333n72; Blue Shirts and, 301–2; Chongqing policy on, 311; designated by Communist Party, 300–301; executions of, 301, 302, 341n184; extortion of taxes by, 314, 336n108; four great traitors of Guangdong, 323; in Japanese-occupied Shanghai, 302–3; for Jurchen Jin dynasty, 299; Korean and Taiwanese, 328n24; merchants as, 305, 313–14, 379; during Ming and Qing, 299–300, 308, 324, 326nn8,9; natives of Subei as, 302–3; origins and meanings of term, 20, 298–99, 300, 326n1, 327n13; and peace, 312–13; after Pearl Harbor, 321–23; published lists of, 314, 336n113; relatives of, 309–11, 333n75, 334n85, 335n102; repentant, 311; and transgression by outsiders, 299, 303, 328n24, 336n110; trials of, 323–24. *See also* assassinations; collaboration; terrorism
Hankou, 99, 107, 114, 120, 126, 133n129; drugstores in, 89; merchants in, 121, 191, 194
Hanyu da cidian, 298, 363n35
Hatamen cigarettes, 54
Hauptmann, Gerhart, 42
Hay, John, 74
Hayhoe, Ruth, 147
He Bingru Gong tang, 206
He Feiguang, *The Light of East Asia,* 396n1
He Jintang, 213
He lineage: Huicheng, 205, 223n67, 225n101; Shawan, 211, 225n95
He Naizhong, 225n92
He Ruoshan, 25n101
He Wenyan (fictional character), 382–83, 389, 392
He Wenyi Gong tang, 223n67
He Xiongxiang, 205, 223n67
He Yanggao, 225n94
He Yingqin, 323
Health Authorities of the Foreign Settlement, 86
heavenly principle (*tianli*), 234, 255n10

Heavenly Spring Dream (Tang Xiaodan), 391, 395
Hebei Normal School, 184
Hebei Normal University, 184
Hebei University, 184
Hecheng native bank, 206
Hefeng shuyuan (Hefeng Academy), 225n92
Hegel, Georg Wilhelm Friedrich, 235
Heini (fictional character), 291–92
Hell, 265–66, 267, 268–69, 271, 283, 294n20, 297n74
heroes, 18, 20–21, 24
Hetang, 224n86
hidden transcripts (Scott), 359
hierarchy, 13–14, 16, 163, 164, 169–70, 173–74, 185
higher education, 166, 167, 170, 171–72, 176, 187–88n3, 189n23; reform of, 146–47, 149; during Sino-Japanese War, 177. *See also* Gong Shang College
Hinduism, 346
history. *See* evolutionary history
Hitchcock, Alfred, 396
H.M.S. *Nemesis,* 300
Hobbes, Thomas, 41
Hobson, John, 41
Hoffman, Stanley, 333n74
Holmes, Sherlock, 268, 295n28
Homer, 42
Hong Chengchou, 299
Hong Kong, 82, 90, 101, 112, 212
Hongwanzihui. *See* Red Swastika Society
Hou, Chi-ming, 72
Hou Fangyu, 308
Hsia, C. T., 281, 282
Hsia, T. A., 270
Hsiao Kung-chuan, 220n39
Hu Feng, 284, 287
Hu Shi, 36, 40, 112, 120, 123, 124
Hu Zhenggu, 331n58
Huai River, 145
Huan, Duke of Qi, 315
Huang, Philip, 201
Huang Chujiu: advertising by, 63, 64, 70–72, 73, 75, 77, 80, 81, 84; and buildings in Shanghai, 79; and calendar poster, 7, 53, 73–75; death of, 87; early years, 63; and Green Gang members, 85–86; Japanese models for, 67, 69–70, 71; and popularization of images of the elite, 78, 90–91; and regulation of new medicines, 85–86; reputation as slippery, 65. *See also* Ailuo Brain Tonic; Human Elixir

Text:	10/12 Baskerville
Display:	Baskerville
Composition:	Impressions, Inc.
	Birdtrack Press
Printing and binding:	Edwards Brothers, Inc.